Gleim Publications, Inc., offers five university-level study systems:

Auditing & Systems Exam Questions and Explanations with Test Prep Software
Business Law/Legal Studies Exam Questions and Explanations with Test Prep Software
Federal Tax Exam Questions and Explanations with Test Prep Software
Financial Accounting Exam Questions and Explanations with Test Prep Software
Cost/Managerial Accounting Exam Questions and Explanations with Test Prep Software

The following is a list of Gleim examination review systems:

CIA Review: Part 1, The Internal Audit Activity's Role in Governance, Risk, and Control
CIA Review: Part 2, Conducting the Internal Audit Engagement
CIA Review: Part 3, Business Analysis and Information Technology
CIA Review: Part 4, Business Management Skills
CIA Review: A System for Success

CMA Review: Part 1, Financial Planning, Performance, and Control
CMA Review: Part 2, Financial Decision Making
CMA Review: A System for Success

CPA Review: Financial
CPA Review: Auditing
CPA Review: Business
CPA Review: Regulation
CPA Review: A System for Success

EA Review: Part 1, Individuals
EA Review: Part 2, Businesses
EA Review: Part 3, Representation, Practices, and Procedures
EA Review: A System for Success

An order form is provided at the back of this book or contact us at www.gleim.com or (800) 874-5346.

REVIEWERS AND CONTRIBUTORS

Garrett Gleim, B.S., CPA (not in public practice), is a graduate of the Wharton School at the University of Pennsylvania. Mr. Gleim coordinated the production staff, reviewed the manuscript, and provided production assistance throughout the project.

Grady M. Irwin, J.D., is a graduate of the University of Florida College of Law, and he has taught in the University of Florida College of Business. Mr. Irwin provided substantial editorial assistance throughout the project.

John F. Rebstock, B.S.A., is a graduate of the Fisher School of Accounting at the University of Florida. He has passed the CIA and CPA exams. Mr. Rebstock reviewed portions of the manuscript.

Kristina M. Rivet, CPA, graduated *cum laude* from Florida International University. She has extensive public accounting experience in the areas of financial accounting, tax, and consulting. Ms. Rivet provided substantial editorial assistance throughout the project.

Stewart B. White, B.M., *cum laude*, University of Richmond, B.S., Virginia Commonwealth University, has passed the CPA, CIA, and CISA exams and has worked in the fields of retail management, financial audit, IT audit, COBOL programming, and data warehouse management. Mr. White provided substantial editorial assistance throughout the project.

A PERSONAL THANKS

This manual would not have been possible without the extraordinary effort and dedication of Jacob Brunny, Julie Cutlip, Kate Devine, Eileen Nickl, Teresa Soard, Joanne Strong, and Candace Van Doren, who typed the entire manuscript and all revisions and drafted and laid out the diagrams and illustrations in this book.

The authors appreciate the production and editorial assistance of Katie Anderson, Alexander Karnazes, Katie Larson, Cary Marcous, Jean Marzullo, Shane Rapp, Drew Sheppard, Katie Wassink, and Martha Willis.

The authors also appreciate the critical reading assistance of Brett Babir, Ellen Buhl, Lauren Bull, Reed Daines, Lawrence Lipp, and Kristina Schoen.

Finally, we appreciate the encouragement, support, and tolerance of our families throughout this project.

SIXTEENTH EDITION

GLEIM

CMA Review

Part 2
Financial Decision Making

by

Irvin N. Gleim, Ph.D., CPA, CIA, CMA, CFM

and

Dale L. Flesher, Ph.D., CPA, CIA, CMA, CFM

ABOUT THE AUTHORS

Irvin N. Gleim is Professor Emeritus in the Fisher School of Accounting at the University of Florida and is a member of the American Accounting Association, Academy of Legal Studies in Business, AICPA, Association of Government Accountants, Florida Institute of CPAs, The IIA, and the IMA. He has had articles published in the *Journal of Accountancy*, *The Accounting Review*, and *The American Business Law Journal* and is author/coauthor of numerous accounting and aviation books and CPE courses.

Dale L. Flesher is the Arthur Andersen Alumni Professor in the School of Accountancy at the University of Mississippi and has written over 300 articles for business and professional journals, including *Management Accounting*, *Journal of Accountancy*, and *The Accounting Review*, as well as numerous books. He is a member of the IMA, AICPA, The IIA, American Accounting Association, and American Taxation Association. He is a past editor of *The Accounting Historians' Journal* and is a trustee and past president of the Academy of Accounting Historians. He is currently the vice president of finance for the American Accounting Association. In 2011, he received the AICPA's highest award for educators, The Distinguished Performance in Accounting Education Award, which is a lifetime achievement award. Previously, in 1990, he received The Institute of Internal Auditors Radde Award as the Outstanding Auditing Educator worldwide.

iv

Gleim Publications, Inc.
P.O. Box 12848
University Station
Gainesville, Florida 32604
(800) 87-GLEIM or (800) 874-5346
(352) 375-0772
Fax: (352) 375-6940
Internet: www.gleim.com
Email: admin@gleim.com

For updates to the first printing of the sixteenth edition of *CMA Review: Part 2*

Go To: www.gleim.com/updates

Or: Scan code with your mobile device

Or: Email update@gleim.com with **CMA 2 16-1** in the subject line. You will receive our current update as a reply.

Updates are available until the next edition is published.

ISSN: 2152-6419

ISBN: 978-1-58194-201-9

Copyright © 2012 by Gleim Publications, Inc.

First Printing: July 2012

ACKNOWLEDGMENTS

The authors are indebted to the Institute of Certified Management Accountants (ICMA) for permission to use problem materials from past CMA examinations. Questions and unofficial answers from the Certified Management Accountant Examinations, copyright © 1982 through 2008 by the Institute of Certified Management Accountants, are reprinted and/or adapted with permission.

The authors are also indebted to The Institute of Internal Auditors, Inc. for permission to use Certified Internal Auditor Examination Questions and Suggested Solutions, copyright © 1985 through 1996 by The Institute of Internal Auditors, Inc.

The authors also appreciate and thank the American Institute of Certified Public Accountants, Inc. Material from Uniform Certified Public Accountant Examination questions and unofficial answers, copyright © 1981-2012 by the American Institute of Certified Public Accountants, Inc., is reprinted and/or adapted with permission.

This publication was printed and bound by Corley Printing Company, St. Louis, MO, a registered ISO-9002 company. More information about Corley Printing Company is available at www.corleyprinting.com or by calling (314) 739-3777.

Visit www.gleim.com for the latest updates and information on all of our products.

This publication is designed to provide accurate and authoritative information with regard to the subject matter covered. It is sold with the understanding that the publisher is not engaged in rendering legal, accounting, or other professional service.

If legal advice or other expert assistance is required, the services of a competent professional person should be sought.

(From a declaration of principles jointly adopted by a Committee of the American Bar Association and a Committee of Publishers.)

TABLE OF CONTENTS

PREFACE FOR CMA PART 2 CANDIDATES

The purpose of this book is to help **you** prepare **yourself** to pass Part 2 of the two-part CMA examination. The overriding consideration is to provide an inexpensive, effective, and easy-to-use study program. This manual

1. Explains how to optimize your grade by focusing on Part 2 of the CMA exam.

2. Defines the subject matter tested on Part 2 of the CMA exam.

3. Outlines all of the subject matter tested on Part 2 in 10 easy-to-use-and-complete study units.

4. Presents multiple-choice and essay questions from past CMA examinations to prepare you for questions in future CMA exams. The multiple-choice answer explanations are presented to the immediate right of each question for your convenience. Use a piece of paper to cover our explanations as you study the questions.

5. Suggests exam-taking and question-answering techniques to help you maximize your exam score.

The outline format, the spacing, and the question-and-answer formats in this book are designed to facilitate readability, learning, understanding, and success on the CMA exam. Our most successful candidates use the Gleim CMA Review System*, which includes books, Test Prep Software, Audio Review, Gleim Online, Essay Wizard, FREE Practice Exams (available Summer 2012), and access to a Personal Counselor; or a group study CMA review program. (Check our website for live courses we recommend.) This review book and all Gleim CMA Review materials are compatible with other CMA review materials and courses that are based on the ICMA's Content Specification Outlines.

To maximize the efficiency and effectiveness of your CMA review program, augment your studying with *CMA Review: A System for Success*. This booklet has been carefully written and organized to provide important information to assist you in passing the CMA examination.

Thank you for your interest in our materials. We deeply appreciate the thousands of letters and suggestions we have received from CIA, CMA, CPA, and EA candidates and accounting students and faculty during the past 5 decades.

If you use Gleim materials, we want YOUR feedback immediately after the exam and as soon as you have received your grades. The CMA exam is NONDISCLOSED, and you must maintain the confidentiality and agree not to divulge the nature or content of any CMA question or answer under any circumstances. We ask only for information about our materials, i.e., the topics that need to be added, expanded, etc.

Please go to www.gleim.com/feedbackCMA2 to share your suggestions on how we can improve this edition.

Good Luck on the Exam,

Irvin N. Gleim
Dale L. Flesher
July 2012

PREPARING FOR AND TAKING THE CMA EXAM

TRANSITION TO TWO-PART EXAM

In 2010, the ICMA changed the CMA program from a four-part to a two-part exam. Candidates are now able to enter only into the two-part program; i.e., old exam Parts 1, 2, 3, and 4 are no longer available to complete.

Candidates who previously began the four-part exam process can transition to the new exam. If they passed old Part 2, they only have to pass new Part 2 to complete the CMA. If they passed old Part 3, they only have to pass new Part 1 to complete the CMA. If both old Parts 2 and 3 were passed, a 2-hour transition exam must be taken to complete the CMA. The Transition Exam will be available until February 28, 2013.

FOLLOW THESE STEPS TO PASS THE EXAM

1. Read this **Introduction** to familiarize yourself with the content and structure of Part 2 of the CMA exam. In the following pages, you will find

    a. An **overview of Part 2** and what it generally tests, including the ICMA's Content Specification Outlines (CSOs)

    b. A detailed plan with **steps to obtain your CMA certification**, including

        1) The order in which you should apply, register, schedule your exam, and buy your study materials

        2) The studying tactics on which you should focus

        3) How to organize your study schedule to make the most out of each resource in the Gleim CMA Review System (i.e., books, Test Prep Software Download, Audio Review, Gleim Online, Essay Wizard, Diagnostic Quizzes, Practice Exams, etc.)

    c. Tactics for your **actual test day**, including

        1) Time budgeting, so you complete all questions with time to review
        2) Question-answering techniques to obtain every point you can
        3) An explanation of how to be in control of your CMA exam

2. Scan the Gleim *CMA Review: A System for Success* booklet and note where to revisit later in your studying process to obtain a deeper understanding of the CMA exam.

    a. *CMA Review: A System for Success* has seven study units:

    Study Unit 1: The CMA Examination: An Overview and Preparation Introduction
    Study Unit 2: ICMA Content Specification Outlines
    Study Unit 3: Content Preparation, Test Administration, and Performance Grading
    Study Unit 4: Multiple-Choice Questions
    Study Unit 5: Essay Questions
    Study Unit 6: Preparing to Pass the CMA Exam
    Study Unit 7: How to Take the CMA Exam

3. BEFORE you begin studying, take a **Diagnostic Quiz** at www.gleim.com/cmadiagnosticquiz or use our **Gleim Diagnostic Quiz App** for iPhone, iPod Touch, and Android.

    a. The Diagnostic Quiz includes a representative sample of 40 multiple-choice questions and will determine your weakest areas in Part 2.

    b. When you are finished, one of our **Personal Counselors** will consult with you to better focus your review on any areas in which you have less confidence.

4. Follow the steps outlined on page 8, "How to Study a Study Unit Using the Gleim CMA Review System." This is the **study plan** that our most successful candidates adhere to. Study until you have reached your **desired proficiency level** (e.g., 75%) for each study unit in Part 2.

    a. As you proceed, be sure to check any **Updates** that may have been released.

        1) Gleim Online and Essay Wizard are updated automatically.

        2) Test Prep Software is updated by the Online Library Updates system in the Tools menu of your Test Prep. You can (and should) set your Test Prep to automatically update at least once a month.

        3) Book updates can be viewed at www.gleim.com/updates, or you can have them emailed to you. See the information box in the top right corner of page iv for details.

    b. **Review the *CMA Review: A System for Success* booklet** and become completely comfortable with what will be expected from you on test day.

5.   Shortly before your test date, take a **Practice Exam** (complimentary with the purchase of the complete Gleim CMA Review System!) at www.gleim.com/cmapracticeexam (available Summer 2012).

   a.   This timed and scored exam emulates the actual CMA exam and tests you not only on the content you have studied, but also on the question-answering and time-management techniques you have learned throughout the Gleim study process.

   b.   When you have completed the exam, study your results to discover where you should **focus your review during the final days before your exam**.

6.   **Take and PASS** Part 2 of the CMA exam!

   a.   When you have completed the exam, please contact Gleim with your **suggestions, comments, and corrections**. We want to know how well we prepared you for your testing experience.

INTRODUCTION TO CMA

CMA is the acronym for Certified Management Accountant. The CMA examination is developed and offered by the Institute of Certified Management Accountants (ICMA) in numerous domestic and international locations.

According to the IMA, the "CMA is the advanced professional certification specifically designed to measure the accounting and financial management skills that drive business performance."

OVERVIEW OF THE CMA EXAMINATION

The total exam is 8 hours of testing. It is divided into two parts, as follows:

Part 1 – Financial Planning, Performance, and Control
Part 2 – Financial Decision Making

Each part consists of 100 multiple-choice questions and 2 essay scenarios, and testing lasts 4 hours (3 hours for the multiple-choice questions plus 1 hour for the essays). The exams are only offered during the following three testing windows: January/February, May/June, and September/October.

The CMA exam is computerized to facilitate easier testing. Prometric, the testing company that the IMA contracts to proctor the exams, has hundreds of testing centers worldwide. The Gleim Test Prep Software, Gleim Online, Gleim Essay Wizard, and Gleim CMA Practice Exams provide exact exam emulations of the Prometric computer screens and procedures to prepare you to PASS.

SUBJECT MATTER FOR PART 2

Below, we have provided the ICMA's abbreviated Content Specification Outline (CSO) for Part 2. The percentage coverage of each topic is indicated to its right. We adjust the content of our materials to any changes in the CSO.

Candidates for the CMA designation are expected to have a minimum level of business knowledge that transcends both examination parts. This minimum level includes knowledge of basic financial statements, time value of money concepts, and elementary statistics. Specific discussion of the ICMA's Levels of Performance (A, B, and C) is provided in Appendix C, which is a reprint of the ICMA's discussion of "Types and Levels of Exam Questions."

Part 2: Financial Decision Making

Financial Statement Analysis	25%
Corporate Finance	25%
Decision Analysis and Risk Management	25%
Investment Decisions	20%
Professional Ethics	5%

Appendix A contains the CSOs in their entirety as well as cross-references to the subunits in our text where topics are covered. Remember that we have studied and restudied the CSOs in developing our *CMA Review* materials. Accordingly, you do not need to spend time with Appendix A. Rather, it should give you confidence that Gleim *CMA Review* is the best review source available to help you PASS the CMA exam.

LEARNING OUTCOME STATEMENTS

In addition to the Content Specification Outlines, the ICMA has published Learning Outcome Statements (LOSs) that specify in detail what skills a candidate should possess. Before you study our knowledge transfer outline, read the LOS at the beginning of each study unit. This will alert you to what is expected and required of you.

WHICH PRONOUNCEMENTS ARE TESTED?

New pronouncements are eligible to be tested on the CMA exam in the testing window beginning 1 year after a pronouncement's effective date.

HOW ETHICS ARE TESTED

Ethical issues and considerations are tested from the perspective of the individual in Part 1 and from the perspective of the organization in Part 2. Candidates will be expected to evaluate the issues involved and make recommendations for the resolution of the situation.

NONDISCLOSED EXAM

As part of the ICMA's nondisclosure policy and to prove each candidate's willingness to adhere to this policy, a confidentiality agreement must be accepted by each candidate before each part is taken. This statement is reproduced here to remind all CMA candidates about the ICMA's strict policy of nondisclosure, which Gleim consistently supports and upholds.

I hereby attest that I will not divulge the content of this examination, nor will I remove any examination materials, notes or other unauthorized materials from the examination room. I understand that failure to comply with this attestation may result in invalidation of my grades and disqualification from future examinations. For those already certified by the Institute of Certified Management Accountants, failure to comply with the statement will be considered a violation of the IMA's Statement of Ethical Professional Practice and could result in revocation of the certification.

THE ICMA'S REQUIREMENTS FOR CMA DESIGNATIONS

The CMA designation is granted only by the ICMA. Candidates must complete the following steps to become a CMA:

1. Become a member of the IMA, enter the certification program, and register for the part(s) you are going to take. The *CMA Review: A System for Success* booklet contains concise instructions on the membership and certification application and registration processes and a useful worksheet to help you keep track of your process and organize what you need for exam day. Detailed instructions and screenshots for those steps can also be found at www.gleim.com/accounting/cma/steps.
2. Pass both parts of the exam within 3 years.
3. Satisfy the education requirement.
4. Satisfy the experience requirement.
5. Comply with the IMA's *Statement of Ethical Professional Practice*.

Upon completion of all requirements, the ICMA will issue a numbered CMA certificate. To keep the certificate, a CMA must (1) maintain active membership in the IMA and pay the annual CMA maintenance fee, (2) fulfill the requirements for continuing professional education, and (3) continue to comply with the IMA's *Statement of Ethical Professional Practice* and all applicable state laws.

CMA EXAM FEES

1. IMA Membership Fees: IMA membership is required for all CMA candidates. There are four types of membership: Regular, Student, Young Professional, and Academic. Fees for IMA members include a one-time membership application fee (for all new members except Students and Young Professionals) and an annual membership renewal fee. Members who have passed the CMA exam will also need to pay an annual maintenance fee, due at the same time as the renewal fee.

    Go to www.gleim.com/CMAfees for the most current IMA membership fees.

2. CMA Certification Fees:

	Entrance Fee	Exam Fee One Part/Window	Exam Fee Both Parts/Window	Rescheduling/ Cancelation Fee *
Regular	$225	$350	$300	$50
Student	$75	$175	$125	$50
Academic	$75	$175	$125	$50

*This fee is applicable to candidates who reschedule/cancel their exam within 30 days of their appointment. Prior to 30 days, there is no penalty.

MAINTAINING YOUR CMA DESIGNATION

When you have completed all requirements, you will be issued a numbered CMA certificate. This certificate is the property of the ICMA and must be returned upon request. To maintain your certificate, membership in the IMA is required. The annual CMA maintenance fee for regular members is $30. You are also required to comply with the IMA's *Statement of Ethical Professional Practice*. The final requirement is continuing professional education (CPE).

Beginning the calendar year after successful completion of the CMA exams, 30 hours of CPE must be completed, which is about 4 days per year. Qualifying topics include management accounting, corporate taxation, statistics, computer science, systems analysis, management skills, marketing, business law, and insurance. All CMAs are required to complete 2 hours of CPE on the subject of ethics as part of their 30-hour annual requirement.

ELIGIBILITY PERIOD

Candidates must register for an exam part within the first 12 months after being admitted to the Certification Program. In addition, all candidates are required to pass both parts of the exam within 3 years of being admitted to the CMA program. If a candidate is not able to pass both parts within this time period, the Certification Entrance Fee will have to be repaid and the passed part will have to be retaken.

STEPS TO BECOME A CMA

1. Become knowledgeable about the exam, and decide which part you will take first.
2. Purchase the Gleim CMA Review System (including books, Test Prep Software Download, Audio Review, Gleim Online, Essay Wizards, Practice Exams, and access to a Personal Counselor) to thoroughly prepare for the CMA exam. Commit to systematic preparation for the exam as described in our review materials, including *CMA Review: A System for Success.*
3. Communicate with your Personal Counselor to design a study plan that meets your needs. Call (800) 874-5346 or email CMA@gleim.com.
4. Apply for membership in the IMA and the Certification Program.
5. Register online to take the desired part of the exam in the next available window.
6. Upon receipt of authorization to take the exam, schedule your test with Prometric.
7. Work systematically through each study unit in the Gleim CMA Review System.
8. Sit for and PASS the CMA exam while you are in control, as described in Study Unit 7 of *CMA Review: A System for Success.* Gleim will make it easy.
9. Contact Gleim with your comments on our study materials and how well they prepared you for the exam.
10. Enjoy your career, pursue multiple certifications (CIA, CPA, EA, etc.), recommend Gleim to others who are also taking these exams, and stay up-to-date on your continuing professional education with Gleim CPE.

More specifically, you should focus on the following **system for success** on the CMA exam:

1. **Understand the exam, including its purpose, coverage, preparation, format, administration, grading, and pass rates.**

   a. The better you understand the examination process from beginning to end, the better you will perform.

   b. Study the Gleim *CMA Review: A System for Success.* Please be sure you have a copy of this useful booklet (also available online at www.gleim.com/sfs).

2. **Learn and understand the subject matter tested.** The ICMA's CSOs for Part 2 are the basis for the study outlines that are presented in each of the 10 study units that make up this book.* You will also learn and understand the material tested on the CMA exam by answering numerous multiple-choice and essay questions from previous CMA exams.

3. **Practice answering past exam questions to perfect your question-answering techniques.** Answering past exam questions helps you understand the standards to which you will be held. This motivates you to learn and understand while studying (rather than reading) the outlines in each of the 10 study units.

   a. Question-answering techniques are suggested for multiple-choice and essay questions in Study Unit 4 and Study Unit 5, respectively, of *CMA Review: A System for Success.*

   b. Our **CMA Test Prep** Software contains thousands of additional multiple-choice questions that are not offered in our books. Additionally, CMA Test Prep Software has many useful features, including documentation of your performance and the ability to simulate the CMA exam environment.

   c. Our **CMA Gleim Online** is a powerful Internet-based program that allows CMA candidates to learn in an interactive environment and provides feedback to candidates to encourage learning. It includes multiple-choice and essay questions in Prometric's format. Each CMA Gleim Online candidate has access to a Personal Counselor, who helps organize study plans that work with busy schedules.

   d. Additionally, each candidate should utilize the Gleim CMA Essay Wizard online courses for even more practice on essays in an exam-like environment. The Essay Wizard courses provide 40 additional essays that can be answered and graded for an accurate indication of how well-prepared you are for the CMA's essays.

4. **Plan and practice exam execution.** Anticipate the exam environment and prepare yourself with a plan: When to arrive? How to dress? What exam supplies to bring? How many questions and what format? Order of answering questions? How much time to spend on each question? See Study Unit 7 in *CMA Review: A System for Success.*

   a. Expect the unexpected and adjust! Remember, your sole objective when taking an examination is to maximize your score. You must outperform your peers, and being as comfortable and relaxed as possible gives you an advantage!

5. **Be in control.** Develop confidence and ensure success with a controlled preparation program followed by confident execution during the examination.

---

*Please fill out our online feedback form (www.gleim.com/feedbackCMA2) IMMEDIATELY after you take the CMA exam so we can adapt to changes in the exam. Our approach has been approved by the ICMA.

PRELIMINARY TESTING: GLEIM CMA DIAGNOSTIC QUIZZES

The five Gleim CMA Diagnostic Quizzes provide a representative sample of 40 multiple-choice questions for each exam part to identify your preliminary strengths and any weaknesses before you start preparing in earnest for the CMA exam. They also provide you with the actual exam experience, i.e., what you will encounter when you take the CMA exam at Prometric.

When you have completed each quiz, one of our Personal Counselors will consult with you to better focus your review on any areas in which you have less confidence. After your consultation, you will be able to access a Review Session, where you can study answer explanations for the correct and incorrect answer choices of the questions you answered incorrectly.

For smart phone users, there is also a Gleim Diagnostic Quiz App for iPhone, iPod Touch, and Android. See our website (www.gleim.com/cmadiagnosticquiz) for more information.

HOW TO STUDY A STUDY UNIT USING THE GLEIM REVIEW SYSTEM

To ensure that you are using your time effectively, we recommend that you follow the steps listed below when using all of the CMA Review System materials together (books, Test Prep Software, Audio Review, Gleim Online, and Essay Wizard):

1. (30 minutes, plus 10 minutes for review) In the CMA Gleim Online course, complete Multiple-Choice Quiz #1 in 30 minutes. It is expected that your scores will be lower on the first quiz.

   a. Immediately following the quiz, you will be prompted to review the questions you marked and/or answered incorrectly. For each question, analyze and understand why you were unsure or answered it incorrectly. This step is an essential learning activity.

2. (30 minutes) Use the audiovisual presentation for an overview of the study unit. The Gleim CMA Review Audios can be substituted for audiovisual presentations and can be used while driving to work, exercising, etc.

3. (45 minutes) Complete the 30-question True/False quiz. It provides immediate feedback and is most effective if used prior to studying the Knowledge Transfer Outline.

4. (60 minutes) Study the Knowledge Transfer Outline, particularly the troublesome areas identified from the multiple-choice questions in the Gleim Online course. The Knowledge Transfer Outlines can be studied either online or from the books.

5. (30 minutes, plus 10 minutes for review) Complete Multiple-Choice Quiz #2 in the Gleim Online course.

   a. Immediately following the quiz, you will be prompted to review the questions you marked and/or answered incorrectly. For each question, analyze and understand why you were unsure or answered it incorrectly. This step is an essential learning activity.

6. (60 minutes) Complete two 20-question quizzes while in Test Mode from the CMA Test Prep Software. Review as needed.

7. (30 minutes) Complete and review the essay question in Gleim Online.

When following these steps, you will complete all 10 units in about 50 hours. Then spend about 10-20 hours using the CMA Test Prep Software to create customized tests for the problem areas that you identified. When you are ready, create 20-question quizzes that draw questions from all 10 study units. Continue taking 20-question quizzes until you approach a 75%+ proficiency level.

The times mentioned above and on the previous page are recommendations based on prior candidate feedback and how long you will have to answer questions on the actual exam. Each candidate's time spent in any area will vary depending on proficiency and familiarity with the subject matter.

CMA GLEIM ONLINE

CMA Gleim Online is a versatile, interactive, self-study review program delivered via the Internet. It is divided into two courses (one for each part of the CMA exam) and emulates the CMA exam.

Each course is broken down into 10 individual, manageable study units. Completion time per study unit will be about 4 hours. Each study unit in the course contains an audiovisual presentation, 30 true/false study questions, 10-20 pages of Knowledge Transfer Outlines, two 20-question multiple-choice quizzes, and an essay question.

CMA Gleim Online provides you with a Personal Counselor, a real person who will provide support to ensure your competitive edge. CMA Gleim Online is a great way to get confidence as you prepare with Gleim. This confidence will continue during and after the exam.

GLEIM ESSAY WIZARD

The Gleim Essay Wizard is a training program that focuses on the essay questions that appear in both parts of the CMA exam. This online course provides two essay questions per study unit, as well as test-taking tips from Dr. Gleim to help you stay in control.

I was just informed I received The ICMA Bronze Medal for the January-February 2012 testing window. The Gleim materials were excellent. They helped me pass by dedicating less than 100 hours of study which I think is quite amazing. I will recommend Gleim to anyone who needs to study for CMA!

- Saif Lalani, CMA

GLEIM BOOKS

This edition of the CMA Part 2 Review book has the following features to make studying easier:

1. **Examples:** Longer, illustrative examples, both hypothetical and those drawn from actual events, are set off in shaded, bordered boxes.

EXAMPLE of Translation Gains and Losses

On December 15, Year 1, Boise Co. purchased electronic components from Kinugasa Corporation. Boise must pay Kinugasa ¥15,000,000 on January 15, Year 2. The exchange rate in effect on December 15, Year 1, was $.01015 per yen, giving the transaction a value on Boise's books of $152,250 (¥15,000,000 × $.01015).

Transaction Date:

Inventory	$152,250	
Accounts payable		$152,250

The exchange rate on December 31, Year 1, Boise's reporting date, has fallen to $.01010 per yen. The balance of the payable must be adjusted (and a gain in OCI recognized) in the amount of $750 [(¥15,000,000 × ($.01015 – $.01010)].

Reporting Date:

Accounts payable	$750	
Foreign currency translation adjustment		$750

The exchange rate on January 15, Year 2, has risen to $.01020 per yen. To settle the payable, the balance must be adjusted (and a loss in OCI recognized) in the amount of $1,500 [¥15,000,000 × ($.01010 – $.01020)].

Settlement Date:

Accounts payable ($152,250 – $750)	$151,500	
Foreign currency translation adjustment	1,500	
Cash		$153,000

---

2. **Gleim Success Tips:** These tips supplement the core exam material by suggesting how certain topics might be presented on the exam or how you should prepare for an issue.

CMA candidates need to be prepared to answer ethical questions, which can be integrated with any topic tested on Part 2: Financial Decision Making. Ethics may be tested in the multiple-choice section, the essay section, or both. Like all other topics, Ethics is eligible to be tested at all three levels of difficulty, requiring you to (1) recall aspects of the Foreign Corrupt Practices Act and IMA Statement of Management Accounting and (2) evaluate and apply the different aspects as they relate to typical business situations. It is also important to understand the differences between illegal and unethical behavior by an organization.

---

3. **Core Concepts:** Core concepts are included at the end of each subunit. The core concepts provide an overview of the key points of each subunit that serve as the foundation for learning. As part of your review, you should make sure that you understand each of them.

CMA TEST PREP SOFTWARE

Twenty-question tests in the **CMA Test Prep** Software will help you to focus on your weaker areas. Make it a game: How much can you improve?

Our CMA Test Prep (in test mode) forces you to commit to your answer choice before looking at answer explanations; thus, you are preparing under true exam conditions. It also keeps track of your time and performance history for each study unit, which is available in either a table or graphical format.

STUDYING WITH BOOKS AND SOFTWARE

Simplify the exam preparation process by following our suggested steps listed below. DO NOT omit the step in which you diagnose the reasons for answering questions incorrectly; i.e., learn from your mistakes while studying so you avoid making similar mistakes on the CMA exam.

1. In test mode, answer a 20-question diagnostic test from each study unit before studying any other information.

2. Study the Knowledge Transfer Outline for the corresponding study unit in your Gleim book.

   a. Place special emphasis on the weaker areas that you identified with the initial diagnostic test in Step 1.

3. Take two or three 20-question tests in test mode after you have studied the Knowledge Transfer Outline.

4. Immediately following each practice test, you will be prompted to review the questions you marked and/or answered incorrectly. For each question, analyze and understand why you were unsure or answered it incorrectly. This step is an essential learning activity.

5. Continue this process until you approach a predetermined proficiency level, e.g., 75%+.

6. Modify this process to suit your individual learning process.

   a. Learning from questions you answer incorrectly is very important. Each question you answer incorrectly should be viewed as an **opportunity** to avoid missing actual test questions on your CMA exam. Thus, you should carefully study the answer explanations provided until you understand why you chose the incorrect answer so you can avoid similar errors on your exam. This study technique is clearly the difference between passing and failing for many CMA candidates.

   b. Also, you **must** determine why you answered questions incorrectly and learn how to avoid the same error in the future. Reasons for missing questions include:

      1) Misreading the requirement (stem)
      2) Not understanding what is required
      3) Making a math error
      4) Applying the wrong rule or concept
      5) Being distracted by one or more of the answers
      6) Incorrectly eliminating answers from consideration
      7) Not having any knowledge of the topic tested
      8) Employing bad intuition when guessing

   c. It is also important to verify that you answered correctly for the right reasons (i.e., read the discussion provided for the correct answer). Otherwise, if the material is tested on the CMA exam in a different manner, you may not answer it correctly.

   d. It is imperative that you complete your predetermined number of study units per week so you can review your progress and realize how attainable a comprehensive CMA review program is when using Gleim CMA Review System. Remember to meet or beat your schedule to give yourself confidence.

GLEIM AUDIO REVIEWS

Gleim CMA Audio Reviews provide an average of 30 minutes of quality review for each study unit. Each review provides an overview of the Knowledge Transfer Outline for each study unit in the *CMA Review* book. The purpose is to get candidates "started" so they can relate to the questions they will answer before reading the study outlines in each study unit.

The audios get to the point, as does the entire Gleim System for Success. We are working to get you through the CMA exam with the minimum time, cost, and frustration. You can listen to two short sample audio reviews on our website at www.gleim.com/accounting/demos/.

FINAL REVIEW: GLEIM CMA PRACTICE EXAM - available Summer 2012

Take a CMA Practice Exam (complimentary with your complete CMA Review System) shortly before you take the actual exam to gain experience in the computer-based exam environment. The Practice Exam is 4 hours (240 minutes) long and contains 100 multiple-choice and 2 essay questions, just like the CMA exam. Therefore, it tests you not only on the content you have studied, but also on the question-answering and time-management techniques you have learned.

For the most realistic practice exam experience, we suggest you complete the entire exam in one sitting, just like the actual CMA exam. Once you have completed the Practice Exam and received your grade, you will be provided with a Review Session that shows which questions were answered incorrectly. Additionally, you will be able to study answer explanations and suggested essay responses to assist you in learning the topics.

TIME-BUDGETING AND QUESTION-ANSWERING TECHNIQUES FOR THE EXAM

Expect 100 multiple-choice questions and 2 essay questions on each part with a 240-minute total time allocation (180 minutes max for multiple-choice questions and at least 60 minutes for the essays). See Study Units 4 and 5 in *CMA Review: A System for Success* for additional discussion of how to maximize your score on multiple-choice questions and essays.

1. **Budget your time.**
   a. We make this point with emphasis. Just as you would fill up your gas tank prior to reaching empty, so too should you finish your exam before time expires.
   b. You have 180 minutes to answer the 100 multiple-choice questions, i.e., 1.8 minutes per question. We suggest you allocate 1.5 minutes per question. This would result in completing 100 questions in 150 minutes to give you 30 minutes to review questions that you have marked.
   c. Before beginning the multiple-choice questions, prepare a Gleim Time Management Sheet as recommended in Study Unit 7 of *CMA Review: A System for Success*.
2. **Answer the questions in consecutive order.**
   a. Do **not** agonize over any one item. Stay within your time budget.
   b. Mark any questions you are unsure of and return to them later as time allows.
   c. Never leave a multiple-choice question unanswered. Make your best educated guess in the time allowed. Remember that your score is based on the number of correct responses. You will not be penalized for guessing incorrectly.

3. **For each multiple-choice question,**

    a. **Try to ignore the answer choices.** Do not allow the answer choices to affect your reading of the question.

        1) If four answer choices are presented, three of them are incorrect. These choices are called **distractors** for good reason. Often, distractors are written to appear correct at first glance until further analysis.

        2) In computational items, the distractors are carefully calculated such that they are the result of making common mistakes. Be careful, and double-check your computations if time permits.

    b. **Read the question** carefully to determine the precise requirement.

        1) Focusing on what is required enables you to ignore extraneous information, to focus on the relevant facts, and to proceed directly to determining the correct answer.

            a) Be especially careful to note when the requirement is an **exception**; e.g., "All of the following statements regarding a company's internal rate of return are true **except**:"

    c. **Determine the correct answer** before looking at the answer choices.

    d. **Read the answer choices carefully.**

        1) Even if the first answer appears to be the correct choice, do **not** skip the remaining answer choices. Questions often ask for the "best" of the choices provided. Thus, each choice requires your consideration.

        2) Treat each answer choice as a true/false question as you analyze it.

    e. **Click on the best answer.**

        1) You have a 25% chance of answering the question correctly by blindly guessing.

        2) For many multiple-choice questions, two answer choices can be eliminated with minimal effort, thereby increasing an educated guess to a 50-50 proposition.

    f. As you answer a question, you can mark it by pressing the "Mark" button or unmark a marked question by pressing the "Marked" button. After you have answered, marked, or looked at and not answered all 100 questions, you will be presented with a review screen that shows how many questions you did not answer and how many you marked. You then have the option of revisiting all of the unanswered questions and "marked" questions.

        1) Go back to the marked questions and finalize your answer choices.

        2) Verify that all questions have been answered.

    g. **If you don't know the answer:**

        1) Again, guess; but make it an educated guess, which means select the best possible answer. First, rule out answers that you think are incorrect. Second, speculate on what the ICMA is looking for and/or the rationale behind the question. Third, select the best answer or guess between equally appealing answers. Your first guess is usually the most intuitive. If you cannot make an educated guess, read the stem and each answer and pick the best or most intuitive answer. It's just a guess!

        2) Make sure you accomplish this step within your predetermined time budget per testlet.

ESSAY QUESTIONS

Each part of the CMA exam contains two essays. You have at least 1 hour to complete both. If you finish your multiple-choice questions section in less than 3 hours, your remaining time will be carried over to the essay section and added to the standard 1-hour allocation. Essay questions that require a purely written answer will have a box in which to type your response. For certain problems that require quantitative responses, you will be able to use a spreadsheet tool to present your calculations. Complete instructions and the ICMA's recommendations regarding the use of the spreadsheet function can be found at www.prometric.com/ICMA/demo.htm.

The following example shows a typical essay question that does not require a quantitative answer.

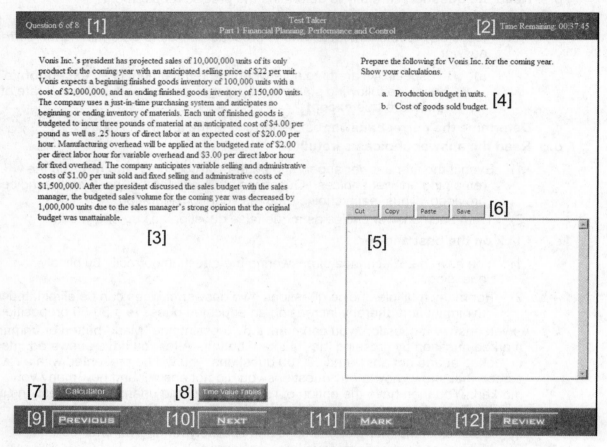

1.   Question Number: The question number indicates which question the candidate is answering out of the total questions in both scenarios.

2.   Time Remaining: This information box displays to the candidate how long (s)he has remaining to complete and review the essays. Consistently check the amount of time remaining in order to stay on schedule.

3.   Scenario: This section displays the content of the current essay's scenario.

4.   Question: This section displays the content of the current question the candidate is answering.

5.   Answer Box: This area is where the candidate types in his/her response to the current question.

6.   Word Processing Tools: These icons, when selected, enable the candidate to cut, copy, paste, and save the content of his/her response (much like a standard word processing program).

7.   Calculator: The calculator provided is a basic tool for simple computations. It is similar to calculators used in common software programs.

8.   Time Value Tables: This function allows the examinee to access Present/Future Time Value Tables as needed.

9.   Previous: This navigation button allows the candidate to move back to the previous question.

10. Next: This navigation button allows the candidate to move ahead to the next question.

11. Mark: This button allows the candidate to mark a question for later review.

12. Review: Clicking this button takes the candidate to the Review screen, which contains a scrollable listing of all the question numbers and indicates if the question has been marked for review, completed, or skipped.

The following example shows a typical essay question that requires a quantitative answer. Note that many of the buttons and functions are the same as in the non-quantitative questions; these have not been explained again below.

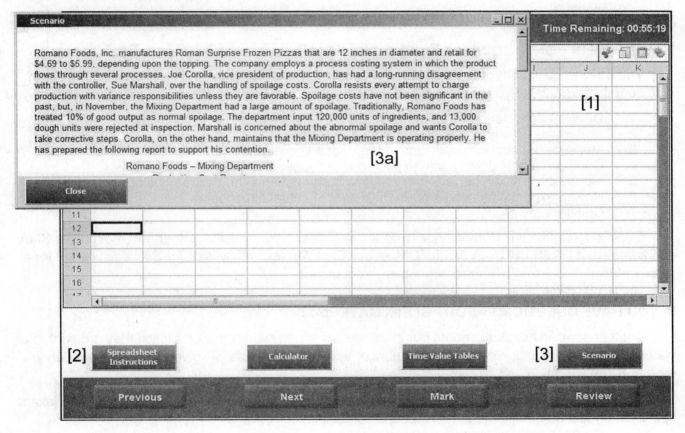

1.   CMA Spreadsheet: This is the area where the candidate types in his/her response to a question that requires computations. Remember that the CMA spreadsheet is NOT Excel. Therefore, even candidates who are extremely proficient in Excel need to practice with the CMA spreadsheets.

2.   Spreadsheet Instructions: The spreadsheet instructions detail the different functions and tools available in the CMA spreadsheet.

3.   Scenario: Clicking this button opens a pop-up window (see [3a]) that shows the content of the current essay's scenario.

ESSAY GRADING

The written-response questions will not be graded online, and therefore, you will not immediately receive your grade. The questions will be graded by subject matter experts, and partial credit will be given. For example, if you are asked to give three reasons why a selected alternative action is good for a business and you provide only two correct reasons, you will receive partial credit for these two responses. Likewise, for questions requiring a calculated response, partial credit will be given for a correct formula even though a mathematical error may have been made in the final number.

The ICMA grades candidates on both subject matter and writing skills on the essay portion of the CMA exam. For writing skills to be graded, the response must be relevant to the question asked. The specific criteria for the ICMA's grading are as follows:

Use of standard English – includes proper grammar, punctuation, and spelling.

Organization – response is arranged logically and coherently.

Clarity – analysis is clearly communicated with well-constructed sentences and appropriate vocabulary.

HOW TO BE IN CONTROL WHILE TAKING THE EXAM

You have to be in control to be successful during exam preparation and execution. Control can also contribute greatly to your personal and other professional goals. Control is a process whereby you

1. Develop expectations, standards, budgets, and plans
2. Undertake activity, production, study, and learning
3. Measure the activity, production, output, and knowledge
4. Compare actual activity with expected and budgeted activity
5. Modify the activity, behavior, or study to better achieve the desired outcome
6. Revise expectations and standards in light of actual experience
7. Continue the process or restart the process in the future

Exercising control will ultimately develop the confidence you need to outperform most other CMA candidates and PASS the CMA exam! Obtain our *CMA Review: A System for Success* booklet for a more detailed discussion of control and other exam tactics.

IF YOU HAVE QUESTIONS ABOUT GLEIM MATERIALS

Content-specific questions about our materials will be answered most rapidly if they are sent to us via email to accounting@gleim.com. Our team of accounting experts will give your correspondence thorough consideration and a prompt response.

Questions regarding the information in this Introduction (study suggestions, studying plans, exam specifics) should be emailed to personalcounselor@gleim.com.

Questions concerning orders, prices, shipments, or payments should be sent via email to customerservice@gleim.com and will be promptly handled by our competent and courteous customer service staff.

For technical support, you may use our automated technical support service at www.gleim.com/support, email us at support@gleim.com, or call us at (800) 874-5346.

STUDY UNIT ONE
ETHICS FOR THE ORGANIZATION
AND BASIC FINANCIAL STATEMENTS

(27 pages of outline)

Organizational Ethics

Ethical issues and considerations are tested in both parts of the CMA exam. In Part 1, ethics is tested from the perspective of the individual, and in Part 2, it is tested from the perspective of the organization. Ethics may be tested in conjunction with any topic area.

Financial Statement Analysis

Management accountants deal with aspects of external financial reporting and thus need to be able to prepare and understand the principal financial statements of a business and to know the limitations of financial statement information. Areas tested on the CMA exam include asset and liability recognition and measurement, equity recognition and measurement, revenue, expenses, extraordinary items, and earnings per share. Knowledge of the SEC and its reporting requirements is also tested, as are annual report contents.

This study unit is the **first of three** on **financial statement analysis**. The relative weight assigned to this major topic in Part 2 of the exam is **25%**. The three study units are

Study Unit 1: Ethics for the Organization and Basic Financial Statements
Study Unit 2: Ratio Analysis
Study Unit 3: Profitability Analysis and Analytical Issues

A portion of this study unit is on **professional ethics**. The relative weight assigned to this major topic in Part 2 of the exam is **5%**.

After studying the outline and answering the questions in this study unit, you will have the skills necessary to address the following topics listed in the ICMA's Learning Outcome Statements:

Ethics may be tested in conjunction with any topic area.

Part 2 – Section E.1. Ethical considerations for the organization

The candidate should be able to:

   a.   identify the purpose of the U.S. Foreign Corrupt Practices Act
   b.   identify the practices that the U.S. Foreign Corrupt Practices Act prohibits, and explain how to apply this Act to typical business situations
   c.   apply relevant provisions of IMA's Statement on Management Accounting, "Values and Ethics: From Inception to Practice" to typical business situations
   d.   discuss corporate responsibility for ethical conduct
   e.   explain why it is important for an organization to have a code of conduct
   f.   demonstrate an understanding of the ways ethical values benefit an organization
   g.   demonstrate an understanding of the differences between ethical and legal behavior
   h.   demonstrate an understanding of role of "leadership by example" or "tone at the top" in determining an organization's ethical environment
   i.   explain the importance of human capital to an organization in creating a climate where "doing the right thing" is expected (i.e., hiring the right people, providing them with training, and practicing consistent values-based leadership)
   j.   explain how an organization's culture impacts its behavioral values
   k.   explain the importance of an organization's core values in explaining its ethical behavior
   l.   discuss the importance of employee training to maintaining an ethical organizational culture
   m.   identify who should receive the employee training, what its focus should be, and what topics the training should cover
   n.   describe the following methods to monitor ethical compliance: human performance feedback loop and survey tools
   o.   explain the importance of a whistleblowing framework (e.g., ethics helpline) to maintaining an ethical organizational culture
   p.   identify the requirements of SOX Section 406 -- Code of Ethics for Senior Financial Officers
   q.   discuss the issues organizations face in applying their values and ethical standards internationally
   r.   demonstrate an understanding of the relationship between ethics and internal controls (comprehensive framework of corporate ethical behavior is a prerequisite for an effective system of internal control)
   s.   describe three tools that can be used to identify process controls related to ethical and behavioral issues

Part 2 – Section A.1. Basic financial statement analysis

For the statement of financial position (balance sheet), the statement of earnings (income statement), statement of cash flows, and the statement of changes in shareholders' equity, the candidate should be able to:

   a.   identify the users of these financial statements and their needs
   b.   demonstrate an understanding of the purposes and uses of each statement
   c.   identify the major components and classifications of each statement
   d.   identify the limitations of each financial statement
   e.   identify, describe, and calculate how a financial transaction affects the elements of each of the financial statements and the resulting impact on financial ratios
   f.   for the statement of cash flows, demonstrate an understanding of the differences between the "direct" and "indirect" methods

g.   for the balance sheet and income statement, prepare and analyze common-size financial statements

h.   for the balance sheet and income statement, prepare and analyze common base-year financial statements (percentage of assets and sales, respectively)

i.   for the balance sheet and income statement, calculate growth of key financial line items

j.   prepare a Statement of Cash Flows using the indirect method

Part 2 – Section A.4. Analytical issues in financial accounting

d.   prepare and/or reconcile the statement of cash flows to the income statement and the balance sheet using the indirect method

 CMA candidates need to be prepared to answer ethical questions, which can be integrated with any topic tested on Part 2: Financial Decision Making. Ethics may be tested in the multiple-choice section, the essay section, or both. Like all other topics, Ethics is eligible to be tested at all three levels of difficulty, requiring you to (1) recall aspects of the Foreign Corrupt Practices Act and IMA Statement of Management Accounting and (2) evaluate and apply the different aspects as they relate to typical business situations. It is also important to understand the differences between illegal and unethical behavior by an organization.

1.1 CORPORATE ETHICS AND LEGISLATION

BACKGROUND to Foreign Corrupt Practices Act

During the Watergate investigations of 1973-74, it was brought to light that U.S. companies were in the practice of handing out bribes to government officials, politicians, and political parties in foreign countries.

The Securities and Exchange Commission (SEC) began its own investigation and, eventually, over 400 U.S. companies admitted paying out an estimated total of over $300 million from secret "slush funds." The most notable firm involved was the aerospace giant Lockheed, which was found to have paid bribes in West Germany, Italy, Japan, the Netherlands, and Saudi Arabia since the late 1950s to ensure purchase by those governments of the company's fighter planes and passenger jets.

The Foreign Corrupt Practices Act (FCPA) was passed by Congress in 1977 in response to these disclosures.

1.   **Foreign Corrupt Practices Act of 1977 (FCPA)**

   a.   The FCPA contains two sets of provisions:

      1)   All public companies must devise and maintain a system of internal accounting control, regardless of whether they have foreign operations.

         a)   This provision has a particular impact on internal and external auditors.

      2)   No domestic concern, including any person acting on its behalf, whether or not doing business overseas and whether or not registered with the SEC, may offer or authorize corrupt payments to any foreign official, foreign political party or official thereof, or candidate for political office in a foreign country.

         a)   Note that only payments to foreign officials and politicians are prohibited; payments to foreign business owners or corporate officers are not addressed by the FCPA.

   b.   Corrupt payments are payments for the purpose of inducing the recipient to act or refrain from acting so that the domestic concern might obtain or retain business.

      1)   The FCPA prohibits a mere offer or promise of a bribe, even if it is not consummated.

         a)   The Act prohibits payment of anything of value; de minimis gifts and tokens of hospitality are acceptable.

      2)   Payments are prohibited if the person making them knew or should have known that some or all of them would be used to influence a governmental official.

3) Individuals found in violation of the FCPA are subject to both fine and imprisonment. A corporation may be assessed a fine as well.

    a) Fines imposed upon individuals may not be paid directly or indirectly by an employer.

c. The FCPA contains an unusual provision that reflects the culturally determined nature of ethics.

  1) During the various investigations leading to passage of the FCPA, it became clear that some of the bribes had been distributed, not to gain unfair advantage, but simply to compete at all.

    a) In some countries, government officials expect to be paid by foreign companies just to perform the duties that would be considered a routine part of their job in the U.S.

  2) Congress became convinced that being prohibited from making such payments would put U.S. firms at a disadvantage.

    a) The antibribery section of the FCPA therefore contains a provision that permits facilitation or "grease" payments when the purpose is to get paperwork processed, secure a license, receive utility service, etc.

  3) Also see item 10. in Subunit 1.2.

BACKGROUND to Sarbanes-Oxley Act

About 25 years after the passage of the FCPA, business ethics were even more in the news than in the mid-1970s. In late 2001 and early 2002, a wave of improper practices came to light. The following table summarizes some of the more prominent ones:

Scandal Became Public	Company	Details
Oct 2001	Enron	Hid debt of over $1 billion in improper off-the-books partnerships
Nov 2001	Arthur Andersen	Shredded documents related to audit of scandal-plagued client Enron
Feb 2002	Global Crossing	Inflated revenues, shredded accounting-related documents
Feb 2002	Qwest	Inflated revenues
Mar 2002	WorldCom	Booked operating expenses as capital expenses; large off-the-books payments to founder
Apr 2002	Adelphia	Booked operating expenses as capital expenses; hid debt
Jun 2002	Xerox	Inflated revenues

2. **Sarbanes-Oxley Act of 2002 (SOX)**

a. In response to the scandals described above, SOX imposes extensive new responsibilities on issuers of publicly traded securities and their auditors.

b. The most significant provision of SOX regarding ethics is Section 406(a), which requires any company issuing securities

*...to disclose whether or not, and if not, the reason therefor, such issuer has adopted a **code of ethics for senior financial officers**, applicable to its principal financial officer and comptroller or principal accounting officer, or persons performing similar functions.*

    c.   Section 406(c) defines "code of ethics" as

> *...such standards as are reasonably necessary to promote (1) honest and ethical conduct, including the ethical handling of actual or apparent conflicts of interest between personal and professional relationships; (2) full, fair, accurate, timely, and understandable disclosure in the periodic reports required to be filed by the issuer; and (3) compliance with applicable governmental rules and regulations.*

    d.   Note that SOX does not define "ethics" itself; it simply takes an understanding of the concept for granted. This reflects the difficulty of legislating a sense of ethics.

Stop and review! You have completed the outline for this subunit. Study multiple-choice questions 1 through 6 beginning on page 44.

1.2 CORPORATE RESPONSIBILITY FOR ETHICAL BEHAVIOR

IMA's Statement on Management Accounting "Values and Ethics: From Inception to Practice," published in 2008, is a useful document for understanding ethical concepts in an organizational context. Quotations from this document are integrated into the outline below and on the following pages.

1.   The **organization has a responsibility** to foster a sense of ethics in its employees and agents. All organizations need a code of conduct.

> *If no defined code of conduct and ethical behavior is developed, employees will act on their own beliefs and values, or they will observe and emulate the behavior they see around them on a daily basis. (II. Introduction)*

2.   A pervasive sense of ethical values can **benefit an organization**.

> *In the past, quality compliance and industrially engineered output expectations helped exert a high level of control over direct-production employees ...*
>
> *In today's service economy, control often involves developing management systems that include the flowcharting, mapping, and documentation of processes, activities, and tasks so that individuals know what to do "on the job." This works well when everything proceeds as anticipated, but what does an employee do when unplanned events occur? What reference does an individual look to for help in making decisions? To take a phrase from the pioneering work done in process management by Geary Rummler and Alan Brache (1995), what does one do "in the white spaces"? In most cases, an organization relies on the judgment of the individual and/or direct supervisor to develop a course of action that they feel represents the "policy" of the organization. This is why it is important to have a defined set of organizational values and code of ethics — they create the "touchstone" against which every unanticipated decision must be judged. Failure to have every individual in the organization know and understand these values and ethical code leads to inconsistency and, in the worst cases, unethical or fraudulent behavior. (IV. Values, Ethics, and Accounting)*

3.   A sense of ethics requires an ability to **distinguish between ethical and merely legal behavior**.

> *Many individuals at the center of corporate scandals [of the late 20th and early 21st Century] have professed the belief that they were innocent of any wrongdoing, including Kenneth Lay of Enron or Conrad Black of Hollinger. The problem is that these individuals did not define their behavior by what most of society would see as "reasonable," but rather they followed their own particular code—in some cases, limiting the definition of ethical behavior to require compliance with the law and nothing more. (II. Introduction)*

4. **"Leadership by example,"** or "tone at the top," plays an important role in determining an organization's ethical environment.

    Ethical behavior is not something that applies to someone else — every single individual is responsible for behaving ethically. Nowhere is this more important than the demonstration of ethical behavior that managers and supervisors exhibit in the way they execute their day-to-day work ...

    Many of us in today's workforce have seen organizations operating with a lack of ethical commitment. As a result, there often is a high level of skepticism toward what is said by those in management and leadership positions: People tend to believe what they see rather than what they are told in the company "pep talk." In order for a code of ethics to be effective, its application must be demonstrated by those in positions of power and leadership. Leaders must be seen living and managing by the code of ethics. (VI. Leadership by Example)

5. **The concept of "human capital"** is important to an organization in creating a climate where "doing the right thing" is expected.

    In most organizations today, labor costs constitute the majority of operating expenses. Efforts to reduce overhead have led to decentralization of operating decisions and the slimming down of supervision. The result is that employees cannot be watched and controlled in every aspect of their work, and an organization must, to a great degree, trust that its employees are acting in its best interests. Human "capital" is a critical asset. Humans create the innovation that generates new products or services and finds unique ways to undertake work in more cost-effective ways. They bring knowledge to the workplace and share it with coworkers. People develop relationships with each other and with suppliers, clients, and others on whom the organization depends. Top leadership in particular creates a climate and culture in which such productive applications of human skills can be optimized to the highest level.

    In organizations where capital investment is a key component of activity ... [a]ccountants would think little of carrying out detailed DCF/ROI calculations and developing models, spreadsheets, and simulations to verify the asset's potential performance. The goal of this planning and analysis is to optimize the investment and reduce the risk of a poor decision. If hiring decisions and employee orientation and training fail to address the alignment of individual values and ethics with organizational expectations, the result can be an equal, if not greater, negative impact on an organization's performance. Unmotivated employees can poison the atmosphere and reduce the teamwork and cooperation required for knowledge transfer and innovation, and they can have a significant negative impact on relationships with suppliers and customers. (IV. Values, Ethics, and Accounting)

    An organizational code of ethics must therefore be used as a benchmark for hiring decisions. This ensures candidates have a personal code that aligns with the organizational expectations. (VI. Leadership by Example)

6.   An **organization's culture** impacts its behavioral values.

*Every organization already has a culture. In smaller companies —
particularly family-owned businesses — the culture reflects the personal
values and business methods of the owners and primary operators. In larger
companies, it is more difficult to convey the proper culture from the top. One
of the most significant risks in very large organizations, in fact, is that the
culture (and, by definition, the values and ethics) that the board of directors
and senior management believe to exist within the company may be different
from the actual culture experienced by employees, clients, and suppliers. In
other words, upper management's perception of the culture is not reality.*

*Step one in establishing an ethical culture must be an assessment of the
existing organizational values and culture and the development of a set of
statements that define the principles the organization believes in and should
act upon. These statements and principles can be developed by the
shareholders, the board, or a governing body within the organization.
(V. Defining and Developing the Organization's Behavioral Values)*

7.   **Employee training** is important to maintaining an ethical organizational culture.

*Although orientation must be provided to every employee at the time of
hiring, it is not enough to maintain awareness and commitment to the
application of a code of ethics in the workplace. Every existing member of
staff should receive ongoing training, starting at the board level and
cascading down throughout the organization ... Ethics training for employees
should focus on covering ethical concepts, the organization's code, and
compliance. To achieve this, training should include:*

• Ethical concepts and thinking: What is "behind" the issue of ethical action?
• The organization's code of ethics and any supporting "rules"
(VIII. Practical Application: Converting Intent into Operational Reality)

8.   **Two methods for monitoring** ethical compliance are

   a.   **Human performance feedback loop**

*Performance review and development systems must be fully aligned
with the requirements for ethical conduct. Competencies, job
descriptions, and objectives should include ethical expectations, and
the regular employee review systems (conducted on an annual basis at
minimum) must assess employees against the same criteria. If the
code of ethics dictates that employees treat all others with dignity and
respect, then the review process must include 360° input — including
both internal and external responses — in order to assess whether that
is truly happening. Key Performance Indicators (KPIs) must include
tracking of employees against ethical training requirements. Examples
include:*

*   • The number of new hires and percentage who completed orientation
      within required time frame*
*   • Percentage of employees who completed annual refresher training
      on ethical conduct*
*   • Number of employees scoring "achieved" and "exceeded" on annual
      reviews in ethics criteria*
*   • Number of employees given an award for noted ethical conduct*
(IX. Measuring and Improving Ethical Compliance)

b.   **Survey tools**

> *Ongoing surveys are very valuable tools for assessing ethical performance, especially in areas such as management and leadership. Surveys can be created using the organization's code of ethics and asking employees to rate how well the organization is following the contents...*
>
> *Respondents can be asked to rate each statement on a scale of 1 through 5 or from "Strongly Disagree" to "Strongly Agree." The results become the basis for developing ongoing compliance indicators and can be used to stimulate dialogue with employees about their concerns and the possible courses of action that could be taken to improve ethical compliance. This turns the company into learning and developing organization. (IX. Measuring and Improving Ethical Compliance)*

9.   A **whistleblowing framework** (e.g., an ethics helpline) is an important component in maintaining an ethical organizational culture.

> *An effective feedback system includes having a confidential framework for employees to report possible violations of the organization's code of ethics and to receive advice on the ethical aspects of challenging decisions. Statistics show that a large number of occupational fraud cases are detected through an employee "hotline" or other reporting method ...*
>
> *Whichever approach an organization chooses, the collection, analysis, and summarization of ethics issues can provide insight into the operation of its code of ethics and the degree to which employees are following it. In addition, tracking and monitoring issues raised through a whistleblowing framework creates opportunities to enhance and improve internal controls. Management accountants need to ensure that such processes are in place, that they operate on a fully confidential basis, and that they are capable of generating statistical or event-based reporting through which insight into ethical practice can be created. (IX. Measuring and Improving Ethical Compliance)*

10.   Organizations face particular challenges in applying their values and ethical standards **internationally**.

> *When groups share the same cultural background, they tend to share the same values as well. Consequently, the basis for decision making and actions, including alignment with a code of ethical conduct, will be similar. When immigration combines groups from dissimilar countries or backgrounds, the impact can be significant, and the values and decision making processes may not be the same. It has nothing to do with a person being "good" or "bad," but rather is a matter of differing "norms" of behavior based on the society in which that person grew up. This situation is also observable when individuals go abroad to receive an education.*
>
> *... The challenge of conflicting values becomes greatest in cases where a society has, for example, a limited separation of "state and religion." While most of the Western world professes to maintain a barrier between church and state, a number of countries in other parts of the world have a far greater integration of the two. In many cases, this creates national conflict when the two find themselves in disagreement on various issues.*
>
> *All of these changes lead to a melting pot of personal values within societies and organizations, creating profound challenges for leaders and resulting in a new aspect of risk management for organizations. If organizations fail to make the effort to clearly define their expectations of ethical behavior and provide support and encouragement for complying with them, then the vacuum that is left will lead to unpredictable results. (II. Introduction)*

11. A comprehensive framework of corporate **ethical behavior** is a prerequisite for an effective system of **internal control**.

> *CEOs and CFOs have to place their own integrity on the line by attesting to compliance with an adequate level of internal controls (as well as all other certifications). Creating a thorough, integrated system for developing, implementing, sustaining, and monitoring ethical performance within the organization will allow executives to make such declarations with confidence that a code of ethics is the foundation of the organization's culture and is fully integrated into the thinking process of every employee and business partner. (IX. Measuring and Improving Ethical Compliance)*

12. **Three tools** that can be used to identify process controls related to ethical and behavioral issues

- **Business Process Reengineering** *(BPR), which became popular in the 1990s, provides a structured view of organizational processes and reveals the existence of tasks and activities that are carried out in order to transform inputs into outputs. At each task and activity level, there are potential risks that the management accountant will want to consider. In all cases, however, the behavioral aspects must provide a context for the risk and its control.*

- **Quality Management** *provides another view of process management that can provide management accountants with an excellent variety of options that assist in creating greater visibility on process performance and risk. In fact, quality management and management accounting have much in common. The quality manager seeks to ensure that a process achieves "zero defects" by avoiding unplanned mistakes and costly rework. This includes ensuring that any potential risks that can lead to mistakes occurring or not being identified are assessed and evaluated — goals shared by management accountants ...*

  Using this tool and considering risk from a behavioral aspect can assist in identifying what types of controls should be in place and where they would be best provided. Rather than relying on traditional accounting approaches such as control batch totals, authorization and security levels, etc., this approach uses the perspective of behavioral deviation from an anticipated norm.

- **Continual Process Improvement** *(CPI) is the third area that can significantly contribute to identifying process controls related to ethical and behavioral issues. This concept relates to the development of a "learning organization" — where continual monitoring and assessment of process performance leads to the identification of potential process management and control issues ... As an organization progresses — hiring new employees or adapting itself to competitive pressures — the business environment changes. These changes have the potential to make current internal controls ineffective or unacceptable. For example, as the workforce changes, the traditional reliance on the behavior of experienced staff may no longer be sufficient; new staff may not behave in a way that achieves the desired outcomes — especially if there is an inadequate approach to ethical hiring, leadership, and compliance. (VII. Ethics and Internal Controls)*

Stop and review! You have completed the outline for this subunit. Study multiple-choice questions 7 through 9 beginning on page 45.

1.3 BASIC FINANCIAL STATEMENTS AND THEIR USERS

1. **Four Basic Financial Statements**

   a. Statement of financial position ("balance sheet")
   b. Statement of earnings ("income statement")
   c. Statement of cash flows
   d. Statement of changes in shareholders' equity ("statement of retained earnings")

2. **Changes in Equity**

   a. Disclosures of changes in equity and in the number of shares of equity securities are necessary whenever financial position and results of operations are presented.

      1) These disclosures may occur in the basic statements, in the notes thereto, or in separate statements.

   b. **Comprehensive income** must be displayed in a financial statement given the same prominence as the other statements, but no specific format is required.

3. **Features of Financial Statements**

   a. The basic financial statements and notes of a business enterprise serve as vehicles for achieving the objectives of financial reporting.

      1) Supplementary information (e.g., on changing prices) and various other means of financial reporting (such as management's discussion and analysis) are also useful.

   b. The basic financial statements complement each other.

      1) They describe different aspects of the same transactions.
      2) More than one statement is necessary to provide information for a specific economic decision.

   c. The elements of one statement articulate (are interrelated) with those of other statements.

      1) The balance sheet reports assets, liabilities, equity, and investments by owners at a moment in time.

         a) The statement of income and statement of retained earnings report revenues, expenses, gains, losses, and distributions to owners over a period of time.

      2) The elements in the first group are changed by those in the second group and are their cumulative result:

Beginning balance	(Balance sheet)
+/– Changes during the period	(Statements of income and retained earnings)
Ending balance	(Balance sheet)

      3) Accordingly, financial statements that report the first type of elements articulate with those reporting the second type and vice versa.

      4) The notes are considered part of the basic financial statements.

         a) They amplify or explain information recognized in the statements and are an integral part of statements prepared in accordance with GAAP.

         b) Notes should not be used to correct improper presentations.

4. **Users of Financial Statements**

   a. Users may directly or indirectly have an economic interest in a specific business.

      1) Users with direct interests usually invest in or manage the business, and users with indirect interests advise, influence, or represent users with direct interests.

   b. Users with direct interests include

      1) Investors or potential investors
      2) Suppliers and creditors
      3) Employees
      4) Management

   c. Users having indirect interests include

      1) Financial advisers and analysts
      2) Stock markets or exchanges
      3) Regulatory authorities

   d. Internal users use financial statements to make decisions affecting the operations of the business. These users include management, employees, and the board of directors.

      1) Management needs financial statements to assess financial strengths and deficiencies, to evaluate performance results and past decisions, and to plan for future financial goals and steps toward accomplishing them.
      2) Employees want financial information to negotiate wages and fringe benefits based on the increased productivity and value they provide to a profitable firm.

   e. External users use financial statements to determine whether doing business with the firm will be beneficial.

      1) Investors need information to decide whether to increase, decrease, or obtain an investment in a firm.
      2) Creditors need information to determine whether to extend credit and under what terms.
      3) Financial advisers and analysts need financial statements to help investors evaluate particular investments.
      4) Stock exchanges need financial statements to evaluate whether to accept a firm's stock for listing or whether to suspend the stock's trading.
      5) Regulatory agencies may need financial statements to evaluate the firm's conformity with regulations and to determine price levels in regulated industries.

5. **Limitations of Financial Statements**

   a. Balance Sheet

      1) The balance sheet shows a company's financial position at a single point in time; accounts may vary significantly a few days before or after the publication of the balance sheet.
      2) Also, many balance sheet items, such as fixed assets, are valued at historical costs, which may bear no resemblance to the current value of those items. Even those assets reported at their current fair values may not always faithfully represent what a company could sell those items for on an open market.
      3) Also, contingent liabilities are not always shown on the balance sheet; in some cases, liabilities may arise that were not expected.

b.   Income Statement

1)   The income statement does not always show all items of income and expense. For example, some items of "other comprehensive income," such as foreign exchange translation adjustments, are not reported in the calculation of net income.

2)   Instead, these items are reported on a statement of other comprehensive income, which is usually effectively hidden on the statement of stockholders' equity.

c.   Statement of Cash Flows

1)   The accounting frameworks in common use do not always agree on what is an operating flow and what is an investment or financing flow.

2)   In addition, some analysts complain that the option to use the indirect method of reporting cash flows (which is used by approximately 97% of reporting companies) instead of the direct method may be hiding important information.

d.   Statement of Changes in Stockholders' Equity (or Retained Earnings Statement)

1)   This statement is rather straightforward, but many investors ignore it. Thus, the biggest limitation is user ignorance.

2)   Since the statement of stockholders' equity typically includes items of other comprehensive income, it is important that users examine the statement closely.

Stop and review! You have completed the outline for this subunit. Study multiple-choice questions 10 through 15 beginning on page 47.

1.4 STATEMENT OF FINANCIAL POSITION (BALANCE SHEET)

1.   **Purpose, Elements, and Formats**

a.   According to the Financial Accounting Standards Board's (FASB's) Conceptual Framework, the statement of financial position (balance sheet) "provides information about an entity's assets, liabilities, and equity and their relationships to each other at a moment in time."

1)   It helps users to assess "the entity's liquidity, financial flexibility, profitability, and risk."

b.   The elements of the balance sheet make up a detailed presentation of the basic accounting equation for a business enterprise:

$$Assets = Liabilities + Equity$$

1)   The left side of the equation depicts the enterprise's resource structure. The right side depicts the financing structure.

2)   Balance sheet accounts are real (permanent) accounts. Their balances carry over from one period to the next.

3)   The equation is based on the proprietary theory. The owners' equity in an enterprise (residual interest) is what remains after the economic obligations of the enterprise are subtracted from its economic resources.

c.   The format of the balance sheet is not standardized, and any method that promotes full disclosure and understandability is acceptable.

1)   The account (or horizontal) form presents the resource structure on the left and the financing structure on the right.

2)   The report (or vertical) form is also commonly used. It differs from the account form only in that liabilities and equity are below rather than beside assets.

2. **The Resource Structure -- A Firm's Assets**

    a. **Current assets** consist of "cash and other assets or resources commonly identified as reasonably expected to be realized in cash or sold or consumed during the normal operating cycle of the business."

        1) The **operating cycle** is the average time between the acquisition of resources and the final receipt of cash from their sale as the culmination of the entity's revenue-generating activities (discussed in detail in Study Unit 2, Subunit 3).

            a) If the operating cycle is less than a year, 1 year is the basis for defining current and noncurrent assets.

        2) Current assets are usually presented in descending order of liquidity.

Current assets:	
Cash and equivalents	$ 10,000
Short-term investments	586,000
Receivables	22,000
Inventories	112,000
Prepaid expenses	6,000
Total current assets	$736,000

    b. **Noncurrent assets** are usually presented in an order determined by convention rather than by liquidity.

        1) **Long-term investments** and funds typically include

            a) Investments in securities intended to be held on a long-term basis

            b) Restricted funds, such as bond sinking funds or plant expansion funds

            c) Cash surrender value of life insurance policies

            d) Capital assets not used in current operations, such as idle facilities or land held for a future plant site or for speculative purposes

        2) **Property, plant, and equipment (PPE)** consist of tangible items used in operations.

            a) PPE are recorded at cost and are shown net of accumulated depreciation if depreciable. They include

                i) Land and depletable natural resources, e.g., oil and gas reserves

                ii) Buildings, machinery, equipment, furniture, fixtures, leasehold improvements, land improvements, leased assets held under capital leases, and other depreciable assets

        3) **Intangible assets** are defined as nonfinancial assets without physical substance.

            a) Examples are patents, copyrights, trademarks, trade names, franchises, and purchased goodwill.

        4) **Other noncurrent assets** include noncurrent assets not readily classifiable elsewhere. Accordingly, there is little uniformity of treatment. Among the items typically reported as other assets are

            a) Long-term receivables arising from unusual transactions, e.g., loans to officers or employees and sales of capital assets

            b) Bond issue costs

            c) Machinery rearrangement costs (also classifiable as PPE)

            d) Long-term prepayments

            e) Deferred tax assets arising from interperiod tax allocation

5) The category deferred charges (long-term prepayments) appears on some balance sheets.

    a) Many of these items, for example, bond issue costs and rearrangement costs, which involve long-term prepayments, are frequently classified as other assets.

3. **The Financing Structure -- A Firm's Liabilities and Owners' Equity**

  a. **Current liabilities** are "obligations whose liquidation is reasonably expected to require the use of existing resources properly classifiable as current assets, or the creation of other current liabilities."

    1) Their order of presentation is usually governed by nearness to maturity.

Current liabilities:	
Accounts payable	$ 2,181
Wages payable	11,015
Notes payable	10,500
Unearned revenues	6,187
Income taxes payable	9,055
Current maturities of long-term debt	5,000
Total current liabilities	$43,938

    a) Accounts and wages payable result from the acquisition of goods and services.

    b) Notes payable are tools of short-term cash generation.

    c) Unearned revenues represent cash received in advance of the delivery of goods (such as subscriptions) or performance of services (such as a legal retainer fee).

    d) Income taxes payable are liabilities to various levels of government for revenues recognized in the past.

    e) Current maturities of long-term debt are that portion of long-term debt (e.g., bonds issued) that must be retired using current assets.

    2) Because current liabilities require the use of current assets or the creation of other current liabilities, they do not include

      a) Short-term obligations intended to be refinanced on a long-term basis when the ability to consummate the refinancing has been demonstrated

        i) This ability is demonstrated by a post-balance-sheet-date issuance of long-term debt or by entering into a financing agreement that meets certain criteria.

      b) Debts to be paid from funds accumulated in accounts classified as noncurrent assets

        i) Hence, a liability for bonds payable in the next period will not be classified as current if payment is to be from a noncurrent fund.

  b. **Noncurrent liabilities** include the noncurrent portions of the following:

Noncurrent liabilities:	
Long-term notes payable ($100,000 face amount, net of unamortized discount of $12,857)	$ 87,143
Bonds payable ($2,000,000 face amount, net of unamortized premium of $100,000)	2,100,000
Liabilities under capital leases	212,456
Pension obligations	1,277,450
Deferred tax liability arising from interperiod tax allocation	99,011
Obligations under product or service warranty agreements	12,094
Advances for long-term commitments to provide goods or services	6,107
Advances from affiliated entities	6,998
Deferred revenue	1,024
Total noncurrent liabilities	$3,802,283

    c.   **Equity** of a business enterprise is the residual interest after total liabilities are deducted from total assets.

Stockholders' equity:	
Contributed capital:	
Preferred stock, 6% cumulative, no par,	
50,000 shares authorized and outstanding	$2,000,000
Common stock, $1 par, 10,000,000 shares	
authorized, 8,000,000 issued and outstanding	8,000,000
Additional contributed capital	357,000
Total contributed capital	$10,357,000
Retained earnings	1,358,449
Treasury stock, at cost, 500,000 common shares	(645,000)
Accumulated other comprehensive income, net	12,707
Total stockholders' equity	$11,083,156

        1)   Preferred stock (if any) is generally listed first since it stands first in line during liquidation.

            a)   The par value (if any), dividend percentage, cumulative and/or participating status, number of shares authorized, and number of shares outstanding are reported.

        2)   Common stock is issued by every corporation.

            a)   The par value, number of shares authorized, and number of shares outstanding are reported.

        3)   Additional paid-in (contributed) capital is the amount received in excess of par value at the time stock was sold.

            a)   A single total is presented for all classes of stock combined.

        4)   Paid-in (contributed) capital is the total amount provided by the firm's shareholders.

        5)   Retained earnings can be restricted or unrestricted depending on the board of directors' intent.

            a)   Restricted retained earnings do not constitute a pool of resources; they are simply an indication of their unavailability for disbursement as dividends.

        6)   Treasury stock is the firm's own stock that has been repurchased either to shrink the breadth of the firm's ownership base or to have a pool of stock to disburse in the form of dividends.

            a)   Treasury stock is reported either at cost (as a deduction from total equity) or at par (as a direct reduction of the relevant contributed capital account). A corporation can never report its own stock as an asset.

4. **Major Note Disclosures**

    a.   The first footnote accompanying any set of complete financial statements is generally one describing significant accounting policies, such as the use of estimates and rules for revenue recognition.

    b.   Footnote disclosures and schedules specifically related to the balance sheet include

        1)   Investment securities
        2)   Property, plant, and equipment holdings
        3)   Maturity patterns of bond issues
        4)   Significant uncertainties, such as pending litigation
        5)   Details of capital stock issues

Stop and review! You have completed the outline for this subunit. Study multiple-choice questions 16 through 20 beginning on page 49.

1.5 STATEMENT OF INCOME AND STATEMENT OF RETAINED EARNINGS

1. **Elements of Income Statement**

   a. The results of operations are reported in the income statement (statement of earnings) on the accrual basis using an approach oriented to historical transactions.

      1) The traditional income statement reports the results of activities during a period of time.

      Revenues – Expenses + Gains – Losses = Income (Loss)

   b. Revenue and expense accounts are nominal (temporary) accounts. They are zeroed out (closed) periodically and their balances transferred to real (permanent) accounts on the balance sheet.

      1) Revenues and expenses stem from a firm's central and ongoing operations.
      2) Gains and losses report the results of peripheral or incidental transactions.

2. **Transactions Included in Income**

   a. All transactions affecting the net change in equity during the period are included except

      1) Transactions with owners
      2) Prior-period adjustments
      3) Items reported initially in other comprehensive income
      4) Transfers to and from appropriated retained earnings
      5) Adjustments made in a quasi-reorganization

   b. This treatment reflects the all-inclusive approach to reporting income.

3. **Income Statement Formats**

   a. The single-step income statement provides one grouping for revenue items and one for expense items. The single step is the one subtraction necessary to arrive at net income.

Bonilla Company
Income Statement
For Year Ended December 31, Year 1

Revenues:		
Net sales	$XXX	
Other revenues	XXX	
Gains	XXX	
Total revenues		$ XXX
Expenses:		
Costs of goods sold	$XXX	
Selling and administrative expenses	XXX	
Interest expense	XXX	
Losses	XXX	
Income tax expense	XXX	
Total expenses		XXX
Net income		$ XXX
Earnings per common share		$Y.YY

b.   The multiple-step income statement matches operating revenues and expenses in a
     section separate from nonoperating items, enhancing disclosure by presenting
     intermediary totals rather than one net income figure.

Willis Company
Income Statement
For Year Ended December 31, Year 1

Revenues:		
Gross sales		$ XXX
Less: Sales discounts	$XXX	
Sales returns and allowances	XXX	XXX
Net sales		$ XXX
Cost of goods sold:		
Beginning inventory		$XXX
Purchases	$XXX	
Less: Purchase returns and discounts	XXX	
Net purchases	$XXX	
Transportation-in	XXX	XXX
Goods available for sale		$XXX
Less: Ending inventory		XXX
Cost of goods sold		XXX
Gross profit		$ XXX
Operating expenses:		
Selling expenses:		
Sales salaries and commissions	$XXX	
Freight-out	XXX	
Travel	XXX	
Advertising	XXX	
Office supplies	XXX	XXX
Administrative expenses:		
Executive salaries	XXX	
Professional salaries	XXX	
Wages	XXX	
Depreciation	XXX	
Office supplies	XXX	XXX
Total operating expenses		XXX
Income from operations		$ XXX
Other revenues and gains:		
Dividend revenue	$XXX	XXX
Other expenses and losses:		
Interest expense	$XXX	
Loss on disposal of equipment	XXX	XXX
Income before taxes *		$ XXX
Income taxes		XXX
Net income *		$ XXX
Earnings per common share		$Y.YY

* If discontinued operations were being reported, these captions would have been "Income
from continuing operations before taxes" and "Income from continuing operations,"
respectively.

c. The condensed income statement includes only the section totals of the multiple-step format.

Marzullo Company
Income Statement
For Year Ended December 31, Year 1

Net sales		$ XXX
Cost of goods sold		XXX
Gross profit		$ XXX
Selling expenses	$XXX	
Administrative expenses	XXX	XXX
Income from operations		$ XXX
Other revenues and gains		XXX
Other expenses and losses		XXX
Income before taxes *		$ XXX
Income taxes		XXX
Net income *		$ XXX
Earnings per common share		$Y.YY

* If discontinued operations were being reported, these captions would have been "Income from continuing operations before taxes" and "Income from continuing operations," respectively.

4. **Typical Items of Cost and Expense**

a. Cost of Goods

1) **Cost of goods sold** equals cost of goods manufactured (or purchases for a retailer) adjusted for the change in finished goods inventory. Adding beginning inventory to purchases produces goods available for sale.

2) **Cost of goods manufactured** is equivalent to a retailer's purchases. It equals all manufacturing costs incurred during the period, plus beginning work-in-process, minus ending work-in-process. It also may be stated as cost of goods sold, plus ending finished goods inventory, minus beginning finished goods inventory.

b. Other Expenses

1) Selling expenses are those incurred in selling or marketing.

a) Examples include sales representatives' salaries, rent for sales department, commissions, and traveling expense; advertising; sales department salaries and expenses; samples; and credit and collection costs. Shipping costs are also often classified as selling costs.

2) General and administrative expenses are incurred for the direction of the enterprise as a whole and are not related wholly to a specific function, e.g., selling or manufacturing.

a) They include accounting, legal, and other fees for professional services; officers' salaries; insurance; wages of office staff; miscellaneous supplies; and office occupancy costs.

3) Interest expense is recognized based on the passage of time. In the case of bonds, notes, and capital leases, the effective interest method is used.

5. **Reporting Irregular Items**

a. When an enterprise reports discontinued operations or extraordinary items, these must be presented in a separate section after income from continuing operations.

    b. **Discontinued operations** are reported in two components:

        1) Income or loss from operations of the division from the first day of the reporting period until the date of disposal

        2) Gain or loss on the disposal of the divisions

    c. **Extraordinary items** must meet two criteria:

        1) To be considered extraordinary, an item must be both unusual in nature and infrequent in occurrence in the environment in which the entity operates.

        2) Write-downs of receivables and inventories, translation of foreign currency amounts, disposal of a segment, sale of productive assets, effects of strikes, and accruals on long-term contracts can never be considered extraordinary.

    d. Because these items are reported after the presentation of income taxes, they must be shown net of tax.

    e. Appropriate per share amounts must be disclosed, either on the face of the statement or in the accompanying notes.

    f. EXAMPLE of reporting discontinued operations and extraordinary items:

Income from continuing operations		$XXX
Discontinued operations:		
Income from operations of divested division,		
net of applicable income taxes of $XXX	$XXX	
Loss on disposal of divested division,		
net of applicable income taxes of $XXX	XXX	XXX
Income before extraordinary item		$XXX
Extraordinary item:		
Loss from volcanic eruption,		
net of applicable income taxes of $XXX		XXX
Net income		$XXX
Per share of common stock:		
Income from continuing operations		$Y.YY
Income from operations of divested division, net of tax		Y.YY
Loss on disposal of divested division, net of tax		(Y.YY)
Income before extraordinary item		$Y.YY
Extraordinary loss, net of tax		(Y.YY)
Net income		$Y.YY

6. **Results of All Operations**

    a. The income statement and the **statement of retained earnings** (presented separately or combined) are designed to broadly reflect the results of operations.

        1) Most entities report changes in retained earnings in a statement of changes in equity or a separate statement.

        2) The statement of retained earnings consists of beginning retained earnings, plus or minus any prior-period adjustments (net of tax); net income (loss); dividends paid or declared; and certain other rare items, e.g., quasi-reorganizations. The final amount is ending retained earnings.

    b. EXAMPLE of reporting changes in retained earnings:

Retained earnings, Jan. 1, as originally reported	$XXX
Correction for overstatement of depreciation expense	
in prior period	XXX
Retained earnings, Jan. 1, as restated	$XXX
Net income	XXX
Cash dividends paid	(XXX)
Retained earnings, Dec. 31	$XXX

    c.   The retained earnings balance is sometimes divided into appropriated and unappropriated amounts.

        1)   A quasi-reorganization eliminates a deficit in retained earnings through reductions in other capital accounts. It accomplishes in a simpler way the same purpose as a legal reorganization. Elimination of the deficit permits a company to pay dividends.

7.   **Comprehensive Income**

    a.   Certain income items are excluded from the calculation of net income and instead are included in comprehensive income.

        1)   Requiring these items to be included in net income would be misleading. They typically represent valuation adjustments, not independent economic events.

    b.   **Other comprehensive income (OCI)** is the subtotal of all these items of comprehensive income that are not included in net income.

        1)   The three principal items of comprehensive income are typically

            a)   Changes in the fair values of available-for-sale securities

            b)   Foreign currency translation adjustments

            c)   The prior service cost and gains and losses not recognized in pension expense

    c.   All components of comprehensive income must be reported in a financial statement displayed with the same prominence as the other statements.

        1)   No specific format is required, but reporting the components of OCI and comprehensive income below net income is encouraged.

        2)   EXAMPLE of separate statement of comprehensive income

Bonilla Company
Statement of Comprehensive Income
For Year Ended December 31, Year 1

Net income		$XXX
Other comprehensive income (net of tax):		
Foreign currency translation adjustment	$XXX	
Prior service cost not included in pension expense	XXX	
Unrealized holding loss on available-for-sale securities	(XXX)	XXX
Comprehensive income		$XXX

8.   **Major Note Disclosures**

    a.   Note disclosures and schedules specifically related to the income statement include the following:

        1)   Earnings per share
        2)   Depreciation schedules
        3)   Components of income tax expense
        4)   Components of pension expense

Stop and review! You have completed the outline for this subunit. Study multiple-choice questions 21 through 25 beginning on page 50.

1.6 STATEMENT OF CASH FLOWS -- CONTENTS

1. **Purpose**

   a. If an entity reports financial position and results of operations, it must present a statement of cash flows for any period for which results of operations are presented. The statement of cash flows is thus part of a full set of financial statements.

      1) Cash flow per share, however, is not reported.

   b. The primary purpose of a statement of cash flows is to provide information about the cash receipts and payments of an entity during a period. A secondary purpose is to provide information about operating, investing, and financing activities.

   c. The statement of cash flows classifies cash receipts and disbursements into one of three categories.

      1) The proper classification can be generalized as follows:

Classification	Source
Operating activities	Income statement
Investing activities	Investment securities and noncurrent assets
Financing activities	Noncurrent liabilities and equity

2. **Operating Activities**

   a. Operating activities include the effects of transactions involved in the determination of net income. These typically include

      1) Cash receipts from the delivery of goods or the performance of services

      2) Cash payments to suppliers for inventory, employees for wages, and governments for taxes

      3) Cash receipts from interest and dividends on investments and from interest on loans to others (e.g., trade credit extended, bondholders)

         a) Even though these are investing activities, their cash effects are included in operating activities because they go into the calculation of net income.

For the purpose of the CMA exam, you will be expected to demonstrate an understanding of both "direct" and "indirect" methods for statement of cash flows. As a CMA candidate, you will be expected to know the application of both methods. To provide a more focused approach to studying these types of questions and others pertaining to the statement of cash flows, Gleim has divided the theory and calculation questions into two different subunits.

---

   b. The FASB prescribes two approaches to presenting cash flows from operating activities, the direct method and the indirect method. The two methods always produce the same net figure.

      1) The **direct method** lists the separate categories of gross cash receipts and disbursements and reports net cash flow as the difference between them.

      2) The **indirect method** (also called the reconciliation method) begins with accrual-basis net income or the change in net assets and removes items that did not affect operating cash flow.

         a) The FASB expresses a preference for the direct method. However, if the direct method is used, a separate reconciliation based on the indirect method must be provided in a separate schedule.

         b) For this reason, most firms simply employ the indirect method on the face of the statement.

DIRECT METHOD			INDIRECT METHOD		
Cash flows from operating activities:			**Cash flows from operating activities:**		
Cash receipts from:			Accrual-basis net income		**$XX,XXX**
Customers	$XX,XXX		**Additions:**		
Sale of trading securities	XX,XXX		Decrease in receivables	$X,XXX	
Interest earned	XX,XXX		Decrease in inventories	X,XXX	
Dividends on equity investments	XX,XXX		Increase in payables	X,XXX	
Other operating cash receipts	XX,XXX		Depreciation expense	X,XXX	
Net cash inflows		$XXX,XXX	Amortization of bond discount	X,XXX	
Cash disbursements for:			Loss on sale of plant assets	X,XXX	
Inventory	$XX,XXX		Loss on investment in equity-		
Purchase of trading securities	XX,XXX		method investees	X,XXX	
Salaries and wages	XX,XXX		**Net additions**		XX,XXX
Interest expense	XX,XXX		**Subtractions:**		
Taxes	XX,XXX		Increase in receivables	$X,XXX	
Other operating cash payments	XX,XXX		Increase in inventories	X,XXX	
Net cash outflows		(XXX,XXX)	Decrease in payables	X,XXX	
Net cash provided by operating activities		$ X,XXX	Amortization of bond premium	X,XXX	
			Gain on sale of plant assets	X,XXX	
			Income from investment in equity-		
			method investees	X,XXX	
			Net subtractions		(XX,XXX)
			Net cash provided by operating activities		$ X,XXX

3. **Investing Activities**

    a. Investing activities include the effects of transactions involving long-lived assets. These typically include

    1) The purchase and sale of securities of other entities (that are not held for active trading)

    2) The purchase and sale of property, plant, and equipment

    3) The granting and repayment of principal on loans made to other entities

Cash flows from investing activities:		
Purchase of land	$(XX,XXX)	
Purchase of building	(XX,XXX)	
Sale of equipment	XX,XXX	
Purchase of available-for-sale securities	(XX,XXX)	
Sale of held-to-maturity securities	XX,XXX	
Proceeds from note receivable	XX,XXX	
Net cash used in investing activities		$(X,XXX)

4. **Financing Activities**

    a. Financing activities include the effects of transactions involving liabilities and owners' equity. These typically include

    1) Cash receipts from the sale of bonds and the issuance of stock

    2) Cash payments to bondholders for the retirement of debt and to stockholders as dividends (the payment of interest to bondholders is generally classified as an operating activity)

Cash flows from financing activities:		
Issuance of equity securities	$X,XXX,XXX	
Retirement of bonds payable	(XXX,XXX)	
Payment of dividends	(XX,XXX)	
Net cash provided by financing activities		$XXX,XXX

5. **Net Change in Cash for the Year**

   a. The three subtotals arrived at on the previous page are added together.

      1) This amount is the starting point for a reconciliation of the beginning balance of cash to the ending balance.

Net increase in cash	$XXX,XXX
Cash as of January 1, Year 8	XX,XXX
Cash as of December 31, Year 8	$XXX,XXX

6. **Noncash Items**

   a. The final section of the statement of cash flows consists of investing and financing items that affect reported assets and liabilities but that have no effect on cash flow.

   b. These include such items as

      1) Conversions of debt to equity
      2) Assets obtained by assuming liabilities or entering into lease agreements
      3) Capital assets received as gifts
      4) Exchange of a noncash asset or liability for another

   c. Since these items cannot be incorporated into the body of the statement, they are disclosed in a separate section, as shown below:

      Summary of noncash investing and financing activities:
      Converted $500,000 bonds payable into 2,000,000 shares $1 par value common stock
      Obtained equipment in exchange for $60,000 note payable

Stop and review! You have completed the outline for this subunit. Study multiple-choice questions 26 through 30 beginning on page 52.

1.7 STATEMENT OF CASH FLOWS -- CALCULATIONS

Some of the questions pertaining to the statement of cash flows that a candidate will encounter on the CMA exam focus on the mechanics of deriving reported amounts rather than on the theory underlying the statement. This subunit consists entirely of such questions. Please review Subunit 1.6 before attempting to answer the questions in this subunit.

Stop and review! You have completed the outline for this subunit. Study multiple-choice questions 31 through 35 beginning on page 53.

1.8 COMMON-SIZE FINANCIAL STATEMENTS

1. **Percentages and Comparability**

   a. Analyzing the financial statements of steadily growing firms and firms of different sizes within an industry presents certain difficulties.

      1) To overcome this obstacle, common-size statements restate financial statement line items in terms of a percentage of a given amount, such as total assets for a balance sheet or net sales for an income statement.

   b. Items on common-size financial statements are expressed as percentages of net sales (on the income statement) or total assets (on the balance sheet). The base amount is assigned the value of 100%.

      1) Thus, on an income statement, net sales is valued at 100%, while all other amounts are a percentage of net sales. On the balance sheet, total assets are 100%, as is the total of liabilities and stockholders' equity. Each line item can be interpreted in terms of its proportion of the baseline figure.

c.   EXAMPLES:

Income statement External reporting format	Current Year	Prior Year	Income statement Common-size format	Current Year	Prior Year
Net sales	$1,800,000	$1,400,000	Net sales	100.0%	100.0%
Cost of goods sold	(1,650,000)	(1,330,000)	Cost of goods sold	(91.7%)	(95.0%)
Gross profit	150,000	70,000	Gross profit	8.3%	5.0%
Selling expenses	(50,000)	(15,000)	Selling expenses	(2.8%)	(1.1%)
General and admin. expenses	(15,000)	(10,000)	General and admin. expenses	(0.8%)	(0.7%)
Operating income	85,000	45,000	Operating income	4.7%	3.2%
Other revenues and gains	20,000	0	Other revenues and gains	1.1%	0.0%
Other expenses and losses	(35,000)	(10,000)	Other expenses and losses	(1.9%)	(0.7%)
Income before taxes	70,000	35,000	Income before taxes	3.9%	2.5%
Income taxes (40%)	(28,000)	(14,000)	Income taxes (40%)	(1.6%)	(1.0%)
Net income	$ 42,000	$ 21,000	Net income	2.3%	1.5%

Balance sheet External reporting format	Current Year End	Prior Year End	Balance sheet Common-size format	Current Year End	Prior Year End
Assets:			Assets:		
Current assets	$ 760,000	$ 635,000	Current assets	42.2%	39.7%
Noncurrent assets	1,040,000	965,000	Noncurrent assets	57.8%	60.3%
Total assets	$1,800,000	$1,600,000	Total assets	100.0%	100.0%
Liabilities and stockholders' equity:			Liabilities and stockholders' equity:		
Current liabilities	$ 390,000	$ 275,000	Current liabilities	21.7%	17.2%
Noncurrent liabilities	610,000	675,000	Noncurrent liabilities	33.9%	42.2%
Total liabilities	$1,000,000	$ 950,000	Total liabilities	55.6%	59.4%
Stockholders' equity	800,000	650,000	Stockholders' equity	44.4%	40.6%
Total liabilities and stockholders' equity	$1,800,000	$1,600,000	Total liabilities and stockholders' equity	100.0%	100.0%

d.   Preparing common-size statements makes it easier to analyze differences among companies of various sizes or comparisons between a similar company and an industry average.

   1)   For example, comparing the efficiency of a company with $1,800,000 of revenues to a company with $44 billion in revenues is difficult unless the numbers are reduced to a common denominator.

2.   **Vertical and Horizontal Analysis**

   a.   The common-size statements above are an example of vertical analysis (i.e., the percentages are based on numbers above or below in the same column).

   1)   Alternatively, there is a concept known as horizontal analysis wherein the amounts for several periods are stated in percentages of a base-year amount. These are often called trend percentages.

b. One period is designated the base period, to which the other periods are compared. Each line item of the base period is thus 100%.

1) EXAMPLE:

Income statement
External reporting format

	Current Year	Prior Year	2nd Prior Year
Net sales	$1,800,000	$1,400,000	$1,500,000
Cost of goods sold	(1,650,000)	(1,330,000)	(1,390,000)
Gross profit	$ 150,000	$ 70,000	$ 110,000

Income statement
Trend analysis

	Current Year	Prior Year	2nd Prior Year
Net sales	120.0%	93.3%	100.0%
Cost of goods sold	118.7%	95.7%	100.0%
Gross profit	**136.4%**	**63.6%**	**100.0%**

2) Even though sales and cost of goods sold declined only slightly from the base year to the next year, gross profit plunged (on a percentage basis). By the same token, when sales recovered in the current year, the gain in gross profit was (proportionally) greater than the increases in its two components.

c. There is also a form of horizontal analysis that does not use common sizes. This method is used to calculate the growth (or decline) of key financial line items.

1) For example, if a company's sales increased from $100,000 to $120,000, there would be a third column showing the percentage increase, which in this case was 20%.

2) This is another form of management by exception. Managers can look at the third column (the percentage change column) and see which accounts have experienced the most change since the previous period.

Stop and review! You have completed the outline for this subunit. Study multiple-choice questions 36 and 37 on page 55.

1.9 CORE CONCEPTS

Corporate Ethics and Legislation

- The **Foreign Corrupt Practices Act of 1977** (FCPA) contains two sets of provisions:
  - All public companies must devise and maintain a system of internal accounting control, regardless of whether they have foreign operations.
  - No domestic concern may offer or authorize corrupt payments to any foreign official, foreign political party or official thereof, or candidate for political office in a foreign country.
- Individuals found in violation of the FCPA are subject to both **fine and imprisonment**. A corporation may be assessed a **fine** as well.
- The **Sarbanes-Oxley Act of 2002** (SOX) imposed extensive new responsibilities on issuers of publicly traded securities and their auditors.
  - The most significant provision of SOX regarding ethics is Section 406(a), which requires any company issuing securities to adopt a code of ethics for senior financial officers.

Corporate Responsibility for Ethical Behavior

- IMA's Statement on Management Accounting **"Values and Ethics: From Inception to Practice"** is a useful document for understanding ethical concepts in an organizational context.
- The **organization has a responsibility** to foster a sense of ethics in its employees and agents. All organizations need a code of conduct.
- A pervasive sense of ethical values can **benefit an organization**.
- A sense of ethics requires an ability to **distinguish between ethical and merely legal behavior**.
- **"Leadership by example,"** or "tone at the top," plays an important role in determining an organization's ethical environment.
- The concept of **"human capital"** is important to an organization in creating a climate where "doing the right thing" is expected.
- An **organization's culture** impacts its behavioral values.
- **Employee training** is important to maintaining an ethical organizational culture.
- **Two methods for monitoring** ethical compliance are **human performance feedback loop** and **survey tools**.
- A **whistleblowing framework** (e.g., an ethics helpline) is an important component in maintaining an ethical organizational culture.
- Organizations face particular challenges in applying their values and ethical standards **internationally**.
- A comprehensive framework of corporate **ethical behavior** is a prerequisite for an effective system of **internal control**.
- **Three tools** that can be used to identify process controls related to ethical and behavioral issues are business process reengineering, quality management, and continual process improvement.

Basic Financial Statements and Their Users

- The **elements** of one statement **articulate** (are interrelated) with those of other statements.
- The **notes** are considered part of the basic financial statements.
- **Users** of financial statements have direct and indirect interests and can be internal or external.
  - Users with **direct** interests include investors or potential investors, suppliers and creditors, employees, and management.
  - Users having **indirect** interests include financial advisers and analysts, stock markets or exchanges, and regulatory authorities.
  - **Internal** users use financial statements to make decisions affecting the operation of the business. These include management, employees, and the board of directors.
  - **External** users use financial statements to determine whether doing business with the firm will be beneficial. These include investors, creditors, financial advisers and analysts, stock exchanges, and regulatory agencies.

Statement of Financial Position

- The statement of financial position (balance sheet) "provides information about an entity's **assets, liabilities, and equity** and their relationships to each other at a moment in time."
- The items in the balance sheet represent the **resources** of the entity and **claims** to those resources.
- **Current assets** are usually presented in descending order of liquidity. **Noncurrent assets** are usually presented in an order determined by convention rather than by liquidity.

Statement of Income and Statement of Retained Earnings

- The items in the statements of income and retained earnings represent the **effects of transactions** and other events and circumstances that result in changes in the entity's resources and claims to those resources.
- The statement of income can be presented in the **single-step**, **multi-step**, or **condensed** format.
- The results of **discontinued operations** and the effects of **extraordinary items** are presented **separately** after income from continuing operations.

Statement of Cash Flows

- The **primary purpose** of a statement of cash flows is to provide relevant information about the cash receipts and payments of an entity during a period.
  - **Operating activities** include the effects of transactions involved in the determination of net income.
  - **Investing activities** include the effects of transactions involving long-lived assets.
  - **Financing activities** include the effects of transactions involving liabilities and owners' equity.
- Cash flows from operating activities can be displayed using the **direct method** (income statement approach) or the **indirect method** (reconciliation approach).
  - If the **direct method** is used for reporting operating activities, a **reconciliation** that mimics the indirect method **must be disclosed**.
- The **net change in cash** for the year is calculated by adding the cash flows provided by/used in operating, investing, and financing activities. This is the starting point for a reconciliation of the beginning balance of cash to the ending balance.
- The final section of the statement of cash flows consists of investing and financing items that affect reported assets and liabilities but that have **no effect on cash flow** (the summary of noncash investing and financing activities).

Common-Size Financial Statements

- Common-size statements restate financial statement line items in terms of a percentage of a given amount, such as total assets for a balance sheet or net sales for an income statement (this is called **vertical analysis**).
- In **horizontal analysis**, the amounts for several periods are stated in percentages of a base-year amount. These are often called trend percentages. Another form of horizontal analysis does not use common sizes. This method is used to calculate the growth (or decline) of key financial line items.

QUESTIONS

1.1 Corporate Ethics and Legislation

1. The Foreign Corrupt Practices Act prohibits

    A. Bribes to all foreigners.

    B. Small bribes to foreign officials that serve as facilitating or grease payments.

    C. Bribery only by corporations and their representatives.

    D. Bribes to foreign officials to influence official acts.

Answer (D) is correct. *(Publisher, adapted)*
    REQUIRED: The action prohibited by the Foreign Corrupt Practices Act.
    DISCUSSION: The Foreign Corrupt Practices Act (FCPA) prohibits any U.S. firm from making bribes to foreign officials to influence official acts. The businesses subject to the FCPA include corporations, partnerships, limited partnerships, business trusts, and unincorporated organizations. Violations of the FCPA are federal felonies. The penalties are up to 5 years in prison or up to a $100,000 fine or both for an officer, director, or shareholder who helps make the bribe.
    Answer (A) is incorrect. Bribes to all foreigners is not covered by the provisions in the FCPA. Answer (B) is incorrect. Small bribes to foreign officials that serve as facilitating or grease payments is not covered by the provisions in the FCPA. Answer (C) is incorrect. All U.S. firms are subject to the anti-bribery provisions.

2. A major impact of the Foreign Corrupt Practices Act of 1977 is that registrants subject to the Securities Exchange Act of 1934 are now required to

    A. Keep records that reflect the transactions and dispositions of assets and to maintain a system of internal accounting controls.

    B. Provide access to records by authorized agencies of the federal government.

    C. Prepare financial statements in accord with international accounting standards.

    D. Produce full, fair, and accurate periodic reports on foreign commerce and/or foreign political party affiliations.

Answer (A) is correct. *(CMA, adapted)*
    REQUIRED: The major impact of the Foreign Corrupt Practices Act of 1977.
    DISCUSSION: The main purpose of the Foreign Corrupt Practices Act of 1977 is to prevent bribery by firms that do business in foreign countries. A major ramification is that it requires all companies that must register with the SEC under the Securities Exchange Act of 1934 to maintain adequate accounting records and a system of internal accounting control.
    Answer (B) is incorrect. Authorized agents of the federal government already have access to records of SEC registrants. Answer (C) is incorrect. Although some international accounting standards have been promulgated, they are incomplete and have not gained widespread acceptance. Answer (D) is incorrect. There are no requirements for providing periodic reports on foreign commerce or foreign political party affiliations.

3. What law prohibits U.S. companies from paying bribes to foreign officials for the purpose of obtaining or retaining business?

    A. Federal Ethical Standards Act.

    B. Robinson-Patman Act.

    C. Foreign Corrupt Practices Act.

    D. North American Free Trade Agreement.

Answer (C) is correct. *(Publisher, adapted)*
    REQUIRED: The law that prohibits bribes to foreign officials.
    DISCUSSION: The Foreign Corrupt Practices Act of 1977 prohibits bribes to foreign officials for purposes of obtaining or retaining business. The Act also requires companies to maintain effective systems of internal control.
    Answer (A) is incorrect. The Federal Ethical Standards Act does not deal with international payments. Answer (B) is incorrect. The Robinson-Patman Act of 1936 prohibits price discrimination. Answer (D) is incorrect. The North American Free Trade Agreement (NAFTA), passed in 1993, provides for free trade among the nations of Canada, Mexico, and the U.S.

4. Which of the following is **not** an aspect of the Foreign Corrupt Practices Act of 1977?

    A. It subjects management to fines and imprisonment.

    B. It prohibits bribes to foreign officials.

    C. It requires the establishment of independent audit committees.

    D. It requires an internal control system to be developed and maintained.

Answer (C) is correct. *(Publisher, adapted)*
    REQUIRED: The false statement with respect to the Foreign Corrupt Practices Act.
    DISCUSSION: The Foreign Corrupt Practices Act of 1977 prohibits bribes to foreign officials and requires firms to have adequate systems of internal control. Violation of the Act subjects individual managers to fines and/or imprisonment. The Act does not specifically require the establishment of audit committees, but many firms have established audit committees as one means of dealing with the internal control provisions of the Act.

5. Firms subject to the reporting requirements of the Securities Exchange Act of 1934 are required by the Foreign Corrupt Practices Act of 1977 to maintain satisfactory internal control. The role of the independent auditor relative to this Act is to

A. Report clients with unsatisfactory internal control to the SEC.

B. Provide assurances to users as part of the traditional audit attest function that the client is in compliance with the present legislation.

C. Express an opinion on the sufficiency of the client's internal control to meet the requirements of the Act.

D. Attest to the financial statements.

Answer (D) is correct. *(Publisher, adapted)*
REQUIRED: The role of the independent auditor relative to the Foreign Corrupt Practices Act.
DISCUSSION: Whether a client is in conformity with the Foreign Corrupt Practices Act is a legal question. Auditors cannot be expected to provide clients or users of the financial statements with legal advice. The role of the auditor is to assess control risk in the course of an engagement to attest to the fair presentation of the financial statements.
Answer (A) is incorrect. The auditor is not required to report violations of the Act to the SEC, although a duty to disclose outside the client may exist in some circumstances; e.g., the client's failure to take remedial action regarding an illegal act may constitute a disagreement that it must report on Form 8-K (AU 317). Answer (B) is incorrect. The traditional attest function does not involve compliance auditing. Answer (C) is incorrect. The FCPA contains no requirement that an auditor express an opinion on internal control.

6. The requirement of the Foreign Corrupt Practices Act of 1977 to devise and maintain adequate internal control is assigned in the Act to the

A. Chief financial officer.

B. Board of directors.

C. Director of internal auditing.

D. Company as a whole with no designation of specific persons or positions.

Answer (D) is correct. *(CMA, adapted)*
REQUIRED: The person in a company responsible for compliance with the FCPA.
DISCUSSION: The accounting requirements apply to all public companies that must register under the Securities Exchange Act of 1934. The responsibility is thus placed on companies, not individuals.
Answer (A) is incorrect. Compliance with the FCPA is not the specific responsibility of the chief financial officer. Answer (B) is incorrect. Compliance with the FCPA is not the specific responsibility of the board of directors. Answer (C) is incorrect. Compliance with the FCPA is not the specific responsibility of the director of internal auditing.

1.2 Corporate Responsibility for Ethical Behavior

7. IMA's Statement on Management Accounting "Values and Ethics: From Inception to Practice" recommends a defined code of conduct and ethical behavior for all organizations. One advantage of having such a code is that it

A. Provides employees with guidance for handling unfamiliar situations.

B. Ensures ethical behavior by all employees.

C. Shields the organization from liability in cases of loss of stockholder value due to fraud.

D. Eases the investigative process performed by police and prosecutors in cases of suspected fraud.

Answer (A) is correct. *(Publisher, adapted)*
REQUIRED: The advantage to the organization of having a code of conduct.
DISCUSSION: "Values and Ethics: From Inception to Practice" states, in part, "... what does an employee do when unplanned events occur? What reference does an individual look to for help in making decisions? ... This is why it is important to have a defined set of organizational values and code of ethics – they create the "touchstone" against which every unanticipated decision must be judged. Failure to have every individual in the organization know and understand these values and ethical code leads to inconsistency and, in the worst cases, unethical or fraudulent behavior." (IV. Values, Ethics, and Accounting.)
Answer (B) is incorrect. A code of conduct cannot guarantee ethical behavior by employees. Answer (C) is incorrect. A code of conduct cannot guarantee that an organization will be shielded from liability in cases of fraud. Answer (D) is incorrect. A code of conduct does not ease law enforcement's investigative process.

8. Which one of the following is a true statement regarding organizational ethics?

A. As long as officer and employee behavior meet the requirements of the law, the organization can be considered to have a functioning system of ethical behavior.

B. A strong sense of ethics on the part of employees who are in the best position to appropriate cash and other assets is the most vital part of a functioning system of ethical behavior.

C. If an organization has a strong code of ethical conduct in place, the role of employee training can be downplayed.

D. Paying attention to "whistleblowers" plays a significant role in maintaining an effective ethical atmosphere.

Answer (D) is correct.   *(Publisher, adapted)*
REQUIRED: The true statement regarding organizational ethics.
DISCUSSION: "Values and Ethics: From Inception to Practice" states, in part, "A whistleblowing framework (e.g., an ethics helpline) is an important component in maintaining an ethical organizational culture. An effective feedback system includes having a confidential framework for employees to report possible violations of the organization's code of ethics and to receive advice on the ethical aspects of challenging decisions. Statistics show that a large number of occupational fraud cases are detected through an employee "hotline" or other reporting method ... " (IX. Measuring and Improving Ethical Compliance.)
Answer (A) is incorrect. A sense of ethics requires an ability to distinguish between ethical and merely legal behavior. "Values and Ethics: From Inception to Practice" states, in part, "Many individuals at the center of corporate scandals [of the late 20th and early 21st Century] have professed the belief that they were innocent of any wrongdoing, including Kenneth Lay of Enron or Conrad Black of Hollinger. The problem is that these individuals did not define their behavior by what most of society would see as 'reasonable,' but rather they followed their own particular code – in some cases, limiting the definition of ethical behavior to require compliance with the law and nothing more." (II. Introduction.) Answer (B) is incorrect. "Values and Ethics: From Inception to Practice" states, in part, "Ethical behavior is not something that applies to someone else – every single individual is responsible for behaving ethically. Nowhere is this more important than the demonstration of ethical behavior that managers and supervisors exhibit in the way they execute their day-to-day work..." This phenomenon is referred to as the "tone at the top." (VI. Leadership by Example.) Answer (C) is incorrect. Employee training is important to maintaining an ethical organizational culture. "Values and Ethics: From Inception to Practice" states, in part, "Every existing member of staff should receive ongoing training, starting at the board level and cascading down throughout the organization ... Ethics training for employees should focus on covering ethical concepts, the organization's code, and compliance. To achieve this, training should include: ethical concepts and thinking: What is 'behind' the issue of ethical action?; [and] the organization's code of ethics and any supporting 'rules.'" (VIII. Practical Application: Converting Intent into Operational Reality.)

9. Which one of the following is a true statement regarding organizational ethics?

A. A comprehensive framework of corporate ethical behavior is a prerequisite for an effective system of internal control.

B. An effective system of internal control is a prerequisite for corporate ethical behavior.

C. If a functioning system of ethical behavior is in place, an organization is able to devote fewer resources to developing human capital.

D. "Organizational culture" is determined mostly by the industry(ies) in which the firm operates.

Answer (A) is correct. *(Publisher, adapted)*
    REQUIRED: The true statement regarding organizational ethics.
    DISCUSSION: A comprehensive framework of corporate ethical behavior is a prerequisite for an effective system of internal control. "Values and Ethics: From Inception to Practice" states, in part, "CEOs and CFOs have to place their own integrity on the line by attesting to compliance with an adequate level of internal controls (as well as all other certifications). Creating a thorough, integrated system for developing, implementing, sustaining, and monitoring ethical performance within the organization will allow executives to make such declarations with confidence that a code of ethics is the foundation of the organization's culture and is fully integrated into the thinking process of every employee and business partner." (IX. Measuring and Improving Ethical Compliance.)
    Answer (B) is incorrect. It is more nearly true to state the opposite. Answer (C) is incorrect. The concept of "human capital" is important to an organization in creating a climate where "doing the right thing" is expected. In most organizations today, labor costs constitute the majority of operating expenses. "Values and Ethics: From Inception to Practice" states, in part, "...an organization must, to a great degree, trust that its employees are acting in its best interests. Human 'capital' is a critical asset ... Unmotivated employees can poison the atmosphere and reduce the teamwork and cooperation required for knowledge transfer and innovation, and they can have a significant negative impact on relationships with suppliers and customers." (IV. Values, Ethics, and Accounting.) Answer (D) is incorrect. "Values and Ethics: From Inception to Practice" states, in part, "Every organization already has a culture ... Step one in establishing an ethical culture must be an assessment of the existing organizational values and culture and the development of a set of statements that define the principles the organization believes in and should act upon. These statements and principles can be developed by the shareholders, the board, or a governing body within the organization." (V. Defining and Developing the Organization's Behavioral Values.)

1.3 Basic Financial Statements and Their Users

10. The basic financial statements include a

A. Balance sheet, income statement, statement of retained earnings, and statement of changes in retained earnings.

B. Statement of financial position, income statement, statement of retained earnings, and statement of changes in retained earnings.

C. Balance sheet, statement of financial position, income statement, and statement of changes in retained earnings.

D. Statement of financial position, income statement, statement of cash flows, and statement of retained earnings.

Answer (D) is correct. *(CMA, adapted)*
    REQUIRED: The statements included in the basic financial statements.
    DISCUSSION: Under GAAP, the basic required statements are the statements of financial position, income, cash flows, and retained earnings. Changes in equity must be disclosed in the basic statements, the notes, or a separate statement. A statement of cash flows is now a required part of a full set of financial statements of all business entities (both publicly held and privately held). Moreover, comprehensive income must be displayed in a financial statement given the same prominence as other statements, but no specific format is required as long as net income is displayed as a component of comprehensive income in the statement.

11. Financial statement users with a direct economic interest in a specific business include

A. Financial advisers.

B. Regulatory bodies.

C. Stock markets.

D. Suppliers.

Answer (D) is correct. *(Publisher, adapted)*
    REQUIRED: The financial statement users with direct economic interests.
    DISCUSSION: Users with direct interests include investors or potential investors, suppliers and creditors, employees, and management.
    Answer (A) is incorrect. Financial advisers have indirect interests. Answer (B) is incorrect. Regulatory bodies have indirect interests. Answer (C) is incorrect. Stock markets have indirect interests.

12. A primary objective of external financial reporting is

    A. Direct measurement of the value of a business enterprise.

    B. Provision of information that is useful to present and potential investors, creditors, and others in making rational financial decisions regarding the enterprise.

    C. Establishment of rules for accruing liabilities.

    D. Direct measurement of the enterprise's stock price.

Answer (B) is correct. *(CMA, adapted)*
    REQUIRED: The primary objective of external financial reporting.
    DISCUSSION: According to the FASB's Conceptual Framework, the objectives of external financial reporting are to provide information that (1) is useful to present and potential investors, creditors, and others in making rational financial decisions regarding the enterprise; (2) helps those parties in assessing the amounts, timing, and uncertainty of prospective cash receipts from dividends or interest and the proceeds from sale, redemption, or maturity of securities or loans; and (3) concerns the economic resources of an enterprise, the claims thereto, and the effects of transactions, events, and circumstances that change its resources and claims thereto.
    Answer (A) is incorrect. Financial reporting is not designed to measure directly the value of a business. Answer (C) is incorrect. While rules for accruing liabilities are a practical concern, the establishment of such rules is not a primary objective of external reporting. Answer (D) is incorrect. The objectives of financial accounting are unrelated to the measurement of stock prices; stock prices are a product of stock market forces.

13. Notes to financial statements are beneficial in meeting the disclosure requirements of financial reporting. The notes should not be used to

    A. Describe significant accounting policies.

    B. Describe depreciation methods employed by the company.

    C. Describe principles and methods peculiar to the industry in which the company operates, when these principles and methods are predominantly followed in that industry.

    D. Correct an improper presentation in the financial statements.

Answer (D) is correct. *(CMA, adapted)*
    REQUIRED: The improper use of notes in financial statements.
    DISCUSSION: Financial statement notes should not be used to correct improper presentations. The financial statements should be presented correctly on their own. Notes should be used to explain the methods used to prepare the financial statements and the amounts shown. The first footnote typically describes significant accounting policies.

14. Which of the following is not a need of financial statement users?

    A. Financial advisers and analysts need financial statements to help investors evaluate particular investments.

    B. Stock exchanges need financial statements to set a firm's stock price.

    C. Regulatory agencies need financial statements to evaluate price changes for regulated industries.

    D. Employees need financial information to negotiate wages and fringe benefits.

Answer (B) is correct. *(Publisher, adapted)*
    REQUIRED: The item not a need of financial statement users.
    DISCUSSION: Investors' purchases and sales set stock prices. Stock exchanges need financial statements to evaluate whether to accept a firm's stock for listing or whether to suspend trading in the stock.
    Answer (A) is incorrect. Financial advisers use financial statements for evaluating investments. Answer (C) is incorrect. Regulatory agencies use financial statements for rate making. Answer (D) is incorrect. Employees use financial statements for labor negotiations.

15. The management of ABC Corporation is analyzing the financial statements of XYZ Corporation because ABC is strongly considering purchasing a block of XYZ common stock that would give ABC significant influence over XYZ. Which financial statement should ABC primarily use to assess the amounts, timing, and uncertainty of future cash flows of XYZ Company?

    A. Income statement.

    B. Statement of retained earnings.

    C. Statement of cash flows.

    D. Balance sheet.

Answer (C) is correct. *(CIA, adapted)*
    REQUIRED: The financial statement used to assess the amounts, timing, and uncertainty of future cash flows.
    DISCUSSION: The primary purpose of a statement of cash flows is to provide information about the cash receipts and cash payments of a business enterprise during a period. This information helps investors, creditors, and other users to assess (1) the enterprise's ability to generate net cash inflows; (2) its ability to meet its obligations, and pay dividends; (3) its needs for external financing; (4) the reasons for the differences between net income and net cash flow; and (5) the effects of cash and noncash financing and investing activities.
    Answer (A) is incorrect. The statement of income is prepared on an accrual basis and is not meant to report cash flows. Answer (B) is incorrect. The statement of retained earnings merely shows the reasons for changes in retained earnings during the reporting period. Answer (D) is incorrect. The balance sheet reports on financial position at a moment in time. It does not provide information about future cash flows.

1.4 Statement of Financial Position (Balance Sheet)

16. The primary purpose of the statement of financial position is to reflect

    A. The fair value of the firm's assets at some moment in time.

    B. The status of the firm's assets in case of forced liquidation of the firm.

    C. The success of a company's operations for a given amount of time.

    D. Items of value, debt, and net worth.

Answer (D) is correct. *(CMA, adapted)*
    REQUIRED: The primary purpose of the statement of financial position.
    DISCUSSION: The balance sheet presents three major financial accounting elements: assets (items of value), liabilities (debts), and equity (net worth). According to the FASB's Conceptual Framework, assets are probable future economic benefits resulting from past transactions or events. Liabilities are probable future sacrifices of economic benefits arising from present obligations as a result of past transactions or events. Equity is the residual interest in the assets after deduction of liabilities.
    Answer (A) is incorrect. The measurement attributes of assets include but are not limited to fair value. Answer (B) is incorrect. Financial statements reflect the going concern assumption. Hence, they usually do not report forced liquidation values. Answer (C) is incorrect. The income statement provides this type of information.

17. Prepaid expenses are valued on the statement of financial position at the

    A. Cost to acquire the asset.

    B. Face amount collectible at maturity.

    C. Cost to acquire minus accumulated amortization.

    D. Cost less expired or used portion.

Answer (D) is correct. *(CMA, adapted)*
    REQUIRED: The means of valuing prepaid expenses on the balance sheet.
    DISCUSSION: Prepaid expenses, such as supplies, prepaid rent, and prepaid insurance, are reported on the balance sheet at cost minus the expired or used portion. These are typically current assets.
    Answer (A) is incorrect. The cost must be reduced by the expired or used portion of the prepaid asset. Answer (B) is incorrect. Prepaid expenses will not be collected at maturity. Answer (C) is incorrect. Prepaid expenses are not depreciated; they expire.

18. A statement of financial position allows investors to assess all of the following **except** the

A. Efficiency with which enterprise assets are used.

B. Liquidity and financial flexibility of the enterprise.

C. Capital structure of the enterprise.

D. Net realizable value of enterprise assets.

Answer (D) is correct. *(CMA, adapted)*
   REQUIRED: The attribute not assessable using a statement of financial position.
   DISCUSSION: Assets are usually measured at original historical cost in a statement of financial position, although some exceptions exist. For example, some short-term receivables are reported at their net realizable value. Thus, the statement of financial position cannot be relied upon to assess NRV.
   Answer (A) is incorrect. Efficiency of asset use is assessed by calculating liquidity, leverage, and asset management ratios. These ratios require balance sheet data. Answer (B) is incorrect. Liquidity and financial flexibility are assessed by calculating liquidity, leverage, and asset management ratios. These ratios require balance sheet data. Answer (C) is incorrect. The capital structure of the enterprise is reported in the equity section of the statement of financial position.

19. The accounting equation *(assets – liabilities = equity)* reflects the

A. Entity point of view.

B. Fund theory.

C. Proprietary point of view.

D. Enterprise theory.

Answer (C) is correct. *(CMA, adapted)*
   REQUIRED: The concept on which the basic accounting equation is based.
   DISCUSSION: The equation is based on the proprietary theory. Equity in an enterprise is what remains after the economic obligations of the enterprise are deducted from its economic resources.
   Answer (A) is incorrect. The entity concept limits accounting information to that related to a specific entity (possibly not the same as the legal entity). Answer (B) is incorrect. Fund theory stresses that assets equal obligations (equity and liabilities are sources of assets). Answer (D) is incorrect. The enterprise concept stresses ownership of the assets; that is, the emphasis is on the credit side of the balance sheet.

20. Abernathy Corporation uses a calendar year for financial and tax reporting purposes and has $100 million of mortgage bonds due on January 15, Year 2. By January 10, Year 2, Abernathy intends to refinance this debt with new long-term mortgage bonds and has entered into a financing agreement that clearly demonstrates its ability to consummate the refinancing. This debt is to be

A. Classified as a current liability on the statement of financial position at December 31, Year 1.

B. Classified as a long-term liability on the statement of financial position at December 31, Year 1.

C. Retired as of December 31, Year 1.

D. Considered off-balance-sheet debt.

Answer (B) is correct. *(CMA, adapted)*
   REQUIRED: The balance sheet treatment of maturing long-term debt that is to be refinanced on a long-term basis.
   DISCUSSION: Short-term obligations expected to be refinanced should be reported as current liabilities unless the firm both plans to refinance and has the ability to refinance the debt on a long-term basis. The ability to refinance on a long-term basis is evidenced by a post-balance-sheet date issuance of long-term debt or a financing arrangement that will clearly permit long-term refinancing.
   Answer (A) is incorrect. The company intends to refinance the debt on a long-term basis. Answer (C) is incorrect. The debt has not been retired. Answer (D) is incorrect. The debt is on the balance sheet.

1.5 Statement of Income and Statement of Retained Earnings

21. An income statement for a business prepared under the current operating performance concept would include only the recurring earnings from its normal operations and

A. No other items.

B. Any extraordinary items.

C. Any prior-period adjustments.

D. Any gains or losses from extinguishment of debt.

Answer (A) is correct. *(CMA, adapted)*
   REQUIRED: The items included in a current operating performance income statement.
   DISCUSSION: The current operating performance concept emphasizes the ordinary, normal, recurring operations of the entity during the current period. In this view, the inclusion of extraordinary items or prior-period adjustments is believed to impair the significance of net income. (The current operating performance concept is not recognized under U.S. GAAP.)
   Answer (B) is incorrect. Extraordinary items are excluded under the current operating performance concept. Answer (C) is incorrect. Prior-period adjustments are excluded under the current operating performance concept. Answer (D) is incorrect. Gains and losses from extinguishment of debt are extraordinary.

22. In a multiple-step income statement for a retail company, all of the following are included in the operating section **except**

    A. Sales.

    B. Cost of goods sold.

    C. Dividend revenue.

    D. Administrative and selling expenses.

Answer (C) is correct. *(CMA, adapted)*
    REQUIRED: The item excluded from the operating section of a multiple-step income statement of a retailer.
    DISCUSSION: The operating section of a retailer's income statement includes all revenues and costs necessary for the operation of the retail establishment, e.g., sales, cost of goods sold, administrative expenses, and selling expenses. Dividend revenue, however, is classified under other revenues. In a statement of cash flows, cash dividends received are considered an operating cash flow.
    Answer (A) is incorrect. Sales is part of the normal operations of a retailer. Answer (B) is incorrect. Cost of goods sold is part of the normal operations of a retailer. Answer (D) is incorrect. Administrative and selling expenses are part of the normal operations of a retailer.

23. In Hopkins Co.'s Year 3 single-step income statement, the section titled *Revenues* consisted of the following:

Net sales revenue		$187,000
Results from discontinued operations:		
Income from operations of		
component (including gain on		
disposal of $21,600)	$18,000	
Income tax	(6,000)	12,000
Interest revenue		10,200
Gain on sale of equipment		4,700
Cumulative change in Year 1 and Year 2		
income due to change in depreciation		
method (net of $750 tax effect)		1,500
Total revenues		$215,400

In the revenues section of the Year 3 income statement, Hopkins should have reported total revenues of

    A. $217,800

    B. $215,400

    C. $203,700

    D. $201,900

Answer (D) is correct. *(Publisher, adapted)*
    REQUIRED: The total revenues for financial reporting purposes.
    DISCUSSION: Revenue is a component of income from continuing operations. Results of discontinued operations is a classification in the income statement separate from continuing operations. The cumulative effect of a change in accounting principle is not reported in the income statement. Hence, total revenues were $201,900 ($215,400 – $12,000 results from discontinued operations – $1,500 cumulative-effect type change). Alternatively, total revenues consist of net sales of $187,000, plus interest revenue of $10,200, plus gain on sale of equipment (which is not an extraordinary item) of $4,700.
    Answer (A) is incorrect. The amount of $217,800 equals $215,400 reported total revenues, plus the $2,400 loss from operations of the segment. Answer (B) is incorrect. The amount of $215,400 improperly includes the results from discontinued operations and the cumulative-effect type change. Answer (C) is incorrect. The amount of $203,700 improperly subtracts interest revenue and does not adjust for the results from discontinued operations.

24. When reporting extraordinary items,

    A. Each item (net of tax) is presented on the face of the income statement separately as a component of net income for the period.

    B. Each item is presented exclusive of any related income tax.

    C. Each item is presented as an unusual item within income from continuing operations.

    D. All extraordinary gains or losses that occur in a period are summarized as total gains and total losses, then offset to present the net extraordinary gain or loss.

Answer (A) is correct. *(CMA, adapted)*
    REQUIRED: The true statement about the reporting of extraordinary items.
    DISCUSSION: Extraordinary items are reported net of tax after discontinued operations.
    Answer (B) is incorrect. Extraordinary items are to be reported net of the related tax effect. Answer (C) is incorrect. Extraordinary items are not reported in the continuing operations section of the income statement. Answer (D) is incorrect. Each extraordinary item is to be reported separately.

25. Which one of the following items is included in the determination of income from continuing operations?

    A. Discontinued operations.

    B. Extraordinary loss.

    C. Cumulative effect of a change in an accounting principle.

    D. Unusual loss from a write-down of inventory.

Answer (D) is correct. *(CMA, adapted)*
    REQUIRED: The item included in the computation of income from continuing operations.
    DISCUSSION: Certain items ordinarily are not to be treated as extraordinary gains and losses. Rather, they are included in the determination of income from continuing operations. These gains and losses include those from write-downs of receivables and inventories, translation of foreign currency amounts, disposal of a business segment, sale of productive assets, strikes, and accruals on long-term contracts. A write-down of inventory is therefore included in the computation of income from continuing operations.
    Answer (A) is incorrect. Discontinued operations are reported separately from income from continuing operations. Answer (B) is incorrect. Extraordinary loss is reported separately from income from continuing operations. Answer (C) is incorrect. A cumulative effect of a change in an accounting principle is not reported in the income statement.

1.6 Statement of Cash Flows -- Contents

26. When preparing the statement of cash flows, companies are required to report separately as operating cash flows all of the following **except**

    A. Interest received on investments in bonds.

    B. Interest paid on the company's bonds.

    C. Cash collected from customers.

    D. Cash dividends paid on the company's stock.

Answer (D) is correct. *(CMA, adapted)*
    REQUIRED: The item not reported separately as an operating cash flow on a statement of cash flows.
    DISCUSSION: In general, the cash flows from transactions and other events that enter into the determination of income are to be classified as operating. Cash receipts from sales of goods and services, from interest on loans, and from dividends on equity securities are from operating activities. Cash payments to suppliers for inventory; to employees for wages; to other suppliers and employees for other goods and services; to governments for taxes, duties, fines, and fees; and to lenders for interest are also from operating activities. However, distributions to owners (cash dividends on a company's own stock) are cash flows from financing, not operating, activities.
    Answer (A) is incorrect. Interest received from investments is an operating cash flow. Answer (B) is incorrect. Interest paid on bonds is an operating cash flow. Answer (C) is incorrect. Customer collections is an operating cash flow.

27. A statement of cash flows is intended to help users of financial statements

    A. Evaluate a firm's liquidity, solvency, and financial flexibility.

    B. Evaluate a firm's economic resources and obligations.

    C. Determine a firm's components of income from operations.

    D. Determine whether insiders have sold or purchased the firm's stock.

Answer (A) is correct. *(CMA, adapted)*
    REQUIRED: The reason companies are required to prepare a statement of cash flows.
    DISCUSSION: The primary purpose of a statement of cash flows is to provide information about the cash receipts and payments of an entity during a period. If used with information in the other financial statements, the statement of cash flows should help users to assess the entity's ability to generate positive future net cash flows (liquidity), its ability to meet obligations (solvency) and pay dividends, the need for external financing, the reasons for differences between income and cash receipts and payments, and the cash and noncash aspects of the investing and financing activities.
    Answer (B) is incorrect. The statement of cash flows deals with only one resource: cash. Answer (C) is incorrect. The income statement shows the components of income from operations. Answer (D) is incorrect. The identity of stock buyers and sellers is not shown.

28. Which of the following items is specifically included in the body of a statement of cash flows?

    A. Operating and nonoperating cash flow information.

    B. Conversion of debt to equity.

    C. Acquiring an asset through a capital lease.

    D. Purchasing a building by giving a mortgage to the seller.

Answer (A) is correct. *(CMA, adapted)*
    REQUIRED: The information specifically included within the body of a statement of cash flows.
    DISCUSSION: All noncash transactions are excluded from the body of the statement of cash flows to avoid undue complexity and detraction from the objective of providing information about cash flows. Information about all noncash financing and investing activities affecting recognized assets and liabilities shall be reported in related disclosures.

29. Depreciation expense is added to net income under the indirect method of preparing a statement of cash flows in order to

    A. Report all assets at gross carrying amount.

    B. Ensure depreciation has been properly reported.

    C. Reverse noncash charges deducted from net income.

    D. Calculate net carrying amount.

Answer (C) is correct. *(CMA, adapted)*
    REQUIRED: The reason depreciation expense is added to net income under the indirect method.
    DISCUSSION: The indirect method begins with net income and then removes the effects of past deferrals of operating cash receipts and payments, accruals of expected future operating cash receipts and payments, and net income items not affecting operating cash flows (e.g., depreciation).
    Answer (A) is incorrect. Assets other than cash are not shown on the statement of cash flows. Answer (B) is incorrect. Depreciation is recorded on the income statement. On the statement of cash flows, depreciation is added back to net income because it was previously deducted on the income statement. Answer (D) is incorrect. Net carrying amount of assets is reported on the balance sheet, not the statement of cash flows.

30. All of the following should be classified under the operating section in a statement of cash flows **except** a

    A. Decrease in inventory.

    B. Depreciation expense.

    C. Decrease in prepaid insurance.

    D. Purchase of land and building in exchange for a long-term note.

Answer (D) is correct. *(CMA, adapted)*
    REQUIRED: The item not classified as an operating item in a statement of cash flows.
    DISCUSSION: Operating activities include all transactions and other events not classified as investing and financing activities. Operating activities include producing and delivering goods and providing services. Cash flows from such activities are usually included in the determination of net income. However, the purchase of land and a building in exchange for a long-term note is an investing activity. Because this transaction does not affect cash, it is reported in related disclosures of noncash investing and financing activities.

1.7 Statement of Cash Flows -- Calculations

31. The net income for Cypress, Inc., was $3,000,000 for the year ended December 31. Additional information is as follows:

Depreciation on fixed assets	$1,500,000
Gain from cash sale of land	200,000
Increase in accounts payable	300,000
Dividends paid on preferred stock	400,000

The net cash provided by operating activities in the statement of cash flows for the year ended December 31 should be

    A. $4,200,000

    B. $4,500,000

    C. $4,600,000

    D. $4,800,000

Answer (C) is correct. *(CMA, adapted)*
    REQUIRED: The net cash provided by operations.
    DISCUSSION: Net operating cash flow may be determined by adjusting net income. Depreciation is an expense not directly affecting cash flows that should be added back to net income. The increase in accounts payable is added to net income because it indicates that an expense has been recorded but not paid. The gain on the sale of land is an accrual-basis item affecting net income and thus should be subtracted. The dividends paid on preferred stock are cash outflows from financing, not operating, activities and do not require an adjustment. Thus, net cash flow from operations is $4,600,000 ($3,000,000 + $1,500,000 − $200,000 + $300,000).
    Answer (A) is incorrect. This amount equals net cash provided by operating activities minus the $400,000 financing activity. Answer (B) is incorrect. This amount equals net income, plus depreciation. Answer (D) is incorrect. This amount equals net income, plus depreciation, plus the increase in accounts payable.

Questions 32 through 34 are based on the following information. Royce Company had the following transactions during the fiscal year ended December 31, Year 2:

- Accounts receivable decreased from $115,000 on December 31, Year 1, to $100,000 on December 31, Year 2.
- Royce's board of directors declared dividends on December 31, Year 2, of $.05 per share on the 2.8 million shares outstanding, payable to shareholders of record on January 31, Year 3. The company did not declare or pay dividends for fiscal Year 1.

- Sold a truck with a net carrying amount of $7,000 for $5,000 cash, reporting a loss of $2,000.
- Paid interest to bondholders of $780,000.
- The cash balance was $106,000 on December 31, Year 1, and $284,000 on December 31, Year 2.

32. Royce Company uses the direct method to prepare its statement of cash flows at December 31, Year 2. The interest paid to bondholders is reported in the

A. Financing section, as a use or outflow of cash.

B. Operating section, as a use or outflow of cash.

C. Investing section, as a use or outflow of cash.

D. Debt section, as a use or outflow of cash.

Answer (B) is correct. *(CMA, adapted)*
REQUIRED: The proper reporting of interest paid.
DISCUSSION: Payment of interest on debt is considered a cash outflow from an operating activity, although repayment of debt principal is a financing activity.
Answer (A) is incorrect. Interest paid on bonds is an operating cash flow. Answer (C) is incorrect. Investing activities include the lending of money and the acquisition, sale, or other disposal of securities that are not cash equivalents and the acquisition, sale, or other disposal of long-lived productive assets. Answer (D) is incorrect. The statement of cash flows does not contain a debt section.

33. Royce Company uses the indirect method to prepare its Year 2 statement of cash flows. It reports a(n)

A. Source or inflow of funds of $5,000 from the sale of the truck in the financing section.

B. Use or outflow of funds of $140,000 in the financing section, representing dividends.

C. Deduction of $15,000 in the operating section, representing the decrease in year-end accounts receivable.

D. Addition of $2,000 in the operating section for the $2,000 loss on the sale of the truck.

Answer (D) is correct. *(CMA, adapted)*
REQUIRED: The correct presentation of an item on a statement of cash flows prepared under the indirect method.
DISCUSSION: The indirect method determines net operating cash flow by adjusting net income. Under the indirect method, the $5,000 cash inflow from the sale of the truck is shown in the investing section. A $2,000 loss was recognized and properly deducted to determine net income. This loss, however, did not require the use of cash and should be added to net income in the operating section.
Answer (A) is incorrect. The $5,000 inflow should be shown in the investing section. Answer (B) is incorrect. No outflow of cash dividends occurred in Year 2. Answer (C) is incorrect. The decrease in receivables should be added to net income.

34. The total of cash provided (used) by operating activities plus cash provided (used) by investing activities plus cash provided (used) by financing activities is

A. Cash provided of $284,000.

B. Cash provided of $178,000.

C. Cash used of $582,000.

D. Equal to net income reported for fiscal year ended December 31, Year 2.

Answer (B) is correct. *(CMA, adapted)*
REQUIRED: The net total of cash provided and used.
DISCUSSION: The total of cash provided (used) by the three activities (operating, investing, and financing) should equal the increase or decrease in cash for the year. During Year 2, the cash balance increased from $106,000 to $284,000. Thus, the sources of cash must have exceeded the uses by $178,000.
Answer (A) is incorrect. This amount is the ending cash balance, not the change in the cash balance; it ignores the beginning balance. Answer (C) is incorrect. The cash balance increased during the year. Answer (D) is incorrect. Net income must be adjusted for noncash expenses and other accruals and deferrals.

35. The following information was taken from the accounting records of Oak Corporation for the year ended December 31:

Proceeds from issuance of preferred stock F	$4,000,000
Dividends paid on preferred stock F	400,000
Bonds payable converted to common stock	2,000,000
Payment for purchase of machinery	500,000
Proceeds from sale of plant building	1,200,000
2% stock dividend on common stock	300,000
Gain on sale of plant building	200,000

The net cash flows from investing and financing activities that should be presented on Oak's statement of cash flows for the year ended December 31 are, respectively,

A. $700,000 and $3,600,000.

B. $700,000 and $3,900,000.

C. $900,000 and $3,900,000.

D. $900,000 and $3,600,000.

Answer (A) is correct. *(CMA, adapted)*
REQUIRED: The respective net cash flows from investing and financing activities.
DISCUSSION: The relevant calculations are as follows:

Proceeds from sale of plant building	$1,200,000
Payment for purchase of machinery	(500,000)
Net cash provided by investing activities	$ 700,000

Proceeds from issuance of preferred stock	$4,000,000
Dividends paid on preferred stock	(400,000)
Net cash provided by financing activities	$3,600,000

Answer (B) is incorrect. The stock dividend has no effect on cash flows from financing activities. Answer (C) is incorrect. The gain on the sale of the building is double counted in determining the net cash flow from investing activities. Answer (D) is incorrect. The gain on the sale of the building is double counted in determining the net cash flow from investing activities.

1.8 Common-Size Financial Statements

36. In financial statement analysis, expressing all financial statement items as a percentage of base-year amounts is called

A. Horizontal common-size analysis.

B. Vertical common-size analysis.

C. Trend analysis.

D. Ratio analysis.

Answer (A) is correct. *(CMA, adapted)*
REQUIRED: The term for expressing all financial statement items as a percentage of base-year amounts.
DISCUSSION: Expressing financial statement items as percentages of corresponding base-year figures is a horizontal form of common-size (percentage) analysis that is useful for evaluating trends. The base amount is assigned the value of 100%, and the amounts for other years are denominated in percentages compared to the base year.
Answer (B) is incorrect. Vertical common-size (percentage) analysis presents figures for a single year expressed as percentages of a base amount on the balance sheet (e.g., total assets) and on the income statement (e.g., sales). Answer (C) is incorrect. The term "trend analysis" is most often applied to the quantitative techniques used in forecasting to fit a curve to given data. Answer (D) is incorrect. It is a general term.

37. On a common-size balance sheet, what would represent 100%?

A. Total current assets.

B. Total assets.

C. Total liabilities.

D. Total stockholders' equity.

Answer (B) is correct. *(Publisher, adapted)*
REQUIRED: The financial statement element that equals 100% on a common-size balance sheet.
DISCUSSION: On a common-size balance sheet, all amounts are converted to percentages with total assets representing 100%. Of course, if the balance sheet is in balance, the total of liabilities plus stockholders' equity will also equal 100%.

Use the Gleim **CMA Test Prep** Software for interactive testing with **additional multiple-choice questions!**

*Page
Intentionally
Left Blank*

1.10 ESSAY QUESTIONS

Scenario for Essay Questions 1, 2

A large American corporation participates in a highly competitive industry. To meet this competition and achieve profit goals, the company has chosen the decentralized form of organization. Each manager of a decentralized profit center is measured on the basis of profit contribution, market penetration, and return on investment. Failure to meet the objectives established by corporate management for these measures was not accepted and usually resulted in demotion or dismissal of a profit center manager.

An anonymous survey of managers in the company revealed that the managers felt the pressure to compromise their personal ethical standards to achieve the corporate objectives. For example, at certain plant locations, there was pressure to reduce quality control to a level that could not ensure that all unsafe products would be rejected. Also, sales personnel were encouraged to use questionable sales tactics to obtain orders, including gifts and other incentives to purchasing agents.

The chief executive officer is disturbed by the survey findings. In his opinion, such behavior cannot be condoned by the company. He concludes that the company should do something about this problem.

Questions

1. Discuss what might be the causes for the ethical problems described.
2. Outline a program that could be instituted by the company to help reduce the pressures on managers to compromise personal ethical standards in their work.

Essay Questions 1, 2 — Unofficial Answers

1. Corporate management has established an environment in which there is an incompatibility (lack of goal congruence) between the achievement of corporate objectives and personal ethics. Under the current situation, severe penalties have been imposed by top management whenever subordinates do not achieve the high levels of performance established by the predetermined objectives. This has caused lower level management to take unethical courses of action.

    Corporate management apparently utilizes an authoritarian, nonparticipative management style that does not consider contributions from lower level management. As a result of this type of management style, top management may have established unreasonable expectations and may not recognize the need to change the expectations in light of changing circumstances. These factors may result in subordinates choosing any means to reach the objectives.

    The penalty and reward system appears to be inappropriate. There is no positive feedback or encouragement for effective performance, and the penalties are heavy for failure to meet objectives. No code of ethics exists, and penalties are apparently nonexistent or minor for violation of acceptable business practices that are compatible with personal ethical standards.

2. A company program to reduce the pressures on lower level management who violate the personal ethical standards and acceptable business practices might include the following actions:

    a. Adopt a participative style of management. Encourage each lower level manager to contribute to the establishment of the goals by which (s)he is to be judged.
    b. Expand the feedback system to recognize and reward good performance, allow for investigation and explanation for substandard performance, and adjust for changing conditions.
    c. Adopt a corporate code of ethics or code of acceptable business practices.
    d. Display top management support for the code evidenced by words and actions.

Use **CMA Gleim Online** and **Essay Wizard** to practice additional essay questions in an exam-like environment.

STUDY UNIT TWO
RATIO ANALYSIS

(17 pages of outline)

This study unit is the **second of three** on **financial statement analysis**. The relative weight assigned to this major topic in Part 2 of the exam is **25%**. The three study units are

Study Unit 1: Ethics for the Corporation and Basic Financial Statements
Study Unit 2: Ratio Analysis
Study Unit 3: Profitability Analysis and Analytical Issues

After studying the outline and answering the questions in this study unit, you will have the skills necessary to address the following topics listed in the ICMA's Learning Outcome Statements:

Part 2 – Section A.2. Financial performance metrics – Financial ratios

The candidate should be able to:

Liquidity
a. calculate current assets, current liabilities, and net working capital
b. analyze working capital by calculating the current ratio, the quick (acid test) ratio, the cash ratio, the cash flow ratio, and the net working capital ratio
c. explain how changes in one or more of the elements of current assets, current liabilities, or unit sales can change the liquidity ratios and calculate that impact
d. demonstrate an understanding of the liquidity of current liabilities

Leverage
e. define solvency
f. define operating leverage and financial leverage
g. calculate degree of operating leverage and degree of financial leverage
h. demonstrate an understanding of the effect on the capital structure and solvency of a company with a change in the composition of debt vs. equity by calculating leverage ratios
i. calculate and interpret the financial leverage ratio, and determine the effect of a change in capital structure on this ratio
j. calculate and interpret the following ratios: total debt to total capital, debt to equity, long-term debt to equity, and debt to total assets
k. define, calculate, and interpret the following ratios: fixed charge coverage (earnings to fixed charges), interest coverage (times interest earned), and cash flow to fixed charges
l. discuss how capital structure decisions affect the risk profile of a firm

Activity
m. calculate and interpret accounts receivable turnover, inventory turnover, and accounts payables turnover
n. calculate and interpret days' sales outstanding in receivables, days' sales in inventory, and days' purchases in accounts payable
o. define and calculate the operating cycle and cash cycle of a firm
p. calculate and interpret total assets turnover and fixed asset turnover

2.1 LIQUIDITY RATIOS -- CALCULATIONS

1. **Elements of Liquidity**

   a. Liquidity is a firm's ability to pay its current obligations as they come due and thus remain in business in the short run. Liquidity reflects the ease with which assets can be converted to cash.

      1) Liquidity ratios measure this ability by relating a firm's liquid assets to its current liabilities.

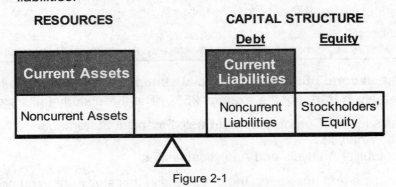

Figure 2-1

   b. **EXAMPLE** of a balance sheet:

RESOURCES	Current Year End	Prior Year End	FINANCING	Current Year End	Prior Year End
CURRENT ASSETS:			**CURRENT LIABILITIES:**		
Cash and equivalents	$ 325,000	$ 275,000	Accounts payable	$ 150,000	$ 75,000
Available-for-sale securities	165,000	145,000	Notes payable	50,000	50,000
Accounts receivable (net)	120,000	115,000	Accrued interest on note	5,000	5,000
Notes receivable	55,000	40,000	Current maturities of L.T. debt	100,000	100,000
Inventories	85,000	55,000	Accrued salaries and wages	15,000	10,000
Prepaid expenses	10,000	5,000	Income taxes payable	70,000	35,000
Total current assets	**$ 760,000**	**$ 635,000**	**Total current liabilities**	**$ 390,000**	**$ 275,000**
NONCURRENT ASSETS:			**NONCURRENT LIABILITIES:**		
Equity-method investments	$ 120,000	$ 115,000	Bonds payable	$ 500,000	$ 600,000
Property, plant, and equipment	1,000,000	900,000	Long-term notes payable	90,000	60,000
Less: accum. depreciation	(85,000)	(55,000)	Employee-related obligations	15,000	10,000
Goodwill	5,000	5,000	Deferred income taxes	5,000	5,000
Total noncurrent assets	**$1,040,000**	**$ 965,000**	**Total noncurrent liabilities**	**$ 610,000**	**$ 675,000**
			Total liabilities	**$1,000,000**	**$ 950,000**
			STOCKHOLDERS' EQUITY:		
			Preferred stock, $50 par	$ 120,000	$ 0
			Common stock, $1 par	500,000	500,000
			Additional paid-in capital	110,000	100,000
			Retained earnings	70,000	50,000
			Total stockholders' equity	**$ 800,000**	**$ 650,000**
Total assets	**$1,800,000**	**$1,600,000**	**Total liabilities and stockholders' equity**	**$1,800,000**	**$1,600,000**

c.   Current assets are the most liquid. They are expected to be converted to cash, sold, or consumed within 1 year or the operating cycle, whichever is longer. Ratios involving current assets thus measure a firm's ability to continue operating in the short run.

   1)   Current assets include, in descending order of liquidity: cash and equivalents; marketable securities; receivables; inventories; and prepaid items.

d.   Current liabilities, by the same token, are ones that must be settled the soonest. Specifically, they are expected to be settled or converted to other liabilities within 1 year or the operating cycle, whichever is longer.

   1)   Current liabilities include accounts payable, notes payable, current maturities of long-term debt, unearned revenues, taxes payable, wages payable, and other accruals.

e.   Net working capital reports the resources the company would have to continue operating in the short run if it had to liquidate all of its current liabilities at once.

Net Working Capital

Current assets – Current liabilities

   1)   EXAMPLE: Current Year: $760,000 – $390,000 = $370,000
                  Prior Year: $635,000 – $275,000 = $360,000

      a)   Although the company's current liabilities increased, its current assets increased by $10,000 more.

2.   **Liquidity Ratios**

a.   The **current ratio** is the most common measure of liquidity.

Current Ratio

$$\frac{Current\ assets}{Current\ liabilities}$$

   1)   EXAMPLE: Current Year: $760,000 ÷ $390,000 = 1.949
                  Prior Year: $635,000 ÷ $275,000 = 2.309

      a)   Although working capital increased in absolute terms ($10,000), current assets now provide less proportional coverage of current liabilities than in the prior year.

   2)   A low ratio indicates a possible solvency problem. An overly high ratio indicates that management may not be investing idle assets productively.

   3)   The general principle is that the current ratio should be proportional to the operating cycle. Thus, a shorter cycle may justify a lower ratio.

      a)   For example, a grocery store has a short operating cycle and can survive with a lower current ratio than could a gold mining company, which has a much longer operating cycle.

   4)   The quality of accounts receivable and merchandise inventory should be considered before evaluating the current ratio. A low receivables turnover (net credit sales ÷ average accounts receivable) and a low inventory turnover (cost of sales ÷ average inventory) indicate a need for a higher current ratio.

   5)   Use of LIFO lowers the current ratio.

b.   The **quick (acid test) ratio** excludes inventories and prepaids from the numerator, recognizing that those assets are difficult to liquidate at their stated values. The quick ratio is thus a more conservative measure than the basic current ratio.

Quick (Acid Test) Ratio

$$\frac{Cash\ +\ Marketable\ securities\ +\ Net\ receivables}{Current\ liabilities}$$

1)   EXAMPLE:
Current Year: ($325,000 + $165,000 + $120,000 + $55,000) ÷ $390,000 = 1.705
Prior Year: ($275,000 + $145,000 + $115,000 + $40,000) ÷ $275,000 = 2.091

   a)   In spite of its increase in total working capital, the company's position in its most liquid assets deteriorated significantly.

2)   This ratio measures the firm's ability to easily pay its short-term debts and avoids the problem of inventory valuation.

3)   A less conservative variation divides the difference between current assets and inventory by current liabilities.

c.   The **cash ratio** is an even more conservative variation.

Cash Ratio

$$\frac{Cash\ +\ Marketable\ securities}{Current\ liabilities}$$

1)   EXAMPLE: Current Year: ($325,000 + $165,000) ÷ $390,000 = 1.256
Prior Year: ($275,000 + $145,000) ÷ $275,000 = 1.527

   a)   In this working capital measure, the company's position declined, but coverage is still positive, i.e., the ratio is greater than 1.

d.   The **cash flow ratio** reflects the significance of cash flow for settling obligations as they become due.

Cash Flow Ratio

$$\frac{Cash\ flow\ from\ operations}{Current\ liabilities}$$

1)   EXAMPLE: The company's cash flows from operations for the two most recent years were $382,000 and $291,000 respectively.

Current Year: $382,000 ÷ $390,000 = 0.979
Prior Year: $291,000 ÷ $275,000 = 1.058

   a)   Unlike the prior year, the cash flows generated by the company in the most recent year were not sufficient to cover current liabilities.

e.   The **net working capital ratio** is the most conservative of the working capital ratios.

Net Working Capital Ratio

$$\frac{Current\ assets\ -\ Current\ liabilities}{Total\ assets}$$

1)   EXAMPLE: Current Year: ($760,000 − $390,000) ÷ $1,800,000 = 0.206
Prior Year: ($635,000 − $275,000) ÷ $1,600,000 = 0.225

   a)   Current liabilities are taking a bigger "bite" out of working capital than in the prior year.

3. **Liquidity of Current Liabilities**

    a. The liquidity of current liabilities is the ease with which a firm can issue new debt or raise new structured (convertible, puttable, callable, etc.) funds.

        1) The liquidity of current liabilities indicates the ease of funding or availability of sources of funding. A firm's ability to borrow in the financial markets is generally a function of its size, reputation, creditworthiness, and capital levels.

        2) Raising liquidity during an adverse situation often requires a combination of both asset liquidity and liability liquidity.

Stop and review! You have completed the outline for this subunit. Study multiple-choice questions 1 through 8 beginning on page 76.

2.2 LIQUIDITY RATIOS -- EFFECTS OF TRANSACTIONS

Some of the questions pertaining to liquidity ratios that a candidate will encounter on the CMA exam focus on the effects that typical business transactions have on a firm's liquidity rather than on the mechanics of calculating the ratios. This subunit consists entirely of such questions. Please review Subunit 2.1 before attempting to answer the questions in this subunit.

Stop and review! You have completed the outline for this subunit. Study multiple-choice questions 9 through 16 beginning on page 78.

2.3 ACTIVITY MEASURES

1. **Income Statement to Balance Sheet**

    a. Activity ratios measure how quickly the two major noncash assets are converted to cash.

        1) Whereas the ratios calculated in Subunit 2.1 report condition at a balance sheet date, the activity ratios measure results over a period of time, and thus draw information from the firm's income statement as well.

    b. EXAMPLE of an income statement:

	Current Year	Prior Year
Net sales	$1,800,000	$1,400,000
Cost of goods sold	(1,650,000)	(1,330,000)
Gross profit	$ 150,000	$ 70,000
SG&A expenses	(65,000)	(25,000)
Operating income	$ 85,000	$ 45,000
Other revenues and losses	(5,000)	0
Earnings before interest and taxes	$ 80,000	$ 45,000
Interest expense	(10,000)	(10,000)
Earnings before taxes	$ 70,000	$ 35,000
Income taxes (40%)	(28,000)	(14,000)
Net income	$ 42,000	$ 21,000

2.   **Receivables**

    a.   Accounts receivable turnover measures the efficiency of accounts receivable collection.

Accounts Receivable Turnover

$$\frac{Net\ credit\ sales}{Average\ accounts\ receivable}$$

        1)   EXAMPLE: All of the company's sales are on credit. Accounts receivable at the balance sheet date of the second prior year were $105,000.

            Current Year: $1,800,000 ÷ [($120,000 + $115,000) ÷ 2] = 15.3 times
            Prior Year: $1,400,000 ÷ [($115,000 + $105,000) ÷ 2] = 12.7 times

            a)   The company turned over its accounts receivable balance 2.6 more times during the current year, even as receivables were growing in absolute terms. Thus, the company's effectiveness at collecting accounts receivable has improved noticeably.

        2)   If a business is highly seasonal, a simple average of beginning and ending balances is inadequate. The monthly balances should be averaged instead.

        3)   A high turnover means that customers are paying their accounts promptly.

        4)   Since sales is in the numerator, higher sales without an increase in receivables will result in better turnover. Since receivables are in the denominator, encouraging customers to pay quickly (thereby lowering the balance in receivables) also results in a higher turnover ratio.

    b.   Days' sales outstanding in receivables (also called the average collection period) measures the average number of days it takes to collect a receivable.

Days' Sales Outstanding in Receivables

$$\frac{Days\ in\ year}{Accounts\ receivable\ turnover}$$

        1)   EXAMPLE: Current Year: 365 days ÷ 15.3 times = 23.9 days*
                         Prior Year: 365 days ÷ 12.7 times = 28.7 days

        *Uses rounded number (15.3 times). The result, 23.9 days, will be used in later figures.

            a)   Since the denominator (calculated in item 2.a.1)) increased and the numerator is a constant, days' sales will necessarily decrease. In addition to improving its collection practices, the company also may have become better at assessing the creditworthiness of its customers.

        2)   Besides 365, other possible numerators are 360 (for simplicity) and 300 (the number of business days in a year).

        3)   Days' sales outstanding in receivables can be compared with the firm's credit terms to determine whether the average customer is paying within the credit period.

3.   **Inventory**

   a.   Inventory turnover measures the efficiency of inventory management.

Inventory Turnover

$$\frac{Cost\ of\ goods\ sold}{Average\ inventory}$$

   1)   EXAMPLE: The balance in inventories at the balance sheet date of the second
        prior year was $45,000.

   Current Year: $1,650,000 ÷ [($85,000 + $55,000) ÷ 2] = 23.6 times
   Prior Year: $1,330,000 ÷ [($55,000 + $45,000) ÷ 2] = 26.6 times

   a)   The company did not turn over its inventories as many times during the
        current year. This is to be expected during a period of growing sales (and
        building inventory level) and so is not necessarily a sign of poor inventory
        management.

   2)   As with receivables turnover, if a business is highly seasonal, a simple average
        of beginning and ending balances is inadequate. The monthly balances should
        be averaged instead.

   3)   A high turnover implies that the firm is not carrying excess levels of inventory or
        inventory that is obsolete.

   4)   The ratio of a firm that uses LIFO may not be comparable with that of a firm with
        a higher inventory valuation.

   5)   Since cost of goods sold is in the numerator, higher sales without an increase in
        inventory balances will result in better turnover.

   6)   Since inventory is in the denominator, keeping inventory levels as low as
        possible also results in a higher turnover ratio.

   7)   The ideal level for inventory turnover is industry specific, with the nature of the
        inventory items impacting the ideal ratio. For example, spoilable items such as
        meat and dairy products will mandate a higher turnover ratio than would natural
        resources such as gold, silver, and coal. Thus, a grocery store should have a
        much higher inventory turnover ratio than a uranium mine or a jewelry store.

   b.   Days' sales in inventory measures the efficiency of the company's inventory
        management practices.

Days' Sales in Inventory

$$\frac{Days\ in\ year}{Inventory\ turnover}$$

   1)   EXAMPLE: Current Year: 365 days ÷ 23.6 times = 15.5 days
                   Prior Year: 365 days ÷ 26.6 times = 13.7 days

   a)   Since the numerator is a constant, the decreased inventory turnover
        calculated meant that days' sales tied up in inventory would increase.
        This is a common phenomenon during a period of increasing sales.
        However, it can also occur during periods of declining sales.

4.   **Payables**

a.   Accounts payable turnover measures the efficiency with which a firm manages the payment of vendors' invoices.

Accounts Payable Turnover

$$\frac{Purchases}{Average\ accounts\ payable}$$

1)   EXAMPLE: The company had current and prior year purchases of $1,760,000 and $1,440,000 respectively. Net accounts payable at the balance sheet date of the 2nd prior year were $65,000.

Current Year: $1,760,000 ÷ [($150,000 + $75,000) ÷ 2] = 15.6 times
Prior Year: $1,440,000 ÷ [($75,000 + $65,000) ÷ 2] = 20.6 times

a)   The company is now carrying a much higher balance in payables, so it is not surprising that the balance is turning over less often. It also may be the case that the company was paying invoices too soon in the prior year.

2)   If a business is highly seasonal, a simple average of beginning and ending balances is inadequate. The monthly balances should be averaged instead.

b.   Days' purchases in accounts payable measures the average number of days it takes to settle a payable.

Days' Purchases in Accounts Payable

$$\frac{Days\ in\ year}{Accounts\ payable\ turnover}$$

1)   EXAMPLE: Current Year: 365 days ÷ 15.6 times = 23.4 days*
                Prior Year: 365 days ÷ 20.6 times = 17.7 days

*The rounded number, 15.6, yields 23.4 days, which will be used in later calculations.

a)   The slower turnover lowers the denominator, thereby increasing the days' purchases in payables. This substantially extended period reflects mostly the fact that the balance in payables has doubled. It also may imply that the company was paying its suppliers too quickly in the prior year.

2)   The days' purchases in accounts payable can be compared with the average credit terms offered by a company's suppliers to determine whether the firm is paying its invoices on a timely basis (or too soon).

5.   **Operating Cycle**

a.   A firm's operating cycle is the amount of time that passes between the acquisition of inventory and the collection of cash on the sale of that inventory.

Operating Cycle

Days' sales in receivables + Days' sales in inventory

1)   EXAMPLE: Current Year: 23.9 days + 15.5 days = 39.4 days
                Prior Year: 28.7 days + 13.7 days = 42.4 days

a)   The company has managed to slightly reduce its operating cycle, even while increasing sales and building inventories.

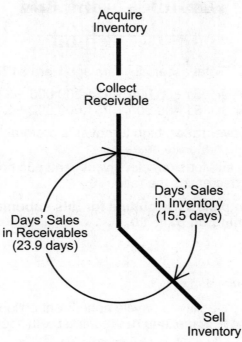

**Operating Cycle
39.4 Days**

Acquire
Inventory

Collect
Receivable

Days' Sales
in Inventory
(15.5 days)

Days' Sales
in Receivables
(23.9 days)

Sell
Inventory

Figure 2-2

6. **Cash Cycle**

   a. The cash cycle is that portion of the operating cycle that is not accounted for by days' purchases in accounts payable.

      1) This is somewhat counterintuitive because the cash cycle is the portion of the operating cycle when the company does <u>not</u> have cash, i.e., when cash is tied up in the form of inventory or accounts receivable.

      Operating cycle – Days' purchases in payables

      2) EXAMPLE: Current Year: 39.4 days – 23.4 days = 16.0 days
                  Prior Year: 42.4 days – 17.7 days = 24.7 days

         a) Of the company's total operating cycle of 39.4 days, cash is held for the 23.4 days that payables are outstanding. The 16.0 days of the cash cycle represent the period when cash is tied up as other forms of current assets.

7. **Other Activity Concepts**

   a. The fixed assets turnover ratio measures how efficiently the company is deploying its investment in plant to generate revenues.

      <u>Fixed Assets Turnover Ratio</u>

      $$\frac{Net\ sales}{Average\ net\ property,\ plant,\ and\ equipment}$$

      1) EXAMPLE: Two years ago, net property, plant, and equipment was $860,000.

         Current Year: $1,800,000 ÷ [($915,000 + $845,000) ÷ 2] = 2.05 times
         Prior Year: $1,400,000 ÷ [($845,000 + $860,000) ÷ 2] = 1.64 times

      2) This ratio is largely affected by the capital intensiveness of the company and its industry, by the age of the assets, and by the depreciation method used.

      3) A high turnover is preferable to a low turnover.

b.   The total assets turnover ratio measures how efficiently the company is deploying the totality of its resources to generate revenues.

Total Assets Turnover Ratio

$$\frac{Net\ sales}{Average\ total\ assets}$$

1)   EXAMPLE: Total assets 2 years ago were $1,520,000.

Current Year: $1,800,000 ÷ [($1,800,000 + $1,600,000) ÷ 2] = 1.06 times
Prior Year: $1,400,000 ÷ [($1,600,000 + $1,520,000) ÷ 2] = .897 times

2)   For all turnover ratios, high turnover is preferable because it implies effective use of assets to generate sales.

3)   Certain assets, for example, investments, do not relate to net sales. Their inclusion decreases the ratio.

Stop and review! You have completed the outline for this subunit. Study multiple-choice questions 17 through 24 beginning on page 80.

2.4 SOLVENCY

1.   **Elements of Solvency**

a.   Solvency is a firm's ability to pay its noncurrent obligations as they come due and thus remain in business in the long run (contrast with liquidity).

1)   The key ingredients of solvency are the firm's capital structure and degree of leverage.

b.   A firm's capital structure includes its sources of financing, both long- and short-term. These sources can be in the form of debt (external sources) or equity (internal sources).

1)   Capital structure decisions affect the risk profile of a firm. For example, a company with a higher percent of debt capital will be riskier than a firm with a high percentage of equity capital. Thus, when there is a lot of debt, equity investors will demand a higher rate of return on their investments to compensate for the risk brought about by the high use of financial leverage.

2)   Alternatively, a company with a high level of equity capital will be able to borrow at lower rates because debt holders will accept lower interest in exchange for the lower risk indicated by the equity cushion.

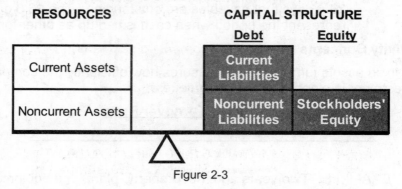

Figure 2-3

c. Debt is the creditor interest in the firm.

  1) The firm is contractually obligated to repay debtholders. The terms of repayment (i.e., timing of interest and principal) are specified in the debt agreement.

  2) As long as the return on debt capital exceeds the amount of interest paid, the use of debt financing is advantageous to a firm. This is due to the fact that interest payments on debt are tax-deductible.

  3) The tradeoff is that an increased debt load makes a firm riskier (since debt must be paid regardless of whether the company is profitable). At some point, either a firm will have to pay a higher interest rate than its return on debt or creditors will simply refuse to lend any more money.

d. Equity is the ownership interest in the firm.

  1) Equity is the permanent capital of an enterprise, contributed by the firm's owners in the hopes of earning a return.

  2) However, a return on equity is uncertain because equity embodies only a residual interest in the firm's assets (residual because it is the claim left over after all debt has been satisfied).

  3) Periodic returns to owners of excess earnings are referred to as dividends. The firm may be contractually obligated to pay dividends to preferred stockholders but not to common stockholders.

2. **Capital Structure Ratios**

a. These ratios report the relative proportions of debt and equity in a firm's capital structure at a given reporting date.

b. The total debt to total capital ratio measures the percentage of the firm's capital structure provided by creditors.

Total Debt to Total Capital Ratio

$$\frac{Total\ debt}{Total\ capital}$$

  1) EXAMPLE: Current Year: \$1,000,000 ÷ \$1,800,000 = 0.556
     Prior Year: \$950,000 ÷ \$1,600,000 = 0.594

     a) The company became slightly less reliant on debt in its capital structure during the current year. Although total debt rose, equity rose by a greater percentage. The company is thus less leveraged than before.

  2) When total debt to total capital is low, it means more of the firm's capital is supplied by the stockholders. Thus, creditors prefer this ratio to be low as a cushion against losses.

c. The debt to equity ratio is a direct comparison of the firm's debt load versus its equity stake.

Debt to Equity Ratio

$$\frac{Total\ debt}{Stockholders'\ equity}$$

  1) EXAMPLE: Current Year: \$1,000,000 ÷ \$800,000 = 1.25
     Prior Year: \$950,000 ÷ \$650,000 = 1.46

     a) The amount by which the company's debts exceed its equity stake declined in the current year.

  2) Like the previous ratio, the debt to equity ratio reflects long-term debt-payment ability. Again, a low ratio means a lower relative debt burden and thus better chances of repayment of creditors.

d.   The long-term debt to equity ratio reports the long-term debt burden carried by a company per dollar of equity.

Long-Term Debt to Equity Ratio

$$\frac{Long\text{-}term\ debt}{Stockholders'\ equity}$$

1)   EXAMPLE: Current Year: $610,000 ÷ $800,000 = 0.763
                        Prior Year: $675,000 ÷ $650,000 = 1.038

    a)   The company has greatly improved its long-term debt burden. It now carries less than one dollar of long-term debt for every dollar of equity.

    b)   A low ratio means a firm will have an easier time raising new debt (since its low current debt load makes it a good credit risk).

e.   The debt to total assets ratio (also called the debt ratio) reports the long-term debt burden carried by a company per dollar of assets.

Debt to Total Assets Ratio

$$\frac{Total\ liabilities}{Total\ assets}$$

1)   EXAMPLE: Current Year: $1,000,000 ÷ $1,800,000 = 0.556
                        Prior Year: $950,000 ÷ $1,600,000 = 0.594

    a)   Although total liabilities increased in absolute terms, this ratio improved because total assets increased even more.

2)   Numerically, this ratio is identical to the debt to total capital ratio.

3.   **Earnings Coverage**

a.   These ratios are a creditor's best measure of a firm's ongoing ability to generate the earnings that will allow it to satisfy its long-term debts and remain solvent.

b.   The times interest earned ratio is an income statement approach to evaluating a firm's ongoing ability to meet the interest payments on its debt obligations.

Times Interest Earned Ratio

$$\frac{EBIT}{Interest\ expense}$$

1)   EXAMPLE: Current Year: $80,000 ÷ $10,000 = 8.00 times
                        Prior Year: $45,000 ÷ $10,000 = 4.50 times

    a)   The company is less able to comfortably pay interest expense. In the prior year EBIT was twelve and a half times interest expense, but in the current year, it is only eight and a third times.

2)   For the ratio to be meaningful, net income cannot be used in the numerator. Since what is being measured is the ability to pay interest, earnings before interest and taxes is appropriate.

3)   The most accurate calculation of the numerator includes only earnings expected to recur. Consequently, unusual or infrequent items, extraordinary items, discontinued operations, and the effects of accounting changes should be excluded.

4)   The denominator should include capitalized interest.

c. The earnings to fixed charges ratio (also called the fixed charge coverage ratio) extends the times interest earned ratio to include the interest portion associated with long-term lease obligations.

Earnings to Fixed Charges Ratio

$$\frac{EBIT + Interest\ portion\ of\ operating\ leases}{Interest\ expense + Interest\ portion\ of\ operating\ leases + Dividends\ on\ preferred\ stock}$$

1) This is a more conservative ratio since it measures the coverage of earnings over all fixed charges, not just interest expense.

d. The cash flow to fixed charges ratio removes the difficulties of comparing amounts prepared on an accrual basis.

Cash Flow to Fixed Charges Ratio

$$\frac{Pre\text{-}tax\ operating\ cash\ flow}{Interest\ expense + Interest\ portion\ of\ operating\ leases + Dividends\ on\ preferred\ stock}$$

Stop and review! You have completed the outline for this subunit. Study multiple-choice questions 25 through 32 beginning on page 83.

2.5 LEVERAGE

For the purpose of the CMA exam, be sure that you understand and can calculate both leverage ratios. However, calculating these ratios is just one aspect of how you could be tested on this topic. Candidates should be fully prepared to apply these calculations and demonstrate an understanding through multiple-choice or essay questions of how changes in cost structure may affect these ratios. Ensure that you understand what risks and advantages are associated with high operating or financial leverage.

1. **Types of Leverage**

   a. Leverage is the relative amount of fixed cost in a firm's overall cost structure. Leverage creates risk because fixed costs must be covered, regardless of the level of sales.

      1) **Operating leverage** arises from the use of a high level of plant and machinery in the production process, revealed through charges for depreciation, property taxes, etc.

      2) **Financial leverage** arises from the use of a high level of debt in the firm's financing structure, revealed through amounts paid out for interest.

   b. Thus, although leverage arises from items on the balance sheet, it is measured by examining its effects on the income statement. A general statement of leverage is

$$Degree\ of\ leverage = \frac{Pre\text{-}fixed\text{-}cost\ income\ amount}{Post\text{-}fixed\text{-}cost\ income\ amount}$$

2. **Degree of Operating Leverage (DOL)**

   a. Calculation of the DOL requires financial information prepared on the variable-costing basis, since variable costing isolates the use of fixed costs in the firm's ongoing operations.

Degree of Operating Leverage (DOL) -- Single-Period Version

$$\frac{Contribution\ margin}{Operating\ income\ or\ EBIT}$$

b. A firm's DOL varies with the level of sales, as shown in the following example:

1) EXAMPLE:

Degree of Operating Leverage at Various Levels of Sales

Sales volume:	100 Units	250 Units	500 Units	750 Units	1,000 Units
Net sales ($1,000 per unit)	$ 100,000	$ 250,000	$ 500,000	$ 750,000	$1,000,000
Variable costs ($800 per unit)	(80,000)	(200,000)	(400,000)	(600,000)	(800,000)
Contribution margin	$ 20,000	$ 50,000	$ 100,000	$ 150,000	$ 200,000
Fixed costs	(100,000)	(100,000)	(100,000)	(100,000)	(100,000)
Operating income (loss)	$ (80,000)	$ (50,000)	$ 0	$ 50,000	$ 100,000
Degree of operating leverage (DOL)	**(0.25)**	**(1.00)**	**Undef.**	**3.00**	**2.00**

2) This firm breaks even at sales of 500 units.

3) As the example demonstrates, DOL is not a meaningful measure when the firm incurs an operating loss.

c. Two versions of DOL are in common use.

1) The version shown on the previous page compares contribution margin and variable-basis operating income in a single reporting period.

2) The percentage-change version of DOL measures the changes in income statement amounts from one period to another.

Degree of Operating Leverage (DOL) -- Percentage-Change Version

$$\frac{\%\Delta \text{ in operating income or EBIT}}{\%\Delta \text{ in sales}}$$

a) The percentage-change version is necessary when the only financial reports available are those prepared on the absorption basis.

b) Note that, in this version, the numerator and denominator are different from those in the single-period version.

3) EXAMPLE:

Degree of Operating Leverage
Period-to-Period Percentage Change

	Current Year	Prior Year
Net sales	$1,800,000	$1,400,000
Cost of goods sold	(1,450,000)	(1,170,000)
Gross margin	$ 350,000	$ 230,000
SG&A expenses	(160,000)	(80,000)
Operating income	$ 190,000	$ 150,000
Other income and loss	(40,000)	(25,000)
Earnings before interest and taxes	$ 150,000	$ 125,000
Interest expense	(15,000)	(10,000)
Earnings before taxes	$ 135,000	$ 115,000
Income taxes (40%)	(54,000)	(46,000)
Net income	$ 81,000	$ 69,000

Numerator: %Δ in EBIT = ($150,000 – $125,000) ÷ $125,000   = 20.00%
Denominator: %Δ in sales = ($1,800,000 – $1,400,000) ÷ $1,400,000 = 28.57%

Degree of operating leverage (DOL) = 20.00% ÷ 28.57% = 0.7%

a) Every 1% change in sales generates a 0.7% change in EBIT.

d. A firm with high operating leverage necessarily carries a greater degree of risk because fixed costs must be covered regardless of the level of sales.

1) However, such a firm is also able to expand production rapidly in times of higher product demand. Thus, the more leveraged a firm is in its operations, the more sensitive operating income is to changes in sales volume.

3. **Degree of Financial Leverage (DFL)**

   a. The DFL also results from a pre-fixed-cost income to post-fixed-cost income comparison, this time on the firm's financing structure.

Degree of Financial Leverage (DFL) -- Single-Period Version

$$\frac{Earnings\ before\ interest\ and\ taxes\ (EBIT)}{Earnings\ before\ taxes\ (EBT)}$$

   1) This formula isolates the effects of interest as the only truly fixed financing cost.
   2) EXAMPLE:

Degree of Financial Leverage
Single-Period Version

	Current Year	Prior Year
Net sales	$1,800,000	$1,400,000
Cost of goods sold	(1,450,000)	(1,170,000)
Gross margin	$ 350,000	$ 230,000
SG&A expenses	(160,000)	(80,000)
Operating income	$ 190,000	$ 150,000
Other income and loss	(40,000)	(25,000)
Earnings before interest and taxes	**$ 150,000**	**$ 125,000**
Interest expense	(15,000)	(10,000)
Earnings before taxes	**$ 135,000**	**$ 115,000**
Income taxes (40%)	(54,000)	(46,000)
Net income	$ 81,000	$ 69,000

Degree of financial leverage
Current year: $150,000 ÷ $135,000 = 1.11   The company needs $1.11 of EBIT to
Prior year: $125,000 ÷ $115,000 = 1.09   generate $1.00 of EBT. Last year, only
$1.09 of EBIT was needed to generate
$1.00 of EBT.

   b. Two versions of DFL are in common use.

   1) The version shown above compares EBIT and EBT from a single reporting period.
   2) The percentage-change version examines the changes in income statement amounts over two periods.

Degree of Financial Leverage (DFL) -- Percentage-Change Version

$$\frac{\%\Delta\ in\ net\ income}{\%\Delta\ in\ EBIT}$$

   a) Note that, in the percentage-change version, the numerator and denominator are different from those in the single-period version.

   3) EXAMPLE:

Numerator: %Δ in net income = ($81,000 – $69,000) ÷ $69,000 = 17.39%
Denominator: %Δ in EBIT = ($150,000 – $125,000) ÷ $125,000   = 20.00%

Degree of financial leverage (DFL) = 17.39% ÷ 28.57% = 0.8696%

   a) Every 1% change in EBIT generates a 0.8696% change in net income.

   c. A firm with high financial leverage necessarily carries a greater degree of risk because debt must be serviced regardless of the level of earnings.

   1) However, if such a firm is profitable, there is more residual profit for the shareholders after debt service (interest on debt is tax-deductible), reflected in higher earnings per share. Furthermore, debt financing permits the current equity holders to retain control.

Stop and review! You have completed the outline for this subunit. Study multiple-choice questions 33 through 35 beginning on page 86.

2.6 CORE CONCEPTS

Liquidity Ratios

- **Liquidity** is a firm's ability to pay its current obligations as they come due and thus remain in business in the short run. Liquidity measures the ease with which assets can be converted to cash.
- **Liquidity ratios** measure this ability by relating a firm's liquid assets to its current liabilities.
  - The **current ratio**

    Current assets ÷ Current liabilities

  - The **quick (acid test) ratio**

    (Cash and equivalents + Marketable securities + Net receivables) ÷ Current liabilities

  - The **cash ratio**

    (Cash and equivalents + Marketable securities) ÷ Current liabilities

  - The **cash flow ratio**

    Cash flow from operations ÷ Current liabilities

  - The **net working capital ratio**

    (Current assets – Current liabilities) ÷ Total assets

- The **liquidity of current liabilities** is the ease with which a firm can issue new debt or raise new structured (convertible, puttable, callable, etc.) funds.

Activity Measures

- **Activity ratios** measure how quickly the two major noncash assets are converted to cash. They measure results over a period of time and thus draw information from the firm's income statement.
  - **Accounts receivable turnover**

    Net credit sales ÷ Average accounts receivable

  - **Days' sales outstanding in receivables**

    Days in year ÷ Accounts receivable turnover

  - **Inventory turnover**

    Cost of goods sold ÷ Average inventory

  - **Days' sales in inventory**

    Days in year ÷ Inventory turnover

  - **Accounts payable turnover**

    Purchases ÷ Average accounts payable

  - **Days' purchases in accounts payable**

    Days in year ÷ Accounts payable turnover

- A firm's **operating cycle** is the amount of time that passes between the acquisition of inventory and the collection of cash on the sale of that inventory.

  Days' sales in receivables + Days' sales in inventory

- The **cash cycle** is that portion of the operating cycle that is not days' purchases in accounts payable. This is somewhat counterintuitive because the cash cycle is the portion of the operating cycle when the company does not have cash, i.e., when cash is tied up in the form of inventory or accounts receivable.

  Operating cycle – Days' purchases in payables

- **Other Activity Ratios**
  - **Fixed assets turnover**

    Net sales ÷ Average net fixed assets
  - **Total assets turnover**

    Net sales ÷ Average total assets

Solvency

- **Solvency** is a firm's ability to pay its noncurrent obligations as they come due and thus remain in business in the long run (contrast with liquidity). The key ingredients of solvency are the firm's capital structure and degree of leverage.
- A firm's **capital structure** includes its sources of financing, both long- and short-term. These sources can be in the form of debt (external sources) or equity (internal sources). Debt is the creditor interest in the firm. Equity is the ownership interest in the firm.
- **Capital structure ratios** report the relative proportions of debt and equity in a firm's capital structure.
  - The **total debt to total capital ratio**

    Total debt ÷ Total capital
  - The **debt to equity ratio**

    Total debt ÷ Stockholders' equity
  - The **long-term debt to equity capital ratio** (also called the debt to equity ratio)

    Long-term debt ÷ Stockholders' equity
  - The **debt to total assets ratio** (also called the debt ratio)

    Total liabilities ÷ Total assets
- **Earnings coverage** is a creditor's best measure of a firm's ongoing ability to generate the earnings that will allow it to satisfy its long-term debts and remain solvent.
  - The **times interest earned ratio** is an income statement approach to evaluating a firm's ongoing ability to meet the interest payments on its debt obligations.

    EBIT ÷ Interest expense
  - The **earnings to fixed charges ratio** (also called the fixed charge coverage ratio) extends the times interest earned ratio to include the interest portion associated with long-term lease obligations.
  - The **cash flow to fixed charges ratio** removes the difficulties of comparing amounts prepared on an accrual basis.

Leverage

- A firm's **leverage** is the relative amount of the fixed cost in a firm's overall cost structure. Leverage, by definition, creates risk because fixed costs must be covered, regardless of the level of sales.
  - **Degree of operating leverage**

    Single-period: Contribution margin ÷ EBIT
    Percentage-change: %Δ in operating income or EBIT ÷ %Δ in sales
  - **Degree of financial leverage**

    Single-period: EBIT ÷ EBT
    Percentage-change: %Δ in net income or EBIT ÷ %Δ in EBIT

QUESTIONS

2.1 Liquidity Ratios -- Calculations

1. Given an acid test ratio of 2.0, current assets of $5,000, and inventory of $2,000, the value of current liabilities is

    A. $1,500

    B. $2,500

    C. $3,500

    D. $6,000

Answer (A) is correct. *(CIA, adapted)*
    REQUIRED: The value of current liabilities given the acid test ratio, current assets, and inventory.
    DISCUSSION: The acid test, or quick, ratio equals the quick assets (cash, marketable securities, and accounts receivable) divided by current liabilities. Current assets equal the quick assets plus inventory and prepaid expenses. (This question assumes that the entity has no prepaid expenses.) Given current assets of $5,000, inventory of $2,000, and no prepaid expenses, the quick assets must be $3,000. Because the acid test ratio is 2.0, the quick assets are double the current liabilities. Current liabilities therefore are equal to $1,500 ($3,000 quick assets ÷ 2.0).
    Answer (B) is incorrect. Dividing the current assets by 2.0 results in $2,500. Current assets includes inventory, which should not be included in the calculation of the acid test ratio. Answer (C) is incorrect. Adding inventory to current assets rather than subtracting it results in $3,500. Answer (D) is incorrect. Multiplying the quick assets by 2 instead of dividing by 2 results in $6,000.

Questions 2 through 4 are based on the following information.

Tosh Enterprises reported the following account information:

Accounts receivable	$400,000	Inventory	$800,000
Accounts payable	160,000	Land	500,000
Bonds payable, due in 10 years	600,000	Notes payable, due in 6 months	100,000
Cash	200,000	Prepaid expense	80,000
Interest payable, due in 3 months	20,000		

The company has a normal operating cycle of 6 months.

---

2. The current ratio for Tosh Enterprises is

    A. 1.68

    B. 2.14

    C. 5.00

    D. 5.29

Answer (D) is correct. *(Publisher, adapted)*
    REQUIRED: The current ratio.
    DISCUSSION: The current ratio equals current assets divided by current liabilities. Current assets consist of cash, accounts receivable, inventory, and prepaid expenses, a total of $1,480,000 ($400,000 + $200,000 + $800,000 + $80,000). Current liabilities consist of accounts payable, interest payable, and notes payable, a total of $280,000 ($160,000 + $20,000 + $100,000). Hence, the current ratio is 5.29 ($1,480,000 ÷ $280,000).
    Answer (A) is incorrect. The figure of 1.68 includes long-term bonds payable among the current liabilities. Answer (B) is incorrect. The figure of 2.14 is the quick ratio. Answer (C) is incorrect. The figure of 5.00 excludes prepaid expenses from current assets.

---

3. What is Tosh Enterprises' quick (acid test) ratio?

    A. 0.68

    B. 1.68

    C. 2.14

    D. 2.31

Answer (C) is correct. *(Publisher, adapted)*
    REQUIRED: The quick ratio.
    DISCUSSION: The quick (acid test) ratio equals the quick assets divided by current liabilities. For Tosh, quick assets consist of cash ($200,000) and accounts receivable ($400,000), a total of $600,000. Current liabilities consist of accounts payable ($160,000), interest payable ($20,000), and notes payable ($100,000), a total of $280,000. Hence, the quick ratio is 2.14 ($600,000 ÷ $280,000).
    Answer (A) is incorrect. This ratio includes long-term bonds payable among the current liabilities. Answer (B) is incorrect. This ratio includes long-term bonds payable among the current liabilities and inventory and prepaid expenses among the quick assets. Answer (D) is incorrect. This ratio excludes interest payable from the current liabilities.

4. Tosh Enterprises' amount of working capital is

A. $600,000

B. $1,120,000

C. $1,200,000

D. $1,220,000

Answer (C) is correct. *(Publisher, adapted)*
   REQUIRED: The amount of working capital.
   DISCUSSION: Working capital equals current assets minus current liabilities. For Tosh Enterprises, current assets consist of cash, accounts receivable, inventory, and prepaid expenses, a total of $1,480,000 ($400,000 + $200,000 + $800,000 + $80,000). Current liabilities consist of accounts payable, interest payable, and notes payable, a total of $280,000 ($160,000 + $20,000 + $100,000). Accordingly, working capital is $1,200,000 ($1,480,000 − $280,000).
   Answer (A) is incorrect. The amount of $600,000 includes long-term bonds payable among the current liabilities.
   Answer (B) is incorrect. The amount of $1,120,000 excludes prepaid expenses from current assets. Answer (D) is incorrect. The amount of $1,220,000 excludes interest payable from current liabilities.

Questions 5 and 6 are based on the following information. The selected data pertain to Tilghman Company at December 31:

Quick assets	$208,000
Acid test ratio	2.6 to 1
Current ratio	3.5 to 1
Net sales for the year	$1,800,000
Cost of sales for the year	$990,000
Average total assets for the year	$1,200,000

5. Tilghman Company's current liabilities at December 31 equal

A. $59,429

B. $80,000

C. $134,857

D. $187,200

Answer (B) is correct. *(CIA, adapted)*
   REQUIRED: The current liabilities at year end.
   DISCUSSION: Current liabilities can be calculated using the following relationship:

$$\text{Acid test ratio} = \text{Quick assets} \div \text{Current liabilities}$$
$$2.6 = \$208,000 \div \text{Current liabilities}$$
$$\text{Current liabilities} \times 2.6 = \$208,000$$
$$\text{Current liabilities} = \$208,000 \div 2.6$$
$$= \$80,000$$

6. Tilghman Company's inventory balance at December 31 is

A. $72,000

B. $187,200

C. $231,111

D. $282,857

Answer (A) is correct. *(CIA, adapted)*
   REQUIRED: The inventory balance at year end.
   DISCUSSION: Ending inventory can be calculated using the following relationships:

$$\text{Acid test ratio} = \text{Quick assets} \div \text{Current liabilities}$$
$$2.6 = \$208,000 \div \text{Current liabilities}$$
$$\text{Current liabilities} \times 2.6 = \$208,000$$
$$\text{Current liabilities} = \$208,000 \div 2.6$$
$$= \$80,000$$

$$\text{Current assets} \div \text{Current liabilities} = \text{Current ratio}$$
$$\text{Current assets} \div \$80,000 = 3.5$$
$$\text{Current assets} = \$280,000$$

Assuming that Tilghman has no prepaid expenses, inventory is the only difference between current assets and quick assets. Thus, the ending balance of inventory must be $72,000 ($280,000 − $208,000).

7. A financial analyst has obtained the following data from Kryton Industries' financial statements:

Cash	$ 200,000
Marketable securities	100,000
Accounts receivable, net	300,000
Inventories, net	480,000
Prepaid expenses	120,000
Total current assets	$1,200,000
Accounts payable	$250,000
Income taxes	50,000
Accrued liabilities	100,000
Current portion of	
long-term debt	200,000
Total current liabilities	$600,000

In order to determine Kryton's ability to pay current obligations, the financial analyst would calculate Kryton's cash ratio as

A. .50

B. .80

C. 1.00

D. 1.20

Answer (A) is correct. *(CMA, adapted)*
    REQUIRED: The cash ratio given relevant information.
    DISCUSSION: The cash ratio, a more conservative measure of liquidity than the quick ratio, is calculated as follows:

Cash ratio = (Cash + Marketable securities) ÷ Current liabilities
         = ($200,000 + $100,000) ÷ $600,000
         = 0.5

    Answer (B) is incorrect. Improperly including only inventories in the numerator results in a ratio of .80. Answer (C) is incorrect. Improperly including accounts receivable in the numerator results in a ratio of 1.00. Answer (D) is incorrect. Improperly including accounts receivable and prepaid expenses in the numerator results in a ratio of 1.20.

8. The following financial information applies to Sycamore Company:

Cash	$ 10,000
Marketable securities	18,000
Accounts receivable	120,000
Inventories	375,000
Prepaid expenses	12,000
Accounts payable	75,000
Long-term debt -- current portion	20,000
Long-term debt	400,000
Sales	1,650,000

What is the acid test (or quick) ratio for Sycamore?

A. 1.56

B. 1.97

C. 2.13

D. 5.63

Answer (A) is correct. *(CMA, adapted)*
    REQUIRED: The acid test ratio given relevant information.
    DISCUSSION: The acid test (quick) ratio equals the quick assets (cash, marketable securities, and accounts receivable) divided by current liabilities. Sycamore's acid test ratio is thus 1.558 [($10,000 + $18,000 + $120,000) ÷ ($75,000 + $20,000)].
    Answer (B) is incorrect. Improperly leaving the current portion of long-term debt from the denominator results in 1.9. Answer (C) is incorrect. Improperly including prepaid expenses in the numerator and leaving the current portion of long-term debt out of the denominator results in 2.13. Answer (D) is incorrect. Improperly including inventories and prepaid expenses in the numerator results in 5.63.

2.2 Liquidity Ratios -- Effects of Transactions

9. Windham Company has current assets of $400,000 and current liabilities of $500,000. Windham Company's current ratio will be increased by

A. The purchase of $100,000 of inventory on account.

B. The payment of $100,000 of accounts payable.

C. The collection of $100,000 of accounts receivable.

D. Refinancing a $100,000 long-term loan with short-term debt.

Answer (A) is correct. *(CMA, adapted)*
    REQUIRED: The transaction that will increase a current ratio of less than 1.0.
    DISCUSSION: The current ratio equals current assets divided by current liabilities. An equal increase in both the numerator and denominator of a current ratio less than 1.0 causes the ratio to increase. Windham Company's current ratio is .8 ($400,000 ÷ $500,000). The purchase of $100,000 of inventory on account would increase the current assets to $500,000 and the current liabilities to $600,000, resulting in a new current ratio of .833.
    Answer (B) is incorrect. This transaction decreases the current ratio. Answer (C) is incorrect. The current ratio would be unchanged. Answer (D) is incorrect. This transaction decreases the current ratio.

Questions 10 through 15 are based on the following information. Depoole Company is a manufacturer of industrial products that uses a calendar year for financial reporting purposes. Assume that total quick assets exceeded total current liabilities both before and after the transaction described. Further assume that Depoole has positive profits during the year and a credit balance throughout the year in its retained earnings account.

10. Depoole's payment of a trade account payable of $64,500 will

   A. Increase the current ratio, but the quick ratio would not be affected.

   B. Increase the quick ratio, but the current ratio would not be affected.

   C. Increase both the current and quick ratios.

   D. Decrease both the current and quick ratios.

Answer (C) is correct. *(CMA, adapted)*
   REQUIRED: The effect of paying a trade account payable on the current and quick ratios.
   DISCUSSION: Current assets consist of more assets than quick assets; thus, if quick assets exceed current liabilities, then current assets do also. It can also be concluded that both ratios are greater than 1. An equal reduction in the numerator and the denominator, such as a payment of a trade payable, will cause each ratio to increase.

11. Depoole's purchase of raw materials for $85,000 on open account will

   A. Increase the current ratio.

   B. Decrease the current ratio.

   C. Increase net working capital.

   D. Decrease net working capital.

Answer (B) is correct. *(CMA, adapted)*
   REQUIRED: The effect of a credit purchase of raw materials on the current ratio or working capital.
   DISCUSSION: The purchase increases both the numerator and denominator of the current ratio by adding inventory to the numerator and payables to the denominator. Because the ratio before the purchase was greater than 1, the ratio is decreased.
   Answer (A) is incorrect. The current ratio is decreased. Answer (C) is incorrect. The purchase of raw materials on account has no effect on working capital (current assets and current liabilities change by the same amount). Answer (D) is incorrect. The purchase of raw materials on account has no effect on working capital (current assets and current liabilities change by the same amount).

12. Depoole's collection of a current accounts receivable of $29,000 will

   A. Increase the current ratio.

   B. Decrease the current ratio and the quick ratio.

   C. Increase the quick ratio.

   D. Not affect the current or quick ratios.

Answer (D) is correct. *(CMA, adapted)*
   REQUIRED: The effect of collection of a current account receivable on the current and quick ratios.
   DISCUSSION: Collecting current accounts receivable has no effect on either the current ratio or the quick ratio because assets (both current and quick) are reduced for the collection of receivables and increased by the same amount for the receipt of cash. Current liabilities are unchanged by the transaction.

13. Obsolete inventory of $125,000 was written off by Depoole during the year. This transaction

   A. Decreased the quick ratio.

   B. Increased the quick ratio.

   C. Increased net working capital.

   D. Decreased the current ratio.

Answer (D) is correct. *(CMA, adapted)*
   REQUIRED: The effect of writing off obsolete inventory.
   DISCUSSION: Writing off obsolete inventory reduces current assets, but not quick assets (cash, marketable securities, and accounts receivable). Thus, the current ratio was reduced and the quick ratio was unaffected.
   Answer (A) is incorrect. The quick ratio was not affected. Answer (B) is incorrect. The quick ratio was not affected. Answer (C) is incorrect. Working capital was decreased.

14. Refer to the information on the preceding page(s). Depoole's issuance of serial bonds in exchange for an office building, with the first installment of the bonds due late this year,

- A. Decreases net working capital.
- B. Decreases the current ratio.
- C. Decreases the quick ratio.
- D. Affects all of the answers as indicated.

Answer (D) is correct. *(CMA, adapted)*
REQUIRED: The effect of issuing serial bonds with the first installment due late this year.
DISCUSSION: The first installment is a current liability; thus the amount of current liabilities increases with no corresponding increase in current assets. The effect is to decrease working capital, the current ratio, and the quick ratio.
Answer (A) is incorrect. The bond issuance would also decrease the current ratio and the quick ratio. Answer (B) is incorrect. The bond issuance would also decrease net working capital and the quick ratio. Answer (C) is incorrect. The bond issuance would also decrease net working capital and the current ratio.

15. Refer to the information on the preceding page(s). Depoole's early liquidation of a long-term note with cash affects the

- A. Current ratio to a greater degree than the quick ratio.
- B. Quick ratio to a greater degree than the current ratio.
- C. Current and quick ratio to the same degree.
- D. Current ratio but not the quick ratio.

Answer (B) is correct. *(CMA, adapted)*
REQUIRED: The effect of an early liquidation of a long-term note with cash.
DISCUSSION: The numerators of the quick and current ratios are decreased when cash is expended. Early payment of a long-term liability has no effect on the denominator (current liabilities). Since the numerator of the quick ratio, which includes cash, net receivables, and marketable securities, is less than the numerator of the current ratio, which includes all current assets, the quick ratio is affected to a greater degree.

16. Peters Company has a 2-to-1 current ratio. This ratio would increase to more than 2 to 1 if

- A. A previously declared stock dividend were distributed.
- B. The company wrote off an uncollectible receivable.
- C. The company sold merchandise on open account that earned a normal gross margin.
- D. The company purchased inventory on open account.

Answer (C) is correct. *(CMA, adapted)*
REQUIRED: The transaction that would increase a current ratio that is greater than 1.
DISCUSSION: The current ratio equals current assets divided by current liabilities. Thus, an increase in current assets or a decrease in current liabilities, by itself, increases the current ratio. The sale of inventory at a profit increases current assets without changing liabilities. Inventory decreases, and receivables increase by a greater amount. Thus, total current assets and the current ratio increase.
Answer (A) is incorrect. The distribution of a stock dividend affects only stockholders' equity accounts (debit common stock dividend distributable and credit common stock). Answer (B) is incorrect. Writing off an uncollectible receivable does not affect total current assets. The allowance account absorbs the bad debt. Thus, the balance of net receivables is unchanged. Answer (D) is incorrect. The purchase of inventory increases current assets and current liabilities by the same amount. The transaction reduces a current ratio in excess of 1.0 since the numerator and denominator of the ratio increase by the same amount.

2.3 Activity Measures

17. When a balance sheet amount is related to an income statement amount in computing a ratio,

- A. The balance sheet amount should be converted to an average for the year.
- B. The income statement amount should be converted to an average for the year.
- C. Both amounts should be converted to market value.
- D. Comparisons with industry ratios are not meaningful.

Answer (A) is correct. *(CMA, adapted)*
REQUIRED: The true statement about relating balance sheet to income statement amounts in a ratio.
DISCUSSION: In ratios that relate the income statement to the balance sheet (e.g., inventory turnover, asset turnover, receivables turnover, and return on assets), the balance sheet figure should be an average. The reason is that the income statement amounts represent activity over a period of time. Thus, the balance sheet figure should be adjusted to reflect assets available for use throughout the period.
Answer (B) is incorrect. The income statement amount is a single figure for an entire year; there is nothing to average. Answer (C) is incorrect. Traditional financial statements and the ratios computed from the data they present are mostly stated in historical cost terms. Answer (D) is incorrect. Comparison is the purpose of ratio usage. All ratios are meaningless unless compared to something else, such as an industry average.

18. Accounts receivable turnover ratio will normally decrease as a result of

    A. The write-off of an uncollectible account (assume the use of the allowance for doubtful accounts method).

    B. A significant sales volume decrease near the end of the accounting period.

    C. An increase in cash sales in proportion to credit sales.

    D. A change in credit policy to lengthen the period for cash discounts.

Answer (D) is correct. *(CMA, adapted)*
    REQUIRED: The event that will cause the accounts receivable turnover ratio to decrease.
    DISCUSSION: The accounts receivable turnover ratio equals net credit sales divided by average receivables. Hence, it will decrease if a company lengthens the credit period or the discount period because the denominator will increase as receivables are held for longer times.
    Answer (A) is incorrect. Write-offs do not reduce net receivables (gross receivables – the allowance) and will not affect the receivables balance and therefore the turnover ratio if an allowance system is used. Answer (B) is incorrect. A decline in sales near the end of the period signifies fewer credit sales and receivables, and the effect of reducing the numerator and denominator by equal amounts is to increase the ratio if the fraction is greater than 1.0. Answer (C) is incorrect. An increase in cash sales with no diminution of credit sales will not affect receivables.

19. Which one of the following inventory cost flow assumptions will result in a higher inventory turnover ratio in an inflationary economy?

    A. FIFO.

    B. LIFO.

    C. Weighted average.

    D. Specific identification.

Answer (B) is correct. *(CMA, adapted)*
    REQUIRED: The cost flow assumption that will result in a higher inventory turnover ratio in an inflationary economy.
    DISCUSSION: The inventory turnover ratio equals the cost of goods sold divided by the average inventory. LIFO assumes that the last goods purchased are the first goods sold and that the oldest goods purchased remain in inventory. The result is a higher cost of goods sold and a lower average inventory than under other inventory cost flow assumptions if prices are rising. Because cost of goods sold (the numerator) will be higher and average inventory (the denominator) will be lower than under other inventory cost flow assumptions, LIFO produces the highest inventory turnover ratio.

20. The days' sales in receivables ratio will be understated if the company

    A. Uses a natural business year for its accounting period.

    B. Uses a calendar year for its accounting period.

    C. Uses average receivables in the ratio calculation.

    D. Does not use average receivables in the ratio calculation.

Answer (A) is correct. *(CMA, adapted)*
    REQUIRED: The reason the days' sales in receivables ratio will be understated.
    DISCUSSION: The days' sales in receivables ratio equals the days in the year divided by the receivables turnover ratio (sales ÷ average receivables). Days' sales may also be computed based only on ending receivables. In either case, use of the natural business year tends to understate the ratio because receivables will usually be at a low point at the beginning and end of the natural year. For example, a ski resort may close its books on May 31, a low point in its operating cycle.
    Answer (B) is incorrect. Using a calendar year will not necessarily affect the usefulness of the days' sales ratio. Answer (C) is incorrect. Using average receivables would not always understate the ratio. The ratio could be higher or lower depending on changes in sales volume or the percentage of credit to cash sales, or other factors. Answer (D) is incorrect. The ratio could be higher or lower depending on changes in sales volume or the percentage of credit to cash sales, or other factors.

Questions 21 and 22 are based on the following information. The information below pertains to Devlin Company.

Statement of Financial Position as of May 31 (in thousands)		
	Year 2	Year 1
Assets		
Current assets		
Cash	$ 45	$ 38
Trading securities	30	20
Accounts receivable (net)	68	48
Inventory	90	80
Prepaid expenses	22	30
Total current assets	$255	$216
Investments, at equity	38	30
Property, plant, and equipment (net)	375	400
Intangible assets (net)	80	45
Total assets	$748	$691
Liabilities		
Current liabilities		
Notes payable	$ 35	$ 18
Accounts payable	70	42
Accrued expenses	5	4
Income taxes payable	15	16
Total current liabilities	$125	$ 80
Long-term debt	35	35
Deferred taxes	3	2
Total liabilities	$163	$117
Equity		
Preferred stock, 6%, $100 par value, cumulative	$150	$150
Common stock, $10 par value	225	195
Additional paid-in capital -- common stock	114	100
Retained earnings	96	129
Total equity	$585	$574
Total liabilities and equity	$748	$691

Income Statement for the year ended May 31 (in thousands)		
	Year 2	Year 1
Net sales	$480	$460
Costs and expenses		
Costs of goods sold	330	315
Selling, general, and administrative	52	51
Interest expense	8	9
Income before taxes	$ 90	$ 85
Income taxes	36	34
Net income	$ 54	$ 51

21. Devlin Company's inventory turnover for the year ended May 31, Year 2, was

A. 3.67 times.

B. 3.88 times.

C. 5.33 times.

D. 5.65 times.

Answer (B) is correct. *(CMA, adapted)*
REQUIRED: The inventory turnover.
DISCUSSION: Inventory turnover equals cost of goods sold divided by average inventory. Hence, the inventory turnover is 3.88 times per year {$330 COGS ÷ [($90 + $80) ÷ 2]}.
Answer (A) is incorrect. The figure of 3.67 is based on ending inventory. Answer (C) is incorrect. The figure of 5.33 equals sales divided by ending inventory. Answer (D) is incorrect. The figure of 5.65 is based on sales, not cost of goods sold.

22. Devlin Company's asset turnover for the year ended May 31, Year 2, was

A. 0.08 times.

B. 0.46 times.

C. 0.67 times.

D. 0.83 times.

Answer (C) is correct. *(CMA, adapted)*
REQUIRED: The asset turnover.
DISCUSSION: Asset turnover equals net sales divided by average total assets. Consequently, the asset turnover is .67 times per year {$480 net sales ÷ [($748 + $691) ÷ 2]}.
Answer (A) is incorrect. The figure of 0.08 is based on net income. Answer (B) is incorrect. The figure of 0.46 uses cost of goods sold in the numerator. Answer (D) is incorrect. The figure of 0.83 is based on average total shareholders' equity.

23. To determine the operating cycle for a retail department store, which one of the following pairs of items is needed?

   A. Days' sales in accounts receivable and average merchandise inventory.

   B. Cash turnover and net sales.

   C. Accounts receivable turnover and inventory turnover.

   D. Asset turnover and return on sales.

Answer (C) is correct. *(CMA, adapted)*
   REQUIRED: The pair of items needed to determine the operating cycle for a retailer.
   DISCUSSION: The operating cycle is the time needed to turn cash into inventory, inventory into receivables, and receivables back into cash. For a retailer, it is the time from purchase of inventory to collection of cash. Thus, the operating cycle of a retailer is equal to the sum of the number of days' sales in inventory and the number of days' sales in receivables. Inventory turnover equals cost of goods sold divided by average inventory. The days' sales in inventory equals 365 (or another period chosen by the analyst) divided by the inventory turnover. Accounts receivable turnover equals net credit sales divided by average receivables. The days' sales in receivables equals 365 (or other number) divided by the accounts receivable turnover.
   Answer (A) is incorrect. Cost of sales must be known to calculate days' sales in inventory. Answer (B) is incorrect. These items are insufficient to permit determination of the operating cycle. Answer (D) is incorrect. These items are insufficient to permit determination of the operating cycle.

24. Carson Corporation computed the following items from its financial records for the current year:

Current ratio	2 to 1
Inventory turnover	54 days
Accounts receivable turnover	24 days
Current liabilities turnover	36 days

The number of days in Carson's operating cycle for the current year was

   A. 60

   B. 90

   C. 78

   D. 42

Answer (C) is correct. *(CMA, adapted)*
   REQUIRED: The number of days in the operating cycle.
   DISCUSSION: The operating cycle is the time needed to turn cash into inventory, inventory into receivables, and receivables back into cash. It is equal to the sum of the number of days' sales in inventory and the number of days' sales in receivables. The number of Carson's days' sales in inventory is given as 54 days. The number of days' sales in receivables is given as 24. Therefore, the number of days in the operating cycle is 78 (54 + 24).
   Answer (A) is incorrect. The sum of the number of days' sales in receivables and the number of days' purchases in accounts payable is 60. Answer (B) is incorrect. The sum of the number of days' sales in inventory and the number of days' purchases in payables is 90. Answer (D) is incorrect. The sum of the number of days' sales in inventory and the number of days' sales in receivables minus the number of days' purchases in payables is 42.

2.4 Solvency

25. A debt to equity ratio is

   A. About the same as the debt to assets ratio.

   B. Higher than the debt to assets ratio.

   C. Lower than the debt to assets ratio.

   D. Not correlated with the debt to assets ratio.

Answer (B) is correct. *(CMA, adapted)*
   REQUIRED: The true statement comparing the debt to equity and debt to assets ratios.
   DISCUSSION: Because debt plus equity equals assets, a debt to equity ratio would have a lower denominator than a debt to assets ratio. Thus, the debt to equity ratio would be higher than the debt to assets ratio.
   Answer (A) is incorrect. The ratios would always be different unless either debt or equity equaled zero. Answer (C) is incorrect. The lower denominator in the debt to equity ratio means that it would always be higher than the debt to assets ratio. Answer (D) is incorrect. The two ratios are related in that they always move in the same direction.

26. The relationship of the total debt to the total equity of a corporation is a measure of

A. Liquidity.

B. Profitability.

C. Creditor risk.

D. Solvency.

Answer (C) is correct. *(CMA, adapted)*
REQUIRED: The characteristic measured by the relationship of total debt to total equity.
DISCUSSION: The debt to equity ratio is a measure of risk to creditors. It indicates how much equity cushion is available to absorb losses before the interests of debt holders would be impaired. The less leveraged the company, the safer the creditors' interests.
Answer (A) is incorrect. Liquidity concerns how quickly cash can be made available to pay debts as they come due. Answer (B) is incorrect. The debt to equity ratio evaluates a company's capital structure and is thus oriented toward the balance sheet. It does not measure the use (profits) made of assets. Answer (D) is incorrect. Solvency is the availability of assets to service debt. Technically, whenever the debt to equity ratio can be computed with a meaningful answer, it can be said that the firm is solvent because assets, by definition, have to exceed debts.

Questions 27 and 28 are based on the following information.

Selected data from Ostrander Corporation's financial statements for the years indicated are presented in thousands.

	Year 2 Operations
Net credit sales	$4,175
Cost of goods sold	2,880
Interest expense	50
Income tax	120
Gain on disposal of a segment (net of tax)	210
Administrative expense	950
Net income	385

	December 31	
	Year 2	Year 1
Cash	$ 32	$ 28
Trading securities	169	172
Accounts receivable (net)	210	204
Merchandise inventory	440	420
Tangible fixed assets	480	440
Total assets	1,397	1,320
Current liabilities	370	368
Total liabilities	790	750
Common stock outstanding	226	210
Retained earnings	381	360

---

27. The times interest earned ratio for Ostrander Corporation for Year 2 is

A. .57 times.

B. 7.70 times.

C. 3.50 times.

D. 6.90 times.

Answer (D) is correct. *(CMA, adapted)*
REQUIRED: The times interest earned ratio for Year 2.
DISCUSSION: The interest coverage ratio is computed by dividing earnings before interest and taxes by interest expense. Net income of $385, minus the disposal gain of $210, is added to income taxes of $120 and interest expense of $50 to produce a ratio numerator of $345. Dividing $345 by $50 results in an interest coverage of 6.90 times.
Answer (A) is incorrect. This figure is the debt ratio. Answer (B) is incorrect. This figure is based on net income from operations after taxes and interest. Answer (C) is incorrect. This figure results from not adding interest and taxes to net income after the gain on disposal is subtracted.

28. The total debt to equity ratio for Ostrander Corporation in Year 2 is

A. 3.49

B. 0.77

C. 2.07

D. 1.30

Answer (D) is correct. *(CMA, adapted)*
REQUIRED: The total debt to equity ratio for Year 2.
DISCUSSION: Total equity consists of the $226 of capital stock and $381 of retained earnings, or $607. Debt is given as the $790 of total liabilities. Thus, the ratio is 1.30 ($790 ÷ $607).
Answer (A) is incorrect. Total liabilities divided by common stock outstanding equals 3.49. Answer (B) is incorrect. Equity divided by debt equals 0.77. Answer (C) is incorrect. Total liabilities divided by retained earnings equals 2.07.

	Ramer	Matson	Industry Average
Current ratio	3.50	2.80	3.00
Accounts receivable turnover	5.00	8.10	6.00
Inventory turnover	6.20	8.00	6.10
Times interest earned	9.00	12.30	10.40
Debt to equity ratio	0.70	0.40	0.55
Return on investment	0.15	0.12	0.15
Dividend payout ratio	0.80	0.60	0.55
Earnings per share	$3.00	$2.00	--

29. Which one of the following is correct if both companies have the same total assets and the same sales?

A. Ramer has more cash than Matson.

B. Ramer has fewer current liabilities than Matson.

C. Matson is more effectively using financial leverage.

D. Matson has a shorter operating cycle than Ramer.

Answer (D) is correct. *(CMA, adapted)*
REQUIRED: The correct statement assuming that both firms have the same total assets and total sales.
DISCUSSION: Ramer's accounts receivable turnover and inventory turnover are much lower than Matson's. Because Matson is collecting its receivables more quickly and holding inventory for a shorter time, it has a much shorter operating cycle than Ramer. Matson's operating cycle is about 91.7 days [(365 ÷ 8.1) + (365 ÷ 8.0)]. Ramer's operating cycle is about 131.2 days [(365 ÷ 5.0) + (365 ÷ 6.2)].
Answer (A) is incorrect. The amount of cash is not determinable from these facts. Answer (B) is incorrect. The amount of current liabilities is not determinable from these facts. Answer (C) is incorrect. Matson is not as highly leveraged, and no information is given about rate of return on shareholders' equity.

30. The attitudes of both Ramer and Matson concerning risk are best explained by the

A. Current ratio, accounts receivable turnover, and inventory turnover.

B. Dividend payout ratio and earnings per share.

C. Current ratio and earnings per share.

D. Debt to equity ratio and times interest earned.

Answer (D) is correct. *(CMA, adapted)*
REQUIRED: The statement that best explains the companies' attitudes toward risk.
DISCUSSION: Matson is the more conservative company because it is less highly leveraged (lower debt to equity ratio and a higher interest coverage). Moreover, it also pays out a smaller portion of its earnings in the form of dividends (lower dividend payout ratio). These ratios reflect management intent.
Answer (A) is incorrect. These are liquidity ratios that do not concern risk incurrence. Answer (B) is incorrect. EPS does not indicate management's intent with respect to risk. Answer (C) is incorrect. The current ratio and EPS are not indicators of the level of risk accepted.

31. Some of the ratios and data for Ramer and Matson are affected by income taxes. Assuming no interperiod income tax allocation, which of the following items would be directly affected by income taxes for the period?

A. Current ratio and debt to equity ratio.

B. Accounts receivable turnover and inventory turnover.

C. Return on investment and earnings per share.

D. Debt to equity ratio and dividend payout ratio.

Answer (C) is correct. *(CMA, adapted)*
REQUIRED: The ratios directly affected by income taxes.
DISCUSSION: Income taxes are an expense of the business and affect rates of return and earnings per share. Any ratio that uses net income as a part of the calculation is affected, e.g., return on investment, EPS, and dividend payout.
Answer (A) is incorrect. Neither ratio is based on net income. Answer (B) is incorrect. These turnover ratios are based on asset accounts and figures at the top of the income statement, not net income. Answer (D) is incorrect. The debt to equity ratio is not affected by taxes.

32. All of the following financial indicators are measures of liquidity and activity **except** the

A. Average collection period in days.

B. Merchandise inventory turnover.

C. Accounts receivable turnover.

D. Times interest earned ratio.

Answer (D) is correct. *(CMA, adapted)*
REQUIRED: The ratio not a measure of liquidity and activity.
DISCUSSION: Liquidity ratios measure a firm's ability to pay its obligations in the short term and thus to continue operations. Examples include the current ratio and acid test (quick) ratio. Activity ratios measure the firm's use of assets to generate revenue and income. Examples include inventory turnover, average collection period, and receivables turnover. Times interest earned is a ratio that measures the firm's ability to cover its interest burden.
Answer (A) is incorrect. Average collection period in days is an activity ratio. Answer (B) is incorrect. Merchandise inventory turnover is an activity ratio. Answer (C) is incorrect. Accounts receivable turnover is an activity ratio.

2.5 Leverage

Question 33 is based on the following information. The data presented below show actual figures for selected accounts of McKeon Company for the fiscal year ended May 31, Year 1, and selected budget figures for the Year 2 fiscal year. McKeon's controller is in the process of reviewing the Year 2 budget and calculating some key ratios based on the budget. McKeon Company monitors yield or return ratios using the average financial position of the company. (Round all calculations to three decimal places if necessary.)

	5/31/Year 2	5/31/Year 1
Current assets	$210,000	$180,000
Noncurrent assets	275,000	255,000
Current liabilities	78,000	85,000
Long-term debt	75,000	30,000
Common stock ($30 par value)	300,000	300,000
Retained earnings	32,000	20,000

	Year 2 Operations
Sales*	$350,000
Cost of goods sold	160,000
Interest expense	3,000
Income taxes (40% rate)	48,000
Dividends declared and paid in Year 2	60,000
Administrative expense	67,000

*All sales are credit sales.

	Current Assets	
	5/31/Year 2	5/31/Year 1
Cash	$ 20,000	$10,000
Accounts receivable	100,000	70,000
Inventory	70,000	80,000
Prepaid expenses	20,000	20,000

33. The degree of financial leverage to be employed by McKeon Company in Year 2 is

A. 1.640

B. 1.600

C. 1.025

D. 0.600

Answer (C) is correct. *(CMA, adapted)*
REQUIRED: The budgeted degree of financial leverage.
DISCUSSION: The degree of financial leverage for a reporting period equals earnings before interest and taxes (EBIT) divided by earnings before taxes (EBT). McKeon's can be calculated as follows:

Sales	$ 350,000
Cost of goods sold	(160,000)
Administrative expenses	(67,000)
EBIT	$ 123,000
Interest expense	(3,000)
EBT	$ 120,000
Income taxes	(48,000)
Net income	$ 72,000

DFL = $123,000 ÷ $120,000 = 1.025

34. This year, Nelson Industries increased earnings before interest and taxes (EBIT) by 17%. During the same period, net income after tax increased by 42%. The degree of financial leverage that existed during the year is

- A. 1.70
- B. 4.20
- C. 2.47
- D. 5.90

Answer (C) is correct. *(CMA, adapted)*
REQUIRED: The degree of financial leverage.
DISCUSSION: The percentage-change version of the degree of financial leverage equals the percentage change in net income over the percentage change in EBIT. Accordingly, Nelson's degree of financial leverage is 2.47 (42% ÷ 17%).

35. A firm with a higher degree of operating leverage when compared to the industry average implies that the

- A. Firm has higher variable costs.
- B. Firm's profits are more sensitive to changes in sales volume.
- C. Firm is more profitable.
- D. Firm is less risky.

Answer (B) is correct. *(CMA, adapted)*
REQUIRED: The effect of a higher degree of operating leverage (DOL).
DISCUSSION: Operating leverage is a measure of the degree to which fixed costs are used in the production process. A company with a higher percentage of fixed costs (higher operating leverage) has greater risk than one in the same industry that relies more heavily on variable costs. However, such a firm is also able to expand production rapidly in times of higher product demand. Thus, the more leveraged a firm is in its operations, the more sensitive operating income is to changes in sales volume.
Answer (A) is incorrect. A firm with higher operating leverage has higher fixed costs and lower variable costs. Answer (C) is incorrect. A firm with higher leverage will be relatively more profitable than a firm with lower leverage when sales are high. The opposite is true when sales are low. Answer (D) is incorrect. A firm with higher leverage is more risky. Its reliance on fixed costs is greater.

2.7 ESSAY QUESTIONS

Scenario for Essay Questions 1, 2

The accounting staff of CCB Enterprises has completed the preparation of financial statements for Fiscal Year 5. The Statement of Income for the current year and the Comparative Statement of Financial Position for Year 5 and Year 4 are reproduced below and on the next page.

The accounting staff calculates selected financial ratios after the financial statements are prepared. Average balance sheet account balances are used in computing ratios involving income statement accounts. Ending balance sheet account balances are used in computing ratios involving only balance sheet items. The ratios have not been calculated for Year 5. Financial ratios that were calculated for Year 4 and their respective values are as follows:

• Times interest earned	5.16 times
• Return on total assets	12.5%
• Return on operating assets	20.2%
• Return on common stockholders' equity	29.1%

CCB Enterprises
Statement of Income
Year Ended December 31, Year 5
($000 omitted)

Revenue:		
Net sales	$800,000	
Other	60,000	
Total revenue		$860,000
Expenses:		
Cost of goods sold	$540,000	
Research and development	25,000	
Selling and administrative	155,000	
Interest	20,000	
Total expenses		(740,000)
Income before income taxes		$120,000
Income taxes		(48,000)
Net income		$ 72,000

CCB Enterprises
Comparative Statement of Financial Position
December 31, Year 5 and Year 4
($000 omitted)

Assets	Year 5	Year 4
Current assets:		
Cash and short-term investments	$ 26,000	$ 21,000
Receivables, less allowance for doubtful accounts		
($1,100 in Year 5 and $1,400 in Year 4)	48,000	50,000
Inventories, at lower of FIFO cost or market	65,000	62,000
Prepaid items and other current assets	5,000	3,000
Total current assets	$144,000	$136,000
Other assets:		
Investments, at cost	$106,000	$106,000
Deposits	10,000	8,000
Total other assets	$116,000	$114,000
Property, plant, and equipment:		
Land	$ 12,000	$ 12,000
Buildings and equipment, less accumulated		
depreciation ($126,000 in Year 5 and $122,000 in Year 4)	268,000	248,000
Total property, plant, and equipment	$280,000	$260,000
Total assets	$540,000	$510,000

Liabilities and Stockholders' Equity		
Current liabilities:		
Short-term loans	$ 22,000	$ 24,000
Accounts payable	72,000	71,000
Salaries, wages, and other	26,000	27,000
Total current liabilities	$120,000	$122,000
Long-term debt	160,000	171,000
Total liabilities	$280,000	$293,000
Stockholders' equity:		
Common stock, at par	$ 44,000	$ 42,000
Paid-in capital in excess of par	64,000	61,000
Total paid-in capital	$108,000	$103,000
Retained earnings	152,000	114,000
Total stockholders' equity	$260,000	$217,000
Total liabilities and stockholders' equity	$540,000	$510,000

Questions

1. Explain how the use of financial ratios can be advantageous to management.

2. Calculate the following financial ratios for Year 5 for CCB Enterprises (round your answer to three decimal places):

   a. Times interest earned
   b. Receivables turnover ratio
   c. Inventory turnover
   d. Days' sales in inventory
   e. Total debt ratio
   f. Total debt/equity ratio
   g. Current ratio
   h. Quick (acid test) ratio

Essay Questions 1, 2 — Unofficial Answers

1. Financial ratios relate financial statement line items to each other. By calculating standardized ratios, management can assess the firm's liquidity, financial activity, solvency, and profitability. Management can also compare the firm's performance to that of others in its industry.

2. Year 5 financial ratios:

    a. Times interest earned = Earnings before interest and taxes (EBIT) ÷ Interest expense
        = ($120,000 + $20,000) ÷ $20,000
        = 7 times

    b. Receivables turnover ratio = Net credit sales ÷ Average receivables
        = $800,000 ÷ [($48,000 + $50,000) ÷2]
        = $800,000 ÷ $49,000
        = 16.327 times

    c. Inventory turnover ratio = Cost of goods sold ÷ Average inventory
        = $540,000 ÷ [($65,000 + $62,000) ÷ 2]
        = $540,000 ÷ $63,500
        = 8.504 times

    d. Days' sales in inventory = Days in year ÷ Inventory turnover ratio
        = 365 days ÷ 8.504
        = 42.921 days

    e. Total debt ratio = Total liabilities ÷ Total assets
        = $280,000 ÷ $540,000
        = 51.9%

    f. Total debt to equity ratio = Total liabilities ÷ Total stockholders' equity
        = $280,000 ÷ $260,000
        = 1.08

    g. Current ratio = Current assets ÷ Current liabilities
        = $144,000 ÷ $120,000
        = 1.2

    h. Quick (acid test) ratio = (Cash + Marketable securities + Net receivables) ÷ Current liabilities
        = ($26,000 + $48,000) ÷ $120,000
        = 0.62

Use **CMA Gleim Online** and **Essay Wizard** to practice additional essay questions in an exam-like environment.

STUDY UNIT THREE
PROFITABILITY ANALYSIS AND ANALYTICAL ISSUES

(34 pages of outline)

This study unit is the **last of three** on **financial statement analysis**. The relative weight assigned to this major topic in Part 2 of the exam is **25%**. The three study units are

Study Unit 1: Ethics for the Organization and Basic Financial Statements
Study Unit 2: Ratio Analysis
Study Unit 3: Profitability Analysis and Analytical Issues

After studying the outline and answering the questions in this study unit, you will have the skills necessary to address the following topics listed in the ICMA's Learning Outcome Statements:

Part 2 – Section A.2. Financial performance metrics – Financial ratios

The candidate should be able to:

Statements a. through p. are covered in Study Unit 2.

Profitability

q. calculate and interpret gross profit margin percentage, operating profit margin percentage, net profit margin percentage and earnings before interest, taxes, depreciation, and amortization (EBITDA) margin percentage

r. calculate and interpret return on assets (ROA) and return on equity (ROE)

Market

s. calculate and interpret the market/book ratio, the price/earnings ratio, and price to EBITDA ratio

t. calculate and interpret book value per share

u. identify and explain the limitations of book value per share

v. calculate and interpret basic and diluted earnings per share

w. calculate and interpret earnings yield, dividend yield, dividend payout ratio, and shareholder return

General

x. identify the limitations of ratio analysis

y. demonstrate a familiarity with the sources of financial information about public companies and industry ratio averages

z. evaluate the performance of an entity based on multiple ratios

Part 2 – Section A.3. Profitability analysis

The candidate should be able to:

a.   demonstrate an understanding of the factors that contribute to inconsistent definitions of "equity," "assets," and "return" when using ROA and ROE

b.   analyze return on assets and return on equity using the DuPont model

c.   calculate ROE based on the DuPont model

d.   describe how the DuPont model enhances the analysis of ROE calculations

e.   determine the effect on return on total assets of a change in one or more elements of the financial statements

f.   disaggregate return on common equity (ROCE) into profit margin (net margin) on sales, total asset turnover, and equity multiplier (leverage) and calculate these ratios

g.   identify factors to be considered in measuring income, including estimates, accounting methods, disclosure incentives, and the different needs of users

h.   explain the importance of the source, stability, and trend of sales and revenue

i.   demonstrate an understanding of the relationship between revenue and receivables and revenue and inventory

j.   determine the effect on revenue of changes in revenue recognition and measurement methods

k.   analyze company cost of sales by calculating and interpreting the gross profit margin

l.   distinguish between gross profit margin, operating profit margin, and net profit margin, and analyze the effects of changes in the components of each

m.   define and perform a variation analysis (percentage change over time)

n.   calculate and interpret sustainable equity growth

Part 2 – Section A.4. Analytical issues in financial accounting

*Note: The focus of this section is analysis of financial statements. With the exception of the statement of cash flows, preparation of financial statements will **not** be required.*

The candidate should be able to:

a.   demonstrate an understanding of the impact of foreign exchange fluctuations

   1.   identify and explain issues in the accounting for foreign operations (e.g., historical vs. current rate and the treatment of translation gains and losses)

   2.   define functional currency

   3.   distinguish between translation (all-current method) and remeasurement (temporal method) and describe the effects on the income statement and the balance sheet

   4.   calculate the financial ratio impact of a change in exchange rates

   5.   determine the impact on reported cash flow of a change in exchange rates

   6.   discuss the possible impact on management and investor behavior of volatility in reported earnings

b.   demonstrate an understanding of the impact of inflation on financial ratios and the reliability of financial ratios

   c.   off-balance sheet financing

       1.   define and explain off-balance sheet financing

       2.   identify and describe the following forms of off-balance sheet financing: (i) leases; (ii) special purpose entities; (iii) sale of receivables; and (iv) joint ventures

       3.   explain why companies use off-balance sheet financing

       4.   calculate the impact of off-balance sheet financing on the debt-to-equity ratio

Statement d. is covered in Study Unit 1.

   e.   describe how to adjust financial statements for changes in accounting treatments (changes, estimates, and errors) and how these adjustments impact financial ratios

   f.   major differences in reported financial results when using GAAP vs. IFRS and the impact on analysis

       1.   identify and describe the following differences between U.S. GAAP and IFRS: (i) revenue recognition, with respect to the sale of goods, services, deferred receipts and construction contracts; (ii) expense recognition, with respect to share-based payments and employee benefits; (iii) intangible assets, with respect to development costs and revaluation; (iv) inventories, with respect to costing methods, valuation, and write-downs (e.g., LIFO); (v) leases, with respect to leases of land and buildings; (vi) long-lived assets, with respect to revaluation, depreciation, and capitalization of borrowing costs; (vii) impairment of assets, with respect to determination, calculation, and reversal of loss; and (viii) financial statement presentation, with respect to extraordinary items and changes in equity

       2.   determine the correct accounting treatment under U.S. GAAP and under IFRS for each of the differences above

       3.   calculate the impact on income, assets, liabilities, and equity, as well as financial ratios, of a change from U.S. GAAP to IFRS for the differences listed above

   g.   fair value accounting

       1.   describe how the disclosure of fair value can supplement ratio analysis

       2.   explain fair value accounting (mark-to-market) and discuss the advantages and disadvantages of this method compared to the historical method

       3.   compare financial ratios based on historical cost to those based on fair value

   h.   distinguish between book value and market value; and distinguish between accounting profit and economic profit

   i.   identify the determinants and indicators of earnings quality

3.1 PROFITABILITY RATIOS

1. **Income Statement Percentages**

   a.   Gross profit margin is what percentage of gross revenues remains with the firm after paying for merchandise. The key analysis with respect to the gross profit margin is whether it is keeping up with the increase or decrease in sales.

       1)   For example, a 10% increase in sales should be accompanied by at least a 10% increase in the gross profit margin.

   b.   Operating profit margin is what percentage remains after selling and general and administrative expenses have been paid.

c.   **Net profit margin** is what percentage remains after other gains and losses (including interest expense) and income taxes have been added or deducted.

1)   EXAMPLE:

	Dollars	Percent
Net sales	$1,800,000	100.0%
Cost of goods sold	(1,650,000)	(91.7%)
Gross margin	**$ 150,000**	**8.3%**
SG&A expenses	(65,000)	(3.6%)
Operating income	**$ 85,000**	**4.7%**
Other income and loss	(5,000)	(0.3%)
Earnings before interest and taxes	$ 80,000	4.4%
Interest expense	(10,000)	(0.6%)
Earnings before taxes	$ 70,000	3.8%
Income taxes (40%)	(28,000)	(1.6%)
Net income	**$ 42,000**	**2.4%** (Net profit margin)

d.   **Earnings before interest, taxes, depreciation, and amortization (EBITDA)** is a commonly used performance measure that approximates accrual-basis profits from ongoing operations.

1)   EBITDA is arrived at by adding back the two major noncash expenses to EBIT.

EBITDA Margin Percentage

$$\frac{EBITDA}{Net\ sales}$$

2.   **Measures of Return on Investment**

NOTE: These examples use denominator amounts from the sample balance sheet on page 60.

a.   Return on assets, or ROA (also called return on total assets, or ROTA), is a straightforward measure of how well management is deploying the firm's assets in the pursuit of a profit.

Return on Assets (ROA)

$$\frac{Net\ income}{Average\ total\ assets}$$

1)   EXAMPLE:

Return on assets (ROA) = Net income ÷ Average total assets
= $42,000 ÷ [($1,800,000 + $1,600,000) ÷ 2]
= $42,000 ÷ $1,700,000
= 2.47%

b.   Return on equity (ROE) measures the return per owner dollar invested.

Return on Equity (ROE)

$$\frac{Net\ income}{Average\ total\ equity}$$

1)   EXAMPLE:

Return on equity (ROE) = Net income ÷ Average total equity
= $42,000 ÷ [($800,000 + $650,000) ÷ 2]
= $42,000 ÷ $725,000
= 5.79%

c.   The difference in the two denominators is total liabilities. ROE will therefore always be greater than ROA.

Stop and review! You have completed the outline for this subunit. Study multiple-choice questions 1 through 5 beginning on page 125.

3.2 PROFITABILITY ANALYSIS

Determining the profitability of a business is an important aspect of a management accountant's role within the organization. As a CMA, you will need to be able to calculate ROE and ROA using the DuPont model along with explaining how it enhances analysis. Remember, the CMA exam requires you to demonstrate several levels of knowledge. You not only need to demonstrate that you know these formulas, but that you are able to properly apply, analyze, and evaluate based on a given set of data. Additionally, pay close attention to the discussion on inconsistent definitions as you will be expected to understand the factors that contribute to these inconsistencies.

1. **Inconsistent Definitions**

   a. Under various return ratios, the numerator ("return") may be adjusted by

      1) Subtracting preferred dividends to leave only income available to common stockholders

      2) Adding back minority interest in the income of a consolidated subsidiary (when invested capital is defined to include the minority interest)

      3) Adding back interest expense

      4) Adding back both interest expense and taxes so that the numerator is EBIT; this results in the basic earning power ratio, which enhances comparability of firms with different capital structures and tax planning strategies

   b. The denominator ("equity" or "assets") may be adjusted by

      1) Excluding nonoperating assets, such as investments, intangible assets, and the other asset category

      2) Excluding unproductive assets, such as idle plant, intangible assets, and obsolete inventories

      3) Excluding current liabilities to emphasize long-term capital

      4) Excluding debt and preferred stock to arrive at equity capital

      5) Stating invested capital at market value

2. **The DuPont Model -- ROA**

   a. The DuPont model begins with the standard equation for ROA and breaks it down into two component ratios, one that focuses on the income statement and one that relates income to the balance sheet.

DuPont Model for Return on Assets

$$\frac{Net\ income}{Average\ total\ assets} = \frac{Net\ income}{Net\ sales} \times \frac{Net\ sales}{Average\ total\ assets}$$

$$= Net\ profit\ margin \times Total\ asset\ turnover$$

NOTE: All examples in this subunit are based on the balance sheet data found on page 60.

   1) EXAMPLE:

Return on assets (ROA) = Net profit margin × Total asset turnover
= (Net income ÷ Net sales) × (Net sales ÷ Average total assets)
= ($42,000 ÷ $1,800,000) × {$1,800,000 + [($1,800,000 + $1,600,000) ÷ 2]}
= 2.33% × 1.06
= 2.47%

   2) This breakdown emphasizes that shareholder return may be explained in terms of both profit margin and the efficiency of asset management.

    b.   The two components of the DuPont equation are interrelated since they both involve net sales.

        1)   Profit margin on sales is another name for the net profit margin calculated in the DuPont model.

            a)   If net sales increase and all other factors remain the same, the net profit margin worsens because more sales are only generating the same bottom line.

        2)   Total asset turnover measures the level of capital investment relative to sales volume.

            a)   If net sales increase and all other factors remain the same, the asset turnover ratio improves because more sales are being produced by the same amount of assets.

3.   **The DuPont Model -- ROE**

    a.   To examine the **return on equity (ROE) ratio**, it can be subdivided by the DuPont model into three different efficiency components.

DuPont Model for Return on Equity

$$ROE = \frac{Net\ income}{Net\ sales} \times \frac{Net\ sales}{Average\ total\ assets} \times \frac{Average\ total\ assets}{Average\ total\ equity}$$

$$= Net\ profit\ margin \times Assets\ turnover \times Equity\ multiplier$$

        1)   EXAMPLE:

$$ROE = \frac{\$42,000}{\$1,800,000} \times \frac{\$1,800,000}{[(\$1,800,000 + \$1,600,000) \div 2]} \times \frac{[(\$1,800,000 + \$1,600,000) \div 2]}{[(\$800,000 + \$650,000) \div 2]}$$

$$= 0.023 \times 1.06 \times 2.345$$

$$= 5.79\%$$

            a)   The net profit margin component examines a company's efficiency in generating earnings from sales. It measures the amount of earnings that the company makes from every $1 of sales.

            b)   The assets turnover component examines how efficiently the company is deploying the totality of its resources to generate revenues. It measures how much sales a company generates from each $1 of assets.

            c)   The equity multiplier measures a company's financial leverage. High financial leverage means that the company relies more on debt to finance its assets. So, on the one hand, by raising capital with debt, the company can increase its equity multiplier and improve its return on equity. But, on the other hand, taking on additional debt may worsen the company's solvency and increase the risk of going bankrupt.

4.   **Return on Common Equity (ROCE)**

    a.   ROCE is a more conservative measure than return on total equity.

Return on Common Equity (ROCE)

$$\frac{Net\ income - Preferred\ dividends}{Average\ common\ equity}$$

        1)   EXAMPLE: The company's preferred stock pays an 8% dividend.

$$ROCE = [\$42,000 - (\$120,000 \times 8\%)] \div [(\$680,000 + \$650,000) \div 2]$$

$$= \$32,400 \div \$665,000$$

$$= 4.87\%$$

b. Using only common equity in the denominator focuses attention on the equity stake provided by the common shareholders, who are the firm's (residual) owners.

1) ROCE can be disaggregated into three components, similar to the DuPont model for ROE.

a) Net income minus preferred dividends can be thought of as income available to common shareholders (IACS).

DuPont Model for Return on Common Equity (ROCE)

$$ROCE = \frac{IACS}{Net\ sales} \times \frac{Net\ sales}{Average\ total\ assets} \times \frac{Average\ total\ assets}{Average\ common\ equity}$$

$$= Net\ profit\ margin \times Total\ asset\ turnover \times Common\ equity\ multiplier$$

2) The equity multiplier is also sometimes called leverage. This is consistent with the earlier discussion of leverage because the equity multiplier indirectly measures the proportion of debt in the capital structure.

3) EXAMPLE:

$$ROCE = \frac{\$42,000 - (\$120,000 \times 8\%)}{[(\$680,000 + \$650,000) \div 2]} = \frac{32,400}{665,000} = 1.80\%$$

$$= \frac{\$32,400}{\$665,000} \times \frac{\$1,800,000}{[(\$1,800,000 + \$1,600,000) \div 2]} \times \frac{[(\$1,800,000 + \$1,600,000) \div 2]}{[(\$680,000 + \$650,000) \div 2]}$$

$$= 1.80\% \times 1.06 \times 2.56$$

5. **Other Measures**

a. The **sustainable equity growth rate** is the highest growth rate a company can sustain without increasing leverage.

Sustainable Equity Growth Rate

$$ROCE \times (1 - Dividend\ payout\ ratio)$$

1) The expression (1 – dividend payout ratio) is also called the plowback rate, i.e., the rate at which earnings are plowed back into the company rather than distributed to the shareholders.

b. The net profit margin on sales equals net income divided by sales (see item 1.c. in Subunit 3.1).

1) The numerator may also be stated in terms of the net income available to common shareholders.

2) Another form of the ratio excludes nonrecurring items from the numerator, e.g., unusual or infrequent items, discontinued operations, extraordinary items, and effects of accounting changes. The result is sometimes called the net profit margin. This adjustment may be made for any ratio that includes net income.

a) Still other numerator refinements are to exclude equity-based earnings and items in the other income and other expense categories.

c. The ratio of net operating income to sales (see item 1.c. in Subunit 3.1) may also be defined as earnings before interest and taxes (EBIT) divided by net sales.

1) Use of EBIT emphasizes operating results and more nearly approximates cash flows than other income measures.

Stop and review! You have completed the outline for this subunit. Study multiple-choice questions 6 through 10 beginning on page 126.

3.3 MARKET VALUATION MEASURES

1. **Fundamental Valuation Multiples**

   a. Book value per share is the amount of net assets attributable to the common shareholders per share outstanding.

   Book Value per Share

   $$\frac{Total\ equity\ -\ Liquidation\ value\ of\ preferred\ equity}{Common\ shares\ outstanding}$$

   1) When preferred stock is cumulative and in arrears or participating, liquidation value will exceed the carrying amount of the preferred stock.

   2) Book value per share is ordinarily based on historical cost expressed in nominal dollars. Accordingly, it may be misleading because book values ordinarily differ materially from fair market values.

      a) Market value is what a share sells for on the open market. Book value may be materially higher or lower than market value.

   b. A high market/book ratio reflects the stock market's positive assessment of the firm's asset management. It measures how much an investor must spend to "own" a dollar of net assets.

   Market/Book Ratio

   $$\frac{Market\ price\ per\ share}{Book\ value\ per\ share}$$

   c. A high price/earnings ratio reflects the stock market's positive assessment of the firm's earnings quality and persistence. It measures how much an investor must spend to "buy" a dollar of earnings.

   Price/Earnings Ratio

   $$\frac{Market\ price\ per\ share}{Diluted\ earnings\ per\ share}$$

   d. A high price/EBITDA ratio reflects the stock market's positive assessment of the firm's generation of profits through ongoing operations. It measures how much an investor must spend to "buy" a dollar of EBITDA.

   Price/EBITDA Ratio

   $$\frac{Market\ price\ per\ share}{EBITDA}$$

   1) The origin of the EBITDA measure can be traced back to the technology boom of the 1990s. High tech companies were producing very little income, so investment bankers became creative in how they defined profits.

      a) Under the guise of comparability, the argument was that a company with debt that was paying interest expense should not be compared on a profit basis with a closely related company that operated without debt.

         i)   In other words, two companies could be selling the same product at the same prices and have the same cost structure and operating income, but the company with debt would have a lower net income.

      b) The investment bankers' answer to this problem was to simply compare the operating earnings before deducting non-cash expenses.

   2) There are numerous benefits to using EBITDA, including operational comparability and as a proxy for cash flows. However, the disadvantages outweigh the advantages.

3) Disadvantages of EBITDA

    a) While EBITDA offers some benefits in comparing a broader set of companies across industries, the metric also carries some drawbacks.

    b) Overstates income: EBITDA distorts reality. From a stockholder's standpoint, investors are most concerned with the level of income and cash flow available after all expenses, including interest expense, depreciation expense, and income tax expense.

    c) Neglects working capital requirements: EBITDA may actually be a decent proxy for cash flows for many companies; however, this profit measure does not account for the working capital needs of a business. For example, companies reporting high EBITDA figures may actually have dramatically lower cash flows once working capital requirements (i.e., inventories, receivables, payables) are tabulated.

    d) Not effective for valuation: Investment bankers push for more generous EBITDA valuation multiples because it serves the bankers' and clients' best interests. However, companies with debt do deserve lower valuations compared to their debt-free counterparts.

4) Despite EBITDA's comparability benefits, and as much as investment bankers would like to use this metric, beware of EBITDA's shortcomings. Although most analysts are looking for the one-size-fits-all number, the reality of the situation is a variety of methods need to be used to gain a more accurate financial picture of a company.

Stop and review! You have completed the outline for this subunit. Study multiple-choice questions 11 through 16 beginning on page 129.

3.4 EARNINGS PER SHARE AND DIVIDEND PAYOUT

1. **Earnings per Share (EPS)**

    a. EPS is probably the most heavily relied-upon performance measure used by investors. EPS states the amount of current-period earnings that can be associated with a single share of a corporation's common stock.

        1) EPS is only calculated for common stock because common shareholders are the residual owners of a corporation. Since preferred shareholders have superior claim to the firm's earnings, amounts associated with preferred stock must be removed during the calculation of EPS.

    b. A corporation is said to have a simple capital structure if one of the following two conditions applies:

        1) The firm has only common stock; i.e., there are no preferred shareholders with a superior claim to earnings in the form of dividends; or

        2) The firm has no dilutive potential common stock.

            a) Potential common stock (PCS) is a security or other contract that may entitle the holder to obtain common stock. Examples include convertible securities, stock options and warrants, and contingently issuable common stock.

            b) Potential common stock is said to be dilutive if its inclusion in the calculation of EPS results in a reduction of EPS.

c.   A firm with a simple capital structure only has to report a single category of EPS, called basic earnings per share (BEPS).

1)   A firm with preferred stock or dilutive potential common stock must report two categories of EPS, BEPS and diluted earnings per share (DEPS).

Basic Earnings Per Share (BEPS)

$$\frac{Income\ available\ to\ common\ shareholders\ (IACS)}{Weighted\text{-}average\ number\ of\ common\ shares\ outstanding}$$

a)   Two BEPS amounts are reported, one using income from continuing operations and one using net income.

b)   The numerator (income available to common shareholders) equals the relevant income amount (income from continuing operations or net income) minus dividends on preferred stock.

c)   The denominator is determined by weighting the shares for the portion of the reporting period that they were outstanding.

d.   **Diluted Earnings Per Share (DEPS)**

1)   The numerator is increased by the amounts that would not have had to be paid if dilutive potential common stock had been converted, namely, dividends on convertible preferred stock and after-tax interest on convertible debt.

2)   The denominator is increased by the weighted-average number of additional shares of common stock that would have been outstanding if dilutive potential common stock had been converted.

e.   If EPS is used as part of a ratio calculation (e.g., price-earnings), DEPS should be used if available.

2.   **Other Market-Based Measures**

a.   Increasing shareholder wealth is the fundamental goal of any corporation. Three common ratios measure the degree of success toward this goal.

b.   Earnings yield is the rate of return on the purchase price of a share of common stock. It is the reciprocal of the P/E ratio and thus measures the amount of earnings an investor expects to receive per dollar invested.

Earnings Yield

$$\frac{Earnings\ per\ share}{Market\ price\ per\ share}$$

1)   The earnings yield can be compared by investors to other types of investments to determine whether a given stock is comparable to other stocks in the industry or to alternative uses of the investment money.

c.   The dividend payout ratio measures what portion of accrual-basis earnings was actually paid out to common shareholders in the form of dividends.

Dividend Payout Ratio

$$\frac{Dividends\ to\ common\ shareholders}{IACS}$$

1)   Growth companies tend to have a low payout, preferring to use earnings to continue growing the firm.

    d.   A related ratio is the dividend yield.

Dividend Yield

$$\frac{Dividend\ per\ share}{Market\ price\ per\ share}$$

        1)   Various investors have different desires with respect to dividend yield. Historically, many long-term investors wanted a low dividend yield because capital gains were taxed at a lower tax rate than dividends; thus, letting the earnings accumulate within the company resulted in a lower overall tax expense.

            a)   However, in recent years, the tax rate on dividends has been as low or lower than that on capital gains; thus, a high dividend yield has come into vogue.

        2)   Also, investors in different circumstances have different perspectives on dividend yield. For example, a retiree wants regular income and therefore wants to see a high dividend yield. A person who is years away from retirement would prefer a lower dividend yield with the earnings reinvested in the business.

Stop and review! You have completed the outline for this subunit. Study multiple-choice questions 17 through 21 beginning on page 131.

3.5 RATIOS IN GENERAL

    1.   **Inherent Limitations of Ratio Analysis**

        a.   Development of ratios for comparison with **industry averages** is more useful for firms that operate within a particular industry than for conglomerates (firms that operate in a variety of industries).

            1)   Because of the problem with conglomerates, the FASB issued Statement No. 14 (later amended) that required companies to provide segment information. Analysts can now determine whether a company's overall ratios are comparable to any of the industries in which the company operates. With such information available, an analyst may be able to find bargains wherein a company's stock is selling at a lower multiple of earnings than it would if its individual businesses were each spun off.

            2)   For comparison purposes, industry averages can be obtained from industry journals and sources, such as Robert Morris Associates and Standard & Poor's.

        b.   The effects of **inflation** on fixed assets and depreciation, inventory costs, long-term debt, and profitability cause misstatement of a firm's balance sheet and income statement. For example, fixed assets and depreciation will be understated, and inventory also will be understated, if LIFO is used. Moreover, the interest rate increases that accompany inflation will decrease the value of outstanding long-term debt. Many assets are recorded at historical cost, so their fair value may not be reflected on the balance sheet.

        c.   Ratio analysis may be affected by **seasonal factors**. For example, inventory and receivables may vary widely, and year-end balances may not reflect the averages for the period.

        d.   A firm's management has an incentive to **window dress** financial statements to improve results. For example, if the current or quick ratio is greater than 1.0, paying liabilities on the last day of the year will increase the ratio.

        e.   Comparability of financial statement amounts and the ratios derived from them is impaired if different firms choose different **accounting policies**. Also, changes in a firm's own accounting policies may create some distortion in the comparison of the results over a period of years.

    f.   Generalizations regarding which ratios are strong indicators of a firm's financial position may change from industry to industry, firm to firm, and division to division.

    g.   Ratios are constructed from accounting data, much of which is subject to estimation. Also, **accounting profit** differs from **economic profit**. Economic profit is the excess of revenues over the costs of land, labor, and capital. Accountants, however, do not subtract the cost of investors' capital.

        1)   Many studies have found a relationship between accounting data and stock prices. Thus, managers may be induced to manipulate accounting data as a means of enhancing stock prices.

        2)   One reason for manipulation is the observed tendency of the stock price of a public company to continue to move upward or downward for months after an earnings announcement, depending on whether the report was favorable or unfavorable, respectively.

        3)   The ability of unscrupulous managers to deceive the market is supported by evidence that investors may be able to beat the market by purchasing shares of companies with high ratios of net operating cash flows to net income.

    h.   Current performance and trends may be misinterpreted if sufficient years of historical analysis are not considered.

    i.   Ratio analysis may be distorted by failing to use an average or weighted average.

    j.   Misleading conclusions may result if improper comparisons are selected.

    k.   Whether a certain level of a ratio is favorable depends on the underlying circumstances. For example, a high quick ratio indicates high liquidity, but it may also imply that excessive cash is being held.

    l.   Different ratios may yield opposite conclusions about a firm's financial health. Thus, the net effects of a set of ratios should be analyzed.

    m.   **Earnings quality** is a measure of how useful reported earnings are as a performance indicator. It is the inverse of the variance in earnings. If earnings have a high degree of variability, many ratios will become less meaningful.

        1)   Consistency of earnings is an aspect of quality. A company that has widely varying earnings levels from year to year will be said to have a low level of earnings quality because looking at a single year's earnings will not really tell you anything about the long-term aspects of the company.

        2)   Analysts also look at a company's accounting policies when assessing earnings quality. For example, during a period of inflation, a company using LIFO will be said to have a higher level of earnings quality than would a company with FIFO because LIFO presents more conservative numbers on both the income statement and the balance sheet.

    n.   Industry averages may include data from capital-intensive and labor-intensive firms. They may also include data from firms with greatly divergent policies regarding leverage.

    o.   Some industry averages may be based on small samples.

    p.   Different sources of information may compute ratios differently.

    q.   Some data may be presented either before or after taxes.

    r.   Comparability among firms may be impaired if they have different fiscal years.

    s.   The geographical locations of firms may affect comparability because of differences in labor markets, price levels, governmental regulation, taxation, and other factors.

    t.   Size differentials among firms affect comparability because of differences in access to and cost of capital, economies of scale, and width of markets.

Stop and review! You have completed the outline for this subunit. Study multiple-choice questions 22 and 23 beginning on page 133.

3.6 FACTORS AFFECTING REPORTED PROFITABILITY

1. **Factors Involved**

   a. Among the many factors involved in measuring profitability are the definition of income; the stability, sources, and trends of revenue; revenue relationships; and expenses, including cost of sales. This analysis attempts to answer questions about the relevant income measure, income quality, the persistence of income, and the firm's earning power.

2. **Income**

   a. Estimates are necessary to calculate income, for example, allocations of revenue and expense over accounting periods, useful lives of assets, and amounts of future liabilities.

   b. Income is measured in accordance with a selection from among generally accepted accounting principles.

   c. Incentives for disclosure about the income measure vary with the interest group: financial analysts, auditors, accountants, management, directors, shareholders, competitors, creditors, and regulators. The pressures from some groups may lead to suboptimal financial reporting.

   d. Users have different needs, but financial statements are general purpose. For example, investors are interested in profitability, but creditors are interested in security.

3. **Revenues**

   a. Revenues are inflows or other enhancements of assets of the firm or settlements of its liabilities from delivering or producing goods, rendering services, or other activities that constitute the firm's ongoing major or central operations.

   b. Understanding the sources of revenue is especially important in diversified firms. Common-size analysis is useful when markets and product lines have differing rates of growth, potential, and profitability.

   c. Trend percentage analysis and evaluation of management's discussion and analysis (MD&A) in the firm's annual report are useful techniques for assessing the persistence of the firm's revenues.

4. **Receivables and Inventories**

   a. The relationship of revenues and receivables helps to assess earnings quality. Thus, if revenues (sales) are growing more slowly than receivables, the analyst should consider management's incentives, the relative leniency of credit policies, and collectibility issues.

   b. The relationship of revenues and inventories is also useful. For example, if materials and work-in-process inventories are falling while finished goods inventories are rising, future output and sales are likely to decline.

5. **Recognition Principles**

   a. Recognition of revenues, expenses, gains, losses, and changes in related assets and liabilities involves, among other things, the application of pervasive expense recognition principles: associating cause and effect, systematic and rational allocation, and immediate recognition.

      1) The FASB's Conceptual Framework defines matching, a term that has been given a variety of meanings in accounting literature, as essentially synonymous with associating cause and effect.

      2) Matching "is simultaneous or combined recognition of the revenues and expenses that result directly and jointly from the same transactions or other events." Such a direct relationship is found when revenue for sales of goods is recognized in the same period as the cost of the goods sold.

    b.   Systematic and rational allocation procedures do not directly relate costs and revenues but are applied when a causal relationship is "generally, but not specifically, identified."

        1)   This expense recognition principle is appropriate when an asset provides benefits over several periods (its estimated useful life), the asset is used up as a result of events affecting the entity, and the expense resulting from such wastage is indirectly (not directly and traceably) related to specific revenues and particular periods. The usual example is depreciation.

    c.   Immediate recognition is the applicable principle when costs cannot be directly or feasibly related to specific revenues and their benefits are used up in the period in which they are incurred. Utilities expense is a common example.

    d.   According to the revenue recognition principle, revenue should be recognized when (1) realized or realizable and (2) earned.

        1)   Revenues are realized when goods or services have been exchanged for cash or claims to cash.

        2)   Revenues are realizable when goods or services have been exchanged for assets that are readily convertible into cash or claims to cash.

        3)   Revenues are earned when the earning process has been substantially completed and the entity is entitled to the resulting benefits or revenues.

        4)   The two conditions are usually met when goods are delivered or services are rendered, that is, at the time of sale, which is customarily the time of delivery.

    e.   As a reflection of the accounting profession's conservatism, expenses and losses have historically been subject to less stringent recognition criteria than revenues and gains.

        1)   Expenses and losses are not subject to the realization criterion.

        2)   Rather, expenses and losses are recognized when a consumption of economic benefits occurs during the entity's primary activities or when the ability of existing assets to provide future benefits has been impaired.

           a)   An expense or loss may also be recognized when a liability has been incurred or increased without the receipt of corresponding benefits; a probable and reasonably estimable contingent loss is an example.

        3)   Long-lived assets, such as equipment, buildings, and intangibles, are depreciated or amortized over their useful lives. Natural resources are depleted, usually on a units-of-production basis.

    f.   The following are exceptions to the basic revenue recognition rules:

        1)   Revenues from long-term contracts may be recognized using the percentage-of-completion method. This method allows for revenue to be recognized at various stages of the contract although the entire job is not complete.

        2)   The completion-of-production method is an appropriate basis for recognition if products or other assets are readily realizable, e.g., precious metals and some agricultural products.

        3)   If the collectibility of assets is relatively uncertain, revenues and gains may be recognized as cash is received using the installment sales method or the cost recovery method.

6. Cost of Goods Sold and Gross Profit

a. Cost of goods sold is the single largest cost element for any seller of merchandise and thus has the greatest impact on profitability. A company's gross profit margin is the percentage of its net sales that it is able to keep after paying for merchandise.

1) EXAMPLE:

	Current Year		Prior Year	
Gross sales	$1,827,000	100.0%	$1,418,000	100.0%
Sales discounts	(15,000)	(0.8%)	(10,000)	(0.7%)
Sales return and allowances	(12,000)	(0.7%)	(8,000)	(0.6%)
Net sales	$1,800,000	98.5%	$1,400,000	98.7%
Cost of goods sold	(1,650,000)	(90.3%)	(1,330,000)	(93.8%)
Gross profit	$ 150,000	8.2%	$ 70,000	4.9%

b. A change in the gross profit margin can indicate that the firm has priced its products differently while maintaining the same cost structure or that it has changed the way it controls the costs of production and/or inventory management.

7. Trends in Expenses

a. Analyzing trends in expenses is facilitated by the use of percentages, i.e., a detailed analysis of the expense line items found on the common-size income statements.

1) EXAMPLE:

	Current Year		Prior Year	
Net sales	$1,800,000	100.0%	$1,400,000	100.0%
Selling expenses:				
Sales salaries and commissions	$ 12,000	0.67%	$ 1,000	0.07%
Freight-out	16,000	0.89%	5,000	0.36%
Travel	10,000	0.56%	5,000	0.36%
Advertising	8,000	0.44%	3,000	0.21%
Office supplies	4,000	0.22%	1,000	0.07%
Total selling expenses	$ 50,000	2.78%	$ 15,000	1.07%
Administrative expenses:				
Executive salaries	$ 6,000	0.33%	$ 4,000	0.29%
Professional salaries	4,000	0.22%	4,000	0.29%
Wages	2,000	0.11%	1,000	0.07%
Depreciation	1,000	0.06%	500	0.04%
Office supplies	2,000	0.11%	500	0.04%
Total administrative expenses	$ 15,000	0.83%	$ 10,000	0.73%
Total operating expenses	$ 65,000	3.61%	$ 25,000	1.80%

2) The company's operating expenses increased overall; this would be expected during a period of rising sales. However, not every expense line item increased proportionally. The company devoted much more effort to moving product out the door by increasing the proportion of sales salaries and commissions and freight-out.

3) Also note that, while professional salaries were the same absolute amount in both years, they were a smaller proportion of all administrative expenses in the current year because of the greater amount spent overall.

8.   **Major Categories of Expenses for a Company**

   a.   Selling expenses are incurred in selling or marketing. Examples include sales representatives' salaries, rent for sales department, commissions, and traveling expenses; advertising; selling department salaries and expenses; samples; and credit and collection costs, including bad debt expenses. Shipping (i.e., freight-out) costs are also often classified as selling costs.

   b.   General and administrative expenses are incurred for the direction of the enterprise as a whole and are not related wholly to a specific function, e.g., selling or manufacturing. They include accounting, legal, and other fees for services; officers' salaries; insurance; wages of office staff; miscellaneous supplies; and office occupancy costs.

   c.   Depreciation is the allocation of the costs of office equipment that benefit subsequent periods. Usually, the cost of a fixed asset minus salvage or residual value is expensed over the asset's useful life. Because of the noncash nature and relatively fixed amount of depreciation, it is not extremely meaningful except in relation to depreciable assets. This ratio may detect changes in the composite rate.

      1)   Depreciation on equipment used in the production of merchandise for sale is considered a product cost and is thus included in cost of goods sold, not administrative expenses.

   d.   Maintenance and repairs expense varies with the amount of plant and equipment and the extent of output. It also has fixed and variable components and does not vary directly with revenues. Moreover, this expense is discretionary and is therefore a means of smoothing income. Thus, it relates to earnings quality.

      1)   Maintenance is also a factor in estimating assets' useful lives and the calculation of depreciation.

   e.   Interest expense is recognized based on the passage of time. In the case of bonds, notes, and capital leases, the effective interest method is used. A typical analytical tool is the calculation of the trend of the average effective interest rate for the firm and comparison with the rates for other firms. It is generally reported on the income statement under other expenses and losses.

   f.   Amortization of special costs such as those of intangible assets is usefully analyzed by comparison of trends with respect to revenues, unamortized special costs, and net property and equipment.

   g.   Income tax expense is an important item in financial statements because of its magnitude. Accrual accounting for income taxes is characterized by interperiod tax allocation that matches tax expense with accrual income. The analysis must be aware of both temporary and permanent tax differences between accrual accounting and tax law.

      1)   Intraperiod tax allocation allocates tax to the components of income (continuing operations, discontinued operations, extraordinary items, and cumulative effect of changes in accounting principles).

      2)   The analysis should extend to comparisons of effective tax rates (expense ÷ pre-tax income) over time.

9. **Effects of Accounting Changes**

    a. The types of accounting changes are changes in (1) accounting principle, (2) accounting estimates, and (3) the reporting entity. Accounting changes and error corrections affect financial ratios.

        1) A change in accounting principle or the reporting entity is retrospectively applied to financial statements of prior periods presented comparatively. Error corrections related to prior periods result in restatement. After retrospective application or restatement, the comparative financial statements and ratios should be comparable and consistent.

        2) However, changing prior years' net income and related EPS figures may undermine shareholders' confidence in the accounting methods.

    b. A change in accounting principle occurs when an entity (1) adopts a generally accepted principle different from the one previously used, (2) changes the **method** of applying a generally accepted principle, or (3) changes to a generally accepted principle when the principle previously used is no longer generally accepted.

        1) Retrospective application, if practicable, is required for all direct effects and the related income tax effects of a change in principle.

            a) An example of a direct effect is an adjustment of an inventory balance to implement a change in the method of measurement.

        2) Retrospective application requires that carrying amounts of (a) assets, (b) liabilities, and (c) retained earnings at the beginning of the first period reported be adjusted for the cumulative effect of the new principle on all periods not reported.

            a) All periods reported must be individually adjusted for the period-specific effects of applying the new principle.

    c. A change in accounting estimate results from new information and a reassessment of the future benefits and obligations represented by assets and liabilities. Its effects should be accounted for only in the period of change and any future periods affected, i.e., prospectively.

        1) A change in estimate inseparable from (effected by) a change in principle is accounted for as a change in estimate. An example is a change in a method of depreciation, amortization, or depletion of long-lived, nonfinancial assets.

    d. A change in reporting entity is retrospectively applied to interim and annual statements.

        1) A change in reporting entity does not result from a business combination or consolidation of a variable interest entity.

    e. An accounting error results from (1) a mathematical mistake, (2) a mistake in the application of GAAP, or (3) an oversight or misuse of facts existing when the statements were prepared. A change to a generally accepted accounting principle from one that is not is an error correction, not an accounting change.

        1) An accounting error related to a prior period is reported as a prior-period adjustment by restating the prior-period statements. Restatement requires the same adjustments as retrospective application of a new principle.

Stop and review! You have completed the outline for this subunit. Study multiple-choice question 24 on page 134.

3.7 EFFECTS OF FOREIGN EXCHANGE FLUCTUATIONS

1. **Definitions**

    a. The **reporting currency** is the currency in which an entity prepares its financial statements.

    b. **Foreign currency translation** expresses in the reporting currency amounts that (1) are denominated in (fixed in units of) a different currency or (2) are measured in a different currency. For example, a U.S. entity may have a liability denominated in (fixed in) euros that it measures in U.S. dollars.

        1) A consolidated entity may consist of separate entities operating in different economic and currency environments. Translation is necessary in these circumstances so that consolidated amounts are presented in one currency.

    c. The **functional currency** is the currency of the primary economic environment in which the entity operates. Normally, that environment is the one in which it primarily generates and expends cash. For example, the functional currency of a foreign subsidiary is more likely to be the parent's currency if its cash flows directly and currently affect the parent's cash flows.

    d. **Foreign currency transactions** are fixed in a currency other than the functional currency. They result when an entity

        1) Buys or sells on credit;
        2) Borrows or lends;
        3) Is a party to a derivative instrument; or,
        4) For other reasons, acquires or disposes of assets, or incurs or settles liabilities, fixed in a foreign currency.

    e. A **foreign currency** is any currency other than the entity's functional currency.

    f. The **current exchange rate** is the rate used for currency conversion.

    g. The **spot rate** is the rate for immediate exchange of currencies.

    h. The **transaction date** is the time when a transaction is recorded under GAAP.

    i. A **transaction gain (loss)** results from a change in exchange rates between the functional currency and the currency in which the transaction is denominated. It is the change in functional currency cash flows

        1) Actually realized on settlement and
        2) Expected on unsettled transactions.

2. **Aspects of Cross-Border Transactions**

    a. Transactions are recorded at the spot rate in effect at the transaction date.

    b. Transaction gains and losses are recorded at each balance sheet date and at the date the receivable or payable is settled. The gains or losses ordinarily are included in the determination of net income.

    c. When the amount of the functional currency exchangeable for a unit of the currency in which the transaction is fixed increases, a transaction gain or loss is recognized on a receivable or payable, respectively. The opposite occurs when the exchange rate (functional currency to foreign currency) decreases.

3. **Exchange Rate Exposure**

   a. When a U.S. firm purchases from, or sells to, an entity in a foreign country, the transaction is recorded in U.S. dollars (the firm's domestic currency).

   Foreign sale:

Accounts receivable	$100,000	
Sales		$100,000

   Foreign purchase:

Inventory	$100,000	
Accounts payable		$100,000

   1) The dollar, however, might not be the currency in which the transaction will have to be settled (typically 30 days later).

   2) If the exchange rate of the two currencies (i.e., the units of one currency required to purchase a single unit of the other) is fixed, the existence of a foreign-denominated receivable or payable raises no measurement issue.

   b. If the exchange rate is not fixed, however, as is the case with most pairs of currencies in today's managed-float exchange rate environment (see Study Unit 7, Subunit 5), it is extremely rare for the two currencies to still have the same exchange rate at the end of the deferral period as they had at the beginning.

   1) It is highly likely, then, that the firm will incur a gain or loss on this transaction arising from a change in the exchange rates.

   c. The gains and losses arising from exchange rate fluctuations are of two types:

   1) The gain or loss incurred at the settlement date, which affects the firm's cash flows, is termed a transaction gain or loss.

      a) Transaction gains and losses, and their associated risk-mitigation techniques, are the subject of Study Unit 7, Subunit 5.

   2) The other type of gain or loss, which does not affect cash flows, is termed a translation gain or loss.

      a) Translation gains and losses arise from the use of accrual-basis accounting and must be calculated whenever financial statements are prepared during the payment deferral period.

4.   **Accounting for Translation Gains and Losses**

    a.   Two exchange rates are needed to calculate translation gains and losses:

        1)   The rate in effect on the date of the transaction, called the historical rate

        2)   The rate in effect on the reporting date, called the current rate

    b.   The carrying amount of the foreign-denominated receivable or payable is adjusted for the difference between the historical rate and the current rate.

        1)   The translation gain or loss bypasses earnings and is instead reported as a component of other comprehensive income (OCI).

EXAMPLE of Translation Gains and Losses

On December 15, Year 1, Boise Co. purchased electronic components from Kinugasa Corporation. Boise must pay Kinugasa ¥15,000,000 on January 15, Year 2. The exchange rate in effect on December 15, Year 1, was $.01015 per yen, giving the transaction a value on Boise's books of $152,250 (¥15,000,000 × $.01015).

Transaction Date:

Inventory	$152,250	
Accounts payable		$152,250

The exchange rate on December 31, Year 1, Boise's reporting date, has fallen to $.01010 per yen. The balance of the payable must be adjusted (and a gain in OCI recognized) in the amount of $750 [(¥15,000,000 × ($.01015 – $.01010)].

Reporting Date:

Accounts payable	$750	
Foreign currency translation adjustment		$750

The exchange rate on January 15, Year 2, has risen to $.01020 per yen. To settle the payable, the balance must be adjusted (and a loss in OCI recognized) in the amount of $1,500 [¥15,000,000 × ($.01010 – $.01020)].

Settlement Date:

Accounts payable ($152,250 – $750)	$151,500	
Foreign currency translation adjustment	1,500	
Cash		$153,000

---

    c.   The occurrence of translation gains and losses can be summarized as follows:

Effects of Exchange Rate Fluctuations

Transaction That Will Be Settled in a Foreign Currency	Results in a Foreign-Denominated	Foreign Currency Appreciates	Foreign Currency Depreciates
Sale	Receivable	Translation gain	Translation loss
Purchase	Payable	Translation loss	Translation gain

5.   **Three Relevant Currencies**

    a.   The firm's reporting currency is the one in which the financial statements will be presented. For a foreign subsidiary of a U.S. parent, this is the U.S. dollar.

    b.   The firm's functional currency is the currency of the primary economic environment in which the firm operates, i.e., the environment in which it primarily generates and expends cash.

        1)   The functional currency of a foreign subsidiary is probably the currency of the country in which it operates.

        2)   However, if the subsidiary gets the bulk of its financing from U.S. sources and has mostly U.S. suppliers and customers, the functional currency could be the dollar.

    c.   The firm may keep its accounting records in a currency other than reporting and/or functional currency, for instance, the local currency of the country in which it operates.

6. **Remeasurement and Translation**

a. If the currency in which the firm keeps its accounting records differs from the functional currency, all unsettled transactions must be remeasured in the functional currency at each reporting date.

1) Remeasurement involves use of the temporal method (item 7. below).

b. If the firm's reporting currency differs from its functional currency, all unsettled transactions must be translated into the reporting currency at each reporting date.

1) Translation involves use of the all-current method (item 8. on the next page).

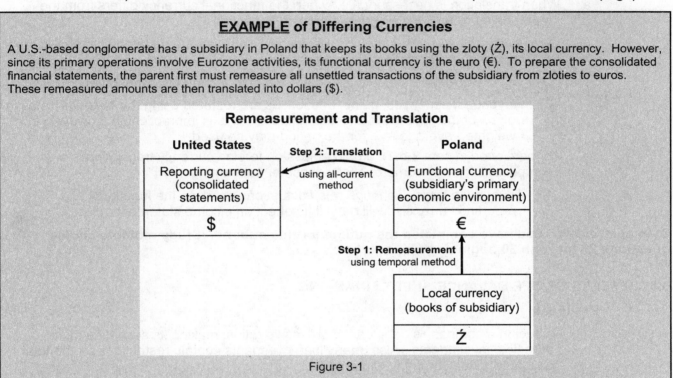

EXAMPLE of Differing Currencies

A U.S.-based conglomerate has a subsidiary in Poland that keeps its books using the zloty (Ż), its local currency. However, since its primary operations involve Eurozone activities, its functional currency is the euro (€). To prepare the consolidated financial statements, the parent first must remeasure all unsettled transactions of the subsidiary from zloties to euros. These remeasured amounts are then translated into dollars ($).

Figure 3-1

7. **Remeasurement (Temporal Method)**

a. When remeasurement is necessary (i.e., when the currency of the accounting records differs from the functional currency), the temporal method is applied.

b. The essence of the temporal method is to make the financial statement items look as if the underlying transactions had been recorded in the functional currency to begin with.

1) Balance sheet items carried at historical cost are remeasured at the historical rate, i.e., the exchange rate in effect on the day of the transaction that gave rise to them.

a) Balance sheet items carried at their current or future values (e.g., present value or net realizable value) are remeasured using the current rate on the reporting date.

2) Revenues, expenses, gains, and losses are restated using historical rates.

    c.   Any net remeasurement gain or loss arising from application of the temporal method is recognized on the income statement as a component of income from continuing operations.

        1)   As a result, maintaining the books of a subsidiary in a local currency other than the functional currency increases earnings volatility.

        2)   Thus, all ratios that use current earnings or components thereof are affected by exchange rate fluctuations arising during the remeasurement process.

8.   **Translation (All-Current Method)**

    a.   When translation is necessary (i.e., when the functional currency differs from the reporting currency), the all-current method is applied.

        1)   Under the all-current method, assets and liabilities are restated using the current exchange rate on the reporting date.

            a)   Stockholders' equity items are restated at their historical rates.

        2)   Revenues, expenses, gains, and losses are restated using the historical rates in effect at the time they were recognized. If this is impracticable, however, a weighted-average rate for the period may be used.

    b.   As mentioned in item 3.b.1), a gain or loss on foreign currency translation is a component of other comprehensive income, not earnings.

        1)   Thus, even large exchange rate fluctuations between the functional and reporting currencies will have little effect on income statement ratios.

Stop and review! You have completed the outline for this subunit. Study multiple-choice questions 25 through 30 beginning on page 134.

3.8 EFFECTS OF OFF-BALANCE-SHEET FINANCING

1.   **Purposes**

    a.   Reducing a company's debt load improves its ratios, making its securities more attractive investments. Also, many loan covenants contain restrictions on the total debt load that a company is permitted to carry.

        1)   However, reducing debt and hiding it are two very different things. Firms that carry extensive debt financing but attempt to disguise the fact are engaging in off-balance-sheet financing.

        2)   Eliminating debt from the balance sheet through off-balance-sheet financing will improve a company's debt to equity ratio because there will be less debt reported.

    b.   Off-balance-sheet financing takes four principal forms.

2.   **Investments in Unconsolidated Subsidiaries**

    a.   Any equity ownership of less than 50% in a subsidiary results in the parent firm reporting the equity investment as an asset.

    b.   The result is that the subsidiary's debts, for which the parent could be substantially responsible, are not reflected as liabilities of the parent.

    c.   Establishing a joint venture will accomplish the same purpose as an unconsolidated subsidiary because joint ventures are usually accounted for on the equity basis since none of the ventures are typically considered to hold control.

3. **Special Purpose Entities**

   a. A firm may create another firm for the sole purpose of keeping the liabilities associated with a specific project off the parent firm's books.

   b. For example, when a company wishes to construct a factory, large amounts of new debt must be taken on. A special purpose entity (SPE) can be established solely to build and operate the new plant while absorbing the debt incurred during construction.

      1) Once the plant is complete, the parent firm will often establish a take-or-pay contract with the SPE. Under a take-or-pay arrangement, the company agrees to either buy all the output of the factory or to make guaranteed payments.

      2) This way, the financial solvency of the SPE is ensured and the company has acquired a steady source of supply without taking on a large debt burden.

   c. In late 2001, the national media revealed that Enron Corporation had hidden a huge amount of debt for which it was responsible by "off-loading" it onto the balance sheets of SPEs. These SPEs had been deliberately structured so that Enron would not have to consolidate them.

      1) In 2003, the FASB responded to these abuses by issuing pronouncements on variable interest entities (VIEs). Any arrangement that meets the criteria of a VIE must be reported on a consolidated basis with another entity.

4. **Operating Leases**

   a. A long-term contract to acquire property or equipment may be structured in such a way that the full amount of the debt does not appear on the firm's balance sheet.

5. **Factoring Receivables with Recourse**

   a. Factoring (selling) accounts receivable to a finance company is a strategy used by firms who need to accelerate their cash flows or who simply do not wish to maintain a collection operation.

      1) If the factoring transaction is "with recourse," the firm remains contingently liable to the finance company in the case of debtor default. This contingent liability does not have to be reported on the company's balance sheet.

Stop and review! You have completed the outline for this subunit. Study multiple-choice question 30 on page 136.

3.9 EFFECTS OF IFRS

BACKGROUND to IFRS

In the early 1970s, financial reporting and the accounting profession worldwide were in a period of substantial change. Among other developments in 1971, the U.S. had gone off the gold standard; that is, it ended the federal government's guaranteed conversion of paper dollars into gold bullion. In 1973, the same year the FASB was formed in the U.S., the International Accounting Standards Committee (IASC) was established in London, England, with the goal of preparing a set of global accounting standards.

The principal benefit of such a single set of global standards is that multinational companies do not have to rewrite their statements in (or perform a complex reconciliation to) the local GAAP in order to trade their stock on the local exchange. Foreign investment is thereby made much easier and the cost of capital is lowered.

During its existence, the IASC issued 41 **International Accounting Standards (IASs)**:

IAS 1	*Presentation of Financial Statements*		**IAS 23**	*Borrowing Costs*
IAS 2	*Inventories*		**IAS 24**	*Related Party Disclosures*
IAS 3	*-Superseded-*		**IAS 25**	*-Superseded-*
IAS 4	*-Withdrawn-*		**IAS 26**	*Accounting and Reporting by Retirement Benefit Plans*
IAS 5	*-Superseded-*			
IAS 6	*-Superseded-*		**IAS 27**	*Consolidated and Separate Financial Statements*
IAS 7	*Statement of Cash Flows*			
IAS 8	*Accounting Policies, Changes in Accounting Estimates, and Errors*		**IAS 28**	*Investments in Associates*
			IAS 29	*Financial Reporting in Hyperinflationary Economies*
IAS 9	*-Superseded-*			
IAS 10	*Events after the Reporting Period*		**IAS 30**	*-Superseded-*
IAS 11	*Construction Contracts*		**IAS 31**	*Interests in Joint Ventures*
IAS 12	*Income Taxes*		**IAS 32**	*-Superseded-*
IAS 13	*-Superseded-*		**IAS 33**	*Earnings per Share*
IAS 14	*Segment Reporting*		**IAS 34**	*Interim Financial Reporting*
IAS 15	*-Withdrawn-*		**IAS 35**	*-Superseded-*
IAS 16	*Property, Plant, and Equipment*		**IAS 36**	*Impairment of Assets*
IAS 17	*Leases*		**IAS 37**	*Provisions, Contingent Liabilities, and Contingent Assets*
IAS 18	*Revenue*			
IAS 19	*Employee Benefits*		**IAS 38**	*Intangible Assets*
IAS 20	*Accounting for Government Grants and Disclosure of Government Assistance*		**IAS 39**	*-Superseded-*
			IAS 40	*Investment Property*
IAS 21	*The Effects of Changes in Foreign Exchange Rates*		**IAS 41**	*Agriculture*
IAS 22	*-Superseded-*			

Disagreements among accountants across the world over the source of the IASC's authority and the direction of its standards led to the creation in 2001 of the IASC Foundation, a not-for-profit, private sector organization governed by "22 trustees, individuals with senior executive experience from diverse geographical and professional backgrounds, in both the private and public sectors."

The IASC Foundation changed its name to the IFRS Foundation in July 2010. As reported on the Foundation's website (www.ifrs.org/The+organisation/IASCF+and+IASB.htm), the first of the Foundation's principal objectives is

to develop a single set of high quality, understandable, enforceable and globally accepted international financial reporting standards (IFRSs) through its standard-setting body, the IASB.

The website goes on to describe the IASB (International Accounting Standards Board) as follows:

The IASB is the independent standard-setting body of the IFRS Foundation. Its members (currently 15 full-time members) are responsible for the development and publication of IFRSs... All meetings of the IASB are held in public and webcast. In fulfilling its standard-setting duties the IASB follows a thorough, open and transparent due process of which the publication of consultative documents, such as discussion papers and exposure drafts, for public comment is an important component. The IASB engages closely with stakeholders around the world, including investors, analysts, regulators, business leaders, accounting standard-setters and the accountancy profession.

-- Continued on next page --

BACKGROUND -- Continued

The IASB has issued 13 **International Financial Reporting Standards (IFRS)**:

IFRS 1	*First-Time Adoption of International Financial Reporting Standards*
IFRS 2	*Share-based Payment*
IFRS 3	*Business Combinations*
IFRS 4	*Insurance Contracts*
IFRS 5	*Non-current Assets Held for Sale and Discontinued Operations*
IFRS 6	*Exploration for and Evaluation of Mineral Resources*
IFRS 7	*Financial Instruments: Disclosures*
IFRS 8	*Operating Segments*
IFRS 9	*Financial Instruments* (replacement of IAS 39)
IFRS 10	*Consolidated Financial Statements*
IFRS 11	*Joint Arrangements*
IFRS 12	*Disclosure of Interests in Other Entities*
IFRS 13	*Fair Value Measurement*

---

1. **Aspects of IFRS**

    a. IFRS are not binding. Their authority is restricted to the willingness of national authorities to adopt them.

       1) IFRS were recognized by the European Union as of January 1, 2005.

    b. IFRS are used as a benchmark by some countries that issue their own standards. They also are used by some countries as a basis for their own standards, by some stock exchanges and regulatory agencies that allow enterprises to present statements in accordance with the IFRS, by many enterprises themselves, and by the European Commission, which has stated that it is relying on the IASB to develop standards meeting the requirements of capital markets.

    c. The IASB's approach to standard setting recognizes a need to formulate and publish standards that will have worldwide acceptance. Accordingly, IFRS are principles-based.

       1) IFRS tend to be less detailed than U.S. GAAP, with few exceptions and little interpretive and implementation guidance. Thus, they require a greater exercise of professional judgment regarding the application of the principles to the economic substance of transactions.

          a) In contrast, U.S. GAAP are sometimes criticized as stressing adherence to the letter of accounting rules rather than their substance (the detailed nature of U.S. GAAP arose from the specific legal culture and regulatory environment of the U.S.). For this reason and as part of its convergence initiatives, the FASB has been considering a more principles-based approach to standard setting.

    d. The FASB and IASB are working closely to eliminate the differences between U.S. GAAP and IFRS, with the goal of easing the process of adoption by U.S. companies.

       1) In February 2012, Mary Schapiro, Chairman of the Securities and Exchange Commission, announced that she felt no need to compel U.S.-based companies to adopt IFRS against their will.

          a) "I feel pressure to do the right thing for U.S. markets and U.S. investors," she explained.

       2) In April 2012, the FASB and IASB released a Joint Update Note that stated, in part, that of the major convergence projects they were working through, three remained incomplete: leases, revenue recognition, and financial instruments.

       3) These factors make it unlikely that either total convergence between U.S. GAAP and IFRS or across-the-board adoption of IFRS by U.S. firms will take place in the foreseeable future.

2.   **Major Differences between U.S. GAAP and IFRS**

   a.   **Revenue Recognition -- The General Rule**

      1)   Under U.S. GAAP, revenue is recognized when it is realized or realizable (when goods or services have been exchanged for cash or other assets), and earned (when the earning process has been substantially completed).

      2)   Under IFRS, revenue is recognized when it is probable that the economic benefits will flow to the company; revenue and transaction costs can be reliably measured; and when (a) for the sale of goods, the risk and rewards of ownership have been transferred and the company has no effective control over the goods, and (b) for rendering services, when the stage of completion can be reliably measured, the revenue is recognized using the percentage-of-completion method.

   b.   **Revenue Recognition -- Construction Contracts**

      1)   Under both U.S. GAAP and IFRS, revenue is recognized based on the percentage-of-completion method. However, when the percentage-of-completion method is inappropriate because the outcome of a construction contract or the stage of completion cannot be estimated reliably/reasonably:

         a)   Under U.S. GAAP, the completed-contract method is used.

         b)   Under IFRS, the completed-contract method is not permitted. Revenue recognition is limited to recoverable costs incurred.

   c.   **Expense Recognition -- Share-Based Payments**

      1)   Transactions with Employees

         a)   Under both U.S. GAAP and IFRS, the services received are measured based on the equity instruments (share options, etc.) granted at the grant date.

      2)   Transactions with Nonemployees

         a)   Under U.S. GAAP, nonemployee share-based payment transactions are measured based on the fair value of the equity instruments issued or the consideration received, whichever is more reliably measurable.

         b)   Under IFRS, nonemployee share-based payment transactions are measured at the fair value of services or goods received.

   d.   **Intangible Assets -- Research and Development (R&D) Costs**

      1)   Under U.S. GAAP, R&D costs are expensed as incurred and are not capitalized.

      2)   Under IFRS,

         a)   Costs incurred during the research phase of an internal project are expensed as incurred and are not capitalized.

         b)   Costs incurred during the development phase of an internal project can be capitalized and recognized as an intangible asset if, and only if, the company can demonstrate all of the following:

            i)   The technical feasibility to complete the intangible asset

            ii)   Its intention to complete the intangible asset and use or sell it

            iii)   Its ability to use or sell the intangible asset

            iv)   Availability of resources to complete and use or sell the intangible asset

            v)   The way in which the asset will generate probable future economic benefits

            vi)   Its ability to measure reliably expenditures attributable to the asset

      c)   Examples of development activities are the design, construction, and testing of (1) pre-production or pre-use prototypes and models and (2) a chosen alternative for new or improved materials, devices, products, processes, systems or services, etc.

e.   **Intangible Assets -- Measurement**

    1)   Under U.S. GAAP, an intangible asset is carried at historical cost minus accumulated amortization and impairment losses (cost model in IFRS). The revaluation model is not permitted.

    2)   Under IFRS, the company must choose either the cost model or the revaluation model to account for the entire class of intangible assets.

        a)   Under the revaluation model, if an intangible asset has an active market, it must be carried subsequent to initial recognition at a revalued amount. This amount is fair value at the date of the revaluation minus any subsequent accumulated amortization and impairment losses.

f.   **Inventories -- Costing Methods**

    1)   Under U.S. GAAP, the company can use the following cost flow methods to determine the cost of inventory: first-in, first-out (FIFO); weighted-average; last-in, first-out (LIFO); and specific identification.

    2)   Under IFRS, the last-in, first-out (LIFO) method is prohibited. Only the FIFO, weighted-average, and specific identification methods are permitted.

g.   **Inventories -- Valuation and Write-Down**

    1)   Under U.S. GAAP, inventory is measured at the lower of cost or market.

        a)   Market is the current cost to replace inventory; it should not (1) exceed a ceiling equal to net realizable value (NRV) or (2) be less than a floor equal to NRV reduced by an allowance for an approximately normal profit margin.

        b)   When the market is lower than the cost, a write-down for the difference should be recognized as a loss in the current period. Reversals of write-downs of inventory are prohibited in subsequent periods.

    2)   Under IFRS, inventory is measured at the lower of cost or NRV. NRV is the estimated selling price in the ordinary course of business minus costs of completion and disposal.

        a)   When the NRV is lower than the cost, a write-down for the difference should be recognized.

        b)   A write-down may be reversed in subsequent periods but not above the original cost. The write-down and reversal are recognized in profit or loss.

h.   **Leases**

    1)   Essentially, the criteria to classify a lease as an operating lease or as a capital lease (finance lease in IFRS) are the same under IFRS and U.S. GAAP.

        a)   The major difference is that, under IFRS, the classification depends on the substance of the transaction rather than the form of the contract.

    2)   In leases involving land and buildings,

        a)   Under U.S. GAAP, if the fair value of the land is less than 25% of the total fair value of the leased property, land and building elements are accounted for as a single unit.

        b)   Under IFRS, land and building elements are accounted for separately unless the land element is not material.

i.   **Long-Lived Assets -- Measurement and Depreciation**

1)   Under U.S. GAAP, a long-lived asset is carried at historical cost minus accumulated depreciation and impairment losses (cost model in IFRS). The revaluation model is not permitted.

2)   Under IFRS, the company must choose either the cost model or the revaluation model to account for an entire class of long-lived assets.

   a)   Under the revaluation model, if the fair value of an asset can be reliably measured, it must be carried subsequent to initial recognition at a revalued amount.

   b)   This amount is fair value at the date of the revaluation minus any subsequent accumulated depreciation and impairment losses.

3)   Under IFRS, a company is required to depreciate separately each significant part of a long-lived asset. Under U.S. GAAP, such a requirement generally does not exist.

j.   **Impairment of Assets**

1)   Under U.S. GAAP, testing for impairment occurs when events or changes in circumstances indicate that the carrying amount may not be recoverable.

   a)   U.S. GAAP requires the following two-step impairment test:

      i)   Recoverability test. The carrying amount is not recoverable if it exceeds the sum of undiscounted cash flows expected from the use and disposition of the asset.

      ii)   If the carrying amount is not recoverable and is greater than the fair value of the asset, an impairment loss is recognized. The loss equals the excess of the carrying amount of the asset over its fair value. The loss is recognized immediately in income from continuing operations and must not be reversed in subsequent periods.

2)   Under IFRS, the company assesses at each reporting date whether an indication of impairment exists. Given such an indication, IFRS requires a one-step impairment test.

   a)   The carrying amount of the asset is compared with its recoverable amount. An impairment loss is recognized equal to the excess of the carrying amount over the recoverable amount.

   b)   The recoverable amount is the greater of an asset's

      i)   Fair value minus cost to sell or

      ii)   Value in use, which is the present value of cash flows expected from the use and disposition of the asset.

k.   **Financial Statement Presentation -- Extraordinary Items**

1)   Under U.S. GAAP, material transactions that are both unusual in nature and infrequent in occurrence in the environment in which the company operates are classified as extraordinary items. Extraordinary items are reported individually in a separate section in the income statement, net of tax, after results of discontinued operations.

2)   Under IFRS, no item is classified as extraordinary.

Stop and review! You have completed the outline for this subunit. Study multiple-choice questions 31 through 34 beginning on page 136.

3.10 EFFECTS OF FAIR VALUE ACCOUNTING

1. **Historical Cost as a Measurement Basis**

   a. In its Statement of Financial Accounting Concepts No. 5, issued in December 1984, the Financial Accounting Standards Board (FASB) listed the following five measurement attributes for assets and liabilities in current use:

      1) Historical cost (for assets) or historical proceeds (for liabilities)
      2) Current cost
      3) Current market value
      4) Net realizable value (for assets) or net settlement value (for liabilities)
      5) Present (i.e., discounted) value of future cash flows.

   b. The appropriate measurement basis for a given asset or liability might not always be obvious because the reporting goals of reliability and relevance are sometimes in conflict.

      1) For example, the historical cost of a piece of productive equipment may not have much relevance for a financial statement user. If the machine is vital to the firm's continuing operations, replacement cost might be more meaningful.

         a) However, selecting an appropriate replacement cost is a process subject to a great degree of judgment and subjectivity, and it might vary significantly over time.

      2) In this case, the reporting goal of reliability is considered to predominate, so historical cost is required for the reporting of property, plant, and equipment.

         a) Likewise, net realizable value is considered the appropriate measurement basis for accounts receivable.

2. **Fair Value as a Measurement Basis**

   a. For investment securities, which are often sold within weeks or days of being purchased, historical cost is not considered a useful basis for measurement.

      1) This situation was acknowledged by the FASB in its Statement of Financial Accounting Standards No. 12, issued in December 1975.
      2) This standard required a portfolio of marketable equity securities to be reported at the lower of average cost or market as of the reporting date.

   b. A more sophisticated reporting regimen was established in May 1993 when the FASB issued its Statement of Financial Accounting Standards No. 115. This standard created a three-way classification system for individual investment securities: held-to-maturity, trading, and available-for-sale.

      1) Trading and available-for-sale securities must be remeasured at fair value at every reporting date.
      2) The unrealized gain or loss associated with the adjustment is a component of net income for trading securities and of other comprehensive income for available-for-sale securities.

   c. The fair value option was instituted by the FASB in its Statement of Financial Accounting Standards No. 159, issued in February 2007.

      1) Under this practice, the firm can elect to measure a security in any of the three categories at fair value, with the unrealized holding gains and losses passing through net income.

         a) The decision to adopt the fair value option must be made on an instrument-by-instrument basis and can only be made for the entire instrument.
         b) Once elected, the fair value option is irrevocable for that instrument.

2)   The fair value option has not been met with universal approval.

    a)   While some believe it is a step toward constant reporting of the most up-to-date information possible (in the spirit of mark-to-market accounting), others believe that its case-by-case nature allows firms to manipulate earnings by cherry picking which instruments to measure at fair value.

3.   **Fair Value's Effect on Financial Statement Analysis**

a.   Although trading and available-for-sale securities must be reported on the face of the balance sheet at fair value, many firms disclose the original cost in the notes to the financial statements.

    1)   A typical such reporting arrangement might look like the following:

Balance sheet

Current assets:
  Trading securities (Note 4) $10,895

Noncurrent assets:
  Held-to-maturity securities (at amortized cost) $5,346
  Available-for-sale securities (Note 5)   2,100

Notes to the financial statements

Note 4: Trading securities are reported at fair value.

	Cost	Fair Value Adjustments	Fair Value
Debt securities	$8,100	$ 950	$ 9,050
Equity securities	2,000	(155)	1,845
Totals		$ 795	$10,895

Note 5: Available-for-sale securities consist of an equity investment with a cost of $2,600 and a credit fair value adjustment of $500.

b.   Having access to historical cost information can supplement the process of financial statement analysis.

    1)   During a rising securities market, liquidity ratios based on fair value will report better performance than those using historical cost.

        a)   Improved-looking liquidity could make it easier for the firm to obtain credit.

    2)   During a falling securities market, liquidity ratios based on fair value will report worse performance than those using historical cost.

        a)   If the deterioration is substantial, the firm may violate certain loan covenants, making debts come due sooner than anticipated. At the same time, falling securities prices will make ready cash harder to come by, continuously worsening the firm's situation.

        b)   This kind of self-reinforcing liquidity crisis could start the firm on a "death spiral."

    3)   Also, as noted above in reference to the fair value option for reporting, the use of fair value approaches the practice of mark-to-market accounting, which some financial statement users consider the ideal.

Stop and review! You have completed the outline for this subunit. Study multiple-choice question 35 on page 137.

3.11 CORE CONCEPTS

<u>Profitability Ratios</u>

- Four percentages are used to measure profitability directly from the income statement:
  - **Gross profit margin** is what percentage of gross revenues remains to the firm after paying for merchandise (gross profit ÷ net sales).
  - **Operating profit margin** is what percentage remains after selling and general and administrative expenses have been paid (operating income ÷ net sales).
  - **Net profit margin** is what percentage remains after other gains and losses (including interest expense) and income taxes have been added or deducted (net income ÷ net sales).
  - **EBITDA** approximates accrual-basis profits from ongoing operations. The EBITDA margin percentage relates it to sales (EBITDA ÷ net sales).
- The return generated for a corporation's owners is measured with two widely used ratios:
  - **Return on assets (ROA)**

    `Net income ÷ Average total assets`
  - **Return on equity (ROE)**

    `Net income ÷ Average total equity`

<u>Profitability Analysis</u>

- **Inconsistent definitions** complicate comparisons of ROI. The wide variety of definitions in use for the terms "return" and "investment" creates difficulties in comparability.
- The **DuPont model** begins with the standard equation for return on assets and breaks it down into two component ratios, one that focuses on the income statement and one that relates income to the balance sheet.

  `ROA = Net profit margin × Total asset turnover`
- The DuPont model can also be used to **disaggregate return on equity (ROE)**.

  `ROE = Net profit margin × Total asset turnover × Equity multiplier`
- **Return on common equity (ROCE)** is probably the most common adjusted ROI measure.

  `(Net income - Preferred dividends) ÷ Average common equity`
- **Return on common equity can be disaggregated** into three components, similar to the DuPont model's two for ROA. The numerator (net income minus preferred dividends) can be thought of as income available to common shareholders (IACS).

  `Net profit margin × Total asset turnover × Common equity multiplier`
- The **sustainable equity growth rate** is the highest growth rate a company can sustain without increasing leverage.

  `ROCE × (1 - Dividend payout ratio)`

<u>Market Valuation Measures</u>

- Fundamental Valuation Multiples
  - **Book value per share** is the amount of net assets attributable to the common shareholders per share outstanding.

    `(Total equity - Liquidation value of preferred equity) ÷ Common shares outstanding`
  - A high **market/book ratio** reflects the stock market's positive assessment of the firm's asset management. It measures how much an investor must spend to "own" a dollar of net assets.

    `Market price per share ÷ Book value per share`

- A high **price/earnings ratio** reflects the stock market's positive assessment of the firm's earnings quality and persistence. It measures how much an investor must spend to "buy" a dollar of earnings.

  Market price per share ÷ Earnings per share

- A high **price/EBITDA ratio** reflects the stock market's positive assessment of the firm's generation of profits through ongoing operations. It measures how much an investor must spend to "buy" a dollar of EBITDA.

  Market price per share ÷ EBITDA

- EBITDA measures should be used with caution because they do not consider all types of expenses.

Earnings per Share and Dividend Payout

- **Earnings per share (EPS)** is probably the most heavily relied-upon performance measure used by investors. EPS states the amount of current-period earnings that can be associated with a single share of a corporation's common stock.

  - EPS is only calculated for common stock because common shareholders are the residual owners of a corporation.

- **Basic Earnings Per Share (BEPS):**

  $$\frac{Income\ available\ to\ common\ shareholders\ (IACS)}{Weighted\text{-}average\ number\ of\ common\ shares\ outstanding}$$

  - Two BEPS amounts are reported, one using income from continuing operations and one using net income.

- **Diluted Earnings Per Share (DEPS)**

  - The numerator is increased by the amounts that would not have had to be paid if dilutive potential common stock had been converted, namely, dividends on convertible preferred stock and after-tax interest on convertible debt.

  - The denominator is increased by the weighted-average number of additional shares of common stock that would have been outstanding if dilutive potential common stock had been converted.

- **Other Market-Based Measures**

  - **Earnings yield** is the rate of return on the fair value of a share of common stock. It is the reciprocal of the price-earnings ratio and thus measures the amount of earnings an investor expects to receive per dollar invested.

    Earnings per share ÷ Market price per share

  - The **dividend payout ratio** measures what portion of accrual-basis earnings was actually paid out to common shareholders in the form of dividends.

    Dividends to common shareholders ÷ IACS

  - A related ratio is the **dividend yield**

    Dividend per share ÷ Market price per share

Ratios in General

- Although ratio analysis provides useful information pertaining to the efficiency of operations and the stability of financial conditions, it has **inherent limitations**.

  - Comparison with industry averages is more useful for firms that operate within a particular industry than for conglomerates.

  - The effects of inflation on fixed assets and depreciation, inventory costs, long-term debt, and profitability cause misstatement of a firm's balance sheet and income statement.

  - Ratio analysis may be affected by seasonal factors.

- A firm's management has an incentive to window dress financial statements to improve results.
- Comparability of financial statement amounts and the ratios derived from them is impaired if different firms choose different accounting policies.
- Generalizations regarding which ratios are strong indicators of a firm's financial position may change from industry to industry, firm to firm, and division to division.
- Ratios are based on accounting data, much of which is subject to estimation.
- Managers may be induced to manipulate accounting data as a means of enhancing stock prices.
- Earnings quality is a measure of how useful reported earnings are as a performance indicator. It is the inverse of the variance in earnings. If earnings have a high degree of variability, many ratios will become less meaningful.

Factors Affecting Reported Profitability

- **Profitability analysis** must address the many factors involved in measuring the firm's income; the stability, sources, and trends of revenue; revenue relationships; and expenses, including cost of sales. This analysis attempts to answer questions about the relevant income measure, income quality, the persistence of income, and the firm's earning power.
- **Income** equals the sum of revenues and gains minus the sum of expenses and losses.
- **Cost of goods sold** is the **single largest cost element** for any seller of merchandise and thus has the greatest impact on profitability. A company's gross profit margin is the percentage of its net sales that it is able to keep after paying for merchandise.
- Three common percentages **measure profitability** directly from the income statement: gross profit margin, operating profit margin, and net profit margin is what percentage remains after other gains and losses (including interest expense) and income taxes have been added or deducted.

Effects of Foreign Exchange Fluctuations

- A firm with a sale transaction that must be settled in a foreign currency will have a **foreign-denominated receivable** on its books. Likewise, a firm with a purchase that must be settled in a foreign currency will have a **foreign-denominated payable**.
    - Fluctuations in the exchange rate between the foreign currency and the firm's domestic currency give rise to translation gains and losses.
- The carrying amount of the foreign-denominated receivable or payable is adjusted for the difference between the historical rate and the current rate. The **translation gain or loss** bypasses earnings and is instead reported as a component of other comprehensive income (OCI).
- If the currency in which the firm keeps its accounting records differs from the firm's functional currency, all unsettled transactions must be **remeasured** in the functional currency at each reporting date using the **temporal method**.
    - Balance sheet items carried at historical cost are remeasured at the historical rate, i.e., the exchange rate in effect on the day of the transaction that gave rise to them.
    - Balance sheet items carried at their current or future values (e.g., present value or net realizable value) are remeasured using the current rate on the reporting date.
    - Revenues, expenses, gains, and losses are restated using historical rates.
    - Any net remeasurement gain or loss arising from application of the temporal method is recognized on the income statement as a component of income from continuing operations.
- If the firm's reporting currency differs from its functional currency, all unsettled transactions must be **translated** into the reporting currency at each reporting date using the **all-current method**.
    - Assets and liabilities are restated using the current exchange rate on the reporting date.

- Stockholders' equity items are restated at their historical rates.
- Revenues, expenses, gains, and losses are restated using the historical rates in effect at the time they were recognized (or a weighted-average in some cases).
- The net gain or loss on foreign currency translation is a component of other comprehensive income, not earnings.

Effects of Off-Balance-Sheet Financing

- Reducing a company's debt load improves its ratios, making its securities more attractive investments. Also, many loan covenants contain restrictions on the total debt load that a company is permitted to carry.
- However, **reducing debt** and **hiding it** are two very different things. Firms that carry extensive debt financing but attempt to disguise the fact are engaging in **off-balance-sheet financing**.
- Off-balance-sheet financing takes **four principal forms**: investments in unconsolidated subsidiaries, special purpose entities (SPEs)/variable interest entities (VIEs), operating leases, and factoring receivables with recourse.

Effects of IFRS

- Despite the IASB's attempts at harmonization, **differences** exist between U.S. GAAP and the requirements of IFRS. For example, IFRS tend to be less detailed than FASB pronouncements and may allow choices prohibited by U.S. GAAP.
- Many countries require conformity between tax accounting and book accounting, which is not a requirement in the U.S. or under IFRS.
- Unlike U.S. GAAP, IFRS do not permit the reporting of extraordinary items.
- Unlike U.S. GAAP, IFRS do not permit the use of the completed-contract method of accounting for long-term construction contracts.
- Under U.S. GAAP, business combinations must be accounted for using the purchase method. Under IFRS, the pooling-of-interests method (called uniting-of-interests) is permitted when the acquirer cannot be identified.
- Under U.S. GAAP, research and development costs are expensed as incurred. Under IFRS, development costs may be capitalized.

Effects of Fair Value Accounting

- Because of the fair value disclosures mandated by SFAS 157, investors have a supplemental tool that can be used in addition to ratio analysis. Also, it should be noted that ratios will likely differ depending upon whether they are based on **historical cost** amounts or **fair value** amounts.
- Much of the recent opposition to fair values that has been expressed by bankers was because of the effect that fair value measurements have on ratios. Bankers were fearful that the lower values shown by fair value would lower liquidity ratios to such an extent that they would be in violation of regulatory requirements. Thus, investors must be aware of how the use of fair values will impact ratios as compared to the same ratios using historical costs.
- In 2007, SFAS 159 permitted companies to choose to measure financial instruments and certain other items at fair value. The objective was to improve financial reporting by providing organizations with the opportunity to mitigate volatility in reported earnings caused by measuring related assets and liabilities differently without having to apply hedge accounting provisions. SFAS 159 expanded the use of fair value measurements.
- The fair value option allows entities to (1) measure most financial instruments at fair value and (2) report unrealized gains and losses in earnings. In effect, the fair value option permits an entity to account for eligible items in the same way as trading securities.
- The entity may elect the fair value option for most recognized financial assets and liabilities.

QUESTIONS

3.1 Profitability Ratios

Questions 1 and 2 are based on the following information. The financial statements for Dividendosaurus, Inc., for the current year are as follows:

Balance Sheet		Statement of Income and Retained Earnings	
Cash	$100	Sales	$ 3,000
Accounts receivable	200	Cost of goods sold	(1,600)
Inventory	50	Gross profit	$ 1,400
Net fixed assets	600	Operations expenses	(970)
Total	$950	Operating income	$ 430
		Interest expense	(30)
Accounts payable	$140	Income before tax	$ 400
Long-term debt	300	Income tax	(200)
Capital stock	260	Net income	$ 200
Retained earnings	250	Add: Jan. 1 retained earnings	150
Total	$950	Less: dividends	(100)
		Dec. 31 retained earnings	$ 250

1. Dividendosaurus has return on assets of

- A. 21.1%
- B. 39.2%
- C. 42.1%
- D. 45.3%

Answer (A) is correct. *(CIA, adapted)*
REQUIRED: The return on assets.
DISCUSSION: The return on assets is the ratio of net income to total assets. For Dividendosaurus, it equals 21.1% ($200 net income ÷ $950 total assets).
Answer (B) is incorrect. The ratio of net income to common equity is 39.2%. Answer (C) is incorrect. The ratio of income before tax to total assets is 42.1%. Answer (D) is incorrect. The ratio of income before interest and tax to total assets is 45.3%.

2. Dividendosaurus has a profit margin of

- A. 6.67%
- B. 13.33%
- C. 14.33%
- D. 46.67%

Answer (A) is correct. *(CIA, adapted)*
REQUIRED: The profit margin.
DISCUSSION: The profit margin is the ratio of net income to sales. For Dividendosaurus, it equals 6.67% ($200 net income ÷ $3,000 sales).
Answer (B) is incorrect. The ratio of income before tax to sales is 13.33%. Answer (C) is incorrect. The ratio of income before interest and taxes to sales is 14.33%. Answer (D) is incorrect. The ratio of gross profit to sales is 46.67%.

3. White Knight Enterprises is experiencing a growth rate of 9% with a return on assets of 12%. If the debt ratio is 36% and the market price of the stock is $38 per share, what is the return on equity?

- A. 7.68%
- B. 9.0%
- C. 12.0%
- D. 18.75%

Answer (D) is correct. *(Publisher, adapted)*
REQUIRED: The return on equity.
DISCUSSION: Assume that the firm has $100 in assets, with debt of $36 and equity of $64. Income (return) is $12. The $12 return on assets equates to an 18.75% return on equity ($12 ÷ $64).
Answer (A) is incorrect. This percentage is based on 64% of the ROA. Answer (B) is incorrect. This percentage is the growth rate, not a return. Answer (C) is incorrect. This percentage is the return on assets, not return on equity.

4. In Year 3, Newman Manufacturing's gross profit margin remained unchanged from Year 2. But, in Year 3, the company's net profit margin declined from the level reached in Year 2. This could have happened because, in Year 3,

- A. Corporate tax rates increased.
- B. Cost of goods sold increased relative to sales.
- C. Sales increased at a faster rate than operating expenses.
- D. Common share dividends increased.

Answer (A) is correct. *(CMA, adapted)*
REQUIRED: The factor that could bring about a reduction in net profit margin with no change in gross profit margin.
DISCUSSION: Gross profit margin is net sales minus cost of goods sold. Net profit margin is gross profit margin minus all remaining expenses and losses, one of which is income taxes. If corporate tax rates increased, net profit margin would decrease, leaving gross profit margin unchanged.
Answer (B) is incorrect. A change in cost of goods sold would have affected gross profit margin. Answer (C) is incorrect. Sales increasing faster than operating expenses would have resulted in an increase, not a decrease, to net profit margin. Answer (D) is incorrect. Any impact on dividends cannot be determined from the information given.

5. Colonie, Inc., expects to report net income of at least $10 million annually for the foreseeable future. Colonie could increase its return on equity by taking which of the following actions with respect to its inventory turnover and the use of equity financing?

	Inventory Turnover	Use of Equity Financing
A.	Increase	Increase
B.	Increase	Decrease
C.	Decrease	Increase
D.	Decrease	Decrease

Answer (B) is correct. *(CMA, adapted)*
REQUIRED: The actions that would increase return on equity.
DISCUSSION: Return on equity, in the most general terms, is the ratio of net income to total equity. Increasing inventory turnover raises the numerator, and decreasing equity financing lowers the denominator. This combination is thus the only effective means of increasing return on equity.
Answer (A) is incorrect. Increasing equity financing raises the denominator, lowering the overall return on equity ratio.
Answer (C) is incorrect. Decreasing inventory turnover lowers the numerator, lowering the overall return on equity ratio.
Answer (D) is incorrect. Decreasing inventory turnover lowers the numerator, lowering the overall return on equity ratio.

3.2 Profitability Analysis

6. The following information pertains to Andrew Co. for the year ended December 31:

Sales	$720,000
Net income	120,000
Average total assets	480,000

Which one of the following formulas depicts the use of the DuPont model to calculate Andrew's return on assets?

A. (720,000 ÷ 480,000) × (720,000 ÷ 120,000)

B. (480,000 ÷ 720,000) × (720,000 ÷ 120,000)

C. (720,000 ÷ 480,000) × (120,000 ÷ 720,000)

D. (480,000 ÷ 720,000) × (120,000 ÷ 720,000)

Answer (C) is correct. *(Publisher, adapted)*
REQUIRED: The formula used to compute ROA.
DISCUSSION: The DuPont model depicts return on assets as total asset turnover (sales divided by average total assets) times the profit margin (net income divided by sales). Therefore, Andrew's ROA calculation uses the formula [($720,000 ÷ $480,000) × ($120,000 ÷ $720,000)].

7. The Intelinet Corporation and Comp, Inc., have assets of $100,000 each and a return on common equity of 17%. Intelinet has twice the debt of Comp while Comp has half the sales of Intelinet. If Intelinet has net income of $10,000 and a total assets turnover ratio of 3.5, what is Comp Inc.'s profit margin?

A. 3.31%

B. 7.71%

C. 10.00%

D. 13.50%

Answer (B) is correct. *(Publisher, adapted)*
REQUIRED: The profit margin percentage for Comp.
DISCUSSION: Since Intelinet's ROCE, net income, assets, and debt (in terms of Comp's debt) are known, they can be plugged into the formula for return on common equity to determine Comp's debt level:

$$ROCE = (\text{Net income} - \text{Preferred dividends}) ÷ \text{Average common equity}$$
$$.17 = (\$10,000 - \$0) ÷ (\$100,000 - 2D)$$
$$.17 × (\$100,000 - 2D) = \$10,000$$
$$\$17,000 - .34D = \$10,000$$
$$.34D = \$7,000$$
$$D = \$20,588$$

Now that Comp's debt is known, it can be substituted in the ROCE formula to find net income:

$$ROCE = (\text{Net income} - \text{Preferred dividends}) ÷ \text{Average common equity}$$
$$.17 = (NI - \$0) ÷ (\$100,000 - \$20,588)$$
$$= NI ÷ \$79,412$$
$$NI = \$13,500$$

Since Comp's sales are one-half those of Intelinet, they amount to $175,000 ($350,000 ÷ 2). Therefore, Comp's profit margin percentage is $13,500 ÷ $175,000, or 7.71%.
Answer (A) is incorrect. This percentage is based on the wrong income. Answer (C) is incorrect. This percentage is the return on assets for Intelinet Corp. Answer (D) is incorrect. This percentage is the return on assets for Comp.

Question 8 is based on the following information. The information below pertains to Devlin Company.

Statement of Financial Position as of May 31
(in thousands)

	Year 2	Year 1
Assets		
Current assets		
Cash	$ 45	$ 38
Trading securities	30	20
Accounts receivable (net)	68	48
Inventory	90	80
Prepaid expenses	22	30
Total current assets	$255	$216
Investments, at equity	38	30
Property, plant, and equipment (net)	375	400
Intangible assets (net)	80	45
Total assets	$748	$691
Liabilities		
Current liabilities		
Notes payable	$ 35	$ 18
Accounts payable	70	42
Accrued expenses	5	4
Income taxes payable	15	16
Total current liabilities	$125	$ 80
Long-term debt	35	35
Deferred taxes	3	2
Total liabilities	$163	$117
Equity		
Preferred stock, 6%, $100 par value, cumulative	$150	$150
Common stock, $10 par value	225	195
Additional paid-in capital -- common stock	114	100
Retained earnings	96	129
Total equity	$585	$574
Total liabilities and equity	$748	$691

Income Statement for the year ended May 31
(in thousands)

	Year 2	Year 1
Net sales	$480	$460
Costs and expenses		
Costs of goods sold	330	315
Selling, general, and administrative	52	51
Interest expense	8	9
Income before taxes	$ 90	$ 85
Income taxes	36	34
Net income	$ 54	$ 51

8. Assuming there are no preferred stock dividends in arrears, Devlin Company's return on common equity for the year ended May 31, Year 2, was

A. 6.3%

B. 7.5%

C. 7.8%

D. 10.5%

Answer (D) is correct. *(CMA, adapted)*
REQUIRED: The return on common equity.
DISCUSSION: Return on common equity (ROCE) equals income available to common shareholders divided by average common equity. Devlin's income available to common shareholders is $45 [$54 net income – ($150 par value of preferred stock × 6%)], and its average common equity is $429.5 {[$574 beginning total equity – $150 beginning preferred stock) + ($585 ending total equity – $150 ending preferred stock)] ÷ 2}. Thus, the return is 10.5% ($45 ÷ $429.5).
Answer (A) is incorrect. Average total assets are based on 6.3%. Answer (B) is incorrect. Net income divided by average total assets equals 7.5%. Answer (C) is incorrect. Net income divided by beginning total assets equals 7.8%.

9. If Company A has a higher rate of return on assets than Company B, the reason may be that Company A has a <List A> profit margin on sales, a <List B> asset turnover ratio, or both.

	List A	List B
A.	Higher	Higher
B.	Higher	Lower
C.	Lower	Higher
D.	Lower	Lower

Answer (A) is correct. *(CIA, adapted)*
REQUIRED: The reason for a higher rate of return on assets.
DISCUSSION: The DuPont model treats the return on assets as the product of the profit margin and the asset turnover:

$$Return\ on\ assets\ =\ Profit\ margin\ \times\ Asset\ turnover$$

$$\frac{Net\ income}{Assets} = \frac{Net\ income}{Sales} \times \frac{Sales}{Assets}$$

If one company has a higher return on assets than another, it may have a higher profit margin, a higher asset turnover, or both.

Question 10 is based on the following information. The Statement of Financial Position for King Products Corporation for the fiscal years ended June 30, Year 2, and June 30, Year 1, is presented below. Net sales and cost of goods sold for the year ended June 30, Year 2, were $600,000 and $440,000, respectively.

King Products Corporation
Statement of Financial Position
(in thousands)

	June 30	
	Year 2	Year 1
Cash	$ 60	$ 50
Marketable securities (at market)	40	30
Accounts receivable (net)	90	60
Inventories (at lower of cost or market)	120	100
Prepaid items	30	40
Total current assets	$ 340	$280
Land (at cost)	$ 200	$190
Building (net)	160	180
Equipment (net)	190	200
Patents (net)	70	34
Goodwill (net)	40	26
Total long-term assets	$ 660	$630
Total assets	$1,000	$910
Notes payable	$ 46	$ 24
Accounts payable	94	56
Accrued interest	30	30
Total current liabilities	$ 170	$110
Notes payable, 10% due 12/31/Year 7	$ 20	$ 20
Bonds payable, 12% due 6/30/Year 10	30	30
Total long-term debt	$ 50	$ 50
Total liabilities	$ 220	$160
Preferred stock -- 5% cumulative, $100 par, nonparticipating, authorized, issued and outstanding, 2,000 shares	$ 200	$200
Common stock -- $10 par, 40,000 shares authorized, 30,000 shares issued and outstanding	300	300
Additional paid-in capital -- common	150	150
Retained earnings	130	100
Total equity	$ 780	$750
Total liabilities & equity	$1,000	$910

10. Assuming that King Products Corporation's net income for the year ended June 30, Year 2, was $70,000 and there are no preferred stock dividends in arrears, King Products Corporation's return on common equity was

A. 7.8%

B. 10.6%

C. 10.9%

D. 12.4%

Answer (B) is correct. *(CMA, adapted)*
REQUIRED: The return on common equity for Year 2.
DISCUSSION: Return on common equity (ROCE) equals income available to common shareholders divided by the average common equity. King's preferred stock dividend requirement is $10,000 ($200,000 par value × 5%), so the income available to common shareholders is $60,000 ($70,000 net income – $10,000). Given that preferred equity was $200,000 at all relevant times, beginning and ending common equity was $550,000 ($750,000 total – $200,000) and $580,000 ($780,000 total – $200,000), an average of $565,000 [($580,000 + $550,000) ÷ 2]. The return on common equity was therefore 10.6% ($60,000 ÷ $565,000).

Answer (A) is incorrect. The percentage 7.8% includes preferred equity in the denominator. Answer (C) is incorrect. Using beginning-of-the-year equity results in 10.9%. Answer (D) is incorrect. Not subtracting the preferred dividend requirement from net income results in 12.4%.

3.3 Market Valuation Measures

11. The issuance of new shares in a five-for-one split of common stock

    A. Decreases the book value per share of common stock.

    B. Increases the book value per share of common stock.

    C. Increases total shareholders' equity.

    D. Decreases total shareholders' equity.

Answer (A) is correct. *(CMA, adapted)*
    REQUIRED: The effect of a five-for-one split of common stock on book value and shareholders' equity.
    DISCUSSION: Given that five times as many shares of stock are outstanding, the book value per share of common stock is one-fifth of the former value after the split.
    Answer (B) is incorrect. The book value per share is decreased. Answer (C) is incorrect. The stock split does not change the amount of shareholders' equity. Answer (D) is incorrect. The stock split does not change the amount of shareholders' equity.

> Question 12 is based on the following information. Depoole Company is a manufacturer of industrial products that uses a calendar year for financial reporting purposes. Assume that total quick assets exceeded total current liabilities both before and after the transaction described. Further assume that Depoole has positive profits during the year and a credit balance throughout the year in its retained earnings account.

12. Depoole's issuance of new shares in a five-for-one split of common stock

    A. Decreases the book value per share of common stock.

    B. Increases the book value per share of common stock.

    C. Increases total equity.

    D. Decreases total equity.

Answer (A) is correct. *(CMA, adapted)*
    REQUIRED: The effect of a five-for-one split of common stock.
    DISCUSSION: Given that five times as many shares of stock are outstanding, the book value per share of common stock is one-fifth of the former value after the split.
    Answer (B) is incorrect. The book value per share is decreased. Answer (C) is incorrect. The stock split does not change the amount of equity. Answer (D) is incorrect. The stock split does not change the amount of equity.

13. Book value per common share represents the amount of equity assigned to each outstanding share of common stock. Which one of the following statements about book value per common share is true?

    A. Market price per common share usually approximates book value per common share.

    B. Book value per common share can be misleading because it is based on historical cost.

    C. A market price per common share that is greater than book value per common share is an indication of an overvalued stock.

    D. Book value per common share is the amount that would be paid to shareholders if the company were sold to another company.

Answer (B) is correct. *(CMA, adapted)*
    REQUIRED: The true statement about book value per common share.
    DISCUSSION: Book value is based on the financial statements, which are stated in terms of historical cost and nominal dollars. The figure can be misleading because fair values may differ substantially from book figures.
    Answer (A) is incorrect. Market price may be more or less than book value. Answer (C) is incorrect. Fair value may be more accurate than the carrying values if the historical cost figures are out of date. Answer (D) is incorrect. The amount another company would pay would be based on fair values, not book values.

14. Consider the following financial statement:

Larsen Manufacturing, Inc.
Statement of Financial Position
December 31 (in thousands)

Assets

Current assets	$ 8,018
Long-term assets	10,308
Total assets	$18,326

Liabilities

Current liabilities	$ 998
Long-term debt	3,394
Total liabilities	$ 4,392

Shareholders' equity

Preferred – 6% cumulative, $100 par, authorized, issued, and outstanding 35,000 shares	$ 3,500
Common – $5 par, 3,000,000 shares authorized, 1,050,000 shares issued and outstanding	5,250
Additional paid-in capital – common	2,625
Retained earnings	2,559
Total shareholders' equity	$13,934
Total liabilities and equity	$18,326

Based on the above financial data and assuming that Larsen had no preferred stock dividends in arrears, the company's book value per share at December 31 of the current year is

A. $5.00

B. $7.50

C. $9.94

D. $13.27

Answer (C) is correct. *(CMA, adapted)*
REQUIRED: The book value per share given the statement of financial position.
DISCUSSION: Book value per share is calculated with the following ratio:

$$\frac{Total\ equity\ -\ Liquidation\ value\ of\ preferred\ equity}{Common\ shares\ outstanding}$$

For Larsen, the calculation is as follows:

Book value per share = ($13,934,000 – $3,500,000) ÷ 1,050,000
= $10,434,000 ÷ 1,050,000
= $9.937

Answer (A) is incorrect. Improperly counting only the value of common stock in the numerator results in $5.00. Answer (B) is incorrect. Improperly including only common stock and additional paid-in capital on common stock in the numerator results in $7.50. Answer (D) is incorrect. Failing to deduct the liquidation value of preferred stock from the numerator results in $13.27.

15. Which one of the following statements about the price-earnings (P/E) ratio is true?

A. A company with high growth opportunities ordinarily has a high P/E ratio.

B. A P/E ratio has more meaning when a firm has losses than when it has profits.

C. A P/E ratio has more meaning when a firm has abnormally low profits in relation to its asset base.

D. A P/E ratio expresses the relationship between a firm's market price and its net sales.

Answer (A) is correct. *(CMA, adapted)*
REQUIRED: The true statement about the P/E ratio.
DISCUSSION: A company with high growth opportunities typically has a high P/E ratio because investors are willing to pay a price for the stock higher than that justified by current earnings. In effect, they are trading current earnings for potential future earnings.
Answer (B) is incorrect. A P/E ratio cannot be computed when a firm has losses. Answer (C) is incorrect. A firm with abnormally low profits could have an extremely high, and thus meaningless, P/E ratio. Answer (D) is incorrect. The P/E ratio expresses the relationship between market price and a firm's EPS.

16. Information concerning Hamilton's common stock is presented below for the fiscal year ended May 31, Year 2.

Common stock outstanding	750,000
Stated value per share	$15.00
Market price per share	45.00
Year 1 dividends paid per share	4.50
Year 2 dividends paid per share	7.50
Basic earning per share	11.25
Diluted earnings per share	9.00

The price-earnings ratio for Hamilton's common stock is

A. 3.0 times.

B. 4.0 times.

C. 5.0 times.

D. 6.0 times.

Answer (C) is correct. *(CMA, adapted)*
REQUIRED: The price-earnings ratio for the common stock.
DISCUSSION: The price-earnings ratio is calculated by dividing the current market price of the stock by the earnings per share. Diluted earnings per share is used if disclosed. Thus, Hamilton's price-earnings ratio is 5.0 ($45 market price ÷ $9 DEPS).
Answer (A) is incorrect. The figure of 3.0 is based on use of the stated value per share as the denominator. Answer (B) is incorrect. The figure of 4.0 is based on erroneously using the basic earnings per share as the denominator. Answer (D) is incorrect. The figure of 6.0 is derived by using Year 2 dividends per share as the denominator.

3.4 Earnings per Share and Dividend Payout

17. Baylor Company paid out one-half of last year's earnings in dividends. Baylor's earnings increased by 20%, and the amount of its dividends increased by 15% in the current year. Baylor's dividend payout ratio for the current year was

A. 50%

B. 57.5%

C. 47.9%

D. 78%

Answer (C) is correct. *(CMA, adapted)*
REQUIRED: The dividend payout ratio given earnings and dividend increases.
DISCUSSION: The prior-year dividend payout ratio was 50%. Hence, if prior-year net income was X, the total dividend payout would have been 50%X. If earnings increase by 20%, current-year income will be 120%X. If dividends increase by 15%, the total dividends paid out will be 57.5%X (115% × 50%X), and the new dividend payout ratio will be 47.9% (57.5%X ÷ 120%X).
Answer (A) is incorrect. The prior-year payout ratio is 50%. Answer (B) is incorrect. The figure of 57.5% is 115% of the prior-year payout ratio. Answer (D) is incorrect. The figure of 78% equals 65% of 120%.

18. Appalachian Outfitters, Inc., a mail order supplier of camping gear, is putting together its current-year statement of cash flow. A comparison of the company's year-end balance sheet with the prior year's balance sheet shows the following changes from a year ago.

Assets

Cash & marketable securities	$ (600)
Accounts receivable	200
Inventories	(100)
Gross fixed assets	4,600
Accumulated depreciation	(500)
Total	$3,600

Liabilities & Net Worth

Accounts payable	$ 250
Accruals	50
Long-term note	(300)
Long-term debt	1,400
Common stock	0
Retained earnings	2,200
Total	$3,600

The firm's payout ratio is 20%. During the current year, net cash provided by operations amounted to

A. $2,900

B. $3,050

C. $3,450

D. $4,050

Answer (C) is correct. *(CMA, adapted)*
REQUIRED: The net cash provided by operations.
DISCUSSION: The net profit after taxes equals the change in retained earnings divided by 1 minus the dividend payout ratio, or $2,750 [$2,200 ÷ (1.0 – 0.2)]. Adjusting this amount for noncash items yields the net cash provided by operations. Depreciation is a noncash expense that should be added. To adjust for the difference between cost of goods sold and purchases, the inventory decrease is added (COGS exceeded purchases). To adjust for the difference between purchases and cash paid to suppliers, the increase in accounts payable is also added (purchases exceeded cash paid to suppliers). The increase in accounts receivable is subtracted because it indicates that accrued revenues were greater than cash collections. Finally, the increase in accrued liabilities is added. Thus, the net cash provided by operations is $3,450 ($2,750 + $500 + $100 + $250 – $200 + $50).
Answer (A) is incorrect. The amount of $2,900 excludes the adjustments for depreciation and accruals of liabilities other than accounts payable. Answer (B) is incorrect. The amount of $3,050 excludes the adjustments for inventory, accounts payable, and accruals. Answer (D) is incorrect. The amount of $4,050 results from adding the $600 decrease in cash and marketable securities.

Questions 19 and 20 are based on the following information. Rinker Corporation had 40,000 shares of common stock outstanding on November 30, Year 1. On May 20, Year 2, a 10% stock dividend was declared and distributed. On June 1, Year 2, Rinker issued options to its existing stockholders giving them the immediate right to acquire one additional share of stock for each share of stock held. The option price of the additional share was $6 per share, and no options have been exercised as of year end. The average price of Rinker's common stock for the year was $20 per share. The price of the stock as of November 30, Year 2, the end of the fiscal year, was $30 per share, and the company's net income for the fiscal year was $229,680. Rinker had no outstanding debt during the year, and its tax rate was 30%.

19. The basic earnings per share (rounded to the nearest cent) of Rinker common stock for the fiscal year ended November 30, Year 2, was

A. $5.22 per share.

B. $3.82 per share.

C. $5.74 per share.

D. $3.38 per share.

Answer (A) is correct. *(CMA, adapted)*
REQUIRED: The basic earnings per share (BEPS).
DISCUSSION: BEPS is net income available to common shareholders divided by the weighted average number of common shares outstanding during the year. The denominator will include the 40,000 shares already outstanding plus the 4,000-share stock dividend (stock dividends and stock splits are deemed to have occurred at the beginning of the earliest period presented). Thus, 44,000 shares are considered to have been outstanding throughout the year. The stock options have no effect on the weighted-average shares outstanding because they were not exercised in the current period. BEPS is $5.22 ($229,680 ÷ 44,000).

20. The diluted earnings per share (rounded to the nearest cent) of Rinker common stock for the fiscal year ended November 30, Year 2, was

A. $5.22 per share.

B. $3.19 per share.

C. $3.07 per share.

D. $3.73 per share.

Answer (D) is correct. *(CMA, adapted)*
REQUIRED: The diluted earnings per share (DEPS).
DISCUSSION: DEPS is net income available to common shareholders divided by the number of common shares outstanding after adjustment for all dilutive securities that could possibly be issued. DEPS is always equal to or less than BEPS. In this problem, the difference between BEPS and DEPS is the price used in the assumed treasury stock purchase. Under the "if-converted" method, the purchase of treasury stock from the hypothetical proceeds of the exercise of the 44,000 rights is presumed to be at the year-end market price, if higher than the average market price for the year. Thus, the $264,000 (44,000 shares × $6) available for treasury stock purchases will buy only 8,800 shares at the year-end price of $30 per share. Consequently, because 8,800 is 20% of the actual shares outstanding, no hypothetical proceeds must be used to reduce debt or purchase securities, and no numerator adjustment of net income is needed. The denominator will consist of the 44,000 actual shares assumed to be outstanding all year, plus 17,600 additional shares [(44,000 new shares − 8,800 treasury shares) × (6/12)]. The weighted average denominator of 61,600 shares is divided into the $229,680 of net income to give DEPS of $3.73.

21. Watson Corporation computed the following items from its financial records for the year:

Price-earnings ratio	12
Payout ratio	.6
Asset turnover ratio	.9

The dividend yield on Watson's common stock is

A. 5.0%

B. 7.2%

C. 7.5%

D. 10.8%

Answer (A) is correct. *(CMA, adapted)*
REQUIRED: The dividend yield given the P/E ratio, payout ratio, and asset turnover ratio.
DISCUSSION: Dividend yield is computed by dividing the dividend per share by the market price per share. The payout ratio (.6) is computed by dividing dividends by net income per share (EPS). The P/E ratio (12) is computed by dividing the market price per share by net income per share. Thus, assuming that net income per share (EPS) is $X, the market price must be $12X and the dividends per share $.6X (.6 × $X net income per share). Consequently, the dividend yield is 5.0% ($.6X dividend ÷ $12X market price per share).
Answer (B) is incorrect. This percentage equals 12% times the payout ratio. Answer (C) is incorrect. This percentage equals asset turnover divided by the P/E ratio. Answer (D) is incorrect. This percentage equals 12% times the asset turnover ratio.

3.5 Ratios in General

22. Marge Halifax, chief financial officer of Strickland Construction, has been tracking the activities of the company's nearest competitor for several years. Among other trends, Halifax has noticed that this competitor is able to take advantage of new technology and bring new products to market more quickly than Strickland. In order to determine the reason for this, Halifax has been reviewing the following data regarding the two companies:

	Strickland	Competitor
Accounts receivable turnover	6.85	7.35
Return on assets	15.34	14.74
Times interest earned	15.65	12.45
Current ratio	2.11	1.23
Debt/equity ratio	42.16	55.83
Degree of financial leverage	1.06	1.81
Price/earnings ratio	26.56	26.15

On the basis of this information, which one of the following is the best initial strategy for Halifax to follow in attempting to improve the flexibility of Strickland?

A. Seek cost cutting measures that would increase Strickland's profitability.

B. Investigate ways to improve asset efficiency and turnover times to improve liquidity.

C. Seek additional sources of outside financing for new product introductions.

D. Increase Strickland's investment in short-term securities to increase the current ratio.

Answer (C) is correct. *(CMA, adapted)*
REQUIRED: The best initial strategy to improve flexibility.
DISCUSSION: Strickland's times interest earned, debt/equity ratio, and degree of financial leverage all reveal that Strickland is less leveraged than its competitor. The two firms' price-earnings ratios are comparable, so Strickland should be able to raise new capital fairly easily, either debt or equity. Thus, Strickland should seek additional sources of outside financing for new product introductions.
Answer (A) is incorrect. Cutting costs makes it harder to take advantage of new opportunities or to innovate. Cost cutting is a last resort and Strickland's return on assets is already better than its competitor's. Answer (B) is incorrect. The receivables turnover is not much different than that of the competitor. Answer (D) is incorrect. Increasing investment in short-term securities would not change the current ratio.

23. Grand Savings Bank has received loan applications from three companies in the plastics manufacturing business and currently has the funds to grant only one of these requests. Specific data shown below has been selected from these applications for review and comparison with industry averages.

	Springfield	Reston	Herndon	Industry
Total sales (millions)	$4.27	$3.91	$4.86	$4.30
Net profit margin	9.55%	9.85%	10.05%	9.65%
Current ratio	1.82	2.02	1.96	1.95
Return on assets	12.0%	12.6%	11.4%	12.4%
Debt/equity ratio	52.5%	44.6%	49.6%	48.3%
Financial leverage	1.30	1.02	1.56	1.33

Based on the information above, select the strategy that should be the most beneficial to Grand Savings.

A. Grand should not grant any loans, as none of these companies represents a good credit risk.

B. Grant the loan to Springfield, as all the company's data approximate the industry average.

C. Grant the loan to Reston, as both the debt/equity ratio and degree of financial leverage are below the industry average.

D. Grant the loan to Herndon, as the company has the highest net profit margin and degree of financial leverage.

Answer (C) is correct. *(CMA, adapted)*
REQUIRED: The most beneficial strategy.
DISCUSSION: Grand's primary concern is the customer's ability to pay a loan back. Crucial in deciding the likelihood of payback is how much of the customer's capital structure is made up of debt currently, that is, before the loan is made. Reston's is well below the industry average (a few percentage points can mean the difference between a good credit risk and a poor one) and is the lowest of the three potential customers. Also, Reston is clearly the least leveraged of the three by far, as revealed by its low degree of financial leverage.
Answer (A) is incorrect. Reston is a good credit risk. Answer (B) is incorrect. Debt makes up more than half of Springfield's capital structure; "approximating industry averages" is meaningless when just a few percentage points can mean the difference between a good credit risk and a poor one. Answer (D) is incorrect. While a high profit margin may be indicative of the ability to pay back a loan, a high degree of financial leverage indicates the opposite, and Herndon's is well above the industry average.

3.6 Factors Affecting Reported Profitability

24. In assessing the financial prospects for a firm, financial analysts use various techniques. An example of vertical, common-size analysis is

- A. An assessment of the relative stability of a firm's level of vertical integration.
- B. A comparison in financial ratio form between two or more firms in the same industry.
- C. Advertising expense is 2% greater compared with the previous year.
- D. Advertising expense for the current year is 2% of sales.

Answer (D) is correct. *(CMA, adapted)*
   REQUIRED: The example of vertical, common-size analysis.
   DISCUSSION: Vertical, common-size analysis compares the components within a set of financial statements. A base amount is assigned a value of 100%. For example, total assets on a common-size balance sheet and net sales on a common-size income statement are valued at 100%. Common-size statements permit evaluation of the efficiency of various aspects of operations. An analyst who states that advertising expense is 2% of sales is using vertical, common-size analysis.
   Answer (A) is incorrect. Vertical integration occurs when a corporation owns one or more of its suppliers or customers. Answer (B) is incorrect. Vertical, common-size analysis restates financial statements amounts as percentages. Answer (C) is incorrect. A statement that advertising expense is 2% greater than in the previous year results from horizontal analysis.

3.7 Effects of Foreign Exchange Fluctuations

25. If an entity's books of account are not maintained in its functional currency, U.S. GAAP require remeasurement into the functional currency prior to the translation process. An item that should be remeasured by use of the current exchange rate is

- A. An investment in bonds to be held until maturity.
- B. A plant asset and the associated accumulated depreciation.
- C. A patent and the associated accumulated amortization.
- D. The revenue from a long-term construction contract.

Answer (A) is correct. *(CMA, adapted)*
   REQUIRED: The item that should be remeasured into the functional currency using the current exchange rate.
   DISCUSSION: When remeasurement is necessary, the temporal method is applied. The essence of the temporal method is to make the financial statement items look as if the underlying transactions had been recorded in the functional currency to begin with. Balance sheet items carried at their future values, such as held-to-maturity investments in bonds, are remeasured using the current rate on the reporting date.
   Answer (B) is incorrect. Property, plant, and equipment is remeasured at the historical rate. Answer (C) is incorrect. Intangible assets are remeasured at the historical rate. Answer (D) is incorrect. Revenues, expenses, gains, and losses are remeasured using historical rates.

26. U.S. GAAP require the application of the functional currency concept. Before the financial statements of a foreign subsidiary may be translated into the parent company's currency, the functional currency of the foreign subsidiary must be determined. All of the following factors indicate that a foreign subsidiary's functional currency is the foreign currency rather than the parent's currency **except** when

- A. Its cash flows are primarily in foreign currency and do not affect the parent's cash flows.
- B. Its sales prices are responsive to exchange rate changes and to international competition.
- C. Its labor, material, and other costs are obtained in the local market of the foreign subsidiary.
- D. Its financing is primarily obtained from local foreign sources and from the subsidiary's operations.

Answer (B) is correct. *(CMA, adapted)*
   REQUIRED: The factor not indicating that a foreign subsidiary's functional currency is the foreign currency rather than the parent's currency.
   DISCUSSION: A company's functional currency is that of the primary economic environment in which an entity operates, i.e., the currency in which the company primarily generates and expends cash. Sales prices that are responsive to exchange rate fluctuations and international competition suggest that the functional currency is the parent's currency.
   Answer (A) is incorrect. Cash flows primarily being in that foreign currency that does not affect the parent's cash flows is generally an indicator that the functional currency is the foreign currency. Answer (C) is incorrect. Labor, material, and other costs being obtained in the local market of the foreign subsidiary is generally an indicator that the functional currency is the foreign currency. Answer (D) is incorrect. Subsidiary financing being obtained from local foreign sources and from the subsidiary's operations is generally an indicator that the functional currency is the foreign currency.

27. U.S. GAAP define foreign currency transactions as those denominated in other than an entity's functional currency. Transaction gains and losses are reported as

    A. Extraordinary items.

    B. Adjustments to the beginning balance of retained earnings.

    C. A component of equity.

    D. A component of income from continuing operations.

Answer (D) is correct. *(CMA, adapted)*
    REQUIRED: The proper treatment of foreign currency transaction gains (losses).
    DISCUSSION: When a foreign currency transaction gives rise to a receivable or a payable, a change in the exchange rate between the measurement currency and the currency in which the transaction is denominated is a foreign currency transaction gain or loss that should be included as a component of income from continuing operations.
    Answer (A) is incorrect. Transaction gains (losses) are not so unusual as to warrant extraordinary status. Answer (B) is incorrect. Adjustments to retained earnings are made only for prior-period adjustments, and transaction gains (losses) do not meet the criteria for such treatment. Answer (C) is incorrect. Foreign currency translation gains and losses (not transaction gains and losses) are reported in other comprehensive income, a component of equity.

28. Unrealized foreign currency gains and losses included in the other comprehensive income section of a consolidated balance sheet represent

    A. Foreign currency transaction gains and losses.

    B. The amount resulting from translating foreign currency financial statements into the reporting currency.

    C. Remeasurement gains and losses.

    D. Accounting not in accordance with U.S. generally accepted accounting principles.

Answer (B) is correct. *(CMA, adapted)*
    REQUIRED: The meaning of unrealized foreign currency gains and losses reported as other comprehensive income.
    DISCUSSION: U.S. GAAP require that foreign currency translation adjustments resulting from translation of an entity's financial statements into the reporting currency be reported on the balance sheet in other comprehensive income.
    Answer (A) is incorrect. Transaction gains and losses (as opposed to translation gains and losses) are recognized in the income statement as they occur. Answer (C) is incorrect. Remeasurement gains and losses are included in net income. Answer (D) is incorrect. The practice described is in accordance with U.S. GAAP.

29. When restating financial statements originally recorded in a foreign currency,

    A. Income taxes are ignored in calculating and disclosing the results of foreign currency translations.

    B. A component of annual net income, "Adjustment from Foreign Currency Translation," should be presented in the notes to the financial statements or in a separate schedule.

    C. The aggregate transaction gain or loss included in net income should be disclosed in the financial statements or in the notes to the financial statements.

    D. The financial statements should be adjusted for a rate change that occurs after the financial statement date but prior to statement issuance.

Answer (C) is correct. *(CMA, adapted)*
    REQUIRED: The true statement about restating financial statements originally recorded in a foreign currency.
    DISCUSSION: Foreign currency transaction gains or losses are ordinarily recognized in the income statement of the period in which the exchange rate changes. Accordingly, the aggregate transaction gain or loss included in earnings should be disclosed.
    Answer (A) is incorrect. Allocation of income tax expense is required, including those income taxes related to translation adjustments and those transaction gains and losses recorded in a separate component of equity. Answer (B) is incorrect. The adjustment for foreign currency translation is reported in other comprehensive income. Answer (D) is incorrect. An enterprise's financial statements are not adjusted for rate changes after their effective date or after the date of foreign currency statements of a foreign entity if they are consolidated, combined, or accounted for under the equity method in the enterprise's financial statements.

3.8 Effects of Off-Balance-Sheet Financing

30. Careful reading of an annual report will reveal that off-balance-sheet debt includes

A. Amounts due in future years under operating leases.

B. Transfers of accounts receivable without recourse.

C. Current portion of long-term debt.

D. Amounts due in future years under capital leases.

Answer (A) is correct. *(CMA, adapted)*
REQUIRED: The off-balance-sheet debt.
DISCUSSION: Off-balance-sheet debt includes any type of liability for which the company is responsible but that does not appear on the balance sheet. The most common example is the amount due in future years on operating leases. Under U.S. GAAP, operating leases are not capitalized; instead, only the periodic payments of rent are reported when actually paid. Capital leases (those similar to a purchase) must be capitalized and reported as liabilities.
Answer (B) is incorrect. Transfers of accounts receivable without recourse do not create a liability for the company. This transaction is simply a transfer of receivables for cash.
Answer (C) is incorrect. The current portion of long-term debt is shown on the balance sheet as a current liability. Answer (D) is incorrect. Amounts due in future years under capital leases are required to be recognized under U.S. GAAP.

3.9 Effects of IFRS

31. The International Accounting Standards Board (IASB)

A. Directly influences governmental legislation regarding accounting standards.

B. Develops binding pronouncements for its members.

C. Meets in private to encourage open and honest discussion.

D. Establishes uniform accounting standards to eliminate reporting differences among nations.

Answer (D) is correct. *(Publisher, adapted)*
REQUIRED: The correct statement about the IASB.
DISCUSSION: Of the four principal objectives listed by the IFRS Foundation, the first is "to develop a single set of high quality, understandable, enforceable and globally accepted international financial reporting standards (IFRS) through its standard-setting body, the IASB." However, IASB pronouncements are not binding.
Answer (A) is incorrect. The IASB has no direct influence on governmental legislation. Answer (B) is incorrect. The IASB's authority is restricted to the willingness of participating and other countries to adopt its standards. Answer (C) is incorrect. All meetings of the IASB are held in public and webcast.

32. Which of the following statements regarding International Financial Reporting Standards (IFRS) is **false**? IFRS

A. Are required as GAAP in member countries.

B. Are intended to lead to harmonization of principles.

C. Are formulated by a body that engages with interested parties around the world.

D. Cannot be enforced by the IASB.

Answer (A) is correct. *(Publisher, adapted)*
REQUIRED: The false statement regarding IFRS.
DISCUSSION: IFRS are designed to lead to harmonization of principles worldwide, but ratified standards are not mandatory. The IASB has no enforcement authority.
Answer (B) is incorrect. IFRS are intended to lead to harmonization of principles. Answer (C) is incorrect. The IASB, which formulates IFRS, engages closely with stakeholders around the world, including investors, analysts, regulators, and others. Answer (D) is incorrect. IFRS cannot be enforced by the IASB.

33. Under IFRS, an entity that acquires an intangible asset may use the revaluation model for subsequent measurement only if

A. The useful life of the intangible asset can be reliably determined.

B. An active market exists for the intangible asset.

C. The cost of the intangible asset can be measured reliably.

D. The intangible asset is a monetary asset.

Answer (B) is correct. *(CPA, adapted)*
REQUIRED: The condition for use of the revaluation model for subsequent measurement of an intangible asset.
DISCUSSION: An intangible asset is carried at cost minus any accumulated amortization and impairment losses, or at a revalued amount. The revaluation model is similar to that for items of PPE (initial recognition of an asset at cost). However, fair value must be determined based on an active market.
Answer (A) is incorrect. An intangible asset may have an indefinite life. Answer (C) is incorrect. Initial recognition of an intangible asset is at cost. Recognition is permitted only when it is probable that the entity will receive the expected economic benefits, and the cost is reliably measurable. Answer (D) is incorrect. An intangible asset is nonmonetary.

34. A company determined the following values for its inventory as of the end of the fiscal year:

Historical cost	$100,000
Current replacement cost	70,000
Net realizable value	90,000
Net realizable value minus a normal profit margin	85,000
Fair value	95,000

Under IFRS, what amount should the company report as inventory on its balance sheet?

A. $70,000

B. $85,000

C. $90,000

D. $95,000

Answer (C) is correct. *(CPA, adapted)*
REQUIRED: The year-end inventory.
DISCUSSION: Inventory is measured at the lower of cost or NRV (estimated selling price in the ordinary course of business – estimated costs of completion and sale). Given cost of $100,000 and NRV of $90,000, inventory should be reported at $90,000. The write-down of $10,000 is recognized as a loss in the current period.
Answer (A) is incorrect. Current replacement cost ($70,000) is neither cost nor NRV. Answer (B) is incorrect. The lower of cost or market ($85,000) is the appropriate measure under GAAP. Answer (D) is incorrect. Fair value is greater than NRV.

3.10 Effects of Fair Value Accounting

35. An investment in trading securities is measured on the statement of financial position at the

A. Cost to acquire the asset.

B. Accumulated income minus accumulated dividends since acquisition.

C. Lower of cost or market.

D. Fair value.

Answer (D) is correct. *(CMA, adapted)*
REQUIRED: The means of valuing trading securities on the balance sheet.
DISCUSSION: Under U.S. GAAP, trading securities are those held principally for sale in the near term. They are classified as current and consist of debt securities and equity securities with readily determinable fair values. Unrealized holding gains and losses on trading securities are reported in earnings. Hence, these securities are reported at fair value.
Answer (A) is incorrect. Cost is adjusted for changes in fair value. Answer (B) is incorrect. An equity-based investment is adjusted for the investor's share of the investee's earnings, minus dividends received. Answer (C) is incorrect. Lower of cost or market is applied by U.S. GAAP to inventories, not trading securities.

Use the Gleim **CMA Test Prep** Software for interactive testing with **additional multiple-choice questions!**

3.12 ESSAY QUESTIONS

Scenario for Essay Questions 1, 2, 3

Easecom Company is a manufacturer of highly specialized products for networking video-conferencing equipment. Production of specialized units is, to a large extent, performed under contract, with standard units manufactured to marketing projections. Maintenance of customer equipment is an important area of customer satisfaction. With the recent downturn in the computer industry, the video-conferencing equipment segment has suffered, causing a slide in Easecom's performance. Easecom's income statement for the fiscal year ended October 31, Year 1, is presented below.

```
                Easecom Company
                Income Statement
        For the Year Ended October 31, Year 1
                ($000 omitted)

Net sales:
  Equipment                              $6,000
  Maintenance contracts                   1,800
    Total net sales                      $7,800

Expenses:
  Cost of goods sold                     $4,600
  Customer maintenance                    1,000
  Selling expense                           600
  Administrative expense                    900
  Interest expense                          150
    Total expenses                       $7,250
  Income before income taxes            $  550
    Income taxes                            220
  Net income                            $  330
```

Easecom's return on sales before interest and taxes was 9% in Fiscal Year 1 while the industry average was 12%. Easecom's total asset turnover was three times, and its return on average assets before interest and taxes was 27%, both well below the industry average. In order to improve performance and raise these ratios near to, or above, industry averages, Bill Hunt, Easecom's president, established the following goals for Fiscal Year 2:

- Return on sales before interest and taxes   11%
- Total asset turnover   4 times
- Return on average assets before interest and taxes 35%

To achieve Hunt's goals, Easecom's management team took into consideration the growing international video-conferencing market and proposed the following actions for Fiscal Year 2:

- Increase equipment sales prices by 10%.
- Increase the cost of each unit sold by 3% for needed technology and quality improvements, and increased variable costs.
- Increase maintenance inventory by $250,000 at the beginning of the year and add two maintenance technicians at a total cost of $130,000 to cover wages and related travel expenses. These revisions are intended to improve customer service and response time. The increased inventory will be financed at an annual interest rate of 12%; no other borrowings or loan reductions are contemplated during Fiscal Year 2. All other assets will be held to Fiscal Year 1 levels.
- Increase selling expenses by $250,000 but hold administrative expenses at Year 1 levels.
- The effective rate for Year 2 federal and state taxes is expected to be 40%, the same as Year 1.

It is expected that these actions will increase equipment unit sales by 6%, with a corresponding 6% growth in maintenance contracts.

Questions

1. Prepare a pro forma income statement for Easecom Company for the fiscal year ending October 31, Year 2, on the assumption that the proposed actions are implemented as planned and that the increased sales objectives will be met. (All numbers should be rounded to the nearest thousand, i.e., $000 omitted.)

2. Calculate the following ratios for Easecom Company for Fiscal Year 2 and determine whether Bill Hunt's goals will be achieved:

   a. Return on sales before interest and taxes.
   b. Total asset turnover.
   c. Return on average assets before interest and taxes.

3. Discuss the limitations and difficulties that can be encountered in using ratio analysis, particularly when making comparisons to industry averages.

Essay Questions 1, 2, 3 — Unofficial Answers

1. The pro forma income statement for Easecom Company for the fiscal year ended October 31, Year 2, assuming all of management's proposed actions are implemented and the increased sales objectives are met, is presented below.

Easecom Company Pro Forma Income Statement For the Year Ending October 31, Year 2 ($000 omitted)	
Net sales:	
Equipment ($6,000 × 1.06 × 1.10)	$6,996
Maintenance ($1,800 × 1.06)	1,908
Total net sales	$8,904
Expenses:	
Cost of goods sold ($4,600 × 1.03 × 1.06)	$5,022
Customer maintenance ($1,000 + $130)	1,130
Selling expense ($600 + $250)	850
Administrative expense	900
Interest expense [$150 + ($250 × .12)]	180
Total expenses	$8,082
Income before income taxes	$ 822
Income taxes	329
Net income	$ 493

2. a. Return on sales before interest and taxes = Income before interest and taxes ÷ Sales
    $$= (\$493 + \$329 + \$180) \div \$8,904$$
    $$= 11.25\%$$

    The goal of 11% return on sales before interest and taxes would be exceeded by .25%.

    b. Total asset turnover = Sales ÷ Average assets
    $$= \$8,904 \div (\$2,600^* + \$250)$$
    $$= 3.12$$

    *Year 1 average assets = Year 1 sales ÷ Year 1 turnover of average assets
    $$= \$7,800 \div 3$$
    $$= \$2,600$$

    The goal of total asset turnover of four times would not be achieved (3.12 is less than 4).

    c. Return on average assets
    before interest and taxes = Income before interest and taxes ÷ Average assets
    $$= (\$493 + \$329 + \$180) \div (\$2,600 + \$250)$$
    $$= 35.16\%$$

    The goal of 35% return on average assets before interest and taxes would be exceeded by .16%.

3. The limitations and difficulties that can be encountered in using ratio analyses include the following:

    - Various techniques are used in the analysis of financial data to emphasize the comparative and relative importance of data presented and to evaluate the position of the firm. These techniques include ratio analysis, common-size analysis, examination of relative size among firms, etc. The information derived from these types of analyses should be blended. No one type of analysis is best or sufficient to support overall findings or to serve all types of users.

    - The nature of the general business environment and direct competition in a company's geographical area can result in special situations not encountered throughout the industry, which creates deviations from the industry norm.

    - Identical companies may use different valuation or expense methods (e.g., LIFO, FIFO, average cost, standard costs, different depreciation methods, etc.). Consequently, footnotes to the financial statements must be carefully analyzed to determine comparability.

Use **CMA Gleim Online** and **Essay Wizard** to practice additional essay questions in an exam-like environment.

STUDY UNIT FOUR
INVESTMENT RISK AND PORTFOLIO MANAGEMENT

(15 pages of outline)

Corporate Finance

The area of corporate finance is a heavily tested area on the CMA exam. Candidates must know the types of risk, measures of risk, elements of portfolio management, the use of options and futures contracts, and the types of capital instruments available for long-term financing. Dividend policy is also covered, as are factors influencing the optimum capital structure, the cost of capital, and the effective and efficient management and financing of working capital.

This study unit is the **first of four** on **corporate finance**. The relative weight assigned to this major topic in Part 2 of the exam is **25%**. The four study units are

Study Unit 4: Investment Risk and Portfolio Management
Study Unit 5: Financial Instruments and Cost of Capital
Study Unit 6: Managing Current Assets
Study Unit 7: Raising Capital, Corporate Restructuring, and International Finance

After studying the outline and answering the questions in this study unit, you will have the skills necessary to address the following topics listed in the ICMA's Learning Outcome Statements:

Part 2 – Section B.1. Risk and return

The candidate should be able to:

a. calculate rates of return
b. identify and demonstrate an understanding of systematic (market) risk and unsystematic (company) risk
c. identify and demonstrate an understanding of credit risk, foreign exchange risk, interest rate risk, market risk, industry risk, and political risk
d. demonstrate an understanding of the relationship between risk and return
e. calculate expected return, standard deviation of return, and coefficient of variation
f. distinguish between individual security risk and portfolio risk
g. demonstrate an understanding of diversification
h. define beta and how a change in beta impacts a security's price
i. demonstrate an understanding of the capital asset pricing model (CAPM) and calculate the expected risk-adjusted returns using CAPM
j. identify the arbitrage pricing theory (APT) and the Fama-French model as alternatives to CAPM (calculations not required)

Part 2 – Section B.2. Managing financial risk

The candidate should be able to:

   a.   describe and calculate business risk

   b.   explain how operating leverage can increase return and business risk concurrently

   c.   describe and calculate financial risk

   d.   explain how financial leverage can increase return and financial risk concurrently

   e.   explain how portfolio theory can be used to decrease the financial risk of a business

   f.   demonstrate an understanding of how individual business activities can affect the business's portfolio risk

   g.   demonstrate an understanding of how individual securities affect portfolio risk

   h.   define a natural hedge and other forms of hedging and demonstrate how hedging can be used to manage financial risk

   i.   demonstrate an understanding of how the concept of correlation is used in risk management

   j.   explain the significance of a positive or a negative covariance or correlation of stocks within a two-stock portfolio

   k.   evaluate alternative strategies and select the strategy that is designed to minimize risk and/or maximize reward

4.1 RISK AND RETURN

1. **Rate of Return**

   a.   A return is the amount received by an investor as compensation for taking on the risk of the investment.

$$Return\ on\ investment = Amount\ received - Amount\ invested$$

      1)   EXAMPLE: An investor paid $100,000 for an investment that returned $112,000. The investor's return is $12,000 ($112,000 – $100,000).

   b.   The rate of return is the return stated as a percentage of the amount invested.

$$Rate\ of\ return = \frac{Return\ on\ investment}{Amount\ invested}$$

      1)   EXAMPLE: The investor's rate of return is 12% ($12,000 ÷ $100,000).

2. **Two Basic Types of Investment Risk**

   a.   **Systematic risk**, also called **market risk**, is the risk faced by all firms. Changes in the economy as a whole, such as the business cycle, affect all players in the market.

      1)   For this reason, systematic risk is sometimes referred to as undiversifiable risk. Since all investment securities are affected, this risk cannot be offset through portfolio diversification.

   b.   **Unsystematic risk**, also called **company risk**, is the risk inherent in a particular investment security. This type of risk is determined by the issuer's industry, products, customer loyalty, degree of leverage, management competence, etc.

      1)   For this reason, unsystematic risk is sometimes referred to as diversifiable risk. Since individual securities are affected differently by economic conditions, this risk can be offset through portfolio diversification.

3. **Other Types of Investment Risk**

    a. Credit risk is the risk that the issuer of a debt security will default. This risk can be gauged by the use of credit-rating agencies (see Study Unit 5, Subunit 1).

    b. Foreign exchange risk is the risk that a foreign currency transaction will be affected by fluctuations in exchange rates (see Study Unit 7, Subunit 5).

    c. Interest rate risk is the risk that an investment security will fluctuate in value due to changes in interest rates. In general, the longer the time until maturity, the greater the degree of interest rate risk.

    d. Industry risk is the risk that a change will affect securities issued by firms in a particular industry. For example, a spike in fuel prices will negatively affect the airline industry.

    e. risk is the probability of loss from actions of governments, such as from changes in tax laws or environmental regulations or from expropriation of assets.

    f. Liquidity risk is the risk that a security cannot be sold on short notice for its market value.

4. **Relationship Between Risk and Return**

    a. Whether the expected return on an investment is sufficient to entice an investor depends on its risk, the risks and returns of alternative investments, and the investor's attitude toward risk.

        1) Most serious investors are risk averse. They have a diminishing marginal utility for wealth. In other words, the utility of additional increments of wealth decreases. The utility of a gain for serious investors is less than the disutility of a loss of the same amount. Due to this risk aversion, risky securities must have higher expected returns.

        2) A risk neutral investor adopts an expected value approach because (s)he regards the utility of a gain as equal to the disutility of a loss of the same amount. Thus, a risk-neutral investor has a purely rational attitude toward risk.

        3) A risk-seeking investor has an optimistic attitude toward risk. (S)he regards the utility of a gain as exceeding the disutility of a loss of the same amount.

5. **Financial Instruments**

    a. Financial managers may select from a wide range of financial instruments in which to invest and with which to raise money.

    b. Ranked from the lowest rate of return to the highest (and thus the lowest **risk** to the highest), the following is a short list of widely available long-term financial instruments:

        1) U.S. Treasury bonds
        2) First mortgage bonds
        3) Second mortgage bonds
        4) Subordinated debentures
        5) Income bonds
        6) Preferred stock
        7) Convertible preferred stock
        8) Common stock

    c. These instruments also are ranked according to the level of security backing them. An unsecured financial instrument is much riskier than an instrument that is secured. Thus, the riskier asset earns a higher rate of return.

        1) Mortgage bonds are secured by assets, but common stock is completely unsecured. Accordingly, common stock will earn a higher rate of return than mortgage bonds.

        2) For more on long-term financing, see Study Unit 5.

    d. Short-term financial instruments increase the liquidity of an entity. For a discussion of the asset management aspects of short-term instruments, see Study Unit 6.

6.   **Measures of Risk – Standard Deviation and Variance**

    a.   The **expected rate of return ($\overline{R}$)** on an investment is determined using an expected value calculation. It is an average of the possible outcomes weighted according to their probabilities.

$$Expected\ rate\ of\ return\ (\overline{R}) = \sum (Possible\ rate\ of\ return \times Probability)$$

EXAMPLE

A company is considering investing in the common stock of one of two firms, Xatalan Corp. and Yarmouth Co. The expected rates of return on the two securities based on the weighted-averages of their probable outcomes are calculated as follows:

Xatalan Corporation Stock						Yarmouth Company Stock				
Rate of Return %		Probability %		Weighted Average		Rate of Return %		Probability %		Weighted Average
80 %	×	60%	=	48 %		30 %	×	70%	=	21 %
(50)%	×	40%	=	(20)%		(10)%	×	30%	=	(3)%
Expected rate of return ($\overline{R}$)				**28 %**		**Expected rate of return ($\overline{R}$)**				**18 %**

The expected rate of return on Xatalan Corporation stock is higher, but the risk of each investment also should be measured.

---

    b.   Risk is the chance that the actual return on an investment will differ from the expected return. One way to measure risk is with the standard deviation (variance) of the distribution of an investment's return.

$$Standard\ deviation\ (\sigma) = \sqrt{\sum [\,(R_i - \overline{R})^2 \times Probability\,]} = \sqrt{Variance}$$

        Where: R_i = Possible rate of return
                 $\overline{R}$ = Expected rate of return

      1)   The **standard deviation** measures the tightness of the distribution and the riskiness of the investment.

          a)   A large standard deviation reflects a broadly dispersed probability distribution, meaning the range of possible returns is wide. Conversely, the smaller the standard deviation, the tighter the probability distribution and the lower the risk.

          b)   Thus, the following general statement can be made: The greater the standard deviation, the riskier the investment.

EXAMPLE

The following measures the risk of the investments from the previous example using standard deviation.

Xatalan Corporation Stock

$$Standard\ deviation\ (\sigma) = \sqrt{[(80\% - 28\%)^2 \times 60\%] + [(-50\% - 28\%)^2 \times 40\%]} = \sqrt{4,056} = \mathbf{63.69\%}$$

Yarmouth Company Stock

$$Standard\ deviation\ (\sigma) = \sqrt{[(30\% - 18\%)^2 \times 70\%] + [(-10\% - 18\%)^2 \times 30\%]} = \sqrt{336} = \mathbf{18.33\%}$$

Although the investment in Xatalan stock has a higher expected return than the investment in Yarmouth stock (28% > 18%), it also is riskier than Yarmouth because its standard deviation is greater (63.69% > 18.33%). Therefore, to determine which investment is the better choice in terms of the risk-return tradeoff, we must measure the coefficient of variation (CV) of the expected returns on the two investments.

---

    c.   The **coefficient of variation (CV)** is useful when the rates of return and standard deviations of two investments differ. It measures the risk per unit of return.

$$\text{Coefficient of variation} = \frac{\textit{Standard deviation}}{\textit{Expected rate of return}}$$

$$CV = \sigma \div \overline{R}$$

The lower the ratio, the better the risk-return tradeoff is.

EXAMPLE

The coefficients of variation for the expected return of the two potential investments are calculated as follows:

		Coefficient of Variation
Xatalan Corporation Stock: $\sigma \div \overline{R}$ = 63.69% ÷ 28% =		**2.275**
Yarmouth Company Stock: $\sigma \div \overline{R}$ = 18.33% ÷ 18% =		**1.018**

The investment in Yarmouth has a better risk-return tradeoff since its coefficient of variation (CV) is lower than that of the investment in Xatalan (1.018 < 2.275).

---

    d.   When comparing the risk of multiple investments, it is important to recognize that using the standard deviation alone can be misleading. Calculating the coefficient of variation gives you a better basis for comparison because it measures the risk per unit of return.

7.   **Security Risk vs. Portfolio Risk**

    a.   The calculations in this subunit apply to investments in individual securities. When a portfolio is held, however, additional considerations apply. Risk and return should be evaluated for the entire portfolio, not for individual assets.

    b.   The expected return on a portfolio is the weighted average of the returns on the individual securities.

    c.   However, the risk of the portfolio is usually not an average of the standard deviations of the particular securities. Thanks to the diversification effect, combining securities results in a portfolio risk that is less than the average of the standard deviations because the returns are imperfectly correlated.

        1)   The **correlation coefficient (r)** has a range from 1.0 to −1.0. It measures the degree to which any two variables, e.g., two stocks in a portfolio, are related.

            a)   Perfect positive correlation (1.0) means that the two variables always move together, and perfect negative correlation (−1.0) means that the two variables always move in the opposite direction.

            b)   Given perfect positive correlation, risk for a two-stock portfolio with equal investments in each stock would be the same as that for the individual assets.

            c)   Given perfect negative correlation, risk would in theory be eliminated.

        2)   In practice, the existence of market risk makes perfect correlation nearly impossible.

            a)   The normal range for the correlation of two randomly selected stocks is .50 to .70. The result is a reduction in, but not elimination of, risk.

    d.   The measurement of the standard deviation of a portfolio's returns is based on the same formula as that for a single security.

8.   **Covariance**

   a.   The correlation coefficient of two securities can be combined with their standard deviations to arrive at their covariance, a measure of their mutual volatility.

Covariance of a Two-Stock Portfolio

Correlation coefficient × Standard deviation $_1$ × Standard deviation $_2$

   1)   EXAMPLE: The coefficient of correlation of Xatalan Corporation stock and Yarmouth Company stock is 0.6 (given), meaning they move in the same direction 60% of the time. The covariance of a portfolio consisting entirely of these two stocks is calculated as follows:

$$\text{Covariance of two-stock portfolio} = 0.6 \times 6.337 \times 8.831$$
$$= 33.58$$

9.   **Diversification and Beta**

   a.   Portfolio theory concerns the composition of an investment portfolio that is efficient in balancing the risk with the rate of return of the portfolio.

   b.   Asset allocation is a key concept in financial planning and money management. It is the process of dividing investments among different kinds of assets, such as stocks, bonds, real estate, and cash, to optimize the risk-reward tradeoff based on specific situations and goals. The rationale is that the returns on different types of assets are not perfectly positively correlated. Asset allocation is especially useful for such institutional investors as pension fund managers, who have a duty to invest with prudence.

   c.   The expected rate of return of a portfolio is the weighted average of the expected returns of the individual assets in the portfolio.

   d.   The variability (risk) of a portfolio's return is determined by the correlation of the returns of individual portfolio assets.

   1)   To the extent the returns are not perfectly positively correlated, variability is decreased.

   e.   **Specific risk**, also called diversifiable risk, unsystematic risk, residual risk, and unique risk, is the risk associated with a specific investee's operations: new products, patents, acquisitions, competitors' activities, etc.

   1)   Specific risk is the risk that can be potentially eliminated by diversification.

   a)   The relevant risk of an individual security held in a portfolio is its contribution to the overall risk of the portfolio. When much of a security's risk can be eliminated by diversification, its relevant risk is low.

   2)   In principle, diversifiable risk should continue to decrease as the number of different securities held increases.

   a)   In practice, however, the benefits of diversification become extremely small when more than about 20 to 30 different securities are held. Moreover, commissions and other transaction costs increase with greater diversification.

    f.   **Market risk**, also called undiversifiable risk and systematic risk, is the risk of the stock market as a whole. Some conditions in the national economy affect all businesses, which is why equity prices so often move together.

        1)   The effect of an individual security on the volatility of a portfolio is measured by its sensitivity to movements by the overall market. This sensitivity is stated in terms of a stock's **beta coefficient (β)**.

            a)   An average-risk stock has a beta of 1.0 because its returns are perfectly positively correlated with those on the market portfolio. For example, if the market return increases by 20%, the return on the security increases by 20%.

            b)   A beta of less than 1.0 means that the security is less volatile than the market; e.g., if the market return increases by 20% and the security's return increases only 10%, the security has a beta of .5.

            c)   A beta over 1.0 indicates a volatile security; e.g., if the return increases 30% when the market return increases by 15%, the security has a beta of 2.0.

        2)   The word beta is derived from the regression equation for regressing the return of an individual security (the dependent variable) to the overall market return. The beta coefficient is the slope of the regression line.

            a)   The beta for a security may also be calculated by dividing the covariance of the return on the market and the return on the security by the variance of the return on the market.

        3)   Beta is the best measure of the risk of an individual security held in a diversified portfolio because it determines how the security affects the risk of the portfolio.

        4)   The beta of a portfolio is the weighted average of the betas of the individual securities.

            a)   Portfolio insurance is a strategy of hedging a stock portfolio against market risk by selling stock index futures short or buying stock index put options. A stock index futures contract is an agreement to deliver the cash equivalent of a group of stocks on a specified date. This cash equivalent equals a given stock index value, for example, the S&P 500, times a cash amount. Thus, if the stock index falls (rises), a seller of stock index futures gains (loses) and a buyer loses (gains).

10. **Capital Asset Pricing Model (CAPM)**

    a.   Investors want to reduce their risk and therefore take advantage of diversification by holding a portfolio of securities. In order to measure how a particular security contributes to the risk and return of a diversified portfolio, investors can use the capital asset pricing model (CAPM).

    b.   The CAPM quantifies the required return on an equity security by relating the security's level of risk to the average return available in the market (portfolio).

    c.   The CAPM formula is based on the idea that the investor must be compensated for his/her investment in two ways: time value of money and risk.

        1)   The time value component is the risk-free rate (denoted R_F in the formula). It is the return provided by the safest investments, e.g., U.S. Treasury securities.

    2) The risk component consists of

        a) The market risk premium (denoted $R_M - R_F$), which is the return provided by the market over and above the risk-free rate, weighted by

        b) A measure of the security's risk, called beta (β) (see page 149).

            i) Thus, the beta of the market portfolio equals 1, and the beta of U.S. Treasury securities is 0.

CAPM Formula

$$Required\ rate\ of\ return = R_F + \beta(R_M - R_F)$$

Where: R_F = Risk-free return
R_M = Market return
β = Measure of the systematic risk or volatility of the individual security in comparison to the market (diversified portfolio)

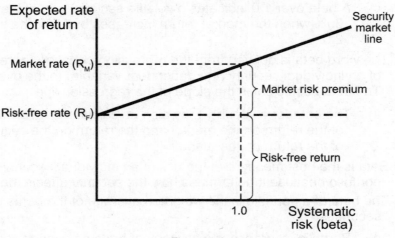

Figure 4-1

    d. The market risk premium varies in direct proportion to beta. Therefore, all investments (securities) must lie on the security market line.

EXAMPLE

An investor is considering the purchase of a stock with a beta value of 1.2. Treasury bills are currently paying 8.6%, and the expected average return on the market is 10.1%. (Remember, U.S. Treasuries are considered as close to a risk-free investment as there can be.) To be induced to buy this stock, the return that the investor must receive is calculated as follows:

$$
\begin{aligned}
Required\ rate\ of\ return &= R_F + \beta(R_M - R_F) \\
&= 8.6\% + 1.2(10.1\% - 8.6\%) \\
&= 8.6\% + 1.8\% \\
&= 10.4\%
\end{aligned}
$$

---

    e. There are two practical problems with the use of CAPM:

        1) It is hard to estimate the risk-free rate of return on projects under different economic environments.

        2) The CAPM is a single-period model. It should not be used for projects lasting more than 1 year.

11. **Arbitrage Pricing Theory (APT)**

    a.   APT is based on the assumption that an asset's return is a function of multiple systematic risk factors. In contrast, the CAPM is a model that uses just one systematic risk factor to explain the asset's return. That factor is the expected return on the market portfolio, i.e., the market-valued weighted-average return for all securities in the market.

        1)   The difference between actual and expected returns on an asset is attributable to systematic and unsystematic risks. Investors must be paid a risk premium to compensate for systematic (market) risk.

    b.   Accordingly, APT provides for a separate beta and a separate risk premium for each systematic risk factor identified in the model. Examples of the many potential systematic risk factors are the gross domestic product (GDP), inflation, and real interest rates. The APT for a three-factor model may be formulated as follows:

Arbitrage Pricing Theory (APT)

$$Expected\ rate\ of\ return = R_F + \beta_1 k_1 + \beta_2 k_2 + \beta_3 k_3$$

    Where: R_F = risk-free rate
             $\beta_{1,2,3}$ = individual factor beta coefficients
             $k_{1,2,3}$ = individual factor risk premiums

    c.   EXAMPLE: Assume R_F = 9%
                        k_1 = 2% β_1 = .6
                        k_2 = 5% β_2 = .4
                        k_3 = 8% β_3 = .2

        Applying these values to the formula, the expected rate of return is .09 + (.6)(.02) + (.4)(.05) + (.2)(.08), or 13.8%.

    d.   R also may be estimated by adding a percentage of the firm's long-term cost of debt. A 3% to 5% premium is frequently used.

    e.   An advantage of ATP is that it can provide more exact information. However, the disadvantage is that it is potentially more difficult to calculate.

12. **Fama-French Three-Factor Model**

    a.   The Fama-French three-factor model, another alternative to CAPM, recognizes that two classes of stocks typically perform better than the stock market as a whole. Those classes are small-cap stocks and stocks with a high book-to-market ratio (also known as value stocks). This model explains over 90% of the diversified portfolio's returns, compared to the average 70% given by CAPM.

Fama-French Model

$$Expected\ rate\ of\ return = \beta_M r_M + \beta_S r_S + \beta_{B/M} r_{B/M}$$

    Where: β_M = market beta r_M = market factor
             β_S = size beta r_S = size factor
             $\beta_{B/M}$ = book-to-market beta $r_{B/M}$ = book-to-market factor

NOTE: Candidates should understand the arbitrage pricing theory and the Fama-French model but will not need to calculate them on the actual exam.

Stop and review! You have completed the outline for this subunit. Study multiple-choice questions 1 through 28 beginning on page 158.

4.2 MANAGING FINANCIAL RISK

In Study Unit 2, we discussed and demonstrated how to calculate operating and financial leverage. This study unit will discuss how being over- or under-leveraged can affect return and both business and financial risk.

1. **Two Types of Risk**

    a. **Business risk** is the risk of an adverse outcome based on a change in the firm's particular context. Examples include changes in input prices, changes in consumer tastes, and changes in the regulatory environment.

        1) **Operating leverage** relates directly to business risk. The degree of a firm's operating leverage increases as it uses more fixed costs in its ongoing operations.

        2) A firm with high operating leverage necessarily carries a greater degree of risk because fixed costs must be covered regardless of the level of sales. However, such a firm is also able to expand production rapidly in times of higher product demand.

            a) Thus, the more leveraged a firm is in its operations, the more sensitive operating income is to changes in input prices, consumer tastes, and the regulatory environment.

        3) EXAMPLE: A farming organization could incur a fixed cost in the form of a new tractor, or it could accomplish the same work by hiring neighboring workers who bring their own mules. The tractor could plow 40 acres in a day, while each mule and his owner could plow 5 acres in a day.

            The tractor represents high operating leverage, while the mules represent low operating leverage. If the company only needs 5 acres plowed, the best option would be to use the mules; if the company needs 40 acres plowed, then the tractor is the better alternative. The firm with a tractor would be over leveraged if demand for its products were low. Alternatively, if only mules were available, then the company would be under leveraged if demand increased and the farmer wanted to plow more acres.

            Management must determine whether it wants to incur the high costs of a tractor and be able to respond quickly to increases in demand, without incurring additional costs, or whether it wants to incur low costs when demand is low and higher costs when demand increases.

    b. **Financial risk** is the risk of an adverse outcome based on a change in the financial markets. Examples include changes in interest rates and changes in investors' desired rates of return.

        1) **Financial leverage** relates directly to financial risk. The degree of a firm's financial leverage increases as it uses more fixed costs (i.e., debt and preferred stock) in its financial structure.

        2) A firm with high financial leverage necessarily carries a greater degree of risk because debt must be serviced regardless of profits. However, if such a firm is profitable, there is more residual profit for the shareholders after debt service (interest on debt is tax-deductible), reflected in higher earnings per share. Furthermore, debt financing permits the current equity holders to retain control.

            a) Thus, the more leveraged a firm is in its financing, the more sensitive net income is to changes in interest rates and desired rates of return.

2. **Portfolio Management**

   a. An investor wants to maximize return and minimize risk when choosing a portfolio of investments. A feasible portfolio that offers the highest expected return for a given risk or the least risk for a given expected return is an efficient portfolio. A portfolio that is selected from the efficient set of portfolios because it is tangent to the investor's highest indifference curve is the optimal portfolio.

   b. An **indifference curve** represents combinations of portfolios having equal utility to the investor. Given that risk and returns are plotted on the horizontal and vertical axes, respectively, and that the investor is risk averse, the curve has an increasingly positive slope. As risk increases, the additional required return per unit of additional risk also increases.

      1) The steeper the slope of an indifference curve, the more risk averse an investor is.

      2) The higher the curve, the greater is the investor's level of utility.

      3) In the diagram below, A, B, C, D, and E are indifference curves. A represents the highest level of utility and E the lowest. On a given curve, each point represents the same total utility to a risk-averse investor. For example, points 1, 2, and 3 are different combinations of risk and return that yield the same utility. The investor is indifferent as to which combination is chosen.

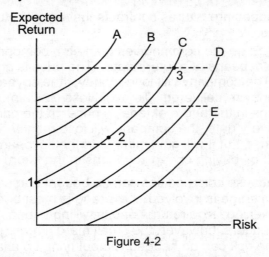

Figure 4-2

   c. Two important decisions are involved in managing a company's portfolio:

      1) The amount of money to invest
      2) The securities in which to invest

   d. The investment in securities should be based on expected net cash flows and cash flow uncertainty evaluations.

      1) Arranging a portfolio so that the maturity of funds will coincide with the need for funds will maximize the average return on the portfolio and provide increased flexibility.

         a) **Maturity matching** ensures that securities will not have to be sold unexpectedly.

      2) If its cash flows are relatively uncertain, a security's marketability and market risk are important factors to be considered. Transaction costs are also a consideration.

         a) Higher-yield long-term securities provide less certainty.

      3) When cash flows are relatively certain, the maturity date becomes the most important concern.

3.   **Hedging**

a.   Hedging is the process of using offsetting commitments to minimize or avoid the impact of adverse price movements. Hedging transactions are often used to protect positions in (1) commodity buying, (2) foreign currency, and (3) securities.

  1)   Thus, the purchase or sale of a derivative or other instrument is a hedge if it is expected to neutralize the risk of a recognized asset or liability, an unrecognized firm commitment, a forecasted transaction, etc.

    a)   For example, if a flour company buys and uses 1 million bushels of wheat each month, it may wish to guard against increases in wheat costs when it has committed to sell at a price related to the current cost of wheat. If so, the company will purchase wheat futures contracts that will result in gains if the price of wheat increases (offsetting the actual increased costs).

    b)   Public futures markets for commodities were established to allow for transparent and efficient hedging of agricultural products. There are also markets for precious metals, foreign currencies, and interest-rate fluctuations.

  2)   Long hedges are futures contracts that are purchased to protect against price increases.

  3)   Short hedges are futures contracts that are sold to protect against price declines.

  4)   EXAMPLE: In the commodities market, a company may contract with a farmer to buy soybeans at a future date. The price is agreed upon as the current price. The company will lose money if the soybean prices decline before the soybeans are delivered. To avoid loss (or gain), the company may sell soybeans in the future at today's price. If the price of soybeans declines before the delivery date, the company will lose money on the soybeans bought from the farmer, but it will gain money on the soybeans sold through the futures contract by buying cheap soybeans in the future to cover the delivery.

    a)   Because commodities can be bought and sold **on margin**, considerable leverage is involved. Leverage is most beneficial to the speculator who is seeking large returns and is willing to bear proportionate risk. For hedgers, however, the small margin requirement is useful only because the risk can be hedged without tying up a large amount of cash.

  5)   A natural hedge is a method of reducing financial risk by investing in two different items whose performance tends to cancel each other. A natural hedge is unlike other types of hedges in that it does not require the use of sophisticated financial tools, such as derivatives. However, natural hedges are not perfect in that they do not eliminate all risk. Buying insurance is a natural hedge.

    a)   Pair trading is a type of natural hedge. Pair trading involves buying long and short positions in highly correlated stocks.

    b)   Investing in both stocks and bonds is sometimes viewed as a natural hedge, since the performance of one offsets the other.

4. **Interest Rate Futures Contracts**

   a. Interest rate futures contracts involve risk-free securities such as Treasury bonds, T-bills, and money market certificates.

      1) The quantity traded is either $100,000 or $1,000,000, depending on which market is used.

      2) EXAMPLE: If a corporation wants to borrow money in 6 months for a major project, but the lender refuses to commit itself to an interest rate, the interest rate futures market can be used to hedge the risk that interest rates might increase in the interim. The company agrees to sell Treasury bonds in 6 months. If interest rates do increase over the period, the value of the Treasury bonds will decline. The company can buy Treasury bonds in 6 months and use them to cover the delivery that it had promised in the futures contract. Because the price of Treasury bonds has declined over the period, the company will make a profit on their delivery. The interest rates that the company will have to pay on the upcoming loan will be higher, however. It has cost the company money to wait 6 months for the loan. The profit from the futures contract should approximately offset the loss resulting from the higher interest loan. If interest rates had declined, the company would have had the benefit of a lower interest loan but would have lost money on the Treasury bonds. The goal of any such hedging operation is to break even on the change in interest rates.

         a) By hedging, the financial manager need not worry about fluctuations in interest rates but can concentrate instead on the day-to-day operations of the company.

5. **Duration Hedging**

   a. Duration hedging involves hedging interest-rate risk. Duration is the weighted average of the periods of time to interest and principal payments. If duration increases, the volatility of the price of the debt instrument increases.

      1) The goal of duration hedging is not to equate the duration of assets and the duration of liabilities but for the following relationship to apply:

$$(Value\ of\ assets) \times (Duration\ of\ assets) = (Value\ of\ liabilities) \times (Duration\ of\ liabilities)$$

         a) The firm is immunized against interest-rate risk when the total price change for assets equals the total price change for liabilities

      2) Assets have positive duration numbers and liabilities have negative numbers. If the duration is positive, then we are exposed to rising interest rates. Likewise, if the duration is negative, we are exposed to falling interest rates.

      3) Duration hedging does not provide a perfect hedge. For example, Gator Company has $4,000,000 of net assets with a net duration of 4 years. This could be hedged by raising the duration of liabilities in any combination to achieve a duration match, such as $4,000,000 of 4.0 years net duration liabilities; or $8,000,000 of 2.0 year net duration liabilities or $2,000,000 of 8.0 year net duration liabilities, etc.

Stop and review! You have completed the outline for this subunit. Study multiple-choice questions 29 through 36 beginning on page 167.

4.3 CORE CONCEPTS

Risk and Return

- A **return** is the amount received by an investor as compensation for taking on the risk of the investment. The **rate of return** is the return stated as a percentage of the amount invested, calculated as follows: (amount received – amount invested) ÷ amount invested.

- **Systematic risk**, also called market risk, is the risk faced by all firms; this risk cannot be offset through portfolio diversification. **Unsystematic risk**, also called company risk, is the risk inherent in a particular investment security; this risk can be offset through portfolio diversification.

- **Other types** of investment risks include credit risk, foreign exchange risk, interest rate risk, industry risk, political risk, and liquidity risk.

- **Riskier investments** have higher potential rates of return.

- A **risk averse** investor is one with a diminishing marginal utility for wealth; i.e., the potential gain is not worth the additional risk. A **risk neutral** investor adopts an expected value approach. A **risk-seeking** investor has an optimistic attitude toward risk.

- The **expected rate of return** on an investment is determined using an **expected value** calculation. It is an average of the outcomes weighted according to their probabilities.

- The **greater the standard deviation** of the expected return, the **riskier the investment**.

- The **coefficient of variation** is useful when the rates of return and standard deviations of two investments differ. It measures the risk per unit of return because it divides the standard deviation by the expected rate of return.

- **Risk and return** should be evaluated for a firm's **entire portfolio**, not for individual assets.

- Thanks to the diversification effect, **combining securities** results in a **portfolio risk that is less** than the average of the standard deviations because the returns are imperfectly correlated.

- Given **perfect negative correlation** of the prices of two stocks, risk would in theory be eliminated.

- An important measurement used in portfolio analysis is the **covariance**. It measures the **volatility** of returns together with their correlation with the returns of other securities (correlation coefficient × standard deviation$_1$ × standard deviation$_2$).

- **Portfolio theory** concerns the composition of an investment portfolio that is efficient in balancing the risk with the rate of return of the portfolio. **Asset allocation** is a key concept in financial planning and money management.

- **Specific risk**, also called diversifiable risk, unsystematic risk, residual risk, and unique risk, is the risk associated with a specific investee's operations: new products, patents, acquisitions, competitors' activities, etc. Specific risk is the risk that can be **potentially eliminated by diversification**.

- **Market risk**, also called undiversifiable risk and systematic risk, is the risk of the stock market as a whole. Some conditions in the national economy **affect all businesses**, which is why equity prices so often move together.

- The effect of an individual security on the volatility of a portfolio is measured by its sensitivity to movements by the overall market. This sensitivity is stated in terms of a stock's **beta coefficient**.

- The stock can have the same **volatility** as the overall market (beta = 1.0), be more volatile than average (beta > 1.0), or be less volatile than average (beta < 1.0).

- Three principal **techniques for asset pricing** are
  - The capital asset pricing model (CAPM):

    $$Expected\ rate\ of\ return\ =\ R_F\ +\ \beta\,(R_M\ -\ R_F)$$

  - Arbitrage pricing theory (APT):

    $$Expected\ rate\ of\ return\ =\ R_F\ +\ \beta_1 k_1\ +\ \beta_2 k_2\ +\ \beta_3 k_3$$

  - The Fama-French model:

    $$Expected\ rate\ of\ return\ =\ \beta_M r_M\ +\ \beta_s r_s\ +\ \beta_{B/M} r_{B/M}$$

Managing Financial Risk

- **Business risk** is the risk of an adverse outcome based on a change in the firm's particular context. **Operating leverage** relates directly to business risk. The degree of a firm's operating leverage increases as it uses more fixed costs in its ongoing operations.
- **Financial risk** is the risk of an adverse outcome based on a change in the financial markets. **Financial leverage** relates directly to financial risk. The degree of a firm's financial leverage increases as it uses more fixed costs (i.e., debt and preferred stock) in its financial structure.
- A feasible portfolio that offers the highest expected return for a given risk or the least risk for a given expected return is an **efficient portfolio**. A portfolio that is selected from the efficient set of portfolios because it is tangent to the investor's highest indifference curve is the **optimal portfolio**.
- A company's investment in securities should be based on **expected net cash flows** and **cash flow uncertainty evaluations**. Arranging a portfolio so that the maturity of funds will coincide with the need for funds will maximize the average return on the portfolio and provide increased flexibility.
- **Hedging** is the process of using offsetting commitments to minimize or avoid the impact of adverse price movements. Hedging transactions are often used to protect positions in (1) commodity buying, (2) foreign currency, and (3) securities.
  - **Long hedges** are futures contracts that are purchased to protect against price increases.
  - **Short hedges** are futures contracts that are sold to protect against price declines.
  - A **natural hedge** is a method of reducing financial risk by investing in two different items whose performance tends to cancel each other.
- **Interest rate futures contracts** involve risk-free securities such as Treasury bonds, T-bills, and money market certificates.
- **Duration hedging** involves hedging interest-rate risk. **Duration** is the weighted average of the periods of time to interest and principal payments. If duration increases, the volatility of the price of the debt instrument increases.

QUESTIONS
4.1 Risk and Return

1. The type of risk that is not diversifiable and affects the value of a portfolio is

    A. Purchasing-power risk.

    B. Market risk.

    C. Nonmarket risk.

    D. Interest-rate risk.

Answer (B) is correct. *(Publisher, adapted)*
    REQUIRED: The term for the type of risk that is not diversifiable.
    DISCUSSION: Prices of all stocks, even the value of portfolios, are correlated to some degree with broad swings in the stock market. Market risk is the risk that changes in a stock's price will result from changes in the stock market as a whole. Market risk is commonly referred to as nondiversifiable risk.
    Answer (A) is incorrect. Purchasing-power risk is the risk that a general rise in the price level will reduce the quantity of goods that can be purchased with a fixed sum of money. Answer (C) is incorrect. Nonmarket risk is the risk that is influenced by an individual firm's policies and decisions. Nonmarket risk is diversifiable since it is specific to each firm. Answer (D) is incorrect. Interest-rate risk is the risk that the value of an asset will fluctuate due to changes in the interest rate.

2. When purchasing temporary investments, which one of the following best describes the risk associated with the ability to sell the investment in a short period of time without significant price concessions?

    A. Interest-rate risk.

    B. Purchasing-power risk.

    C. Financial risk.

    D. Liquidity risk.

Answer (D) is correct. *(CMA, adapted)*
    REQUIRED: The risk associated with the ability to sell investments in a short period of time without significant price concessions.
    DISCUSSION: Liquidity risk is the possibility that an asset cannot be sold on short notice for its market value. If an asset must be sold at a high discount; it is said to have a substantial amount of liquidity risk.
    Answer (A) is incorrect. Interest-rate risk is caused by fluctuations in the value of an asset as interest rates change. Its components are price risk and reinvestment-rate risk. Answer (B) is incorrect. Purchasing-power risk is the risk that a general rise in the price level (inflation) will reduce what can be purchased with a fixed sum of money. Answer (C) is incorrect. Financial risk is the risk borne by shareholders, in excess of basic business risk that arises from use of financial leverage (issuance of fixed income securities, i.e., debt and preferred stock).

3. Political risk may be reduced by

    A. Entering into a joint venture with another foreign company.

    B. Making foreign operations dependent on the domestic parent for technology, markets, and supplies.

    C. Refusing to pay higher wages and higher taxes.

    D. Financing with capital from a foreign country.

Answer (B) is correct. *(Publisher, adapted)*
    REQUIRED: The way to reduce political risk.
    DISCUSSION: Political risk is the risk that a foreign government may act in a way that will reduce the value of the company's investment. Political risk may be reduced by making foreign operations dependent on the domestic parent for technology, markets, and supplies.
    Answer (A) is incorrect. Political risk may be reduced by entering into a joint venture with a company from the host country rather than from a foreign country. Answer (C) is incorrect. Refusing to pay higher wages and higher taxes will only increase political risk. Answer (D) is incorrect. Political risk may be reduced by financing with local capital, rather than foreign capital.

4. The risk of loss because of fluctuations in the relative value of foreign currencies is called

   A. Expropriation risk.

   B. Multinational beta.

   C. Exchange rate risk.

   D. Undiversifiable risk.

Answer (C) is correct. *(CIA, adapted)*
REQUIRED: The risk of loss because of fluctuations in the relative value of foreign currencies.
DISCUSSION: When amounts to be paid or received are denominated in a foreign currency, exchange rate fluctuations may result in exchange gains or losses. For example, if a U.S. firm has a receivable fixed in terms of units of a foreign currency, a decline in the value of that currency relative to the U.S. dollar results in a foreign exchange loss.
Answer (A) is incorrect. Expropriation risk is the risk that the sovereign country in which the assets backing an investment are located will seize the assets without adequate compensation. Answer (B) is incorrect. The beta value in the capital asset pricing model for a multinational firm is the systematic risk of a given multinational firm relative to that of the market as a whole. Answer (D) is incorrect. The beta value in the capital asset pricing model for a multinational firm is the systematic risk of a given multinational firm relative to that of the market as a whole. It is an undiversifiable risk.

5. An investment security with high risk will have a(n)

   A. Low expected return.

   B. Lower price than an asset with low risk.

   C. Increasing expected rate of return.

   D. High standard deviation of returns.

Answer (D) is correct. *(Publisher, adapted)*
REQUIRED: The characteristic of an asset with high risk.
DISCUSSION: The greater the standard deviation of the expected return, the riskier the investment. A large standard deviation implies that the range of possible returns is wide; i.e., the probability distribution is broadly dispersed. Conversely, the smaller the standard deviation, the tighter the probability distribution and the lower the risk.
Answer (A) is incorrect. An investment security with high risk will have a high expected return to compensate for the additional risk. Answer (B) is incorrect. An investment security with high risk will not necessarily have a lower price than an investment security with low risk. For example, two bond issues with different risk levels might be sold at the same price but have different interest rates. Answer (C) is incorrect. An expected rate of return by definition is a constant expected return.

6. Catherine & Co. has extra cash at the end of the year and is analyzing the best way to invest the funds. The company should invest in a project only if the

   A. Expected return on the project exceeds the return on investments of comparable risk.

   B. Return on investments of comparable risk exceeds the expected return on the project.

   C. Expected return on the project is equal to the return on investments of comparable risk.

   D. Return on investments of comparable risk equals the expected return on the project.

Answer (A) is correct. *(Publisher, adapted)*
REQUIRED: The rule for deciding whether to invest in a project.
DISCUSSION: Investment risk is analyzed in terms of the probability that the actual return on an investment will be lower than the expected return. Comparing a project's expected return with the return on an asset of similar risk helps determine whether the project is worth investing in. If the expected return on a project exceeds the return on an asset of comparable risk, the project should be pursued.

7. The marketable securities with the **least** amount of default risk are

   A. Federal government agency securities.

   B. U.S. Treasury securities.

   C. Repurchase agreements.

   D. Commercial paper.

Answer (B) is correct. *(CMA, adapted)*
REQUIRED: The marketable securities with the least default risk.
DISCUSSION: The marketable securities with the lowest default risk are those issued by the federal government because they are backed by the full faith and credit of the U.S. government and are therefore the least risky form of investment.
Answer (A) is incorrect. Securities issued by a federal agency are first backed by that agency and secondarily by the U.S. government. Agency securities are issued by agencies and corporations created by the federal government, such as the Federal Housing Administration. Answer (C) is incorrect. Repurchase agreements could become worthless if the organization agreeing to make the repurchase goes bankrupt. Answer (D) is incorrect. Commercial paper is unsecured.

8. The best example of a marketable security with minimal risk would be

A.   Municipal bonds.

B.   The common stock of a AAA-rated company.

C.   The commercial paper of a AAA-rated company.

D.   Stock options of a AAA-rated company.

Answer (C) is correct.   *(CMA, adapted)*
REQUIRED: The best example of a marketable security with minimal risk.
DISCUSSION: Of the choices given, the commercial paper of a top-rated (most creditworthy) company has the least risk. Commercial paper is preferable to stock or stock options because the latter represent only a residual equity in a corporation. Commercial paper is debt and thus has priority over stockholders' claims. Also, commercial paper is a very short-term investment. The maximum maturity allowed without SEC registration is 270 days. However, it can be sold only to sophisticated investors without registration.
Answer (A) is incorrect. Municipal bonds are rarely considered marketable securities in that they constitute long-term debt. Answer (B) is incorrect. Common stock does not have as high a priority in company assets as commercial paper or other debt. Answer (D) is incorrect. Common stock does not have as high a priority in company assets as commercial paper or other debt.

9. Which of the following classes of securities are listed in order from lowest risk/opportunity for return to highest risk/opportunity for return?

A.   U.S. Treasury bonds; corporate first mortgage bonds; corporate income bonds; preferred stock.

B.   Corporate income bonds; corporate mortgage bonds; convertible preferred stock; subordinated debentures.

C.   Common stock; corporate first mortgage bonds; corporate second mortgage bonds; corporate income bonds.

D.   Preferred stock; common stock; corporate mortgage bonds; corporate debentures.

Answer (A) is correct.   *(CIA, adapted)*
REQUIRED: The correct listing of classes of securities from lowest to highest risk/opportunity for return.
DISCUSSION: The general principle is that risk and return are directly correlated. U.S. Treasury securities are backed by the full faith and credit of the federal government and are therefore the least risky form of investment. However, their return is correspondingly lower. Corporate first mortgage bonds are less risky than income bonds or stock because they are secured by specific property. In the event of default, the bondholders can have the property sold to satisfy their claims. Holders of first mortgages have rights paramount to those of any other parties, such as holders of second mortgages. Income bonds pay interest only in the event the corporation earns income. Thus, holders of income bonds have less risk than shareholders because meeting the condition makes payment of interest mandatory. Preferred shareholders receive dividends only if they are declared, and the directors usually have complete discretion in this matter. Also, shareholders have claims junior to those of debtholders if the enterprise is liquidated.
Answer (B) is incorrect. The proper listing is mortgage bonds, subordinated debentures, income bonds, and preferred stock. Debentures are unsecured debt instruments. Their holders have enforceable claims against the issuer even if no income is earned or dividends declared. Answer (C) is incorrect. The proper listing is first mortgage bonds, second mortgage bonds, income bonds, and common stock. The second mortgage bonds are secured, albeit junior, claims. Answer (D) is incorrect. The proper listing is mortgage bonds, debentures, preferred stock, and common stock. Holders of common stock cannot receive dividends unless the holders of preferred stock receive the stipulated periodic percentage return, in addition to any averages if the preferred stock is cumulative.

10. From the viewpoint of the investor, which of the following securities provides the **least** risk?

A. Mortgage bond.

B. Subordinated debenture.

C. Income bond.

D. Debentures.

Answer (A) is correct. *(CIA, adapted)*
REQUIRED: The least risky security from the viewpoint of the investor.
DISCUSSION: A mortgage bond is secured with specific fixed assets, usually real property. Thus, under the rights enumerated in the bond indenture, creditors will be able to receive payments from liquidation of the property in case of default. In a bankruptcy proceeding, these amounts are paid before any transfers are made to other creditors, including those preferences. Hence, mortgage bonds are less risky than the others listed.
Answer (B) is incorrect. A debenture is long-term debt that is not secured (collateralized) by specific property. Subordinated debentures have a claim on the debtor's assets that may be satisfied only after senior debt has been paid in full. Debentures of either kind are therefore more risky than mortgage bonds. Answer (C) is incorrect. An income bond pays interest only if the debtor earns it. Such bonds are also more risky than secured debt. Answer (D) is incorrect. Unsecured debt is riskier than a mortgage bond.

11. City Development, Inc., is considering a new investment project that will involve building a large office block in Frankfurt-am-Main. The firm's financial analysis department has estimated that the proposed investment has the following estimated rate of return distributions.

Rate of Return	Probability
(5%)	30%
10%	50%
20%	20%

Calculate the expected rate of return.

A. 5.5%

B. 7.5%

C. 10.5%

D. 11.7%

Answer (B) is correct. *(CMA, adapted)*
REQUIRED: The expected rate of return for an investment project
DISCUSSION: The expected rate of return of an investment can be calculated by weighting each potential rate of return by its probability of occurrence and summing the results. City Development's expected rate of return for this development is thus derived as follows:

Rate of Return	Probability	Expected Rate of Return
(5.0)%	30.0%	(1.5)%
10.0%	50.0%	5.0%
20.0%	20.0%	4.0%
		7.5%

Answer (A) is incorrect. This percentage is a nonsense result. Answer (C) is incorrect. This percentage results from improperly treating the negative 5% return as a positive number. Answer (D) is incorrect. This percentage results from treating the negative return as a positive number and weighting the three possible results equally.

12. Russell, Inc., is evaluating four independent investment proposals. The expected returns and standard deviations for each of these proposals are presented below.

Investment Proposal	Expected Returns	Standard Deviation
I	16%	10%
II	14%	10%
III	20%	11%
IV	22%	15%

Which one of the investment proposals has the **least** relative level of risk?

A. Investment I.

B. Investment II.

C. Investment III.

D. Investment IV.

Answer (C) is correct. *(CMA, adapted)*
REQUIRED: The investment proposal with the least relative risk.
DISCUSSION: The coefficient of variation is useful when the rates of return and standard deviations of investments differ. It measures the risk per unit of return because it divides the standard deviation (σ) by the expected return ($\hat{k}$). The coefficients of variation of Russell's four investment proposals can thus be calculated as follows:

	Expected Returns	Standard Deviation	Coefficient of Variation
Investment I	16%	10%	0.625
Investment II	14%	10%	0.714
Investment III	20%	11%	0.550
Investment IV	22%	15%	0.682

Answer (A) is incorrect. The coefficient of variation for Investment I is 0.625 (10% ÷ 16%), which is not the lowest coefficient of the four. Answer (B) is incorrect. Investment II has the highest relative level of risk with a coefficient of variation of 0.714 (10% ÷ 14%). Answer (D) is incorrect. The coefficient of variation for Investment IV is 0.682 (15% ÷ 22%), which is not the lowest coefficient of the four.

13. The expected rate of return for the stock of Cornhusker Enterprises is 20%, with a standard deviation of 15%. The expected rate of return for the stock of Mustang Associates is 10%, with a standard deviation of 9%. The riskier stock is

A. Cornhusker because the return is higher.

B. Cornhusker because the standard deviation is higher.

C. Mustang because the standard deviation is higher.

D. Mustang because the coefficient of variation is higher.

Answer (D) is correct. *(CMA, adapted)*
REQUIRED: The riskier stock.
DISCUSSION: The coefficient of variation is useful when the rates of return and standard deviations of two investments differ. It measures the risk per unit of return because it divides the standard deviation by the expected return. The coefficient of variation is much higher for Mustang (.09 ÷ .10 = .9) than for Cornhusker (.15 ÷ .20 = .75).
Answer (A) is incorrect. The existence of a higher return is not necessarily indicative of high risk. Answer (B) is incorrect. The higher standard deviation must be viewed relative to the mean of the population; the absolute level of the standard deviation is meaningless without a knowledge of the mean. Answer (C) is incorrect. Mustang does not have the higher standard deviation.

Questions 14 through 16 are based on the following information. The state of the economy has a strong effect on the expected returns for Techspace, Inc., as shown below:

State of the Economy	Probability	Techspace Returns
Recession	.35	–10%
Stable	.40	10%
Expansion	.25	30%

14. What is the expected rate of return on Techspace, Inc., stock?

A. 8%

B. 10%

C. 15%

D. 30%

Answer (A) is correct. *(Publisher, adapted)*
REQUIRED: The expected rate of return on a stock given probabilities for different situations and corresponding returns.
DISCUSSION: The expected rate of return on an investment is the sum of the weighted averages of the possible outcomes weighted by their probabilities. For Techspace, the computation is performed as follows:

State of the Economy	Possible Rate of Return		Probability		Weighted Averages
Recession	(10)%	×	35%	=	(3.5)%
Stable	10%	×	40%	=	4.0%
Expansion	30%	×	25%	=	7.5%
Expected rate of return					8.0%

Answer (B) is incorrect. This percentage is a simple average of the returns. Answer (C) is incorrect. This percentage results from adding, rather than subtracting, the average for the recession state. Answer (D) is incorrect. This percentage results from failing to weight the rates of return by their probabilities.

15. Given an expected rate of return on Techspace, Inc., stock of 8.0%, the standard deviation (σ) is

A. 2.36%

B. 8.12%

C. 8.0%

D. 15.36%

Answer (D) is correct. *(Publisher, adapted)*
REQUIRED: The variance on a stock given probabilities for different situations and corresponding returns.
DISCUSSION: Techspace's total weighted squared variances can be calculated in two steps. First, the individual variances are computed:

State of the Economy	Possible Rate of Return		Expected Rate		Variances
Recession	(10)%	–	8%	=	(18)%
Stable	10%	–	8%	=	2%
Expansion	30%	–	8%	=	22%

The total weighted squared variances is arrived at by squaring, weighting, and summing the individual variances:

State of the Economy	Variances	Variances Squared		Probability		Weighted Squared Variances
Recession	(18)%	3.24%	×	35%	=	1.134%
Stable	2%	0.04%	×	40%	=	0.016%
Excession	22%	4.84%	×	25%	=	1.210%
Total weighted squared variances						2.360%

The standard deviation (σ) of Techspace returns is the square root of this number ($\sqrt{2.36\%}$ = 15.36%).
Answer (A) is incorrect. The standard deviation (σ) is the square root of this percentage. Answer (B) is incorrect. This percentage results from failing to weight the squared variances. Answer (C) is incorrect. The expected rate of return is 8.0%.

16. Given that the standard deviation (σ) of Techspace returns is 15.36% and the expected rate of return is 8%, the coefficient of variation is

A. 1.0%

B. 1.23%

C. 1.92%

D. 2.36%

Answer (C) is correct. *(Publisher, adapted)*
REQUIRED: The coefficient of variation of Techspace returns.
DISCUSSION: The coefficient of variation is useful when the rates of return and standard deviations of two investments differ. It measures the risk per unit of return.

$$Coefficient\ of\ variation\ =\ \frac{Standard\ deviation\ (\sigma)}{Expected\ rate\ of\ return}$$

Techspace's is calculated as follows:

Coefficient of variation = 15.36% ÷ 8%
= 1.92%

Answer (A) is incorrect. One is the upper limit of the value for the beta coefficient of a security. Answer (B) is incorrect. This percentage results from multiplying, rather than dividing, the standard deviation and expected rate of return. Answer (D) is incorrect. This percentage is the total weighted squared variance.

17. If the covariance of Stock A with Stock B is −.0076, then what is the covariance of Stock B with Stock A?

A. +.0076

B. −.0076

C. Greater than .0076.

D. Less than −.0076.

Answer (B) is correct. *(Publisher, adapted)*
REQUIRED: The covariance of two stocks.
DISCUSSION: The covariance measures the volatility of returns together with their correlation with the returns of other securities. It equals the coefficient of correlation of the securities being compared times the standard deviations of the securities. The covariance of two stocks is the same regardless of which stock is compared to the other.

18. Standard deviation and expected return information for four investments selling for the same price is as follows:

Investment	Standard Deviation	Expected Return
A	25%	20%
B	20%	18%
C	12%	8%
D	10%	10%

What investment is the best choice in terms of the risk/return relationship?

A. Investment A.

B. Investment B.

C. Investment C.

D. Investment D.

Answer (D) is correct. *(CPA, adapted)*
REQUIRED: Calculation of the best investment.
DISCUSSION: The coefficient of variation is useful when the rates of return and standard deviations of two investments differ. It measures the risk per unit of return because it divides the standard deviation by the expected return. Thus, the risk per unit of return for Investment D is 1.00 (.10 ÷ .10), which is the lowest of the given investments.
Answer (A) is incorrect. Investment A has a risk per unit of return of 1.25 (.25 ÷ .20), which is higher than that of Investment D. Answer (B) is incorrect. Investment B has a risk per unit of return of 1.11 (.20 ÷ .18), which is higher than that of Investment D. Answer (C) is incorrect. Investment C has a risk per unit of return of 1.50 (.12 ÷ .08), which is higher than that of Investment D.

Questions 19 and 20 are based on the following information. The following information is known about three common stocks:

	Stock A	Stock B	Stock C
Expected rate of return	3%	4%	2%
Weighted squared variances of returns	6	5	4

19. Using only the standard deviation of projected returns, which stock is riskiest?

A. Stock A.

B. Stock B.

C. Stock C.

D. Cannot be determined from information given.

Answer (A) is correct. *(Publisher, adapted)*
REQUIRED: The riskiest stock.
DISCUSSION: The risk of a stock can be measured using the standard deviation of its projected returns. This standard deviation is the square root of the sum of all the probability-weighted squared variances of the projected returns. Thus, the standard deviations of the three stocks presented are, respectively, 2.45, 2.24, and 2.00. The highest of these, indicating the riskiest stock, is 2.45, Stock A.
Answer (B) is incorrect. Stock B's standard deviation is lower than that of Stock A. Answer (C) is incorrect. Stock C's standard deviation is lower than that of Stock A. Answer (D) is incorrect. Stock A has the highest standard deviation.

20. The coefficient of variation is useful when the rates of return and standard deviations of investments differ because it measures risk per unit of return. Which stock is riskiest based on a coefficient of variation analysis?

A. Stock A.

B. Stock B.

C. Stock C.

D. Stocks A and C have equal risk when analyzed on a per-unit of return basis.

Answer (C) is correct. *(Publisher, adapted)*
REQUIRED: The riskiest stock based on a coefficient of variation analysis.
DISCUSSION: The coefficient of variation of an investment is calculated by dividing the standard deviation by the expected rate of return. This standard deviation is the square root of the sum of all the probability-weighted squared variances of the projected returns. Thus, the standard deviations of the three stocks presented are, respectively, 2.45, 2.24, and 2.00. Dividing each by the expected rate of return gives the coefficient of variation (Stock A: 2.45 ÷ 3% = 81.7; Stock B: 2.24 ÷ 4% = 56.0; Stock C: 2.00 ÷ 2% = 100). Stock C is therefore the riskiest on a per-unit of return basis.
Answer (A) is incorrect. The coefficient of variation for Stock A is 2.45, which is higher than that for Stock C. Answer (B) is incorrect. The coefficient of variation for Stock B is 2.24, which is higher than that for Stock C. Answer (D) is incorrect. The variation for Stock A is 2.45, which is higher than that for Stock C.

21. An optimal portfolio of investments is

A. Efficient because it offers the highest expected return.

B. Any portfolio chosen from the efficient set of portfolios.

C. Any portfolio chosen from the feasible set of portfolios.

D. Tangent to the investor's highest indifference curve.

Answer (D) is correct. *(Publisher, adapted)*
  REQUIRED: The description of an optimal portfolio.
  DISCUSSION: An investor wants to maximize expected return and minimize risk when choosing a portfolio. A feasible portfolio that offers the highest expected return for a given risk or the least risk for a given expected return is an efficient portfolio. A portfolio that is selected from the efficient set of portfolios because it is tangent to the investor's highest indifference curve is the optimal portfolio.
  Answer (A) is incorrect. A portfolio is efficient if it offers the highest return for a given risk or the least risk for a given return. Answer (B) is incorrect. The optimal portfolio is tangent to the investor's highest indifference curve. Thus, it is the efficient portfolio with the highest utility. Answer (C) is incorrect. The optimal portfolio is efficient as well as feasible.

22. The returns on two stocks can be correlated in values **except** those that are

A. Positive.

B. Negative.

C. Neutral.

D. Skewed.

Answer (D) is correct. *(Publisher, adapted)*
  REQUIRED: The range of correlation between two stocks.
  DISCUSSION: The correlation coefficient (*r*) measures the degree to which any two variables are related. It ranges from −1.0 to 1.0. Perfect positive correlation (1.0) means that the two variables always move together. Perfect negative correlation (−1.0) means that the two variables always move inversely to one another. A neutral correlation, or no correlation, is 0.0. Skewed is a nonsense concept in this context.

23. A market analyst has estimated the equity beta of Modern Homes, Inc., to be 1.4. This beta implies that the company's

A. Systematic risk is lower than that of the market portfolio.

B. Systematic risk is higher than that of the market portfolio.

C. Unsystematic risk is higher than that of the market portfolio.

D. Total risk is higher than that of the market portfolio.

Answer (B) is correct. *(CMA, adapted)*
  REQUIRED: The implications of a beta greater than 1.
  DISCUSSION: Systematic risk, also called market risk and undiversifiable risk, is the risk of the stock market as a whole. Some conditions in the national economy affect all businesses, which is why equity prices so often move together. The effect of an individual security on the volatility of a portfolio is measured by its sensitivity to movements by the overall market. This sensitivity is stated in terms of a stock's beta coefficient. An average-risk stock has a beta of 1.0 because its returns are perfectly positively correlated with those on the market portfolio.
  Answer (A) is incorrect. A beta of less than 1.0 means that the market, or systematic, risk is lower than that of the market portfolio. Answer (C) is incorrect. Unsystematic risk is the risk that is influenced by an individual firm's policies and decisions. The beta does not concern unsystematic risk. Answer (D) is incorrect. Only a portion of the risk, not the total risk, is higher than that of the market portfolio.

24. A measure that describes the risk of an investment project relative to other investments in general is the

A. Coefficient of variation.

B. Beta coefficient.

C. Standard deviation.

D. Expected return.

Answer (B) is correct. *(CIA, adapted)*
  REQUIRED: The measure of the risk of an investment relative to investments in general.
  DISCUSSION: The required rate of return on equity capital in the capital asset pricing model is the risk-free rate (determined by government securities), plus the product of the market risk premium times the beta coefficient (beta measures the firm's risk). The market risk premium is the amount above the risk-free rate that will induce investment in the market. The beta coefficient of an individual stock is the correlation between the volatility (price variation) of the stock market and that of the price of the individual stock. For example, if an individual stock goes up 15% and the market only 10%, beta is 1.5.
  Answer (A) is incorrect. The coefficient of variation compares risk with expected return (standard deviation ÷ expected return). Answer (C) is incorrect. Standard deviation measures dispersion (risk) of project returns. Answer (D) is incorrect. Expected return does not describe risk.

25. The benefits of diversification decline to near zero when the number of securities held increases beyond

   A. 4

   B. 6

   C. 10

   D. 40

Answer (D) is correct.   *(Publisher, adapted)*
   REQUIRED: The number of securities beyond which the benefits of diversification decline to near zero.
   DISCUSSION: The benefits of diversification become extremely small when more than 20 to 30 different securities are held. Moreover, commissions and other transaction costs increase with greater diversification.

Question 26 is based on the following information. DQZ Telecom is considering a project for the coming year that will cost $50 million. DQZ plans to use the following combination of debt and equity to finance the investment.

● Issue $15 million of 20-year bonds at a price of $101, with a coupon rate of 8%, and flotation costs of 2% of par.

● Use $35 million of funds generated from earnings.

● The equity market is expected to earn 12%. U.S. Treasury bonds are currently yielding 5%. The beta coefficient for DQZ is estimated to be .60. DQZ is subject to an effective corporate income tax rate of 40%.

---

26. The capital asset pricing model (CAPM) computes the expected return on a security by adding the risk-free rate of return to the incremental yield of the expected market return, which is adjusted by the company's beta. Compute DQZ's expected rate of return.

   A. 9.20%

   B. 12.20%

   C. 7.20%

   D. 12.00%

Answer (A) is correct.   *(CMA, adapted)*
   REQUIRED: The expected rate of return using the capital asset pricing model (CAPM).
   DISCUSSION: The market return (R_M), given as 12%, minus the risk-free rate (R_F), given as 5%, is the market risk premium. It is the rate at which investors must be compensated to induce them to invest in the market. The beta coefficient (β) of an individual stock, given as 60%, is the correlation between volatility (price variation) of the stock market and the volatility of the price of the individual stock. Consequently, the expected rate of return is 9.20% $[R_F + \beta (R_M - R_F) = .05 + .6(.12 - .05)]$.
   Answer (B) is incorrect. This percentage equals the risk-free rate plus 60% of market rate. Answer (C) is incorrect. This percentage results from multiplying both the market rate premium and the risk-free rate by 60%. Answer (D) is incorrect. This percentage is the market rate.

27. Using the capital asset pricing model (CAPM), the required rate of return for a firm with a beta of 1.25 when the market return is 14% and the risk-free rate is 6% is

   A. 6.0%

   B. 7.5%

   C. 17.5%

   D. 16.0%

Answer (D) is correct.   *(CMA, adapted)*
   REQUIRED: The required rate of return using the capital asset pricing model.
   DISCUSSION: The CAPM adds the risk-free rate to the product of the beta coefficient and the difference between the market return and the risk-free rate. The market-risk premium is the amount above the risk-free rate for which investors must be compensated to induce them to invest in the company. The beta coefficient of an individual stock is the correlation between volatility (price variation) of the stock market and the volatility of the price of the individual stock. Thus, the required rate is 16% $[6\% + 1.25 (14\% - 6\%)]$.
   Answer (A) is incorrect. This percentage is the risk-free rate based on insured government securities and bears no relation to the return of the stock market. Answer (B) is incorrect. This percentage is calculated by multiplying the beta times the risk-free rate; the beta should be multiplied times the risk premium that is required by investors. Answer (C) is incorrect. This percentage is calculated by multiplying the market rate times beta. This ignores the risk premium. The beta should be multiplied times the risk premium that is desired by investors.

28. An analyst covering Guilderland Mining Co. common stock estimates the following information for next year:

Expected return on the market portfolio	12%
Expected return on Treasury securities	5%
Expected beta of Guilderland	2.2

Using the CAPM, the analyst's estimate of next year's risk premium for Guilderland's stock is closest to

   A. 7.0%

   B. 10.4%

   C. 15.4%

   D. 21.4%

Answer (C) is correct. *(CMA, adapted)*
   REQUIRED: The expected risk-adjusted premium of a stock based on the capital asset pricing model.
   DISCUSSION: The capital asset pricing model derives the risk premium of a particular stock (that is, the excess of the rate of return on the stock over the risk-free rate) by multiplying the stock's beta by the excess of the market rate of return over the risk-free rate. Mathematically, this is expressed as

$$(R_{Stock} - R_{Risk\text{-}free}) = \beta \times (R_{Market} - R_{Risk\text{-}free})$$

For Guilderland Mining, this calculation looks like this:

$$
\begin{aligned}
(R_{Stock} - 5\%) &= 2.2 \times (12\% - 5\%) \\
(R_{Stock} - 5\%) &= 2.2 \times 7\% \\
(R_{Stock} - 5\%) &= 15.4\% \\
R_{Stock} &= 20.4\%
\end{aligned}
$$

   Answer (A) is incorrect. This percentage is the difference between the overall market rate of return and the risk-free rate. Answer (B) is incorrect. This percentage results from improperly subtracting the risk-free rate from the intermediate answer rather than adding. Answer (D) is incorrect. This percentage is based on using the market rate instead of the risk premium when multiplying times beta.

4.2 Managing Financial Risk

29. A firm must select from among several methods of financing arrangements when meeting its capital requirements. To acquire additional growth capital while attempting to maximize earnings per share, a firm should normally

   A. Attempt to increase both debt and equity in equal proportions, which preserves a stable capital structure and maintains investor confidence.

   B. Select debt over equity initially, even though increased debt is accompanied by interest costs and a degree of risk.

   C. Select equity over debt initially, which minimizes risk and avoids interest costs.

   D. Discontinue dividends and use current cash flow, which avoids the cost and risk of increased debt and the dilution of EPS through increased equity.

Answer (B) is correct. *(CIA, adapted)*
   REQUIRED: The financing arrangement that should be selected to acquire additional growth capital while attempting to maximize earnings per share.
   DISCUSSION: Earnings per share will ordinarily be higher if debt is used to raise capital instead of equity, provided that the firm is not over-leveraged. The reason is that the cost of debt is lower than the cost of equity because interest is tax deductible. However, the prospect of higher EPS is accompanied by greater risk to the firm resulting from required interest costs, creditors' liens on the firm's assets, and the possibility of a proportionately lower EPS if sales volume fails to meet projections.
   Answer (A) is incorrect. EPS is not a function of investor confidence and is not maximized by concurrent proportional increases in both debt and equity. EPS is usually higher if debt is used instead of equity to raise capital, at least initially. Answer (C) is incorrect. Equity capital is initially more costly than debt. Answer (D) is incorrect. Using only current cash flow to raise capital is usually too conservative an approach for a growth-oriented firm. Management is expected to be willing to take acceptable risks to be competitive and attain an acceptable rate of growth.

30. Duration hedging involves hedging interest-rate risk by matching the duration of assets with the duration of liabilities. Which of the following is a true statement about duration hedging?

   A. If duration increases, the volatility of the price of a debt instrument decreases.

   B. The goal of duration hedging is to equate the duration of assets with the duration of liabilities.

   C. The firm is immunized against interest-rate risk when the total price change for assets equals the total price change for liabilities.

   D. Duration is higher if the nominal rate on a debt instrument is higher.

Answer (C) is correct. *(Publisher, adapted)*
   REQUIRED: The true statement about duration hedging.
   DISCUSSION: The goal of duration hedging is not to equate the duration of assets and the duration of liabilities but for the following relationship to apply:

(Value of assets) × (Duration of assets) =

(Valuation of liabilities) × (Duration of liabilities)

The firm is immunized against interest-rate risk when the total price change for assets equals the total price change for liabilities.
   Answer (A) is incorrect. If duration increases, the volatility of the price of a debt instrument. Answer (B) is incorrect. The goal is to equate the total price change for assets and the total price change for liabilities. Answer (D) is incorrect. Duration is lower if the nominal rate on a debt instrument is higher.

31. Business risk is the risk inherent in a firm's operations that excludes financial risk. It depends on all of the following factors **except** the

A. Amount of financial leverage.

B. Sales price variability.

C. Demand variability.

D. Input price variability.

Answer (A) is correct. *(Publisher, adapted)*
REQUIRED: The factor not affecting business risk of a firm.
DISCUSSION: Business risk is the risk of fluctuations in earnings before interest and taxes or in operating income when the firm uses no debt. It depends on factors such as demand variability, sales price variability, input price variability, and the amount of operating leverage. Financial leverage affects financial risk and is not a factor affecting business risk.
Answer (B) is incorrect. Sales price variability is a factor affecting business risk. Answer (C) is incorrect. Demand variability is a factor affecting business risk. Answer (D) is incorrect. Input price variability is a factor affecting business risk.

32. A higher degree of operating leverage compared with the industry average implies that the firm

A. Has higher variable costs.

B. Has profits that are more sensitive to changes in sales volume.

C. Is more profitable.

D. Is less risky.

Answer (B) is correct. *(CMA, adapted)*
REQUIRED: The effect of a higher degree of operating leverage (DOL).
DISCUSSION: Operating leverage is a measure of the degree to which fixed costs are used in the production process. A company with a higher percentage of fixed costs (higher operating leverage) has greater risk than one in the same industry that relies more heavily on variable costs. The DOL equals the percentage change in net operating income divided by the percentage change in sales. Thus, profits become more sensitive to changes in sales volume as the DOL increases.
Answer (A) is incorrect. A firm with higher operating leverage has higher fixed costs and lower variable costs. Answer (C) is incorrect. A firm with higher leverage will be relatively more profitable than a firm with lower leverage when sales are high. The opposite is true when sales are low. Answer (D) is incorrect. A firm with higher leverage is more risky. Its reliance on fixed costs is greater.

33. Business risk excludes such factors as

A. Financial risk.

B. Amount of operating leverage.

C. Demand variability.

D. Fluctuations in suppliers' prices.

Answer (A) is correct. *(Publisher, adapted)*
REQUIRED: The factor excluded from business risk.
DISCUSSION: Business risk is the risk of fluctuations in earnings before interest and taxes or in operating income when the firm uses no debt. It is the risk inherent in its operations that excludes financial risk, which is the risk to the shareholders from the use of financial leverage. Business risk depends on factors such as demand variability, sales price variability, input price variability, and amount of operating leverage.
Answer (B) is incorrect. Business risk depends on such factors as amount of operating leverage. Answer (C) is incorrect. Business risk depends on such factors as demand variability. Answer (D) is incorrect. Business risk depends on such factors as fluctuations in suppliers' prices.

34. Sylvan Corporation has the following capital structure:

Debenture bonds	$10,000,000
Preferred equity	1,000,000
Common equity	39,000,000

The financial leverage of Sylvan Corporation would increase as a result of

A. Issuing common stock and using the proceeds to retire preferred stock.

B. Maintaining the same dollar level of cash dividends as the prior year, even though earnings have increased by 7%.

C. Financing its future investments with a higher percentage of bonds.

D. Financing its future investments with a higher percentage of equity funds.

Answer (C) is correct. *(CMA, adapted)*
REQUIRED: The event that would increase the company's financial leverage.
DISCUSSION: Financial leverage is the use of borrowed money to earn money for the benefit of shareholders. The expectation is that investment earnings will be greater than the interest paid on the borrowed funds. Increasing debt (such as bonds) increases financial leverage.
Answer (A) is incorrect. The issuance of common stock does not increase financial leverage. No increase in borrowed capital and fixed interest charges occurs when equity is issued. Answer (B) is incorrect. A decrease in the dividend payout ratio would result in increased owners' equity (retained earnings), and would not increase debt capital and financial leverage. Answer (D) is incorrect. Using equity funds to finance new investments decreases financial leverage.

35. An indifference curve represents combinations of portfolios having equal utility to the investor. Given that risk and returns are plotted on the horizontal and vertical axes, respectively, and that the investor is risk averse, the curve has

    A. An increasingly steeper slope if the investor is less risk averse.

    B. A decreasingly negative slope if the investor's utility increases.

    C. An increasingly positive slope.

    D. A decreasingly positive slope.

Answer (C) is correct. *(Publisher, adapted)*
    REQUIRED: The true statement about the slope of an indifference curve.
    DISCUSSION: An indifference curve represents combinations of portfolios having equal utility to the investor. Given that risk and returns are plotted on the horizontal and vertical axes, respectively, and that the investor is risk averse, the curve has an increasingly positive slope. As risk increases, the additional required return per unit of additional risk also increases. The steeper the slope of an indifference curve, the more risk averse an investor is. The higher the curve, the greater is the investor's level of utility.
    Answer (A) is incorrect. The slope is less steep if the investor is less risk averse. The increase in the required additional return per unit of additional risk is lower. Answer (B) is incorrect. The higher the curve, the greater is the investor's level of utility. Moreover, the slope is positive, not negative. Answer (D) is incorrect. The slope is increasingly positive.

36. An automobile company that uses the futures market to set the price of steel to protect a profit against price increases is an example of

    A. A short hedge.

    B. A long hedge.

    C. Selling futures to protect the company from loss.

    D. Selling futures to protect against price declines.

Answer (B) is correct. *(Publisher, adapted)*
    REQUIRED: The example of the use of the futures market to protect a profit.
    DISCUSSION: A change in prices can be minimized or avoided by hedging. Hedging is the process of using offsetting commitments to minimize or avoid the impact of adverse price movements. The automobile company desires to stabilize the price of steel so that its cost to the company will not rise and cut into profits. Accordingly, the automobile company uses the futures market to create a long hedge, which is a futures contract that is purchased to protect against price increases.
    Answer (A) is incorrect. A short hedge is a futures contract that is sold to protect against price declines. The automobile company wishes to protect itself against price increases. Answer (C) is incorrect. The automobile company needs to purchase futures in order to protect itself from loss, not sell futures. Selling futures protects against price declines. Answer (D) is incorrect. It is the definition of a short hedge, which is used for avoiding price declines. The automobile company wants to protect itself against price increases.

Use the Gleim **CMA Test Prep** Software for interactive testing with **additional multiple-choice questions!**

Page
Intentionally
Left Blank

4.4 ESSAY QUESTION

Scenario for Essay Question 1

Clewash Linen Supply Co. provides laundered items to various commercial and service establishments in a large metropolitan city. Clewash is scheduled to acquire some new cleaning equipment in mid-Year 2 that should provide some operating efficiencies. The new equipment would enable Clewash to increase the volume of laundry it handles without any increase in labor costs. In addition, the estimated maintenance costs in terms of pounds of laundry processed would be reduced slightly with the new equipment.

The new equipment was justified not only on the basis of reduced cost but also on the basis of expected increase in demand starting in late Year 2. However, since the original forecast was prepared, several potential new customers have either delayed or discontinued their own expansion plans in the market area that is serviced by Clewash. The most recent forecast indicates that no great increase in demand can be expected until late Year 3 or early Year 4.

Question

1. Identify and explain the factors Clewash Linen Supply Co. should consider in deciding whether or not to delay the investment in the new cleaning equipment. In the presentation of your response, distinguish between those factors that tend to indicate that the investment should be made as scheduled versus those that tend to indicate that the investment should be delayed.

Essay Question 1 — Unofficial Answers

1. Some of the factors that affect the decision of whether or not to delay the investment in new cleaning equipment are given below. Each factor can have two sides, i.e., delay versus no delay, depending upon the circumstances involved.

   - Unemployment, inflation rate, and business conditions in general.
        Business outlook improving -- do not delay.
        Business outlook deteriorating -- delay.
   Unemployment, inflation rate, and business conditions all affect the climate for business and should be considered.
   - Difficulty associated with acquisition and installation of equipment and training of operators.
        Great difficulty -- do not delay.
        Little difficulty -- delay.
   The greater the lead time involved, the sooner the equipment should be acquired so that it is ready when needed.
   - Extent of operating efficiency improvements.
        Great -- do not delay.
        Little -- delay.
   The greater the efficiency, the less the delay because costs will be saved even though volume does not increase.
   - Inflation rate in cost of equipment.
        Cost of equipment expected to increase drastically -- do not delay.
        Cost of equipment not expected to increase drastically -- delay.
   Company wants to minimize its initial cost outlay.
   - Dependability of present equipment and likelihood of breakdowns.
        Dependability is not good -- do not delay.
        Dependability is good -- delay.
   Company could defer or have to go ahead with investment due to condition of present equipment.
   - Chance for technological advances in equipment.
        No chance -- do not delay.
        Good -- delay.
   If there is a chance that technological advances will develop in the design of the equipment, the company might want to take advantage of the new design.
   - Ability to obtain market advantage by providing better quality service at same or lower price.
        Good -- do not delay.
        Poor/neutral -- delay.
   Better service means more customers or justifies higher rates.
   - Competitors' plans for obtaining similar equipment and achieving market advantage.
        High probability -- do not delay.
        Low probability -- delay.
   Company wants to maintain competitive advantage or meet competition.
   - Ability to predict timing and increased volume of demand from new or increased customers.
        Good -- better quality of decision could defer switch longer.
        Low -- less reliable criteria for decision.
   The better a company is able to predict new business, the more certain it can be of its decision and, possibly, the longer it can wait to make a change.

Use **CMA Gleim Online** and **Essay Wizard** to practice additional essay questions in an exam-like environment.

STUDY UNIT FIVE
FINANCIAL INSTRUMENTS AND COST OF CAPITAL

(29 pages of outline)

This study unit is the **second of four** on **corporate finance**. The relative weight assigned to this major topic in Part 2 of the exam is **25%**. The four study units are:

Study Unit 4: Investment Risk and Portfolio Management

Study Unit 5: Financial Instruments and Cost of Capital

Study Unit 6: Managing Current Assets

Study Unit 7: Raising Capital, Corporate Restructuring, and International Finance

After studying the outline and answering the questions in this study unit, you will have the skills necessary to address the following topics listed in the ICMA's Learning Outcome Statements:

Part 2 – Section B.3. Financial instruments

The candidate should be able to:

a. describe the term structure of interest, and explain why it changes over time

b. define and identify characteristics of common stock and preferred stock

c. identify and describe the basic features of a bond such as maturity, par value, coupon rate, provisions for redeeming, conversion provisions, covenants, options granted to the issuer or investor, indentures, and restrictions

d. identify and evaluate debt issuance or refinancing strategies

e. value bonds, common stock, and preferred stock using discounted cash flow methods

f. demonstrate an understanding of duration as a measure of bond interest rate sensitivity

g. explain how income taxes impact financing decisions

h. define and demonstrate an understanding of derivatives and their uses

i. identify and describe the basic features of futures and forwards

j. distinguish a long position from a short position

k. define options and distinguish between a call and a put by identifying the characteristics of each

l. define exercise price, strike price, option premium, and intrinsic value

m. demonstrate an understanding of the interrelationship of the variables that comprise the value of an option; e.g., relation between exercise price and strike price, and value of call

n. calculate total profit on a combined option position

o. define swap and calculate net payment on interest rate and foreign exchange swaps

p. demonstrate a basic understanding of the Black-Scholes and the binomial option-valuation models and how a change in one variable will affect the value of the option (calculation not required)

q. define and identify characteristics of other sources of long-term financing, such as leases, convertible securities, warrants, and retained earnings

r. demonstrate an understanding of the relationship among inflation, interest rates, and the prices of financial instruments

Part 2 – Section D.6. Valuation

The candidate should be able to:

a. identify the key variables that should be used in valuing stocks and companies

b. demonstrate how discounted cash flow analysis can be used to analyze stocks, acquisitions, and divestitures

c. demonstrate an understanding of required rate of return concepts

d. explain the importance of beta and the CAPM in valuation

e. calculate a required rate of return using the capital asset pricing model (CAPM)

f. explain the concept of a risk premium and why discount rates higher (or lower) than the weighted average cost of capital might be appropriate in valuation

g. explain the importance of growth in valuation

h. explain the importance of cash flows (and earnings) in valuation

i. analyze financial statements to develop operating cash flows and forecast growth in cash flows

j. explain how changes in the discount rate will affect the valuation for stocks, acquisitions, or divestitures

l. use the constant growth dividend discount model to value stocks and demonstrate an understanding of the two-stage dividend discount model

m. demonstrate an understanding of relative or comparable valuation methods, such as price-earnings (P/E) ratios, market-book ratios, and price-sales ratios

n. value a business, a business segment, and a business combination using discounted cash flow methods

o. value a business using relative or comparable valuation methods (P/E ratios, etc.)

p. explain how income taxes impact valuation

r. evaluate a proposed business combination and make a recommendation based on both quantitative and qualitative considerations

Statements k. and q. are covered in Study Unit 10.

Part 2 – Section B.4. Cost of capital

The candidate should be able to:

a. define the cost of capital and demonstrate an understanding of its applications in capital structure decisions

b. determine the weighted average (historical) cost of capital and the cost of its individual components

c. calculate the marginal cost of capital

d. explain the importance of using marginal cost as opposed to historical cost

e. demonstrate an understanding of the use of the cost of capital in capital investment decisions

f. demonstrate an understanding of how income taxes impact capital structure and capital investment decisions

5.1 BONDS

1. The **term structure of interest rates** is the relationship between yield to maturity and time to maturity.

    a. It is important to corporate treasurers, who must decide whether to issue short- or long-term debt, and to investors, who must decide whether to buy short- or long-term debt.

    b. Therefore, it is important to understand how the long- and short-term rates are related and what causes shifts in their positions. The term structure is graphically depicted by a yield curve.

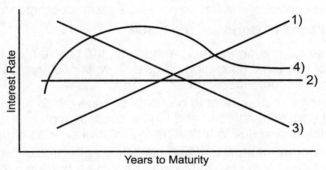

Years to Maturity

Figure 5-1

    c. The graph above illustrates four common yield curves. In most years, long-term rates have been higher than short-term rates, so the yield curve is usually upward sloping. However, other shapes do occur sometimes. Thus, the various shapes are as follows:

    1) Upward sloping
    2) Flat
    3) Downward sloping
    4) Humped

    d. When plotting a yield curve, several factors are held constant:

    1) Default risk of instruments
    2) Taxability of the instruments
    3) Callability of the instruments
    4) Sinking fund provisions

2. **Aspects of Bonds**

    a. Bonds are the principal form of long-term debt financing for corporations and governmental bodies.

    1) A bond is a formal contractual obligation to pay an amount of money (called the **par value**, **maturity amount**, or **face amount**) to the holder at a certain date, plus, in most cases, a series of cash interest payments based on a specified percentage (called the **stated rate** or **coupon rate**) of the face amount at specified intervals.

    2) All of the terms of the agreement are stated in a document called an **indenture**.

    b. Bringing a bond issue to market requires extensive legal and accounting work. The expense of this process is rarely worthwhile for bonds with maturities of less than 5 years.

    1) In general, the longer the term of a bond, the higher will be the return (yield) demanded by investors to compensate for increased risk.

    c.   A bond indenture may require the issuer to establish and maintain a bond **sinking fund**. The objective of making payments into the fund is to segregate and accumulate sufficient assets to pay the bond principal at maturity.

        1)   The amounts transferred plus the revenue earned on investments provide the necessary funds.

    d.   **Advantages of Bonds to the Issuer**

        1)   Interest paid on debt is tax deductible. This is by far the most significant advantage of debt. For a corporation facing a 40%-50% marginal tax rate, the tax savings produced by the deduction of interest can be substantial.

        2)   Basic control of the firm is not shared with debtholders.

    e.   **Disadvantages of Bonds to the Issuer**

        1)   Unlike returns on equity investments, the payment of interest and principal on debt is a legal obligation. If cash flow is insufficient to service debt, the firm could become insolvent.

        2)   The legal requirement to pay debt service raises a firm's risk level. Shareholders will consequently demand higher capitalization rates on retained earnings, which may result in a decline in the market price of the stock.

        3)   The long-term nature of bond debt also affects risk profiles. Debt originally appearing to be profitable may become a burden if interest rates fall and the firm is unable to refinance.

        4)   Certain managerial prerogatives are usually given up in the contractual relationship outlined in the bond's indenture contract. For example, specific ratios must be kept above a certain level during the term of the loan.

        5)   The amount of debt financing available to the individual firm is limited. Generally accepted standards of the investment community will usually dictate a certain debt-equity ratio for an individual firm. Beyond this limit, the cost of debt may rise rapidly, or debt may not be available.

3.   **Types of Bonds**

    a.   Maturity Pattern

        1)   A **term bond** has a single maturity date at the end of its term.
        2)   A **serial bond** matures in stated amounts at regular intervals.

    b.   Valuation

        1)   **Variable rate bonds** pay interest that is dependent on market conditions.
        2)   **Zero-coupon** or **deep-discount bonds** bear no stated rate of interest and thus involve no periodic cash payments; the interest component consists entirely of the bond's discount.
        3)   **Commodity-backed bonds** are payable at prices related to a commodity such as gold.

    c.   Redemption Provisions

        1)   **Callable bonds** may be repurchased by the issuer at a specified price before maturity.
        2)   **Convertible bonds** may be converted into equity securities of the issuer at the option of the holder under certain conditions.

    d.   Securitization

        1)   **Mortgage bonds** are backed by specific assets, usually real estate.
        2)   **Debentures** are backed by the borrower's general credit but not by specific collateral. Thus, debentures are riskier to investors than secured bonds.

e. Ownership

1) **Registered bonds** are issued in the name of the holder. Only the registered holder may receive interest and principal payments.

2) **Bearer bonds** are not individually registered. Interest and principal are paid to whomever presents the bond.

f. Priority

1) **Subordinated debentures** and **second mortgage bonds** are junior securities with claims inferior to those of senior bonds.

g. Repayment Provisions

1) **Income bonds** pay interest contingent on the issuer's profitability.

2) **Revenue bonds** are issued by governmental units and are payable from specific revenue sources.

4. **Bond Ratings**

a. Investors can judge the creditworthiness of a bond issue by consulting the rating assigned by a credit-rating agency. The higher the rating, the more likely the firm is to make good its commitment to pay the interest and principal.

b. This field is dominated by the three largest firms: Moody's, Standard & Poor's, and Fitch.

1) Investment-grade bonds are considered safe investments and thus have the lowest yields. The highest rating assigned is "triple-A." Some fiduciary organizations (such as banks and insurance companies) are only allowed to invest in investment-grade bonds.

2) Non-investment grade bonds, also called speculative-grade bonds, high-yield bonds, or junk bonds, carry high risk. They exploit the tax deductibility of their large interest payments. They are often used to finance leveraged buyouts and mergers.

5. **Bond Valuation**

a. Of primary concern to a bond issuer is the amount of cash that (s)he will receive from investors on the day the bonds are sold.

1) This amount is equal to the **present value of the cash flows** associated with the bonds discounted at the interest rate prevailing in the market at the time (called the market rate or effective rate).

a) The cash flow associated with bonds are

i) Face amount
ii) Interest payments

2) Using the effective interest rate method ensures that the bonds' **yield to maturity** (that is, their ultimate rate of return to the investor) is equal to the rate of return prevailing in the market at the time of the sale.

b. This present value calculation can result in cash proceeds equal to, less than, or greater than the face amount of the bonds, depending on the relationship of the bonds' stated rate of interest to the market rate.

1) If the bonds' stated rate happens to be the same as the market rate at the time of sale, the present value of the bonds will exactly equal their face amount, and the bonds are said to be sold "at par." It is rare, however, for the coupon rate to precisely match the market rate at the time the bonds are ready for sale.

2)   If the bonds' **stated rate is lower than the market rate**, investors must be offered an incentive to buy the bonds, since the bonds' periodic interest payments are lower than those currently available in the market.

a)   In this case, the issuer receives less cash than the par value and the bonds are said to be sold at a **discount**.

EXAMPLE

An entity issues 200 6%, 5-year, $5,000 bonds when the prevailing interest rate in the market is 8%. The total face amount of bonds issued is therefore $1,000,000 ($5,000 face amount × 200 bonds). Annual cash interest payments of $60,000 ($1,000,000 face amount × 6% stated rate) will be made at the end of each year. The present value of the cash flows associated with this bond issue, discounted at the market rate of 8%, is calculated as follows:

Present value of face amount ($1,000,000 × 0.68058)	$680,580
Present value of cash interest ($60,000 × 3.99271)	239,563 (rounded)
Cash proceeds from bond issue	$920,143

Because the bonds are issued at a discount, the cash proceeds are less than the face amount. The issuer records the following entry:

Cash (present value of cash flows)	$920,143	
Discount on bonds payable (difference)	79,857	
Bonds payable (face amount)		$1,000,000

---

3)   If the bonds' **stated rate is higher than the market rate**, investors are willing to pay more for the bonds, since their periodic interest payments are higher than those currently available in the market.

a)   In this case, the issuer receives more cash than the par value and the bonds are said to be sold at a **premium**.

EXAMPLE

An entity issues 200 8%, 5-year, $5,000 bonds when the prevailing interest rate in the market is 6%. The total face amount of bonds issued is therefore $1,000,000 ($5,000 face amount × 200 bonds). Annual cash interest payments of $80,000 ($1,000,000 face amount × 8% stated rate) will be made at the end of each year. The present value of the cash flows associated with this bond issue, discounted at the market rate of 6%, is calculated as follows:

Present value of face amount ($1,000,000 × 0.74726)	$ 747,260
Present value of cash interest ($80,000 × 4.21236)	336,989 (rounded)
Cash proceeds from bond issue	$1,084,249

Because the bonds are issued at a premium, the cash proceeds exceed the face amount. The issuer records the following entry:

Cash (present value of cash flows)	$1,084,249	
Bonds payable (face amount)		$1,000,000
Premium on bonds payable (difference)		84,249

---

c.   Using the **effective rate** to determine the bonds' present value ensures that, upon maturity, they will be valued at their face amount.

d.   When bonds are traded among investors in the secondary market, the issuer is not a party to the transaction and receives no infusion of cash.

1)   The amount that changes hands between the old and new bondholders is determined by the interest rate prevailing in the market at the time of the trade; i.e., the bonds are priced to achieve a new yield.

Stop and review! You have completed the outline for this subunit. Study multiple-choice question 1 through 7 beginning on page 201.

5.2 EQUITY

1. **Common Stock**

    a. The common shareholders are the **owners of the corporation**, and their rights as owners, although reasonably uniform, depend on the laws of the state in which the firm is incorporated.

        1) Equity ownership involves risk because holders of common stock are not guaranteed a return and are last in priority in a liquidation. Shareholders' capital provides the cushion for creditors if any losses occur on liquidation.

    b. **Advantages to the Issuer**

        1) Common stock does not require a fixed dividend; dividends are paid from profits when available.

        2) There is no fixed maturity date for repayment of the capital.

        3) The sale of common stock increases the creditworthiness of the firm by providing more equity.

        4) Common stock is frequently more attractive to investors than debt because it grows in value with the success of the firm. The higher the common stock value, the more advantageous equity financing is compared with debt financing.

    c. **Disadvantages to the Issuer**

        1) Cash dividends on common stock are not tax-deductible and so must be paid out of after-tax profits.

        2) Control (voting rights) is usually diluted as more common stock is sold. (While this aspect is disadvantageous to existing shareholders, management of the corporation may view it as an advantage.)

        3) New common stock sales dilute earnings per share available to existing shareholders.

        4) Underwriting costs are typically higher for common stock issues.

        5) Too much equity may raise the average cost of capital of the firm above its optimal level.

    d. Common shareholders ordinarily have preemptive rights. Preemptive rights give common shareholders the right to purchase any additional stock issuances in proportion to their current ownership percentages.

        1) If applicable state law or the corporate charter does not provide preemptive rights, the firm may nevertheless sell to the existing common shareholders in a rights offering.

        2) Each shareholder is issued a certificate or warrant that is an option to buy a certain number of shares at a fixed price.

    e. As the corporation's owners, the common shareholders have voting rights, that is, they select the firm's board of directors and vote on resolutions.

    f. A stock's par value represents legal capital. It is an arbitrary value assigned to stock before the stock is issued. It also represents the maximum liability of a shareholder.

2. **Preferred Stock**

   a. Preferred stock is a **hybrid of debt and equity**. It has a fixed charge and increases leverage, but payment of dividends is not a legal obligation.

      1) Also, preferred shareholders stand ahead of common shareholders in priority in the event of corporate bankruptcy.

   b. **Advantages to the Issuer**

      1) It is a form of equity and therefore builds the creditworthiness of the firm.
      2) Control is still held by common shareholders.
      3) Superior earnings of the firm are usually still reserved for the common shareholders.

   c. **Disadvantages to the Issuer**

      1) Cash dividends on preferred stock are not deductible as a tax expense and are paid with after-tax income. The result is a substantially greater cost relative to bonds.
      2) In periods of economic difficulty, accumulated unpaid dividends (called dividends in arrears) may create major managerial and financial problems for the firm.

   d. **Typical Provisions of Preferred Stock Issues**

      1) Priority in assets and earnings. If the firm goes bankrupt, the preferred shareholders have priority over common shareholders.
      2) Accumulation of dividends. If preferred dividends are cumulative, dividends in arrears must be paid before any common dividends can be paid.
      3) Convertibility. Preferred stock issues may be convertible into common stock at the option of the shareholder.
      4) Participation. Preferred stock may participate with common in excess earnings of the company. For example, 8% participating preferred stock might pay a dividend each year greater than 8% when the corporation is extremely profitable, but nonparticipating preferred stock will receive no more than is stated on the face of the stock.
      5) Par value. Par value is the liquidation value, and a percentage of par equals the preferred dividend.
      6) Redeemability. Some preferred stock may be redeemed at a given time or at the option of the holder or otherwise at a time not controlled by the issuer. This feature makes preferred stock more nearly akin to debt, particularly in the case of transient preferred stock, which must be redeemed within a short time (e.g., 5 to 10 years). The SEC requires a separate presentation of redeemable preferred, nonredeemable preferred, and common stock.
      7) Voting rights. These may be conferred if preferred dividends are in arrears for a stated period.
      8) Callability. The issuer may have the right to repurchase the stock. For example, the stock may be noncallable for a stated period, after which it may be called if the issuer pays a call premium (an amount exceeding par value).
      9) Maturity. Preferred stock may have a sinking fund that allows for the purchase of a given annual percentage of the outstanding shares.

   e. Holding preferred stock rather than bonds provides corporations a major tax advantage. At least 70% of the dividends received from preferred stock is tax deductible, but all bond interest received is taxable. The dividends-received deduction also applies to common stock.

3.   **Stock Valuation**

a.   The method of valuing a bond shown in item 5.b. in Subunit 5.1 can also be used for preferred stock.

1)   If the preferred dividend rate is less than what is prevalent in the market, then the preferred stock will sell at less than its par value.

2)   A dividend rate higher than the market average (based on a similar risk level) will result in the preferred stock selling at a premium.

3)   The discount rate used would normally be higher than that used for a bond valuation because a preferred stock is slightly more risky than a bond but has few additional advantages (other than the aforementioned advantage that preferred dividends are sometimes taxed at lower tax rates than bond interest).

b.   Common stocks can be valued in the same way, but the return is based on earnings per share rather than dividend level. Also, with common stocks, the future returns are pure estimates, so there is usually a heavy risk premium incorporated into the calculation.

1)   For example, if a bond could be sold at its face value based on an 8% interest rate, a similar preferred stock might necessitate a 10% return because of the increased risk.

2)   At the same time, a common stock might have to be valued on an assumed return of 20%. Because investors in common stock fear the risk of ever getting future returns, a high risk premium must be used to calculate the common stock's value.

c.   Corporate valuation methods are discussed in greater detail in Subunit 5.3.

4.   **Effect of Inflation**

a.   With any financial instrument, investors in an inflationary environment require higher real and nominal rates of return.

Stop and review! You have completed the outline for this subunit. Study multiple-choice questions 8 through 11 beginning on page 203.

5.3 CORPORATE/STOCK VALUATION METHODS

1.   **The Dividend Discount Model**

a.   The dividend discount model (also known as the dividend growth model) is a method of arriving at the value of a stock by using expected dividends per share and discounting them back to present value. The formula is as follows:

$$\frac{Dividend\ per\ share}{Cost\ of\ capital\ -\ dividend\ growth\ rate}$$

This method is used when dividends are expected to grow at a constant rate. If the value obtained using this formula is greater than the stock's current fair market value, then the stock is considered to be undervalued (meaning it is worth more than its fair market value).

1) EXAMPLE: A company recently paid an annual dividend of $10. Dividends have grown steadily at a rate of 5% and are expected to continue indefinitely. Investors require a 12% rate of return (cost of capital) for similar investments. The value of this stock can be calculated as

$$\frac{\$10 \times (1 + .05)}{.12 - .05} = \$150$$

NOTE: Given only the amount of the last annual dividend paid, it is important to adjust it to the expected dividend using the growth rate of the company in order to calculate the correct dividend per share amount.

If the fair market value of this stock was $100, then this stock would be considered a good investment. However, if the fair market value of the stock was $200, the opposite would be true.

2. **Preferred Stock Valuation**

a. Preferred stock usually pays a fixed dividend. When this is the case, the value of the stock can be calculated as follows:

$$\frac{Dividend\ per\ share}{Cost\ of\ capital}$$

This formula can also be used when dividends on common stock are not expected to grow.

1) EXAMPLE: Several years ago, a company issued preferred stock that pays a fixed dividend each year of $12. Investors require a 15% rate of return (cost of capital) for similar preferred stock. The value of this stock can be calculated as

$$\frac{\$12}{.15} = \$80$$

3. **Common Stock with Variable Dividend Growth**

a. Dividends do not always grow at a constant rate. When this occurs, stock valuation becomes more difficult. Many companies experience a two-stage growth. In the initial phase, growth can be very rapid and unstable. In the second phase, growth slows down and stabilizes. In these situations, the **two-stage dividend discount model** can be used to effectively calculate the stock value. This calculation requires three steps:

1) Calculate and sum the present value of dividends in the period of high growth.
2) Calculate the present value of the stock based on the period of steady growth, discounting the value back to Year 1.
3) Sum the totals calculated in Step 1 and Step 2.

b. EXAMPLE: Rapido Company expects to pay an annual dividend of $5 at the end of this year. Annual growth is expected to be at 20% for the next 3 years, after which growth is expected to stabilize at 8%. Investors require a 12% rate of return (cost of capital) for similar stock.

Step 1: Calculate and sum the present value of dividends in the period of high growth.

End of Year	Dividend	PV Factor @ 12%	PV of Dividend
1	$5.00	.893	$ 4.47
2	$5 × (1 + .20) = $6.00	.797	4.78
3	$6 × (1+.20) = $7.20	.712	5.13
		Total PV of Dividends	$14.38

Step 2: Calculate the present value of the stock based on the period of steady growth and discount it back to Year 1. This is done using the dividend discount method. The end of Year 4 dividend is $7.78, calculated by taking the end of Year 3 dividend and multiplying it by 1 plus the Year 4 rate [$7.20 × (1 + .08)].

$$\frac{Dividend\ per\ share}{Cost\ of\ capital\ -\ Dividend\ growth\ rate}$$

$$\frac{\$7.78}{.12 - .08} = \$194.50$$

Then discount the value back to Year 1, using the present value factor from Year 3.

$$\$194.50 \times .712 = \$138.48$$

Step 3: Sum the totals calculated in Step 1 and Step 2.

$$\$14.38 + \$138.48 = \$152.86$$

Based on the two-stage dividend discount model, $152.86 is an appropriate value for this stock, given the projected dividends per share and cost of capital.

4. **Per-Share Ratios**

   a. **Earnings per share (EPS)** equals net income available to common shareholders divided by the average number of shares outstanding for the period.

   $$\frac{Net\ income\ available\ to\ common\ shareholders}{Average\ shares\ outstanding}$$

      1) Net income available to common shareholders is usually net income minus preferred dividends.
      2) Both basic and diluted EPS must be presented.

   b. **Book value per share** equals the amount of net assets available to the shareholders of a given type of stock divided by the number of those shares outstanding.

   $$\frac{Shareholders'\ equity}{Shares\ outstanding}$$

      1) When a company has preferred as well as common stock outstanding, the computation of book value per common share must consider potential claims by preferred shareholders, such as whether the preferred stock is cumulative and in arrears, or participating. It must also take into account whether the call price (or possibly the liquidation value) exceeds the carrying amount of the preferred stock.

   c. **Dividend yield** equals the annual dividend payment divided by the market value per share.

   $$\frac{Dividend\ per\ share}{Market\ value\ per\ share}$$

      1) A related ratio is the **dividend payout**, which equals dividends per common share divided by EPS.

d.   The **price-earnings (P/E) ratio** equals the market price per share of common stock divided by EPS.

$$\frac{Market\ price}{EPS}$$

1)   Most analysts prefer to use diluted EPS. The diluted EPS is usually a more accurate reflection of a company's earning power. **Earning power** is defined as a company's ability to generate income from normal operations.

2)   Growth companies are likely to have high P/E ratios. A high ratio may also indicate that the firm is relatively low risk or that its choice of accounting methods results in a conservative EPS.

3)   Because of the widespread use of the P/E ratio and other measures, the relationship between accounting data and stock prices is crucial. Thus, managers have an incentive to "manage earnings," sometimes by fraudulent means.

e.   **Price-book ratio** (also called the market-to-book ratio).

$$\frac{Market\ price\ per\ share}{Book\ value\ per\ share}$$

1)   Well-managed firms should sell at high multiples of their book value, which reflects historical cost.

f.   **Price-sales ratio** is preferred by some analysts over profit ratios.

$$\frac{Market\ price\ per\ share}{Sales\ per\ share}$$

1)   Analysts who use the price-sales ratio believe that strong sales are the basic ingredient of profits and that sales are the item on the financial statements least subject to manipulation.

Stop and review! You have completed the outline for this subunit. Study multiple-choice questions 12 through 14 beginning on page 204.

5.4 DERIVATIVES

1.   **Overview**

a.   A **derivative instrument** is an investment transaction in which the parties' gain or loss is derived from some other economic event, for example, the price of a given stock, a foreign currency exchange rate, or the price of a certain commodity.

1)   One party enters into the transaction to speculate (incur risk), and the other enters into it to hedge (avoid risk).

b.   Derivatives are a type of financial instrument, along with cash, accounts receivable, notes receivable, bonds, preferred shares, common shares, etc. Derivatives are not, however, claims on business assets, such as those represented by equity securities.

2.   **Hedging**

a.   Hedging is the process of using offsetting commitments to minimize or avoid the impact of adverse price movements.

b.   A person who would like to sell an asset in the future has a **long position** in the asset because (s)he benefits from a rise in value of the asset.

1)   To protect against a decline in value, the owner can enter into a short hedge, i.e., obtain an instrument whose value will rise if the asset's value falls.

      2) EXAMPLE: A soybean farmer hopes that the price of soybeans will rise by the time his crop is ready to go to market. The farmer is thus long in soybeans. To protect against the possibility that the price will fall in the meantime, he can obtain a short hedge.

  c. A person who would like to buy an asset in the future has a **short position** in the asset because (s)he benefits from a fall in value of the asset.

      1) To protect against a rise in value, the party can enter into a long hedge, i.e., obtain an instrument whose value will rise if the asset's value rises.

      2) EXAMPLE: An agricultural wholesaler hopes that the price of soybeans will fall by the time farmers are bringing their harvests to the warehouse. The wholesaler is thus short in soybeans. To protect against the possibility that the price will rise in the meantime, the wholesaler can obtain a long hedge.

3. **Options**

  a. Options are the most common form of derivative.

      1) A party who buys an option has bought the right to demand that the counterparty (the seller or "writer" of the option) perform some action on or before a specified future date.

      2) The exercise of an option is always at the discretion of the option holder (the buyer) who has, in effect, bought the right to exercise the option or not. The seller of an option has no choice; (s)he must perform if the holder chooses to exercise.

  b. An option has an expiration date after which it can no longer be exercised.

      1) An option that can be exercised only on its expiration date is referred to as a European option.

      2) An option that grants the buyer the right to exercise anytime on or before expiration is an American option.

  c. Determining the correct price for an option is a complex calculation, discussed in item 7 in this subunit.

      1) The exercise price (or strike price) is the price at which the owner can purchase or sell the asset underlying the option contract.

      2) The option price, also called option premium, is the amount the buyer pays to the seller to acquire an option.

  d. An option can be covered or uncovered.

      1) A covered option is one in which the seller (writer) already has possession of the underlying.

      2) A naked (uncovered) option is a speculative instrument; since the writer does not hold the underlying, (s)he may have to acquire it at an unknown price in the future to satisfy his/her obligations under the option contract.

  e. Options can be classified by their underlying assets.

      1) A stock option is an option whose underlying asset is a traded stock.

      2) An index option is an option whose underlying asset is a market index. If exercised, settlement is made by cash since delivery of the underlying is impossible.

      3) Long-term equity anticipation securities (LEAPS) are examples of long-term stock options or index options, with expiration dates up to 3 years away.

      4) Foreign currency options give the holder the right to buy a specific foreign currency at a designated exchange rate.

4.   **Call Options**

a.   A call option gives the buyer (holder) the **right to purchase** (i.e., the right to "call" for) the underlying asset (stock, currency, commodity, etc.) at a fixed price.

   1)   If the price of the underlying rises above the exercise price, the option is said to be "in-the-money." The holder can exercise his/her option and buy the underlying at a bargain price.

   2)   If the value of the underlying is less than the exercise price of the option, the option is "out-of-the-money," or not worth exercising.

   3)   If the value of the underlying is equal to the exercise price of the option, the option is said to be "at-the-money."

b.   Thus, a call option represents a long position to the holder because the holder benefits from a price increase.

   1)   The seller (writer) of a call option obviously hopes the price of the underlying will remain below the exercise price since (s)he must make the underlying available to the holder at the strike price, regardless of how much the seller must pay to obtain it. The seller of a call option is thus taking a short position.

c.   The buyer's gain (loss) necessarily mirrors the seller's loss (gain). The amount of gain and loss on a call option can be calculated as follows:

   1)   Buyer/holder (long position):

   Units of underlying × (Excess of market price over exercise price − Option price)

   2)   Seller/writer (short position):

   Units of underlying × (Option price − Excess of market price over exercise price)

d.   EXAMPLE of an in-the-money call option: Tapworth Co. bought call options giving it the right to buy 100 shares of PanGlobal Corp. stock in 30 days at $100 per share. Smith Co. sold these options to Tapworth for $3 per share. On Day 30, PanGlobal stock is trading at $105 and Tapworth exercises all of its options (since the options give Tapworth the right to buy PanGlobal stock at a better-than-market price). Tapworth's and Smith's respective gains and losses on the transaction can be calculated as follows:

   Buyer's gain(loss) = 100 call options × [($105 − $100) − $3] = $200 gain
   Seller's gain(loss) = 100 call options × [$3 − ($105 − $100)] = $(200) loss

e.   EXAMPLE of an out-of-the-money call option: On Day 30, PanGlobal stock is trading at $97 and Tapworth's options are worthless (since having the right to buy PanGlobal at $100 gives Tapworth no advantage over buying on the open market). Tapworth's and Smith's respective gains and losses on the transaction can be calculated as follows:

   Buyer's gain(loss) = 100 call options × ($0 − $3) = $(300) loss
   Seller's gain(loss) = 100 call options × ($3 − $0) = $300 gain

f. These relationships can be depicted in the following diagram:

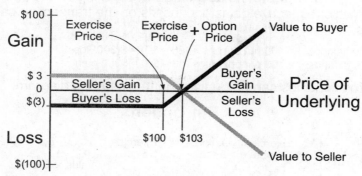

Figure 5-2

Clearly, the accurate valuation of options is crucial.

5. **Put Options**

a. A put option gives the buyer (holder) the **right to sell** (i.e., the right to "put" onto the market) the underlying asset (stock, currency, commodity, etc.) at a fixed price.

1) If the price of the underlying falls below the exercise price, the option is said to be "in-the-money." The holder can exercise his/her option and compel the counterparty to buy the underlying at a price higher than that prevailing in the market.

2) If the value of the underlying is higher than the exercise price of the option, the option is "out-of-the-money," or not worth exercising.

3) If the value of the underlying is equal to the exercise price of the option, the option is said to be "at-the-money."

b. Thus, a put option represents a short position to the holder because the holder benefits from a price decrease.

1) The seller (writer) of a put option obviously hopes the price of the underlying will remain above the exercise price, since (s)he must buy from the holder at the strike price, regardless of the fact that the same underlying can be obtained for less in the open market. The seller of a put option is thus taking a long position.

c. The buyer's gain(loss) necessarily mirrors the seller's loss(gain). The amount of gain and loss on a put option can be calculated as follows:

1) Buyer/holder (short position):

Units of underlying × (Excess of exercise price over market price − Option price)

2) Seller/writer (long position):

Units of underlying × (Option price − Excess of exercise price over market price)

d. EXAMPLE of an in-the-money put option: Tapworth Co. bought put options giving it the right to sell 100 shares of PanGlobal Corp. stock in 30 days at $100 per share. Smith Co. sold these options to Tapworth for $3 per share. On Day 30, PanGlobal stock is trading at $92 and Tapworth exercises all of its options (since the options give Tapworth the right to sell PanGlobal stock at a price higher than the one prevailing in the market). Tapworth's and Smith's respective gains and losses on the transaction can be calculated as follows:

Buyer's gain(loss) = 100 put options × [($100 − $92) − $3] = $500 gain
Seller's gain(loss) = 100 put options × [$3 − ($100 − $92)] = $(500) loss

e.   EXAMPLE of an out-of-the-money put option: On Day 30, PanGlobal stock is trading
at $104 and Tapworth's options are worthless (since having options to sell PanGlobal
at $100 gives Tapworth no advantage over selling on the open market). Tapworth's
and Smith's respective gains and losses on the transaction can be calculated as
follows:

Buyer's gain(loss) = 100 put options × ($0 – $3) = $(300) loss
Seller's gain(loss) = 100 put options × ($3 – $0) = $300 gain

f.   These relationships can be depicted in the following diagram:

Put Options

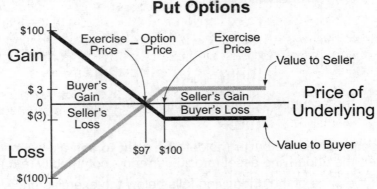

Figure 5-3

6.   Put-Call Parity

a.   The put-call parity theorem mathematically depicts the combinations of investment
strategies that can be devised using European options (i.e., those with a single
exercise date). The two sides of this equation represent combinations with identical
outcomes (given identical exercise prices for the put and the call and identical
expiration dates):

Value of call + PV of exercise price* = Value of put + Value of underlying

* Discounted at the risk-free rate

1)   Look first at the left side of the equation. The buyer of a call may wish to hedge
against the loss that (s)he will incur if the market price of the underlying fails to
rise sufficiently. The buyer can do this by investing the present value of the
exercise price in a safe investment. If the option is out-of-the-money on the
expiration date, the option holder has the return from this safe investment to
make up for the loss.

2)   Look next at the right side of the equation. The buyer of a put may wish to
hedge against the loss that (s)he will incur if the market price of the underlying
fails to fall sufficiently. The buyer can do this by buying the underlying at the
same time as the option. If the option is out-of-the-money on the expiration
date, the option holder can simply sell the underlying at the going market price
to make up for the loss.

b.   The basic formula can be restated to depict the investment strategy that provides a
risk-free return:

PV of exercise price = Value of put + Value of underlying – Value of call

1)   In other words, the combination of buying a put option, buying the underlying,
and selling a call option provides the same return as investing the present value
of the exercise price at the risk-free rate. Knowledge of these relationships can
help investors devise appropriate option strategies.

7. **Valuing an Option**

    a.   The two most well-known models for valuing options are the Black-Scholes formula for call options and the binomial method. The equations themselves are extremely complex and beyond the scope of an accounting text, but some general statements can be made about the factors that affect the outcomes.

        1) **Exercise price.** In general, the buyer of a call option benefits from a low exercise price. Likewise, the buyer of a put option generally benefits from a high exercise price.

            a)   Thus, an increase in the exercise price of an option results in a decrease in the value of a call option and an increase in the value of a put option.

        2) **Price of underlying.** As the price of the underlying increases, the value of a call option also will increase; the exercise price is more and more of a bargain with each additional dollar in the price of the underlying.

            a)   By the same token, the value of a put option will decrease as the price of the underlying increases since there is no advantage in selling at a lower-than-market price.

        3) **Interest rates.** Buying a call option is like buying the underlying on credit. The purchase of the option is a form of down payment. If the option is exercised in a period of rising interest rates, the exercise price is paid in inflated dollars, making it more attractive for the option holder.

            a)   A rise in interest rates will therefore result in a rise in the value of a call option and a fall in the value of a put option.

        4) **Time until expiration.** The more time that passes, the riskier any investment is.

            a)   Thus, an increase in the term of an option (both calls and puts) will result in an increase in the value of the option.

        5) **Volatility of price of underlying.** The price of an asset can drop no lower than zero. Thus, there is a natural limit to the potential downside loss for either party to an option transaction. On the upside, however, there is much greater flexibility. Thus, parties to an option transaction will prefer volatility.

            a)   An increase in the volatility of the price of the underlying will result in an increase in the value of the option (both calls and puts).

    b.   These factors and their effects can be summarized as follows:

Increase in	Value of call option will	Value of put option will
Exercise price of option	Decrease	Increase
Price of underlying	Increase	Decrease
Interest rates	Increase	Decrease
Time until expiration	Increase	Increase
Volatility of price of underlying	Increase	Increase

8. Forward Contracts

a. One method of mitigating risk is the simple forward contract. The two parties agree that, at a set future date, one of them will perform and the other will pay a specified amount for the performance.

   1) A common example is that of a retailer and a wholesaler who agree in September on the prices and quantities of merchandise that will be shipped to the retailer's stores in time for the winter holiday season. The retailer has locked in a price and a source of supply, and the wholesaler has locked in a price and a customer.

b. The party that has contracted to buy the underlying at a future date has taken a long position, and the party that has contracted to deliver the underlying has taken a short position. The payoff structure is similar to that for options:

   1) If the market price of the underlying on the delivery date is higher than the contractual price, the party that has taken the long position benefits, since (s)he has locked in a lower price.

   2) If the market price of the underlying on the delivery date is lower than the contractual price, the party that has taken the short position benefits, since (s)he is entitled to receive higher payment for the underlying than the amount currently prevailing in the market.

c. Note the significant difference between a forward contract and an option: In a contract, both parties must meet their contractual obligations, i.e., to deliver merchandise and to pay. Neither has the option of nonperformance.

9. Futures Contracts

a. A forward contract like the one described above is appropriate for a retailer and a wholesaler, who are exchanging very specific merchandise and can take the time to address all the facets of the contract.

   1) Traders in undifferentiated commodities, such as grains, metals, fossil fuels, and foreign currencies, often do not have this luxury. The trading process of these products is eased by the use of futures contracts.

   2) A futures contract is a commitment to buy or sell an asset at a fixed price during a specific future month; unlike with a forward contract, the counterparty is unknown.

b. Futures contracts are actively traded on futures exchanges.

   1) Because futures contracts are for delivery during a given month, not a specific day, they are more flexible arrangements than forward contracts.

   2) The clearinghouse randomly matches sellers who will deliver during a given month with buyers who are seeking delivery during the same month.

c. Because futures contracts are actively traded, the result is a liquid market in futures that permits buyers and sellers to net out their positions.

   1) For example, a party who has sold a contract can net out his/her position by buying a futures contract. In contrast, a person holding a forward contract does not enjoy this liquidity.

d. Another distinguishing feature of futures contracts is that their prices are marked to market every day at the close of the day to each person's account. Thus, the market price is posted at the close of business each day.

   1) A mark-to-market provision minimizes a futures contract's chance of default because profits and losses on the contracts must be received or paid each day through a clearinghouse.

   2) This requirement of daily settlement minimizes default and is necessary because futures contracts are sold on margin (i.e., they are highly leveraged).

e. Another difference is that a party to a forward contract typically expects actual delivery; futures contracts are generally used as financial tools to offset the risks of changing economic conditions. Thus, the two parties simply exchange the difference between the contracted price and the market price prior to the expiration date.

1) This is why a trader who does not want to accidentally have to settle in a certain month buys a future for the following month.

10. **Swaps**

a. Swaps are contracts by which the parties exchange cash flows. Three types are common:

1) **Interest rate swaps** are agreements to exchange interest payments based on one interest structure for payments based on another structure.

a) For example, a firm that has fixed debt service charges may enter into a swap with a counterparty that agrees to supply the first party with interest payments based on a floating rate that more closely tracks the first party's revenues.

b) These agreements are highly customized.

2) **Currency swaps** are agreements to exchange cash flows denominated in one currency for cash flows denominated in another.

a) For example, a U.S. firm with revenues in euros has to pay suppliers and workers in dollars, not euros. To minimize exchange-rate risk, it might agree to exchange euros for dollars held by a firm that needs euros.

b) The exchange rate will be an average of the rates expected over the life of the agreement.

3) **Credit default swaps** are agreements whereby one of the parties indemnifies the other against default by a third party.

a) For example, a large bank may agree to pay a constant stream of cash to another bank as long as one of the first bank's major debtors remains current on its loans. If the customer defaults, the second bank covers the first bank's loss. One of the parties is, in effect, providing loan default insurance to the other party.

b) Unlike interest rate swaps, these agreements are usually bundled into large portfolios.

b. The swap spread is the market-determined additional yield that compensates counterparties who receive fixed payments in a swap for the credit risk involved in the swap. The swap spread will differ with the creditworthiness of the counterparty.

c. Most swaps are priced to be at-the-money at inception, meaning that the value of the two sets of cash flows being exchanged is the same. Naturally, as interest rates, currency exchange rates, and credit risks change, the values of the swaps will change.

11. Options can be invested in as a speculative form of investment. Alternatively, if they are combined with other positions, they can also be used in hedging.

Stop and review! You have completed the outline for this subunit. Study multiple-choice questions 15 through 22 beginning on page 205.

5.5 OTHER SOURCES OF LONG-TERM FINANCING

1. **Leases**

   a. A lease is a long-term, contractual agreement in which the owner of property (the lessor) allows another party (the lessee) the right to use the property for a stated period in exchange for a stated payment.

      1) Leases are a well-structured and widely used tool for obtaining the use of long-lived assets without tying up the large amounts of capital that would be needed for an outright purchase (U.S. airlines routinely lease anywhere from one-quarter to one-half of their passenger jets).

   b. A lease can be a purchase-and-financing arrangement (a capital lease) or merely a long-term rental contract (an operating lease). The annual cash outflow is the same, but there is a significant advantage to the lessee in structuring the lease as an operating lease: The total liability for the entire term of the lease need not be reported as a liability on the balance sheet.

2. **Convertible Securities**

   a. Convertible securities are debt or preferred stock securities that contain a provision allowing the holder to convert the securities into some specified number of common shares after a specified time has elapsed.

      1) The conversion feature is an enticement to potential investors that allows the corporation to raise capital at a cost lower than a straight new common equity issue.

3. **Stock Purchase Warrants**

   a. A stock purchase warrant is, in effect, a call option on the corporation's common stock. After a specified time has elapsed, the holder of the warrant can exchange the warrant plus a specified amount of cash for some number of shares of common stock.

      1) Attaching warrants to a debt or preferred stock issue can make the securities more attractive to investors.

4. **Retained Earnings**

   a. Retained earnings is the cumulative accrual-basis income of the corporation minus amounts paid out in cash dividends minus amounts reclassified as additional paid-in capital from stock dividends.

      1) Retained earnings are the lowest-cost form of capital (all internally generated, no issue costs).

Stop and review! You have completed the outline for this subunit. Study multiple-choice question 23 on page 208.

5.6 COST OF CAPITAL -- CURRENT

1.   **Overview**

   a.   Investors provide funds to corporations with the understanding that management will deploy those funds in such a way that the investor will ultimately receive a return.

   1)   If management does not generate the **investors' required rate of return**, the investors will take their funds out of the corporation and redirect them to more profitable ventures.

   2)   For this reason, the investors' required rate of return (also called their opportunity cost of capital) in turn becomes the firm's cost of capital.

   b.   A firm's cost of capital is typically used to discount the future cash flows of long-term projects, since investments with a return higher than the cost of capital will increase the value of the firm, i.e., shareholders' wealth. (The cost of capital is not used in connection with working capital since short-term needs are met with short-term funds.)

2.   **Component Costs of Capital**

   a.   As described in Subunits 5.1 and 5.2, a firm's financing structure consists of three components: long-term debt, preferred equity, and common equity (retained earnings are treated as part of common equity in this analysis for reasons given below). The rate of return demanded by holders of each is the component cost for that form of capital.

   1)   The component cost of **debt** is the after-tax interest rate on the debt (interest payments are tax-deductible by the firm):

   Effective rate × (1.0 - Marginal tax rate)

   2)   The component cost of **preferred stock** is computed using the dividend yield ratio:

   Cash dividend on preferred stock ÷ Market price of preferred stock

   3)   The component cost of **common stock** is also computed using the dividend yield ratio:

   Cash dividend on common stock ÷ Market price of common stock

   NOTE: If all the relative components are known, the cost of capital can also be computed using the capital asset pricing model (CAPM). (See page 149.)

   4)   The component cost of **retained earnings** is considered to be the same as that for common stock (if the firm cannot find a profitable use for retained earnings, it should be distributed to the common shareholders in the form of dividends so that they can find their own alternative investments).

b.   Providers of equity capital are exposed to more risk than are lenders because (1) the firm is not legally obligated to pay them a return and (2) in case of liquidation, equity investors trail creditors in priority. To compensate for this higher level of risk, equity investors demand a higher return, making equity financing more expensive than debt.

Through understanding the cost of capital and how it is applied in capital structure decisions, CMA candidates will need to be able to determine the weighted-average cost of capital (WACC). Additionally, you should be able to calculate the marginal cost of capital. On the CMA exam you will be expected to calculate and demonstrate that you understand how they will affect investment decisions for a business.

3.   **Weighted-Average Cost of Capital**

a.   Corporate management usually designates a **target capital structure** for the firm, i.e., the proportions that each component of capital should comprise in the overall combination. An example might be 10% debt, 20% preferred stock, and 70% common stock.

1)   EXAMPLE: The following is excerpted from a firm's most recent balance sheet:

Component	Carrying Amount	Proportions
11.4% Bonds Payable	$ 2,000,000	10.42%
11.5% Preferred Stock	4,000,000	20.83%
Common Stock	12,000,000	62.50%
Retained Earnings	1,200,000	6.25%
Totals	**$19,200,000**	**100.00%**

b.   A firm's **weighted-average cost of capital (WACC)** is a single, composite rate of return on its combined components of capital. The weights are based on the components' respective market values, not book values, because market value provides the best information about investors' expectations.

1)   EXAMPLE: In order to calculate its WACC, the firm must first determine the component costs of long-term debt and preferred equity. The company has historically provided a 16% return on common equity. The firm is in a 35% marginal tax bracket.

Component cost of long-term debt = Effective rate × (1.0 – Marginal tax rate)
= 11.4% × (1.0 – .35)
= 7.41%

Component cost of preferred equity = Cash dividend ÷ Market price of stock
= ($4,000,000 × 11.5%) ÷ $4,600,000
= 10.0%

The firm can now determine its WACC by multiplying the cost of each component of capital by the proportion of total market value represented by that component.

Component	(1) Market Value	(2) Weight		(3) Component Cost		(2) × (3) Weighted Cost
11.4% Bonds Payable	$ 2,200,000	10.00%	×	7.41%	=	0.7410%
11.5% Preferred Stock	4,600,000	20.91%	×	10.0%	=	2.0909%
Common Stock	14,000,000	63.64%	×	16.0%	=	10.1824%
Retained Earnings	1,200,000	5.45%	×	16.0%	=	0.8727%
Totals	**$22,000,000**	**100.00%**				**13.8870%**

The firm will invest in projects that have an expected return that is greater than 13.8870% (firm's WACC). These projects will generate additional free cash flow and will create positive net present value for the shareholders.

c.   A formula to calculate the after-tax WACC where there is no preferred stock is

$$WACC = \frac{E}{V} \times R_e + \frac{D}{V} \times R_d \times (1 - T)$$

R_e = Cost of equity
R_d = Cost of debt
E   = Market value of the firm's equity
D   = Market value of the firm's debt
T   = Corporate tax rate
$V = D + E$ = Capital used to generate profits

EXAMPLE

The firm provides the following information:

Capital used to generate profits

50% debt, 50% equity	$1,200
Cost of equity	15%
Cost of debt	5%
Corporate tax rate	40%

$$WACC = \frac{(1{,}200 \times 50\%)}{1{,}200} \times 15\% + \frac{(1{,}200 \times 50\%)}{1{,}200} \times 5\% \times (1 - 40\%) = 0.09 = 9\%$$

---

d.   Standard financial theory provides a model for the **optimal capital structure** of every firm. This model holds that shareholder wealth-maximization results from **minimizing the weighted-average cost of capital**. Thus, the focus of management should not be on maximizing earnings per share (EPS can be increased by taking on more debt, but debt increases risk).

1)   The relevant relationships are depicted below:

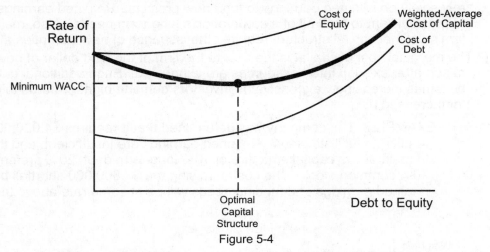

Figure 5-4

Ordinarily, firms cannot identify this optimal point precisely. Thus, they should attempt to find an optimal range for the capital structure.

4.   **Impact of Income Taxes on Capital Structure and Capital Decisions**

a.   Taxes are an important consideration because they can be anywhere from 25% to 50% of all costs.

b.   Corporate capital gains are taxed at regular rate, and the capital gains of individuals are currently 16% or less.

c.   A dividends-received deduction renders anywhere from 70% to 100% of dividends received by one company from investments in the stock of another company free from taxation. This deduction prevents or reduces double taxation. It also encourages one company to invest in the stock of another company. However, a conflict may arise between the desires of corporate owners and individual owners in that individuals may sometimes prefer capital gains, while corporate owners would prefer dividends.

d.   Interest is a tax-deductible expense of the debtor company, but dividends are not deductible. Thus, a company needing capital would prefer to issue bonds rather than stock because the interest would be deductible. As a result, the issuer would prefer to issue debt because the interest is deductible, but the investor would prefer stock because interest on debt is fully taxable while the return on stock is only partially taxable or taxable at special low rates. Similarly, a corporation may be reluctant to issue common stock because it does not want to share control of the company, but the investor may prefer stock because of the favorable tax treatment.

e.   Multinational corporations frequently derive income from several countries. The government of each country in which a corporation does business may enact statutes imposing one or more types of tax on the corporation, so any capital decision affecting multiple countries must consider the tax provisions of each nation.

Stop and review! You have completed the outline for this subunit. Study multiple-choice questions 24 through 29 beginning on page 208.

5.7 COST OF CAPITAL -- NEW

1.   **Marginal Cost of Capital**

a.   While internally generated capital is the least expensive form of capital, a firm cannot rely solely on retained earnings to fund new projects. Retained earnings alone are rarely sufficient to fund all of a corporation's long-term needs. Also, maintaining the firm's optimal capital structure requires the issuance of new securities at some point.

b.   The marginal cost of capital is the cost to the firm of the next dollar of new capital raised after existing internal sources are exhausted. Each additional dollar raised becomes increasingly expensive as investors demand higher returns to compensate for increased risk.

1)   EXAMPLE: The company has determined that it requires $4,000,000 of new funding to fulfill its plans. Retained earnings are insufficient, and the firm wants to maintain its capital structure of 10% long-term debt, 20% preferred stock, 70% common stock. The cost of raising the $2,800,000 shortfall between retained earnings and funding needs will be at some rate above the current WACC.

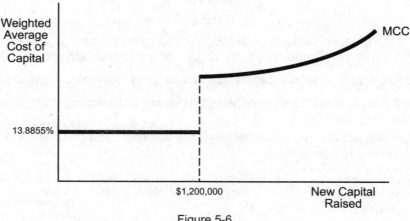

Figure 5-6

2.   **Cost of New Capital**

    a.   The cost of new capital (also called external capital) is the ratio of what the firm must pay to what the firm gets.

        1)   Because of interest rate fluctuations, the **cost of new debt** will rarely be the historical, or embedded, rate. Also, if the firm's debt load is already considerable, new debtholders will demand a higher interest rate to compensate for the increased risk.

Annual interest ÷ Net issue proceeds

            As tax rates rise, the deductibility of interest makes debt a more attractive financing option.

        2)   All new issues of equity securities involve the payment of flotation costs, which reduce the proceeds received, thereby raising the cost of capital. The **cost of new preferred stock** is thus calculated:

Next dividend ÷ Net issue proceeds

        3)   The **cost of new common stock** employs a form of the dividend growth model, which anticipates that common shareholders will demand steadily increasing dividends over time (while assuming that the dividend payout ratio will remain constant).

(Next dividend ÷ Net issue proceeds) + Dividend growth rate

            An issue of new common stock is used mostly by young, growing companies. Mature firms rarely issue new common stock to the general public because of the issue costs involved and the depressing influence a new issue can have on the stock's price.

    b.   EXAMPLE: Retained earnings are sufficient to cover 30% of the firm's new capital needs ($1,200,000 ÷ $4,000,000). The rest must come from the other three components of capital.

        The company can issue new debt at a cost of 12.6%. The firm can also sell $100 par value preferred stock that pays a 14% dividend and has $5-per-share flotation costs. The $1,200,000 balance of retained earnings will be used, and the remainder will come from an issue of common stock. The new common stock will pay an $8 dividend that is expected to grow 2% annually. The company's common stock is currently trading at $55 per share, and the new issue will have $3-per-share flotation costs.

            Cost of new long-term debt = 12.6% (given)

            Cost of new preferred stock = Next dividend ÷ Net issue proceeds
                              = $14 ÷ ($100 − $5)
                              = 14.7%

            Cost of new common stock = (Next dividend ÷ Net issue proceeds) + Dividend growth rate
                              = [$8 ÷ ($55 − $3)] + 2%
                              = 15.4% + 2%
                              = 17.4%

        If the company maintains its current capital structure, the weighed-average cost of capital for this round of capital formation is calculated as follows:

Component	Weight		Cost of Capital		Weighted Cost
New long-term debt	10%	×	12.6%	=	1.26%
New preferred stock	20%	×	14.7%	=	2.94%
New common stock	40%	×	17.4%	=	6.96%
Retained earnings	30%	×	16.0%	=	4.80%
Total					**15.96%**

Stop and review! You have completed the outline for this subunit. Study multiple-choice questions 30 through 37 beginning on page 210.

5.8 CORE CONCEPTS

Bonds

- A bond is a **formal contractual obligation** to pay an amount of money (called the par value, maturity amount, or face amount) to the holder at a certain date, plus, in most cases, a series of cash interest payments based on a specified percentage (called the stated rate or coupon rate) of the face amount at specified intervals.

    - **Advantages** of bonds to the issuer: Interest paid on debt is tax deductible; basic control of the firm is not shared with debtholders.

    - **Disadvantages** of bonds to the issuer: The payment of interest and principal on debt is a legal obligation; the legal requirement to pay debt service raises a firm's risk level; certain managerial prerogatives are usually given up in the contractual relationship outlined in the bond's indenture contract.

- Bonds come in several **types**: term bond vs. serial bond; variable rate bonds vs. zero-coupon or deep-discount bonds vs. commodity-backed bonds; callable bonds and convertible bonds; mortgage bonds vs. debentures; registered bonds vs. bearer bonds; subordinated debentures vs. second mortgage bonds; income bonds and revenue bonds

- Investors can judge the **creditworthiness** of a bond issue by consulting the **rating** assigned by a bond-rating agency. Investment-grade bonds are considered safe investments and thus have the lowest yields. The highest rating assigned is "triple-A."

- Of primary concern to a bond issuer is the **amount of cash** that (s)he will receive from investors on the day the bonds are sold.

    - If the bonds' stated rate is lower than the market rate, the issuer receives less cash than the par value and the bonds are said to be sold at a **discount**.

    - If the bonds' stated rate is higher than the market rate, the issuer receives more cash than the par value and the bonds are said to be sold at a **premium**.

Common Stock

- The common shareholders are the **owners of the corporation**, and their rights as owners, although reasonably uniform, depend on the laws of the state in which the firm is incorporated. Equity ownership involves risk because holders of common stock are not guaranteed a return and are last in priority in a liquidation.

    - **Advantages** to the issuer: Common stock does not require a fixed dividend; dividends are paid from profits when available; common stock is frequently more attractive to investors than debt because it grows in value with the success of the firm.

    - **Disadvantages** to the issuer: Cash dividends on common stock are not tax-deductible and so must be paid out of after-tax profits; control (voting rights) is usually diluted as more common stock is sold; new common stock sales dilute earnings per share available to existing shareholders; underwriting costs are typically higher for common stock issues.

- Common shareholders ordinarily have **preemptive rights**. Preemptive rights give common shareholders the right to purchase any additional stock issuances in proportion to their current ownership percentages.

- As the corporation's owners, the common shareholders have **voting rights**, that is, they select the firm's board of directors and vote on resolutions.

<u>Preferred Stock</u>

- Preferred stock is a hybrid of debt and equity. It has a fixed charge and increases leverage, but payment of dividends is not an obligation. Also, preferred shareholders stand ahead of common shareholders in priority in the event of corporate bankruptcy.

    • **Advantages:** It is a form of equity and therefore builds the creditworthiness of the firm; control is still held by common shareholders; superior earnings of the firm are usually still reserved for the common shareholders.

    • **Disadvantages:** Cash dividends on preferred stock are not deductible as a tax expense and are paid with taxable income; in periods of economic difficulty, dividends in arrears may create major managerial and financial problems for the firm.

<u>Corporate/Stock Valuation Methods</u>

- **Per-share ratios** relate company financial information to the market price per share.
- **Earnings per share** equals net income available to common shareholders divided by the average number of shares outstanding for the period.
- **Book value per share** equals the amount of net assets available to the shareholders of a given type of stock divided by the number of those shares outstanding.
- **Dividend yield** equals the annual dividend payment divided by the market value per share.
- The **price-earnings (P/E)** ratio equals the market price per share of common stock divided by EPS.
- **Price-book ratio** equals the market price per share of common stock divided by the book value per share.
- **Price-sales ratio** equals the market price per share of common stock divided by sales per share.

<u>Derivatives</u>

- A **derivative instrument** is an investment transaction in which the parties' gain or loss is **derived** from some other economic event, for example, the price of a given stock, a foreign currency exchange rate, or the price of a certain commodity.

- **Hedging** is the process of using offsetting commitments to minimize or avoid the impact of adverse price movements.

    • A person who would like to sell an asset in the future has a **long position** in the asset because (s)he benefits from a rise in value of the asset. To protect against a decline in value, the owner can enter into a short hedge, i.e., obtain an instrument whose value will rise if the asset's value falls.

    • A person who would like to buy an asset in the future has a **short position** in the asset because (s)he benefits from a fall in value of the asset. To protect against a rise in value, the party can enter into a long hedge, i.e., obtain an instrument whose value will rise if the asset's value rises.

- **Options** are the most common form of derivative. A party who buys an option has bought the right to demand that the counterparty (the seller or "writer" of the option) perform some action on or before a specified future date.

    • A **call option** gives the buyer (holder) the **right to purchase** (i.e., the right to "call" for) the underlying asset (stock, currency, commodity, etc.) at a fixed price. Thus, a call option represents a long position to the holder because the holder benefits from a price increase.

    • A **put option** gives the buyer (holder) the **right to sell** (i.e., the right to "put" onto the market) the underlying asset (stock, currency, commodity, etc.) at a fixed price. Thus, a put option represents a short position to the holder because the holder benefits from a price decrease.

- Put-call parity for European options.

  - The basic formula for **put-call parity** is

    Value of call + PV of exercise price = Value of put + Value of underlying

  - This basic formula can be restated to depict a **risk-free return**:

    PV of exercise price = Value of put + Value of underlying − Value of call

- The two most well-known models for **valuing options** are the Black-Scholes formula for call options and the binomial method.

- These factors and their effects can be summarized as follows:

Increase in	Value of call option will	Value of put option will
Exercise price of option	Decrease	Increase
Price of underlying	Increase	Decrease
Interest rates	Increase	Decrease
Time until expiration	Increase	Increase
Volatility of price of underlying	Increase	Increase

- One method of mitigating risk is the **simple forward contract**. The two parties agree that, at a set future date, one of them will perform and the other will pay a specified amount for the performance. The party that has contracted to **buy** the underlying at a future date has taken a **long position**, and the party that has contracted to **deliver** the underlying has taken a **short position**.

- A **futures contract** is a commitment to buy or sell an asset at a fixed price during a specific future month; unlike with a forward contract, the counterparty is unknown. Futures contracts are actively traded on futures exchanges.

- **Swaps** are contracts by which the parties exchange cash flows. Three types are common: interest rate swaps, currency swaps, and credit default swaps.

Other Sources of Long-Term Financing

- A **lease** is a long-term, contractual agreement in which the owner of property (the lessor) allows another party (the lessee) the right to use the property for a stated period in exchange for a stated payment.

- **Convertible securities** are debt or preferred stock securities that contain a provision allowing the holder to convert the securities into some specified number of common shares after a specified time has elapsed.

- A **stock purchase warrant** is, in effect, a call option on the corporation's common stock. After a specified time has elapsed, the holder of the warrant can exchange the warrant plus a specified amount of cash for some number of shares of common stock.

- **Retained earnings** is the cumulative accrual-basis income of the corporation minus amounts paid out in cash dividends minus amounts reclassified as additional paid-in capital from stock dividends.

Cost of Capital -- Current

- A corporation's investors' required rate of return (also called their opportunity cost of capital) in turn becomes the **firm's cost of capital**.

  - The component cost of **debt** is the after-tax interest rate on the debt:

    Coupon rate × (1.0 − Marginal tax rate)

  - The component cost of **preferred stock** is computed using the dividend yield ratio:

    Cash dividend ÷ Market price of stock

- The component cost of **common stock** is also computed using the dividend yield ratio:

  Cash dividend ÷ Market price of stock

- The component cost of **retained earnings** is considered to be the same as that for common stock.

■ Corporate management usually designates a **target capital structure** for the firm; i.e., the proportions that each component of capital should comprise in the overall combination. An example might be 10% debt, 20% preferred stock, and 70% common stock.

■ A firm's **weighted-average cost of capital (WACC)** is a single, composite rate of return on its combined components of capital. The weights are based on the components' respective **market values**, not book values, because market value provides the best information about investors' expectations.

■ Standard financial theory provides a model for the **optimal capital structure** of every firm. This model holds that shareholder wealth-maximization results from **minimizing the weighted-average cost of capital**.

Cost of Capital -- New

■ The **marginal cost of capital** is the cost to the firm of the next dollar of new capital raised after existing internal sources are exhausted. Each additional dollar raised becomes increasingly expensive as investors demand higher returns to compensate for increased risk.

■ The cost of **new capital** (also called **external capital**) is the ratio of what the firm must pay to what the firm gets.

- Because of interest rate fluctuations, the **cost of new debt** will rarely be the historical, or embedded, rate.

  Annual interest ÷ Net issue proceeds

- The **cost of new preferred stock** is thus calculated:

  Next dividend ÷ Net issue proceeds

- The **cost of new common stock** employs a form of the dividend growth model:

  (Next dividend ÷ Net issue proceeds) + Dividend growth rate

QUESTIONS

5.1 Bonds

1. Short-term interest rates are

   A. Usually lower than long-term rates.

   B. Usually higher than long-term rates.

   C. Lower than long-term rates during periods of high inflation only.

   D. Not significantly related to long-term rates.

Answer (A) is correct. *(CMA, adapted)*

REQUIRED: The true statement about short-term interest rates.

DISCUSSION: Historically, one facet of the term structure of interest rates (the relationship of yield and time to maturity) is that short-term interest rates have ordinarily been lower than long-term rates. One reason is that less risk is involved in the short run. Moreover, future expectations concerning interest rates affect the term structure. Most economists believe that a long-term interest rate is an average of future expected short-term interest rates. For this reason, the yield curve will slope upward if future rates are expected to rise, downward if interest rates are anticipated to fall, and remain flat if investors think the rate is stable. Future inflation is incorporated into this relationship. Another consideration is liquidity preference: investors in an uncertain world will accept lower rates on short-term investments because of their greater liquidity, whereas business debtors often prefer to pay higher rates on long-term debt to avoid the hazards of short-term maturities.

Answer (B) is incorrect. Short-term rates are usually lower than long-term rates. Answer (C) is incorrect. Short-term rates are more likely to be greater than long-term rates if current levels of inflation are high. Answer (D) is incorrect. Long-term rates may be viewed as short-term rates adjusted by a risk factor.

2. Which one of the following characteristics distinguishes income bonds from other bonds?

   A. The bondholder is guaranteed an income over the life of the security.

   B. By promising a return to the bondholder, an income bond is junior to preferred and common stock.

   C. Income bonds are junior to subordinated debt but senior to preferred and common stock.

   D. Income bonds pay interest only if the issuing company has earned the interest.

Answer (D) is correct. *(CMA, adapted)*
   REQUIRED: The characteristic of income bonds.
   DISCUSSION: An income bond is one that pays interest only if the issuing company has earned the interest, although the principal must still be paid on the due date. Such bonds are riskier than normal bonds.
   Answer (A) is incorrect. Bondholders will receive an income only if the issuing company earns sufficient income to pay the interest. Answer (B) is incorrect. All bonds have priority over preferred and common stock. Answer (C) is incorrect. Subordinated debt is junior to nonsubordinated debt.

3. If Brewer Corporation's bonds are currently yielding 8% in the marketplace, why is the firm's cost of debt lower?

   A. Market interest rates have increased.

   B. Additional debt can be issued more cheaply than the original debt.

   C. There should be no difference; cost of debt is the same as the bonds' market yield.

   D. Interest is deductible for tax purposes.

Answer (D) is correct. *(CMA, adapted)*
   REQUIRED: The reason a firm's cost of debt is lower than its current market yield.
   DISCUSSION: Because interest is deductible for tax purposes, the actual cost of debt capital is the net effect of the interest payment and the offsetting tax deduction. The actual cost of debt equals the interest rate times (1 – the marginal tax rate). Thus, if a firm with an 8% market rate is in a 40% tax bracket, the net cost of the debt capital is 4.8% [8% × (1.0 – .40)].
   Answer (A) is incorrect. The tax deduction always causes the market yield rate to be higher than the cost of debt capital. Answer (B) is incorrect. Additional debt may or may not be issued more cheaply than earlier debt, depending upon the interest rates in the market place. Answer (C) is incorrect. The cost of debt is less than the yield rate given that bond interest is tax deductible.

4. Debentures are

   A. Income bonds that require interest payments only when earnings permit.

   B. Subordinated debt and rank behind convertible bonds.

   C. Bonds secured by the full faith and credit of the issuing firm.

   D. A form of lease financing similar to equipment trust certificates.

Answer (C) is correct. *(CMA, adapted)*
   REQUIRED: The true statement about debentures.
   DISCUSSION: Debentures are unsecured bonds. Although no assets are mortgaged as security for the bonds, debentures are secured by the full faith and credit of the issuing firm. Debentures are a general obligation of the borrower. Only companies with the best credit ratings can issue debentures because only the company's credit rating and reputation secure the bonds.
   Answer (A) is incorrect. Debentures must pay interest regardless of earnings levels. Answer (B) is incorrect. Debentures are not subordinated except to the extent of assets mortgaged against other bond issues. Debentures are a general obligation of the borrower and rank equally with convertible bonds. Answer (D) is incorrect. Debentures have nothing to do with lease financing. Debentures are not secured by assets.

5. Serial bonds are attractive to investors because

   A. All bonds in the issue mature on the same date.

   B. The yield to maturity is the same for all bonds in the issue.

   C. Investors can choose the maturity that suits their financial needs.

   D. The coupon rate on these bonds is adjusted to the maturity date.

Answer (C) is correct. *(CMA, adapted)*
   REQUIRED: The reason serial bonds are attractive to investors.
   DISCUSSION: Serial bonds have staggered maturities; that is, they mature over a period (series) of years. Thus, investors can choose the maturity date that meets their investment needs. For example, an investor who will have a child starting college in 16 years can choose bonds that mature in 16 years.
   Answer (A) is incorrect. Serial bonds mature on different dates. Answer (B) is incorrect. Bonds maturing on different dates may have different yields, or they may be the same. Usually, the earlier date maturities carry slightly lower yields than the later maturities. Answer (D) is incorrect. The coupon rate is the same for all bonds; only the selling price and yield differ.

6. From an investor's viewpoint, the **least** risky type of bond in which to invest is a(n)

    A. Debenture bond.

    B. Deep discount bond.

    C. Income bond.

    D. Secured bond.

Answer (D) is correct. *(CMA, adapted)*
    REQUIRED: The least risky type of bond from an investor's viewpoint.
    DISCUSSION: A secured bond is backed by tangible property, making it the safest type for the investor of the four listed.
    Answer (A) is incorrect. A debenture bond is backed only by the borrower's general credit, not by specific collateral. Answer (B) is incorrect. A deep discount bond is a bond sold for much less than its face value. Answer (C) is incorrect. An income bond pays interest only if the issuing company has earnings; such bonds are riskier than other bonds.

7. All of the following may reduce the coupon rate on a bond issued at par except a

    A. Sinking fund.

    B. Call provision.

    C. Change in rating from Aa to Aaa.

    D. Conversion option.

Answer (B) is correct. *(CMA, adapted)*
    REQUIRED: The item that will not reduce the coupon rate on a bond issued at par.
    DISCUSSION: A bond issued at par may carry a lower coupon rate than other similar bonds in the market if it has some feature that makes it more attractive to investors. For example, a sinking fund reduces default risk. Hence, investors may require a lower risk premium and be willing to accept a lower coupon rate. Other features attractive to investors include covenants in the bond indenture that restrict risky undertakings by the issuer and an option to convert the debt instruments to equity securities. The opportunity to profit from appreciation of the firm's stock justifies a lower coupon rate. An improvement in a bond's rating from Aa to Aaa (the highest possible) also justifies reduction in the risk premium and a lower coupon rate. However, a call provision is usually undesirable to investors. The issuer may take advantage of a decline in interest rates to recall the bond and stop paying interest before maturity.

5.2 Equity

8. In general, it is more expensive for a company to finance with equity capital than with debt capital because

    A. Long-term bonds have a maturity date and must therefore be repaid in the future.

    B. Investors are exposed to greater risk with equity capital.

    C. Equity capital is in greater demand than debt capital.

    D. Dividends fluctuate to a greater extent than interest rates.

Answer (B) is correct. *(CMA, adapted)*
    REQUIRED: The reason equity financing is more expensive than debt financing.
    DISCUSSION: Providers of equity capital are exposed to more risk than are lenders because the firm is not obligated to pay them a return. Also, in case of liquidation, creditors are paid before equity investors. Thus, equity financing is more expensive than debt because equity investors require a higher return to compensate for the greater risk assumed.
    Answer (A) is incorrect. The obligation to repay at a specific maturity date reduces the risk to investors and thus the required return. Answer (C) is incorrect. The demand for equity capital is directly related to its greater cost to the issuer. Answer (D) is incorrect. Dividends are based on managerial discretion and may rarely change; interest rates, however, fluctuate daily based upon market conditions.

9. The par value of a common stock represents

    A. The estimated market value of the stock when it was issued.

    B. The liability ceiling of a shareholder when a company undergoes bankruptcy proceedings.

    C. The total value of the stock that must be entered in the issuing corporation's records.

    D. A theoretical value of $100 per share of stock with any differences entered in the issuing corporation's records as discount or premium on common stock.

Answer (B) is correct. *(CMA, adapted)*
    REQUIRED: The amount represented by the par value of common stock.
    DISCUSSION: Par value represents a stock's legal capital. It is an arbitrary value assigned to stock before it is issued. Par value represents a shareholder's liability ceiling because, as long as the par value has been paid in to the corporation, the shareholders obtain the benefits of limited liability.
    Answer (A) is incorrect. Par value is rarely the same as market value. Normally, market value will be equal to or greater than par value, but there is no relationship between the two. Answer (C) is incorrect. All assets received for stock must be entered into a corporation's records. The amount received is very rarely the par value. Answer (D) is incorrect. Par value can be any amount more or less than $100.

10. The equity section of Smith Corporation's Statement of Financial Position is presented below.

Preferred stock, $100 par	$12,000,000
Common stock, $5 par	10,000,000
Paid-in capital in excess of par	18,000,000
Retained earnings	9,000,000
Net worth	$49,000,000

The common shareholders of Smith Corporation have preemptive rights. If Smith Corporation issues 400,000 additional shares of common stock at $6 per share, a current holder of 20,000 shares of Smith Corporation's common stock must be given the option to buy

- A. 1,000 additional shares.
- B. 3,774 additional shares.
- C. 4,000 additional shares.
- D. 3,333 additional shares.

Answer (C) is correct. *(CMA, adapted)*
REQUIRED: The new shares that a shareholder may buy given preemptive rights.
DISCUSSION: Common shareholders usually have preemptive rights, which means they have first right to purchase any new issues of stock in proportion to their current ownership percentages. The purpose of a preemptive right is to allow stockholders to maintain their current percentages of ownership. Given that Smith had 2,000,000 shares outstanding ($10,000,000 ÷ $5 par), an investor with 20,000 shares has a 1% ownership. Hence, this investor must be allowed to purchase 4,000 (400,000 shares × 1%) of the additional shares.
Answer (A) is incorrect. To arrive at 1,000 additional shares, the number of shares currently outstanding was incorrectly calculated as 8,000,000 [($12,000,000 + $10,000,000 + $18,000,000) ÷ $5]. Answer (B) is incorrect. The investor would be allowed to purchase 1% of any new issues. Answer (D) is incorrect. The investor would be allowed to purchase 1% of any new issues.

11. A financial manager usually prefers to issue preferred stock rather than debt because

- A. Payments to preferred stockholders are not considered fixed payments.
- B. The cost of fixed debt is less expensive since it is tax deductible even if a sinking fund is required to retire the debt.
- C. The preferred dividend is often cumulative, whereas interest payments are not.
- D. In a legal sense, preferred stock is equity; therefore, dividend payments are not legal obligations.

Answer (D) is correct. *(CMA, adapted)*
REQUIRED: The reason a financial manager usually would rather issue preferred stock instead of debt.
DISCUSSION: For a financial manager, preferred stock is preferable to debt because dividends do not have to be paid on preferred stock, but failure to pay interest on debt could lead to bankruptcy. Thus, preferred stock is less risky than debt. However, debt has some advantages over preferred stock, the most notable of which is that interest payments are tax deductible. Preferred stock dividends are not.
Answer (A) is incorrect. Preferred dividends are viewed as fixed payments since they must be made before any dividends or distributions in liquidation can be made to common shareholders. Answer (B) is incorrect. It states a reason to issue debt, not preferred stock. Answer (C) is incorrect. In the sense that they cannot be avoided, interest payments are cumulative.

5.3 Corporate/Stock Valuation Methods

12. The equity section of Smith Corporation's Statement of Financial Position is presented below.

Preferred stock, $100 par	$12,000,000
Common stock, $5 par	10,000,000
Paid-in capital in excess of par	18,000,000
Retained earnings	9,000,000
Net worth	$49,000,000

The book value per share of Smith Corporation's common stock is

- A. $18.50
- B. $5.00
- C. $14.00
- D. $100

Answer (A) is correct. *(CMA, adapted)*
REQUIRED: The book value per share of common stock.
DISCUSSION: The book value per common share equals the net assets (equity) attributable to common shareholders divided by the common shares outstanding, or $18.50 [($10,000,000 common stock + $18,000,000 additional paid-in capital + $9,000,000 RE) ÷ ($10,000,000 ÷ $5 par)].
Answer (B) is incorrect. The amount of $5.00 is the par value per share. Answer (C) is incorrect. The amount of $14.00 fails to include retained earnings in the portion of equity attributable to common shareholders. Answer (D) is incorrect. The amount of $100 is the par value of a preferred share.

Questions 13 and 14 are based on the following information. The Dawson Corporation projects the following for the year:

Earnings before interest and taxes	$35 million
Interest expense	$5 million
Preferred stock dividends	$4 million
Common stock dividend-payout ratio	30%
Common shares outstanding	2 million
Effective corporate income tax rate	40%

13. The expected common stock dividend per share for Dawson Corporation is

A. $2.34

B. $2.70

C. $1.80

D. $2.10

Answer (D) is correct. *(CMA, adapted)*
REQUIRED: The expected common stock dividend per share.
DISCUSSION: The company's net income is $18,000,000 [($35,000,000 EBIT – $5,000,000 interest) × (1.0 – .4 tax rate)]. Thus, the earnings available to common shareholders equal $14,000,000 ($18,000,000 – $4,000,000 preferred dividends), and EPS is $7 ($14,000,000 ÷ 2,000,000 common shares). Given a dividend-payout ratio of 30%, the dividend to common shareholders is expected to be $2.10 per share ($7 × 30%).
Answer (A) is incorrect. The amount of $2.34 results from treating preferred dividends as tax deductible. Answer (B) is incorrect. The amount of $2.70 ignores the effect of preferred dividends. Answer (C) is incorrect. The amount of $1.80 is based on a 60% effective tax rate and ignores the effect of preferred dividends.

14. If Dawson Corporation's common stock is expected to trade at a price-earnings ratio of 8, the market price per share (to the nearest dollar) would be

A. $104

B. $56

C. $72

D. $68

Answer (B) is correct. *(CMA, adapted)*
REQUIRED: The market price per share given the P-E ratio.
DISCUSSION: Net income is $18,000,000 [($35,000,000 EBIT – $5,000,000 interest) × (1.0 – .4 tax rate)], and EPS is $7 [($18,000,000 NI – $4,000,000 preferred dividends) ÷ 2,000,000 common shares]. Consequently, the market price is $56 ($7 EPS × 8 P-E ratio).
Answer (A) is incorrect. The amount of $104 ignores income taxes. Answer (C) is incorrect. The amount of $72 ignores the effect of preferred dividends. Answer (D) is incorrect. The amount of $68 ignores the deductibility of interest.

5.4 Derivatives

15. An automobile company that uses the futures market to set the price of steel to protect a profit against price increases is an example of

A. A short hedge.

B. A long hedge.

C. Selling futures to protect the company from loss.

D. Selling futures to protect against price declines.

Answer (B) is correct. *(Publisher, adapted)*
REQUIRED: The example of the use of the futures market to protect a profit.
DISCUSSION: A change in prices can be minimized or avoided by hedging. Hedging is the process of using offsetting commitments to minimize or avoid the impact of adverse price movements. The automobile company desires to stabilize the price of steel so that its cost to the company will not rise and cut into profits. Accordingly, the automobile company uses the futures market to create a long hedge, which is a futures contract that is purchased to protect against price increases.
Answer (A) is incorrect. A short hedge is a futures contract that is sold to protect against price declines. The automobile company wishes to protect itself against price increases. Answer (C) is incorrect. The automobile company needs to purchase futures in order to protect itself from loss, not sell futures. Selling futures protects against price declines. Answer (D) is incorrect. It is the definition of a short hedge, which is used for avoiding price declines. The automobile company wants to protect itself against price increases.

16. The use of derivatives to either hedge or speculate results in

- A. Increased risk regardless of motive.
- B. Decreased risk regardless of motive.
- C. Offsetting risk when hedging and increased risk when speculating.
- D. Offsetting risk when speculating and increased risk when hedging.

Answer (C) is correct. *(Publisher, adapted)*
REQUIRED: The effects on risk of hedging and speculating.
DISCUSSION: Derivatives, including options and futures, are contracts between the parties who contract. Unlike stocks and bonds, they are not claims on business assets. A futures contract is entered into as either a speculation or a hedge. Speculation involves the assumption of risk in the hope of gaining from price movements. Hedging is the process of using offsetting commitments to minimize or avoid the impact of adverse price movements.
Answer (A) is incorrect. Hedging decreases risk by using offsetting commitments that avoid the impact of adverse price movements. Answer (B) is incorrect. Speculation involves the assumption of risk in the hope of gaining from price movements. Answer (D) is incorrect. Speculating increases risk while hedging offsets risk.

Questions 17 and 18 are based on the following information. AA Company has purchased one ordinary share of QQ Company and one put option. It has also sold one call option. The options are written on one ordinary share of QQ Company and have the same maturity date and exercise price. The exercise price (US $40) is the same as the share price. Moreover, the options are exercisable only at the expiration date.

---

17. Assume that the value of a share of QQ Company common stock at the expiration date is either $30 or $45. The difference in the net payoff on the portfolio because of a difference in the stock price at the maturity date is

- A. $10.00
- B. $7.50
- C. $5.00
- D. $0

Answer (D) is correct. *(Publisher, adapted)*
REQUIRED: The difference in the net payoff on the portfolio because of a difference in the stock price at the maturity date.
DISCUSSION: If the stock price at the maturity date is $30, AA Company will have a share of stock worth $30 and a put option worth $10 ($40 exercise price – $30 stock price). The call option will be worthless. Hence, the net payoff is $40 ($30 + $10). If the stock price at the maturity date is $45, the share of stock will be worth $45, the put will be worthless, and the loss on the call will be $5 ($45 – $40). Thus, the net payoff will be $40 ($45 – $5). Consequently, the difference in the net payoff on the portfolio because of a difference in the stock price at the maturity date is $0 ($40 – $40). The portfolio has the same value at the maturity date regardless of the price of the stock.

---

18. Assuming the present value of the exercise price is $36 and the value of the call is $4.50, the value of the put in accordance with the put-call parity theorem is

- A. $4.50
- B. $4.00
- C. $.50
- D. $0

Answer (C) is correct. *(Publisher, adapted)*
REQUIRED: The value of the put in accordance with the put-call parity theorem.
DISCUSSION: For European options, given market equilibrium for all relevant prices (no arbitrage possibilities), equal exercise prices for the put and the call, and the same expiration date, the put-call parity theorem states that a fixed relationship applies to the market values of the put and call options on a security. For example, a strategy of selling one call option, buying one share of the stock, and buying one put option should result in a risk-free return. The gain (loss) from the stock and the put should equal the gain (loss) on the call. If V_S is the value of the stock, V_P is the value of the put, V_C is the value of the call, and PV_E is the present value of the exercise price (the time interval is the time to expiration), the formula for put-call parity may be stated as follows:

$$PV_E = V_P + V_S - V_C$$

Accordingly, the value of the put is $.50 ($36 + $4.50 – $40).
Answer (A) is incorrect. The amount of $4.50 is the value of the call. Answer (B) is incorrect. The amount of $4.00 is the difference between the exercise price and its present value. Answer (D) is incorrect. The put has a value of $.50.

19. A forward contract involves a commitment today to purchase a product

A. On a specific future date at a price to be determined some time in the future.

B. At some time during the current day at its present price.

C. On a specific future date at a price determined today.

D. Only when its price increases above its current exercise price.

20. If a corporation holds a forward contract for the delivery of U.S. Treasury bonds in 6 months and, during those 6 months, interest rates decline, at the end of the 6 months the value of the forward contract will have

A. Decreased.

B. Increased.

C. Remained constant.

D. Any of the answers may be correct, depending on the extent of the decline in interest rates.

21. When a firm finances each asset with a financial instrument of the same approximate maturity as the life of the asset, it is applying

A. Working capital management.

B. Return maximization.

C. Financial leverage.

D. A hedging approach.

22. On October 1, Year 1, Bordeaux, Inc., a calendar-year-end firm, invested in a derivative designed to hedge the risk of changes in fair value of certain assets, currently valued at $1.5 million. The derivative is structured to result in an effective hedge. However, some ineffectiveness may result. On December 31, Year 1, the fair value of the hedged assets has decreased by $350,000; the fair value of the derivative has increased by $325,000. Bordeaux should recognize a net effect on Year 1 earnings of

A. $0

B. $25,000

C. $325,000

D. $350,000

Answer (C) is correct. *(Publisher, adapted)*
REQUIRED: The terms of a forward contract.
DISCUSSION: A forward contract is an executory contract in which the parties involved agree to the terms of a purchase and a sale, but performance is deferred. Accordingly, a forward contract involves a commitment today to purchase a product on a specific future date at a price determined today.
Answer (A) is incorrect. The price of a future contract is determined on the day of commitment, not some time in the future. Answer (B) is incorrect. Performance is deferred in a future contract, and the price of the product is not necessarily its present price. The price can be any price determined on the day of commitment. Answer (D) is incorrect. A forward contract is a firm commitment to purchase a product. It is not based on a contingency. Also, a forward contract does not involve an exercise price (exercise price is in an option contract).

Answer (B) is correct. *(Publisher, adapted)*
REQUIRED: The impact of an interest rate decline on the value of a forward contract.
DISCUSSION: Interest rate futures contracts involve risk-free bonds, such as U.S. Treasury bonds. When interest rates decrease over the period of a forward contract, the value of the bonds and the forward contract increase.
Answer (A) is incorrect. The value of the forward contract will increase when interest rates decrease. Answer (C) is incorrect. The value of the forward contract will increase when interest rates decrease. Answer (D) is incorrect. Any decline in interest rates increases the value of the bonds.

Answer (D) is correct. *(CMA, adapted)*
REQUIRED: The technique used when a firm finances a specific asset with a financial instrument having the same approximate maturity as the life of the asset.
DISCUSSION: Maturity matching, or equalizing the life of an asset and the debt instrument used to finance that asset, is a hedging approach. The basic concept is that the company has the entire life of the asset to recover the amount invested before having to pay the lender.
Answer (A) is incorrect. Working capital management is short-term asset management. Answer (B) is incorrect. Return maximization is more aggressive than maturity matching. It entails using the lowest cost forms of financing. Answer (C) is incorrect. Financial leverage is the relationship between debt and equity financing.

Answer (B) is correct. *(Publisher, adapted)*
REQUIRED: The net effect on earnings of a partially effective hedge of changes in fair value of a recognized asset.
DISCUSSION: A hedge of an exposure to changes in the fair value of a recognized asset or liability is classified as a fair value hedge. Gains and losses arising from changes in fair value of a derivative classified as a fair value hedge are included in the determination of earnings in the period of change. They are offset by losses or gains on the hedged item attributable to the risk being hedged. Thus, earnings of the period of change are affected only by the net gain or loss attributable to the ineffective aspect of the hedge. The ineffective portion is equal to $25,000 ($350,000 – $325,000).
Answer (A) is incorrect. The effect on earnings is equal to the ineffective portion of the hedge. Answer (C) is incorrect. It is the gross effect of the increase in fair value of the derivative. Answer (D) is incorrect. It is the gross effect of the decrease in fair value of the hedged assets.

5.5 Other Sources of Long-Term Financing

23. A major use of warrants in financing is to

A. Lower the cost of debt.

B. Avoid dilution of earnings per share.

C. Maintain managerial control.

D. Permit the buy-back of bonds before maturity.

Answer (A) is correct. *(CMA, adapted)*
REQUIRED: The major use of warrants in financing.
DISCUSSION: Warrants are long-term options that give holders the right to buy common stock in the future at a specific price. If the market price goes up, the holders of warrants will exercise their rights to buy stock at the special price. If the market price does not exceed the exercise price, the warrants will lapse. Issuers of debt sometimes attach stock purchase warrants to debt instruments as an inducement to investors. The investor then has the security of fixed-return debt plus the possibility for large gains if stock prices increase significantly. If warrants are attached, debt can sell at an interest rate slightly lower than the market rate.
Answer (B) is incorrect. Outstanding warrants dilute earnings per share. They are included in the denominator of the EPS calculation even if they have not been exercised. Answer (C) is incorrect. Warrants can, if exercised, result in a dilution of management's holdings. Answer (D) is incorrect. A call provision in a bond indenture, not the use of warrants, permits the buyback of bonds.

5.6 Cost of Capital -- Current

24. The theory underlying the cost of capital is primarily concerned with the cost of

A. Long-term funds and old funds.

B. Short-term funds and new funds.

C. Long-term funds and new funds.

D. Short-term funds and old funds.

Answer (C) is correct. *(CMA, adapted)*
REQUIRED: The true statement about the theory underlying the cost of capital.
DISCUSSION: The theory underlying the cost of capital is based primarily on the cost of long-term funds and the acquisition of new funds. The reason is that long-term funds are used to finance long-term investments. For an investment alternative to be viable, the return on the investment must be greater than the cost of the funds used. The objective in short-term borrowing is different. Short-term loans are used to meet working capital needs and not to finance long-term investments.
Answer (A) is incorrect. The concern is with the cost of new funds; the cost of old funds is a sunk cost and of no relevance for decision-making purposes. Answer (B) is incorrect. The cost of short-term funds is not usually a concern for investment purposes. Answer (D) is incorrect. The cost of old funds is a sunk cost and of no relevance for decision-making purposes. Similarly, short-term funds are used for working capital or other temporary purposes, and there is less concern with the cost of capital and the way it compares with the return earned on the assets borrowed.

25. Osgood Products has announced that it plans to finance future investments so that the firm will achieve an optimum capital structure. Which one of the following corporate objectives is consistent with this announcement?

A. Maximize earnings per share.

B. Minimize the cost of debt.

C. Maximize the net worth of the firm.

D. Minimize the cost of equity.

Answer (C) is correct. *(CMA, adapted)*
REQUIRED: The consistent corporate objective.
DISCUSSION: Financial structure is the composition of the financing sources of the assets of a firm. Traditionally, the financial structure consists of current liabilities, long-term debt, retained earnings, and stock. For most firms, the optimum structure includes a combination of debt and equity. Debt is cheaper than equity, but excessive use of debt increases the firm's risk and drives up the weighted-average cost of capital.
Answer (A) is incorrect. The maximization of EPS may not always suggest the best capital structure. Answer (B) is incorrect. The minimization of debt cost may not be optimal; as long as the firm can earn more on debt capital than it pays in interest, debt financing may be indicated. Answer (D) is incorrect. Minimizing the cost of equity may signify overly conservative management.

Questions 26 and 27 are based on the following information.

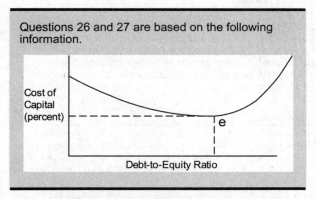

26. In referring to the graph of a firm's cost of capital, if e is the optimal position, which one of the following statements best explains the saucer or U-shaped curve?

A. The composition of debt and equity does not affect the firm's cost of capital.

B. The cost of capital is almost always favorably influenced by increases in financial leverage.

C. The cost of capital is almost always negatively influenced by increases in financial leverage.

D. Use of at least some debt financing will enhance the value of the firm.

Answer (D) is correct. *(CMA, adapted)*
REQUIRED: The best explanation of the U-shaped curve in a cost-of-capital graph.
DISCUSSION: The U-shaped curve indicates that the cost of capital is quite high when the debt-to-equity ratio is quite low. As debt increases, the cost of capital declines as long as the cost of debt is less than that of equity. Eventually, the decline in the cost of capital levels off because the cost of debt ultimately rises as more debt is used. Additional increases in debt (relative to equity) will then increase the cost of capital. The implication is that some debt is present in the optimal capital structure because the cost of capital initially declines when debt is added. However, a point is reached (e) at which debt becomes excessive and the cost of capital begins to rise.
Answer (A) is incorrect. The composition of the capital structure affects the cost of capital since the components have different costs. Answer (B) is incorrect. The cost of debt does not remain constant as financial leverage increases. Eventually, that cost also increases. Answer (C) is incorrect. Increased leverage is initially favorable.

27. In referring to the graph of a firm's cost of capital, if e is the optimal position, which one of the following statements best explains the saucer or U-shaped curve?

A. The cost of capital is almost always favorably influenced by increases in financial leverage.

B. The cost of capital is almost always negatively influenced by increases in financial leverage.

C. The financial markets will penalize firms that borrow even in moderate amounts.

D. Use of at least some debt financing will enhance the value of the firm.

Answer (D) is correct. *(CMA, adapted)*
REQUIRED: The best explanation of the U-shaped curve in a cost-of-capital graph.
DISCUSSION: The U-shaped curve indicates that the cost of capital is quite high when the debt-to-equity ratio is quite low. As debt increases, the cost of capital declines as long as the cost of debt is less than that of equity. Eventually, the decline in the cost of capital levels off because the cost of debt ultimately rises as more debt is used. Additional increases in debt (relative to equity) will then increase the cost of capital. The implication is that some debt is present in the optimal capital structure because the cost of capital initially declines when debt is added. However, a point is reached (e) at which debt becomes excessive and the cost of capital begins to rise.
Answer (A) is incorrect. The cost of debt does not remain constant as financial leverage increases. Eventually, that cost also increases. Answer (B) is incorrect. Increased leverage is initially favorable. Answer (C) is incorrect. The initial decline in the U-shaped graph indicates that the financial markets reward moderate levels of debt.

28. If k is the cost of debt and t is the marginal tax rate, the after-tax cost of debt, k_i, is best represented by the formula

A. $k_i = k \div t$

B. $k_i = k \div (1 - t)$

C. $k_i = k(t)$

D. $k_i = k(1 - t)$

Answer (D) is correct. *(CMA, adapted)*
REQUIRED: The formula representing the after-tax cost of debt.
DISCUSSION: The after-tax cost of debt is the cost of debt times the quantity one minus the tax rate. For example, the after-tax cost of a 10% bond is 7% [10% × (1 – 30%)] if the tax rate is 30%.
Answer (A) is incorrect. The after-tax cost of debt is the cost of debt times the quantity one minus the tax rate. Answer (B) is incorrect. The after-tax cost of debt is the cost of debt times the quantity one minus the tax rate. Answer (C) is incorrect. The cost of debt times the marginal tax rate equals the tax savings from issuing debt.

29. Hi-Tech, Inc., has determined that it can minimize its weighted average cost of capital (WACC) by using a debt-equity ratio of 2/3. If the firm's cost of debt is 9% before taxes, the cost of equity is estimated to be 12% before taxes, and the tax rate is 40%, what is the firm's WACC?

A. 6.48%

B. 7.92%

C. 9.36%

D. 10.80%

Answer (C) is correct. *(CMA, adapted)*
REQUIRED: The firm's weighted-average cost of capital.
DISCUSSION: A firm's weighted-average cost of capital (WACC) is derived by weighting the (after-tax) cost of each component of the financing structure by its proportion of the financing structure as a whole. Hi-Tech's WACC can be calculated as follows:

Component	Weight		Component Cost		Totals
Debt	40%	×	5.4%	=	2.16%
Equity	60%	×	12.0%	=	7.20%
					9.36%

$$\text{WACC} = 9.36\% = \left(\frac{3}{5} \times 12\%\right) + \left\{\frac{2}{5} \times \left[9\% \times (1 - 0.4)\right]\right\}$$

Answer (A) is incorrect. Improperly subtracting the effect of taxes from the cost of equity results in 6.48%. Answer (B) is incorrect. Improperly subtracting the effect of taxes from equity, but not from debt, results in 7.92%. Answer (D) is incorrect. Improperly using the before-tax cost of debt results in 10.80%.

5.7 Cost of Capital -- New

30. A firm's new financing will be in proportion to the market value of its current financing shown below.

	Carrying Amount ($000 Omitted)
Long-term debt	$7,000
Preferred stock (100,000 shares)	1,000
Common stock (200,000 shares)	7,000

The firm's bonds are currently selling at 80% of par, generating a current market yield of 9%, and the corporation has a 40% tax rate. The preferred stock is selling at its par value and pays a 6% dividend. The common stock has a current market value of $40 and is expected to pay a $1.20 per share dividend this fiscal year. Dividend growth is expected to be 10% per year, and flotation costs are negligible. The firm's weighted-average cost of capital is (round calculations to tenths of a percent)

A. 13.0%

B. 8.13%

C. 9.6%

D. 9.0%

Answer (C) is correct. *(CMA, adapted)*
REQUIRED: The weighted-average cost of capital.
DISCUSSION: The first step is to determine the component costs of each form of capital. Multiplying the current yield of 9% (since the coupon rate is not given) times one minus the tax rate (1.0 – .40 = .60) results in an after-tax cost of debt of 5.4% (9% × .60). Since the preferred stock is trading at par, the component cost is 6% (the annual dividend rate). The component cost of common equity is calculated using the dividend growth model, which combines the dividend yield with the growth rate. Dividing the $1.20 dividend by the $40 market price produces a dividend yield of 3%. Adding the 3% dividend yield and the 10% growth rate gives a 13% component cost of common equity.
Once the costs of the three types of capital have been computed, the next step is to weight them according to their current market values. The market value of the long-term debt is 80% of its carrying amount, or $5,600,000 ($7,000,000 × 80%). The $1,000,000 of preferred stock is selling at par. The common stock has a current market value of $8,000,000 (200,000 shares × $40).

Long-term debt	$ 5,600,000	×	5.4%	=	$ 302,400
Preferred stock	1,000,000	×	6.0%	=	60,000
Common stock	8,000,000	×	13.0%	=	1,040,000
Totals	$14,600,000				$1,402,400

Thus, the weighted-average cost of capital is 9.6% ($1,402,000 ÷ $14,600,000).
Answer (A) is incorrect. This percentage is the cost of equity. Answer (B) is incorrect. This percentage is the simple average. Answer (D) is incorrect. This percentage is based on carrying amounts.

31. A preferred stock is sold for $101 per share, has a face value of $100 per share, underwriting fees of $5 per share, and annual dividends of $10 per share. If the tax rate is 40%, the cost of funds (capital) for the preferred stock is

A. 4.2%

B. 6.25%

C. 10.0%

D. 10.4%

Answer (D) is correct. *(CMA, adapted)*
REQUIRED: The cost of capital for a preferred stock issue.
DISCUSSION: The cost of capital for new preferred stock is equal to the dividend on the stock divided by the net issue proceeds [$10 ÷ ($101 – $5) = 10.4%]. Because dividends on preferred stock are not deductible for tax purposes, the income tax rate is irrelevant.
Answer (A) is incorrect. This figure results from improperly multiplying the dividends by the tax rate. Answer (B) is incorrect. This figure results from improperly multiplying the dividends by the tax rate. Answer (C) is incorrect. This figure results from improperly basing the calculation on par value funds received.

Questions 32 and 33 are based on the following information. DQZ Telecom is considering a project for the coming year that will cost $50 million. DQZ plans to use the following combination of debt and equity to finance the investment.

- Issue $15 million of 20-year bonds at a price of $101, with a coupon rate of 8%, and flotation costs of 2% of par.
- Use $35 million of funds generated from earnings.
- The equity market is expected to earn 12%. U.S. Treasury bonds are currently yielding 5%. The beta coefficient for DQZ is estimated to be .60. DQZ is subject to an effective corporate income tax rate of 40%.

32. The before-tax cost of DQZ's planned debt financing, net of flotation costs, in the first year is

A. 11.80%

B. 8.08%

C. 10.00%

D. 7.92%

Answer (B) is correct. *(CMA, adapted)*
REQUIRED: The before-tax cost of the planned debt financing, net of flotation costs.
DISCUSSION: The cost of new debt equals the annual interest divided by the net issue proceeds. The annual interest is $1.2 million ($15,000,000 × .08 coupon rate). The proceeds amount to $14,850,000 [($15,000,000 × 1.01) market price – ($15,000,000 × .02) flotation costs]. Thus, the company is paying $1.2 million annually for the use of $14,850,000, a cost of 8.08% ($1,200,000 ÷ $14,850,000).
Answer (A) is incorrect. The contract rate is 8% annually. Answer (C) is incorrect. This percentage is the sum of the coupon rate and the flotation rate. Answer (D) is incorrect. This percentage ignores the 2% flotation costs.

33. Assume that the after-tax cost of debt is 7% and the cost of equity is 12%. Determine the weighted-average cost of capital to DQZ.

A. 10.50%

B. 8.50%

C. 9.50%

D. 6.30%

Answer (A) is correct. *(CMA, adapted)*
REQUIRED: The weighted-average cost of capital given the costs of debt and equity.
DISCUSSION: The 7% debt cost and the 12% equity cost should be weighted by the proportions of the total investment represented by each source of capital. The total project costs $50 million, of which debt is $15 million, or 30% of the total. Equity capital is the other 70%. Consequently, the weighted-average cost of capital is 10.5% [(30% × 7%) + (70% × 12%)].
Answer (B) is incorrect. This percentage reverses the weights. Answer (C) is incorrect. This percentage assumes debt and equity are equally weighted. Answer (D) is incorrect. This percentage assumes that 7% is the before-tax cost of debt and that equity is tax deductible.

34. Enert, Inc.'s current capital structure is shown below. This structure is optimal, and the company wishes to maintain it.

Debt   25%
Preferred equity 5
Common equity   70

Enert's management is planning to build a $75 million facility that will be financed according to this desired capital structure. Currently, $15 million of cash is available for capital expansion. The percentage of the $75 million that will come from a new issue of common stock is

- A. 52.50%
- B. 50.00%
- C. 70.00%
- D. 56.00%

Answer (D) is correct. *(CMA, adapted)*
REQUIRED: The percentage of the new financing needed that will come from a new issue of common stock.
DISCUSSION: Because $15 million is already available, the company must finance $60 million ($75 million – $15 million). Of this amount, 70%, or $42 million, should come from the issuance of common stock to maintain the current capital structure. The $42 million represents 56% of the total $75 million.
Answer (A) is incorrect. The 70% desired common stock percentage multiplied by the original $75 million is $52.5. Answer (B) is incorrect. This is a bogus percentage. Answer (C) is incorrect. The new issue of common stock will fund 70% of the financed amount, not 70% of the total project cost. The financed amount is $60 million ($75 million – $15 million cash).

35. Which one of a firm's sources of new capital usually has the lowest after-tax cost?

- A. Retained earnings.
- B. Bonds.
- C. Preferred stock.
- D. Common stock.

Answer (B) is correct. *(CMA, adapted)*
REQUIRED: The source of new capital that normally has the lowest after-tax cost.
DISCUSSION: Debt financing, such as bonds, normally has a lower after-tax cost than does equity financing. The interest on debt is tax deductible, whereas the dividends on equity are not. Also, bonds are slightly less risky than stock because the bond holders have a first right to assets at liquidation.
Answer (A) is incorrect. The cost to the company of equity instruments is in the form of dividends. Because dividends are not deductible for tax purposes, equity sources of capital have a higher after-tax cost than debt sources. Answer (C) is incorrect. Preferred stock has a higher after-tax cost than debt. Answer (D) is incorrect. Common stock has a higher after-tax cost than debt.

36. Maylar Corporation has sold $50 million of $1,000 par value, 12% coupon bonds. The bonds were sold at a discount and the corporation received $985 per bond. If the corporate tax rate is 40%, the after-tax cost of these bonds for the first year (rounded to the nearest hundredth percent) is

- A. 7.31%
- B. 4.87%
- C. 12.00%
- D. 7.09%

Answer (A) is correct. *(CMA, adapted)*
REQUIRED: The after-tax cost of bonds for the first year.
DISCUSSION: Interest is 12%, and the annual interest payment on one bond is $120. Thus, the effective rate is 12.18% ($120 ÷ $985). Reducing this rate by the 40% tax savings lowers the cost to 7.31%.
Answer (B) is incorrect. Multiplying the pretax effective rate 12.18% ($120 ÷ $985) by the tax rate of .40 instead of by (1 – .40) results in 4.87%. Answer (C) is incorrect. The nominal interest rate is 12%. Answer (D) is incorrect. The after-tax cost of the bonds equals the effective rate times the tax effect.

37. Acme Corporation is selling $25 million of cumulative, non-participating preferred stock. The issue will have a par value of $65 per share with a dividend rate of 6%. The issue will be sold to investors for $68 per share, and issuance costs will be $4 per share. The cost of preferred stock to Acme is

- A. 5.42%
- B. 5.74%
- C. 6.00%
- D. 6.09%

Answer (D) is correct. *(CMA, adapted)*
REQUIRED: The cost of financing by issuing preferred stock.
DISCUSSION: Acme's cost of capital for its new preferred stock is calculated as follows:

Cost of new preferred stock = Dividend ÷ Net issue proceeds
= ($65 × 6%) ÷ ($68 – $4)
= $3.90 ÷ $64
= 6.09%

Answer (A) is incorrect. Improperly dividing the annual dividend by the sum of the issue price and the issue costs results in 5.42%. Answer (B) is incorrect. Improperly dividing the annual dividend by the issue price results in 5.74%. Answer (C) is incorrect. Improperly dividing the annual dividend by the par value results in 6.00%.

5.9 ESSAY QUESTIONS

Scenario for Essay Questions 1, 2, 3

Safe-T-Systems (STS) has developed safety devices marketed to manufacturing facilities in the Midwest. STS's limited product line has been well accepted, and the company is experiencing favorable profits and cash flow. The research staff is developing four new products that it believes will gain market acceptance. The marketing staff advised that there is good revenue potential for each proposed product where anticipated revenues and profits are equal relative to the level of investment. These products are independent of each other so that STS can invest in any combination of the four products or only in a single product. The investment required for each project is as follows:

Product	Investment (in millions)
Foot pedal release	$ 2.4
Power tool safety lock	1.7
Stationary machine retraction	4.6
Overhead machine retraction	3.3
Total	$12.0

STS's capital structure is currently composed of 60% long-term debt and 40% common equity (common stock and retained earnings), and management believes these contemplated transactions will maintain these capital ratios in the future. The weighted average cost of capital in this capital structure is 13.2%. The annual cost of internally generated funds from operations is 12%.

STS's cash flow in the current year will generate an estimated $2 million of funds that will be used first for product investment. STS can raise $3 million through privately placed short-term notes at a constant interest rate of 9%. Any product investments beyond $5 million ($2 million of current year cash flow and $3 million of privately placed notes) would have to be financed by a combination of long-term bonds and issuance of additional common stock. STS's effective tax rate is 40%.

	Proportion	Cost
Long-term debt	60	10%
Common stock	40	13

Questions

1.   a. Explain the difference between weighted-average cost of capital and weighted marginal cost of capital.

     b. Explain why the weighted marginal cost of capital should be used instead of the weighted-average cost of capital when evaluating product investment opportunities in discounted cash flow analyses.

2. If Safe-T-Systems plans to invest up to $5 million in the development of new products during the current year, calculate the weighted marginal cost of capital for this transaction.

3. Assume Safe-T-Systems (STS) already invested $5 million in power tool safety locks and overhead machine retraction devices this year. STS is now considering investing additional funds at the same debt to equity proportions in foot pedal releases and stationary machine retraction devices. Calculate the cost of capital STS should use in its analysis.

Essay Questions 1, 2, 3 — Unofficial Answers

1.   a.   The weighted-average cost of capital is based on historical costs and thus reflects a composite rate of past financing decisions. The marginal cost of capital measures the cost of new, additional capital at current rates.

   b.   When evaluating product investment opportunities in discounted cash flow analyses, the marginal cost of capital should be used where the concern is what rates are presently available and can be used for future new investments rather than how the capital was raised in the past. The weighted-average cost of capital reflects historical rates from past decisions as well as present rates, whereas the marginal cost of capital reflects current market conditions in obtaining incremental financing and allows an evaluation of capital structure based on future events and opportunity costs.

2.   The marginal cost of capital for the first $5 million of new funds is 8.04%, calculated as follows:

Component	Weight		Component Cost		Weighted Cost
Long-term debt [9% × (1.0 − .40)]	60	×	5.4%	=	3.24%
Retained earnings	40	×	12.0%	=	4.80%
Marginal cost of capital					8.04%

3.   The marginal cost of capital that STS should use in evaluating foot pedal releases and stationary machine retraction devices is 8.80%, calculated as follows:

Component	Weight		Component Cost		Weighted Cost
Long-term debt [10% × (1.0 − .40)]	60	×	6.0%	=	3.60%
Common stock	40	×	13.0%	=	5.20%
Marginal cost of capital					8.80%

The marginal cost of capital for an investment in excess of the first $5 million has increased because of the higher market cost of new equity capital and additional long-term bonds. In order to increase the firm's value, foot pedal releases and stationary machine retraction devices would have to earn a return that exceeds 8.80%, the incremental marginal cost of capital.

Use **CMA Gleim Online** and **Essay Wizard** to practice additional essay questions in an exam-like environment.

STUDY UNIT SIX
MANAGING CURRENT ASSETS

(22 pages of outline)

This study unit is the **third of four** on **corporate finance**. The relative weight assigned to this major topic in Part 2 of the exam is **25%**. The four study units are

Study Unit 4: Investment Risk and Portfolio Management
Study Unit 5: Financial Instruments and Cost of Capital
Study Unit 6: Managing Current Assets
Study Unit 7: Raising Capital, Corporate Restructuring, and International Finance

After studying the outline and answering the questions in this study unit, you will have the skills necessary to address the following topics listed in the ICMA's Learning Outcome Statements:

Part 2 – Section B.5. Managing current assets

The candidate should be able to:

Working capital

    a.   define working capital and identify its components
    b.   explain the benefit of short-term financial forecasts in the management of working capital

Cash

    c.   identify and describe factors influencing the levels of cash
    d.   identify and explain the three motives for holding cash
    e.   prepare forecasts of future cash flows
    f.   identify methods of speeding up cash collections
    g.   calculate the net benefit of a lockbox system
    h.   define concentration banking and discuss how firms utilize it
    i.   demonstrate an understanding of the uses of compensating balances
    j.   identify methods of slowing down disbursements
    k.   define payable through draft and zero balance account
    l.   demonstrate an understanding of disbursement float and overdraft systems

Marketable securities

    m.   identify and describe reasons for holding marketable securities
    n.   define the different types of marketable securities, including money market instruments, T-bills, Treasury notes, Treasury bonds, repurchase agreements, Federal agency securities, bankers' acceptances, commercial paper, negotiable CDs, Eurodollar CDs, and other marketable securities
    o.   evaluate the trade-offs among the variables in marketable security selections, including safety, marketability, yield, maturity, and taxability
    p.   demonstrate an understanding of the risk and return trade-off

Accounts receivable

q.   identify reasons for carrying accounts receivable and the factors influencing the level of receivables

r.   calculate days sales in receivables (average collection period)

s.   demonstrate an understanding of the impact of changes in credit terms or collection policies on accounts receivable, working capital, and sales volume

t.   define default risk

u.   identify and explain the factors involved in determining an optimal credit policy

Inventory

v.   identify reasons for carrying inventory and the factors influencing its level

w.   identify and calculate the costs related to inventory, including carrying costs, ordering costs, and shortage (stockout) costs, and determine the optimum safety stock level

x.   define lead time and safety stock

y.   demonstrate an understanding of economic order quantity (EOQ) and how a change in one variable would affect the EOQ (calculation not required)

z.   define just-in-time (JIT) inventory management systems

Short-term credit and working capital cost management

aa.   demonstrate an understanding of how risk affects a firm's approach to its current asset financing policy (aggressive, conservative, etc.)

bb.   identify and describe the different types of short-term credit, including trade credit, short-term bank loans, commercial paper, lines of credit, and bankers' acceptances

cc.   estimate the annual cost and effective annual interest rate of not taking a cash discount

dd.   calculate the effective annual interest rate of a bank loan with a compensating balance requirement and/or a commitment fee

ee.   demonstrate an understanding of factoring accounts receivable and calculate the cost of factoring

ff.   explain the maturity matching or hedging approach to financing

gg.   demonstrate an understanding of the factors involved in managing the costs of working capital

General

hh.   recommend a strategy for managing current assets that would fulfill a given objective

6.1 WORKING CAPITAL

1.   **Definitions**

a.   Working capital finance concerns the optimal level, mix, and use of current assets and the means used to acquire them, notably current liabilities. The objective is to minimize the cost of maintaining liquidity (quick convertibility to cash) while guarding against the risk of insolvency.

1)   From a financial analyst's perspective, working capital equals current assets. Its components include cash, marketable securities, receivables, and inventory.

2)   From the accounting perspective, net working capital equals current assets minus current liabilities.

2. **Working Capital Policy**

   a. A firm that adopts a conservative working capital policy seeks to minimize liquidity risk by increasing working capital.

       1) This policy is reflected in a higher current ratio (current assets ÷ current liabilities) and acid test ratio (quick assets ÷ current liabilities). The firm forgoes the potentially higher returns available from using the additional working capital to acquire long-term assets.

       2) To increase profitability, an aggressive policy reduces liquidity and accepts a higher risk of short-term cash-flow problems. This policy is reflected in a lower current ratio and acid test ratio.

   b. Carrying excessive current assets, such as inventories, increases costs.

       1) The carrying costs of inventory usually increase in proportion to the quantity of inventory. Thus, the firm with excess inventory incurs not only the opportunity costs of funds invested in inventory but also the costs of storage and insurance. Also, spoilage and obsolescence costs increase as inventories increase.

   c. The optimal level of current assets varies with the industry in which a firm operates. For example, a grocery store has spoilable inventory and cannot carry more than a few days of sales. Moreover, the grocery has no receivables. It also can operate with lower cash reserves than firms in many industries because its sales do not vary greatly from week to week. In contrast, a uranium mine must have a high level of cash to meet ongoing expenses because its sales may be irregular.

       1) Working capital policy applies to short-term decisions, and capital structure finance applies to long-term decisions.

       2) Working capital ratios are meaningful only in terms of norms and trends. Thus, a firm's ratios must be normal or average ratios from competitors or based on industry averages.

3. **Permanent vs. Temporary Working Capital**

   a. Permanent working capital is the minimum level of current assets maintained by a firm. Temporary working capital, however, fluctuates seasonally.

       1) Permanent working capital is similar to the firm's fixed assets and should increase as the firm grows. It differs because the items included in working capital turn over relatively rapidly although their minimum total is maintained or increased over the long term.

   b. Permanent working capital generally is financed with long-term debt. Financing with short-term debt is risky because (1) assets may not be liquidated in time to pay the debt, (2) interest rates may rise, and (3) loans may not be renewed.

Stop and review! You have completed the outline for this subunit. Study multiple-choice questions 1 through 5 beginning on page 237.

6.2 CASH MANAGEMENT

 A CMA candidate must demonstrate an understanding of effective cash management and its value. By forecasting future cash flows, you should (1) understand how to analyze the cost-benefit for the organization to hold cash and (2) know the motives and be able to weigh those against the lost opportunity costs. CMAs will be expected to evaluate cash budgeting by forecasting cash collection and payments. In addition, you should be able to (1) evaluate whether an organization should change the way it collects payments and (2) provide an analysis of how this should be done and the costs associated.

1.   **Managing the Level of Cash**

 a.   The following are the three motives for holding cash:

  1)   Transactional (as a medium of exchange)
  2)   Precautionary (to provide a reserve for contingencies)
  3)   Speculative (to take advantage of unexpected opportunities)

 b.   The goal of cash management is to determine and maintain the firm's optimal cash balance.

  1)   Because cash does not earn a return, only the amount needed to satisfy current obligations as they come due should be kept.

 c.   The firm's optimal level of cash should be determined by a cost-benefit analysis.

  1)   The motives for holding cash must be balanced against the opportunity cost of missed investments in marketable securities. One approach is the economic order quantity (EOQ) model originally developed for inventory management. The model helps the firm determine the proper mix of cash and marketable securities.

  2)   To apply the model, the firm must determine (a) how much cash will be needed over a period, (b) the cost per security transaction, and (c) the return that can be earned on marketable securities.

EOQ Model Applied to Cash Management

$$Q = \sqrt{\frac{2bT}{i}}$$

Where: Q = optimal cash balance
    b = fixed cost per transaction
    T = total demand for cash for the period
    i = interest rate on marketable securities

  3)   EXAMPLE: A firm projects that it needs $20,000 to pay its obligations during the upcoming month. Every marketable security transaction costs $5, and securities are currently paying 6% annual interest. The optimal cash balance can be determined by applying the EOQ model:

$$Q = \sqrt{\frac{2bT}{i}} = \sqrt{\frac{2 \times \$5 \times \$20{,}000}{6\% \div 12 \text{ months}}} = \sqrt{\frac{\$200{,}000}{.005}} = \$6{,}324$$

The firm's optimal cash balance for the upcoming month is $6,324, and its average balance will be $3,162 ($6,324 ÷ 2).

2. Forecasting Future Cash Flows

a. Managing cash flows begins with the cash budget. It states projected receipts and payments for the purpose of matching inflows and outflows.

b. Cash receipts are based on projected sales, credit terms, and estimated collection rates.

1) EXAMPLE: A firm forecasts the following cash collections for the next 4 months:

	Cash Sales	Credit Sales
July	$40,000	$160,000
August	60,000	220,000
September	80,000	340,000
October	70,000	300,000

On average, 50% of credit sales are paid for in the month of sale, 30% in the month after sale, and 15% in the second month after sale (5% are expected to be uncollectible). The firm's projected cash collections for October can be calculated as follows:

October cash sales		$ 70,000
October credit sales:	$300,000 × 50% =	150,000
September credit sales:	$340,000 × 30% =	102,000
August credit sales:	$220,000 × 15% =	33,000
Total October collections		$355,000

c. Cash payments are based on budgeted purchases and total sales.

1) EXAMPLE: The firm forecasts the following cash payments for the next 4 months:

	Purchases	Total Sales
July	$200,000	$200,000
August	250,000	280,000
September	300,000	420,000
October	350,000	370,000

On average, the firm pays for 50% of purchases in the month of purchase and 25% in each of the 2 following months. Payroll is projected as 10% of that month's sales and operating expenses are 20% of the following month's sales (November's sales are projected to be $280,000). Interest of $5,000 is paid every month. The firm's projected cash payments for October can be calculated as follows:

October purchases:	$350,000 × 50% =	$175,000
September purchases:	$300,000 × 25% =	75,000
August purchases:	$250,000 × 25% =	62,500
October payroll:	$370,000 × 10% =	37,000
October op. expenses	$280,000 × 20% =	56,000
Interest		5,000
Total October disbursements		$410,500

d. The budget is for a specific period, but cash budgeting is an ongoing, cumulative activity. It is re-evaluated constantly to ensure that all objectives are met.

3.   **Speeding Up Cash Collections**

   a.   The period from when a payor mails a check until the funds are available in the payee's bank is float. Firms use various strategies to decrease the float time for receipts (and to increase the float time for payments). The benefit of receiving cash earlier can be quantified:

   Daily cash receipts × Days of reduced float × Opportunity cost of funds

   b.   The product of the daily amount of receipts and the number of days of reduced float is the increase in the average cash balance. This amount is multiplied by an annual rate of return on short-term investments to arrive at the annual benefit.

   1)   EXAMPLE: A firm has $22,000 in daily cash receipts. It is considering a plan that costs $0 and speeds up collections by 2 days. The result is an additional $44,000 in the firm's average cash balance ($22,000 × 2 days). Marketable securities currently pay 6% annually.

   Benefit = $44,000 × 6% = $2,640 annually

   c.   The benefit of any plan to speed up cash collections must exceed the cost.

   1)   EXAMPLE: A firm has daily cash receipts of $150,000. A bank has offered to reduce the collection time by 2 days, increasing the firm's average cash balance by $300,000 ($150,000 × 2 days). The bank will charge a monthly fee of $1,250. Money market funds are expected to average 8% during the year.

   Benefit (loss) = Interest earned − Cost
                  = ($300,000 × 8%) − ($1,250 × 12 months)
                  = $24,000 − $15,000
                  = $9,000 annually

   d.   A lockbox system is the most important means of speeding up cash receipts.

   1)   Customers submit their payments to a mailbox rather than to the firm's offices. Bank personnel remove the envelopes from the mailbox and deposit the checks to the firm's account immediately. The remittance advices must then be transported to the firm for entry into the accounts receivable system. The bank generally charges a flat monthly fee for this service.

   2)   For firms doing business nationwide, a lockbox network is appropriate. The country is divided into regions according to customer population patterns. A lockbox arrangement is then established with a bank in each region.

   e.   A firm with a lockbox network ordinarily engages in concentration banking. The regional banks that provide lockbox services automatically transfer their daily collections to the firm's principal bank where they can be used for payments and short-term investment.

   1)   A depository transfer check (DTC) is often used. A DTC is a nonnegotiable instrument. It is drawn on the regional bank and made payable only to the firm's account at the concentration bank.

   f.   Transfer of funds by wire speeds up cash management. A wire transfer is any electronic funds transfer (EFT) by means of a two-way system, for example, the Federal Reserve Wire Transfer System (Fedwire).

   1)   Automated clearinghouses (ACHs) are electronic networks that facilitate the reading of data among banks. The 32 regional ACH associations guarantee 1-day clearing of checks. Except for the New York ACH, they are operated by the Federal Reserve.

g. Under the Check Clearing for the 21st Century Act, financial institutions may convert paper checks to electronic images (substitute checks that are legal copies of the originals). The paper checks may then be destroyed.

   1) The effect of this conversion has been to speed up check clearing. Consequently, cash collections and payments will be credited or debited, respectively, to the firm's accounts more quickly.

h. A compensating balance is a minimum amount that the bank requires the firm to keep in its account. Compensating balances are noninterest-bearing and are meant to compensate the bank for various services rendered, such as unlimited check writing. These funds are unavailable for short-term investment and thus incur an opportunity cost.

4. **Slowing Cash Payments**

   a. A draft is a three-party instrument in which one person (the drawer) orders a second person (the drawee) to pay money to a third person (the payee).

      1) A check is the most common form of draft. A check is an instrument payable on demand in which the drawee is a bank. Consequently, a draft can be used to delay the outflow of cash.

      2) A draft can be dated on the due date of an invoice and will not be processed by the drawee until that date. This practice eliminates writing a check earlier than the due date or using an EFT. Thus, the outflow is delayed until the check clears the drawee bank.

   b. A payable through draft (PTD) differs from a check because (1) it is not payable on demand, and (2) the drawee is the payor, not a bank. After the payee presents the PTD to a bank, the bank in turn presents it to the issuer. The issuer then must deposit sufficient funds to cover the PTD. Use of PTDs allows a firm to maintain lower cash balances.

      1) Disadvantages are that vendors prefer to receive an instrument that will be paid on demand, and banks generally impose higher processing charges for PTDs.

   c. A zero-balance account (ZBA) has a balance of $0. At the end of each processing day, the bank transfers just enough from the firm's master account to cover all checks presented against the ZBA that day.

      1) This practice allows the firm to maintain higher balances in the master account from which short-term investments can be made. The bank generally charges a fee for this service.

   d. Payment (disbursement) float is the period from when the payor mails a check until the funds are subtracted from the payor's account. To increase payment float, a firm may send checks to its vendors without being certain that it has sufficient funds to cover them all.

      1) For these situations, some banks offer overdraft protection. The bank guarantees (for a fee) to cover any shortage with a transfer from the firm's master account. ·

Stop and review! You have completed the outline for this subunit. Study multiple-choice questions 6 through 12 beginning on page 238.

6.3 MARKETABLE SECURITIES MANAGEMENT

1. **Types of Marketable Securities**

   a.   Idle cash incurs an opportunity cost. To offset this cost, firms invest their idle cash balances in marketable securities.

   b.   Beyond achieving an optimal risk and after-tax return trade-off, the most important aspects of marketable securities management are liquidity and safety. Liquidity is the ability to convert an investment into cash quickly and without a loss of principal. Marketable securities management thus concerns low-yield, low-risk instruments that are traded on highly active markets (money market instruments).

   1)   An entity also must consider whether the maturities of marketable securities match the needs for the cash.

   c.   The money market is the market for short-term investments where firms invest their temporary surpluses of cash. The money market is not formally organized but consists of many financial institutions, firms, and government agencies offering many instruments of various risk levels and short- to medium-range maturities.

   1)   U.S. Treasury obligations are (a) the safest investment, (b) exempt from state and local taxation, and (c) highly liquid.

   a)   Treasury bills (T-bills) have maturities of 1 year or less. Rather than bear interest, they are sold on a discount basis.

   b)   Treasury notes (T-notes) have maturities of 1 to 10 years. They provide the lender with an interest payment every 6 months.

   c)   Treasury bonds (T-bonds) have maturities of 10 years or longer. They provide the lender with an interest payment every 6 months.

   2)   Repurchase agreements (repos) are a means for dealers in government securities to finance their portfolios. When a firm buys a repo, it is temporarily purchasing some of the dealer's government securities. The dealer agrees to repurchase them at a later time for a specific (higher) price. In essence, the firm gives the securities dealer a secured, short-term loan. Maturities vary from overnight to a few days.

   3)   Federal agency securities are backed by either (a) the full faith and credit of the U.S. government or (b) only by the issuing agency.

   a)   Obligations of the Federal Housing Administration (FHA) and the Government National Mortgage Association (Ginnie Mae) are backed by the U.S. Treasury.

   b)   Obligations of such government-sponsored enterprises (GSEs) as the Federal National Mortgage Association (Fannie Mae) and the Federal Home Loan Mortgage Corporation (Freddie Mac), which issue mortgage-backed securities, are officially backed only by the agencies. But they are implicitly guaranteed by the federal government.

   4)   Bankers' acceptances are drafts drawn by a nonfinancial firm on deposits at a bank. One advantage is that the acceptance by the bank is a guarantee of payment at maturity. The payee can rely on the creditworthiness of the bank rather than on that of the (presumably riskier) drawer. A second advantage is that, because they are backed by the prestige of a large bank, these instruments are highly marketable once they have been accepted.

   5)   Commercial paper consists of unsecured, short-term notes issued by large companies that are very good credit risks.

6) Certificates of deposit (CDs) are a form of savings deposit that cannot be withdrawn before maturity without a high penalty. CDs often yield a lower return than commercial paper and bankers' acceptances because they are less risky. Negotiable CDs are typically issued in a denomination of $100,000 and traded in a secondary market under the regulation of the Federal Reserve System.

7) Eurodollars are time deposits of U.S. dollars in banks located abroad.

8) Others

a) Money-market mutual funds invest in short-term, low-risk securities. In addition to paying interest, these funds allow investors to write checks on their balances.

b) State and local governments issue short-term securities exempt from taxation.

Stop and review! You have completed the outline for this subunit. Study multiple-choice questions 13 through 18 beginning on page 240.

6.4 RECEIVABLES MANAGEMENT

1. **Overview**

a. Accounts receivable are carried for competitive and investment purposes.

1) A firm almost always must offer credit if its competitors do.

2) Customers who choose to pay beyond the stated time limit can be charged financing fees (interest income to the firm).

3) Due to the interaction of these two factors, managing accounts receivable must involve the sales, finance, and accounting functions.

b. Factors influencing the level of receivables include the soundness of the

1) Procedures for evaluating customer creditworthiness,
2) Formula for establishing standard credit terms,
3) System for tracking accounts receivable and billing customers, and
4) Procedures for following up on overdue accounts.

c. Default risk is the probability that a particular customer will be unwilling or unable to pay a debt. To manage (not necessarily minimize) default risk, firms often require written agreements to be signed by the customer, outlining the terms of credit and the consequences for nonpayment.

1) Firms often use credit scoring to determine whether to extend credit to a specific customer. Credit scoring assigns numerical values to the elements of credit worthiness.

d. The optimal credit policy does not seek merely to maximize sales. This result could be accomplished by increasing discounts, offering longer payment periods, and accepting riskier customers. But the firm cannot ignore the increase in bad debts and its negative effect on cash inflows.

1) Thus, the firm must balance default risk (bad debt experience) and sales maximization.

e. A common analytical tool is an aging schedule developed from an accounts receivable ledger. It stratifies the accounts depending on time outstanding.

f. The cash conversion cycle is the time that passes, on average, between the firm's payment for a purchase of inventory and the collection of cash from a customer on the sale of that inventory. The operating cycle is the cash cycle plus the time between purchases and payment.

2. **Basic Receivables Formulas**

   a. The most common credit terms offered are 2/10, net 30. This convention means that the customer may either deduct 2% of the invoice amount if the invoice is paid within 10 days, or must pay the entire balance by the 30th day.

      1) Credit terms do not include quantity discounts, which affect the prices of purchases, not financing.

   b. The **average collection period** (also called the days sales outstanding in receivables) is the average number of days that pass between the time of a sale and payment of the invoice. It can be derived by weighting the collection period for each group of receivables by its collection percentage.

      1) EXAMPLE: A firm grants credit terms of 2/10, net 30. The firm's credit department has examined the customers' payment histories and determined that 20% of customers pay on the 10th day, 60% pay on the 30th day, and 20% pay on the 40th day. Thus, a typical account receivable is outstanding for 28 days [(10 days × 20%) + (30 days × 60%) + (40 days × 20%)].

   c. The **average balance in receivables** is the amount the firm has chosen to invest in extending credit rather than in some alternative use.

   Avg. balance in receivables = Daily credit sales × Avg. collection period

      1) EXAMPLE: The firm in the above example has $15,000 in daily sales on credit. The firm's average balance in receivables is thus $420,000 ($15,000 × 28 days).

   d. In many circumstances, the average balance in receivables is more efficiently calculated on an annual basis, i.e., Annual credit sales × (Average collection period ÷ Days in year). A standard accounting convention for the length of a year is 360 days.

      1) EXAMPLE: The firm has annual credit sales of $5,400,000. The firm's average balance in receivables is thus $420,000 [$5,400,000 × (28 days ÷ 360 days)].

   e. The **accounts receivable turnover** ratio is the number of times in a year the average balance of receivables is converted to cash.

   $$\textit{Accounts receivable turnover (using dollars)} = \frac{\textit{Annual net credit sales}}{\textit{Average balance in receivables}}$$

      1) EXAMPLE: The firm turned its accounts receivable over 12.9 times during the year ($5,400,000 ÷ $420,000).

   f. The turnover ratio also can be stated in terms of days without regard to dollar amounts.

   $$\textit{Accounts receivable turnover (using days)} = \frac{\textit{Days in year}}{\textit{Average collection period}}$$

      1) EXAMPLE: The above version of the formula can be proven as follows:

         Accounts receivable turnover = Days in year ÷ Average collection period
         12.9 = 360 days ÷ 28 days
         12.9 = 12.9

3. **Assessing the Impact of a Change in Credit Terms**

   a. Amounts of receivables are an opportunity cost, i.e., the return that could be earned if those amounts were invested elsewhere. A key aspect of any change in credit terms is balancing the competitive need to offer credit with the opportunity cost incurred.

   b. The increased investment in receivables is calculated with this formula:

   $$\textit{Incremental variable costs} \times \frac{\textit{Incremental average collection period}}{\textit{Days in year}}$$

1) EXAMPLE: The firm is evaluating a proposal to relax its credit standards. Under the new plan, credit sales are expected to increase by $600,000. The new customers attracted by this plan are expected to have a 40-day average collection period. Variable costs are 80% of sales.

Increase in sales	$600,000
Times: variable cost ratio	× 80%
Increase in variable costs	$480,000

Increased investment in receivables = $480,000 × (40 days ÷ 360 days)
= $53,333

c. The cost of a change in credit terms is calculated with this formula:

Increased investment in receivables × Opportunity cost of funds

1) Opportunity cost is the maximum benefit forgone by choosing an investment.
2) EXAMPLE: Money market instruments are currently paying 12%.

Increased investment in receivables	$53,333
Times: opportunity cost of funds	× 12%
Cost of new credit plan	$ 6,400

d. The **benefit or loss** resulting from a change in credit terms is calculated with this formula:

Incremental contribution margin − Cost of change

1) EXAMPLE: The firm can now calculate the net benefit from the proposed change in credit policy:

Increase in sales	$600,000
Times: contribution margin ratio	× 20%
Increase in contribution margin	$120,000
Less: cost of new credit plan	(6,400)
Benefit of new credit plan	$113,600

Stop and review! You have completed the outline for this subunit. Study multiple-choice questions 19 through 25 beginning on page 242.

6.5 INVENTORY MANAGEMENT

1. **Overview**

   a. Reasons for carrying inventory include

      1) Hedging against supply uncertainty (vendors may have financial difficulties or shipments may be delayed),
      2) Hedging against demand uncertainty (high levels of inventory allow a firm to take advantage of unexpected customer orders), and
      3) Ensuring that operations are not interrupted by inventory shortages.

         a) A manufacturer needs a certain supply of materials on hand. Just-in-time systems, discussed on page 229, address this issue.

   b. Factors influencing the level of inventory. The optimal level of inventory is the one that (1) considers the three factors above and (2) minimizes total inventory cost.

c.   **Costs related to inventory.** Minimizing total inventory cost involves constant evaluation of the tradeoffs among the four components of the total:

Purchase costs + Carrying costs + Ordering costs + Stockout costs

1) Purchase costs are the actual invoice amounts charged by suppliers. This is also referred to as investment in inventory.

2) Carrying costs are associated with holding inventory: (a) storage, (b) insurance, (c) security, (d) inventory taxes, (e) depreciation or rent of facilities, (f) interest, (g) obsolescence and spoilage, and (h) the opportunity cost of funds invested in inventory.

3) Ordering costs are the fixed costs of placing an order with a vendor. They are independent of the number of units ordered. For internally manufactured units, they are the costs of setting up a production line.

4) Stockout costs are the opportunity cost of missing a customer order. These can also include the costs of expediting a special shipment necessitated by insufficient inventory on hand.

5) EXAMPLE: The following cost data are available for an item of inventory:

Invoice price	$300.00 per unit
Shipping costs	$ 15.00 per unit
Inventory insurance	$ 5.00 per unit
Handling	80.00 per order
Order cost	15.00 per order
Cost of capital	20%

The cost of carrying a unit of inventory can be calculated as follows:

Invoice price	$300
Shipping costs	15
Per-unit purchase cost	$315
Times: cost of capital	× 20%
Opportunity cost	$ 63
Insurance on inventory	5
Per-unit carrying cost	$ 68

d.   The challenge inherent in minimizing total inventory cost is illustrated in the following diagram:

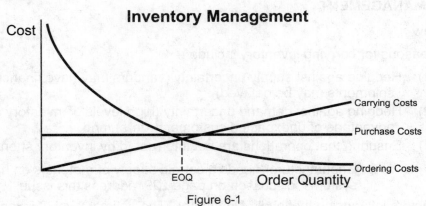

Figure 6-1

e.   Stockout costs can be minimized only by incurring high carrying costs. Carrying costs can be minimized only by incurring the high fixed costs of placing many small orders. Ordering costs can be minimized but only at the cost of storing large quantities. [The economic order quantity (EOQ) model, discussed later, is a widely used aid in meeting this challenge.]

2. **Inventory Replenishment Models**

    a.   Lead time is the time between placing an order with a supplier and receipt of the
         goods. When lead time is known and demand is uniform, goods can be timed to
         arrive just as inventory on hand is exhausted. This is the foundation of the
         just-in-time model, discussed later.

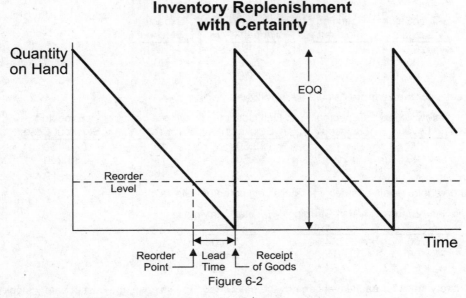

**Inventory Replenishment
with Certainty**

Figure 6-2

    b.   The following is the reorder point equation:

         (Average daily demand × Lead time in days) + Safety stock

    c.   The certainty depicted in the graph above is rare outside of just-in-time systems.
         Accordingly, safety stock is held as a hedge against contingencies. Determining the
         appropriate level of safety stock involves a probabilistic calculation. It balances the
         variability of demand with the acceptable risk of stockout costs.

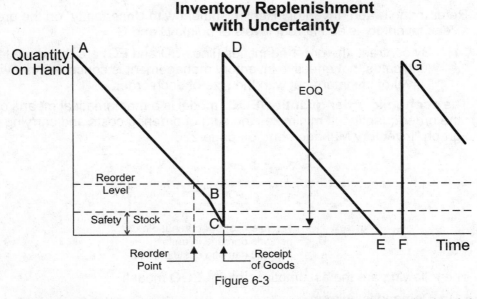

**Inventory Replenishment
with Uncertainty**

Figure 6-3

    d.   The diagram above assumes uncertainty. At point B, during the lead time of an order,
         demand increased, and the safety stock was used. Receipt of the order restored
         quantities to point D. During EF, a stockout occurred because of a delay in receipt of
         the order. Receipt of the order restored quantities to point G.

e.   The total cost of carrying safety stock consists of two components:

Cost of carrying safety stock = Expected stockout cost + Carrying cost

---

EXAMPLE of the Cost of Safety Stock

A firm has prepared the following schedule of the likelihood of stockouts at various levels of safety stock for the upcoming year:

Safety Stock Level	Resulting Stockout		Probability		Expected Stockout
200	0	×	10%	=	0
100	100	×	20%	=	20
0	100	×	15%	=	15

Expected stockout costs for the year are calculated as follows:

Safety Stock Level	Expected Stockout		Unit Cost of Stockout		Orders per Year		Expected Stockout Costs
200	0	×	$3.50	×	18	=	$0
100	20	×	$3.50	×	18	=	$1,260
0	15	×	$3.50	×	18	=	$945

Carrying costs for the various levels of safety stock are calculated as follows:

Safety Stock Level		Unit Carrying Costs		Total Carrying Costs
200	×	$4.00	=	$800
100	×	$4.00	=	$400
0	×	$4.00	=	$0

The annual cost of safety stock for each level can now be calculated. In this case, the cost of safety stock is minimized by holding 200 units.

Safety Stock Level	Expected Stockout Costs		Total Carrying Costs		Total Costs of Safety Stock
200	$0	+	$800	=	$800
100	$1,260	+	$400	=	$1,660
0	$945	+	$0	=	$945

---

3.   **Determining the Order Quantity**

a.   Refer to the graph "Inventory Replenishment with Uncertainty" on the previous page. Peak inventory is at different levels at points D and G.

1)   By contrast, the order quantities (lines CD and FG) are the same length. This indicates that effective inventory management is concerned not with the peak level of inventory but with the size of each order.

b.   The **economic order quantity (EOQ)** model is a mathematical means of determining the order quantity. It minimizes the sum of ordering costs and carrying costs (see the graph "Inventory Management" on page 226).

$$Economic\ order\ quantity\ (EOQ) = \sqrt{\frac{2aD}{k}}$$

Where: a = variable cost per purchase order
D = periodic demand in units
k = periodic carrying costs per unit

c.   The following are the assumptions of the EOQ model:

1)   Demand is uniform.
2)   Order (setup) costs and carrying costs are constant.
3)   No quantity discounts are allowed.
4)   Sales are perfectly predictable.
5)   Deliveries are always on time.

d. A change in any of the variables changes the EOQ solution. If demand or order costs rise, each order must contain more units. If carrying costs rise, each order must contain fewer units.

4. **Just-in-Time and Kanban Inventory Systems**

    a. In a just-in-time (JIT) inventory system, the storage of inventory is treated as a nonvalue-adding activity.

        1) All materials inventories (and their associated carrying costs) are reduced or eliminated entirely. Binding agreements with suppliers ensure that materials arrive exactly when they are needed and not before.

        2) JIT is a pull or demand-driven system. Production of goods does not begin until an order has been received. In this way, finished goods inventories also are eliminated.

    b. Another method of improving inventory flow is the kanban system, developed by the Toyota Motor Corporation (kanban is not characteristic of Japanese industry as a whole).

        1) Kanban means ticket. Tickets (also described as cards or markers) control the flow of production or parts so that they are produced or obtained in the needed amounts at the needed times.

        2) A basic kanban system includes a withdrawal kanban that states the quantity that a later process should withdraw from its predecessor, a production kanban that states the output of the preceding process, and a vendor kanban that tells a vendor what, how much, where, and when to deliver.

Stop and review! You have completed the outline for this subunit. Study multiple-choice questions 26 through 32 beginning on page 244.

6.6 SHORT-TERM FINANCING

1. **Sources**

    a. Types of sources include the following:

        1) Spontaneous sources (those that arise in the normal course of business),
        2) Commercial banks, and
        3) Market-based instruments.

2. **Spontaneous Forms of Financing**

    a. Trade credit resulting in accounts payable is the largest source of credit for small firms. It is created when a firm is offered credit terms by its suppliers as described in item 2.a. in Subunit 6.4.

        1) EXAMPLE: A vendor has delivered goods at a price of $160,000 on terms of net 30. The firm has effectively received a 30-day interest-free loan.

        2) The advantages of trade credit are that it is widely available and is free during the discount period. Another advantage is that not taking the discount sometimes is less costly than alternative sources of financing.

    b. Accrued expenses, such as salaries, wages, interest, dividends, and taxes payable, are other sources of (interest-free) spontaneous financing.

        1) For instance, employees work 5, 6, or 7 days a week but are paid only every 2 weeks. A firm carries on operations constantly but must only remit federal income taxes every quarter.

        2) Accruals have the additional advantage of fluctuating directly with operating activity, satisfying the matching principle.

3. Cost of Not Taking a Discount

    a.   If an early payment discount is offered, the firm ordinarily should take the discount. The annualized cost of not taking a discount can be calculated with the following formula:

$$\frac{Discount\ \%}{100\%\ -\ Discount\ \%}\ \times\ \frac{Days\ in\ year}{Total\ payment\ period\ -\ Discount\ period}$$

        1)   EXAMPLE: A vendor has delivered goods on terms of 2/10, net 30. The firm has chosen to pay on day 30. The effective rate paid by not taking the discount is calculated as follows (using a 360-day year):

            Cost of not taking discount = [2% ÷ (100% – 2%)] × [360 days ÷ (30 days – 10 days)]
                              = (2% ÷ 98%) × (360 days ÷ 20 days)
                              = 2.0408% × 18
                              = 36.73%

        The firm chose to finance $160,000 for 30 days rather than $156,800 ($160,000 × 98%) for 10 days. In effect, the cost is $3,200 ($160,000 – $156,800) to finance the last 20 days. Only companies in dire cash flow situations would incur a 36.73% cost of funds.

4. Short-Term Bank Loans

    a.   Commercial banks offer term loans and lines of credit. These loans are second only to spontaneous credit as a source of short-term financing.

        1)   The advantage is that bank loans provide financing not available from trade credit, etc. Thus, a firm can benefit from growth opportunities. The disadvantages are (a) the increased risk of insolvency, (b) the risk that short-term loans may not be renewed, and (c) the imposition of contractual restrictions, such as a compensating balance requirement.

        2)   A term loan, such as a note, must be repaid by a date certain.

        3)   A line of credit is an informal borrowing arrangement, generally for a 1-year period. It allows the debtor to reborrow amounts up to a maximum, as long as certain minimum payments are made each month (similar to a consumer's credit card). An advantage of a line of credit is that it is often an unsecured loan that is self-liquidating, that is, the assets acquired (e.g., inventory) provide the cash to pay the loan. However, one disadvantage of a line of credit is that it is not a legal commitment to give credit. Accordingly, it might not be renewed. A second is that a bank might require the borrower to "clean up" its debt for a certain period during the year, e.g., for 1 or 2 months.

    b.   The prime interest rate is the rate charged by commercial banks to their best (the largest and financially strongest) business customers. It is traditionally the lowest rate charged by banks.

5. Simple Interest Loans

    a.   A simple interest loan is one in which the interest is paid at the end of the loan term. The effective rate on the loan is the same as the nominal (stated) rate. The relevant formulas are presented here:

$$Amount\ needed\ =\ Invoice\ amount\ \times\ (1.0\ -\ Discount\ \%)$$

$$Interest\ expense\ =\ Amount\ needed\ \times\ Stated\ rate$$

1) EXAMPLE: A firm has received an invoice for $120,000 with terms of 2/10, net 30. The firm's bank can lend it the necessary amount for 30 days at a nominal annual rate of 6%, due at the end of the loan term.

Amount needed = Invoice amount × (1.0 − Discount %)
= $120,000 × (100% − 2%)
= $120,000 × 98%
= $117,600

Interest expense (annualized) = Amount needed × Stated rate
= $117,600 × 6%
= $7,056

6. **Effective Interest Rate on a Loan**

   a. The effective rate on any financing arrangement is the ratio of the amount the firm must pay to the amount the firm can use. The most basic statement of this ratio uses the dollar amounts generated by the equations illustrated on the previous page.

   $$Effective\ interest\ rate = \frac{Net\ interest\ expense}{Usable\ funds}$$

   b. The effective rate and the nominal rate on a simple interest loan are the same.

      1) EXAMPLE: The firm calculates the effective rate on this loan as follows:

      Effective rate = Net interest expense (annualized) ÷ Usable funds
      = $7,056 ÷ $117,600
      = 6.0%

7. **Discounted Loans**

   a. A discounted loan requires the interest to be paid at the beginning of the loan term.

   $$Total\ borrowings = \frac{Amount\ needed}{(1.0 - Stated\ rate)}$$

      1) EXAMPLE: A firm needs to pay a $90,000 invoice. Its bank has offered to make a loan at an 8% nominal rate on a discounted basis.

      Total borrowings = Amount needed ÷ (1.0 − Stated rate)
      = $90,000 ÷ (100% − 8%)
      = $90,000 ÷ 92%
      = $97,826

   b. Because the borrower has the use of a smaller amount, the effective rate on a discounted loan is higher than its nominal rate:

      Effective rate = Net interest expense (annualized) ÷ Usable funds
      = ($97,826 × 8%) ÷ $90,000
      = $7,826 ÷ $90,000
      = 8.696%

   c. As with all financing arrangements, the effective rate can be calculated without reference to dollar amounts:

   $$Effective\ rate\ on\ discounted\ loan = \frac{Stated\ rate}{(1.0 - Stated\ rate)}$$

      1) EXAMPLE: The firm calculates the effective rate on this loan without using dollar amounts.

      Effective rate = Stated rate ÷ (1.0 − Stated rate)
      = 8% ÷ (100% − 8%)
      = 8% ÷ 92%
      = 8.696%

8. **Loans with Compensating Balances**

    a. Rather than charge cash interest, banks sometimes require borrowers to maintain a compensating balance during the term of a financing arrangement.

$$Total\ borrowings\ = \frac{Amount\ needed}{(1.0\ -\ Compensating\ balance\ \%)}$$

    1) EXAMPLE: A firm has received an invoice for $120,000 with terms of 2/10, net 30. The firm's bank will lend it the necessary amount for 30 days at a nominal annual rate of 6% with a compensating balance of 10%.

    Total borrowings = Amount needed ÷ (1.0 – Compensated balance %)
    = ($120,000 × 98%) ÷ (100% – 10%)
    = $117,600 ÷ 90%
    = $130,667

    b. As with a discounted loan, the borrower has access to a smaller amount than the face amount of the loan and so pays an effective rate higher than the nominal rate.

    Effective rate = Net interest expense (annualized) ÷ Usable funds
    = ($130,667 × 6%) ÷ $117,600
    = $7,840 ÷ $117,600
    = 6.667%

    c. Once again, the dollar amounts involved are not needed to determine the effective rate.

$$Effective\ rate\ with\ comp.\ balance\ = \frac{Stated\ rate}{(1.0\ -\ Compensating\ balance\ \%)}$$

    Effective rate = Stated rate ÷ (1.0 – Compensating balance %)
    = 6% ÷ (100% – 10%)
    = 6% ÷ 90%
    = 6.667%

9. **Lines of Credit with Commitment Fees**

    a. A line of credit is the right to draw cash at any time up to a specified maximum. A line of credit may have a definite term, or it may be revolving, that is, the borrower can continuously pay off and reborrow from it. Sometimes a bank charges a borrower a commitment fee on the unused portion.

    1) EXAMPLE: A firm's bank extended a $1,000,000 line of credit at a nominal rate of 8% with a 0.5% commitment fee on the unused portion. The average loan balance during the year was $400,000.

    Annual cost = Interest expense on average balance + Commitment fee on unused portion
    = (Average balance × Stated rate) + [(Credit limit – Average balance) × Commitment fee %]
    = ($400,000 × 8%) + [($1,000,000 – $400,000) × 0.5%]
    = $32,000 + $3,000
    = $35,000

10. **Market-Based Instruments**

    a. Bankers' acceptances were discussed earlier as tools for short-term investment. They also can be sources of short-term financing.

    1) After acceptance, the drawer is no longer the primary responsible party and can sell the instrument to an investor at a discount.

    2) Once the instrument's term is reached after, for example, 90 days, the investor presents it to the accepting bank and demands payment. At that time, the drawer must have sufficient funds to cover it on deposit at the bank. In this way, the drawer obtained financing for 90 days.

    3) Bankers' acceptances are sold on a discount basis. The difference between the face amount and the proceeds received from the investor is interest expense to the drawer.

b.   Commercial paper consists of short-term, unsecured notes payable issued in large denominations ($100,000 or more) by large corporations with high credit ratings to other corporations and institutional investors, such as pension funds, banks, and insurance companies.

1)   Maturities of commercial paper are at most 270 days. No general secondary market exists for commercial paper. Commercial paper is a lower-cost source of funds than bank loans. It is usually issued at below the prime rate.

2)   The advantages of commercial paper are that it (a) provides broad and efficient distribution, (b) provides a great amount of funds (at a given cost), and (c) avoids costly financing arrangements.

3)   The disadvantages are that (a) it is an impersonal market and (b) the total amount of funds available is limited to the excess liquidity of big corporations.

11.   Secured Financing

a.   Loans can be secured by pledging receivables, i.e., committing the proceeds of the receivables to paying off the loan. A bank often lends up to 80% of outstanding receivables, depending upon the average age of the accounts and the probability of collection.

b.   A trust receipt is an instrument issued by a borrower that provides inventory as collateral. It is signed by the borrower and acknowledges that

1)   The inventory is held in trust for the lender, and
2)   Any proceeds of sale are to be paid to the lender.

c.   Warehouse financing gives the lender control over inventory collateral.

1)   A third party, such as a public warehouse, holds the collateral and serves as the creditor's agent. The creditor receives the warehouse receipts as evidence of its rights in the collateral.

2)   A field warehouse is established when the warehouser takes possession of the inventory on the debtor's property. The inventory is released (often from a fenced-in area) as needed for sale. Warehouse receipts may be negotiable or nonnegotiable.

12.   Factoring Receivables

a.   When a firm pledges receivables (described above), it retains ownership of the accounts and simply commits to sending the proceeds to a creditor. Under a factoring arrangement, the firm sells the accounts receivable outright. The financing cost is usually high.

1)   However, a firm that uses a factor can eliminate its credit department and accounts receivable staff. Also, bad debts are eliminated from the balance sheet. These reductions in costs can more than offset the fee charged by the factor. The factor can often operate more efficiently than its clients because of the specialized nature of its service.

b.   Before computers, factoring was often considered a last-resort source of financing, used only when bankruptcy was imminent. However, the factor's computerization of receivables means it can operate a receivables department more economically than most small firms. Factoring is no longer viewed as an undesirable source of financing.

1)   EXAMPLE: A firm that often factors its accounts receivable has an agreement with its finance company that (a) requires it to maintain a 4% reserve and (b) charges a 2% commission on the amount of receivables. The net proceeds are further reduced by an annual interest charge of 10% on the funds advanced. The firm has a $100,000 account that is due in 90 days. It calculates the net proceeds of the transaction as follows:

The first step is to calculate the gross proceeds of the factoring transaction:

Amount of receivables	$100,000
Less: reserve ($100,000 × 4%)	(4,000)
Less: factor fee ($100,000 × 2%)	(2,000)
Gross proceeds	$ 94,000

This amount must be reduced by the interest charged on the gross proceeds:

Gross proceeds	$94,000
Times: annual finance charge	× 10%
Annualized interest expense	$ 9,400
Times: portion of year (90 days ÷ 360 days)	× 25%
Interest expense	$ 2,350

The actual cash received is calculated as follows:

Gross proceeds	$94,000
Less: interest expense	(2,350)
Net proceeds	$91,650

In addition to the $91,650 of immediate proceeds, the firm also receives the $4,000 reserve at the end of the 90-day period if it has not been absorbed by sales returns and allowances. Thus, the total cost to factor the sales is $4,350 ($2,000 factor fee + interest of $2,350). Assuming that the factor has approved the customer's credit in advance, the seller does not incur any bad debts. The total cost of $4,350 should be compared with the cost of (a) operating a credit and collection department and (b) borrowing money that would otherwise be advanced by the factor.

13.   **Other Forms of Short-Term Borrowing**

a.   A chattel mortgage is a loan secured by personal property (movable property such as equipment or livestock). A floating lien is a loan secured by property, such as inventory, the composition of which may be constantly changing.

14.   **Maturity Matching**

a.   Maturity matching equalizes the life of an acquired asset with the debt instrument used to finance it. Because it mitigates financial risk, maturity matching is a hedging approach to financing.

1)   For instance, a debt due in 30 days should be paid with funds currently invested in a 30-day marketable security, not with proceeds from a 10-year bond issue.

2)   Moreover, long-term debt should not be paid with funds needed for day-to-day operations. Careful planning is needed to ensure that dedicated funds are available to retire long-term debt as it matures.

Stop and review! You have completed the outline for this subunit. Study multiple-choice questions 33 through 41 beginning on page 246.

6.7 CORE CONCEPTS

Working Capital

- From a financial analyst's perspective, **working capital** equals current assets. Its components include cash, marketable securities, and inventory. From the accounting perspective, **net working capital** equals current assets minus current liability.
- A firm that adopts a **conservative** working capital policy seeks to minimize liquidity risk by increasing working capital. An **aggressive** policy involves reducing liquidity and accepting a higher risk of short-term cash flow problems in an effort to increase profitability.

Cash Management

- The **three motives** for holding cash are transactional, precautionary, and speculative.
- Managing cash flows begins with the **cash budget**. It states projected receipts and payments for the purpose of matching inflows and outflows.
- The **benefit of receiving cash earlier** can be quantified:

  Daily cash receipts × Days of reduced float × Opportunity cost of funds

- A **lockbox system** is the most important means of speeding up cash receipts. Depository transfer checks and wire transfers also are widely used.
- **Cash payments** can be **slowed** through the use of drafts (such as checks), payables through draft, and zero-balance accounts.
- **Payment float** is the period from when the payor mails a check until the funds are subtracted from the payor's account.

Marketable Securities Management

- **Idle cash** incurs an opportunity cost. To offset this cost, firms invest their idle cash balances in marketable securities. Beyond earning a modest return, the most important aspects of marketable securities management are **liquidity** and **safety**.
- Marketable securities management concerns low-yield, low-risk instruments **(money market instruments)** that are traded on highly active markets. Examples include U.S. Treasury obligations, repurchase agreements, Federal agency securities, bankers' acceptances, commercial paper, and certificates of deposit.

Receivables Management

- The **average balance in receivables** is the amount the firm has chosen to invest in extending credit rather than in some alternative use.

  Daily credit sales × Average collection period

- The **accounts receivable turnover** ratio is the number of times in a year the average balance of receivables is converted to cash. It can be calculated using either dollars or days.

  Using dollars: Average net credit sales ÷ Average balance in receivables

  Using days: Days in year ÷ Average collection period

- A key aspect of any **change in credit terms** is balancing the competitive need to offer credit with the opportunity cost incurred. The **increased investment in receivables** is calculated:

  $$\textit{Incremental variable costs} \times \frac{\textit{Incremental average collection period}}{\textit{Days in year}}$$

- The **cost of a change in credit terms** is calculated:

  Increased investment in receivables × Opportunity cost of funds

- The **benefit or loss** resulting from a change in credit terms is calculated:

  Incremental contribution margin − Cost of change

Inventory Management

- **Minimizing the total cost of inventory** involves constant re-evaluation of the tradeoffs among the four components of the total:

  Purchase costs + Carrying costs + Ordering costs + Stockout costs

- The **reorder point** is calculated:

  (Average daily demand × Lead time in days) + Safety stock

- The total **cost of carrying safety stock** consists of two components:

  Expected stockout cost + Carrying cost

- The **economic order quantity (EOQ) model** is a mathematical tool for determining the order quantity that minimizes the sum of ordering costs and carrying costs (assuming uniform demand, constant order/setup costs, and no quantity discounts):

  $$\textit{Square root of } \frac{\textit{2 × Variable cost per purchase order × Periodic demand}}{\textit{Per unit carrying cost}}$$

Short-Term Financing

- If an early payment discount is offered, it is usually to the firm's advantage to take the discount. The annualized **cost of not taking a discount** is calculated:

  $$\frac{\textit{Discount \%}}{\textit{100\% − Discount \%}} \times \frac{\textit{Days in year}}{\textit{Total payment period − Discount period}}$$

- A **simple interest loan** is one in which the interest is paid at the end of the loan term. The effective rate on the loan is the same as the nominal (stated) rate. The relevant formulas:

  Amount needed = Invoice amount × (1.0 − Discount %)

  Interest expense = Amount needed × Stated rate

- The **effective rate** on any financing arrangement is the ratio of the amount the firm must pay to the amount the firm can use. The most basic statement of this ratio is:

  Effective interest rate = Net interest expense ÷ Usable funds

- A **discounted loan** requires the interest to be paid at the beginning of the loan term.

  Total borrowings = Amount needed ÷ (1.0 − Stated rate)

  Effective rate on discounted loan = Stated rate ÷ (1.0 − Stated rate)

- Rather than charge cash interest, banks sometimes require borrowers to maintain a **compensating balance** during the term of a financing arrangement.

  Total borrowings = Amount needed ÷ (1.0 − Compensating balance %)

  Eff. rate w/ comp. balance = Stated rate ÷ (1.0 − Compensating balance %)

- A **line of credit** is the right to draw cash any time up to a specified maximum. A line of credit may have a definite term, or it may be revolving, that is, the borrower can continuously pay off and reborrow from it. Sometimes a bank will charge a borrower a commitment fee on the unused portion. The **annual cost** of a line of credit can be calculated:

  Interest expense on average balance + Commitment fee on unused portion

  This also can be stated:

  (Average balance × Stated rate) + [(Credit limit − Average balance) × Commitment fee %]

- Firms can obtain short-term financing by issuing such **market-based instruments** as bankers' acceptances and commercial paper. Loans can be secured by **pledging receivables** or using **warehouse inventory** as collateral.

- Under a **factoring** arrangement, the firm **sells** the accounts receivable outright. The financing cost is usually high. However, a firm that uses a factor can eliminate its credit department and accounts receivable staff. Also, bad debts are eliminated from the balance sheet.

QUESTIONS

6.1 Working Capital

1. Net working capital is the difference between

   A. Current assets and current liabilities.
   B. Fixed assets and fixed liabilities.
   C. Total assets and total liabilities.
   D. Shareholders' investment and cash.

Answer (A) is correct. *(CMA, adapted)*
   REQUIRED: The definition of net working capital.
   DISCUSSION: Net working capital is defined by accountants as the difference between current assets and current liabilities. Working capital is a measure of short-term solvency.
   Answer (B) is incorrect. Working capital refers to the difference between current assets and current liabilities; fixed assets are not a component. Answer (C) is incorrect. Total assets and total liabilities are not components of working capital; only current items are included. Answer (D) is incorrect. Shareholders' equity is not a component of working capital; only current items are included in the concept of working capital.

2. Determining the appropriate level of working capital for a firm requires

   A. Changing the capital structure and dividend policy of the firm.
   B. Maintaining short-term debt at the lowest possible level because it is generally more expensive than long-term debt.
   C. Offsetting the benefit of current assets and current liabilities against the probability of technical insolvency.
   D. Maintaining a high proportion of liquid assets to total assets in order to maximize the return on total investments.

Answer (C) is correct. *(CMA, adapted)*
   REQUIRED: The requirement for determining the appropriate level of working capital.
   DISCUSSION: Working capital finance concerns the determination of the optimal level, mix, and use of current assets and current liabilities. The objective is to minimize the cost of maintaining liquidity while guarding against the possibility of technical insolvency. Technical insolvency is defined as the inability to pay debts as they come due.
   Answer (A) is incorrect. Capital structure and dividends relate to capital structure finance, not working capital finance. Answer (B) is incorrect. Short-term debt is usually less expensive than long-term debt. Answer (D) is incorrect. Liquid assets do not ordinarily earn high returns relative to long-term assets, so holding the former will not maximize the return on total assets.

3. Since Marsh, Inc., is experiencing a sharp increase in sales activity and a steady increase in production, the management of Marsh has adopted an aggressive working capital policy. Therefore, the company's current level of net working capital

   A. Would most likely be the same as in any other type of business condition as business cycles tend to balance out over time.
   B. Would most likely be lower than under other business conditions in order that the company can maximize profits while minimizing working capital investment.
   C. Would most likely be higher than under other business conditions so that there will be sufficient funds to replenish assets.
   D. Would most likely be higher than under other business conditions as the company's profits are increasing.

Answer (B) is correct. *(CMA, adapted)*
   REQUIRED: The effect of an aggressive working capital policy.
   DISCUSSION: When a firm has an aggressive working capital policy, management keeps the investment in working capital at a minimum. Thus, a growing company would want to invest its funds in capital goods and not in idle assets. This policy maximizes return on investment at the price of the risk of minimal liquidity.
   Answer (A) is incorrect. The growing firm is more apt to emphasize production rather than protecting against technical insolvency by maintaining a high level of working capital. Answer (C) is incorrect. The company will prefer to expend funds on capital goods. Answer (D) is incorrect. The company needs its profits to invest in new production equipment in order to grow.

4. Which one of the following would increase the net working capital of a firm?

   A. Cash payment of payroll taxes payable.
   B. Purchase of a new plant financed by a 20-year mortgage.
   C. Cash collection of accounts receivable.
   D. Refinancing a short-term note payable with a 2-year note payable.

Answer (D) is correct. *(CMA, adapted)*
   REQUIRED: The transaction that increases working capital.
   DISCUSSION: Net working capital equals current assets minus current liabilities. Refinancing a short-term note with a 2-year note payable decreases current liabilities, thus increasing working capital.
   Answer (A) is incorrect. A cash payment of payroll taxes decreases current assets and current liabilities by equal amounts. Answer (B) is incorrect. Buying a new plant with a 20-year mortgage has no effect on current assets or current liabilities. Answer (C) is incorrect. Cash collection of an account receivable increases one current asset and decreases another by the same amount.

5. The working capital financing policy that subjects the firm to the greatest risk of being unable to meet the firm's maturing obligations is the policy that finances

   A. Fluctuating current assets with long-term debt.

   B. Permanent current assets with long-term debt.

   C. Permanent current assets with short-term debt.

   D. Fluctuating current assets with short-term debt.

Answer (C) is correct. *(CMA, adapted)*
   REQUIRED: The working capital financing policy that subjects a firm to the greatest risk of being unable to meet maturing obligations.
   DISCUSSION: Fluctuating current assets can often be financed with short-term debt because the periodic liquidation of the assets provides funds to pay off the debt. However, financing permanent current assets with short-term debt is a risky strategy because the assets may not be liquidated in time to pay off the debt at maturity.
   Answer (A) is incorrect. It is not particularly risky to finance working capital needs from long-term debt sources. Answer (B) is incorrect. It is not particularly risky to finance working capital needs from long-term debt sources. Answer (D) is incorrect. Financing fluctuating current assets with short-term debt is not as risky as financing permanent current assets with short-term debt.

6.2 Cash Management

6. A consultant recommends that a company hold funds for the following two reasons:

   Reason #1: Cash needs can fluctuate substantially throughout the year.

   Reason #2: Opportunities for buying at a discount may appear during the year.

The cash balances used to address the reasons given above are correctly classified as

	Reason #1	Reason #2
A.	Speculative balances	Speculative balances
B.	Speculative balances	Precautionary balances
C.	Precautionary balances	Speculative balances
D.	Precautionary balances	Precautionary balances

Answer (C) is correct. *(CMA, adapted)*
   REQUIRED: The correct classifications for the reasons for a firm to hold cash.
   DISCUSSION: The three motives for holding cash are as a medium of exchange, as a precautionary measure, and for speculation. Reason #1 can be classified as a precautionary measure, and Reason #2 can be classified as holding cash for speculation.
   Answer (A) is incorrect. Reason #1 is fulfilled by precautionary balances. Answer (B) is incorrect. This combination results from reversing the correct balances. Answer (D) is incorrect. Reason #2 is fulfilled by speculative balances.

7. A firm uses the following model to determine the optimal level of cash balance (Q):

$$Q = \sqrt{\frac{2bT}{i}}$$

Where: b = fixed cost per transaction
       T = total demand for cash over a period of time
       i = interest rate on marketable securities

This formula is a modification of the economic order quantity (EOQ) formula used for inventory management. Assume that the fixed cost of selling marketable securities is $10 per transaction and the interest rate on marketable securities is 6% per year. The company estimates that it will make cash payments of $12,000 over a 1-month period. What is the average cash balance (rounded to the nearest dollar)?

   A. $1,000

   B. $2,000

   C. $3,464

   D. $6,928

Answer (C) is correct. *(CMA, adapted)*
   REQUIRED: The average cash balance.
   DISCUSSION: The EOQ for inventory is a function of ordering cost per order, inventory demand, and carrying cost. In the cash model, the fixed cost per sale of securities is equivalent to the ordering cost, the demand for cash is similar to the demand for inventory, and the interest rate is effectively the cost of carrying a dollar of cash for the period. The formula can be used to determine the optimal level of cash:

$$Q = \sqrt{\frac{2bT}{i}} = \sqrt{\frac{2 \times \$10 \times \$12,000}{6\% \div 12 \text{ months}}} = \sqrt{\frac{\$240,000}{.005}} = \$6,928$$

   Thus, the average cash balance is $3,464 ($6,928 ÷ 2).
   Answer (A) is incorrect. The amount of $1,000 results from using 24%, rather than .5%, in the denominator. Answer (B) is incorrect. The amount of $2,000 results from using 6%, rather than .5%, in the denominator. Answer (D) is incorrect. The amount of $6,928 is the optimal, not the average, cash balance.

8. Newman Products has received proposals from several banks to establish a lockbox system to speed up receipts. Newman receives an average of 700 checks per day averaging $1,800 each, and its cost of short-term funds is 7% per year. Assuming that all proposals will produce equivalent processing results and using a 360-day year, which one of the following proposals is optimal for Newman?

    A. A $0.50 fee per check.

    B. A flat fee of $125,000 per year.

    C. A fee of 0.03% of the amount collected.

    D. A compensating balance of $1,750,000.

Answer (D) is correct. *(CMA, adapted)*
    REQUIRED: The optimal fee structure for a lockbox system.
    DISCUSSION: Multiplying 700 checks times 360 days results in a total of 252,000 checks per year. Accordingly, using a $0.50 fee per check, total annual cost is $126,000 (252,000 × $.50), which is less desirable than a $125,000 flat fee. Given that the annual collections equal $453,600,000 (700 checks × $1,800 × 360 days), a fee of 0.03% of the amount collected is also less desirable because the annual fee would be $136,080 ($453,600,000 × .03%). The best option is therefore to maintain a compensating balance of $1,750,000 when the cost of funds is 7%, resulting in a total cost of $122,500 ($1,750,000 × 7%).
    Answer (A) is incorrect. A $0.50 fee per check will result in an annual cost of $126,000. Answer (B) is incorrect. An annual cost of $125,000 is not optimal. Answer (C) is incorrect. A fee of 0.03% of the amount collected will result in an annual cost of $136,080.

9. Troy Toys is a retailer operating in several cities. The individual store managers deposit daily collections at a local bank in a non-interest bearing checking account. Twice per week, the local bank issues a depository transfer check (DTC) to the central bank at headquarters. The controller of the company is considering using a wire transfer instead. The additional cost of each transfer would be $25; collections would be accelerated by 2 days; and the annual interest rate paid by the central bank is 7.2% (0.02% per day). At what amount of dollars transferred would it be economically feasible to use a wire transfer instead of the DTC? Assume a 360-day year.

    A. It would never be economically feasible.

    B. $125,000 or above.

    C. Any amount greater than $173.

    D. Any amount greater than $62,500.

Answer (D) is correct. *(CMA, adapted)*
    REQUIRED: The amount at which wire transfers are preferable.
    DISCUSSION: To break even, the interest that Troy can earn on the early deposits must at least equal the wire transfer fee.

$$\text{Interest earned} = \text{Cost}$$
$$\text{Transfer amount} \times 2 \text{ days} \times .02\% = \$25$$
$$\text{Transfer amount} \times .04\% = \$25$$
$$\text{Transfer amount} = \$62,500$$

    Answer (A) is incorrect. The $25 transfer fee is covered by the interest on $62,500 for 2 days. Answer (B) is incorrect. The amount of $125,000 is required if collections are accelerated by only 1 day. Answer (C) is incorrect. The interest on $173 for 2 days is less than $.07.

10. An automated clearinghouse (ACH) electronic transfer is a(n)

    A. Electronic payment to a company's account at a concentration bank.

    B. Check that must be immediately cleared by the Federal Reserve Bank.

    C. Computer-generated deposit ticket verifying deposit of funds.

    D. Check-like instrument drawn against the payor and not against the bank.

Answer (A) is correct. *(CMA, adapted)*
    REQUIRED: The definition of an automated clearinghouse (ACH) electronic transfer.
    DISCUSSION: An ACH electronic funds transfer (EFT) is an electronic payment to a company's account at a concentration bank. A concentration bank is a large bank to which a company transfers funds from local depository banks. These local banks operate the company's lockboxes and thus serve as collection points. The transfer of funds to the concentration bank allows the company to take advantage of economies of scale in cash management. The use of ACHs facilitates concentration banking. ACHs are electronic networks operated by the Federal Reserve (except for the New York regional ACH association) that guarantee 1-day clearing.
    Answer (B) is incorrect. A check is not involved in an EFT. Answer (C) is incorrect. An ACH transfer involves the actual transfer of funds electronically; it is not just a computer-generated document. Answer (D) is incorrect. An EFT is not a check-like instrument.

240   SU 6: Managing Current Assets

11. A compensating balance

   A. Compensates a financial institution for services rendered by providing it with deposits of funds.

   B. Is used to compensate for possible losses on a marketable securities portfolio.

   C. Is a level of inventory held to compensate for variations in usage rate and lead time.

   D. Is the amount of prepaid interest on a loan.

Answer (A) is correct. *(CMA, adapted)*
   REQUIRED: The true statement about compensating balances.
   DISCUSSION: A compensating balance is a minimum amount that the bank requires the firm to keep in its demand account. Compensating balances are noninterest-bearing and are meant to compensate the bank for various services rendered, such as unlimited check writing. These funds are obviously unavailable for short-term investment and thus incur an opportunity cost.
   Answer (B) is incorrect. In financial accounting, a valuation allowance is used to reflect losses on marketable securities. Answer (C) is incorrect. Safety stock is held for such purposes. Answer (D) is incorrect. Interest deducted in advance is discount interest.

12. A working capital technique that increases the payable float and therefore delays the outflow of cash is

   A. Concentration banking.

   B. A draft.

   C. Electronic data interchange (EDI).

   D. A lockbox system.

Answer (B) is correct. *(CMA, adapted)*
   REQUIRED: The working capital technique to increase the payable float and delay the outflow of cash.
   DISCUSSION: A draft is a three-party instrument in which one person (the drawer) orders a second person (the drawee) to pay money to a third person (the payee). A check is the most common form of draft. It is an instrument payable on demand in which the drawee is a bank. Consequently, a draft can be used to delay the outflow of cash. A draft can be dated on the due date of an invoice and will not be processed by the drawee until that date, thereby eliminating the necessity of writing a check earlier than the due date or using an EFT. Thus, the outflow is delayed until the check clears the drawee bank.
   Answer (A) is incorrect. Concentration banking, in connection with a lockbox network, is a technique used to accelerate cash receipts. Answer (C) is incorrect. EDI is the communication of electronic documents directly from a computer in one entity to a computer in another entity. Thus, EDI expedites cash payments. The payee receives the money almost instantaneously. Answer (D) is incorrect. A lockbox system is a technique used to accelerate cash receipts.

6.3 Marketable Securities Management

13. Which one of the following is **not** a characteristic of a negotiable certificate of deposit? Negotiable certificates of deposit

   A. Have a secondary market for investors.

   B. Are regulated by the Federal Reserve System.

   C. Are usually sold in denominations of a minimum of $100,000.

   D. Have yields considerably greater than bankers' acceptances and commercial paper.

Answer (D) is correct. *(CMA, adapted)*
   REQUIRED: The item not a characteristic of a negotiable certificate of deposit.
   DISCUSSION: A certificate of deposit (CD) is a form of savings deposit that cannot be withdrawn before maturity without incurring a high penalty. A negotiable CD can be traded. CDs usually have a fairly high rate of return compared with other savings instruments because they are for fixed, usually long-term periods. However, their yield is less than that of commercial paper and bankers' acceptances because they are less risky.
   Answer (A) is incorrect. Negotiable CDs do have a secondary market (i.e., they are negotiable). Answer (B) is incorrect. Negotiable CDs are regulated. Answer (C) is incorrect. Negotiable CDs are typically issued in a denomination of $100,000.

14. In smaller businesses in which the management of cash is but one of numerous functions performed by the treasurer, various cost incentives and diversification arguments suggest that surplus cash should be invested in

    A. Commercial paper.

    B. Bankers' acceptances.

    C. Money market mutual funds.

    D. Corporate bonds.

Answer (C) is correct. *(CMA, adapted)*
    REQUIRED: The most efficient manner in which a small firm could invest short-term surpluses of cash.
    DISCUSSION: A small firm with surplus cash should invest for the highest return and lowest risk. The ability to convert the investment into cash without a loss of principal is also important. Money market mutual funds invest in money market certificates such as treasury bills, negotiable CDs, and commercial paper. Because of diversification, these mutual funds are superior to any single instrument.
    Answer (A) is incorrect. A small firm may not have enough surplus cash to invest in commercial paper, which usually consists of secured or unsecured promissory notes of large corporations. Answer (B) is incorrect. The transactions cost of bankers' acceptances is high. A banker's acceptance is a unique credit instrument used to finance both domestic and international "self-liquidating" transactions. It is usually initiated by a bank's irrevocable letter of credit on behalf of the bank's customer, on which the company doing business with the bank's customer draws a time draft. The company discounts the time draft with the company's local bank and receives immediate payment. The local bank forwards the time draft to the bank customer for payment. Answer (D) is incorrect. An increase in interest rates could cause a substantial loss in principal.

15. When managing cash and short-term investments, a corporate treasurer is primarily concerned with

    A. Maximizing rate of return.

    B. Minimizing taxes.

    C. Investing in Treasury bonds since they have no default risk.

    D. Liquidity and safety.

Answer (D) is correct. *(CMA, adapted)*
    REQUIRED: The primary concern when managing cash and short-term investments.
    DISCUSSION: Cash and short-term investments are crucial to a firm's continuing success. Sufficient liquidity must be available to meet payments as they come due. At the same time, liquid assets are subject to significant control risk. Therefore, liquidity and safety are the primary concerns of the treasurer when dealing with highly liquid assets. Cash and short-term investments are held because of their ability to facilitate routine operations of the company. These assets are not held for purposes of achieving investment returns.
    Answer (A) is incorrect. Most companies are not in business to earn high returns on liquid assets (i.e., they are held to facilitate operations). Answer (B) is incorrect. The holding of cash and cash-like assets is not a major factor in controlling taxes. Answer (C) is incorrect. Investments in Treasury bonds do not have sufficient liquidity to serve as short-term assets.

16. All of the following are alternative marketable securities suitable for investment **except**

    A. U.S. Treasury bills.

    B. Eurodollars.

    C. Commercial paper.

    D. Convertible bonds.

Answer (D) is correct. *(CMA, adapted)*
    REQUIRED: The item that is not a marketable security.
    DISCUSSION: Marketable securities are near-cash items used primarily for short-term investment. Examples include U.S. Treasury bills, Eurodollars, commercial paper, money-market mutual funds with portfolios of short-term securities, bankers' acceptances, floating rate preferred stock, and negotiable CDs of U.S. banks. A convertible bond is not a short-term investment because its maturity date is usually more than 1 year in the future and its price can be influenced substantially by changes in interest rates or by changes in the investee's stock price.
    Answer (A) is incorrect. U.S. Treasury bills are short-term marketable securities. Answer (B) is incorrect. Eurodollars are short-term marketable securities. Answer (C) is incorrect. Commercial paper is a short-term marketable security.

17. Obligations issued by federal agencies other than the U.S. Treasury Department are

    A. Guaranteed by the U.S. government but not by the agency issuing the security.

    B. Guaranteed neither by the agency issuing the security nor by the U.S. government.

    C. Guaranteed by the agency issuing the security but not by the U.S. government.

    D. Not easily marketed.

Answer (C) is correct. *(CMA, adapted)*
    REQUIRED: The true statement about obligations issued by federal agencies other than the U.S. Treasury Department.
    DISCUSSION: Obligations issued by the Treasury Department are insured by the full faith and credit of the U.S. government. However, obligations of other federal agencies (agency securities) are guaranteed only by the issuing agency, not the federal government. Exceptions are securities issued by the Government National Mortgage Association (Ginnie Mae), which have the full backing of the U.S. government.
    Answer (A) is incorrect. Agency obligations are not insured by the U.S. government. Answer (B) is incorrect. Agency obligations are guaranteed by the issuing agency. Answer (D) is incorrect. Agency securities are widely marketed with an active secondary market.

18. The best example of a marketable security with minimal risk would be

    A. Municipal bonds.

    B. The common stock of an Aaa-rated company.

    C. Gold.

    D. The commercial paper of an Aaa-rated company.

Answer (D) is correct. *(CMA, adapted)*
    REQUIRED: The best example of a marketable security with minimal risk.
    DISCUSSION: Of the choices given, the commercial paper of a top-rated (most creditworthy) company has the least risk. Commercial paper is preferable to stock or stock options because the latter represent only a residual equity in a corporation. Commercial paper is debt and thus has priority over shareholders' claims. Also, commercial paper is a very short-term investment. The maximum maturity allowed without SEC registration is 270 days. However, it can be sold only to sophisticated investors without registration.
    Answer (A) is incorrect. Municipal bonds are rarely considered marketable securities in the accounting sense. They constitute long-term debt. Answer (B) is incorrect. Common stock does not have as high a priority in company assets as commercial paper or other debt. Answer (C) is incorrect. Gold is a commodity, not a security. Also, its price fluctuates for many reasons that do not affect the value of commercial paper.

6.4 Receivables Management

19. A change in credit policy has caused an increase in sales, an increase in discounts taken, a reduction in the investment in accounts receivable, and a reduction in the number of doubtful accounts. Based upon this information, we know that

    A. Net profit has increased.

    B. The average collection period has decreased.

    C. Gross profit has declined.

    D. The size of the discount offered has decreased.

Answer (B) is correct. *(CMA, adapted)*
    REQUIRED: The true statement about a change in credit policy that has resulted in greater sales and a reduction in accounts receivable.
    DISCUSSION: An increase in discounts taken accompanied by declines in receivables balances and doubtful accounts all indicate that collections on the increased sales have been accelerated. Accordingly, the average collection period must have declined. The average collection period is a ratio calculated by dividing the number of days in a year (365) by the receivable turnover. Thus, the higher the turnover, the shorter the average collection period. The turnover increases when either sales (the numerator) increase or receivables (the denominator) decrease. Accomplishing both higher sales and a lower receivables increases the turnover and results in a shorter collection period.
    Answer (A) is incorrect. No statement can be made with respect to profits without knowing costs. Answer (C) is incorrect. No statement can be made with respect to profits without knowing costs. Answer (D) is incorrect. The discount may have been increased, which has led to quicker payments.

20. The average collection period for a firm measures the number of days

    A. After a typical credit sale is made until the firm receives the payment.

    B. For a typical check to "clear" through the banking system.

    C. Beyond the end of the credit period before a typical customer payment is received.

    D. Before a typical account becomes delinquent.

Answer (A) is correct. *(CMA, adapted)*
    REQUIRED: The meaning of a firm's average collection period.
    DISCUSSION: The average collection period measures the number of days between the date of sale and the date of collection. It should be related to a firm's credit terms. For example, a firm that allows terms of 2/15, net 30, should have an average collection period of somewhere between 15 and 30 days.
    Answer (B) is incorrect. It describes the concept of float. Answer (C) is incorrect. The average collection period includes the total time before a payment is received, including the periods both before and after the end of the normal credit period. Answer (D) is incorrect. It describes the normal credit period.

21. An aging of accounts receivable measures the

    A. Ability of the firm to meet short-term obligations.

    B. Average length of time that receivables have been outstanding.

    C. Percentage of sales that have been collected after a given time period.

    D. Amount of receivables that have been outstanding for given lengths of time.

Answer (D) is correct. *(CMA, adapted)*
    REQUIRED: The item measured by an aging of accounts receivable.
    DISCUSSION: The purpose of an aging of receivables is to classify receivables by due date. Those that are current (not past due) are listed in one column, those less than 30 days past due in another column, etc. The amount in each category can then be multiplied by an estimated bad debt percentage that is based on a company's credit experience and other factors. The theory is that the oldest receivables are the least likely to be collectible. Aging the receivables and estimating the uncollectible amounts is one method of arriving at the appropriate balance sheet valuation of the accounts receivable account.
    Answer (A) is incorrect. An aging schedule is used for receivables, not liabilities. Answer (B) is incorrect. An aging schedule concerns specific accounts, not averages. Answer (C) is incorrect. An aging schedule focuses on uncollected receivables.

22. An increase in sales resulting from an increased cash discount for prompt payment would be expected to cause

    A. An increase in the operating cycle.

    B. An increase in the average collection period.

    C. A decrease in the cash conversion cycle.

    D. A decrease in purchase discounts taken.

Answer (C) is correct. *(CMA, adapted)*
    REQUIRED: The effect of an increase in sales resulting from an increased cash discount.
    DISCUSSION: If the cause of increased sales is an increase in the cash discount, it can be inferred that the additional customers would pay during the discount period. Thus, cash would be collected more quickly than previously and the cash conversion cycle would be shortened.
    Answer (A) is incorrect. The operating cycle would decrease since the average time from cash disbursement to cash realization would be shorter. Answer (B) is incorrect. The average collection period would decrease since the average time from cash disbursement to cash realization would be shorter. Answer (D) is incorrect. More customers will take discounts.

23. An organization would usually offer credit terms of 2/10, net 30 when

    A. The organization can borrow funds at a rate exceeding the annual interest cost.

    B. The organization can borrow funds at a rate less than the annual interest cost.

    C. The cost of capital approaches the prime rate.

    D. Most competitors are offering the same terms, and the organization has a shortage of cash.

Answer (D) is correct. *(CMA, adapted)*
    REQUIRED: The reason for offering credit terms of 2/10, net 30.
    DISCUSSION: Because these terms involve an annual interest cost of over 36%, a company would not offer them unless it desperately needed cash. Also, credit terms are typically somewhat standardized within an industry. Thus, if most companies in the industry offer similar terms, a firm will likely be forced to match the competition or lose market share.
    Answer (A) is incorrect. If the company does not need cash, it would not offer cash discounts, regardless of its cost of capital, unless required to match competition. Answer (B) is incorrect. The ability to borrow at a lower rate is a reason for not offering cash discounts. Answer (C) is incorrect. The relationship between the cost of capital and the prime rate may not be relevant if the firm cannot borrow at the prime rate.

24. Clauson, Inc., grants credit terms of 1/15, net 30 and projects gross sales for next year of $2,000,000. The credit manager estimates that 40% of their customers pay on the discount date, 40% on the net due date, and 20% pay 15 days after the net due date. Assuming uniform sales and a 360-day year, what is the projected days' sales outstanding (rounded to the nearest whole day)?

A. 20 days.

B. 24 days.

C. 27 days.

D. 30 days.

Answer (C) is correct. *(CMA, adapted)*
REQUIRED: The projected days' sales outstanding.
DISCUSSION: The days' sales outstanding can be determined by weighting the collection period for each group of receivables by its collection percentage. Hence, the projected days' sales outstanding equal 27 days [(15 days × 40%) + (30 days × 40%) + (45 days × 20%)].
Answer (A) is incorrect. Average receivables are outstanding for much more than 20 days. Answer (B) is incorrect. Twenty-four days assumes 40% of receivables are collected after 15 days and 60% after 30 days. Answer (D) is incorrect. More receivables are collected on the 15th day than on the 45th day; thus, the average must be less than 30 days.

25. Best Computers believes that its collection costs could be reduced through modification of collection procedures. This action is expected to result in a lengthening of the average collection period from 28 days to 34 days; however, there will be no change in uncollectible accounts. The company's budgeted credit sales for the coming year are $27,000,000, and short-term interest rates are expected to average 8%. To make the changes in collection procedures cost beneficial, the minimum savings in collection costs (using a 360-day year) for the coming year would have to be

A. $30,000

B. $36,000

C. $180,000

D. $360,000

Answer (B) is correct. *(CMA, adapted)*
REQUIRED: The minimum savings in collection costs that would be necessary to make the lengthened credit period beneficial.
DISCUSSION: If the change is adopted, Best's average balance in receivables will increase by $450,000 {$27,000,000 × [(34 days – 28 days) ÷ 360 days]}. The minimum savings that Best must experience to justify the change is therefore $36,000 ($450,000 × 8%).

6.5 Inventory Management

26. An example of a carrying cost is

A. Disruption of production schedules.

B. Quantity discounts lost.

C. Handling costs.

D. Spoilage.

Answer (D) is correct. *(CMA, adapted)*
REQUIRED: The inventory carrying cost.
DISCUSSION: Inventory costs fall into three categories: order or set-up costs, carrying (holding) costs, and stockout costs. Carrying costs include storage costs for inventory items plus opportunity cost (i.e., the cost incurred by investing in inventory rather than making an income-earning investment). Examples are insurance, spoilage, interest on invested capital, obsolescence, and warehousing costs.
Answer (A) is incorrect. Disruption of production schedules may result from a stockout. Answer (B) is incorrect. Quantity discounts lost are related to ordering costs or inventory acquisition costs. Answer (C) is incorrect. Shipping and handling costs are included in acquisition costs.

27. The ordering costs associated with inventory management include

A. Insurance costs, purchasing costs, shipping costs, and spoilage.

B. Obsolescence, setup costs, quantity discounts lost, and storage costs.

C. Purchasing costs, shipping costs, setup costs, and quantity discounts lost.

D. Shipping costs, obsolescence, setup costs, and capital invested.

Answer (C) is correct. *(CMA, adapted)*
REQUIRED: The items included in ordering costs.
DISCUSSION: Ordering costs are costs incurred when placing and receiving orders. Ordering costs include purchasing costs, shipping costs, setup costs for a production run, and quantity discounts lost.
Answer (A) is incorrect. Insurance costs are a carrying cost. Answer (B) is incorrect. Obsolescence, spoilage, interest on invested capital, and storage costs are carrying costs. Answer (D) is incorrect. Obsolescence, spoilage, interest on invested capital, and storage costs are carrying costs.

28. A major supplier has offered Alpha Corporation a year-end special purchase whereby Alpha could purchase 180,000 cases of sport drink at $10 per case. Alpha normally orders 30,000 cases per month at $12 per case. Alpha's cost of capital is 9%. In calculating the overall opportunity cost of this offer, the cost of carrying the increased inventory would be

A. $32,400

B. $40,500

C. $64,800

D. $81,000

Answer (A) is correct. *(CMA, adapted)*
REQUIRED: The cost of carrying the increased inventory.
DISCUSSION: If Alpha makes the special purchase of 6 months of inventory (180,000 cases ÷ 30,000 cases per month), the average inventory for the 6-month period will be $900,000 [(180,000 × $10) ÷ 2]. If the special purchase is not made, the average inventory for the same period will be the average monthly inventory of $180,000 [(30,000 × $12) ÷ 2]. Accordingly, the incremental average inventory is $720,000 ($900,000 − $180,000), and the interest cost of the incremental 6-month investment is $32,400 [($720,000 × 9%) ÷ 2].
Answer (B) is incorrect. The amount of $40,500 is the result of assuming an incremental average inventory of $900,000. Answer (C) is incorrect. The interest cost for 12 months is $64,800. Answer (D) is incorrect. The amount of $81,000 is the result of assuming an incremental average inventory of $900,000 and a 12-month period.

29. In inventory management, the safety stock will tend to increase if the

A. Carrying cost increases.

B. Cost of running out of stock decreases.

C. Variability of the lead time increases.

D. Variability of the usage rate decreases.

Answer (C) is correct. *(CMA, adapted)*
REQUIRED: The factor that will cause safety stocks to increase.
DISCUSSION: A company maintains safety stocks to protect itself against the losses caused by stockouts. These can take the form of lost sales or lost production time. Safety stock is necessary because of the variability in lead time and usage rates. As the variability in lead time increases, a company will tend to carry larger safety stocks.
Answer (A) is incorrect. An increase in inventory carrying costs makes it less economical to carry safety stocks. Answer (B) is incorrect. If the cost of stockouts declines, the incentive to carry large safety stocks is reduced. Answer (D) is incorrect. A decline in the variability of usage makes it easier to plan orders, and safety stocks will be less necessary.

30. Handy operates a chain of hardware stores across Ohio. The controller wants to determine the optimum safety stock levels for an air purifier unit. The inventory manager compiled the following data:

- The annual carrying cost of inventory approximates 20% of the investment in inventory.
- The inventory investment per unit averages $50.
- The stockout cost is estimated to be $5 per unit.
- The company orders inventory on the average of 10 times per year.
- Total cost = carrying cost + expected stockout cost.
- The probabilities of a stockout per order cycle with varying levels of safety stock are as follows:

Units		
Safety Stock	Resulting Stockout	Probability
200	0	0%
100	100	15%
0	100	15%
0	200	12%

The total cost of safety stock on an annual basis with a safety stock level of 100 units is

A. $1,750

B. $1,950

C. $550

D. $2,000

Answer (A) is correct. *(CMA, adapted)*
REQUIRED: The total cost of safety stock on an annual basis for a given safety stock level.
DISCUSSION: The cost of safety stock is given as carrying cost plus expected stockout cost. At 20% of the $50 unit inventory cost, carrying cost is $10 per unit per year. Thus, carrying cost for 100 units of safety stock is $1,000. A stockout has a 15% probability at this level of safety stock, and stockout costs are $500 (100 × $5) for each occurrence. If the firm orders 10 times per year, the expected number of stockouts is 1.5 (15% × 10). Hence, total expected stockout cost for the year is $750 ($500 × 1.5). Total cost is $1,750 per year ($1,000 + $750).
Answer (B) is incorrect. The amount of $1,950 is the sum of the expected stockout costs for stockouts of 100 units and 200 units. Answer (C) is incorrect. The carrying cost alone is $10 per unit, or $1,000 per year. Answer (D) is incorrect. The amount of $2,000 is the carrying cost of 200 units of safety stock.

31. The result of the economic order quantity (EOQ) formula indicates the

    A. Annual quantity of inventory to be carried.

    B. Annual usage of materials during the year.

    C. Safety stock plus estimated inventory for the year.

    D. Quantity of each individual order during the year.

Answer (D) is correct. *(CMA, adapted)*
    REQUIRED: The indication given by the EOQ formula.
    DISCUSSION: The EOQ model is a deterministic model that calculates the ideal order (or production lot) quantity given specified demand, ordering or setup costs, and carrying costs. The model minimizes the sum of inventory carrying costs and either ordering or production setup costs.
    Answer (A) is incorrect. The annual quantity of inventory demanded is an input into the formula, not the result. Answer (B) is incorrect. Annual usage is a determinant of annual demand, which is an input into the formula. Answer (C) is incorrect. Safety stock is not reflected in the basic EOQ formula.

32. The Stewart Co. uses the economic order quantity (EOQ) model for inventory management. A decrease in which one of the following variables would increase the EOQ?

    A. Annual sales.

    B. Cost per order.

    C. Safety stock level.

    D. Carrying costs.

Answer (D) is correct. *(CMA, adapted)*
    REQUIRED: The variable for which a decrease will lead to an increase in the economic order quantity (EOQ).
    DISCUSSION: The EOQ model minimizes the total of ordering and carrying costs. The EOQ is calculated as follows:

$$\sqrt{\frac{2\,(Demand)\,(Order\ costs)}{Carrying\ costs\ per\ unit}}$$

Increases in the numerator (demand or ordering costs) will increase the EOQ, whereas decreases in demand or ordering costs will decrease the EOQ. Similarly, a decrease in the denominator (carrying costs) will increase the EOQ.
    Answer (A) is incorrect. A decrease in demand (annual sales), which is in the numerator, will decrease the EOQ. Answer (B) is incorrect. A decrease in ordering costs will encourage more orders, or a decrease in the EOQ. Answer (C) is incorrect. A decrease in safety stock levels will not affect the EOQ, although it might lead to a different ordering point.

6.6 Short-Term Financing

33. Which one of the following provides a spontaneous source of financing for a firm?

    A. Accounts payable.

    B. Mortgage bonds.

    C. Accounts receivable.

    D. Debentures.

Answer (A) is correct. *(CMA, adapted)*
    REQUIRED: The item that provides a spontaneous source of financing.
    DISCUSSION: Trade credit is a spontaneous source of financing because it arises automatically as part of a purchase transaction. Because of its ease in use, trade credit is the largest source of short-term financing for many firms both large and small.
    Answer (B) is incorrect. Mortgage bonds and debentures do not arise automatically as a result of a purchase transaction. Answer (C) is incorrect. The use of receivables as a financing source requires an extensive factoring arrangement and often involves the creditor's evaluation of the credit ratings of the borrower's customers. Answer (D) is incorrect. Mortgage bonds and debentures do not arise automatically as a result of a purchase transaction.

34. Which one of the following financial instruments generally provides the largest source of short-term credit for small firms?

    A. Installment loans.

    B. Commercial paper.

    C. Trade credit.

    D. Bankers' acceptances.

Answer (C) is correct. *(CMA, adapted)*
    REQUIRED: The largest source of short-term credit for small firms.
    DISCUSSION: Trade credit is a spontaneous source of financing because it arises automatically as part of a purchase transaction. Because of its ease in use, trade credit is the largest source of short-term financing for many firms both large and small.
    Answer (A) is incorrect. Installment loans are usually a longer-term source of financing and are more difficult to acquire than trade credit. Answer (B) is incorrect. Commercial paper is normally used only by large companies with high credit ratings. Answer (D) is incorrect. Bankers' acceptances are drafts drawn on bank deposits; the acceptance is a guarantee of payment at maturity.

35. Maple Motors buys axles in order to produce automobiles. Maple carries an average credit balance of $25,000,000 with its axle supplier. The axle supplier provides credit terms of 1/10 net 25. The nominal annual cost of Maple **not** taking the trade discount is closest to which one of the following? Assume a 360-day year.

    A. 14.4%

    B. 14.5%

    C. 24.0%

    D. 24.2%

Answer (D) is correct. *(CMA, adapted)*
    REQUIRED: The annualized cost of not taking a trade discount.
    DISCUSSION: The annualized cost of not taking a discount can be calculated with this formula:

$$\frac{Discount\ \%}{100\% - Discount\ \%} \times \frac{Days\ in\ year}{Total\ payment\ period - Discount\ period}$$

Cost of not taking discount = [1% ÷ (100% − 1%)] × [360 days ÷ (25 days − 10 days)]
        = (1% ÷ 99%) × (360 days ÷ 15 days)
        = 24 × 1.0101%
        = 24.24%

    Answer (A) is incorrect. This percentage results from failing to take the discount period and discount percentage into account in the two denominators [1% × (360 ÷ 25) = 14.4%]. Answer (B) is incorrect. This percentage results from using a 365-day year. Answer (C) is incorrect. This percentage results from failing to take the discount percentage into account in the denominator of the first fraction [1% × (360 ÷ 15) = 24.0%]

36. Which one of the following responses is **not** an advantage to a corporation that uses the commercial paper market for short-term financing?

    A. This market provides more funds at lower rates than other methods provide.

    B. The borrower avoids the expense of maintaining a compensating balance with a commercial bank.

    C. There are no restrictions as to the type of corporation that can enter into this market.

    D. This market provides a broad distribution for borrowing.

Answer (C) is correct. *(CMA, adapted)*
    REQUIRED: The item not an advantage of using commercial paper for short-term financing.
    DISCUSSION: Commercial paper is a short-term, unsecured note payable issued in large denominations by major companies with excellent credit ratings. Maturities usually do not exceed 270 days. Commercial paper is a lower cost source of funds than bank loans, and no compensating balances are required. Commercial paper provides a broad and efficient distribution of debt, and costly financing arrangements are avoided. But the market is not open to all companies because only major corporations with high credit ratings can participate.
    Answer (A) is incorrect. Lower rates are an advantage of commercial paper. Answer (B) is incorrect. Avoidance of compensating balance requirements is an advantage of commercial paper. Answer (D) is incorrect. Broad debt distribution is an advantage of commercial paper.

37. On January 1, Scott Corporation received a $300,000 line of credit at an interest rate of 12% from Main Street Bank and drew down the entire amount on February 1. The line of credit agreement requires that an amount equal to 15% of the loan be deposited into a compensating balance account. What is the effective annual cost of credit for this loan arrangement?

    A. 11.00%

    B. 12.00%

    C. 12.94%

    D. 14.12%

Answer (D) is correct. *(CMA, adapted)*
    REQUIRED: The effective annual cost of credit.
    DISCUSSION: The effective interest rate on this financing arrangement can be calculated as follows:

Effective rate = Stated rate ÷ (1.0 − Compensating balance %)
        = 12% ÷ (100% − 15%)
        = 12% ÷ 85%
        = 14.12%

The amount of the loan is not needed to calculate the effective rate.
    Answer (A) is incorrect. The nominal rate for 11 months is 11.00%. Answer (B) is incorrect. The nominal rate of interest is 12.00%. Answer (C) is incorrect. This percentage equals $33,000 (11 months of interest) divided by $255,000.

Questions 38 through 41 are based on the following information. The Frame Supply Company has just acquired a large account and needs to increase its working capital by $100,000. The controller of the company has identified the four sources of funds given below.

1. Pay a factor to buy the company's receivables, which average $125,000 per month and have an average collection period of 30 days. The factor will advance up to 80% of the face value of receivables at 10% and charge a fee of 2% on all receivables purchased. The controller estimates that the firm would save $24,000 in collection expenses over the year. Assume the fee and interest are not deductible in advance.
2. Borrow $110,000 from a bank at 12% interest. A 9% compensating balance would be required.
3. Issue $110,000 of 6-month commercial paper to net $100,000. (New paper would be issued every 6 months.)
4. Borrow $125,000 from a bank on a discount basis at 20%. No compensating balance would be required.

Assume a 360-day year in all of your calculations.

---

38. The cost of Alternative 1 to Frame Supply Company is

   A. 10.0%

   B. 12.0%

   C. 13.2%

   D. 16.0%

Answer (D) is correct. *(CMA, adapted)*
   REQUIRED: The annual percentage cost of factoring receivables.
   DISCUSSION: The first step is to calculate the amount the firm will receive from the factoring transaction:

Amount of receivables	$125,000
Times: advance percentage	× 80%
Amount received	$100,000

This amount is the basis for the calculation of interest expense:

Amount advanced	$100,000
Times: annual finance charge	× 10%
Annual interest expense	$ 10,000

The next step is to calculate the annual factor fee:

Amount of receivables	$125,000
Times: factor fee percentage	× 2%
Monthly factor fee	$ 2,500
Times: months	× 12
Annual factor fee	$ 30,000

The annual net cost of this factoring transaction is calculated as follows:

Annual interest expense	$ 10,000
Annual factor fee	30,000
Less: annual savings	(24,000)
Annual net cost	$ 16,000

As with all financing arrangements, the effective rate is the ratio of the amount the firm must pay to the amount the firm gets use of:

$$\text{Effective rate} = \text{Net cost} \div \text{Usable funds}$$
$$= \$16,000 \div \$100,000$$
$$= 16.0\%$$

   Answer (A) is incorrect. The interest rate on the amount advanced is 10%. Answer (B) is incorrect. The sum of the interest rate and the fee percentage is 12%. Answer (C) is incorrect. The cost of Alternative 2 is 13.2%.

39. The cost of Alternative 2 to Frame Supply Company is

A. 9.0%

B. 12.0%

C. 13.2%

D. 21.0%

Answer (C) is correct. *(CMA, adapted)*
  REQUIRED: The annual percentage cost of borrowing with a compensating balance requirement.
  DISCUSSION: The effective interest rate on a loan that requires a compensating balance can be calculated as follows:

$$\text{Effective rate} = \text{Stated rate} \div (1.0 - \text{Compensating balance \%})$$
$$= 12\% \div (100\% - 9\%)$$
$$= 12\% \div 91\%$$
$$= 13.19\%$$

  Answer (A) is incorrect. The compensating balance requirement is 9.0%. Answer (B) is incorrect. The contract rate is 12.0%. Answer (D) is incorrect. This percentage is the sum of the contract rate and the compensating balance requirement.

40. The cost of Alternative 3 to Frame Supply Company is

A. 9.1%

B. 10.0%

C. 18.2%

D. 20.0%

Answer (D) is correct. *(CMA, adapted)*
  REQUIRED: The annual percentage cost of issuing commercial paper.
  DISCUSSION: By issuing commercial paper, the company will receive $100,000 and repay $110,000 every 6 months. Thus, for the use of $100,000 in funds, the company pays $10,000 in interest each 6-month period, or a total of $20,000 per year. The annual percentage rate can therefore be calculated as follows:

$$\text{Effective rate} = \text{Interest expense} \div \text{Usable funds}$$
$$= \$20,000 \div \$100,000$$
$$= 20.0\%$$

  Answer (A) is incorrect. This percentage is the 6-month rate based on the face amount of the paper. Answer (B) is incorrect. The rate for 6 months is 10.0%. Answer (C) is incorrect. This percentage is based on the face amount of the commercial paper.

41. The cost of Alternative 4 to Frame Supply Company is

A. 20.0%

B. 25.0%

C. 40.0%

D. 50.0%

Answer (B) is correct. *(CMA, adapted)*
  REQUIRED: The annual percentage cost of a discounted note.
  DISCUSSION: The company will receive $100,000 ($125,000 × 80%) at an annual cost of $25,000 ($125,000 − $100,000). The effective interest rate on this loan can thus be calculated as follows:

$$\text{Effective rate} = \text{Interest expense} \div \text{Usable funds}$$
$$= \$25,000 \div \$100,000$$
$$= 25.0\%$$

  Answer (A) is incorrect. The effective rate must exceed the contract rate of 20%. Answer (C) is incorrect. This percentage assumes no discount and a 6-month loan term. Answer (D) is incorrect. This percentage assumes a 6-month loan term.

Use the Gleim CMA Test Prep Software for interactive testing with additional multiple-choice questions!

*Page
Intentionally
Left Blank*

6.8 ESSAY QUESTIONS

<u>**Scenario for Essay Questions 1, 2, 3, 4**</u>

Attract-One, Inc. (AOI), a moderately profitable producer of fragrances, has been in business for a number of years and sells its products through its U.S. retailer network. In the last year, AOI has developed and introduced a line of fragrances that has had wide public acceptance. Retailer remittances have grown to an average of $200,000 each business day, with additional collections of $1,250,000 a day for each 4-day period following the special occasions of Valentine's Day, Mother's Day, June graduations, and Christmas.

AOI is continuing to expand its network of retail outlets and introduce new lines of consumer products, fully expecting continued growth of the company. As a result, Steve Louhan, treasurer, has been hired to direct AOI's cash management function. After reviewing the company's centralized operations, Louhan found that retailer remittances take an average of 5 mail days to reach AOI. An additional 2 days are needed for in-house processing before bank deposits are made.

Louhan has investigated various regional lockbox arrangements as a means to accelerate this cash collection process. Louhan determined that with a three-bank system, one each in the eastern, central, and western regions of the U.S., mail times could be reduced by 2 days. In addition, the in-house check processing would be eliminated. The banks would provide AOI with a listing of daily transactions and any supporting documents that retailers submit with payments. The lockbox service charges would be $1,000 per month for each bank, and Louhan estimates that 6% interest could be earned on short-term investments.

Louhan is also considering various ways of investing available funds, including the use of marketable securities. He believes this is particularly important during the peak periods when cash inflows are large.

Questions

1. Briefly describe the responsibilities of the cash management function.

2. Identify and describe at least two motives for a company to hold cash.

3. a. Identify and explain at least three characteristics of marketable securities that a company should consider when investing.

   b. Identify at least three types of financial instruments that would meet Attract-One, Inc.'s cash and investing needs.

4. Recommend whether or not Attract-One, Inc., should implement a lockbox system by preparing an analysis using a 360-day year.

Essay Questions 1, 2, 3, 4 — Unofficial Answers

1. The responsibilities of the cash management function include planning and controlling cash collections, disbursements, and cash balances in order to maintain liquidity, as well as develop banking relationships.

2. At least two motives for a company to hold cash include using cash for

    a. Transactions, since cash is necessary to conduct business, such as purchases, paying wages, taxes, or dividends

    b. Precautions against unexpected needs, as cash inflows and outflows are unpredictable

3. a. At least three characteristics that a firm should consider when investing in marketable securities include

    1) Default risk, as safety of principal is an important concern for investments that are to be included in the short-term portfolio

    2) Marketability, as the securities should be easy to sell for cash liquidity needs

    3) Maturity, as yields are generally higher, but riskier for longer-term investment

    b. At least three types of financial instruments that would meet Attract-One, Inc.'s cash and investing needs include

    1) U.S. Treasury bills
    2) Negotiable certificates of deposit
    3) Prime commercial paper

4. The benefit or loss on a proposed cash management system is found by determining whether the incremental interest income earned will exceed the cost of the new system. If implemented, the new system would accelerate the company's collections by 4 days (2 days mail time + 2 days processing time).

Interest income from average daily balances:	
($200,000 × 4 days saved × .06)	$48,000
Interest income from additional holiday volume:	
[($1,250,000 × 4 days saved × 4 holidays) ÷ 360 days] × .06	3,333
Total incremental interest income	$51,333
Less: cost of lockbox system:	
(3 banks × $1,000 per month × 12 months)	(36,000)
Net benefit from implementing lockbox system	$15,333

NOTE: Interest income from time savings of daily average collections alone exceeds cost of implementation. Interest income associated with holiday savings is an additional benefit. Since the incremental interest income that can be earned from implementing the lockbox system exceeds its cost, the system should be adopted.

Use **CMA Gleim Online** and **Essay Wizard** to practice additional essay questions in an exam-like environment.

STUDY UNIT SEVEN
RAISING CAPITAL, CORPORATE RESTRUCTURING, AND INTERNATIONAL FINANCE

(47 pages of outline)

This study unit is the **last of four** on **corporate finance**. The relative weight assigned to this major topic in Part 2 of the exam is **25%**. The four study units are

Study Unit 4: Investment Risk and Portfolio Management
Study Unit 5: Financial Instruments and Cost of Capital
Study Unit 6: Managing Current Assets
Study Unit 7: Raising Capital, Corporate Restructuring, and International Finance

After studying the outline and answering the questions in this study unit, you will have the skills necessary to address the following topics listed in the ICMA's Learning Outcome Statements:

Part 2 – Section B.6. Raising capital

The candidate should be able to:

a. identify the characteristics of the different types of financial markets and exchanges
b. demonstrate an understanding of the concept of market efficiency, including the strong form, semi-strong form, and weak form of market efficiency
c. describe the role of the credit rating agencies
d. demonstrate an understanding of the roles of investment banks, including underwriting, advice, and trading
e. define offering price and calculate spread
f. identify and define the terms best-efforts distribution, syndicate, and tombstone ad
g. identify the information that must be supplied when registering with the SEC
h. distinguish between a public offering and a private placement
i. define initial public offerings (IPOs)
j. define subsequent/secondary offerings
k. define the different types of dividends, including cash dividends, stock dividends, and stock splits
l. identify and discuss the factors that influence the dividend policy of a firm
m. demonstrate an understanding of the dividend payment process for both common and preferred stock
n. define share repurchase and explain why a firm would repurchase its stock
o. define dividend reinvestment plans
p. define insider trading and explain why it is illegal
q. describe lease financing, explain its benefits and disadvantages, and calculate the net advantage to leasing using discounted cash flow concepts

Part 2 – Section B.7. Corporate restructuring

The candidate should be able to:

    a.   demonstrate an understanding of mergers, acquisitions, and leveraged buyouts

    b.   identify defenses against takeovers

    c.   identify and describe divestiture concepts such as spin-offs, split-ups, equity carve-outs, and tracking stock

    d.   evaluate a company's financial situation and determine if a restructuring would be beneficial to the shareholders

    e.   identify possible synergies in targeted mergers and acquisitions

    f.   define bankruptcy and identify the different types of bankruptcy

    g.   determine the priority of creditors in a bankruptcy proceeding

    h.   differentiate between reorganization and liquidation

Part 2 – Section B.8. International finance

The candidate should be able to:

    a.   demonstrate an understanding of foreign currencies and how prices are determined in the foreign exchange market

    b.   identify the variables that affect exchange rates

    c.   calculate whether a currency has depreciated or appreciated against another currency over a period of time

    d.   demonstrate how currency futures, currency swaps, and currency options can be used to manage exchange rate risk

    e.   calculate the net profit/loss of cross-border transactions

    f.   recommend methods of managing exchange rate risk and calculate the net profit/loss of your strategy

    g.   identify and explain the benefits of international diversification

    h.   identify and explain common trade financing methods, including cross-border factoring, letters of credit, banker's acceptances, forfaiting, and countertrade

    i.   demonstrate an understanding of how transfer pricing is used by multinational firms to manage their effective worldwide tax rate

    j.   define and discuss political risk

7.1 FINANCIAL MARKETS AND SECURITIES OFFERINGS

    1. **Aspects of Financial Markets**

        a.   Financial markets facilitate the creation and transfer of financial assets and obligations. They bring together entities that have funds to invest with entities that have financing needs. The resulting transactions create assets for the former and obligations for the latter.

            1) Transfers of funds may be direct or may be through intermediate entities such as banks. The use of intermediate entities and financial markets improves allocative efficiency because of their special expertise. The result is the availability of relatively rapid and low-cost transfers of capital, an essential feature of a modern economy.

        b.   Financial markets are not particular places but rather the totality of supply and demand for securities. Securities include a very wide variety of instruments. Some of the most basic are stocks, corporate bonds, mortgages, consumer loans, leases, commercial paper, certificates of deposit, governmental securities, and derivatives of many kinds. Moreover, new kinds of securities are continually being developed.

2. **Money Markets and Capital Markets**

   a. Money markets trade debt securities with maturities of less than 1 year. These are dealer-driven markets because most transactions involve dealers who buy and sell instruments at their own risk. The dealer is a principal in most transactions, unlike a stockbroker who acts as an agent. Money markets exist in New York, London, and Tokyo. Money market securities are generally short-term and marketable. They usually have low default risk. Money market securities include

      1) Government Treasury bills
      2) Government Treasury notes and bonds
      3) Federal agency securities
      4) Short-term tax-exempt securities
      5) Commercial paper
      6) Certificates of deposit
      7) Repurchase agreements
      8) Eurodollar CDs
      9) Bankers' acceptances

   b. Capital markets trade long-term debt and equity securities. The New York Stock Exchange is an example of a capital market.

3. **Primary Markets and Secondary Markets**

   a. Primary markets are the markets in which corporations and governmental units raise new capital by making initial offerings of their securities. The issuer receives the proceeds of sale in a primary market.

   b. Secondary markets provide for trading of previously issued securities among investors. Examples of secondary markets include auction markets and dealer markets.

      1) Auction markets like the New York Stock Exchange, the American Stock Exchange, and regional exchanges conduct trading at particular physical sites. Furthermore, share prices are communicated immediately to the public.

         a) Companies that wish to have their shares traded on an exchange must apply for listing and meet certain requirements. For example, the New York Stock Exchange has established requirements relating to the amount and value of shares outstanding, the number of shareholders, earning power, and tangible assets.

            i) Listing is beneficial because it adds to a firm's prestige and increases the liquidity of a firm's securities. However, increased SEC disclosure requirements and the greater risk of an unfriendly takeover are possible disadvantages.

         b) Matching of buy and sell orders communicated to brokerages with seats on the exchange is the essence of exchange trading. To facilitate this process, members known as specialists undertake to make a market in particular stocks. These firms are obliged to buy and sell those stocks.

            i) Accordingly, a specialist maintains an inventory of stocks and sets bid and asked prices (prices at which the specialist will buy or sell, respectively) to keep the inventory in balance.

            ii) The profit margin for the specialist is the spread, or the excess of the asked over the bid price.

c)   Stock exchanges have expanded their role to include trading in derivatives. Moreover, commodities markets, e.g., the Chicago Board of Trade and the Chicago Mercantile Exchange also permit trading in derivatives. Thus, both commodity futures (e.g., in oil, livestock, metals, grains, and fibers) and financial futures (e.g., in U.S. Treasury Securities, foreign currencies, stock indexes, bonds, and certificates of deposit) are now traded on commodity exchanges.

2)   The over-the-counter (OTC) market is a dealer market. It consists of numerous brokers and dealers who are linked by telecommunications equipment that enables them to trade throughout the country. The OTC market conducts transactions in securities not traded on the stock exchanges.

   a)   The OTC market handles transactions involving

      i)   Bonds of U.S. companies
      ii)   Bonds of federal, state, and local governments
      iii) Open-end investment company shares of mutual funds
      iv)   New securities issues
      v)   Most secondary stock distributions, whether or not they are listed on an exchange

   b)   The governing authority for the OTC market is the National Association of Securities Dealers (NASD). Its computerized trading system is the NASD Automated Quotation (NASDAQ) system, which supplies price quotes and volume amounts during the trading day.

   c)   The majority of stocks are traded in the OTC market, but the dollar volume of trading on the exchanges is greater because they list the largest companies.

   d)   Brokers and dealers of OTC securities may also maintain inventories of securities to match buy and sell orders efficiently.

   e)   Trading in the bonds of corporations is primarily done in the OTC market by large institutional investors, such as pension funds, mutual funds, and life insurance companies. Because very large amounts are exchanged among a few investors, dealers in the bond markets can feasibly arrange these transactions. A similar arrangement for trading of stocks would be difficult because they are owned by millions of shareholders.

4.   **Financial Intermediaries**

   a.   Financial intermediaries are specialized firms that help create and exchange the instruments of financial markets. Financial intermediaries increase the efficiency of financial markets through better allocation of financial resources.

      1)   The financial intermediary obtains funds from savers, issues its own securities, and uses the money to purchase an enterprise's securities. Thus, financial intermediaries create new forms of capital. For example, a savings and loan association purchases a mortgage with its funds from savers and issues a savings account or a certificate of deposit.

    b.   Financial intermediaries include

        1)   Commercial banks
        2)   Life insurance companies
        3)   Private pension funds
        4)   Nonbank thrift institutions, such as savings banks and credit unions
        5)   State and local pension funds
        6)   Mutual funds
        7)   Finance companies
        8)   Casualty insurance companies
        9)   Money market funds
        10) Mutual savings banks
        11) Credit unions
        12) Investment bankers

5. Efficient Markets Hypothesis

    a.   The efficient markets hypothesis states that current stock prices immediately and fully reflect all relevant information. Hence, the market is continuously adjusting to new information and acting to correct pricing errors.

        1)   In other words, securities prices are always in equilibrium. The reason is that securities are subject to intense analysis by many thousands of highly trained individuals.

        2)   These analysts work for well-capitalized institutions with the resources to take very rapid action when new information is available.

    b.   The efficient markets hypothesis states that it is impossible to obtain abnormal returns consistently with either fundamental or technical analysis.

        1)   Fundamental analysis is the evaluation of a security's future price movement based upon sales, internal developments, industry trends, the general economy, and expected changes in each factor.

        2)   Technical analysis is the evaluation of a security's future price based on the sales price and number of shares traded in a series of recent transactions.

    c.   Under the efficient markets hypothesis, the expected return of each security is equal to the return required by the marginal investor given the risk of the security. Moreover, the price equals its fair value as perceived by investors. The efficient markets hypothesis has three forms (versions).

        1)   Strong Form

            a)   All public and private information is instantaneously reflected in securities' prices. Thus, insider trading is assumed not to result in abnormal returns.

        2)   Semistrong Form

            a)   All publicly available data are reflected in security prices, but private or insider data are not immediately reflected. Accordingly, insider trading can result in abnormal returns.

        3)   Weak Form

            a)   Current securities prices reflect all recent past price movement data, so technical analysis will not provide a basis for abnormal returns in securities trading.

        4)   Empirical data have refuted the strong form of the efficient markets hypothesis but not the weak and semistrong forms.

    d.   The market efficiently incorporates public information into securities prices. However, when making investment decisions, investors should be aware of economic information about the firm's markets and the strength of the products of the firm.

        1)   Because the possibility exists that all information is not reflected in security prices, there is an opportunity for arbitrage.

6.   Rating Agencies

    a.   A firm must pay to have its debt rated. Standard & Poor's and Moody's are the most frequently used agencies.

        1)   Ratings are based upon the probability of default and the protection for investors in case of default.

    b.   The ratings are determined from corporate information such as financial statements.

        1)   Important factors involved in the analysis include the ability of the issuer to service its debt with its cash flows, the amount of debt it has already issued, the type of debt issued, and the firm's cash flow stability.

        2)   A rating may change because the rating agencies periodically review outstanding securities. A decrease in the rating may increase the firm's cost of capital or reduce its ability to borrow long-term. One reason is that many institutional investors are not allowed to purchase lower-grade securities.

        3)   A rating agency review of existing securities may be triggered by a variety of factors, e.g., a new issue of debt, an intended merger involving an exchange of bonds for stock, or material changes in the economic circumstances of the firm.

    c.   The ratings are significant because higher ratings lower interest costs to issuing firms. Lower ratings incur higher required rates of return.

        1)   The lower the risk of default, the lower the interest rate the market will demand.

    d.   Standard & Poor's rates bonds from very high quality to very poor quality.

        1)   AAA and AA are the highest, signifying little chance of default and high quality.

        2)   A- and BBB-rated bonds are of investment grade. They have strong interest- and principal-paying capabilities. Bonds with these ratings are the lowest-rated securities that many institutional investors are permitted to hold.

        3)   Debt rated BB and below is speculative; such bonds are junk bonds.

            a)   Junk bonds are high-yield or low-grade bonds.

            b)   These high-risk bonds have received much attention in the last decade because of their use in corporate mergers and restructurings and the increase in junk-bond defaults.

        4)   CCC to D are very poor debt ratings. The likelihood of default is significant, or the debt is already in default (D rating).

        5)   Standard & Poor's adjusts its ratings with the use of a plus-minus system. A plus indicates a stronger rating in a category and a minus a weaker rating.

    e.   Moody's rates bonds in a similar manner. Its ratings vary from Aaa for very high quality debt to D for very poor debt.

7. **Investment Banking**

    a.   Investment bankers serve as intermediaries between businesses and the providers of capital.

        1)   Moreover, they not only help to sell new securities but also assist in business combinations, act as brokers in secondary markets, and trade for their own accounts.

    b.   In their traditional role in the sale of new securities, investment bankers help determine the method of issuing the securities and the price to be charged, distribute the securities, provide expert advice, and perform a certification function.

        1)   An issuer of new securities ordinarily selects an investment banker in a negotiated deal. Only a few large issuers seek competitive bids. The reason for the predominance of negotiated deals is that the costs of learning about the issuer and setting an issue price and fees are usually prohibitive unless the investment banker has a high probability of closing the deal.

        2)   A choice must be made as to whether to have the securities underwritten or sold through the best efforts of the investment banker.

            a)   Best efforts sales of securities provide no guarantee that the securities will be sold or that enough cash will be raised. The investment banker receives commissions and is obligated to use its best efforts to sell the securities.

            b)   An underwritten deal or a firm commitment provides a guarantee. The investment banker agrees to purchase the entire issue and resell it.

        3)   Investment bankers contribute to the efficiency with which securities are sold. An investment banker has a professional staff, a network of dealers, and a regular clientele.

        4)   The certification function of an investment banker derives from its reputation capital.

            a)   The expertise, integrity, and experience of the investment banker help to offset the information asymmetry between the management of the issuing firm and potential buyers of the securities. Thus, buyers rely on the investment banker's reputation for pricing the issue fairly.

    c.   A prospective issuer and an investment banker conduct preunderwriting conferences to discuss such basic questions as the amount to be raised, the type of securities to issue, and the nature of their agreement.

        1)   After the parties agree that a flotation will occur, the investment banker conducts an investigation of the issuer. Thus, a firm of public accountants is engaged to audit the issuer and to assist in preparing the registration statement to be filed with the SEC. Attorneys are hired as advisers concerning the legal issues, and other experts are consulted as necessary.

            a)   The investment banker that serves as the managing underwriter will also analyze the issuer's financial condition and prospects.

        2)   The result of this phase is an agreement establishing all of the terms of the arrangement, including the amount of capital to be raised, the type of securities, and the basis for determining the offering price.

    d.   The next step is the filing of a registration statement with the SEC. This process may be necessary whether the issue is an initial public offering (see item 8.) or a seasoned issue (one made by a company whose securities are already publicly traded).

e. Determining the offering price of the securities is crucial. For a seasoned issue, the offering price may be pegged to the price of the existing securities, such as the market price of stock or the yield on bonds. For example, an issue of common stock may be priced at a certain percentage below the closing price on the last day of the registration period.

1) The spread is the difference between the price paid by the investment banker (underwriter) and the offering price paid by investors. It provides a profit and covers the costs of underwriting. For example, if an investment banker buys a firm's stock for $50.00 per share, and the offering price is $53.50, then the underwriter's spread is $3.50 per share ($53.50 – $50.00), or 7% of the offer price.

2) However, if the closing price falls below a certain price (the upset price), the agreement is voided.

3) The issuer and the investment banker obviously have divergent interests regarding price. The investment banker wants to set a price as low as possible to facilitate sale, whereas the issuer desires as high a price as possible to raise the maximum amount of funds.

a) For seasoned issues, recent market prices may provide clear guidelines, but the problem may be acute for an initial public offering.

f. A single investment banker ordinarily does not underwrite an entire issue of securities unless the amount is relatively small. To share the risk of overpricing the issue or of a market decline during the offering period, the investment banker (the lead or managing underwriter) forms an underwriting syndicate with other firms. The members of the syndicate share in the underwriting commission, but their risk is limited to the percentage of their participation.

1) The formation of a syndicate also improves marketing efficiency by combining the efforts of the firms' selling organizations.

2) For a large offering, a selling group is also formed. It consists of the members of the syndicate and other dealers who take small shares of the issue (participations) from the original underwriters. Accordingly, the syndicate members are in effect wholesalers of the securities, and the additional members of the selling group are retailers.

a) The members of the selling group agree to subscribe to the new issue at the public offering price minus the concession they receive as a commission. They also agree not to sell below the public offering price.

3) While the public offering is in force, but not for more than approximately 30 days, the lead underwriter customarily attempts to maintain a stable price for the securities by placing orders to buy in the market.

a) One incidental effect of this operation is that the certificate numbers of repurchased securities are examined to determine whether members of the selling group have violated their agreement not to sell below the public offering price.

g. **Flotation costs**, or the costs of issuing new securities, are relatively lower for large issues than those for small issues. These costs include the following:

1) The underwriting spread is the difference between the price paid by purchasers and the net amount received by the issuer.

2) The issuer incurs expenses for filing fees, taxes, accountants' fees, and attorneys' fees. These costs are essentially fixed.

3) The issuer incurs indirect costs because of management time devoted to the issue.

             4) Announcement of a new issue of seasoned securities usually results in a price decline. One theory is that the announcement is a negative signal to the market. Management may not want to issue new stock when it is undervalued. Moreover, existing owners do not want to share the company's growth with additional owners.

             5) The green shoe option allows underwriters to buy additional shares to compensate for oversubscriptions. A cost is involved because the option will be exercised only when the offer price is lower than the market price.

             6) An offer of unseasoned securities (an initial public offering) tends to be significantly underpriced compared with the price in the aftermarket.

     h. Flotation costs tend to be greater for common stock than for preferred stock and for stocks than for bonds.

8. **Initial Public Offerings (IPOs)**

     a. A firm's first issuance of securities to the public is an initial public offering.

             1) The process by which a closely held corporation issues new securities to the public is called going public. When a firm goes public, it issues its stock on a new issue or initial public offering market.

             2) Later issues of stock by the same company are subsequent offerings.

     b. Advantages of going public include

             1) The ability to raise additional funds
             2) The establishment of the firm's value in the market
             3) An increase in the liquidity of the firm's stock

     c. Disadvantages of going public include

             1) Costs of the reporting requirements of the SEC and other agencies
             2) Access to the company's operating data by competing firms
             3) Access to net worth information of major shareholders
             4) Limitations on self-dealing by corporate insiders, such as officers and major shareholders
             5) Pressure from outside shareholders for earnings growth
             6) Stock prices that do not accurately reflect the true net worth of the company
             7) Loss of control by management as ownership is diversified
             8) Need for improved management control as operations expand
             9) Increased shareholder servicing costs

     d. To have its stock listed (have it traded on a stock exchange), the firm must apply to a stock exchange, pay a fee, and fulfill the exchange's requirements for membership.

             1) Included in the requirements for membership is disclosure of the firm's financial data.

     e. Once the decision to make an initial public offering has been made, the questions are similar to those for seasoned issues: the amount to be raised, the type of securities to sell, and the method of sale. For example, the following matters should be considered in selecting the type of securities to issue:

             1) Should fixed charges be avoided? The issuance of debt would create fixed charges.
             2) Is a maturity date on the security preferable, or is permanent capital more attractive?
             3) Does the firm want a cushion to protect itself from losses to the firm's creditors?
             4) How quickly and easily does the firm want to raise the capital?
             5) Is the firm concerned about losing control of the company?
             6) How does the cost of underwriting differ among the types of securities?

f.   The company's next step is to prepare and file a registration statement and prospectus with the Securities and Exchange Commission (SEC).

1)   The **Securities Act of 1933** prohibits the offer or sale through the use of the mails or any means of interstate commerce of any security unless a registration statement for that security is in effect or an exemption from registration is applicable. Thus, any offer or sale of a security to the public requires registration unless a specific exemption applies.

a)   A registration statement is a complete disclosure to the SEC of all material information with respect to the issuance of the specific securities.

b)   The purpose of registration is to provide adequate and accurate disclosure of financial and other pertinent information with which potential investors may evaluate the merits of the securities. Registration calls for

i)   A description of the registrant's business and property, the significant provisions of the security to be offered for sale, and its relationship to the registrant's other securities

ii)   Information about management

iii)   The most recent audited financial statements

iv)   Disclosure of the principal purposes for which the offering's proceeds will be used

c)   The SEC does not make any judgment on the financial health of an investment or guarantee the accuracy of the information contained in the registration statement.

i)   Registration does not insure investors against loss.

d)   In response to the Emerging Company Marketplace initiative of the American Stock Exchange (Amex), the SEC has proposed rules to simplify the process for small businesses to register securities.

i)   Simpler financial reporting forms are being devised.

ii)   The rules would facilitate active auction-type trading of stock of emerging companies on a branch of the Amex. This could provide greater access to capital than the over-the-counter markets.

2)   The registration process has three distinct periods.

a)   During the prefiling period, the issuer may engage in preliminary negotiations and agreements with underwriters. Offers to buy or sell securities are prohibited during this period.

b)   The waiting period begins when the registration statement is filed. During this time, selling a security is still illegal; however, making an oral offer to buy or sell a security is not.

i)   Information may be published during the waiting period in tombstone ads. These ads must state that they are not offers and must identify

•   The name and the business of the issuer

•   The amount of securities being offered and the price if known

•   The approximate date when the offering will be made

•   The party by whom the orders will be executed and from whom a prospectus may be obtained

ii)   Dealers may make offers to buy from underwriters subject to later acceptance.

       iii) There are no restrictions on oral offers made during the waiting period. Moreover, a preliminary prospectus may be distributed. It contains information similar to that in a registration statement.

- The outside front cover page of the preliminary prospectus must bear, in red ink and printed in large type, the title "preliminary prospectus," the date of issuance, and a required legend.
- The legend states, among other things, that a registration statement has been filed, it has not yet become effective, the securities may not be sold and offers to buy may not be accepted prior to the time the registration statement becomes effective, and the prospectus shall not constitute an offer to sell or the solicitation of an offer to buy.
- A preliminary prospectus is called a red-herring prospectus.

       iv) The SEC uses the 20-day waiting period to review the registration statement. If the registration statement does not substantially comply with the statutory requirements, the SEC will issue detailed comments as to how the statement can be brought into conformity. Any amendments to the registration statement have the effect of starting the 20-day waiting period anew.

  c) The post-effective period begins once a registration statement becomes effective. The underlying securities may then be sold.

       i) The SEC may issue a **bedbug letter** during the 20-day waiting period. In a bedbug letter, the SEC states that the registration statement is poorly prepared or fails to disclose information adequately.

       ii) An issuer who receives a bedbug letter must either redraft the registration statement or cancel the public offering.

       iii) If the registration is not rewritten, the SEC will issue a stop order preventing registration.

       iv) A registration becomes effective 20 days (the waiting period after it is filed, unless the SEC accelerates the effective date or issues a bedbug letter.

3) A **prospectus** must be furnished to any interested investor. Its purpose is to supply sufficient facts to make an informed investment decision.

  a) The prospectus contains material information (financial and otherwise) with respect to the offering and the issuer.

  b) An issuer can amend a prospectus by filing 10 copies of the modified document with the SEC.

  c) The Securities Act of 1933 requires that any prospectus still in use more than 9 months after its effective date be updated so that the information contained in the prospectus is not more than 16 months old.

       i) Developments after the effective date that render the existing prospectus misleading impose an obligation to update the prospectus without regard to the 9-month period.

  d) A disclaimer must be printed on the outside front cover of the prospectus in boldface type. It states that the securities have not been approved or disapproved by the SEC and that the SEC has not passed upon the accuracy or adequacy of the prospectus. It also states that any representation to the contrary is a criminal offense.

4)   The entire allotment of securities ordinarily is made available for purchase on the effective date of the registration statement. An exception is a shelf registration.

 a)   In a **shelf registration** under the SEC's Rule 415, a master registration statement is filed for securities that the company reasonably expects to sell within 2 years. However, they are put "on the shelf" until the most opportune time for offering is determined.

 i)   Shelf registrations allow issuers to respond rapidly in volatile markets and to reduce flotation costs.

 b)   A shelf registration is available only to large, well-established issuers.

 c)   The information in the master registration statement must be updated with a short-form statement just prior to a new issue.

5)   The final price of the stock will be set at the close of the day on which the SEC clears the issuance of the stock.

6)   Investment bankers must pay for underwritten stock by the fourth day after the offering's commencement. Investors must pay by the tenth day.

g.   A public issue of securities may be sold through a cash offer or a rights offer.

1)   A cash offer follows the procedures previously described.

2)   A rights offer gives existing shareholders an option to purchase new shares before they are offered to the public. If the corporate charter provides for a preemptive right, a rights offer is mandatory.

 a)   The rights or options are evidenced by warrants that state the terms of the arrangement, including subscription price, the number of rights required to purchase one share, and the expiration date. Shareholders may exercise the rights, sell them, or allow them to expire.

 b)   Under a standby underwriting arrangement, an underwriter may agree to buy undersubscribed shares. However, granting other shareholders an oversubscription privilege reduces the probability of needing to resort to the underwriter.

3)   A cash offer is made to any interested party, whereas a rights offer is made to current security holders. Debt is normally sold by cash offer, but equity securities may be sold by either means.

4)   An IPO necessarily involves a cash offer because, if existing security holders desired to purchase the new issue, no public offer would be made.

5)   A seasoned equity issue may be sold in a cash offer or a rights offer.

6)   A registered offering of a large block of a previously issued security by a current shareholder is a secondary offering. The proceeds of the sale go to the holder, not the original issuer, and the number of shares outstanding does not change. A secondary offering is also called a secondary distribution.

h.   The ability of a firm to raise capital through an IPO, the issuance of bonds, or by other means significantly depends upon the quality of the information it provides to potential investors, creditors, regulators, and others. One such source of information is a set of audited financial statements accompanied by the opinion of the independent external auditor. This opinion attests to the fairness of the financial statements. The independence and professional reputation of the auditor give the opinion its value. The following are the principal types of external audit opinions. The unqualified opinion provides the highest level of assurance.

1)   An unqualified opinion states that the financial statements present fairly, in all material respects, the financial position, results of operations, and cash flows of the entity in conformity with accounting principles generally accepted in the United States of America.

      i.   Rule 506 implements the private placement exemption from registration for "transactions by an issuer not involving any public offering." Section 4(2) provides for this exemption. Rule 506, unlike Rules 504 and 505, has no ceiling amount. A private placement, also called a non-public offering, is the issuance of securities that are sold without a registered public offering, usually to a small number of private investors. Although these placements are still subject to the Securities Act of 1933, the securities offered do not actually have to be registered with the SEC if the issuance conforms to an exemption from registrations as set forth in the securities acts and SEC rules promulgated thereunder.

           1)   Rule 506 provides a safe harbor for a private placement, but noncompliance with Rule 506 does not necessarily mean that the exemption cannot be claimed.

           2)   The offering may be purchased by an unlimited number of accredited investors.

           3)   The issuer must reasonably believe that there are no more than 35 non-accredited investors/offerees. Each nonaccredited purchaser must have the knowledge and experience in financial and business matters needed to evaluate the merits and risks of the prospective investment, or the issuer must reasonably believe that such purchasers meet this requirement.

           4)   Generally, the issuer requires the purchaser to sign an investment letter stating that (s)he is purchasing for investment only and not for resale. For this reason, shares issued pursuant to Rule 506 are referred to as lettered stock.

Stop and review! You have completed the outline for this subunit. Study multiple-choice questions 1 through 5 beginning on page 300.

7.2 DIVIDEND POLICY AND SHARE REPURCHASE

GLEIM SUCCESS TIPS The CMA exam tests one's understanding of what influences a company's dividends policy along with the importance of a stable policy. Furthermore, a candidate will need to identify the types of dividend payouts and when and how a company would use each.

   1.   **Dividend Policy**

      a.   Dividend policy determines what portion of a corporation's net income is distributed to shareholders and what portion is retained for reinvestment.

          1)   A high dividend rate means a slower rate of growth. A high growth rate usually means a low dividend rate.

      b.   Because both a high growth rate and a high dividend rate are desirable, the financial manager attempts to achieve the balance that maximizes the firm's share price.

      c.   Normally, corporations try to maintain a stable level of dividends, even though profits may fluctuate considerably, because many shareholders buy stock with the expectation of receiving a certain dividend every year. Hence, management tends not to raise dividends if the payout cannot be sustained.

          1)   The desire for stability has led theorists to propound the information content or signaling hypothesis, which states that a change in dividend policy is a signal to the market regarding management's forecast of future earnings. Thus, firms generally have an active policy strategy with respect to dividends.

      d.   This stability often results in a stock that sells at a higher market price because shareholders perceive less risk in receiving their dividends.

2. **Factors Influencing a Company's Dividend Policy**

    a. Legal Restrictions

        1) Dividends ordinarily cannot be paid out of paid-in capital. A corporation must have a balance in its retained earnings account before dividends can be paid.

    b. Stability of Earnings

        1) A company whose earnings fluctuate greatly from year to year will tend to pay out a smaller dividend during good years so that the same dividend can be paid even if profits are much lower. For example, a company with fluctuating earnings might pay out $1 every year whether earnings per share are $10 (10% payout rate) or $1 (100% payout rate).

    c. Rate of Growth

        1) A company with a faster growth rate will have a greater need to finance that growth with retained earnings. Thus, growth companies usually have lower dividend payout ratios. Shareholders hope to be able to obtain larger capital gains in the future.

    d. Cash Position

        1) Regardless of a firm's earnings record, cash must be available before a dividend can be paid. No dividend can be declared if all of a firm's earnings are tied up in receivables and inventories.

    e. Restrictions in Debt Agreements

        1) Restrictive covenants in bond indentures and other debt agreements often limit the dividends that a firm can declare.

    f. Tax Position of Shareholders

        1) In corporations, the shareholders may not want regular dividends because the individual owners are in such high tax brackets. They may want to forgo dividends in exchange for future capital gains or wait to receive dividends in future years when they are in lower tax brackets.

        2) However, an accumulated earnings tax is assessed on a corporation if it has accumulated retained earnings beyond its reasonably expected needs.

    g. Residual Theory of Dividends

        1) The amount (residual) of earnings paid as dividends depends on the available investment opportunities and the debt-equity ratio at which cost of capital is minimized. The rational investor should prefer reinvestment of retained earnings when the return exceeds what the investor could earn on investments of equal risk. However, the firm may prefer to pay dividends when investment opportunities are poor and the use of internal equity financing would move the firm away from its ideal capital structure.

3. **Important Dates Relative to Dividends**

    a. The date of declaration is the date the directors meet and formally vote to declare a dividend. On this date, the dividend becomes a liability of the corporation.

    b. The date of record is the date as of which the corporation determines the shareholders who will receive the declared dividend. Essentially, the corporation closes its shareholder records on this date.

        1) Only those shareholders who own the stock on the date of record will receive the dividend. It typically falls from 2 to 6 weeks after the declaration date.

    c. The date of distribution is the date on which the dividend is actually paid (when the checks are put into the mail to the investors). The payment date is usually from 2 to 4 weeks after the date of record.

    d.   The ex-dividend date is a date established by the stock exchanges, such as 4 business days before the date of record. Unlike the other dates previously mentioned, it is not established by the corporate board of directors.

        1)   The period between the ex-dividend date and the date of record gives the stock exchange members time to process any transactions so that new shareholders will receive the dividends to which they are entitled.

        2)   An investor who buys a share of stock before the ex-dividend date will receive the dividend that has been previously declared. An investor who buys the stock after the ex-dividend date (but before the date of record or payment date) will not receive the declared dividend. Instead, the individual who sold the stock will receive the dividend because (s)he owned it on the ex-dividend date.

        3)   Usually, a stock price will drop on the ex-dividend date by the amount of the dividend because the new investor will not receive it.

4.   **Stock Dividends and Stock Splits**

    a.   Although the cash dividend is the most common type, other types are available.

        1)   Stock dividends and splits involve issuance of additional shares to existing shareholders. Stock shareholders do not really receive any increase in the value of their holdings. The previous holdings are simply divided into more pieces (additional shares).

    b.   A stock dividend is an issuance of stock and entails the transfer of a sum from the retained earnings account to a paid-in capital account.

        1)   Usually, the corporation wants to give something to the shareholders but without paying out a cash dividend because the funds are needed in the business.

        2)   Casual investors may believe they are receiving something of value when in essence their previous holdings are merely being divided into more pieces.

        3)   Stock dividends are often used by growing companies that wish to retain earnings in the business while placating shareholders.

    c.   A stock split does not involve any accounting entries. Instead, the existing shares are divided into more pieces so that the market price per share will be reduced.

        1)   EXAMPLE: If a corporation has 1 million shares outstanding, each of which sells for $90, a 2-for-1 stock split will result in 2 million shares outstanding, each of which sells for about $45.

        2)   Reverse stock splits reduce the shares outstanding.

    d.   Advantages of Issuing Stock Splits and Dividends

        1)   Because more shares will be outstanding, the price per share will be lower. The lower price per share will induce more small investors to purchase the company's stock. Thus, because demand for the stock is greater, the price may increase.

            a)   EXAMPLE: In the example above, the additional investors interested in the company at the lower price may drive the price up to $46 or $47, or slightly higher than the theoretically correct price of $45. Consequently, current shareholders will benefit from the split (or dividend) after all.

        2)   A dividend or split can be a publicity gesture. Because shareholders may believe they are receiving something of value (and may be indirectly), they will have a better opinion of their company.

        3)   Moreover, the more shares a corporation has outstanding, the larger the number of shareholders, who are usually good customers for their own company's products.

e.   On rare occasions, a firm may use a reverse stock split to raise the market price per share. For example, a 1-for-10 stock split would require shareholders to turn in 10 old shares to receive one new share.

5. **Share Repurchases**

a.   A share repurchase takes place when a corporation buys its own stock back on the open market. Once in the firm's possession, these shares are called treasury shares.

b.   Among the motives for a share repurchase are

   1)   Mergers
   2)   Share options
   3)   Stock dividends
   4)   Tax advantages to shareholders (e.g., favorable capital gains rates)
   5)   To increase earnings per share and other ratios
   6)   To prevent a hostile takeover
   7)   To eliminate a particular ownership interest

6. **Dividend Reinvestment Plans (DRPs or DRIPs)**

a.   Any dividends due to shareholders are automatically reinvested in shares of the same corporation's common stock.

   1)   Broker's fees on such purchases of stock are either zero (the costs absorbed by the corporation) or only a few cents per shareholder because only one purchase is made and the total fee is divided among all shareholders participating.

b.   Initially, dividends were reinvested in stock bought by a trustee (typically a large bank) on the open market. Many plans are still of this type.

   1)   More recently, corporations have seen the opportunity to use DRPs as a source of financing. Thus, many plans now involve a sale of newly issued stock to the trustee to fulfill the requirements of the plan. The corporation benefits because it can issue stock at the current market value without incurring underwriting and issue costs.

7. **Insider Trading**

a.   Under the SEC's Rule 10b-5, insider trading is the purchase or sale of any security by an individual who (1) has access to material, nonpublic information; (2) has not disclosed it before trading; and (3) has a fiduciary obligation to the issuer, the shareholders, or any other source of the information. Insiders include (1) officers, (2) directors, (3) consultants, (4) lawyers, (5) engineers, (6) auditors, (7) bankers, (8) reporters, (9) public relations advisors, (10) tippees, and (11) personnel in government agencies entrusted with confidential corporate information for corporate purposes.

   1)   The SEC may bring a civil action against anyone violating the 1934 act by "purchasing or selling a security while in possession of material nonpublic information."
   2)   A private suit for damages may be brought by a contemporaneous purchaser or seller of shares of the same class.

8. **Leases**

   a. A lease is a long-term, contractual agreement in which the owner of property (the lessor) allows another party (the lessee) the right to use the property for a stated period in exchange for a stated payment.

      1) The fundamental issue is whether the lease is a purchase-and-financing arrangement (a capital lease) or merely a long-term rental contract (an operating lease).

         a) Lessees have a strong incentive not to treat leases as purchase-and-financing arrangements, since such contracts require the reporting of large amounts of debt on the balance sheet.

         b) Lessors, on the other hand, would prefer that a lease be treated as a purchase-and-financing, since that allows them to report the long-term receivable.

   b. Discounting the present value of the cash flows associated with a lease using the time value of money allows a firm to determine the type of lease that is most beneficial.

   c. Lease financing must be analyzed by comparing the cost of owning to the cost of leasing. Leasing is a major means of financing because it offers a variety of tax and other benefits. If leases are not accounted for as installment purchases, they provide off-balance-sheet financing. Thus, under an operating lease, the lessee need not record an asset or a liability, and rent expense (not rent) is recognized. The three principal forms of leases are discussed below:

      1) A sale-leaseback is a financing method. A firm seeking financing sells an asset to an investor (creditor) and leases the asset back, usually on a noncancelable lease. The lease payments consist of principal and interest paid by the lessee to the lessor.

      2) Service or operating leases usually include both financing and maintenance services.

      3) Financial leases, which do not provide for maintenance services, are noncancelable and fully amortize the cost of the leased asset over the term of the basic lease contract. They are installment purchases.

Stop and review! You have completed the outline for this subunit. Study multiple-choice questions 6 through 10 beginning on page 301.

7.3 MERGERS AND ACQUISITIONS

1. **Mergers**

   a. A merger is a business transaction in which an acquiring firm absorbs a second firm, and the acquiring firm remains in business as a combination of the two merged firms. A merger is legally straightforward; however, approval of the shareholders of each firm is required.

      1) A consolidation is similar to a merger, but a new entity is formed and neither of the merging entities survives.

   b. Four types of mergers are recognized:

      1) A horizontal merger occurs when two firms in the same line of business combine.

      2) A vertical merger combines a firm with one of its suppliers or customers.

      3) A congeneric merger is a combination of firms with related products or services; however, the firms do not produce the same product or have a producer-supplier relationship.

      4) A conglomerate merger involves two unrelated firms in different industries.

2.   **Acquisitions**

    a.   An acquisition is the purchase of all of another firm's assets or a controlling interest in its stock.

        1)   An acquisition of all of a firm's assets requires a vote of that firm's shareholders. It also entails the costly transfer of legal title, but it avoids the minority interest that may arise if the acquisition is by purchase of stock.

    b.   An acquisition by stock purchase is advantageous because it can be effected when management and the board of directors are hostile to the combination, and it does not require a formal vote of the firm's shareholders. If the acquiring firm's offer is rejected by the acquiree's management, a tender offer may be made directly to the acquiree's shareholders to obtain a controlling interest.

        1)   A tender offer is a general invitation by an individual or a corporation to all shareholders of another corporation to tender their shares for a specified price.

            a)   In 1968, Congress enacted the Williams Act to extend reporting and disclosure requirements under the Securities Exchange Act of 1934 to tender offers.

            b)   Any person or group that acquires more than 5% of a class of registered securities is required, within 10 days of the tender, to file a statement with the SEC and the issuing company.

            c)   The tender offer may be friendly (acceptable to the target corporation's management) or hostile. If it is the latter, the target must also file a statement with the SEC. The target has 10 days in which to respond to the bidder's tender offer. Moreover, a tender offer must be kept open for at least 20 business days.

        2)   Direct solicitation of shareholders when management and the board resist the combination has been called a Saturday night special or a hostile takeover. This solicitation may be by advertisement in the media or, when a shareholder list can be obtained, by a general mailing.

    c.   An acquisition of stock may eventually result in the merger or consolidation of the two firms.

    d.   Takeover is a broad term often used in the description of business combinations. It signifies a shift of control from one set of shareholders to another and may be friendly or hostile. A takeover includes not only mergers and acquisitions but also proxy contests and going private.

        1)   A proxy contest is an attempt by dissident shareholders to gain control of the corporation, or at least to gain influence, by electing directors. A proxy is a power of attorney given by a shareholder that authorizes the holder to exercise the voting rights of the shareholder.

            a)   Ten days prior to mailing a proxy statement to shareholders, the issuer must file a copy with the SEC.

            b)   SEC rules require the solicitor of proxies to furnish shareholders with all material information concerning the matter subject to vote.

            c)   A form by which shareholders may indicate their agreement or disagreement must be provided.

            d)   Proxies solicited for the purpose of voting for directors must be accompanied by an annual report.

2) Going private entails the purchase of the publicly owned stock of a corporation by a small group of private investors, usually including senior managers. Accordingly, the stock is delisted (if it is traded on an exchange) because it will no longer be traded. Such a transaction is usually structured as a leveraged buyout.

    a) A leveraged buyout (LBO) is a financing technique by which a company is purchased using very little equity. The cash-offer price is financed with large amounts of debt. An LBO is often used when a company is sold to management or some other group of employees, but it is also used in hostile takeovers.

        i) The company's assets serve as collateral for a loan to finance the purchase.

- Junk bonds are often issued in an LBO. They are high-risk and therefore high-yield securities that are normally issued when the debt ratio is very high. Thus, the bondholders will have as much risk as the holders of equity securities.
- The tax deductibility of interest paid by the restructured company is an advantage of an LBO. Given a high debt ratio, that is, greater financial leverage, after-tax cash flows increase.

        ii) In addition to greater financial leverage, the firm may benefit from an LBO because of savings in administrative costs from no longer being publicly traded. Furthermore, if the managers become owners, they have greater incentives and greater operational flexibility.

        iii) Characteristics of firms that are candidates for an LBO include

- An established business with proven operating performance
- Stable earnings and cash flows
- Very little outstanding debt
- A quality asset base that can be used as collateral for a new loan
- Stable technology that will not require large expenditures for R&D

        iv) The high degree of risk in LBOs results from the fixed charges for interest on the loan and the lack of cash for expansion.

3) A merger is usually a negotiated arrangement between a single bidder and the acquired firm. Payment is most frequently in stock. Moreover, the bidder is often a cash-rich firm in a mature industry and is seeking growth possibilities. The acquired firm is usually growing and in need of cash.

4) Takeovers effected through tender offers may be friendly or hostile.

    a) When the takeover is friendly, the target is usually a successful firm in a growth industry, payment may be in cash or stock, and management of the target often has a high percentage of ownership.

    b) When the takeover is hostile, the target is usually in a mature industry and is underperforming, more than one bidder may emerge, management ownership is likely to be low, payment is more likely to be in cash, and the initial bidder is probably a corporate raider.

3.   **Opposition to the Combination**

    a.   **Greenmail**

        1)   A targeted repurchase (greenmail) is a defensive tactic used to protect against takeover after a bidder buys a large number of shares on the open market and then makes (or threatens to make) a tender offer.

            a)   If management and the board are opposed to the takeover (a hostile tender offer), the potential acquirer is offered the opportunity to sell his/her already acquired shares back to the corporation at an amount substantially above market value (i.e., paying greenmail).

        2)   In conjunction with greenmail, management may reach a standstill agreement in which the bidder agrees not to acquire additional shares.

    b.   **Staggered Election of Directors**

        1)   Staggered terms for directors requires new shareholders to wait several years before being able to place their own people on the board.

        2)   Another antitakeover amendment to the corporate charter may require a supermajority (e.g., 80%) for approval of a combination.

    c.   **Golden Parachutes**

        1)   So-called golden parachutes are provisions passed by a board of directors requiring large payments to specified executives if their employment is terminated by the acquiring firm following a takeover.

            a)   A 1984 change in the tax law imposed a 20% excise tax on such payments and provided for their nondeductibility by the corporation. It was specifically designed to reduce the use of golden parachutes.

        2)   Shareholders have often been unhappy with golden parachute payoffs and have filed suit to stop such payments.

    d.   **Fair Price Provisions**

        1)   Fair price provisions (shareholder rights plans) have become popular.

        2)   Warrants are issued to shareholders that permit purchase of stock at a small percentage (often half) of market price in the event of a takeover attempt.

        3)   The plan is intended to protect shareholder interests if the corporation is confronted by a coercive or unfair takeover attempt.

        4)   The objective is not to deter takeovers but to ensure that all shareholders are treated equally.

        5)   In the event of a friendly tender offer, the outstanding stock rights (warrants) may be repurchased by the corporation for a few cents per share, thus paving the way for the takeover.

        6)   In many cases, these rights are not even issued in certificate form to shareholders because they are not immediately exercisable and are not traded separately from the common stock.

    e.   **Going Private and LBOs**

        1)   Going private and leveraged buyouts are defensive tactics that have been previously discussed.

    f.   **Poison Pill**

        1)   A target corporation's charter, bylaws, or contracts may include a wide variety of provisions that reduce the value of the target to potential tender offerors. For example, a valuable contract may terminate by its terms upon a specified form of change of ownership of the target. A poison pill is typically a right to purchase shares, at a reduced price, in the merged firm resulting from a takeover.

g. **Flip-over Rights**

  1) The charter of a target corporation may provide for its shareholders to acquire in exchange for their stock (in the target) a relatively greater interest (e.g., twice the shares of stock of equivalent value) in an acquiring entity.

h. **Flip-in Rights**

  1) Acquisition of more than a specified ownership interest (e.g., 25%) in the target corporation by a raider is a contingency, the occurrence of which triggers additional rights in the stock other than the stock acquired by the raider; e.g., each share becomes entitled to two votes.

i. **Issuing Stock**

  1) The target corporation significantly increases the amount of outstanding stock.

j. **Reverse Tender**

  1) The target corporation may respond with a tender offer to acquire control of the tender offeror.

k. **ESOP**

  1) The trustees of an employee stock ownership plan are usually favorable to current management. Thus, they are likely to vote the shares allocated to the ESOP against a raider, who will probably destabilize the target corporation's current structure.

l. **White Knight Merger**

  1) Target management arranges an alternative tender offer with a different acquirer that will be more favorable to incumbent management and shareholders.

m. **Crown Jewel Transfer**

  1) The target corporation sells or otherwise disposes of one or more assets that made it a desirable target.

n. **Legal Action**

  1) A target corporation may challenge one or more aspects of a tender offer. A resulting delay increases costs to the raider and enables further defensive action.

4. **Other Restructurings**

  a. A spin-off is the creation of a new separate entity from another entity, with the new entity's shares being distributed on a pro rata basis to existing shareholders of the parent entity.

   1) Existing shareholders will have the same proportion of ownership in the new entity that they had in the parent.

   2) A spin-off is a type of dividend to existing shareholders.

  b. A divestiture involves the sale of an operating unit of a firm to a third party.

   1) Some writers define the term divestiture to include spin-offs and liquidations.

  c. A liquidation of assets of an operating unit occurs when they are sold piecemeal.

  d. A leveraged cash-out is borrowing heavily to issue a very large dividend which acts as a poison pill.

  e. An equity carve-out involves the sale of a portion of the firm through an equity offering of shares in the new entity to outsiders.

  f. Reasons for spin-offs and divestitures include governmental antitrust litigation, refocusing of a firm's operations, and raising capital for the core business operation.

  g. Letter stock, also known as tracking stock or targeted stock, is created by a conglomerate to separate the cash flows of two or more businesses and allow for separate market valuations.

5.   **Prevalence of Mergers and Acquisitions**

    a.   The level of mergers and acquisitions increased dramatically in the 1980s because of changes in the global and U.S. economies, technological advances, political events, interest and exchange rate fluctuations, the emergence of new financial instruments, etc.

    b.   Some of these factors included

        1)   General undervaluation of stocks in the early 1980s

        2)   High inflation that increased the replacement cost of a firm's assets

        3)   Political acceptance of large mergers, especially in view of greater competition, for example, as a result of the increased strength of large foreign firms, deregulation, the emergence of new financial services, and the development of new technologies

        4)   The decline of the dollar, which facilitated acquisition of U.S. firms by foreign firms

        5)   The belief of oil, gas, and other natural resource companies that reserves could be obtained more cheaply by merger than by exploration

        6)   Reduced marginal corporate and personal tax rates and an increase in the capital gains rate

        7)   Deregulation of numerous industries, e.g., transportation, oil, gas, broadcasting, cable, banking, the S&L industry, and other financial services

        8)   The U.S. government's budget deficits, the nation's trade deficits, high interest rates, and other economic factors

        9)   Defensive combinations by takeover targets

6.   **Motivations**

    a.   Inefficient management may be replaced in a merger or acquisition by the management of the acquiring or merging firm, or the competency of existing management may be improved.

        1)   Undervaluation of the firm to be acquired may result if the market focuses on short-term earnings rather than long-term prospects. Thus, such a firm may be a bargain for the acquirer.

        2)   Another aspect of undervaluation is that a firm's q ratio (market value of the firm's securities ÷ replacement cost of its assets) may be less than one. Hence, an acquiring firm that wishes to add capacity or diversify into new product lines may discover that a combination is less expensive than internal expansion.

    b.   Managerial motivation is an issue because not all business decisions are based purely on economic considerations. Thus, the increased salary, fringe benefits, power, and prestige that often result from managing a larger enterprise may affect a manager's decision to consummate a business combination that is not favorable to the shareholders. Fear of negative personal consequences may also cause a manager to resist a favorable combination, perhaps by entering into another combination that preserves the manager's position by making the firm a less desirable acquisition.

        1)   The inconsistency between a manager's personal goals and the goal of maximizing shareholder wealth has been called the agency problem. It arises from the separation between ownership and control of corporations. When the manager does not own all of the firm's shares, (s)he is an agent for the other shareholders, and a possible conflict of interest exists. Managerial actions will then have costs and benefits that are shared by others. Accordingly, a manager may be more inclined to incur certain costs and less inclined to pursue certain benefits.

2) Ways of addressing the agency problem include tying managerial compensation to the firm's stock price performance; direct shareholder intervention, especially by large institutional investors such as pension funds and insurance companies; and the threat of a hostile takeover, which often results in the ouster of incumbent management.

    a) Shareholders often seek more independence for the board of directors and the ability to introduce a wider range of proposals to be voted on at shareholder meetings.

c. A firm may be a target if its breakup value exceeds the cost of its acquisition. Thus, the acquirer may earn a profit by selling the assets piecemeal.

d. Diversification is sometimes claimed to be an advantage of a combination because it stabilizes earnings and reduces the risks to employees and creditors. Thus, the coinsurance effect applies. If one of the combining firms fails, creditors can be paid from the assets of the other. However, whether shareholders benefit is unclear. The variability of the firm's returns is subject to systematic and unsystematic risk. The former affects all firms and cannot be diversified.

1) Unsystematic risk is unique to the firm and can be diversified in a combination, but shareholders can diversify simply by purchasing shares in a variety of firms. Diversification by individual shareholders is therefore easier and cheaper than by the firm except in the case of closely held firms.

2) Another argument supporting the view that diversification by itself does not benefit shareholders is that the decrease in earnings variability increases the value of debt at the expense of equity. Absent synergy, the value of the combined firm is the same as the total of the values of the separate firms. Because the debt increases in value as a result of the decreased risk of default (the coinsurance effect), the value of the equity must therefore decrease if the total value of debt and equity is unchanged.

3) Nevertheless, the coinsurance effect can be offset by issuing additional debt after the combination, thereby increasing the firm's unsystematic risk and decreasing the value of debt. Moreover, the greater leverage may increase the firm's value. Another possibility is reducing debt prior to the combination at the lower, pre-combination price and reissuing the same amount of debt afterward.

7. **Synergies**

a. Synergy exists if the value of the combined firm exceeds the sum of the values of the separate firms.

1) It can be determined by using the risk-adjusted discount rate (usually the cost of equity of the acquired firm) to discount the incremental cash flows (changes in revenues, costs, taxes, and capital needs) of the newly formed entity.

b. Operational synergy arises because the combined firm may be able to increase its revenues and reduce its costs. For example, the new firm created by a horizontal merger may have a more balanced product line and a stronger distribution system. Furthermore, costs may be decreased because of economies of scale in production, marketing, purchasing, and management.

1) Operating economies also arise from vertical integration because of the improved coordination of successive activities in the production process.

c. Financial synergy may also result from the combination. The cost of capital for both firms may be decreased because the cost of issuing both debt and equity securities is lower for larger firms. Moreover, uncorrelated cash flow streams will provide for increased liquidity and a lower probability of bankruptcy. Another benefit is the availability of additional internal capital. The acquired company is often able to exploit new investment opportunities because the acquiring company has excess cash flows.

d.   Greater market power because of reduced competition might appear to be a benefit of business combinations, but the evidence does not support this conclusion. Antitrust restrictions, the globalization of markets, and the emergence of new forms of competition work against concentration of market power.

e.   A combination may provide not only specific new investment opportunities but also a strategic position that will allow the combined entity to exploit conditions that may arise in the future. For example, the acquisition of a firm in a different industry may provide a beachhead that eventually permits development of a broad product line if circumstances are favorable.

f.   Tax benefits may arise from a combination if the acquired firm has an unusual net operating loss and the acquiring firm is profitable.

   1)   Another advantage is that the combined firm's optimal capital structure may allow for increased use of debt financing, with attendant tax savings from greater interest deductions.

   2)   Furthermore, a combination may be the best use of surplus cash from a tax perspective. Dividends received by individual shareholders are fully taxable, whereas the capital gains from a combination are not taxed until the shares are sold. In addition, amounts remitted from the acquired to the acquiring firm are not taxable.

      a)   An alternative use of surplus cash is a stock repurchase. However, the effect might be to increase the firm's share price above its equilibrium level. The result might be that the repurchase would have an excessive cost. The IRS will disallow this strategy if its sole purpose is to avoid taxes.

      b)   Surplus cash may be invested in short-term fixed-income securities, but the returns from this strategy tend to be low.

      c)   Buying shares in other firms permits the firm to take advantage of the dividends-received deduction, but the IRS may also disallow these benefits if the sole motive is tax avoidance.

Stop and review! You have completed the outline for this subunit. Study multiple-choice questions 11 through 15 beginning on page 302.

7.4 BANKRUPTCY

1.   **Conditions for Bankruptcy**

a.   A firm may be either insolvent when its debts exceed its assets or illiquid when cash flows are insufficient to meet maturing obligations (these concepts were discussed in Study Unit 2, Subunits 1 and 4).

   1)   The early signals of financial distress include late payments, plant closings, negative earnings, employee layoffs, falling stock prices, and dividend reductions.

b.   A firm may respond to insolvency by combining with another firm, selling assets, reducing costs, issuing new debt or equity securities, or negotiating with creditors to restructure its obligations. However, these private workouts may be unlikely to succeed or may already have failed.

c.   Consequently, a formal bankruptcy may be declared either voluntarily by the debtor or involuntarily due to a petition brought by creditors. The two major options are bankruptcy reorganization and liquidation.

2. **Chapter 7 Liquidation**

    a.   A voluntary or an involuntary petition for liquidation may be filed in federal bankruptcy court under the terms of the Bankruptcy Reform Act of 1978.

        1)   An involuntary petition must be joined by three or more creditors with unsecured claims totaling at least $11,625 if the debtor has 12 or more creditors. If there are fewer than 12, one creditor with a claim of at least $11,625 may file.

        2)   A contested involuntary petition will be granted if the debtor is not paying its bills when due or if, within 120 days prior to filing, a custodian took possession of the debtor's property to enforce a lien.

    b.   When the court issues an order for relief, creditors' collection activities must cease immediately. Moreover, the court usually appoints an interim trustee to take control of the debtor's estate.

    c.   At the first creditor's meeting, a permanent trustee may be elected. The trustee notifies creditors, collects the debtor's nonexempt property, distributes that property to creditors, and otherwise administers the bankruptcy estate. Secured creditors are entitled to the proceeds of the sale of specific property pledged for a lien or a mortgage. If the proceeds do not fully satisfy the secured creditors' claims, the balances are treated as claims of general or unsecured creditors. The other assets of the bankruptcy estate are distributed according to the absolute priority rule. A claim with a higher priority is fully satisfied before claims with a lower priority are paid. The following are the classes of priority claims listed in order of rank:

        1)   Claims for administrative expenses and claims for expenses incurred in preserving and collecting the estate

        2)   Claims of tradespeople who extended unsecured credit after an involuntary case has begun but before a trustee is appointed

        3)   Wages due workers if earned within the 90 days preceding the earlier of the filing of the petition or the cessation of business. The amount of wages is limited to $4,650 per person.

        4)   Claims for unpaid contributions to employee benefit plans that were to have been paid within 180 days prior to filing. However, these claims, plus wages, are not to exceed the $4,650 per employee limit.

        5)   Unsecured claims for customer deposits, not to exceed a maximum of $2,100 per individual

        6)   Taxes due to federal, state, and any other governmental agency

        7)   Unfunded pension plan liabilities. These claims are superior to those of the general creditors for an amount up to 30% of the common and preferred equity; any remaining unfunded pension claims rank with those of the general creditors.

        8)   Claims of general or unsecured creditors

        9)   Claims of preferred shareholders, who may receive an amount up to the par value of the issue

        10) Claims of common shareholders

    d.   Individual debtors may receive a discharge under Chapter 7 from most debts that remain unpaid after distribution of the debtor's estate. A corporation or a partnership does not receive a discharge in bankruptcy.

3.   **Chapter 11 Reorganization**

   a.   Reorganization allows a distressed business enterprise to restructure its finances. The primary purpose of the restructuring is usually the continuation of the business.

      1)   Reorganization is a process of negotiation whereby the debtor firm and its creditors develop a plan for the adjustment and discharge of debts. Partnerships, corporations, and any person who may be a debtor under Chapter 7 (except stock and commodity brokers) are eligible debtors under Chapter 11.

      2)   Such a plan may provide for a change of management or liquidation.

   b.   A case under Chapter 11 is commenced by the filing of a petition that may be either voluntary or involuntary.

      1)   The petition may be filed by the debtor or by the creditors.

      2)   Insolvency is not a condition precedent to a voluntary Chapter 11 petition.

      3)   The debtor has the exclusive right to file a plan during the 120 days after the order for relief is issued by the court, unless a trustee has been appointed, and may file a plan of reorganization at any time.

      4)   A plan of reorganization must divide creditors' claims and shareholders' interests into classes, and claims in each class must be treated equally.

         a)   The plan must specify which classes of creditors are impaired creditors and how they will be treated. A class is impaired if its rights are altered under the plan.

   c.   To become effective, the plan ordinarily must be accepted by a certain percentage (usually, at least two-thirds) of persons whose rights as creditors or owners have been impaired, provide for full payment of administration expenses, and be confirmed (approved and put into operation) by the bankruptcy court.

      1)   Confirmation makes the plan binding not only on the debtor but also on creditors, equity security holders, and others.

   d.   A bankruptcy court may force an impaired class of creditors to participate in, and the court may confirm, a plan of reorganization that is fair and equitable to the impaired class.

   e.   In a Chapter 11 reorganization, the court has limited power to appoint a trustee. Instead, to better accomplish the rehabilitative aspirations of a reorganization, a firm seeking protection under Chapter 11 may be permitted to operate its own business as a debtor-in-possession.

      1)   A strong presumption exists that a debtor-in-possession should be permitted to continue to operate the business unless there is evidence of incompetence or mismanagement on the part of the debtor.

      2)   A debtor-in-possession has basically all the same rights and duties as a trustee but does not receive special compensation for performing the function.

      3)   The judge may appoint a trustee upon a sufficient showing of dishonesty or incompetence of the debtor or management. The duties are identical to those of a trustee in a liquidation

      4)   If the court does not appoint a trustee, the court will appoint an examiner to conduct investigations into any allegations of fraud, misconduct, or mismanagement if appointment of an examiner is requested by a party in interest, appointment is in the interests of creditors or equity security holders, and the debtor's fixed, liquidated, unsecured debts exceed $5,000,000.

f.   As soon as practicable after an order for relief has been granted, a committee of unsecured creditors is appointed by the court.

1)   The committee usually consists of persons who hold the seven largest unsecured claims against the debtor, but the court may order the appointment of additional committees of creditors or of equity security holders to assure adequate representation.

2)   The committee may employ attorneys, accountants, and other professionals to perform services on behalf of the committee or to represent it.

3)   The committee may consult with the debtor-in-possession or the trustee, request appointment of a trustee, independently investigate the debtor's affairs, and participate in formulating the plan of reorganization.

g.   A plan can only be put into effect when it is accepted by each class of impaired creditors.

1)   All persons who are entitled to participate in the plan of reorganization have a period of not less than 5 years from the date of the final decree within which to exchange their old securities in the old business organization for new securities in the new business organization.

Stop and review! You have completed the outline for this subunit. Study multiple-choice questions 16 through 20 beginning on page 304.

7.5 CURRENCY EXCHANGE RATES -- SYSTEMS AND CALCULATIONS

Questions pertaining to currency exchange rates on the CMA exam will require the candidate to calculate forward and spot rates. In addition, a candidate should be able to understand how to determine if a currency has appreciated or depreciated and how that will influence purchasing power.

1.   **The Market for Foreign Currency**

a.   When someone buys merchandise, a capital asset, or a financial instrument from another country, the seller wishes to be paid in his/her domestic currency.

1)   Thus, in general, when the demand for a country's merchandise, capital assets, and financial instruments rises, demand for its currency rises.

b.   For these international exchanges to occur, the two currencies involved must be easily convertible at some prevailing exchange rate. The exchange rate is the price of one country's currency in terms of another country's currency.

c.   Four systems for setting exchange rates are in use. Each is described in items 2. through 5. on the following pages.

1)   Fixed rates
2)   Freely floating rates
3)   Managed floating rates
4)   Pegged rates

BACKGROUND to Currency Exchange Rates

The gold standard prevailed from 1876 to 1913, i.e., countries pegged one unit of their currencies to a specified amount of gold. The gold standard was suspended during World War I. Following the war and during the Great Depression, the gold standard's reimplementation did not achieve universal success.

In 1944, during World War II, the United States convened a meeting of delegates from all 45 allied nations in Bretton Woods, New Hampshire. The convention's purpose was to establish a monetary system for the postwar world that would encourage rebuilding and prosperity while avoiding a disastrous repeat of the Great Depression. Under the resulting Bretton Woods Agreement, the U.S. guaranteed convertibility of the dollar into a certain quantity of gold, and all other nations in turn pegged their currencies to the dollar. To ensure stability, governments agreed that they would prevent exchange rates from fluctuating more than 1% plus or minus from their original rates.

This system could not be sustained after about 25 years. It was generally agreed that the U.S. currency was pegged too high, and in August 1971, President Richard Nixon ended direct convertibility of paper dollars into gold. By 1973, it was clear that any governmental intervention in currency markets was unworkable and a floating exchange rate system was established.

---

2. **Fixed Exchange Rate System**

   a. In a fixed exchange rate system, the value of a country's currency in relation to another country's currency is either fixed or allowed to fluctuate only within a very narrow range.

      1) If the forces of supply and demand appear to be causing the value of the currency to fluctuate, the country's government intervenes to maintain it within the specified range (or prints money, generating inflationary pressure).

   b. The one very significant advantage to a fixed exchange rate is that it makes for a high degree of predictability in international trade because the element of uncertainty about gains and losses on exchange rate fluctuations is eliminated.

      1) EXAMPLE: Since July 1986, the Saudi government has allowed its currency to trade within an extremely narrow band surrounding the ratio of 3.75 riyals to 1 U.S. dollar.

         a) Because the U.S. buys a tremendous amount of petroleum from Saudi Arabia, this system has the advantage of adding a degree of stability to the U.S. oil market.

   c. A disadvantage is that a government can manipulate the value of its currency.

      1) EXAMPLE: One of the complaints of authorities in the U.S. with respect to its enormous trade deficit with China is the belief that the Chinese government has held the value of the yuan in an artificially low range in order to make its exports more affordable.

         a) After years of urging by the U.S. government, China allowed its currency to rise almost 18% between 2005 and 2008. After further negotiations, China agreed in June 2010 to allow the yuan to rise even more.

3. **Freely Floating Exchange Rate System**

   a. In a freely floating exchange rate system, the government steps aside and allows exchange rates to be determined entirely by the market forces of supply and demand.

      1) The advantage of such a system is that it tends to automatically correct any disequilibrium in the balance of payments (see item 7. on page 283 for an explanation).

      2) The disadvantage is that a freely floating system makes a country vulnerable to economic conditions in other countries.

4.   **Managed Float Exchange Rate System**

a.   In a managed float exchange rate system, the government allows market forces to determine exchange rates until they move too far in one direction or another. The government will then intervene to maintain the currency within the broad range considered appropriate.

1)   This system is the one currently in use by the major trading nations.

2)   EXAMPLE: In 2000, the so-called G8 nations (Canada, France, Germany, Italy, Japan, the Russian Federation, the United Kingdom, and the United States) agreed on collective action to stop the slide of the euro against the U.S. dollar by selling dollars and buying euros.

b.   The advantage of managed float is that it has the market-response nature of a freely floating system while still allowing for government intervention when necessary.

1)   This system has allowed the network of international trade to be robust in normal times while responding effectively to such crises as the OPEC oil embargo of 1973-74 and the large U.S. budget deficits of the 1980s and '90s.

c.   The criticism of managed float is that it makes exporting countries vulnerable to sudden changes in exchange rates and lacks the self-correcting mechanism of a freely floating system.

5.   **Pegged Exchange Rate System**

a.   In a pegged exchange rate system, a government fixes the rate of exchange for its currency with respect to another country's currency (or to a "basket" of several currencies).

b.   The pegging country then calculates its currency's movement with respect to the currencies of third countries based on the movements of the currency to which it has been pegged.

1)   EXAMPLE: The currencies of Saudi Arabia and China, being essentially fixed with respect to the U.S. dollar, are pegged to the dollar with respect to the currencies of other countries. If the dollar appreciates with respect to the euro, the riyal and yuan also appreciate against the euro.

6.   **Exchange Rate Basics**

a.   The **spot rate** is the number of units of a foreign currency that can be received today in exchange for a single unit of the domestic currency.

1)   EXAMPLE: A currency trader is willing to give 1.652 Swiss francs today in exchange for a single British pound. Today's spot rate for the pound is therefore 1.652 Swiss francs, and today's spot rate for the franc is £0.6053 $(1 \div \text{F}1.652)$.

b.   The **forward rate** is the number of units of a foreign currency that can be received in exchange for a single unit of the domestic currency at some definite date in the future.

1)   EXAMPLE: The currency trader contracts to provide 1.654 Swiss francs in exchange for a single British pound 30 days from now. Today's 30-day forward rate for the pound is therefore 1.654 Swiss francs, and the 30-day forward rate for the franc is £0.6046 $(1 \div \text{F}1.654)$.

c.   If the domestic currency fetches more units of a foreign currency in the forward market than in the spot market, the domestic currency is said to be trading at a **forward premium** with respect to the foreign currency.

1)   EXAMPLE: Since the pound is fetching more francs in the forward market than in the spot market (F1.654 > F1.652), the pound is currently trading at a forward premium with respect to the franc. This reflects the market's belief that the pound is going to increase in value in relation to the franc.

d. If the domestic currency fetches fewer units of a foreign currency in the forward market than in the spot market, the domestic currency is said to be trading at a **forward discount** with respect to the foreign currency.

   1) EXAMPLE: Since the franc is fetching fewer pounds in the forward market than in the spot market (£0.6046 < £0.6053), the franc is currently trading at a forward discount with respect to the pound. This reflects the market's belief that the franc is going to lose value in relation to the pound.

e. The forward premium or discount on one currency with respect to another currency can be calculated by multiplying the percentage spread by the number of forward periods in a year:

Calculation of Forward Premium or Discount

$$\frac{Forward\ rate\ -\ Spot\ rate}{Spot\ rate} \times \frac{Days\ in\ year}{Days\ in\ forward\ period}$$

EXAMPLES

Pound forward premium = [(₣1.654 − ₣1.652) ÷ ₣1.652] × (360 days ÷ 30 days)
= (₣0.002 ÷ ₣1.652) × 12
= 0.00121 × 12
= 1.45%

Franc forward discount = [(£0.6046 − £0.6053) ÷ £0.06053] × (360 days ÷ 30 days)
= (−£0.0007 ÷ £0.6053) × 12
= −0.00121 × 12
= −1.45%

f. The implications of these relationships can be generalized as follows:

If the domestic currency is trading at a forward	Then it is expected to
Premium	Gain purchasing power
Discount	Lose purchasing power

g. A **cross rate** is used when the two currencies involved are not stated in terms of each other. The exchange must be valued in terms of a third currency, very often the U.S. dollar.

$$Cross\ rate = \frac{Domestic\ currency\ per\ U.S.\ dollar}{Foreign\ currency\ per\ U.S.\ dollar}$$

   1) EXAMPLE: A firm in Sweden needs to make a payment of 100,000 yen today. However, the krona is not stated in terms of yen, so a cross rate must be calculated.

      a) The spot rate for a single U.S. dollar at the time of the transaction is 6.8395 kronor and 79.8455 yen.

         Cross rate = kr6.8395 ÷ ¥79.8455
         = 0.0857 kronor per yen

      The company needs kr8,570 to settle its debt (¥100,000 × 0.0857).

7. **Exchange Rates and Purchasing Power**

    a.   The graph below depicts the relationship between the supply of and demand for a foreign currency by consumers and investors who use a given domestic currency:

Exchange Rate Equilibrium

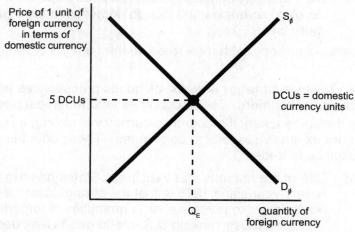

Figure 7-1

        1)   The demand curve for the foreign currency is downward sloping because, when that currency becomes cheaper, goods and services denominated in that currency become more affordable and domestic consumers need more of that currency.

        2)   The supply curve for the foreign currency is upward sloping because, when that currency becomes more expensive, goods and services become more affordable to users of the foreign currency, leading them to inject more of their currency into the domestic market.

    b.   When one currency gains purchasing power with respect to another currency, the first currency is said to have appreciated against the second currency. By the same token, the second currency is said to have depreciated (lost purchasing power) against the first.

        1)   EXAMPLE: A U.S. company buys merchandise from an EU company for €1,000,000, due in 60 days. On the day of the sale, $0.795 is required to buy a single euro. By the 60th day, $0.812 is required to buy a euro.

            a)   The dollar has thus weakened against the euro, and the euro has strengthened against the dollar; i.e., the dollar has lost purchasing power with respect to the euro.

            b)   The U.S. firm only needed $795,000 to pay off a €1,000,000 debt on the date of sale but must now use $812,000 to pay off the €1,000,000 debt.

    c.   This phenomenon has definite implications for international trade.

8. **Foreign Trade and a Country's Balance of Payments**

    a.   A country's balance of payments is the net of all transactions between domestic parties and parties in a particular foreign country.

        1)   The balance of payments consists of two major categories of activities.

            a)   The current account is the net of all cross-border transactions associated with the exchange of goods, services, interest and dividends, and nonreciprocal transfers (foreign aid, remittances to relatives, etc.).

                i)   The net of cross-border transactions associated with goods alone is called the balance of trade.

      b)   The capital account is the net of all cross-border transactions associated with capital assets and financial instruments.

  2)   When a nation has an unfavorable balance of payments, it must keep reserves of its own or other countries' currency sufficient to net the deficit to zero.

      a)   The necessity of holding such reserves depletes the country's reserves of foreign currencies and ties up domestic funds that could be used for other purposes.

b.   The impact of currency exchange rates on the balance of trade can be summarized as follows:

  1)   If a country's currency is weak, its goods and services are more affordable to foreign consumers. These countries tend to have a positive balance of trade.

  2)   By the same token, if a country's currency is strong, its goods and services are more expensive to foreign consumers. These countries tend to have a negative balance of trade.

      a)   One of the reasons that the United States has run a deficit balance of trade every year since 1975 is that the strong dollar has encouraged U.S. consumers to purchase large quantities of imported goods while simultaneously making U.S.-made goods less desirable to foreign consumers.

      b)   This phenomenon can be viewed graphically at www.census.gov/foreign-trade/statistics/graphs/gands.html.

c.   As a short-term measure, a government can attempt to correct a deficit balance of payments by deliberately devaluing its currency. This makes the country's goods more affordable, causing exports to rise.

  1)   However, this approach has its own disadvantages. By making imports more expensive, consumers complain because they have fewer choices.

  2)   Also, over the long run, domestic producers can raise their own prices to match those of the more expensive imported goods.

9.   **Effective Interest Rate on a Foreign Currency Loan**

a.   EXAMPLE: A U.S. company takes out a 1-year, 12,000,000 peso loan at 6.5% to pay a Mexican supplier. After a year, the U.S. company repays the loan with interest but, in the meantime, the peso has experienced a slight appreciation. Thus, the company's effective rate on the loan is higher than the stated rate, calculated as follows:

		Times: Conversion Rate	Equals: Equivalent USD
Amount borrowed	12,000,000 Pesos	0.0921496	$1,105,795
Times: stated rate	6.5%		
Equals: interest charged	780,000 Pesos		
Total repayment	12,780,000 Pesos	0.0940000	1,201,320
Difference			$ 95,525

Effective rate:
Difference ÷ amount borrowed = ($95,525 ÷ $1,105,795)   **8.64%**

Stop and review! You have completed the outline for this subunit. Study multiple-choice questions 21 through 25 beginning on page 305.

7.6 CURRENCY EXCHANGE RATES -- FACTORS AFFECTING RATES AND RISK MITIGATION TECHNIQUES

1. **Factors Affecting Exchange Rates**

    a. The five factors that affect currency exchange rates can be classified as three trade-related factors and two financial factors. Each is discussed in detail in items 2. and 3. below and on the following pages.

        1) Trade-related factors

            a) Relative inflation rates
            b) Relative income levels
            c) Government intervention

        2) Financial factors

            a) Relative interest rates
            b) Ease of capital flow

2. **Trade-Related Factors That Affect Exchange Rates**

    a. **Relative Inflation Rates**

        1) When the rate of inflation in a given country rises relative to the rates of other countries, the demand for that country's currency falls.

            a) This inward shift of the demand curve results from the lowered desirability of that currency, a result of its falling purchasing power.

        2) As investors unload this currency, there is more of it available, reflected in an outward shift of the supply curve.

        3) A new equilibrium point will be reached at a lower price in terms of investors' domestic currencies.

            a) An investor's domestic currency has gained purchasing power in the country where inflation is worse.

Changes in Supply and Demand for the Currency of a Foreign Country Experiencing Higher Relative Inflation

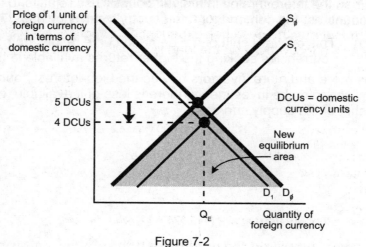

Figure 7-2

b.   **Relative Income Levels**

1)   Citizens with higher incomes look for new consumption opportunities in other countries, driving up the demand for those currencies and shifting the demand curve to the right.

a)   Thus, as incomes rise in one country, the prices of foreign currencies rise as well, and the local currency will depreciate.

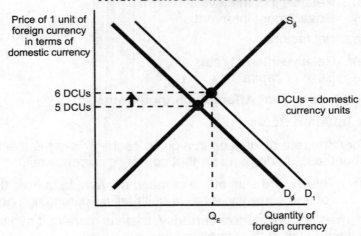

**Changes in Supply and Demand
for the Currency of a Foreign Country
When Domestic Incomes Rise**

Figure 7-3

c.   **Government Intervention**

1)   Actions by national governments, such as trade barriers and currency restrictions, complicate the process of exchange rate determination.

3.   **Financial Factors That Affect Exchange Rates**

a.   **Relative Interest Rates**

1)   When the interest rates in a given country rise relative to those of other countries, the demand for that country's currency rises.

a)   This outward shift of the demand curve results from the influx of other currencies seeking the higher returns available in that country.

2)   As more and more investors buy up the high-interest country's currency with which to make investments, there is less of it available, reflected in an inward shift of the supply curve.

3) A new equilibrium point will be reached at a higher price in terms of investors' domestic currencies.

   a) An investor's domestic currency has lost purchasing power in the country paying higher returns.

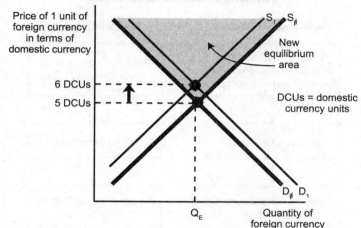

**Changes in Supply and Demand
for the Currency of a Foreign Country
Experiencing Rising Interest Rates**

Figure 7-4

b. **Ease of Capital Flow**

   1) If a country with high real interest rates loosens restrictions against the cross-border movement of capital, the demand for the currency will rise as investors seek higher returns.

EXAMPLE

The ease with which large amounts of capital can quickly flow into and out of countries in a world connected by electronic networks was disastrously displayed in late 1997 during the "Asian contagion" monetary crisis.

From 1985 to 1994, the fastest growing economy in the world was Thailand's. Thai consumers spent down their savings, putting upward pressure on prices for real estate and consumer goods and on interest rates. Because the Thai baht was "pegged" to the U.S. dollar, Thailand was seen as a safe place by investors looking for high returns. Investors reasoned that the linkage between the baht and the dollar ensured that the value of the baht could not suddenly deflate. The huge influx of foreign currency made for a money glut, further driving up real estate prices and inducing Thai banks to make ever riskier loans. Also, the close ties between Thai banks and corporations meant that a degree of skepticism and objectivity was missing from some loan transactions.

In the first half of 1997, the dollar strengthened against the Japanese yen and European currencies, thus making Japanese and European goods attractive to U.S. consumers. But since the baht rose along with the dollar, Thai goods were relatively less attractive, and Thailand's exports fell. Disappointed foreign investors began moving their money out of Thailand. This caused the monetary dominoes to begin falling.

As investors began selling large blocks of baht, it could no longer be realistically pegged to the dollar and was detached in early July. Thailand's central bank desperately tried to prop up the baht by exchanging the country's currency reserves for dollars and using those dollars to buy up the baht. But the enormous quantities of baht being dumped overwhelmed this action and the baht went into free fall, losing over 20% of its value against the dollar in July and August.

Several of the economies of Southeast Asia were closely integrated through mutual trade, and most of them had experienced tremendous growth through the late '80s and early '90s, leaving them vulnerable to an economic crisis experienced by any one of them. Upon seeing that the central bank in Thailand was unable to hold up the value of the baht, investors lost confidence in other Southeast Asian economies as well, and the flight of capital spread across the region. By June 1998, the currencies of Thailand, India, Singapore, Malaysia, Indonesia, the Philippines, Taiwan, and South Korea had fallen anywhere from 15% to 84%.

2)   As the example on the previous page illustrates, this factor has become by far the most important of the five factors listed.

a)   The speed with which capital can be moved electronically and the huge amounts involved in the "wired" global economy easily dominate the effects of the trade-related factors.

4.   **Graphical Depiction**

Exchange Rate Determination

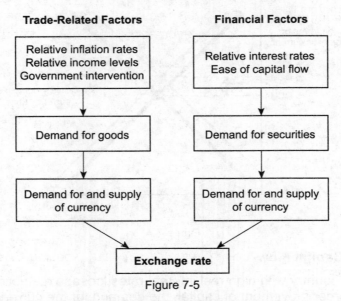

Figure 7-5

5.   **Calculating Simultaneous Effects on Exchange Rates**

a.   Differential Interest Rates

1)   Interest rate parity (IRP) theory holds that exchange rates will settle at an equilibrium point where the difference between the forward rate and the spot rate (i.e., the forward premium or discount) equals the exact amount necessary to offset the difference in interest rates between the two countries.

b.   Differential Inflation Rates

1)   Purchasing power parity (PPP) theory explains differences in exchange rates as the result of the differing inflation rates in the two countries.

c.   International Fisher Effect (IFE) Theory

1)   International Fisher Effect (IFE) theory also focuses on how the spot rate will change over time, but it uses the interplay between real and nominal interest rates to explain the change.

a)   If all investors require a given real rate of return, then differences between currencies can be explained by each country's expected inflation rate.

    d.   Aspects of the Three Theories

        1)   The three theories can be summarized as follows:

Theory	Deals with	Explanatory Variable
Interest rate parity (IRP)	Forward rate	Interest rates
Purchasing power parity (PPP)	Percentage change in spot rate	Inflation rates
International Fisher Effect (IFE)	Percentage change in spot rate	Interest rates

        2)   Each of the three theories isolates a single factor as the principal cause of exchange rate differences. However, as depicted in Figure 7-5 on the previous page, multiple factors are actually at work in the determination of exchange rates.

        3)   With regard to high-inflation currencies,

            a)   IRP theory suggests that they usually trade at large forward discounts.
            b)   PPP and IFE theory suggest that they will weaken over time.
            c)   IFE theory suggests that their economies will have high interest rates.

6. **Exchange Rate Fluctuations over Time**

    a.   Long-term exchange rates are dictated by the purchasing-power parity theorem.

        1)   In the long run, real prices should be the same worldwide (net of government taxes or trade barriers and transportation costs) for a given good. Exchange rates will adjust until purchasing-power parity is achieved.

        2)   In other words, relative price levels determine exchange rates. In the real world, exchange rates do not perfectly reflect purchasing-power parity, but relative price levels are clearly important determinants of those rates.

    b.   Medium-term exchange rates are dictated by the economic activity in a country.

        1)   When the U.S. is in a recession, spending on imports (as well as domestic goods) will decrease. This reduced spending on imports shifts the supply curve for dollars to the left, causing the equilibrium value of the dollar to increase (assuming the demand for dollars is constant); that is, at any given exchange rate, the supply to foreigners is less.

        2)   If more goods are exported because of an increased preference for U.S. goods, the demand curve for dollars shifts to the right, causing upward pressure on the value of the dollar.

        3)   An increase in imports or a decrease in exports will have effects opposite to those described above.

    c.   Short-term exchange rates are dictated by interest rates.

        1)   Big corporations and banks invest their large reserves of cash where the real interest rate is highest. A rise in the real interest rate in a country will lead to an appreciation of the currency because it will be demanded for investment at the higher real interest rate, thereby shifting the demand curve to the right (outward).

        2)   The reverse holds true for a decline in real interest rates because that currency will be sold as investors move their money out of the country.

        3)   However, the interplay of interest rates and inflation must also be considered. Inflation of a currency relative to a second currency causes the first currency to depreciate relative to the second. Moreover, nominal interest rates increase when inflation rates are expected to increase.

Due to exchange rate fluctuations, there are risks involved with international trade. As a CMA candidate, you will need to be able to identify and be prepared to explain the methods used to mitigate the risks. Additionally, you should be able to analyze the best method to manage this risk with supporting calculations.

7. Risks of Exchange Rate Fluctuation

a. When a firm sells merchandise to a foreign customer, the firm's receivable might be denominated in the customer's currency.

   1) The downside risk to a foreign-denominated receivable is that the foreign currency might depreciate against the firm's domestic currency.

   2) If the foreign currency has depreciated by the settlement date, the firm will receive fewer units of its domestic currency than it would have if the transaction had been settled at the time of the sale.

b. Likewise, when a firm buys merchandise from a foreign supplier, the firm's payable might be denominated in the supplier's currency.

   1) The downside risk to a foreign-denominated payable is that the foreign currency might appreciate against the firm's domestic currency.

   2) If the foreign currency has appreciated by the settlement date, the firm will be forced to buy more units of the foreign currency to settle the payable than it would have if the transaction had been settled at the time of the purchase.

Summary of Exchange Rate Risk

Foreign-Denominated Transaction	Results in a Foreign-Denominated	Downside Risk is That Foreign Currency
Sale	Receivable	Depreciates
Purchase	Payable	Appreciates

8. Hedging in Response to Exchange Rate Risk

a. Hedging as a Tool against Uncertainty

   1) When hedging, some amount of possible upside is forgone in order to protect against the potential downside. Hedging thus embodies the old saying, "A bird in the hand is worth two in the bush."

b. Hedging a Foreign-Denominated Receivable

   1) When the downside risk is that the foreign currency will depreciate by the settlement date, the hedge is to sell the foreign currency forward to lock in a definite price.

EXAMPLE

A U.S. company knows that it will be receiving 5,000,000 pesos in 30 days from the sale of some equipment at one of its facilities in Mexico. The spot rate for a peso is $0.77, and the 30-day forward rate is $0.80. The firm wants to be sure that it will be able to sell the pesos it will be receiving in 30 days for $0.80 each. The firm thus hedges by selling 5,000,000 pesos 30 days forward. The company is buying a guarantee that it will be able to sell 5,000,000 pesos in 30 days and receive $4,000,000 (5,000,000 × $0.80) in return.

The spot rate on day 30 turns out to be $0.82. Thus, the U.S. company could have made more money by forgoing the hedge and simply waiting to convert the pesos on day 30. However, this possibility was not worth the risk that the peso might have fallen below $0.80.

The counterparty to the hedge just described (i.e., the buyer of pesos) might also be hedging but could be speculating or simply making a market in the instrument. The two parties are indifferent to each other's goals.

c. Hedging a Foreign-Denominated Payable

   1) When the downside risk is that the foreign currency will appreciate by the settlement date, the hedge is to purchase the foreign currency forward to lock in a definite price.

EXAMPLE

A U.S. company knows that it will need 100,000 Canadian dollars in 60 days to pay an invoice. The firm thus hedges by purchasing 100,000 Canadian dollars 60 days forward. The company is essentially buying a guarantee that it will have C$100,000 available for use in 60 days. The 60-day forward rate for a Canadian dollar is US $0.99. Thus, for the privilege of having a guaranteed receipt of 100,000 Canadian dollars, the company will commit now to paying $99,000 in 60 days.

The counterparty to the hedge just described (i.e., the seller of Canadian dollars) might also be hedging, but could be speculating or simply making a market in the instrument. The two parties are indifferent to each other's goals.

d. Managing Net Receivables and Payables Positions

   1) A firm can reduce its exchange rate risk by maintaining a position in each foreign currency of receivables and payables that net to near zero.

     a) On the other hand, the firm may wish to actively manage its foreign-denominated receivables and payables.

       i) The firm maintains a net receivables position in currencies expected to appreciate and a net payables position in currencies expected to appreciate.

       ii) This speculative approach obviously carries risks of its own.

   2) Large multinational corporations often establish multinational netting centers as special departments to execute whichever strategy is selected.

     a) They enter into foreign currency futures contracts when necessary to achieve balance.

9. **Tools for Mitigating Exchange Rate Risk -- Short-Term**

a. **Money Market Hedges**

   1) The least complex tool for hedging exchange rate risk is the money market hedge.

   2) A firm with a receivable denominated in a foreign currency can borrow the amount and convert it to its domestic currency now, then pay off the foreign loan when the receivable is collected.

   3) A firm with a payable denominated in a foreign currency can buy a money market instrument denominated in that currency that is timed to mature when the payable is due. Exchange rate fluctuations between the transaction date and the settlement date are avoided.

b. **Futures Contracts**

   1) Whereas forward contracts are negotiated individually between the parties on a one-by-one basis, futures contracts are essentially commodities that are traded on an exchange, making them available to more parties.

   2) Futures contracts are only available for generic amounts (e.g, 62,500 British pounds, 100,000 Brazilian reals, 12,500,000 Japanese yen) and with specific settlement dates (typically the third Wednesday in March, June, September, and December).

     a) This rigidity makes them less flexible than forward contracts because forward contracts are customized for the parties.

     b) The largest market in the world for trading currency futures is the Chicago Mercantile Exchange. Information about the sizes and prices of various actively traded futures contracts is available at www.cmegroup.com/trading/fx/.

3)   Because futures contracts are impersonal, the two parties need never know each other's identity.

a)   The exchange clearinghouse randomly matches those wishing to purchase a particular futures contract with someone wishing to sell one. The clearinghouse thus underwrites the contract, removing the risk of nonperformance by either party.

c.   **Currency Options**

1)   A currency option differs from a currency futures contract in that a futures contract is, as the name implies, a binding contract; both parties must perform. An option is exercised only if the party purchasing the option chooses to.

a)   Futures contracts have four settlement dates in the course of a year. Options offer one settlement date every month.

2)   Two types of options are available:

a)   A call option gives the holder the right to buy (i.e., call for) a specified amount of currency in a future month at a specified price. Call options are among the many tools available to hedge payables.

b)   A put option gives the holder the right to sell (i.e., put onto the market) a specified amount of currency in a future month at a specified price. Put options are among the many tools available to hedge receivables.

3)   Currency options are available from two sources: options exchanges (similar to those for futures contracts) and the over-the-counter market.

a)   As with futures contracts, exchange-traded options are only available for predefined quantities of currency.

b)   Options available in over-the-counter markets are provided by commercial banks and brokerage houses.

10.   **Tools for Mitigating Exchange Rate Risk -- Long-Term**

a.   **Forward Contracts**

1)   Large corporations that have close relationships with major banks are able to enter into contracts for individual transactions concerning large amounts. These contracts are unavailable to smaller firms or firms without a history with a particular bank.

2)   The bank guarantees that it will make available to the firm a given quantity of a certain currency at a definite rate at some point in the future. The price charged by the bank for this guarantee is called the premium.

EXAMPLE

A large U.S. firm purchases equipment from a Korean manufacturer for 222,000,000 won, due in 90 days. The exchange rate on the date of sale is $1 to 1,110 won. The U.S. firm suspects that the won may appreciate over the next 90 days and wants to lock in a forward rate of 1-to-1,110. The firm negotiates a contract whereby its bank promises to deliver 222,000,000 won to the firm in 90 days for $200,000. In return for this guarantee, the firm will pay the bank a 2% premium ($200,000 × 2% = $4,000).

---

3)   Clearly, the use of any mitigation strategy carries an opportunity cost.

a)   The firm must execute its part of the contract whether the exchange rate with the won has fluctuated or not. If the won falls in value or rises less than the 2% premium with respect to the dollar, the firm has incurred an economic loss on the transaction.

b. **Currency Swaps**

1) A broker brings together two parties who would like to hedge exchange rate risk by swapping cash flows in each other's currency.

EXAMPLE

The Australian owner of a new office building in Shanghai is currently signing 20-year lease agreements with tenants. At the same time, a Shanghai-based consultant has just signed a 20-year outsourcing contract in Melbourne. The Australian landlord is going to have cash flows denominated in yuan, and the Chinese consultant is going to have cash flows denominated in Australian dollars.

A broker working for a large investment bank engineers an agreement whereby the two will exchange cash flows each month for the next 20 years. A mechanism is agreed upon to determine the appropriate exchange rate.

Stop and review! You have completed the outline for this subunit. Study multiple-choice questions 26 through 30 beginning on page 306.

7.7 INTERNATIONAL TRADE

1. **Analysis of Foreign Investments**

   a. A company planning a foreign investment can either purchase the stock of a foreign corporation or make a **direct foreign investment**. A direct foreign investment involves buying equipment and buildings for a new company. The advantages of a direct foreign investment include

      1) Lower taxes in the foreign nation
      2) Annual depreciation allowances for the amount invested
      3) Access to foreign capital sources

   b. Relevant cash flows are the dividends and possible future sales price of the investment paid to the investor. To this extent, traditional capital budgeting techniques can be used.

   c. Cost of capital for foreign projects is higher because of the increased

      1) Exchange-rate risk
      2) Sovereignty (or political) risk arising from possible expropriation (or other restrictions), with net losses to the parent company
      3) The likelihood of laws requiring financing from certain sources, such as a requirement that foreign subsidiaries must be at least 51% owned by locals.

   d. Foreign operations are more difficult to manage than domestic operations.

   e. Ownership rights in foreign corporations are sometimes evidenced by American depository receipts (ADRs). The foreign stocks are deposited with a large U.S. bank, which in turn issues ADRs representing ownership in the foreign shares. The ADR shares then trade on a U.S. stock exchange, whereas the company's original shares trade in foreign stock markets. ADRs allow foreign companies to develop a U.S. shareholder base without being subject to many SEC restrictions.

   f. Foreign investments are funded by

      1) Parent company resources
      2) Common stock sales in the foreign country
      3) Bond sales in the foreign country
      4) Borrowing in world financial markets

2. **Multinational Corporations**

    a. **Benefits to the home country** include

        1) Improved earnings and exports of products to foreign subsidiaries.

        2) Improved ability to obtain scarce resources.

        3) The typical benefits of free trade, i.e., greater product availability, a better international monetary system, and improved international understanding.

    b. **Adverse effects on the home country** include

        1) Loss of jobs and tax revenues.

        2) Instability caused by reduced flexibility of operation in a foreign political system and the risk of expropriation.

        3) Competitive advantage of multinationals over domestic rivals.

    c. **Benefits to the host country** include

        1) New investment of capital, technology, and management abilities.

        2) Improvements in output and efficiency along with the resulting stronger balance of payments.

        3) Stimulation of competition, increased tax revenues, and higher standard of living.

    d. **Adverse effects on the host country** include

        1) Remittance of royalties, dividends, and profits that can result in a net capital outflow.

        2) Setting of transfer prices among subsidiaries so that profits will be earned where taxes are lowest or restrictions on the export of profits are least stringent.

        3) Multinationals engaging in anticompetitive activities, such as the formation of cartels.

3. **Methods of Financing International Trade**

    a. **Cross-Border Factoring**

        1) A factor purchases receivables and assumes the risk of collection.

        2) Cross-border factoring is a method of consummating a transaction by a network of factors across borders. The exporter's factor contacts correspondent factors in other countries to assist in the collection of accounts receivable.

    b. **Letters of Credit**

        1) Under a letter of credit, an issuer (usually a bank) undertakes with the account party (an importer-buyer that obtains the letter of credit) to verify that the beneficiary (seller-exporter) has performed under the contract, e.g., by shipping goods.

        2) Thus, the issuer pays the beneficiary when it presents documents (such as bills of lading) that provide evidence of performance. The issuer then is reimbursed by the account party.

        3) The process is as follows:

            a) The importer applies to its home country bank (issuer) for a letter of credit. The issuer sends the letter to a correspondent bank in the exporter's country.

            b) The correspondent bank transfers the letter to the exporter, who is thereby assured of payment.

            c) The exporter ships the goods and delivers the shipping documents to the correspondent bank, which pays the exporter if they are in order.

      d)   The correspondent bank sends the shipping documents to the issuer, which reimburses the correspondent bank and charges the importer's account.

      e)   The importer (or its broker) receives the shipping documents and presents them to the carrier to obtain the goods.

  c. **Banker's Acceptances**

    1) Banker's acceptances are time drafts drawn on deposits in a bank. They are short-term credit investments created by a nonfinancial firm and guaranteed (accepted) by a bank as to payment.

    2) Acceptances are traded at discounts in secondary markets. These instruments have been a popular investment for money market funds.

  d. **Forfaiting**

    1) Forfaiting is a form of factoring that involves the sale by exporters of large, medium- to long-term receivables to buyers (forfaiters) who are willing and able to bear the costs and risks of credit and collections.

  e. **Countertrade**

    1) Countertrade at its simplest is barter -- the exchange of goods or services for other goods or services rather than merely for cash.

4. **International Tax Considerations**

  a. Multinational corporations frequently derive income from several countries. The government of each country in which a corporation does business may enact statutes imposing one or more types of tax on the corporation.

  b. **Treaties.** To avoid double taxation, two or more countries may adopt treaties to coordinate or synchronize the effects of their taxing statutes.

    1) Treaties are also used to integrate other governmental goals, e.g., providing incentive for desired investment.

    2) If a U.S. statute and a treaty to which the U.S. is a party conflict, the one enacted or adopted last controls.

    3) A treaty might modify the rules in a country's statutes that designate to which country income is sourced or of which country a firm is a resident.

  c. **Multinational Corporations**

    1) Most countries tax only the income sourced to that country.

    2) The U.S. taxes worldwide income (from whatever source derived) of a domestic corporation. Double taxation is avoided by allowing a credit for income tax paid to foreign countries or by treaty provisions.

    3) In the case of foreign corporations, the U.S. taxes only income sourced to the U.S. Ordinarily, such income is effectively connected with engaging in a trade or business of the U.S. Certain U.S. source income, e.g., gain on the sale of most stock, is not taxed by the U.S.

    4) **Transfer pricing** is an important aspect of the tax calculation for multinational corporations that transfer inventories between branches in different countries. The U.S. tax laws have limits on the amount of profit that can be transferred from a U.S. parent to a foreign subsidiary or branch. Although there are exceptions, the basic transfer pricing rules under the *Internal Revenue Code* limit the amount of taxable income that can be claimed by the foreign subsidiary to no more than 50% of the total taxable income. Thus, transfer prices charged to foreign subsidiaries may differ substantially from those charged to domestic subsidiaries.

5) There are also non-tax aspects of transfer pricing. For example, limitations on taking profits out of a foreign country, or currency restrictions, can be avoided by charging the foreign subsidiary a higher transfer price than that charged to domestic subsidiaries. This is because firms in developing countries are allowed to pay their accounts payable to foreign vendors but are not allowed to distribute profits to foreign owners.

6) The existence of tariffs in the foreign country may necessitate a lower transfer price to reduce a tariff based on the inventory value.

Stop and review! You have completed the outline for this subunit. Study multiple-choice questions 31 through 35 beginning on page 308.

7.8 CORE CONCEPTS

Financial Markets and Securities Offerings

- **Money markets** trade debt securities with maturities of less than 1 year. **Capital markets** trade long-term debt and equity securities.

- **Primary markets** are the markets in which corporations and governmental units raise new capital by making initial offerings of their securities. The issuer receives the proceeds of sale in a primary market. **Secondary markets** provide for trading of previously issued securities among investors.

- The **efficient markets hypothesis (EMH)** states that current stock prices immediately and fully reflect all relevant information. Hence, the market is continuously adjusting to new information and acting to correct pricing errors. In other words, securities prices are always in equilibrium. The EMH has three forms (versions):

  - **Strong form.** All public and private information is instantaneously reflected in securities' prices. Thus, insider trading is assumed not to result in abnormal returns. Empirical data have refuted the strong form of the efficient markets hypothesis but not the weak and semistrong forms.

  - **Semistrong form.** All publicly available data are reflected in security prices, but private or insider data are not immediately reflected. Accordingly, insider trading can result in abnormal returns.

  - **Weak form.** Current securities prices reflect all recent past price movement data, so technical analysis will not provide a basis for abnormal returns in securities trading.

- **Investment bankers** serve as intermediaries between businesses and the providers of capital. Moreover, they not only help to sell new securities but also assist in business combinations, act as brokers in secondary markets, and trade for their own accounts.

- A firm's first issuance of securities to the public is an **initial public offering**. The process by which a closely held corporation issues new securities to the public is called going public. When a firm goes public, it issues its stock on a new issue or initial public offering market. Later issues of stock by the same company are subsequent offerings.

Dividend Policy and Share Repurchase

- **Dividend policy** determines what portion of a corporation's net income is distributed to shareholders and what portion is retained for reinvestment. A high dividend rate means a slower rate of growth. A high growth rate usually means a low dividend rate. Because both a high growth rate and a high dividend rate are desirable, the financial manager attempts to achieve the balance that maximizes the firm's share price.

- The **cash dividend** is the most common type. A **stock dividend** is an issuance of stock and entails the transfer of a sum from the retained earnings account to a paid-in capital account. A **stock split** does not involve any accounting entries. Instead, the existing shares are divided into more pieces so that the market price per share will be reduced.

- A **share repurchase** takes place when a corporation buys its own stock back on the open market. Once in the firm's possession, these shares are called treasury shares.

Mergers and Acquisitions

- A **merger** is a business transaction in which an acquiring firm absorbs a second firm, and the acquiring firm remains in business as a combination of the two merged firms. A merger is legally straightforward; however, approval of the shareholders of each firm is required. A **consolidation** is similar to a merger, but a new entity is formed and neither of the merging entities survives. An **acquisition** is the purchase of all of another firm's assets or a controlling interest in its stock.

- **Opposition** to a business combination can take the form of greenmail, staggered election of boards of directors, golden parachutes, fair price provisions, going private, poison pills, and others.

- **Other forms** of corporate restructuring include spin-offs, divestitures, liquidations, leveraged cash-outs, and equity carve-outs.

Bankruptcy

- A firm may respond to **insolvency** by combining with another firm, selling assets, reducing costs, issuing new debt or equity securities, or negotiating with creditors to restructure its obligations. However, these private workouts may be unlikely to succeed or may already have failed. Consequently, a **formal bankruptcy** may be declared either voluntarily by the debtor or involuntarily due to a petition brought by creditors.

- A firm may be **liquidated** under Chapter 7 of the Federal Bankruptcy Code, or **reorganized** under Chapter 11.

Currency Exchange Rates -- Systems and Calculations

- In general, when the **demand for a country's merchandise**, capital assets, and financial instruments rises, **demand for its currency** rises.

- The **exchange rate** is the price of one country's currency in terms of another country's currency.

  - The exchange rates of most currencies today are set by a **floating exchange rate system**. Despite this, some countries continue to fix their currencies (e.g., the Saudi riyal and the Chinese yuan). The following are four basic exchange rate systems:

    - **Fixed.** The value of a country's currency in relation to another country's currency is either fixed or allowed to fluctuate only within a very narrow range.

    - **Freely floating.** The government steps aside and allows exchange rates to be determined entirely by the market forces of supply and demand.

    - **Managed float.** The government allows market forces to determine exchange rates until they move too far in one direction or another. The government will then intervene to maintain the currency within the broad range considered appropriate.

    - **Pegged.** The government fixes the rate of exchange for its currency with respect to another country's currency (or to a "basket" of several currencies). The pegging country then calculates its currency's movement with respect to the currencies of third countries based on the movements of the currency to which it has been pegged.

- As exchange rates **fluctuate**, buying power rises and falls. Currency appreciates when it can buy more units of another currency. Currency depreciates when it can purchase fewer units of another currency. **Equilibrium exchange rates** in floating markets are determined by the supply of and demand for the currencies.

- The **spot rate** is the number of units of a foreign currency that can be received today in exchange for a single unit of the domestic currency. The **forward rate** is the number of units of a foreign currency that can be received in exchange for a single unit of the domestic currency at some definite date in the future.

  - If the domestic currency fetches more units of a foreign currency in the forward market than in the spot market, the domestic currency is said to be trading at a **forward premium** with respect to the foreign currency.

  - If the domestic currency fetches fewer units of a foreign currency in the forward market than in the spot market, the domestic currency is said to be trading at a **forward discount** with respect to the foreign currency.

  - The forward premium or discount is calculated as the percentage spread times the number of forward periods in a year.

Calculation of Forward Premium or Discount

$$\frac{Forward\ rate - Spot\ rate}{Spot\ rate} \times \frac{Days\ in\ year}{Days\ in\ forward\ period}$$

  - A **cross rate** is used when the two currencies involved are not stated in terms of each other. The exchange must be valued in terms of a third currency, very often the U.S. dollar.

- A country's **balance of payments** is the net of all transactions between domestic parties and parties in a particular foreign country.

  - If a country's currency is weak, its goods and services are more affordable to foreign consumers. These countries tend to have a positive balance of trade.

  - By the same token, if a country's currency is strong, its goods and services are more expensive to foreign consumers. These countries tend to have a negative balance of trade.

Currency Exchange Rates -- Factors Affecting Rates and Risk Mitigation Techniques

- The five factors that affect currency exchange rates can be classified as three trade-related factors and two financial factors.

  - The **trade-related factors** are relative inflation rates, relative income levels, and government intervention.

  - The **financial factors** are relative interest rates and ease of capital flow.

- The **three theories** about currency exchange rates can be summarized as follows:

Theory	Deals with	Explanatory Variable
Interest rate parity (IRP)	Forward rate	Interest rates
Purchasing power parity (PPP)	Percentage change in spot rate	Inflation rates
International Fisher Effect (IFE)	Percentage change in spot rate	Interest rates

- Exchange rate **fluctuations over time** are generally considered to be affected as follows:

  - Long-term exchange rates are dictated by the purchasing-power parity theorem.
  - Medium-term exchange rates are dictated by the economic activity in a country.
  - Short-term exchange rates are dictated by interest rates.

- The **downside risk** of a foreign-denominated receivable is that the foreign currency might depreciate against the firm's domestic currency. Likewise, the downside risk to a foreign-denominated payable is that the foreign currency might appreciate against the firm's domestic currency.

- Tools for hedging these risks in the **short term** include

    - **Money market hedges**, in which a firm with a foreign-denominated payable buys a money market instrument denominated in that currency that is timed to mature when the payable is due.

    - **Futures contracts**, in which a firm can contract for certain generic amounts and with specific settlement dates. While they lack the flexibility of forward contracts, they are impersonal and so can be readily traded.

    - **Currency options**, which give the holder the opportunity (as opposed to a contract, under which the parties have no choice) to buy or sell a quantity of a given currency at a given price.

- Tools for hedging these risks over the **long term** include

    - **Forward contracts**, in which large corporations that have close relationships with major banks can establish precisely customized agreements for the delivery of a quantity of a given currency at a given price.

    - **Currency swaps**, in which two parties who have cash flows in currencies other than their domestic currencies agree to exchange their flows.

International Trade

- A **direct foreign investment** involves buying equipment and buildings in a foreign country for a new company. The advantages of a direct foreign investment include lower taxes in the foreign nation, annual depreciation allowances for the amount invested, and access to foreign capital sources.

- When determining whether to operate a foreign subsidiary, a company must take the following **factors** into account: tax differences, restrictions on remittances, administrative fees, currency fluctuations, salvage value, host-country government policies, and any nonfinancial considerations.

- **Methods of payment** for international trade include prepayment, letters of credit, sight drafts, time drafts, consignment, and open account.

- **Methods of financing** international trade include cross-border factoring, banker's acceptances, forfaiting, and countertrade.

- **Multinational corporations** have both benefits for and adverse effects on both their home and host countries.

- Multinational corporations frequently derive income from several countries. The government of each country in which a corporation does business may enact statutes imposing one or more types of **tax** on the corporation. **Transfer pricing** is an important aspect of the tax calculation for multinational corporations that transfer inventories between branches in different countries.

QUESTIONS

7.1 Financial Markets and Securities Offerings

1. Which of the following financial instruments can be traded in international money markets?

- A. Mortgages.
- B. Preferred stocks.
- C. Government treasury bills.
- D. Government treasury bonds.

Answer (C) is correct. *(CIA, adapted)*
REQUIRED: The instruments traded in international money markets.
DISCUSSION: Funds are borrowed or lent for short periods (less than 1 year) in money markets. Examples of instruments traded in money markets are U.S. Treasury bills, bankers' acceptances, commercial paper, negotiable certificates of deposit, money market mutual funds, Eurodollar market time deposits, and consumer credit loans. Capital markets trade stocks and long-term debt.
Answer (A) is incorrect. Mortgages are long-term, capital market securities. Answer (B) is incorrect. Preferred stocks are long-term, capital market securities. Answer (D) is incorrect. Treasury bonds are long-term, capital market securities.

2. In capital markets, the primary market is concerned with the provision of new funds for capital investments through

- A. New issues of bond and stock securities.
- B. Exchanges of existing bond and stock securities.
- C. The sale of forward or future commodities contracts.
- D. New issues of bond and stock securities and exchanges of existing bond and stock securities.

Answer (A) is correct. *(CMA, adapted)*
REQUIRED: The purpose of the primary market.
DISCUSSION: The primary market is the market for new stocks and bonds. In this market, wherein investment money flows directly to the issuer, securities are initially sold by investment bankers who purchase them from issuers and sell them through an underwriting group. Later transactions occur on securities exchanges or other markets.
Answer (B) is incorrect. Existing securities are traded on a secondary market (e.g., securities exchanges). Answer (C) is incorrect. The futures market is where commodities contracts are sold, not the capital market. Answer (D) is incorrect. Exchanges of existing securities do not occur in the primary market.

3. Financial market efficiency implies that

- A. All securities are perfect substitutes, and that the net present value of any securities investment is zero.
- B. A firm's share price may not be a good estimate of future cash flows because price adjustment to new information is slow.
- C. It is possible to systematically gain or lose abnormal profits from trading on the basis of available public information.
- D. Because of the speculative nature of securities markets, share prices may not be the best benchmark for corporate financial choices.

Answer (A) is correct. *(CFM, adapted)*
REQUIRED: The correct statement about financial market efficiency.
DISCUSSION: The efficient markets hypothesis (EMH) states that current stock prices immediately and fully reflect all relevant information. Hence, the market is continuously adjusting to new information and acting to correct pricing errors. Thus, the price of a security, which reflects an assessment of future cash flows, must equal the present value of those flows (NPV = 0) if the security is accurately priced. Furthermore, if all securities are accurately priced, every security has an NPV of $0, and all securities are therefore perfect substitutes.
Answer (B) is incorrect. Price adjustments are instantaneous under the EMH. Answer (C) is incorrect. Securities prices are always in equilibrium under the EMH, i.e., no abnormal profit with public information. Answer (D) is incorrect. The EMH states that securities prices are, rather than are not, the best benchmark of corporate financial decisions.

4. The semistrong form of the efficient markets hypothesis (EMH) states that current market prices of securities reflect

- A. No pertinent information.
- B. All pertinent information.
- C. Only information contained in past price movements.
- D. Only publicly available information.

Answer (D) is correct. *(CIA, adapted)*
REQUIRED: The information reflected in current market prices under the semistrong form of the EMH.
DISCUSSION: According to the EMH, stock prices are in equilibrium and investors cannot obtain abnormal returns, that is, returns in excess of the riskiness of their investments. The semistrong form of the EMH postulates that current market prices reflect all publicly available information. However, investors with inside information can still earn an abnormal return.
Answer (A) is incorrect. The EMH states that current prices reflect at least the information contained in past price movements. Answer (B) is incorrect. The strong form of the EMH states that current market prices reflect all pertinent information, including insider information. Answer (C) is incorrect. The weak form of the EMH states that current market prices reflect only information contained in past price movements.

5. Moody's and Standard & Poor's debt ratings depend on

A. The chances of default.

B. The size of the company.

C. The size and the type of issue.

D. The firm's industry.

Answer (A) is correct. *(Publisher, adapted)*
REQUIRED: The basis for debt ratings.
DISCUSSION: Debt ratings are based on the probability of default and the protection for investors in case of default.
Answer (B) is incorrect. The size of the company is relevant only insofar as it bears upon the probability of default.
Answer (C) is incorrect. The size and the type of issue are relevant only insofar as they bear upon the probability of default.
Answer (D) is incorrect. The firm's industry is relevant only insofar as it bears upon the probability of default.

7.2 Dividend Policy and Share Repurchase

6. In practice, dividends

A. Usually exhibit greater stability than earnings.

B. Fluctuate more widely than earnings.

C. Tend to be a lower percentage of earnings for mature firms.

D. Are usually changed every year to reflect earnings changes.

Answer (A) is correct. *(CMA, adapted)*
REQUIRED: The true statement about dividends and their relation to earnings.
DISCUSSION: Dividend policy determines the portion of net income distributed to stockholders. Corporations normally try to maintain a stable level of dividends, even though profits may fluctuate considerably, because many stockholders buy stock with the expectation of receiving a certain dividend every year. Thus, management tends not to raise dividends if the payout cannot be sustained. The desire for stability has led theorists to propound the information content or signaling hypothesis: A change in dividend policy is a signal to the market regarding management's forecast of future earnings. This stability often results in a stock that sells at a higher market price because stockholders perceive less risk in receiving their dividends.
Answer (B) is incorrect. Most companies try to maintain stable dividends. Answer (C) is incorrect. Mature firms have less need of earnings to reinvest for expansion; thus, they tend to pay a higher percentage of earnings as dividends. Answer (D) is incorrect. Most companies try to maintain stable dividends.

7. Residco, Inc., expects net income of $800,000 for the next fiscal year. Its targeted and current capital structure is 40% debt and 60% common equity. The director of capital budgeting has determined that the optimal capital spending for next year is $1.2 million. If Residco follows a strict residual dividend policy, what is the expected dividend-payout ratio for next year?

A. 90.0%

B. 66.7%

C. 40.0%

D. 10.0%

Answer (D) is correct. *(CMA, adapted)*
REQUIRED: The expected dividend-payout ratio assuming a strict residual dividend policy.
DISCUSSION: Under the residual theory of dividends, the residual of earnings paid as dividends depends on the available investments and the debt-equity ratio at which cost of capital is minimized. The rational investor should prefer reinvestment of retained earnings when the return exceeds what the investor could earn on investments of equal risk. However, the firm may prefer to pay dividends when investment returns are poor and the internal equity financing would move the firm away from its ideal capital structure. If Residco wants to maintain its current structure, 60% of investments should be financed from equity. Hence, it needs $720,000 ($1,200,000 × 60%) of equity funds, leaving $80,000 of net income ($800,000 NI – $720,000) available for dividends. The dividend-payout ratio is therefore 10% ($80,000 ÷ $800,000 NI).
Answer (A) is incorrect. This percentage is the reinvestment ratio. Answer (B) is incorrect. This percentage is the ratio between earnings and investment. Answer (C) is incorrect. The percentage is the ratio of debt in the ideal capital structure.

8. Brady Corporation has 6,000 shares of 5% cumulative, $100 par value preferred stock outstanding and 200,000 shares of common stock outstanding. Brady's board of directors last declared dividends for the year ended May 31, Year 1, and there were no dividends in arrears. For the year ended May 31, Year 3, Brady had net income of $1,750,000. The board of directors is declaring a dividend for common shareholders equivalent to 20% of net income. The total amount of dividends to be paid by Brady at May 31, Year 3, is

A. $350,000

B. $380,000

C. $206,000

D. $410,000

Answer (D) is correct. *(CMA, adapted)*
REQUIRED: The total amount of dividends to be paid given cumulative preferred stock.
DISCUSSION: If a company has cumulative preferred stock, all preferred dividends for the current and any unpaid prior years must be paid before any dividends can be paid on common stock. The total preferred dividends that must be paid equal $60,000 (6,000 shares × $100 par × 5% × 2 years), and the common dividend is $350,000 ($1,750,000 × 20%), for a total of $410,000.
Answer (A) is incorrect. The amount of $350,000 is the common stock dividend. Answer (B) is incorrect. The amount of $380,000 omits the $30,000 of cumulative dividends for the year ended May 31, Year 2. Answer (C) is incorrect. The amount of $206,000 is based on a flat rate of $1 per share of stock.

9. A 10% stock dividend most likely

A. Increases the size of the firm.

B. Increases shareholders' wealth.

C. Decreases future earnings per share.

D. Decreases net income.

Answer (C) is correct. *(CMA, adapted)*
REQUIRED: The most likely effect of a stock dividend.
DISCUSSION: A stock dividend is a transfer of equity from retained earnings to paid-in capital. The debit is to retained earnings, and the credits are to common stock and additional paid-in capital. Additional shares are outstanding following the stock dividend, but every shareholder maintains the same percentage of ownership. In effect, a stock dividend divides the pie (the corporation) into more pieces, but the pie is still the same size. Hence, a corporation will have a lower EPS and a lower book value per share following a stock dividend, but every shareholder will be just as well off as previously. A stock dividend has no effect except on the composition of the shareholders' equity section of the balance sheet.

10. The purchase of treasury stock with a firm's surplus cash

A. Increases a firm's assets.

B. Increases a firm's financial leverage.

C. Increases a firm's interest coverage ratio.

D. Dilutes a firm's earnings per share.

Answer (B) is correct. *(CMA, adapted)*
REQUIRED: The true statement about a purchase of treasury stock.
DISCUSSION: A purchase of treasury stock involves a decrease in assets (usually cash) and a corresponding decrease in equity. Thus, equity is reduced and the debt-to-equity ratio and financial leverage increase.
Answer (A) is incorrect. Assets decrease when treasury stock is purchased. Answer (C) is incorrect. A firm's interest coverage ratio is unaffected. Earnings, interest expense, and taxes will all be the same regardless of the transaction. Answer (D) is incorrect. The purchase of treasury stock is antidilutive; the same earnings will be spread over fewer shares. Some firms purchase treasury stock for this reason.

7.3 Mergers and Acquisitions

11. A horizontal merger is a merger between

A. Two or more firms from different and unrelated markets.

B. Two or more firms at different stages of the production process.

C. A producer and its supplier.

D. Two or more firms in the same market.

Answer (D) is correct. *(CMA, adapted)*
REQUIRED: The example of a horizontal merger.
DISCUSSION: A horizontal merger is one between competitors in the same market. From the viewpoint of the Justice Department, it is the most closely scrutinized type of merger because it has the greatest tendency to reduce competition.
Answer (A) is incorrect. A merger between firms in different and unrelated markets is a conglomerate merger. Answer (B) is incorrect. A merger between two or more firms at different stages of the production process is a vertical merger. Answer (C) is incorrect. A merger between a producer and a supplier is a vertical merger.

12. The acquisition of a retail shoe store by a shoe manufacturer is an example of

    A. Vertical integration.

    B. A conglomerate.

    C. Market extension.

    D. Horizontal integration.

Answer (A) is correct. *(CMA, adapted)*
    REQUIRED: The type of transaction represented.
    DISCUSSION: The acquisition of a shoe retailer by a shoe manufacturer is an example of vertical integration. Vertical integration is typified by a merger or acquisition involving companies that are in the same industry but at different levels in the supply chain. In other words, one of the companies supplies inputs for the other.
    Answer (B) is incorrect. A conglomerate is a company made up of subsidiaries in unrelated industries. Answer (C) is incorrect. Market extension involves expanding into new market areas. Answer (D) is incorrect. Horizontal integration involves a merger between competing firms in the same industry.

13. A company transferred ownership of one of its divisions to the company's existing shareholders, and the shareholders received new stock representing separate ownership rights in the division. That process is referred to as a

    A. Liquidation.

    B. Spin-off.

    C. Leveraged buyout.

    D. Managerial buyout.

Answer (B) is correct. *(CIA, adapted)*
    REQUIRED: The type of restructuring.
    DISCUSSION: A spin-off is a type of restructuring that is characterized by establishing a new and separate entity and transferring its newly issued stock to the shareholders of the original company.
    Answer (A) is incorrect. In a liquidation, assets are sold piecemeal. Answer (C) is incorrect. In an LBO, the acquirer borrows heavily from third parties to finance the transaction and uses the acquired company's assets as collateral. Answer (D) is incorrect. In a managerial buyout, the managers become the owners.

14. What is a payment to compensate top management after the occurrence of a takeover called?

    A. Greenmail.

    B. A golden parachute.

    C. A poison pill.

    D. Blackmail.

Answer (B) is correct. *(Publisher, adapted)*
    REQUIRED: The payment to compensate top management after the occurrence of a takeover.
    DISCUSSION: A golden parachute provides large payments to specified executives if their employment is terminated by the acquiring firm after a takeover. These provisions are passed by the board of directors. Shareholders are unhappy about golden parachute payoffs and have filed suits because they feel that these payoffs enrich management at their expense. In 1984, a change in the tax law imposed a 20% excise tax on these payoffs and provided for their nondeductibility by the corporation. This law was designed to reduce golden parachutes.
    Answer (A) is incorrect. Greenmail consists of payments to potential bidders to delay or stop unfriendly takeover attempts. Answer (C) is incorrect. A poison pill may be included in a target corporation's charter, by-laws, or contracts to reduce its value to potential tender offerors. Answer (D) is incorrect. Blackmail is obtaining a desired result by threats, such as public exposure of a negative attribute, and is usually not relevant to corporate takeover defenses.

15. Clover, Inc., recently sold a portion of the firm via an offering of shares in the new entity to public investors. This type of sell-off is classified as a(n)

    A. Spin-off.

    B. Equity carve-out.

    C. Leveraged cash-out.

    D. Liquidation.

Answer (B) is correct. *(CFM, adapted)*
    REQUIRED: The type of sell-off when a portion of a firm is sold to public investors.
    DISCUSSION: An equity carve-out involves the sale of a portion of the firm through an equity offering of shares in the new entity to outsiders.
    Answer (A) is incorrect. A spin-off is the creation of a new separate entity from another entity, with the new entity's shares being distributed on a pro rata basis to existing shareholders of the parent entity. Answer (C) is incorrect. A leveraged cash-out is borrowing heavily to issue a very large dividend that acts as a poison pill. Answer (D) is incorrect. In a liquidation, assets are sold piecemeal.

7.4 Bankruptcy

16. Chapter 7 of the Federal Bankruptcy Code will grant a debtor a discharge when the debtor

    A. Is a corporation or a partnership.

    B. Is an entity that could successfully reorganize under Chapter 11 of the Federal Bankruptcy Code.

    C. Is an insurance company.

    D. Unjustifiably destroyed information relevant to the bankruptcy proceeding.

Answer (B) is correct. *(Publisher, adapted)*
    REQUIRED: The basis for granting a discharge to a debtor under Chapter 7 of the Bankruptcy Code.
    DISCUSSION: A general discharge of most debts is provided a person under Chapter 7. Certain entities are not eligible, including railroads, insurance companies, banks, credit unions, and savings and loan associations. Liquidation and discharge under Chapter 7 are not restricted to cases in which Chapter 11 reorganization would not be successful.
    Answer (A) is incorrect. Partnerships and corporations do not receive a general discharge under Chapter 7. They are simply liquidated. Answer (C) is incorrect. Insurance companies are ineligible to file under Chapter 7. Answer (D) is incorrect. Destroying information can result in denial of general discharge. Only if it is justified, e.g., accidental and not to defraud creditors, might it not result in denial of discharge.

17. Which of the following is indicative of insolvency?

    A. Payments to creditors are late.

    B. The market value of the firm's stock has declined substantially.

    C. Operating cash flows of the firm cannot meet current obligations.

    D. Dividends are not declared because of inadequate retained earnings.

Answer (C) is correct. *(Publisher, adapted)*
    REQUIRED: The indicator of insolvency.
    DISCUSSION: A firm is insolvent when its debts exceed its assets (stock-based insolvency) or when its cash flows are inadequate to meet maturing obligations (flow-based insolvency).
    Answer (A) is incorrect. Late payments are an early signal of potential insolvency. Answer (B) is incorrect. A declining share price is an early signal of potential insolvency. Answer (D) is incorrect. Elimination of dividends is an early signal of potential insolvency.

18. A plan of reorganization formulated under Chapter 11 must be submitted to the creditors for acceptance and to the court for confirmation. Which of the following is correct?

    A. The effect of confirmation is to make the plan binding on all parties and to grant the debtor a discharge from claims not protected by the plan.

    B. A plan cannot be confirmed if any impaired class of claims or interests rejects it.

    C. If no class of claims or interests accepts a plan, the court may nevertheless confirm it if the plan is in the best interests of the creditors.

    D. A class that is not impaired is presumed to accept, but more than half of the claims in a class by amount must accept if the class is impaired.

Answer (A) is correct. *(Publisher, adapted)*
    REQUIRED: The correct statement about acceptance and confirmation of a plan.
    DISCUSSION: Confirmation is the court's approval of the plan after notice and a hearing. Confirmation makes the plan binding on the creditors, equity security holders, and debtor, whether or not they accepted the plan. It also operates as a discharge of unprotected debts, except for those claims previously denied discharge in a Chapter 7 case, and vests the estate property in the debtor. Confirmation is contingent upon the plan's feasibility, the good faith in which it was proposed, and the provision for cash payment of certain allowed claims, such as administration expenses.
    Answer (B) is incorrect. An impaired class may be required to accept a plan over its objection if the court finds that the plan is "fair and equitable," for instance, if no junior claim or interest receives anything. Answer (C) is incorrect. At least one class of claims (not ownership interests) must accept. Answer (D) is incorrect. A class of claims accepts if approval is given by more than half the allowed claims, provided they represent at least two-thirds of the claims by amount. A class of interests (shareholders) accepts if approval is given by two-thirds in amount of the allowed interests.

19. Which of the following is **not** an early signal of potential financial distress?

    A. Negative earnings.

    B. Employee layoffs.

    C. Rapidly falling stock prices.

    D. Stagnant cash flows.

Answer (D) is correct. *(Publisher, adapted)*
    REQUIRED: The item not an early signal of financial distress.
    DISCUSSION: Mere stagnation of cash flows does not indicate potential insolvency. Flow-based insolvency occurs when cash flows are inadequate, not when they are simply not growing at the desired rate.
    Answer (A) is incorrect. Negative earnings are an early signal of potential insolvency. Answer (B) is incorrect. Layoffs are an early signal of potential insolvency. Answer (C) is incorrect. A declining share price is an early signal of potential insolvency.

20. A plan of reorganization under Chapter 11

   A. May be filed by any party in interest for 120 days after entry of the order for relief.

   B. Must be filed by the trustee and approved by the creditors within 180 days after entry of the order for relief.

   C. Must treat all classes of claims and ownership interests equally.

   D. Must treat all claims or interests in the same class equally.

Answer (D) is correct. *(Publisher, adapted)*
   REQUIRED: The correct statement about a plan of reorganization.
   DISCUSSION: A Chapter 11 plan must designate classes of creditors' claims and owners' interests; state the treatment to be given each class; indicate which classes will or will not be impaired; allow for equal treatment of the members within a class unless they agree otherwise; and provide for an adequate method of payment. If the debtor is a corporation, the plan must also protect voting rights, state that no nonvoting stock will be issued, and require that selection of officers and directors be effected in a manner to protect the parties in interest.
   Answer (A) is incorrect. Only the debtor may file a plan within 120 days after entry of the order for relief. If the debtor fails to file or if the creditors do not approve of the plan within 180 days of the entry of the order for relief, any party in interest (including the trustee) may file a plan. Answer (B) is incorrect. Only the debtor may file a plan within 120 days after entry of the order for relief. If the debtor fails to file or if the creditors do not approve of the plan within 180 days of the entry of the order for relief, any party in interest (including the trustee) may file a plan. Answer (C) is incorrect. The plan must be fair and equitable but all classes need not be treated the same. However, no party may receive less than the amount that would have been distributed in a liquidation.

7.5 Currency Exchange Rates -- Systems and Calculations

21. In foreign currency markets, the phrase "managed float" refers to the

   A. Tendency for most currencies to depreciate in value.

   B. Discretionary buying and selling of currencies by central banks.

   C. Necessity of maintaining a highly liquid asset, such as gold, to conduct international trade.

   D. Fact that actual exchange rates are set by private business people in trading nations.

Answer (B) is correct. *(CMA, adapted)*
   REQUIRED: The meaning of the phrase "managed float."
   DISCUSSION: Exchange rates "float" when they are set by supply and demand, not by agreement among countries. In a managed float, central banks buy and sell currencies at their discretion to avoid erratic fluctuations in the foreign currency market. The objective of such transactions is to "manage" the level at which a particular currency sells in the open market. For instance, if there is an oversupply of a country's currency on the foreign currency market, the central bank will purchase that currency to support the market.
   Answer (A) is incorrect. Currencies do not have an inherent tendency to depreciate or appreciate. Answer (C) is incorrect. Currencies no longer have to be supported by gold. Answer (D) is incorrect. Central banks, not private business people, manage the quantity of currency on the market.

22. One U.S. dollar is being quoted at 100 Japanese yen on the spot market and at 102.5 Japanese yen on the 90-day forward market; hence, the annual effect in the forward market is that the U.S. dollar is at a

   A. Premium of 10%.

   B. Premium of 2.5%.

   C. Discount of 10%.

   D. Discount of 0.025%.

Answer (A) is correct. *(CMA, adapted)*
   REQUIRED: The annual effect in the forward market of the difference between the current (spot) rate and the 90-day rate.
   DISCUSSION: A forward currency premium or discount is calculated by multiplying the percentage spread by the number of forward periods in a year:

$$\frac{Forward\ rate - Spot\ rate}{Spot\ rate} \times \frac{Days\ in\ year}{Days\ in\ forward\ period}$$

In this case, the calculation is as follows:

$$Forward\ premium = [(¥102.5 - ¥100) \div ¥100] \times (360 \div 90)$$
$$= 0.025 \times 4$$
$$= 10\%$$

   Answer (B) is incorrect. This percentage is the premium for 90 days. Answer (C) is incorrect. The effect is a 10% premium, not discount. Answer (D) is incorrect. The 90-day effect is a 2.5% or 0.025 premium.

23. If the value of the U.S. dollar in foreign currency markets changes from $1 = .75 euros to $1 = .70 euros,

A. The euro has depreciated against the dollar.

B. Products imported from Europe to the U.S. will become more expensive.

C. U.S. tourists in Europe will find their dollars will buy more European products.

D. U.S. exports to Europe should decrease.

Answer (B) is correct. *(CMA, adapted)*
REQUIRED: The effect of a depreciation in the value of the dollar.
DISCUSSION: Since it now takes fewer euros to buy a single dollar, the dollar has declined in value relative to the euro; i.e., the euro has gained purchasing power. As a result, imports from Europe will become more expensive and will tend to decrease.
Answer (A) is incorrect. Since it now takes fewer euros to buy a single dollar, the euro has appreciated (gained purchasing power) relative to the dollar. Answer (C) is incorrect. Since a dollar will now fetch fewer euros than before, U.S. tourists will find European goods more expensive. Answer (D) is incorrect. Since the euro has gained purchasing power against the dollar, U.S. exports should increase.

24. An overvalued foreign currency exchange rate

A. Represents a tax on exports and a subsidy to imports.

B. Represents a subsidy to exports and a tax on imports.

C. Has an effect on capital flows but no effect on trade flows.

D. Has no effect on capital flows but does affect trade flows.

Answer (A) is correct. *(CMA, adapted)*
REQUIRED: The effect of an overvalued exchange rate.
DISCUSSION: If a country's currency is strong, its goods and services are more expensive to foreign consumers. At the same time, foreign goods become relatively more affordable to domestic consumers.
Answer (B) is incorrect. An overvalued domestic currency will have the opposite effect. Answer (C) is incorrect. Both will be affected. Answer (D) is incorrect. Both will be affected.

25. Of the following transactions, the one that would result in worsening the U.S. balance of payments account is the

A. Receipt of dividends by an American corporation from its German subsidiary.

B. Buying of IBM shares by a Kuwaiti investor.

C. U.S. export of military equipment to Saudi Arabia.

D. Expenditure of a U.S. resident vacationing in France.

Answer (D) is correct. *(CMA, adapted)*
REQUIRED: The transaction requiring a debit in the U.S. balance of payments account.
DISCUSSION: A U.S. resident vacationing abroad transfers money to the foreign country, worsening the U.S. balance of payments and improving that of the other country.
Answer (A) is incorrect. A transfer of dividends into the U.S. improves the balance of payments. Answer (B) is incorrect. The purchase of a U.S. financial instrument by a foreigner improves the balance of payments. Answer (C) is incorrect. The purchase of U.S. goods by a foreign country improves the balance of payments.

7.6 Currency Exchange Rates -- Factors Affecting Rates and Risk Mitigation Techniques

26. Assuming exchange rates are allowed to fluctuate freely, which one of the following factors would likely cause a nation's currency to appreciate on the foreign exchange market?

A. A relatively rapid rate of growth in income that stimulates imports.

B. A high rate of inflation relative to other countries.

C. A slower rate of growth in income than in other countries, which causes imports to lag behind exports.

D. Domestic real interest rates that are lower than real interest rates abroad.

Answer (C) is correct. *(CMA, adapted)*
REQUIRED: The factor causing a currency to appreciate given freely fluctuating exchange rates.
DISCUSSION: Assuming that exchange rates are allowed to fluctuate freely, a nation's currency will appreciate if the demand for it is constant or increasing while supply is decreasing. For example, if the nation decreases its imports relative to exports, less of its currency will be used to buy foreign currencies for import transactions and more of its currency will be demanded for export transactions. Thus, the supply of the nation's currency available in foreign currency markets decreases. If the demand for the currency increases or does not change, the result is an increase in (appreciation of) the value of the currency.
Answer (A) is incorrect. An increase in imports drives down the value of the nation's currency. Answer (B) is incorrect. A high rate of inflation devalues a nation's currency. Answer (D) is incorrect. Lower interest rates relative to those in other countries discourage foreign investment, decreases demand for the nation's currency, and reduces its value.

27. If the central bank of a country raises interest rates sharply, the country's currency will likely

    A. Increase in relative value.

    B. Remain unchanged in value.

    C. Decrease in relative value.

    D. Decrease sharply in value at first and then return to its initial value.

Answer (A) is correct. *(CMA, adapted)*
    REQUIRED: The effect on a country's currency if its central bank raises interest rates sharply.
    DISCUSSION: If the interest rates in a given country rise, money will pour in from all over the world in pursuit of that country's higher returns. This increase in demand for the country's currency will boost its purchasing power.
    Answer (B) is incorrect. A currency tends to increase relative to other currencies when interest rates in the country rise sharply. More investors will want to earn the higher rates of return available in that country. Answer (C) is incorrect. A currency tends to increase relative to other currencies when interest rates in the country rise sharply. More investors will want to earn the higher rates of return available in that country. Answer (D) is incorrect. A currency tends to increase relative to other currencies when interest rates in the country rise sharply. More investors will want to earn the higher rates of return available in that country.

28. Which one of the following statements supports the conclusion that the U.S. dollar has gained purchasing power against the Japanese yen?

    A. Inflation has recently been higher in the U.S. than in Japan.

    B. The dollar is currently trading at a premium in the forward market with respect to the yen.

    C. The yen's spot rate with respect to the dollar has just fallen.

    D. Studies recently published in the financial press have shed doubt on the interest rate parity (IRP) theory.

Answer (C) is correct. *(Publisher, adapted)*
    REQUIRED: The statement that supports the conclusion that the U.S. dollar has gained purchasing power against the Japanese yen.
    DISCUSSION: If the yen's spot rate has just fallen, then more yen are required to buy a single dollar. The yen has therefore depreciated, i.e., lost purchasing power. At the same time, the dollar has gained purchasing power.
    Answer (A) is incorrect. This statement reflects a loss, not a gain, of purchasing power for the dollar. Answer (B) is incorrect. No conclusion can be drawn about changes in purchasing power simply from a statement about forward rates. Answer (D) is incorrect. No conclusion can be drawn about changes in purchasing power simply from evidence for or against the interest rate parity (IRP) theory.

29. If the annual U.S. inflation rate is expected to be 5% while the euro is expected to depreciate against the U.S. dollar by 10%, an Italian firm importing from its U.S. parent can expect its euro costs for these imports to

    A. Decrease by about 10%.

    B. Decrease by about 5%.

    C. Increase by about 5%.

    D. Increase by about 16.7%.

Answer (D) is correct. *(CMA, adapted)*
    REQUIRED: The combined effect of inflation and currency depreciation.
    DISCUSSION: Inflation in the U.S. means that $1.05 now has the purchasing power formerly enjoyed by $1.00. The 10% depreciation of the euro means that its purchasing power in dollars has declined to 90%. Dividing the U.S. inflation factor of 1.05 by the new euro value of .90 and subtracting 1 results in a net loss of euro purchasing power against the dollar of 16.67%.
    Answer (A) is incorrect. The euro's loss of purchasing power through depreciation against the dollar outweighs the dollar's loss of purchasing power against all other currencies due to inflation. Thus, euro costs will increase, not decrease. Answer (B) is incorrect. The euro's loss of purchasing power through depreciation against the dollar outweighs the dollar's loss of purchasing power against all other currencies due to inflation. Thus, euro costs will increase, not decrease. Answer (C) is incorrect. This percentage is the difference between the currency depreciation and the inflation rate.

30. An American importer of English clothing has contracted to pay an amount fixed in British pounds 3 months from now. If the importer worries that the U.S. dollar may depreciate sharply against the British pound in the interim, it would be well advised to

    A. Buy pounds in the forward exchange market.

    B. Sell pounds in the forward exchange market.

    C. Buy dollars in the futures market.

    D. Sell dollars in the futures market.

Answer (A) is correct. *(CMA, adapted)*
    REQUIRED: The action to hedge a liability denominated in a foreign currency.
    DISCUSSION: The American importer should buy pounds now. If the dollar depreciates against the pound in the next 90 days, the gain on the forward exchange contract would offset the loss from having to pay more dollars to satisfy the liability.
    Answer (B) is incorrect. Selling pounds would compound the risk of loss for someone who has incurred a liability. However, it would be an appropriate hedge of a receivable denominated in pounds. Answer (C) is incorrect. The importer needs pounds, not dollars. Answer (D) is incorrect. Although buying pounds might be equivalent to selling dollars for pounds, this is not the best answer. This choice does not state what is received for the dollars.

7.7 International Trade

31. All of the following are valid reasons for expansion of international business by U.S. multinational corporations, **except** to

- A. Secure new sources for raw materials.
- B. Find additional areas where their products can be successfully marketed.
- C. Minimize their costs of production.
- D. Protect their domestic market from competition from foreign manufacturers.

Answer (D) is correct. *(CMA, adapted)*
REQUIRED: The statement not a valid reason for a multinational corporation, known as direct foreign investment, expanding into a foreign country.
DISCUSSION: Reasons for international business expansion, known as direct foreign investment, can be both revenue-oriented (seeking new markets or avoiding trade restrictions) and cost-oriented (seeking cheaper inputs or favorable exchange rates). An attempt to protect the firm's domestic market from foreign competition by expanding operations into foreign countries is unlikely.
Answer (A) is incorrect. Securing new sources of raw materials is one of the sound cost-related reasons firms have for international business expansion. Answer (B) is incorrect. Seeking new markets is one of the sound revenue-related reasons firms have for international business expansion. Answer (C) is incorrect. Attempting to minimize the costs of production is one of the sound cost-related reasons firms have for international business expansion.

32. Which one of the following statements concerning American Depository Receipts (ADRs) is **false**?

- A. ADRs facilitate the banking procedures for U.S. multinational firms.
- B. ADRs allow Americans to invest abroad.
- C. ADRs allow foreigners to raise capital in the U.S.
- D. ADRs are securities issued by American banks acting as custodians of shares of foreign firms.

Answer (A) is correct. *(CMA, adapted)*
REQUIRED: The false statement concerning American depository receipts (ADRs).
DISCUSSION: Ownership rights in foreign corporations are sometimes evidenced by American Depository Receipts (ADRs). The foreign stocks are deposited with a large U.S. bank, which in turn issues ADRs representing ownership in the foreign shares. The ADR shares then trade on a U.S. stock exchange, whereas the company's original shares trade in foreign stock markets. ADRs allow foreign companies to develop a U.S. shareholder base without being subject to many SEC restrictions.
Answer (B) is incorrect. The purpose of an ADR is to allow Americans to invest abroad. Answer (C) is incorrect. ADRs are designed to allow foreign firms to raise capital in the U.S. Answer (D) is incorrect. ADRs are securities issued by American banks acting as custodians of shares of foreign firms.

33. A British company currently has domestic operations only. It plans to invest equal amounts of money on projects either in the U.S. or in China. The company will select the country based on risk and return for its portfolio of domestic and international projects taken together. The risk reduction benefits of investing internationally (based on 50% of British domestic operations and 50% foreign operations) will be the greatest when there is perfectly

- A. Positive correlation between the British return and the U.S. return.
- B. Negative correlation between the U.S. return and the Chinese return.
- C. Positive correlation between the U.S. return and the Chinese return.
- D. Negative correlation between the Chinese return and the British return.

Answer (D) is correct. *(CMA, adapted)*
REQUIRED: The correlation yielding the greatest benefits from an international business portfolio.
DISCUSSION: Portfolio theory concerns the composition of an investment portfolio that is efficient in balancing the risk with the rate of return of the portfolio. Diversification reduces risk. This firm's goal is to balance the risk inherent in having 100% of its operations in Britain. This will be accomplished when the foreign investment moves in the opposite direction from the domestic (British) operations.
Answer (A) is incorrect. A positive correlation between the foreign investment and domestic operations will increase risk, not reduce it. Answer (B) is incorrect. The correlation between the U.S. investment and the Chinese investment is irrelevant; the investment must be in one or the other of those two countries. Answer (C) is incorrect. The relevant correlation is one between the domestic (British) operations and one of the two alternatives.

34. Direct foreign investment allows firms to avoid

A. Exposure to political risk.

B. The cost of exchange rate fluctuations.

C. Trade restrictions imposed on foreign companies in the customers' market.

D. Domestic regulations on the use of foreign technology.

Answer (C) is correct. *(CMA, adapted)*
   REQUIRED: The advantage of a direct foreign investment.
   DISCUSSION: Reasons for international business expansion, known as direct foreign investment, can be both revenue-oriented (seeking new markets or avoiding trade restrictions) and cost-oriented (seeking cheaper inputs or favorable exchange rates.
   Answer (A) is incorrect. Direct foreign investment increases exposure to political risk. Answer (B) is incorrect. Direct foreign investment increases exposure to exchange rate risk. Answer (D) is incorrect. A multinational company is subject to its home country's regulations on the use of foreign technology.

35. Technocrat, Inc., located in Belgium currently manufactures products at its domestic plant and exports them to the U.S. since it is less expensive to produce at home. The company is considering the possibility of setting up a plant in the U.S. All of the following factors would encourage the company to consider direct foreign investment in the U.S. **except** the

A. Expectation of more stringent trade restrictions by the U.S.

B. Depreciation of the U.S. dollar against Belgium's currency.

C. Widening the gap in production costs between the United States and Belgium locations.

D. Changing demand for the company's exports to the U.S. due to exchange rate fluctuations.

Answer (C) is correct. *(CMA, adapted)*
   REQUIRED: The factor not an advantage of direct foreign investment.
   DISCUSSION: Production costs in the home country are already lower than those in the U.S. Widening this gap would not serve the firm's interests.
   Answer (A) is incorrect. Avoiding trade restrictions is one of the sound revenue-related reasons firms have for international business expansion. Answer (B) is incorrect. If the foreign currency depreciates against the home country's currency, operations in the foreign country are made even less expensive. Answer (D) is incorrect. Avoiding exchange rate risk is one of the sound cost-related reasons for international business expansion.

Use the Gleim **CMA Test Prep** Software for interactive testing with **additional multiple-choice questions!**

7.9 ESSAY QUESTIONS

Scenario for Essay Questions 1, 2, 3

Atrax Corporation is now a diversified company that was originally founded as a textile and milling company by Adam Traxal. During the 1990s and early 2000s before any diversification, Atrax's earnings had leveled off to about $2.25 per share. The growth possibilities in this industry were limited so that the demand for expansion funds has been low. There were large internal cash flows during this period, and Atrax regularly paid out 65% of its earnings as cash dividends. By the late 1990s, this large dividend payout had become a trademark of Atrax's common stock.

The firm began diversifying into high-technology, growth companies in 2008 in an effort to reduce its business risk from its dependence on a single source of sales. Traxal thought such diversification was essential to maintain Atrax's financial health. The diversification program has been successful as far as Traxal is concerned. Atrax is no longer completely dependent on a single source of sales. The earnings have grown moderately to $2.80 per share since 2008 despite the issuance of additional common shares. The price of the Atrax common stock has increased so that the P/E ratio is slightly higher than it was in 2008. In addition, the 65% cash dividend payout ratio has been maintained during the expansion period.

The diversification program at first was easily financed by the excess funds that were generated internally. Eventually though, the firm began to recognize the need to use external sources – long-term debt and/or additional issues of common stock – to finance its expansion programs. One consequence of the several common stock offerings was to dilute Traxal's control over the firm because he was unable to purchase his pro rata share of the additional offerings due to a shortage of personal funds. The Traxal family holdings amounted to 54% of the firm's stock in 2008 but their ownership has now fallen to around 35%. However, Traxal is still able to maintain effective control over the firm because no other stockholder owns more than 4% of the total stock.

Traxal believes that continued expansion is important for Atrax. Traxal is against any additional issues of common equity because he still cannot generate the personal funds necessary to purchase additional stock to maintain his present equity position. However, further expansion could be greatly hampered if additional issues of common equity are not employed. Traxal has instructed his staff to suggest alternative proposals which would allow him to maintain control of Atrax and still continue the firm's diversification program. A summary of three proposals follows.

Proposal 1

The acquisition program would continue and be financed out of earnings not paid out as dividends and from long-term debt issues and preferred stock issues. The current 65% cash dividend payout ratio would be maintained, and there would be no additional issues of common stocks. However, there would be an increase in long-term debt and preferred stock issues.

Proposal 2

The acquisition program would continue, and cash dividends would be reduced. The staff estimates that acquisitions could be financed with internally generated funds and a minimum amount of long-term debt. No additional common equity would be required. Atrax could probably distribute cash dividends equal to 10%-20% of earnings. This proposal would not significantly change Atrax's present debt to equity relationships. In an attempt to appease stockholders who face a drop in their cash dividends, a stock dividend would be paid.

Proposal 3

The acquisition program would continue and be financed entirely by internally generated funds by reducing the cash dividend payout rate to zero, if necessary. No additional long-term debt or shares of common stock would be employed.

Questions

1. Adam Traxal finds Proposal 1 interesting but wonders what effect this would have on the rest of the firm and on the market value of Atrax Corporation's common stock. Assuming that the price of a firm's stock is in the product of its current earnings per share and its historical price-earnings ratio, indicate the ways in which implementing Proposal 1 would operate to affect the market price of Atrax's common stock.

2. Adam Traxal considers Proposal 3 to be the least attractive because cash dividends might be reduced to zero. Explain what the probable short-term and long-term effects would be on the market price of Atrax's common stock if the acquisition program is dependent upon reducing the cash dividend payout ratio to zero.

3. Adam Traxal considers Proposal 2 the most appealing because dividends would still continue to be distributed.

   a. Would Traxal be able to maintain his current equity position of 35% if stock dividends were distributed? Explain your answer.

   b. Explain how, if at all, the market price of Atrax's common stock would probably be affected if this proposal is adopted.

   c. Compare and contrast Proposal 2 with Proposal 3 in terms of the probable effects on the market price of Atrax's common stock.

Essay Questions 1, 2, 3 — Unofficial Answers

1.   The higher fixed costs associated with the issuance of long-term debt and preferred stock would increase Atrax's degree of financial leverage. When the firm earns a return greater than its cost of capital, earnings per share, and thus the price of Atrax's common stock, would increase by a proportionally greater amount. When the firm loses money, losses will be proportionally greater because of the mandatory interest payments on debt and dividend payments on preferred stock. Thus, earnings per share and the price of Atrax's common stock would become more volatile.

   If this proposal is carried out, then risk is increased and common shareholders will demand that steps be taken to compensate. The diversification program should be an effective step to mitigate the increased business risk.

2.   In the short term, the elimination of a historically dependable dividend on common stock would cause current investors, who are most likely interested in the income stream from the steady dividend, to sell. This would depress the price of the stock. Over the long run, the cash saved by eliminating dividends would be used to expand and continue diversifying the business. Investors who are interested in long-term growth will then become interested in the stock and bid the price back up.

3.   a.   Adam Traxal would be able to maintain his current equity position of 35% in the event a stock dividend is declared. Stock dividends involve the distribution of stock in proportion to each stockholder's current stake.

   b.   In the short term, the reduction of the dividend would be interpreted as a sign of lowered earnings, some current stockholders would sell, and the price of the common stock would be depressed. However, not all current stockholders will sell in expectation that the dividend will eventually fully recover. Also, some current stockholders may be persuaded not to sell by receipt of the stock dividend, interpreting it as some compensation for the lowered cash dividend.

      Over the long run, the stock price will stabilize owing to the continuation of a moderate level of dividend payout. Investors who are interested in long-term growth and capital gains will buy the stock and bid up the price. If the firm's expansion and diversification programs succeed, even more upward pressure will be placed on the stock price.

   c.   In the short term, Proposal 3 would bring about a greater decrease in the stock price than Proposal 2 because Proposal 3 involves the complete elimination of the current dividend, driving away income investors who own the stock for the steady cash dividend. Over the long run, the direction of the stock price is dependent on the success of the expansion and diversification program. If it is successful, Proposal 3 will result in a higher ultimate stock price since all internally-generated funds can be plowed back into the business rather than paid out as dividends.

Use **CMA Gleim Online** and **Essay Wizard** to practice additional essay questions in an exam-like environment.

STUDY UNIT EIGHT
CVP ANALYSIS AND MARGINAL ANALYSIS

(16 pages of outline)

This study unit is the first of two on **decision analysis and risk management**. The relative weight assigned to this major topic in Part 2 of the exam is **25%**. The two study units are:

Study Unit 8: CVP Analysis and Marginal Analysis
Study Unit 9: Decision Analysis and Risk Management

After studying the outlines and answering the questions in this study unit, you will have the skills necessary to address the following topics listed in the ICMA's Learning Outcome Statements:

Part 2 – Section C.1. Cost-volume-profit analysis

The candidate should be able to:

a. demonstrate an understanding of how cost-volume-profit (CVP) analysis (breakeven analysis) is used to examine the behavior of total revenues, total costs, and operating income as changes occur in output levels, selling prices, variable costs per unit, or fixed costs

b. calculate operating income at different operating levels

c. differentiate between costs that are fixed and costs that are variable with respect to levels of output

d. explain why the classification of fixed vs. variable costs is affected by the time frame being considered

e. demonstrate an understanding of the behavior of total revenues and total costs in relation to output within a relevant range

f. calculate contribution margin per unit and total contribution margin

g. calculate the breakeven point in units and dollar sales to achieve targeted operating income or targeted net income

h. demonstrate an understanding of how changes in unit sales mix affect operating income in multiple-product situations

i. calculate multiple-product breakeven points given percentage share of sales and explain why there is no unique breakeven point in multiple-product situations

j. define, calculate, and interpret margin of safety and margin of safety ratio

k. explain how sensitivity analysis can be used in CVP analysis when there is uncertainty about sales

l. analyze and recommend a course of action using CVP analysis

m. demonstrate an understanding of the impact of income taxes on CVP analysis

Part 2 – Section C.2. Marginal analysis

The candidate should be able to:

a. identify and define relevant costs (incremental, marginal, or differential costs), sunk costs, avoidable costs, explicit and implicit costs, and relevant revenues

b. explain why sunk costs are not relevant in the decision-making process

c. demonstrate an understanding of and calculate opportunity costs

d. calculate relevant costs given a numerical scenario

e. differentiate between economic concepts of revenues and costs and accounting concepts of revenues and costs

f. define and calculate marginal cost and marginal revenue

g. identify and calculate total cost, average fixed cost, average variable cost, and average total cost

Statements h. through o. are covered in Study Unit 9.

8.1 COST-VOLUME-PROFIT (CVP) ANALYSIS -- THEORY

1. **Purpose**

   a. Also called **breakeven analysis**, CVP analysis is a tool for understanding the interaction of revenues with fixed and variable costs.

      1) It illuminates how changes in assumptions about cost behavior and the relevant ranges in which those assumptions are valid may affect the relationships among revenues, variable costs, and fixed costs at various production levels.

      2) Thus, CVP analysis allows management to discern the probable effects of changes in sales volume, sales price, product mix, etc.

2. **Simplifying Assumptions of CVP**

   a. Cost and revenue relationships are predictable and linear. These relationships are true over the relevant range of activity and specified time span.

   b. Unit selling prices and market conditions are constant, i.e., reductions in prices are not necessary to increase revenues, and no learning curve effect operates to reduce unit variable labor costs at higher output levels.

   c. Changes in inventory are insignificant in amount, i.e., production equals sales.

   d. Total variable costs change proportionally with volume, but unit variable costs are constant over the relevant range. Raw materials and direct labor are typically variable costs.

   e. Fixed costs remain constant over the relevant range of volume, but unit fixed costs vary indirectly with volume. The classification of fixed versus variable can be affected by the time frame being considered.

   f. The revenue (sales) mix is constant, or the firm makes and sells only one product.

   g. All costs are either fixed or variable relative to a given cost object for a given time span. The longer the time span, the more likely the cost is variable.

   h. Technology and productive efficiency are constant.

   i. Revenues and costs vary only with changes in physical unit volume. Hence, volume is the sole revenue driver and cost driver.

   j. The breakeven point is directly related to costs and inversely related to the budgeted margin of safety and the contribution margin.

   k. The time value of money is ignored.

3. **Definitions**

   a. The **breakeven point** is the level of output at which total revenues equal total expenses, that is, the point at which all fixed costs have been covered and operating income is zero.

   b.   The **margin of safety** is the excess of budgeted sales over breakeven sales. It is the amount by which sales can decline before losses occur.

   c.   Mixed costs (or semivariable costs) are costs with both fixed and variable elements.

   d.   The revenue (sales) mix is the composition of total revenues in terms of various products, i.e., the percentages of each product included in total revenues. It is maintained for all volume changes.

   e.   Sensitivity analysis examines the effect on the outcome of not achieving the original forecast or of changing an assumption.

       1)   The assumptions under which CVP analysis operates, described in item 2. on the previous page, primarily hinge on certainty. However, many decisions must be made even though uncertainty exists. Assigning probabilities to the various outcomes and sensitivity ("what-if") analysis are important approaches to dealing with uncertainty.

   f.   **Unit contribution margin (UCM)** is the unit selling price minus the unit variable cost. It is the contribution from the sale of one unit to cover fixed costs (and possibly a targeted profit).

       1)   It is expressed as either a percentage of the selling price **(contribution margin ratio)** or a dollar amount.

       2)   The UCM is the slope of the total cost curve plotted so that volume is on the x-axis and dollar value is on the y-axis.

4.   **Calculating the Breakeven Point**

   a.   The simplest calculation for breakeven in units is to divide fixed costs by the unit contribution margin (UCM). UCM equals unit selling price minus unit variable cost.

$$\textit{Breakeven point in units} = \frac{\textit{Fixed costs}}{\textit{UCM}}$$

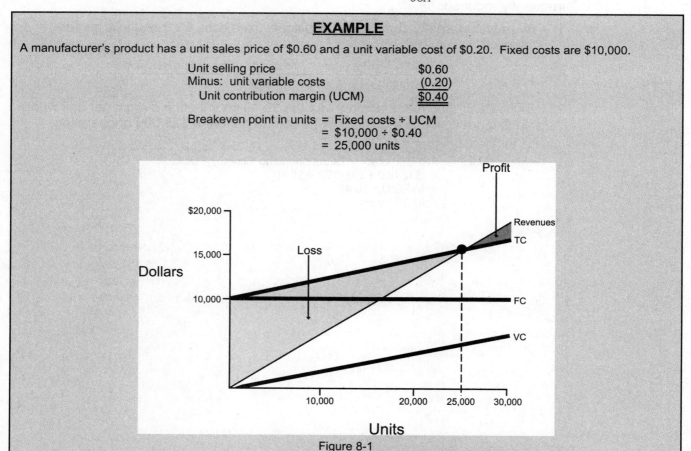

EXAMPLE

A manufacturer's product has a unit sales price of $0.60 and a unit variable cost of $0.20. Fixed costs are $10,000.

Unit selling price	$0.60
Minus: unit variable costs	(0.20)
Unit contribution margin (UCM)	$0.40

Breakeven point in units = Fixed costs ÷ UCM
= $10,000 ÷ $0.40
= 25,000 units

Figure 8-1

b. The breakeven point in sales dollars equals fixed costs divided by the contribution margin ratio (CMR). CMR is the ratio of the unit contribution margin to the unit sales price.

$$Breakeven\ point\ in\ dollars\ =\ \frac{Fixed\ costs}{CMR}$$

1) EXAMPLE: The manufacturer's contribution margin ratio is 66.667% ($0.40 ÷ $0.60).

Breakeven point in dollars = Fixed costs ÷ CMR
                           = $10,000 ÷ .66667
                           = $15,000

Stop and review! You have completed the outline for this subunit. Study multiple-choice questions 1 through 7 beginning on page 328.

8.2 CVP ANALYSIS -- BASIC CALCULATIONS

The ability to apply the mathematical principles of breakeven analysis quickly is a crucial skill on Part 2 of the CMA exam. This subunit consists entirely of questions that "drill" the candidate on this ability. Please review Subunit 8.1 before attempting to answer the questions in this subunit.

Stop and review! You have completed the outline for this subunit. Study multiple-choice questions 8 through 13 beginning on page 330.

8.3 CVP ANALYSIS -- TARGET INCOME CALCULATIONS

1. **Target Operating Income**

    a. An amount of operating income, either in dollars or as a percentage of sales, is frequently required.

        1) By treating target income as an additional fixed cost, CVP analysis can be applied.

$$Target\ unit\ volume\ =\ \frac{Fixed\ costs\ +\ Target\ operating\ income}{UCM}$$

        2) EXAMPLE: The manufacturer with the $0.40 contribution margin per unit wants to find out how many units must be sold to generate $25,000 of operating income.

Target unit volume = (Fixed costs + Target operating income) ÷ UCM
                   = ($10,000 + $25,000) ÷ $0.40
                   = $35,000 ÷ $0.40
                   = 87,500 units

    b.   Other target income situations call for the application of the standard formula for operating income.

Operating income = Sales – Variable costs – Fixed costs

        1)   EXAMPLE: If units are sold at $6.00 and variable costs are $2.00, how many units must be sold to realize operating income of 15% ($6.00 × .15 = $.90 per unit) before taxes, given fixed costs of $37,500?

$$Operating\ income = Sales - Variable\ costs - Fixed\ costs$$
$$\$0.90 \times Q = (\$6.00 \times Q) - (\$2.00 \times Q) - \$37,500$$
$$\$3.10 \times Q = \$37,500$$
$$Q = 12,097\ units$$

           a)   Selling 12,097 units results in $72,582 of revenues. Variable costs are $24,194, and operating income is $10,888 ($72,582 × 15%). The proof is that variable costs of $24,194, plus fixed costs of $37,500, plus operating income of $10,888, equals $72,582 of sales.

  2.   **Target Net Income**

    a.   A variation of this problem asks for net income (an after-tax amount) instead of operating income (a pretax amount).

$$Target\ unit\ volume = \frac{Fixed\ costs + [Target\ net\ income \div (1.0 - tax\ rate)]}{UCM}$$

        1)   EXAMPLE: The manufacturer wants to generate $30,000 of net income. The effective tax rate is 40%.

$$Target\ unit\ volume = \{Fixed\ costs + [Target\ net\ income \div (1.0 - .40)]\} \div UCM$$
$$= [\$10,000 + (\$30,000 \div .60)] \div \$.40$$
$$= 150,000\ units$$

    b.   The operating income formula can also be used in this situation.

        1)   EXAMPLE: If variable costs are $1.20, fixed costs are $10,000, and selling price is $2, and the company targets a $5,000 after-tax profit when the tax rate is 30%, the calculation is as follows:

$$\$\,2Q = [\$5,000 \div (1.0 - 0.3)] + \$1.20Q + \$10,000$$
$$\$.8Q = \$7,142.86 + \$10,000$$
$$\$.8Q = \$17,142.86$$
$$Q = \$17,142.86 \div .8$$
$$Q = 21,428.575\ units$$

        2)   If the company plans to sell 21,429 units at $2 each, revenue will be $42,858. The following is the pro forma income statement for the target net income:

Sales (21,429 × $2)	$ 42,857
Less: variable costs (21,429 × $1.20)	(25,714)
Contribution margin	$ 17,143
Less: fixed costs	(10,000)
Operating income	$ 7,143
Income taxes (30%)	(2,143)
Net income	$ 5,000

Stop and review! You have completed the outline for this subunit. Study multiple-choice questions 14 through 20 beginning on page 333.

8.4 CVP ANALYSIS -- MULTI-PRODUCT CALCULATIONS

1. **Multiple Products (or Services)**

    a. EXAMPLE: A and B account for 60% and 40% of total sales, respectively. The variable costs of A and B are 60% and 85% of individual product sales, respectively. What is the breakeven point, given fixed costs of $150,000?

    $$S = FC + VC$$
    $$S = \$150,000 + .6\ (.6\ S) + .85\ (.4\ S)$$
    $$S = \$150,000 + .36\ S + .34\ S$$
    $$.30\ S = \$150,000$$
    $$S = \$500,000$$

    1) In effect, the result is obtained by calculating a weighted-average contribution margin ratio (100% − 36% − 34% = 30%) and dividing it into the fixed costs to arrive at the breakeven point in sales dollars.

    2) Another approach to multiproduct breakeven problems is to divide fixed costs by the UCM for a composite unit (when unit prices are known) to determine the number of composite units. The number of individual units can then be calculated based on the stated mix.

        a) EXAMPLE: If 150,000 units of X and 300,000 units of Y are expected to be sold, the composite unit consists of 1 unit of X and 2 units of Y. If X and Y have UCMs of $5 and $7, respectively, the composite UCM is $19 ($5 + $7 + $7). Dividing $19 into fixed costs gives the breakeven point in composite units. The units of X and Y equal the number of composite units and twice the number of composite units, respectively.

        b) In a multiple product (or service) problem, the breakeven point in total units varies with the sales mix. The BEP in units will be lower (higher) when the proportion of high (low) CM items is greater. Thus, there is no unique breakeven point in multiple-product situations. The breakeven point depends upon the specific mix of products.

2. **Choice of Product**

    a. When resources are limited, a company may produce only a single product.

    1) A breakeven analysis of the point where the same operating income or loss will result, regardless of the product selected, is calculated by setting the breakeven formulas of the individual products equal to each other.

    2) EXAMPLE: Assume a lessor can rent property to either of two lessees. One lessee offers a rental fee of $100,000 per year plus 2% of revenues. The other lessee offers $20,000 per year plus 5% of revenues. The optimal solution depends on the level of revenues. A typical CMA question asks at what level the lessor will be indifferent. The solution is to equate the two formulas as follows:

    $$\$100,000 + .02\ R = \$20,000 + .05\ R$$
    $$.03\ R = \$80,000$$
    $$R = \$80,000 \div .03$$
    $$R = \$2,666,667$$

    Where: R = revenues

    Thus, if revenues are expected to be less than $2,666,667, the lessor would prefer the larger fixed rental of $100,000 and the smaller variable rental.

3.   **Special Orders**

    a.   Sometimes CVP analysis is applied to special orders. This application is essentially contribution margin analysis.

       1)   EXAMPLE: What is the effect of accepting a special order for 10,000 units at $8.00, given the following operating data?

		Per Unit
Sales		$12.50
Manufacturing costs:		
Variable	$6.25	
Fixed	1.75	(8.00)
Gross profit		$ 4.50
Selling expenses:		
Variable	$1.80	
Fixed	1.45	(3.25)
Operating income		$ 1.25

          a)   Because the variable cost of manufacturing is $6.25, the UCM is $1.75 ($8.00 – $6.25), and the increase in operating income resulting from accepting the special order is $17,500 (10,000 units × $1.75).

          b)   The assumptions are that idle capacity is sufficient to manufacture 10,000 extra units, that sale at $8.00 per unit will not affect the price or quantity of other units sold, and that no additional selling expenses are incurred.

Stop and review! You have completed the outline for this subunit. Study multiple-choice questions 21 through 24 beginning on page 336.

8.5 MARGINAL ANALYSIS

1.   **Accounting Costs vs. Economic Costs**

    a.   The accounting concept of costs includes only explicit costs, i.e., those that represent actual outlays of cash, the allocation of outlays of cash, or commitments to pay cash. Examples include the incurrence of payables, the satisfaction of payables, and the recognition of depreciation.

    b.   The economic concept of costs includes both explicit and implicit costs.

       1)   Implicit in any business decision is opportunity cost, defined as "the contribution to income that is forgone by not using a limited resource in its best alternative use."

    c.   EXAMPLE: A manufacturer's accounting cost for a new product line consists only of the costs associated with the new machinery and personnel, but the economic cost includes the 4.75% return the company could make by simply investing the money in certificates of deposit.

2.   **Explicit vs. Implicit Costs**

    a.   Explicit costs are those requiring actual cash disbursements. For this reason, they are sometimes called out-of-pocket or outlay costs.

       1)   Explicit costs are accounting costs, that is, they are recognized in a concern's formal accounting records.

       2)   For example, an entrepreneur opening a gift shop has to make certain cash disbursements to get the business up and running.

Inventory	$50,000
Display cases	9,000
Rent	4,000
Utilities	1,000
Total explicit costs	**$64,000**

    b.   Implicit costs are those costs not recognized in a concern's formal accounting records.

        1)   Implicit costs are opportunity costs, i.e., the maximum benefit forgone by using a scarce resource for a given purpose and not for the next-best alternative.

        2)   To measure the true economic success or failure of the venture, the entrepreneur in the example on the previous page must tally up more than just the explicit costs that can easily be found in the accounting records.

            a)   The entrepreneur's opportunity costs are the most important implicit costs. (S)he could have simply gone to work for another company rather than open the gift shop.

            b)   The money put into startup costs could have been invested in financial instruments.

            c)   A normal profit is a crucial implicit cost. In this example, the normal profit is the income that the entrepreneur could have earned applying his/her skill to another venture.

Salary forgone	$35,000
Investment income forgone	3,600
Total implicit costs	**$38,600**

    c.   Economic costs are total costs.

        1)   The true hurdle for an economic decision is whether the revenues from the venture will cover all costs, both explicit and implicit.

$$\begin{aligned}
\textbf{Economic costs} &= \text{Total costs} \\
&= \text{Explicit costs} + \text{Implicit costs} \\
&= \$64,000 + \$38,600 \\
&= \mathbf{\$102,600}
\end{aligned}$$

3. **Accounting vs. Economic Profit**

    a.   Accounting profits are earned when the (book) income of an organization exceeds the (book) expenses.

        1)   After the first year of operation, the gift shop owner made a tidy accounting profit.

Sales revenue	$100,000
Explicit costs	(64,000)
Accounting profit	**$ 36,000**

    b.   Economic profits are a significantly higher hurdle. They are not earned until the organization's income exceeds not only costs as recorded in the accounting records, but the firm's implicit costs as well. Economic profit is also called pure profit.

        1)   Once total costs are taken into account, a different picture emerges.

Accounting profit	$ 36,000
Implicit costs	(38,600)
Economic loss	**$ (2,600)**

4. **Marginal Revenue and Marginal Cost**

    a.   Marginal revenue is the additional (also called incremental) revenue produced by generating one additional unit of output. Mathematically, it is the difference in total revenue at each level of output.

        1)   If the product is being sold in a competitive market (i.e., the seller does not have monopoly power), the seller typically must cut its price to sell additional units.

            a)   Thus, while total revenue keeps increasing with the sale of additional units, it increases by ever smaller amounts. This is reflected in a constantly decreasing marginal revenue.

        2)   EXAMPLE: A company has the following revenue data for one of its products:

Units of Output		Unit Price		Total Revenue	Marginal Revenue
1	×	$580	=	$ 580	$580
2	×	575	=	1,150	570
3	×	570	=	1,710	560
4	×	565	=	2,260	550
5	×	560	=	2,800	540
6	×	555	=	3,330	530
7	×	550	=	3,850	520
8	×	545	=	4,360	510
9	×	540	=	4,860	500
10	×	535	=	5,350	490
11	×	530	=	5,830	480
12	×	525	=	6,300	470

            a)   Revenue by itself cannot determine the proper level of output. Cost data must also be considered.

    b.   Marginal cost is the additional (also called incremental) cost incurred by generating one additional unit of output. Mathematically, it is the difference in total cost at each level of output.

        1)   Typically, unit cost decreases for a while as the process becomes more efficient. Past a certain point, however, the process becomes less efficient and unit cost increases.

            a)   Thus, while total cost increases gradually for a while, at some point it begins to increase sharply. This is reflected in a decreasing then increasing marginal cost.

        2)   EXAMPLE: A company has the following cost data for the product (for simplicity, each unit of output requires exactly one unit of input):

Units of Output		Unit Cost		Total Cost	Marginal Cost
1	×	$570	=	$ 570	$570
2	×	405	=	810	240
3	×	340	=	1,020	210
4	×	305	=	1,220	200
5	×	287	=	1,435	215
6	×	279	=	1,675	240
7	×	279	=	1,955	280
8	×	284	=	2,275	320
9	×	295	=	2,655	380
10	×	310	=	3,095	440
11	×	327	=	3,595	500
12	×	347	=	4,165	570

5. Profit Maximization

a. The firm's goal is to maximize profits, not revenues. Thus, marginal revenue data must be compared with marginal cost data to determine the point of profit maximization.

1) This occurs where marginal revenue equals marginal cost. Beyond this point, increasing production results in a level of costs so high that total profit is diminished.

2) EXAMPLE: Comparing its marginal revenue and marginal cost data allows the company to determine the point of profit maximization.

Units of Output	Marginal Revenue		Cost		Profit	Total Revenue		Cost		Profit
1	$580	–	$570	=	$ 10	$ 580	–	$ 570	=	$ 10
2	570	–	240	=	330	1,150	–	810	=	340
3	560	–	210	=	350	1,710	–	1,020	=	690
4	550	–	200	=	350	2,260	–	1,220	=	1,040
5	540	–	215	=	325	2,800	–	1,435	=	1,365
6	530	–	240	=	290	3,330	–	1,675	=	1,655
7	520	–	280	=	240	3,850	–	1,955	=	1,895
8	510	–	320	=	190	4,360	–	2,275	=	2,085
9	500	–	380	=	120	4,860	–	2,655	=	2,205
10	**490**	–	**440**	=	**50**	**5,350**	–	**3,095**	=	**2,255**
11	480	–	500	=	(20)	5,830	–	3,595	=	2,235
12	470	–	570	=	(100)	6,300	–	4,165	=	2,135

a) Beyond the output level of 10 units, marginal profit turns negative. Note that this is, by definition, the point of highest total profit.

3) This is a crucial principle for marginal analysis: Profit is maximized at the output level where marginal revenue equals marginal cost.

Profit Maximization

    Marginal revenue = Marginal cost

6. Short-Run Cost Relationships

a. To make marginal analysis meaningful, total cost must be broken down into its fixed and variable components.

1) EXAMPLE: Cost analysis reveals that the inputs to the company's process have the following cost structure:

Units of Output	Total Costs In Total	Average	Fixed Costs In Total	Average	Variable Costs In Total	Average
1	$ 570	$570	$300	$300	$ 270	$270
2	810	405	300	150	510	255
3	1,020	340	300	100	720	240
4	1,220	305	300	75	920	230
5	1,435	287	300	60	1,135	227
6	1,675	279	300	50	1,375	229
7	1,955	279	300	43	1,655	236
8	2,275	284	300	38	1,975	247
9	2,655	295	300	33	2,355	262
10	3,095	310	300	30	2,795	280
11	3,595	327	300	27	3,295	300
12	4,165	347	300	25	3,865	322

b.   These relationships can be depicted graphically as follows:

Legend
  MC = marginal cost
  ATC = average total cost
  AVC = average variable cost
  AFC = average fixed cost

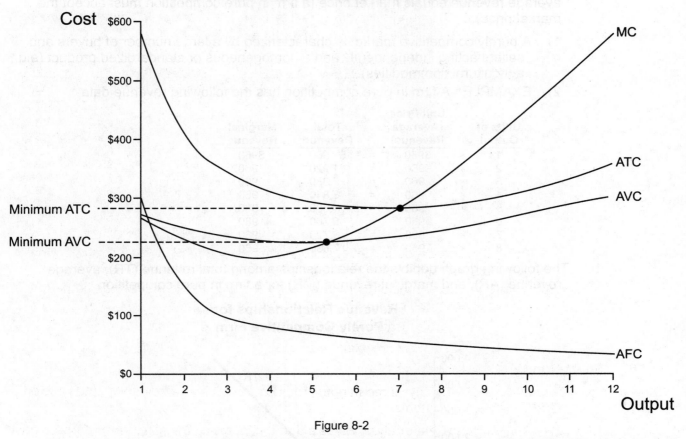

Figure 8-2

1)   Average fixed cost (AFC) declines for as long as production increases. This is because the fixed amount of cost is being spread over more and more units.

     a)   AFC is thus an asymptotic function, always approaching the x-axis without ever intersecting with it.

2)   Average variable cost (AVC) declines quickly and then gradually begins increasing.

     a)   AVC is at its lowest where MC crosses it, between 5 and 6 units. This is confirmed by reference to the data in the tables (MC: $215-$240, AVC: $227-$229).

3)   Average total cost (ATC) behaves similarly. It declines rapidly and then begins a gradual increase.

     a)   ATC also reaches its minimum at the point where MC crosses it, just after 7 units (MC: $280, AVC: $279).

4)   As a general statement, ATC = AFC + AVC.

     a)   Thus, the distance between the ATC and AVC curves is always the same as the distance between the AFC curve and the x-axis.

Stop and review! You have completed the outline for this subunit. Study multiple-choice questions 25 through 29 beginning on page 337.

8.6 SHORT-RUN PROFIT MAXIMIZATION

1. **Pure Competition**

    a.   For a product being sold in a purely competitive market, marginal revenue equals average revenue equals market price (a firm in pure competition must accept the market price).

    1)   A purely competitive market is characterized by a large number of buyers and sellers acting independently and a homogeneous or standardized product (e.g., agricultural commodities).

    2)   EXAMPLE: A firm in pure competition has the following revenue data:

Units of Output		Unit Price (Average Revenue)		Total Revenue	Marginal Revenue
1	×	$960	=	$ 960	$960
2	×	960	=	1,920	960
3	×	960	=	2,880	960
4	×	960	=	3,840	960
5	×	960	=	4,800	960
6	×	960	=	5,760	960
7	×	960	=	6,720	960
8	×	960	=	7,680	960

    b.   The following graph depicts the relationships among total revenue (TR), average revenue (AR), and marginal revenue (MR) for a firm in pure competition.

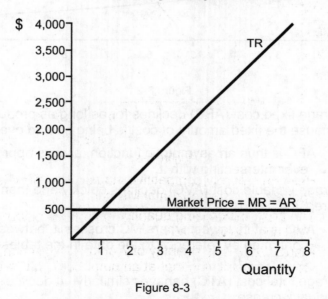

Figure 8-3

    1)   TR is a straight line with a constant positive slope. The price, MR, and AR curves are identical.

c.   As noted in 5.a.3) in Subunit 8.5, short-run profit maximization is achieved when marginal revenue equals marginal cost. As long as the next unit of output adds more in revenue (MR) than in cost (MC), the firm will increase total profit or decrease total losses.

1)   For a purely competitive firm, price = MC is the same as MR = MC.

2)   EXAMPLE: The firm has performed the following marginal analysis:

Units of Output	Revenue		Cost		Profit	
	Total	Marginal	Total	Marginal	Total	Marginal
1	$ 960	$960	$1,800	$1,800	$(840)	$(840)
2	1,920	960	2,500	700	(580)	260
3	2,880	960	3,100	600	(220)	360
4	3,840	960	3,600	500	240	460
5	4,800	960	4,200	600	600	360
6	5,760	960	5,080	880	680	80
7	**6,720**	**960**	**6,040**	**960**	**680**	**0**
8	7,680	960	7,160	1,120	520	(160)

3)   The following graph depicts the short-run profit-maximizing quantity for a firm in pure competition (a "price taker").

Price Taking for a Purely Competitive Firm

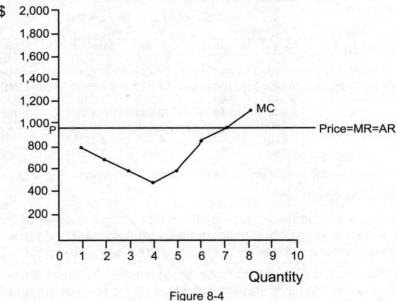

Figure 8-4

a)   Being in a purely competitive industry, the firm has no choice but to find its price along the horizontal MR curve.

b)   The profit-maximizing quantity to produce is found at the point where the MC curve crosses MR.

c)   Point A reveals a quantity of 7 units. This is confirmed by consulting the table and verifying that at an output of 7, MR = MC.

2.   **Monopoly**

    a.   In a monopoly market, the industry consists of one firm and the product has no close substitutes.

       1)   To encourage more sales of its product, a monopolist must lower its price.

       2)   Thus, a monopolist's marginal revenue continuously decreases as it raises output. Past the point where MR = $0, the monopolist's total revenue begins to decrease.

Units of Output		Unit Price (Average Revenue)		Total Revenue	Marginal Revenue
1	×	$960	=	$ 960	$960
2	×	910	=	1,820	860
3	×	860	=	2,580	760
4	×	810	=	3,240	660
5	×	760	=	3,800	560
6	×	710	=	4,260	460
7	×	660	=	4,620	360
8	×	610	=	4,880	260

       3)   The monopolist has the power to set output at the level where profits are maximized, that is, where **MR = MC**. This is called "price searching."

Price Searching for a Monopolist

Units of Output	Revenue		Cost		Profit	
	Total	Marginal	Total	Marginal	Total	Marginal
1	$ 960	$960	$ 800	$ 800	$ 160	$ 160
2	1,820	860	1,480	680	340	180
3	2,580	760	1,980	500	600	260
4	3,240	660	2,320	340	920	320
5	**3,800**	**560**	**2,800**	**480**	**1,000**	**80**
6	4,260	460	3,480	680	780	(220)
7	4,620	360	4,620	1,140	0	(780)
8	4,880	260	5,920	1,300	(1,040)	(1,040)

          a)   Profit is maximized at an output of 5 units.

3.   **Monopolistic Competition**

    a.   An industry in monopolistic competition has a large number of firms. The number is fewer than in pure competition, but it is great enough that firms cannot collude. That is, they cannot act together to restrict output and fix the price.

       1)   To maximize profits (or minimize losses) in the short run or long run, a firm in monopolistic competition produces at the level of output at which MR = MC.

4.   **Oligopoly**

    a.   An oligopoly is an industry with a few large firms. Firms operating in an oligopoly are mutually aware and mutually interdependent. Their decisions as to price, advertising, etc., are to a very large extent dependent on the actions of the other firms.

       1)   Prices tend to be rigid (sticky) because of the interdependence among firms.

Stop and review! You have completed the outline for this subunit. Study multiple-choice questions 30 through 33 beginning on page 339.

8.7 CORE CONCEPTS

<u>Cost-Volume-Profit (CVP) Analysis</u>

- **Cost-volume-profit analysis** (also called breakeven analysis) is a tool for understanding the interaction of revenues with fixed and variable costs.

- The **breakeven point** is the level of output at which total revenues equal total expenses; that is, the point at which operating income is zero. This can be stated mathematically as

  `Sales - Variable costs - Fixed costs = $0`

  - The **breakeven point in units** can be determined by applying this formula:

    `Fixed costs ÷ Unit contribution margin`

  - The **breakeven point in dollars** can be determined by applying the following formula (contribution margin ratio equals contribution margin divided by sales):

    `Fixed costs ÷ Contribution margin ratio`

- The **contribution income statement** with per unit amounts is an integral part of breakeven analysis. Every unit sold contributes a certain percentage of its sales revenue to covering fixed costs. Once fixed costs are fully covered, all additional revenue contributes to profit.

<u>Applications of CVP Analysis</u>

- By treating **desired pretax or after-tax profit** as an additional fixed cost, CVP analysis can be applied as follows:

  `Unit sales = (Fixed costs + Target operating income) ÷ UCM`

  `Unit sales = {Fixed costs + [Target net income ÷ (1.0 - tax rate)]} ÷ UCM`

- The breakeven point can also be calculated for a **multi-product situation** by using a weighted-average composite unit contribution margin in the numerator.

<u>Marginal Analysis</u>

- **Explicit costs (accounting costs)** are those requiring actual cash disbursements. **Implicit costs (opportunity costs)** are those costs not recognized in a concern's formal accounting records. A normal profit is a crucial implicit cost. **Economic costs** are total costs. The true hurdle for an economic decision is whether the revenues from the venture will cover all costs, both explicit and implicit.

  - **Accounting profits** are earned when the (book) income of an organization exceeds the (book) expenses.

  - **Economic profits** are a significantly higher hurdle. They are not earned until the organization's income exceeds not only costs as recorded in the accounting records, but the firm's implicit costs as well.

- In decision making, an organization must focus on only relevant revenues and costs. To be **relevant**, the revenues and costs must (a) be made in the **future** and (b) **differ** among the possible alternative courses of action.

- **Marginal revenue** is the additional (also called incremental) revenue produced by generating one additional unit of output. Mathematically, it is the difference in total revenue at each level of output. **Marginal cost** is the additional (also called incremental) cost incurred by generating one additional unit of output. Mathematically, it is the difference in total cost at each level of output.

- The firm's goal is to **maximize profits, not revenues**. Mathematically, this can be stated as

  `Profit maximization: Marginal revenue = Marginal cost`

Short-Run Profit Maximization

- For a product being sold in a **purely competitive market**, marginal revenue equals average revenue equals market price (a firm in pure competition must accept the market price, called "price taking"). A purely competitive market is characterized by a large number of buyers and sellers acting independently and a homogeneous or standardized product (e.g., agricultural commodities).

- In a **monopoly market**, the industry consists of one firm and the product has no close substitutes. To encourage more sales of its product, a monopolist must lower its price. The monopolist has the power to set output at the level where profits are maximized, that is, where marginal revenue equals marginal cost. This is called "price searching."

- An industry in **monopolistic competition** has a large number of firms. The number is fewer than in pure competition, but it is great enough that firms cannot collude. That is, they cannot act together to restrict output and fix the price. To maximize profits (or minimize losses) in the short run or long run, a firm in monopolistic competition produces at the level of output at which marginal revenue equals marginal cost.

- An **oligopoly** is an industry with a few large firms. Firms operating in an oligopoly are mutually aware and mutually interdependent. Their decisions as to price, advertising, etc., are to a very large extent dependent on the actions of the other firms. Prices tend to be rigid (sticky) because of the interdependence among firms.

QUESTIONS

8.1 Cost-Volume-Profit (CVP) Analysis -- Theory

1. Cost-volume-profit (CVP) analysis is a key factor in many decisions, including choice of product lines, pricing of products, marketing strategy, and use of productive facilities. A calculation used in a CVP analysis is the breakeven point. Once the breakeven point has been reached, operating income will increase by the

- A. Gross margin per unit for each additional unit sold.

- B. Contribution margin per unit for each additional unit sold.

- C. Fixed costs per unit for each additional unit sold.

- D. Variable costs per unit for each additional unit sold.

Answer (B) is correct.   *(CMA, adapted)*
   REQUIRED: The amount by which operating income will increase once the breakeven point has been reached.
   DISCUSSION: At the breakeven point, total revenue equals total fixed costs plus the variable costs incurred at that level of production. Beyond the breakeven point, each unit sale will increase operating income by the unit contribution margin (unit sales price – unit variable cost) because fixed cost will already have been recovered.
   Answer (A) is incorrect. The gross margin equals sales price minus cost of goods sold, including fixed cost. Answer (C) is incorrect. All fixed costs have been covered at the breakeven point. Answer (D) is incorrect. Operating income will increase by the unit contribution margin, not the unit variable cost.

2. One of the major assumptions limiting the reliability of breakeven analysis is that

- A. Efficiency and productivity will continually increase.

- B. Total variable costs will remain unchanged over the relevant range.

- C. Total fixed costs will remain unchanged over the relevant range.

- D. The cost of production factors varies with changes in technology.

Answer (C) is correct.   *(CMA, adapted)*
   REQUIRED: The major assumption limiting the use of breakeven analysis.
   DISCUSSION: One of the inherent simplifying assumptions used in CVP analysis is that fixed costs remain constant over the relevant range of activity.
   Answer (A) is incorrect. Breakeven analysis assumes no changes in efficiency and productivity. Answer (B) is incorrect. Total variable costs, by definition, change across the relevant range. Answer (D) is incorrect. The cost of production factors is assumed to be stable; this is what is meant by relevant range.

3. The margin of safety is a key concept of CVP analysis. The margin of safety is the

    A. Contribution margin rate.

    B. Difference between budgeted contribution margin and breakeven contribution margin.

    C. Difference between budgeted sales and breakeven sales.

    D. Difference between the breakeven point in sales and cash flow breakeven.

Answer (C) is correct. *(CMA, adapted)*
    REQUIRED: The definition of the margin of safety.
    DISCUSSION: The margin of safety measures the amount by which sales may decline before losses occur. It is the excess of budgeted or actual sales over sales at the BEP.
    Answer (A) is incorrect. The contribution margin rate is computed by dividing contribution margin by sales. The contribution margin equals sales minus total variable costs. Answer (B) is incorrect. The margin of safety is expressed in revenue or units, not contribution margin. Answer (D) is incorrect. Cash flow is not relevant.

4. When used in cost-volume-profit analysis, sensitivity analysis

    A. Determines the most profitable mix of products to be sold.

    B. Allows the decision maker to introduce probabilities in the evaluation of decision alternatives.

    C. Is done through various possible scenarios and computes the impact on profit of various predictions of future events.

    D. Is limited because, in cost-volume-profit analysis, costs are not separated into fixed and variable components.

Answer (C) is correct. *(CMA, adapted)*
    REQUIRED: The true statement about sensitivity analysis.
    DISCUSSION: Sensitivity analysis is the process of observing how a mathematical model's outcome is affected when the input parameters are changed. CVP analysis is extremely useful for this kind of exercise.
    Answer (A) is incorrect. CVP analysis assumes either a constant product mix or only one product. Answer (B) is incorrect. Expected value analysis allows the decision maker to introduce probabilities in the evaluation of decision alternatives. Answer (D) is incorrect. To perform cost-volume-profit analysis, costs must be separated into fixed and variable components.

5. Marston Enterprises sells three chemicals: petrol, septine, and tridol. Petrol is the company's most profitable product; tridol is the least profitable. Which one of the following events will definitely decrease the firm's overall breakeven point for the upcoming accounting period?

    A. The installation of new computer-controlled machinery and subsequent layoff of assembly-line workers.

    B. A decrease in tridol's selling price.

    C. An increase in the overall market for septine.

    D. An increase in anticipated sales of petrol relative to sales of septine and tridol.

Answer (D) is correct. *(CMA, adapted)*
    REQUIRED: The event that will decrease the firm's overall breakeven point.
    DISCUSSION: Since petrol is the company's most profitable product, it has a higher unit contribution margin than septine and tridol. Thus, an increase in sales of petrol relative to the other products will result in a higher weighted-average unit contribution margin and a lower breakeven point (fixed costs ÷ weighted-average UCM).
    Answer (A) is incorrect. The acquisition of new machinery will result in greater fixed costs and thus a higher breakeven point. Answer (B) is incorrect. A decrease in selling price reduces the unit contribution margin, which in turn increases the breakeven point. Answer (C) is incorrect. The effect of an increase in the market for septine cannot be determined. The facts given do not indicate whether its unit contribution margin is greater or less than the weighted-average unit contribution margin for all the products.

6. The breakeven point in units increases when unit costs

    A. Increase and sales price remains unchanged.

    B. Decrease and sales price remains unchanged.

    C. Remain unchanged and sales price increases.

    D. Decrease and sales price increases.

Answer (A) is correct. *(CMA, adapted)*
    REQUIRED: The event that causes the breakeven point in units to increase.
    DISCUSSION: The breakeven point in units is calculated by dividing total fixed costs by the unit contribution margin. If selling price is constant and costs increase, the unit contribution margin will decline, resulting in an increase of the breakeven point.
    Answer (B) is incorrect. A decrease in costs will cause the unit contribution margin to increase, lowering the breakeven point. Answer (C) is incorrect. An increase in the selling price will increase the unit contribution margin, resulting in a lower breakeven point. Answer (D) is incorrect. Both a cost decrease and a sales price increase will increase the unit contribution margin, resulting in a lower breakeven point.

7. Which one of the following is true regarding a relevant range?

A. Total variable costs will not change.

B. Total fixed costs will not change.

C. Actual fixed costs usually fall outside the relevant range.

D. The relevant range cannot be changed after being established.

Answer (B) is correct. *(CMA, adapted)*
REQUIRED: The true statement about a relevant range.
DISCUSSION: The relevant range is the range of activity over which unit variable costs and total fixed costs are constant.
Answer (A) is incorrect. Variable costs will change in total, but unit variable costs will be constant across the relevant range. Answer (C) is incorrect. Actual fixed costs should not vary greatly from budgeted fixed costs for the relevant range. Answer (D) is incorrect. The relevant range can change whenever production activity changes; the relevant range is merely an assumption used for budgeting and control purposes.

8.2 CVP Analysis -- Basic Calculations

8. Which of the following would decrease unit contribution margin the most?

A. A 15% decrease in selling price.

B. A 15% increase in variable expenses.

C. A 15% decrease in variable expenses.

D. A 15% decrease in fixed expenses.

Answer (A) is correct. *(CMA, adapted)*
REQUIRED: The change in a CVP variable causing the greatest decrease in UCM.
DISCUSSION: Unit contribution margin (UCM) equals unit selling price minus unit variable costs. It can be decreased by either lowering the price or raising the variable costs. As long as UCM is positive, a given percentage change in selling price must have a greater effect than an equal but opposite percentage change in variable cost. The example below demonstrates this point.

Original: $UCM = SP - UVC$
                   $= \$100 - \$50$
                   $= \$50$

Lower Selling Price: $UCM = (SP \times .85) - UVC$
                   $= \$85 - \$50$
                   $= \$35$

Higher Variable Cost: $UCM = SP - (UVC \times 1.15)$
                   $= \$100 - \$57.50$
                   $= \$42.50$

Since $\$35 < \$42.50$, the lower selling price has the greater effect.
Answer (B) is incorrect. A 15% increase in variable expenses will not decrease the CM as much as a 15% decrease in sales price. Answer (C) is incorrect. A decrease in variable expenses would increase UCM. Answer (D) is incorrect. Fixed expenses have no effect on the contribution margin.

9. Romashka, Inc., plans to introduce a new product. The marketing manager forecasts a unit selling price of $500. The variable cost per unit is estimated to be $100. In addition, there is a total of $110,000 fixed indirect manufacturing costs, and $150,000 in fixed operating costs associated with these units. What quantity will the company have to sell to break even?

A. 220 units.

B. 275 units.

C. 520 units.

D. 650 units.

Answer (D) is correct. *(CMA, adapted)*
REQUIRED: The breakeven quantity given relevant data.
DISCUSSION: The breakeven point in units equals total fixed costs divided by the unit contribution margin. Romashka's breakeven quantity can therefore be derived thusly:

Breakeven point $= (\$110,000 + \$150,000) \div (\$500 - \$100)$
$= \$260,000 \div \$400$
$= 650$ units

Answer (A) is incorrect. Failing to take the $150,000 of fixed operating costs and the $100 of variable per unit cost into account results in 220 units. Answer (B) is incorrect. Failing to take the $150,000 of fixed operating costs into account results in 275 units. Answer (C) is incorrect. Failing to take the $100 of variable per unit cost into account results in 520 units.

Question 10 is based on the following information.

Delphi Company has developed a new project that will be marketed for the first time during the next fiscal year. Although the Marketing Department estimates that 35,000 units could be sold at $36 per unit, Delphi's management has allocated only enough manufacturing capacity to produce a maximum of 25,000 units of the new product annually. The fixed costs associated with the new product are budgeted at $450,000 for the year, which includes $60,000 for depreciation on new manufacturing equipment.

Data associated with each unit of product are presented as follows. Delphi is subject to a 40% income tax rate.

Direct material	$ 7.00
Direct labor	3.50
Manufacturing overhead	4.00
Variable manufacturing cost	$14.50
Selling expenses	1.50
Total variable cost	$16.00

10. The number of units of the new product that Delphi Company must sell during the next fiscal year in order to break even is

A. 20,930

B. 18,140

C. 22,500

D. 25,500

Answer (C) is correct. *(CMA, adapted)*
REQUIRED: The breakeven point in units.
DISCUSSION: The breakeven point in units equals total fixed costs divided by the unit contribution margin. The unit contribution margin is $20 ($36 selling price – $16 unit variable cost). Hence, the breakeven point is 22,500 units ($450,000 ÷ $20).
Answer (A) is incorrect. This figure excludes the $1.50 of variable selling expenses from the unit contribution margin. Answer (B) is incorrect. This figure excludes the $1.50 of variable selling expenses from the unit contribution margin and the depreciation from the fixed costs. Answer (D) is incorrect. This figure adds the $60,000 of depreciation to the fixed costs.

Question 11 is based on the following information. Bruell Electronics Co. is developing a new product, surge protectors for high-voltage electrical flows. The cost information below relates to the product:

	Unit Costs
Direct materials	$3.25
Direct labor	4.00
Distribution	.75

The company will also be absorbing $120,000 of additional fixed costs associated with this new product. A corporate fixed charge of $20,000 currently absorbed by other products will be allocated to this new product.

11. If the selling price is $14 per unit, the breakeven point in units (rounded to the nearest hundred) for surge protectors is

A. 8,500 units.

B. 10,000 units.

C. 15,000 units.

D. 20,000 units.

Answer (D) is correct. *(CMA, adapted)*
REQUIRED: The breakeven point in units.
DISCUSSION: The breakeven point in units for a new product equals total additional fixed costs divided by the unit contribution margin. Unit variable costs total $8 ($3.25 + $4.00 + $.75). Thus, UCM is $6 ($14 unit selling price – $6 unit variable cost), and the breakeven point is 20,000 units ($120,000 ÷ $6).
Answer (A) is incorrect. A breakeven point of 8,500 units ignores variable costs. Answer (B) is incorrect. The breakeven point is 20,000 units when the contribution margin is $6 per unit. Answer (C) is incorrect. This number of units equals fixed costs divided by unit variable cost.

Questions 12 and 13 are based on the following information. Barnes Corporation manufactures skateboards and is in the process of preparing next year's budget. The pro forma income statement for the current year is presented below.

Sales		$1,500,000
Cost of sales:		
Direct materials	$250,000	
Direct labor	150,000	
Variable overhead	75,000	
Fixed overhead	100,000	(575,000)
Gross profit		$ 925,000
Selling and G&A:		
Variable	$200,000	
Fixed	250,000	(450,000)
Operating income		$ 475,000

12. The breakeven point (rounded to the nearest dollar) for Barnes Corporation for the current year is

A. $146,341

B. $636,364

C. $729,730

D. $181,818

Answer (B) is correct. *(CMA, adapted)*
REQUIRED: The breakeven point in dollars.
DISCUSSION: Fixed costs total $350,000 ($100,000 overhead + $250,000 SG&A). Variable costs total $675,000. Given sales of $1,500,000, the contribution margin is $825,000 ($1,500,000 – $675,000). Thus, the contribution margin percentage is 55% ($825,000 ÷ $1,500,000). Dividing the $350,000 of fixed costs by 55% produces a breakeven point of $636,363.64.
Answer (A) is incorrect. This amount does not even cover fixed costs. Answer (C) is incorrect. This amount of sales results in a small profit. Answer (D) is incorrect. This amount does not cover the $350,000 of fixed costs.

13. For the coming year, the management of Barnes Corporation anticipates a 10% increase in sales, a 12% increase in variable costs, and a $45,000 increase in fixed expenses. The breakeven point for next year will be

A. $729,027

B. $862,103

C. $214,018

D. $474,000

Answer (A) is correct. *(CMA, adapted)*
REQUIRED: The breakeven point following an increase in sales, variable costs, and fixed expenses.
DISCUSSION: Sales are expected to be $1,650,000 ($1,500,000 × 1.10), variable costs $756,000 ($675,000 × 1.12), and fixed expenses $395,000 ($350,000 + $45,000). Thus, the contribution margin will be $894,000 ($1,650,000 – $756,000), and the contribution margin percentage is 54.1818%. The breakeven point is therefore $729,027 ($395,000 fixed expenses ÷ .541818).
Answer (B) is incorrect. The contribution margin percentage is computed by dividing the contribution margin (total sales – total variable costs) by total sales, not by dividing the total variable costs by total sales. Answer (C) is incorrect. This amount does not cover fixed costs. Answer (D) is incorrect. This amount barely covers fixed costs.

8.3 CVP Analysis -- Target Income Calculations

14. Associated Supply, Inc., is considering introducing a new product that will require a $250,000 investment of capital. The necessary funds would be raised through a bank loan at an interest rate of 8%. The fixed operating costs associated with the product would be $122,500, while the contribution margin percentage would be 42%. Assuming a selling price of $15 per unit, determine the number of units (rounded to the nearest whole unit) Associated would have to sell to generate earnings before interest and taxes (EBIT) of 32% of the amount of capital invested in the new product.

    A. 35,318 units.

    B. 32,143 units.

    C. 25,575 units.

    D. 23,276 units.

Answer (B) is correct. *(CMA, adapted)*
REQUIRED: The level of sales required to achieve a targeted EBIT given relevant data.
DISCUSSION: Associated has determined it must generate EBIT equal to 32% of the capital invested in this project, or $80,000 ($250,000 × 32%). The number of units it must produce to achieve this level of EBIT can be derived as follows:

$$\text{Breakeven point} = \text{(Fixed costs + EBIT)} \div \text{Unit contribution margin}$$
$$= (\$122{,}500 + \$80{,}000) \div (\$15 \times 42\%)$$
$$= \$202{,}500 \div \$6.30$$
$$= 32{,}142.86 \text{ units}$$

Answer (A) is incorrect. Improperly including interest as a fixed cost results in 35,318. Answer (C) is incorrect. Improperly including interest as a fixed cost and using the cost percentage in the calculation instead of the contribution margin percentage results in 25,575. Answer (D) is incorrect. Improperly using the complement of the contribution margin percentage instead of the contribution margin percentage results in 23,276.

Questions 15 and 16 are based on the following information.

Delphi Company has developed a new project that will be marketed for the first time during the next fiscal year. Although the Marketing Department estimates that 35,000 units could be sold at $36 per unit, Delphi's management has allocated only enough manufacturing capacity to produce a maximum of 25,000 units of the new product annually. The fixed costs associated with the new product are budgeted at $450,000 for the year, which includes $60,000 for depreciation on new manufacturing equipment.

Data associated with each unit of product are presented as follows. Delphi is subject to a 40% income tax rate.

Direct material	$ 7.00
Direct labor	3.50
Manufacturing overhead	4.00
Variable manufacturing cost	$14.50
Selling expenses	1.50
Total variable cost	$16.00

15. The maximum after-tax profit that can be earned by Delphi Company from sales of the new product during the next fiscal year is

    A. $30,000

    B. $50,000

    C. $110,000

    D. $66,000

Answer (A) is correct. *(CMA, adapted)*
REQUIRED: The maximum after-tax profit.
DISCUSSION: Delphi's breakeven point is 22,500 units ($450,000 fixed costs ÷ $20 UCM). The unit contribution margin (UCM) is $20 ($36 selling price – $16 unit variable costs). At the breakeven point, all fixed costs have been recovered. Hence, pretax profit equals the unit contribution margin times unit sales in excess of the breakeven point, or $50,000 [(25,000 unit sales – 22,500 BEP) × $20 UCM]. After-tax profit is $30,000 [$50,000 × (1.0 – .40)].
Answer (B) is incorrect. This amount is the pre-tax profit. Answer (C) is incorrect. This amount fails to include depreciation as a fixed cost and ignores income taxes. Answer (D) is incorrect. This amount fails to include depreciation as a fixed cost.

16. Delphi Company's management has stipulated that it will not approve the continued manufacture of the new product after the next fiscal year unless the after-tax profit is at least $75,000 the first year. The unit selling price to achieve this target profit must be at least

    A. $37.00

    B. $36.60

    C. $34.60

    D. $39.00

Answer (D) is correct. *(CMA, adapted)*
REQUIRED: The unit selling price to achieve a targeted after-tax profit.
DISCUSSION: If X represents the necessary selling price, 25,000 equals maximum sales volume, $16 is the variable cost per unit, $450,000 is the total fixed cost, and $125,000 [$75,000 target after-tax profit ÷ (1.0 – .40)] is the desired pre-tax profit, the following formula may be solved to determine the requisite unit price:

$$25{,}000\,(X - \$16) - \$450{,}000 = \$125{,}000$$
$$25{,}000X - \$400{,}000 - \$450{,}000 = \$125{,}000$$
$$25{,}000X = \$975{,}000$$
$$X = \$39$$

Answer (A) is incorrect. The amount of $37.00 does not consider income taxes. Answer (B) is incorrect. The amount of $36.60 excludes depreciation. Answer (C) is incorrect. The amount of $34.60 does not include depreciation or taxes.

Questions 17 and 18 are based on the following information. Bruell Electronics Co. is developing a new product, surge protectors for high-voltage electrical flows. The cost information below relates to the product:

	Unit Costs
Direct materials	$3.25
Direct labor	4.00
Distribution	.75

The company will also be absorbing $120,000 of additional fixed costs associated with this new product. A corporate fixed charge of $20,000 currently absorbed by other products will be allocated to this new product.

17. How many surge protectors (rounded to the nearest hundred) must Bruell Electronics sell at a selling price of $14 per unit to gain $30,000 additional income before taxes?

    A. 10,700 units.

    B. 12,100 units.

    C. 20,000 units.

    D. 25,000 units.

Answer (D) is correct. *(CMA, adapted)*
    REQUIRED: The number of units to be sold to generate a targeted pre-tax income.
    DISCUSSION: The number of units to be sold to generate a specified pre-tax income equals the sum of total fixed costs and the targeted pre-tax income, divided by the unit contribution margin. Unit variable costs total $8 ($3.25 + $4.00 + $.75), and UCM is $6 ($14 unit selling price – $8). Thus, the desired unit sales level equals 25,000 units [($120,000 + $30,000) ÷ $6].
    Answer (A) is incorrect. This number of units is based on a UCM equal to selling price. Answer (B) is incorrect. A contribution margin of $6 per unit necessitates sales of 25,000 units to produce a $30,000 before-tax profit. Answer (C) is incorrect. This number of units is the breakeven point.

18. How many surge protectors (rounded to the nearest hundred) must Bruell Electronics sell at a selling price of $14 per unit to increase after-tax income by $30,000? Bruell Electronics' effective income tax rate is 40%.

    A. 10,700 units.

    B. 12,100 units.

    C. 20,000 units.

    D. 28,300 units.

Answer (D) is correct. *(CMA, adapted)*
    REQUIRED: The number of units to be sold to generate a specified after-tax income.
    DISCUSSION: The number of units to be sold to generate a specified pre-tax income equals the sum of total fixed costs and the targeted pre-tax income, divided by the unit contribution margin. Given a desired after-tax income of $30,000 and a tax rate of 40%, the targeted pre-tax income must be $50,000 [$30,000 ÷ (1.0 – .40)]. Unit variable costs total $8 ($3.25 + $4.00 + $.75), and UCM is $6 ($14 unit selling price – $8). Hence, the desired unit sales level is 28,333 [($120,000 + $50,000) ÷ $6]. Rounded to the nearest hundred, the answer is $28,300.
    Answer (A) is incorrect. This number of units is based on a UCM equal to selling price and $30,000 of pretax income. Answer (B) is incorrect. A $6 UCM necessitates sales of 28,300 units to produce a $30,000 after-tax profit. Answer (C) is incorrect. This number of units is the breakeven point.

19. BE&H Manufacturing is considering dropping a product line. It currently produces a multi-purpose woodworking clamp in a simple manufacturing process that uses special equipment. Variable costs amount to $6.00 per unit. Fixed overhead costs, exclusive of depreciation, have been allocated to this product at a rate of $3.50 a unit and will continue whether or not production ceases. Depreciation on the special equipment amounts to $20,000 a year. If production of the clamp is stopped, the special equipment can be sold for $18,000; if production continues, however, the equipment will be useless for further production at the end of 1 year and will have no salvage value. The clamp has a selling price of $10 a unit. Ignoring tax effects, the minimum number of units that would have to be sold in the current year to break even on a cash flow basis is

A. 4,500 units.

B. 5,000 units.

C. 20,000 units.

D. 36,000 units.

20. Austin Manufacturing, which is subject to a 40% income tax rate, had the following operating data for the period just ended.

Selling price per unit	$60
Variable cost per unit	$22
Fixed costs	$504,000

Management plans to improve the quality of its sole product by (1) replacing a component that costs $3.50 with a higher-grade unit that costs $5.50, and (2) acquiring a $180,000 packing machine. Austin will depreciate the machine over a 10-year life with no estimated salvage value by the straight-line method of depreciation. If the company wants to earn after-tax income of $172,800 in the upcoming period, it must sell

A. 19,300 units.

B. 21,316 units.

C. 22,500 units.

D. 23,800 units.

Answer (A) is correct. *(CMA, adapted)*
REQUIRED: The breakeven point in units on a cash flow basis.
DISCUSSION: The BEP in units is equal to fixed costs divided by the unit contribution margin ($10 unit selling price – $6 unit variable cost). The $18,000 salvage value, the cash flow that would be received if production is discontinued, is treated as a fixed cost. Hence, the number of units that must be sold to break even on continuation of the product line is 4,500 [$18,000 fixed costs ÷ ($10 – $6)]. Fixed overhead allocated is not considered in this calculation because it is not a cash flow and will continue regardless of the decision.
Answer (B) is incorrect. The BEP is equal to the salvage value (not depreciation) divided by the UCM of $4 ($10 – $6). Depreciation is a non-cash flow and therefore should not be considered in the cash flow breakeven point calculation.
Answer (C) is incorrect. The BEP is equal to the salvage value (not depreciation) divided by the UCM of $4 ($10 – $6). Depreciation is a non-cash flow and therefore should not be considered in the cash flow breakeven point calculation.
Answer (D) is incorrect. Unit fixed costs should not be subtracted in determining the unit contribution margin. The fixed costs will continue regardless so they are not included in the calculation. Therefore, the $18,000 salvage value will be divided by the $4 unit contribution margin in determining the cash flow breakeven point in units.

Answer (C) is correct. *(CMA, adapted)*
REQUIRED: The number of units to be sold to generate a targeted after-tax profit given that variable costs and fixed costs increase.
DISCUSSION: The units to be sold equal fixed costs plus the desired pretax profit, divided by the unit contribution margin. In the preceding year, the unit contribution margin is $38 ($60 selling price – $22 unit variable cost). That amount will decrease by $2 to $36 in the upcoming year because of use of a higher-grade component. Fixed costs will increase from $504,000 to $522,000 as a result of the $18,000 ($180,000 ÷ 10 years) increase in fixed costs attributable to depreciation on the new machine. Dividing the $172,800 of desired after-tax income by 60% (the complement of the tax rate) produces a desired before-tax income of $288,000. Hence, the breakeven point in units is 22,500 [($522,000 + $288,000) ÷ $36].
Answer (A) is incorrect. This number of units does not take income taxes into consideration. Answer (B) is incorrect. This number of units fails to consider the increased variable costs from the introduction of the higher-priced component.
Answer (D) is incorrect. This number of units does not take income taxes into consideration, and it includes the entire cost of the new machine as a fixed cost.

8.4 CVP Analysis -- Multi-Product Calculations

Question 21 is based on the following information.

Moorehead Manufacturing Company produces two products for which the data presented to the right have been tabulated. Fixed manufacturing cost is applied at a rate of $1.00 per machine hour. The sales manager has had a $160,000 increase in the budget allotment for advertising and wants to apply the money to the most profitable product. The products are not substitutes for one another in the eyes of the company's customers.

Per Unit	XY-7	BD-4
Selling price	$4.00	$3.00
Variable manufacturing cost	2.00	1.50
Fixed manufacturing cost	.75	.20
Variable selling cost	1.00	1.00

21. Suppose Moorehead has only 100,000 machine hours that can be made available to produce additional units of XY-7 and BD-4. If the potential increase in sales units for either product resulting from advertising is far in excess of this production capacity, which product should be advertised and what is the estimated increase in contribution margin earned?

A. Product XY-7 should be produced, yielding a contribution margin of $75,000.

B. Product XY-7 should be produced, yielding a contribution margin of $133,333.

C. Product BD-4 should be produced, yielding a contribution margin of $187,500.

D. Product BD-4 should be produced, yielding a contribution margin of $250,000.

Answer (D) is correct. *(CMA, adapted)*
REQUIRED: The more profitable product and the estimated increase in contribution margin.
DISCUSSION: The machine hours are a scarce resource that must be allocated to the product(s) in a proportion that maximizes the total CM. Given that potential additional sales of either product are in excess of production capacity, only the product with the greater CM per unit of scarce resource should be produced. XY-7 requires .75 hours; BD-4 requires .2 hours of machine time (given fixed manufacturing cost applied at $1 per machine hour of $.75 for XY-7 and $.20 for BD-4).
XY-7 has a CM of $1.33 per machine hour ($1 UCM ÷ .75 hours), and BD-4 has a CM of $2.50 per machine hour ($.50 ÷ .2 hours). Thus, only BD-4 should be produced, yielding a CM of $250,000 (100,000 × $2.50). The key to the analysis is CM per unit of scarce resource.
Answer (A) is incorrect. Product XY-7 actually has a CM of $133,333, which is lower than the $250,000 CM for product BD-4. Answer (B) is incorrect. Product BD-4 has a higher CM at $250,000. Answer (C) is incorrect. Product BD-4 has a CM of $250,000.

Questions 22 through 24 are based on the following information. MultiFrame Company has the following revenue and cost budgets for the two products it sells:

	Plastic Frames	Glass Frames
Sales price	$10.00	$15.00
Direct materials	(2.00)	(3.00)
Direct labor	(3.00)	(5.00)
Fixed overhead	(3.00)	(4.00)
Net income per unit	$ 2.00	$ 3.00
Budgeted unit sales	100,000	300,000

The budgeted unit sales equal the current unit demand, and total fixed overhead for the year is budgeted at $975,000. Assume that the company plans to maintain the same proportional mix. In numerical calculations, MultiFrame rounds to the nearest cent and unit.

22. The total number of units MultiFrame needs to produce and sell to break even is

A. 150,000 units.

B. 354,545 units.

C. 177,273 units.

D. 300,000 units.

Answer (A) is correct. *(CMA, adapted)*
REQUIRED: The total units sold at the breakeven point.
DISCUSSION: The calculation of the breakeven point is to divide the fixed costs by the contribution margin per unit. This determination is more complicated for a multi-product firm. If the same proportional product mix is maintained, one unit of plastic frames is sold for every three units of glass frames. Accordingly, a composite unit consists of four frames: one plastic and three glass. For plastic frames, the unit contribution margin is $5 ($10 – $2 – $3). For glass frames, the unit contribution margin is $7 ($15 – $3 – $5). Thus, the composite unit contribution margin is $26 ($5 + $7 + $7 + $7), and the breakeven point is 37,500 packages ($975,000 FC ÷ $26). Because each composite unit contains four frames, the total units sold equal 150,000.

23. The total number of units needed to break even if the budgeted direct labor costs were $2 for plastic frames instead of $3 is

A. 154,028 units.

B. 144,444 units.

C. 156,000 units.

D. 146,177 units.

Answer (B) is correct. *(CMA, adapted)*
REQUIRED: The breakeven point in units if labor costs for the plastic frames are reduced.
DISCUSSION: If the labor costs for the plastic frames are reduced by $1, the composite unit contribution margin will be $27 {($10 − $2 − $2) + [($15 − $3 − $5) × 3]}. Hence, the new breakeven point is 144,444 units [4 units × ($975,000 FC ÷ $27)].

24. The total number of units needed to break even if sales were budgeted at 150,000 units of plastic frames and 300,000 units of glass frames with all other costs remaining constant is

A. 171,958 units.

B. 418,455 units.

C. 153,947 units.

D. 365,168 units.

Answer (C) is correct. *(CMA, adapted)*
REQUIRED: The total number of units needed to break even if the product mix is changed.
DISCUSSION: The unit contribution margins for plastic frames and glass frames are $5 ($10 − $2 − $3) and $7 ($15 − $3 − $5), respectively. If the number of plastic frames sold is 50% of the number of glass frames sold, a composite unit will contain one plastic frame and two glass frames. Thus, the composite unit contribution margin will be $19 ($5 + $7 + $7), and the breakeven point in units will be 153,947 [3 units × ($975,000 ÷ $19)].

8.5 Marginal Analysis

25. During the previous year, Morrison, Inc., produced 200,000 pogo sticks and sold them all for $10 each. The explicit costs of production were $700,000, and the implicit costs of production were $200,000. The firm had

A. An accounting profit of $1.1 million and an economic profit of $0.

B. An accounting profit of $1.3 million and an economic profit of $1.1 million.

C. An accounting profit of $1.3 million and an economic profit of $1.3 million.

D. An accounting profit of $1.3 million and an economic profit of $1.5 million.

Answer (B) is correct. *(Publisher, adapted)*
REQUIRED: The amounts of accounting and economic profits.
DISCUSSION: Implicit costs are amounts that would have been received if self-owned resources had been used outside the firm's business. Economic profit is pure profit, or the excess of revenue over both explicit and implicit costs. Revenues of $2 million minus explicit costs of $700,000 result in accounting income of $1.3 million. That amount is reduced by the $200,000 of implicit costs to arrive at economic profit of $1.1 million.
Answer (A) is incorrect. The $200,000 of implicit costs is not used in computing accounting income. Answer (C) is incorrect. Economic income will be less than accounting income when there are implicit costs. Answer (D) is incorrect. Implicit costs reduce accounting income rather than increase it.

26. A normal profit is

A. The same as an economic profit.

B. The same as the accountant's bottom line.

C. An explicit or out-of-pocket cost.

D. A cost of resources from an economic perspective.

Answer (D) is correct. *(CMA, adapted)*
REQUIRED: The true statement about normal profit.
DISCUSSION: Normal profit is the level of profit necessary to induce entrepreneurs to enter and remain in the market. Economists view this profit as an implicit cost of economic activity.
Answer (A) is incorrect. Economic (pure) profit is the residual return in excess of normal profit. Economic profit equals total revenue minus opportunity costs. These are the sum of explicit and implicit costs, including normal profit. Answer (B) is incorrect. Accounting profit is the excess of total revenue over explicit costs (out-of-pocket payments to outsiders). Answer (C) is incorrect. A normal profit is an implicit cost.

27. A corporation's net income as presented on its income statement is usually

A. More than its economic profits because opportunity costs are not considered in calculating net income.

B. More than its economic profits because economists do not consider interest payments to be costs.

C. Equal to its economic profits.

D. Less than its economic profits because accountants include labor costs, while economists exclude labor costs.

Answer (A) is correct. *(CMA, adapted)*
REQUIRED: The true statement about a corporation's net income.
DISCUSSION: Economic (pure) profit equals total revenue minus economic costs. Economic costs are defined by economists as total costs, which are the sum of outlay costs, and opportunity costs, which are the values of productive resources in their best alternative uses. The return sufficient to induce the entrepreneur to remain in business (normal profit) is an implicit (opportunity) cost. Net income as computed under generally accepted accounting principles considers only explicit costs, not such implicit costs as normal profit and the opportunity costs associated with not using assets for alternative purposes. Thus, net income will be higher than economic profit because the former fails to include a deduction for opportunity costs, for example, the salary forgone by an entrepreneur who chooses to be self-employed.
Answer (B) is incorrect. Both economists and accountants treat interest as a cost. Answer (C) is incorrect. Economic profits will be less than net income. Answer (D) is incorrect. Economic profits will be less than net income.

28. The difference between variable costs and fixed costs is

A. Variable costs per unit fluctuate, and fixed costs per unit remain constant.

B. Variable costs per unit are fixed over the short run, and fixed costs per unit are variable.

C. Total variable costs are variable over the short run and fixed in the long term, while fixed costs never change.

D. Variable costs per unit change in varying increments, while fixed costs per unit change in equal increments.

Answer (B) is correct. *(CMA, adapted)*
REQUIRED: The difference between variable and fixed costs.
DISCUSSION: Fixed costs remain unchanged for a given period despite fluctuations in activity, but per-unit fixed costs do change as the level of activity changes. Thus, fixed costs are fixed in total but vary per unit as activity changes. Total variable costs vary directly with activity. They are fixed per unit but vary in total.
Answer (A) is incorrect. Variable costs are fixed per unit; they do not fluctuate. Fixed costs per unit change as production changes. Answer (C) is incorrect. All costs are variable in the long term. Answer (D) is incorrect. Unit variable costs are fixed in the short term.

29. Which of the following is the best example of a variable cost?

A. The corporate president's salary.

B. Cost of raw material.

C. Interest charges.

D. Property taxes.

Answer (B) is correct. *(CMA, adapted)*
REQUIRED: The item that is a variable cost.
DISCUSSION: Variable costs vary directly with the level of production. As production increases or decreases, material cost increases or decreases, usually in a direct relationship.
Answer (A) is incorrect. The president's salary usually does not vary with production levels. Answer (C) is incorrect. Interest charges are independent of production levels. They are called "fixed" costs and are elements of overhead. Answer (D) is incorrect. Property taxes are independent of production levels. They are called "fixed" costs and are elements of overhead.

8.6 Short-Run Profit Maximization

30. In the short run in perfect competition, a firm maximizes profit by producing the rate of output at which the price is equal to

   A. Total cost.

   B. Total variable cost.

   C. Average fixed costs.

   D. Marginal cost.

Answer (D) is correct. *(CMA, adapted)*
   REQUIRED: The profit-maximizing price in the short run in perfect competition.
   DISCUSSION: A firm should increase production until marginal revenue equals marginal cost. In the short run, this is the same as saying a firm in perfect competition will increase production until marginal cost equals price. The result is the short-run maximization of profits. As long as selling price exceeds marginal cost, a firm should continue producing. In the short run in perfect competition, the market price equals marginal revenue because no firm can affect price by its production decisions.
   Answer (A) is incorrect. There would be no profit when selling price and total costs are the same. Answer (B) is incorrect. Equating selling price to total variable costs leaves nothing to cover fixed costs. Answer (C) is incorrect. Using only average fixed costs ignores variable costs, which increase in total with every unit produced.

31. A characteristic of a monopoly is that

   A. A monopoly will produce when marginal revenue is equal to marginal cost.

   B. There is a unique relationship between the market price and the quantity supplied.

   C. In optimizing profits, a monopoly will increase its supply curve to where the demand curve becomes inelastic.

   D. There are multiple prices for the product to the consumer.

Answer (A) is correct. *(CMA, adapted)*
   REQUIRED: The characteristic of a monopoly.
   DISCUSSION: A monopoly consists of a single firm with a unique product. Such a firm has significant price control. For profit maximization, it increases production until its marginal revenue equals its marginal cost (unless marginal revenue is less than average variable cost, which will cause the firm to shut down). When a monopoly exists, consumers will face higher prices and lower output than in perfect competition.
   Answer (B) is incorrect. The monopolist is in control of the quantity supplied. Thus, the supply can be limited to produce the profit-maximizing price. Answer (C) is incorrect. A monopolist will increase supply as long as the demand curve is inelastic. Inelasticity means that an increase in price will cause a less-than-proportionate decline in demand. Answer (D) is incorrect. There is only one price when a monopoly exists.

32. Monopolistic competition is characterized by a

   A. Relatively large group of sellers who produce differentiated products.

   B. Relatively small group of sellers who produce differentiated products.

   C. Monopolistic market where the consumer is persuaded that there is perfect competition.

   D. Relatively large group of sellers who produce a homogeneous product.

Answer (A) is correct. *(CMA, adapted)*
   REQUIRED: The true statement about monopolistic competition.
   DISCUSSION: Monopolistic competition is characterized by a large number of firms offering differentiated products. Entry into the market is relatively easy, firms have some price control, and substantial nonprice competition exists, such as advertising.
   Answer (B) is incorrect. Monopolistic competition is characterized by a relatively large group of sellers. Answer (C) is incorrect. The market is not monopolistic. There are many sellers. Answer (D) is incorrect. Products are not homogeneous in monopolistic competition; although products may appear to be similar, they have differences in service, quality, or other attributes.

33. The distinguishing characteristic of oligopolistic markets is

   A. A single seller of a homogeneous product with no close substitute.

   B. A single seller of a heterogeneous product with no close substitute.

   C. Lack of entry and exit barriers in the industry.

   D. Mutual interdependence of firm pricing and output decisions.

Answer (D) is correct. *(CMA, adapted)*
   REQUIRED: The distinguishing characteristic of oligopolistic markets.
   DISCUSSION: The oligopoly model is much less specific than the other market structures, but there are typically few firms in the industry. Thus, the decisions of rival firms do not go unnoticed. Products can be either differentiated or standardized. Prices tend to be rigid (sticky) because of the interdependence among firms. Entry is difficult because of either natural or created barriers. Price leadership is typical in oligopolistic industries. Under price leadership, price changes are announced first by a major firm. Once the industry leader has spoken, other firms in the industry match the price charged by the leader. The mutual interdependence of the firms influences both pricing and output decisions.
   Answer (A) is incorrect. Oligopolies contain several firms; a single seller is characteristic of a monopoly. Answer (B) is incorrect. Oligopolies contain several firms; a single seller is characteristic of a monopoly. Answer (C) is incorrect. Oligopolies are typified by barriers to entry; that is the reason the industry has only a few firms.

Use the Gleim **CMA Test Prep** Software for interactive testing with **additional multiple-choice questions**!

8.8 ESSAY QUESTION

Scenario for Essay Questions 1, 2

Don Masters and two of his colleagues are considering opening a law office in a large metropolitan area that would make inexpensive legal services available to those who could not otherwise afford these services. The intent is to provide easy access for their clients by having the office open 360 days per year, 16 hours each day from 7:00 a.m. to 11:00 p.m. The office would be staffed by a lawyer, paralegal, legal secretary, and clerk-receptionist for each of the two 8-hour shifts.

To determine the feasibility of the project, Masters hired a marketing consultant to assist with market projections. The results of this study show that, if the firm spends $500,000 on advertising the first year, the number of new clients expected each day would have the following probability distribution.

Number of New Clients per Day	Probability
20	.10
30	.30
55	.40
85	.20

Masters and his associates believe these numbers are reasonable and are prepared to spend the $500,000 on advertising. Other pertinent information about the operation of the office is given below.

- The only charge to each new client would be $30 for the initial consultation. All cases that warranted further legal work would be accepted on a contingency basis with the firm earning 30% of any favorable settlements or judgments. Masters estimates that 20% of new client consultations will result in favorable settlements or judgments averaging $2,000 each. It is not expected that there will be repeat clients during the first year of operations.

- The hourly wages of the staff are projected to be $25 for the lawyer, $20 for the paralegal, $15 for the legal secretary, and $10 for the clerk-receptionist. Fringe benefit expense will be 40% of the wages paid. A total of 400 hours of overtime is expected for the year; this will be divided equally between the legal secretary and the clerk-receptionist positions. Overtime will be paid at one and one-half times the regular wage, and the fringe benefit expense will apply to the full wage.

- Masters has located 6,000 square feet of suitable office space that rents for $28 per square foot annually. Associated expenses will be $22,000 for property insurance and $32,000 for utilities.

- It will be necessary for the group to purchase malpractice insurance, which is expected to cost $180,000 annually.

- The initial investment in office equipment will be $60,000; this equipment has an estimated useful life of 4 years.

- The cost of office supplies has been estimated to be $4 per expected new client.

Questions

1. Determine how many new clients must visit the law office being considered by Don Masters and his colleagues for the venture to break even during its first year of operations.

2. Using the information provided by the marketing consultant, determine if it is feasible for the law office to achieve breakeven operations.

Essay Questions 1, 2 — Unofficial Answers

1. In order to break even during the first year of operations, 10,220 clients must visit the law office being considered by Don Masters and his colleagues, as calculated below.

Breakeven Calculations for First Year of Operations

Fixed expenses:

Advertising		$ 500,000
Rent (6,000 × $28)		168,000
Property insurance		22,000
Utilities		32,000
Malpractice insurance		180,000
Depreciation ($60,000 ÷ 4)		15,000
Wages & fringe benefits		
Regular wages:		
($25 + $20 + $15 + $10) × 16 hours × 360 days	$403,200	
Overtime wages:		
(200 × $15 × 1.5) + (200 × $10 × 1.5)	7,500	
Total wages	$410,700	
Fringe benefits @ 40%	164,280	574,980
Total fixed expenses		$1,491,980

$$\text{Unit contribution margin} = \text{Unit revenue} - \text{Unit variable cost}$$
$$= [\$30 + (\$2,000 \times .2 \times .3)] - \$4$$
$$= (\$30 + \$120) - \$4$$
$$= \$146$$

$$\text{Breakeven point} = \text{Fixed costs} \div \text{UCM}$$
$$= \$1,491,980 \div \$146$$
$$= 10,219.04 \text{ clients}$$

2. Based on the report of the marketing consultant, the expected number of new clients during the first year is 18,000, as calculated below. Therefore, it is feasible for the law office to break even during the first year of operations as the breakeven point is 10,220 clients.

$$\text{Expected value} = (20 \times .10) + (30 \times .30) + (55 \times .40) + (85 \times .20)$$
$$= 50 \text{ clients per day}$$

$$\text{Annual clients} = 50 \times 360 \text{ days}$$
$$= 18,000 \text{ clients per year}$$

Use **CMA Gleim Online** and **Essay Wizard** to practice additional essay questions in an exam-like environment.

STUDY UNIT NINE
DECISION ANALYSIS AND RISK MANAGEMENT

(30 pages of outline)

This study unit is the second of two on **decision analysis and risk management**. The relative weight assigned to this major topic in Part 2 of the exam is **25%**. The two study units are

Study Unit 8: CVP Analysis and Marginal Analysis
Study Unit 9: Decision Analysis and Risk Management

After studying the outlines and answering the questions in this study unit, you will have the skills necessary to address the following topics listed in the ICMA's Learning Outcome Statements:

Part 2 – Section C.2. Marginal analysis

Statements a. through g. are covered in Study Unit 8.

The candidate should be able to:

h. demonstrate proficiency in the use of marginal analysis for decisions such as (1) introducing a new product or changing output levels of existing products, (2) accepting or rejecting special orders, (3) making or buying a product or service, (4) selling a product or performing additional processes and selling a more value-added product, and (5) adding or dropping a segment

i. calculate the effect on operating income of a decision to accept or reject a special order when there is idle capacity and the order has no long-run implications

j. identify and describe qualitative factors in make-or-buy decisions, such as product quality and dependability of suppliers

k. calculate the effect on operating income of a make-or-buy decision

l. calculate the effects on operating income of a decision to sell or process further; and of a decision to drop or add a segment

m. identify the effects of changes in capacity on production decisions

n. demonstrate an understanding of the impact of income taxes on marginal analysis

o. recommend a course of action using marginal analysis

Part 2 – Section C.3. Pricing

The candidate should be able to:

- a. define market comparables
- b. differentiate between a cost-based approach and a market-based approach to setting prices
- c. calculate selling price using a cost-based approach
- d. demonstrate an understanding of how the pricing of a product or service is affected by the demand for and supply of the product or service, as well as the market structure within which it operates
- e. demonstrate an understanding of the impact of cartels on pricing
- f. demonstrate an understanding of the short-run equilibrium price for the firm in (1) pure competition; (2) monopolistic competition; (3) oligopoly; and (4) monopoly using the concepts of marginal revenue and marginal cost
- g. identify techniques used to set prices based on understanding customers' perceptions of value, competitors' technologies, products, and costs
- h. define and demonstrate an understanding of target pricing and target costing and identify the main steps in developing target prices and target costs
- i. define value engineering
- j. calculate the target operating income per unit and target cost per unit
- k. define and distinguish between a value-added cost and a nonvalue-added cost
- l. define the pricing technique of cost plus target rate of return
- m. calculate the price elasticity of demand using the midpoint formula
- n. define and explain elastic and inelastic demand
- o. estimate total revenue given changes in prices and demand as well as elasticity
- p. discuss how pricing decisions can differ in the short-run and in the long-run
- q. define product life cycle and explain why pricing decisions might differ over the life of a product
- r. evaluate and recommend pricing strategies under specific market conditions

Part 2 – Section C.4. Risk assessment

The candidate should be able to:

- a. identify and explain the different types of risk, including hazard risks, financial risks, operational risks, and strategic risks
- b. define operational risk as the risk of loss from inadequate or failed internal processes, people, and systems
- c. recognize that operational risk includes legal risk and compliance risk
- d. demonstrate an understanding of how volatility and time impact risk
- e. define the concept of capital adequacy (i.e., solvency, liquidity, reserves, sufficient capital, etc.)
- f. explain the use of probabilities in determining exposure to risk and calculate expected loss given a set of probabilities
- g. define the concepts of unexpected loss and maximum possible loss (extreme or catastrophic loss)
- h. identify strategies for risk response (or treatment), including actions to avoid, retain, reduce (mitigate), transfer (share), and exploit (accept) risks
- i. define risk transfer (e.g., purchasing insurance, issuing debt)
- j. demonstrate an understanding of the concept of residual risk and distinguish it from inherent risk
- k. identify and explain the benefits of risk management

l. identify and describe the key steps in the risk management process

m. explain how attitude toward risk might affect the management of risk

n. demonstrate a general understanding of the use of liability/hazard insurance to mitigate risk (detailed knowledge not required)

o. identify methods of managing operational risk

p. identify and explain financial risk management methods

q. identify and explain qualitative risk assessment tools including risk identification, risk ranking, and risk maps

r. identify and explain quantitative risk assessment tools including cash flow at risk, earnings at risk, earnings distributions and earnings per share (EPS) distributions

s. identify and explain Value at Risk (VaR) (calculations not required)

t. define Enterprise Risk Management (ERM) and identify and describe key objectives, components, and benefits of an ERM program and the relationship between them

u. identify and describe the critical elements of an ERM approach to risk management as outlined in one of the major conceptual frameworks (e.g., COSO, Basel II, Casualty Actuarial Society, Australian/New Zealand Risk Standard, etc.)

v. identify event identification techniques and provide examples of event identification within the context of an ERM approach

w. explain the role of corporate governance, risk analytics, and portfolio management in an ERM program

x. evaluate scenarios and recommend risk mitigation strategies

y. prepare a cost-benefit analysis and demonstrate an understanding of its uses in risk assessment and decision making

9.1 DECISION MAKING -- APPLYING MARGINAL ANALYSIS

When applying marginal analysis to decision making, a CMA candidate must be able to easily identify avoidable and unavoidable costs. Unavoidable costs have no relevance to the decision-making process to drop or add a segment. This may seem simple, but a typical CMA exam question will not include whether the costs are relevant or irrelevant, and you must be able to readily identify them as such, calculate the cost, and recommend a course of action. Incorrectly identifying a cost for whatever reason could easily lead to an incorrect calculation and evaluation of the situation.

1. **Relevant vs. Irrelevant Factors**

    a. In decision making, an organization must focus on only relevant revenues and costs. To be relevant, the revenues and costs must

        1) Be made in the future

            a) Costs that have already been incurred or to which the organization is committed, called sunk costs, have no bearing on any future decisions.

            b) EXAMPLE: A manufacturer is considering upgrading its production equipment owing to the obsolescence of its current machinery. The amounts paid for the existing equipment are sunk costs; they make no difference in the decision to modernize.

        2) Differ among the possible alternative courses of action

            a) EXAMPLE: A union contract may require 6 months of wage continuance in case of a plant shutdown. Thus, 6 months of wages must be disbursed, regardless of whether the plant remains open.

    b.   Only avoidable costs are relevant.

        1)   An avoidable cost may be saved by not adopting a particular option. Avoidable costs might include variable raw material costs and direct labor costs.

        2)   An unavoidable cost is one that cannot be avoided if a particular action is taken.

            a)   For example, if a company has a long-term lease on a building, closing out the business in that building will not eliminate the need to pay rent. Thus, the rent is an unavoidable cost.

    c.   Incremental (marginal or differential) costs are inherent in the concept of relevance.

        1)   Throughout the relevant range, the incremental cost of an additional unit of output is the same. Once a certain level of output is reached, however, the current production capacity is insufficient and another increment of fixed costs must be incurred.

    d.   Another pitfall in relevant cost determination is the use of unit revenues and costs.

        1)   The emphasis should be on total relevant revenues and costs because unit data may include irrelevant amounts or may have been computed for an output level different from the one for which the analysis is being made.

2. **Marginal, Differential, or Incremental Analysis**

    a.   The typical problem for which marginal (differential or incremental) analysis can be used involves choices among courses of action.

        1)   EXAMPLE: Sanjay Chandrashakar is driving a 20-year-old automobile that gets poor fuel mileage and is subject to recurring repair bills.

            a)   The car is fully paid for, but a major engine overhaul may or may not be required within the next 12 months. The new car he is considering is a high-performance model and will not get noticeably higher fuel mileage than his current car.

            b)   Sanjay must decide between continuing to drive his current car or purchasing the new one and he now must separate the costs that are relevant to the decision from those that are irrelevant.

Variable costs:	Relevant	Irrelevant
Repairs	✓	
Overhaul	✓	
Fixed costs, recurring:		
Loan	✓	
Insurance	✓	
License Plates		✓
Fixed costs, one-time:		
Trade-in value	✓	

            c)   Each item designated as relevant will both occur in the future and be different depending on which car Sanjay chooses.

    b.   Quantitative analysis emphasizes the ways in which revenues and costs vary with the option chosen. Thus, the focus is on incremental revenues and costs, not the totals of all revenues and costs for the given option.

c. EXAMPLE: A firm produces a product for which it incurs the following unit costs:

Direct materials	$2.00
Direct labor	3.00
Variable overhead	.50
Fixed overhead	.50
Total cost	$6.00

1) The product normally sells for $10 per unit. An application of marginal analysis is necessary if a foreign buyer, who has never before been a customer, offers to pay $5.60 per unit for a special order of the firm's product.

   a) The immediate reaction might be to refuse the offer because the selling price is less than the average cost of production.

2) However, marginal analysis results in a different decision. Assuming that the firm has idle capacity, only the additional costs should be considered.

   a) In this example, the only marginal costs are for direct materials, direct labor, and variable overhead. No additional fixed overhead costs would be incurred.

   b) Because marginal revenue (the $5.60 selling price) exceeds marginal costs ($2 materials + $3 labor + $.50 variable OH = $5.50 per unit), accepting the special order will be profitable.

3) If a competitor bids $5.80 per unit, the firm can still profitably accept the special order while underbidding the competitor by setting a price below $5.80 per unit but above $5.50 per unit.

3. **Qualitative Factors**

   a. Caution always must be used in applying marginal analysis because of the following considerations:

      1) Special price concessions place the firm in violation of the price discrimination provisions of the Robinson-Patman Act of 1936.
      2) Government contract pricing regulations apply.
      3) Sales to a special customer affect sales in the firm's regular market.
      4) Regular customers learn of a special price and demand equal terms.
      5) Disinvestment, such as by dropping a product line, will hurt sales in the other product lines (e.g., the dropped product may have been an unintended loss leader).
      6) An outsourced product's quality is acceptable and the supplier is reliable.
      7) Employee morale may be affected. If employees are laid off or asked to work too few or too many hours, morale may be affected favorably or unfavorably.

4. **Add-or-Drop-a-Segment Decisions**

   a. Disinvestment decisions are the opposite of capital budgeting decisions, i.e., to terminate an operation, product or product line, business segment, branch, or major customer rather than start one.

      1) In general, if the marginal cost of a project exceeds the marginal revenue, the firm should disinvest.

    b.   Four steps should be taken in making a disinvestment decision:

        1)   Identify fixed costs that will be eliminated by the disinvestment decision, e.g., insurance on equipment used.

        2)   Determine the revenue needed to justify continuing operations. In the short run, this amount should at least equal the variable cost of production or continued service.

        3)   Establish the opportunity cost of funds that will be received upon disinvestment (e.g., salvage value).

        4)   Determine whether the carrying amount of the assets is equal to their economic value. If not, reevaluate the decision using current fair value rather than the carrying amount.

    c.   When a firm disinvests, excess capacity exists unless another project uses this capacity immediately. The cost of idle capacity should be treated as a relevant cost.

Stop and review! You have completed the outline for this subunit. Study multiple-choice questions 1 through 4 beginning on page 373.

9.2 DECISION MAKING -- SPECIAL ORDERS

1.   **Special Orders When Excess Capacity Exists**

    a.   When a manufacturer has excess production capacity, there is no opportunity cost involved when accepting a special order.

        1)   The company should accept the order if the minimum price for the product is equal to the variable costs.

        2)   EXAMPLE: Granton Fabricators produces two models of pump for natural gas pipelines. The following price and cost data are available for these products:

	Small Pump		Large Pump	
Selling price		$250		$300
Variable costs:				
Direct materials	$110		$125	
Direct labor	20		25	
Variable overhead	55		50	
Variable S&A	5	(190)	5	(205)
Contribution margin		$ 60		$ 95

            a)   Granton has just received a special, one-time order for 2,000 units of its small pump and has enough unused capacity to produce them. Granton can accept the order if it requires at least a minimum price of $190 (unit variable cost) per pump.

2.   **Special Orders in the Absence of Excess Capacity**

    a.   When a manufacturer lacks excess production capacity, the differential (marginal or incremental) costs of accepting the order must be considered.

        1)   Besides the variable costs of the production run, the firm must consider the opportunity cost of redirecting productive capacity away from (possibly more profitable) products.

        2)   EXAMPLE: Granton has received another special order for 2,000 small pumps, but this month the production line is committed to running at its full capacity. Granton is using all of the 24,000 machine hours available to produce its large pump.

            a)   Each small pump requires 4 hours to produce, and each large pump requires 6 hours. Granton will need to divert 8,000 hours (2,000 small pumps × 4 hours per unit) to run the special order.

b) The opportunity cost of these hours is the contribution margin (CM) that would be earned by devoting them to the higher-margin large pump [the small pump generates a CM of $15 per machine hour ($60 ÷ 4 hours), while the large pump produces a CM of $15.83 per machine hour ($95 ÷ 6 hours)].

Hours needed	8,000	Large pump UCM	$ 95
Hours per large pump	÷ 6	Large pumps forgone	× 1,333
Large pumps forgone	1,333	Opportunity cost	$126,635

c) For the special order to be profitable, Granton must recover (1) the opportunity cost of not producing the large pump and (2) the variable costs of the production run itself.

Large pump margin forgone	$ 126,635
Variable costs of special order (2,000 units × $190)	380,000
Total cost to be recovered	$ 506,635
Size of special order	÷ 2,000
Minimum price per unit	$253.3175

Stop and review! You have completed the outline for this subunit. Study multiple-choice questions 5 through 8 beginning on page 374.

9.3 DECISION MAKING -- MAKE OR BUY

1. **Make-or-Buy Decisions (Insourcing vs. Outsourcing)**

    a. The firm should use available resources as efficiently as possible before outsourcing. Often, an array of products can be produced efficiently if production capacity is available.

        1) If not enough capacity is available to produce all products, those that are produced least efficiently should be outsourced (or capacity should be expanded).

        2) Support services such as computer processing, legal work, accounting, and training may also be outsourced.

        3) Moreover, both products and services may be outsourced internationally. Thus, computer programming, information processing, customer service via telephone, etc., as well as manufacturing tasks, may be not only outsourced but outsourced offshore.

    b. As with a special order, the manager considers only the costs relevant to the investment decision.

        1) The key variable is total relevant costs, not all total costs.

        2) Sunk costs are irrelevant. Hence, a production plant's cost of repairs last year is irrelevant to this year's make-or-buy decision. The carrying amount of old equipment is another example.

        3) Costs that do not differ between two alternatives should be ignored because they are not relevant to the decision being made.

        4) Opportunity costs must be considered when idle capacity is not available. They are of primary importance because they represent the forgone opportunities of the firm.

            a) If the total relevant costs of production are less than the cost to buy the item, it should be insourced.

c.   EXAMPLE: Should a company make or buy an item?

	Make	Buy
Total variable cost	$10	
Allocation of fixed cost	5	
Total unit costs	$15	$13

1)   If the plant has excess capacity, the decision should be to produce the item. Total variable cost ($10) is less than the purchase price.

a)   However, if the plant is running at capacity, the opportunity cost of displaced production becomes a relevant cost that might alter the decision in favor of purchasing the item from a supplier.

2)   The firm also should consider the qualitative aspects of the decision. For example, will product quality be as high if a component is outsourced than if produced internally? Also, how reliable are the suppliers?

Stop and review! You have completed the outline for this subunit. Study multiple-choice questions 9 through 12 beginning on page 376.

9.4 DECISION MAKING -- OTHER SITUATIONS

1.   **Capacity Constraints and Product Mix**

a.   Marginal analysis also applies to decisions about which products and services to sell and in what quantities given the known demand and resource limitations.

1)   For example, if the firm can sell as much as it can produce and has a single resource constraint, the decision rule is to maximize the contribution margin per unit of the constrained resource.

a)   However, given multiple constraints, the decision is more difficult. In that case, sophisticated techniques such as linear programming must be used.

2.   **Sell-or-Process-Further Decisions**

a.   In determining whether to sell a product at the split-off point or process the item further at additional cost, the joint cost of the product is irrelevant because it is a sunk cost.

b.   The sell-or-process decision should be based on the relationship between the incremental costs (the cost of additional processing) and the incremental revenues (the benefits received).

Stop and review! You have completed the outline for this subunit. Study multiple-choice questions 13 through 16 beginning on page 378.

9.5 PRICE ELASTICITY OF DEMAND

1. **Demand -- the Buyer's Side of the Market**

    a. Demand is a schedule of the amounts of a good or service that consumers are willing and able to purchase at various prices during a period of time.

    1) Quantity demanded is the amount that will be purchased at a specific price during a period of time.

Demand Schedule

Price per Unit	Quantity Demanded
$10	0
9	1
8	2
7	3
6	4
5	5
4	6
3	7
2	8
1	9
0	10

2. **Changes in Quantity Demanded**

    a. The law of demand states that if all other factors are held constant *(ceteris paribus)*, the price of a product and the quantity demanded are inversely (negatively) related; i.e., the higher the price, the lower the quantity demanded.

    1) A demand schedule can be graphically depicted as a relationship between the prices of a commodity (on the vertical axis) and the quantity demanded at the various prices (horizontal axis), holding other determinants of demand constant.

Law of Demand

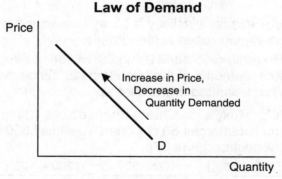

Figure 9-1

    a) As the price of a good falls, consumers have more buying power (also called higher real income). They can buy more of the good with the same amount of money. This is termed the income effect.

    b) As the price of one good falls, it becomes cheaper relative to other goods. Consumers will thus have a tendency to spend money on the cheaper good in preference to the more expensive one. This is termed the substitution effect.

3.   **Changes in Demand**

    a.   Whereas a change in price results in a change in quantity demanded, i.e., movement along a demand curve (depicted in the preceding graph), a change in one of the determinants of demand results in a change in demand, i.e., a shift of the curve itself.

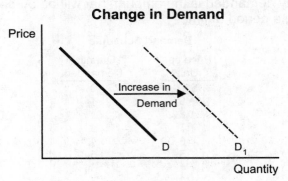

Change in Demand

Figure 9-2

4.   **Price Elasticity of Demand**

    a.   The price elasticity of demand (E_d) measures the sensitivity of the quantity demanded of a product to a change in its price.

$$E_d = \frac{Percentage \; change \; in \; quantity \; demanded}{Percentage \; change \; in \; price}$$

        1)   Elasticity describes the reaction to a change in price from one level to another. Thus, the most accurate way of calculating elasticity is the arc method, which measures elasticity across a range.

$$E_d = \frac{\% \; \Delta \; Q}{\% \; \Delta \; P} = \frac{|Q_1 - Q_2| \;\; \div \;\; |Q_1 + Q_2|}{|P_1 - P_2| \;\; \div \;\; |P_1 + P_2|}$$

        2)   Note that, because elasticity is always measured with a positive number, absolute value is used in the formula.

    b.   Elasticity is also often calculated using the midpoint formula, which involves dividing each of the four elements of the formula by 2. Since the result is mathematically identical, we have omitted this extra step.

        1)   EXAMPLE: Roxy's Ice Cream Shoppe sells 100 quarts of chocolate a day at $6 each. If it charges $3 per quart, it will sell 300 quarts a day. According to the arc formula,

$$E_d = \frac{|100 - 300| \;\; \div \; |100 + 300|}{|\$6 - \$3| \;\; \div \; |\$6 + \$3|} = \frac{|200 \div 400|}{|\$3 \div \$9|} = 1.5$$

           a)   Given a coefficient of 1.5, demand is elastic, and total revenue increases when the price is lowered.

Price Elasticity of Demand

Quantity Demanded	Q1 – Q2	Q1 + Q2	Numerator $\frac{\|Q1 - Q2\|}{\|Q1 + Q2\|}$	Price	P1 – P2	P1 + P2	Denominator $\frac{\|P1 - P2\|}{\|P1 + P2\|}$	Equals Price Elasticity
0	–	–	–	$10	–	–	–	–
1	1	1	1.000	9	$1	$19	0.053	19.000
2	1	3	0.333	8	1	17	0.059	5.667
3	1	5	0.200	7	1	15	0.067	3.000
4	1	7	0.143	6	1	13	0.077	1.857
5	1	9	0.111	5	1	11	0.091	1.222
6	1	11	0.091	4	1	9	0.111	0.818
7	1	13	0.077	3	1	7	0.143	0.538
8	1	15	0.067	2	1	5	0.200	0.333
9	1	17	0.059	1	1	3	0.333	0.176
10	1	19	0.053	0	1	1	1.000	0.053

2) These relationships can be depicted graphically as follows:

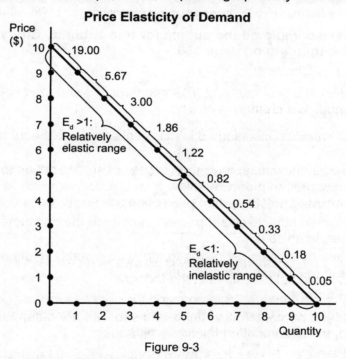

Price Elasticity of Demand

Figure 9-3

c. When the demand elasticity coefficient is

1) **Greater than one**, demand is in a relatively elastic range. A small change in price results in a large change in quantity demanded.

2) **Equal to one**, demand has unitary elasticity (usually a very limited range). A single-unit change in price brings about a single-unit change in quantity demanded.

3) **Less than one**, demand is in a relatively inelastic range. A large change in price results in a small change in quantity demanded.

4) **Infinite**, demand is perfectly elastic (depicted as a horizontal line).

    a) In pure competition, the number of firms is so great that one firm cannot influence the market price. The demand curve faced by a single seller in such a market is perfectly elastic (although the demand curve for the market as a whole has the normal downward slope).

    b) EXAMPLE: Consumers will buy a farmer's total output of soybeans at the market price but will buy none at a slightly higher price. Moreover, the farmer cannot sell below the market price without incurring losses.

5) **Equal to zero**, demand is perfectly inelastic (depicted as a vertical line).

    a) Some consumers' need for a certain product is so high that they will pay whatever price the market sets. The number of these consumers is limited and the amount they desire is relatively fixed.

    b) EXAMPLE: Addiction to illegal drugs tends to result in demand that is unresponsive to price changes. In this example, existing buyers (addicts) will not be driven out of the market by a rise in price, and no new buyers will be induced to enter the market by a reduction in price.

d. Price elasticity of demand is useful for a firm wondering how a change in the price of a product will affect total revenue from that product.

Effect on Total Revenue

	Elastic Range	Unitary Elasticity	Inelastic Range
Price increase	Decrease	No change	Increase
Price decrease	Increase	No change	Decrease

Stop and review! You have completed the outline for this subunit. Study multiple-choice questions 17 through 20 beginning on page 380.

9.6 PRICING -- THEORY

1. **Pricing Objectives**

    a. Profit maximization is assumed in classical economic theory to be the overriding goal of all firms.

    b. Target margin maximization is the process of setting prices to reach a specified percentage ratio of profits to sales.

    c. Volume-oriented objectives set prices to meet target sales volumes or market shares.

    d. Image-oriented objectives set prices to enhance the consumer's perception of the firm's merchandise mix.

    e. Stabilization objectives set prices to maintain a stable relationship between the firm's prices and the industry leader's prices.

2. **Price-Setting Factors**

    a. Supply of and demand for products and services are determined by customers' demand, the actions of competitors, and costs.

    b. Internal Factors

        1) Marketing objectives may include survival, current profit maximization, market-share leadership, or product-quality leadership.

        2) Marketing-mix strategy.

        3) All relevant costs (variable, fixed, and total costs) in the value chain from R&D to customer service affect the amount of a product that the company is willing to supply. Thus, the lower costs are in relation to a given price, the greater the amount supplied.

        4) Organizational locus of pricing decisions.

        5) Capacity.

            a) For example, under peak-load pricing, prices vary directly with capacity usage. Thus, when idle capacity is available, that is, when demand falls, the price of a product or service tends to be lower given a peak-load pricing approach. When demand is high, the price charged will be higher. Peak-load pricing is often used by public utilities.

    c. External Factors

        1) The type of market (pure competition, monopolistic competition, oligopolistic competition, or monopoly) affects the price. For example, a monopolist is usually able to charge a higher price because it has no competitors. However, a company selling a relatively undifferentiated product in a highly competitive market may have no control over price.

        2) Customer perceptions of price and value.

        3) The price-demand relationship.

            a) The demand curve for normal goods is ordinarily downward sloping to the right (quantity demanded increases as the price decreases).

            b) However, over some intermediate range of prices, the reaction to a price increase for prestige goods is an increase, not a decrease, in the quantity demanded. Within this range, the demand curve is upward sloping. The reason is that consumers interpret the higher price to indicate a better or more desirable product. Above some price level, the relation between price and quantity demanded will again become negatively sloped.

            c) If demand is price elastic (inelastic), the ratio of the percentage change in quantity demanded to the percentage change in price is greater (less) than 1.0. For example, if customer demand is price elastic, a price increase will result in the reduction of the seller's total revenue.

        4) Competitors' products, costs, prices, and amounts supplied.

    d. The time dimension for price setting is important. Whether the decision is for the short-term (generally, less than 1 year) or the long-term determines which costs are relevant and whether prices are set to achieve tactical goals or to earn a targeted return on investment. For example, short-term fixed costs may be variable in the long-term, and short-term prices may be raised (lowered) when customer demand is strong (weak).

        1) From the long-term perspective, maintaining price stability may be preferable to responding to short-term fluctuations in demand. A policy of predictable prices is desirable when the company wishes to cultivate long-term customer relationships. This policy is only feasible, however, when the company can predict its long-term costs.

3. **Price Setting by Cartels**

    a. A cartel arises when a group of firms joins together for price-fixing purposes. This practice is illegal except in international markets.

        1) For example, the international diamond cartel DeBeers has successfully maintained the market price of diamonds for many years by incorporating into the cartel almost all major diamond-producing sources.

    b. A cartel is a collusive oligopoly. Its effects are similar to those of a monopoly. Each firm will restrict output, charge a higher (collusive or agreed-to) price, and earn the maximum profit.

        1) Thus, each firm in effect becomes a monopolist, but only because it is colluding with other members of the cartel.

4.   **General Pricing Approaches**

a.   **Cost-Based Pricing** (see item 5.)

b.   **Market-Based Pricing**

1)   This approach involves basing prices on the product's perceived value and competitors' actions rather than on the seller's cost. Nonprice variables in the marketing mix augment the perceived value. Market comparables, which are assets with similar characteristics, are used to estimate the price of a product.

a)   For example, a cup of coffee may have a higher price at an expensive restaurant than at a fast-food outlet.

2)   Market-based pricing is typical when there are many competitors and the product is undifferentiated, as in many commodities markets, e.g., agricultural products or natural gas.

a)   For a significant type of market-based pricing, see item 6.

c.   **Competition-Based Pricing**

1)   Going-rate pricing bases price largely on competitors' prices.

2)   Sealed-bid pricing bases price on a company's perception of its competitors' prices.

d.   **New Product Pricing**

1)   Price skimming is the practice of setting an introductory price relatively high to attract buyers who are not concerned about price and to recover research and development costs.

2)   Penetration pricing is the practice of setting an introductory price relatively low to gain deep market penetration quickly.

e.   **Pricing by Intermediaries**

1)   Using markups tied closely to the price paid for a product

2)   Using markdowns -- a reduction in the original price set on a product

f.   **Price Adjustments**

1)   Geographical Pricing

a)   FOB-origin pricing charges each customer its actual freight costs.

b)   A seller that uses uniform delivered pricing charges the same price, inclusive of shipping, to all customers regardless of their location.

i)   This policy is easy to administer, permits the company to advertise one price nationwide, and facilitates marketing to faraway customers.

c)   Zone pricing sets differential freight charges for customers on the basis of their location. Customers are not charged actual average freight costs.

d)   Basing-point pricing charges each customer the freight costs incurred from a specified city to the destination regardless of the actual point of origin of the shipment.

e)   A seller that uses freight-absorption pricing absorbs all or part of the actual freight charges. Customers are not charged actual delivery costs.

2)   Discounts and Allowances

a)   Cash discounts encourage prompt payment, improve cash flows, and avoid bad debts.

b)   Quantity discounts encourage large volume purchases.

      c)   Trade (functional) discounts are offered to other members of the marketing channel for performing certain services, such as selling.

      d)   Seasonal discounts are offered for sales out of season. They help smooth production.

      e)   Allowances (e.g., trade-in and promotional allowances) reduce list prices.

3)   Discriminatory pricing adjusts for differences among customers, the forms of a product, or locations.

4)   Psychological pricing is based on consumer psychology. For example, consumers who cannot judge quality may assume higher prices correlate with higher quality.

5)   Promotional pricing temporarily reduces prices below list or even cost to stimulate sales.

6)   Value pricing entails redesigning products to improve quality without raising prices or offering the same quality at lower prices.

7)   International pricing adjusts prices to local conditions.

g. **Product-Mix Pricing**

1)   Product-line pricing sets price steps among the products in the line based on costs, consumer perceptions, and competitors' prices.

2)   Optional-product pricing requires the firm to choose which products to offer as accessories and which as standard features of a main product.

3)   Captive-product pricing involves products that must be used with a main product, such as razor blades with a razor. Often the main product is relatively cheap, but the captive products have high markups.

4)   By-product pricing usually sets prices at any amount in excess of storing and delivering by-products. Such prices allow the seller to reduce the costs and therefore the prices of the main products.

5)   Product-bundle pricing entails selling combinations of products at a price lower than the combined prices of the individual items. This strategy promotes sales of items consumers might not otherwise buy if the price is low enough. An example is season tickets for sports events.

h. **Illegal Pricing**

1)   Certain pricing tactics are illegal. For example, pricing products below cost to destroy competitors (predatory pricing) is illegal.

      a)   The U.S. Supreme Court has held that a price is predatory if it is below an appropriate measure of costs and the seller has a reasonable prospect of recovering its losses in the future through higher prices or greater market share.

2)   Also illegal is price discrimination among customers. The Robinson-Patman Act of 1936 makes such pricing illegal if it has the effect of lessening competition, although price discrimination may be permissible if the competitive situation requires it and if costs of serving some customers are lower. The Robinson-Patman Act applies to manufacturers, not service entities.

3)   Another improper form of pricing is collusive pricing. Companies may not conspire to restrict output and set artificially high prices. Such behavior violates antitrust laws.

4)   Still another inappropriate pricing tactic is selling below cost in other countries (dumping), which may trigger retaliatory tariffs and other sanctions.

5. **Cost-Based Pricing**

   a. This process begins with a cost determination followed by setting a price that will recover the value chain costs and provide the desired return on investment.

       1) When an industry is characterized by significant product differentiation, e.g., the automobile industry, cost-based and market-based pricing approaches are combined.

       2) Basing prices on cost assumes that costs can be correctly determined. Thus, cost-behavior patterns, cost traceability, and cost drivers become important determinants of profitability.

   b. A cost-plus price equals the cost plus a markup. Cost may be defined in many ways. Most companies use either absorption manufacturing cost or total cost when calculating the price. Variable costs may be used as the basis for cost, but then fixed costs must be covered by the markup.

Four Common Cost-Plus Pricing Formulas

$Price = Total\ cost + (Total\ cost \times Markup\ percentage)$

$Price = Abs.\ mfg.\ cost + (Abs.\ mfg.\ cost \times Markup\ percentage)$

$Price = Var.\ mfg.\ cost + (Var.\ mfg.\ cost \times Markup\ percentage)$

$Price = Tot.\ var.\ cost + (Tot.\ var.\ cost \times Markup\ percentage)$

   c. The costs of unused capacity in production facilities, distribution channels, marketing organizations, etc., are ordinarily not assignable to products or services on a cause-and-effect basis, so their inclusion in overhead rates may distort pricing decisions.

       1) Including the fixed costs of unused capacity in a cost-based price results in higher prices and in what is known as the downward (black hole) demand spiral.

       2) As higher prices depress demand, unused capacity costs and the fixed costs included in prices will increase. As a result of still higher prices, demand will continue to spiral downward.

           a) One way to avoid this problem is not to assign unused capacity costs to products or services. The result should be better operating decisions and better evaluation of managerial performance.

6. **Target Pricing**

   a. A target price is the expected market price for a product or service, given the company's knowledge of its consumers' perceptions of value and competitors' responses.

       1) The company's contacts with its customers and its market research studies provide information about consumers' perceptions of value.

       2) The company must also gain information about competitors' potential responses by learning about their technological expertise, products, costs, and financial positions. This information may be obtained from competitors' customers, suppliers, employees, and financial reports. Reverse engineering of their products is also possible.

   b. Subtracting the unit target operating income determines the long-term unit target cost. Relevant costs are all future value-chain costs whether variable or fixed.

       1) Because it may be lower than the full cost of the product, the target cost may not be achievable unless the company adopts comprehensive cost-reduction measures.

       2) The Japanese concept of kaizen is relevant to target costing. A policy of seeking continuous improvement in all phases of company activities facilitates cost reduction, often through numerous minor changes.

c. Value engineering is a means of reaching targeted cost levels. It is a systematic approach to assessing all aspects of the value chain cost buildup for a product: R&D, design of products, design of processes, production, marketing, distribution, and customer service. The purpose is to minimize costs without sacrificing customer satisfaction.

1) Value engineering requires identifying value-added and nonvalue-added costs. **Value-added costs** are costs of activities that cannot be eliminated without reducing the quality, responsiveness, or quantity of the output required by a customer or the organization.

2) Value engineering also requires distinguishing between cost incurrence and locked-in costs. Cost incurrence is the actual use of resources, whereas **locked-in (designed-in) costs** will result in use of resources in the future as a result of past decisions. Traditional cost accounting focuses on budget comparisons, but value engineering emphasizes controlling costs at the design stage before they are locked in.

7. **Life-Cycle Costing**

a. The product life cycle begins with R&D, proceeds through the introduction and growth stages, continues into the product's mature stage, and finally ends with the harvest or decline stage and the final provision of customer support. Life-cycle costing is sometimes used as a basis for cost planning and product pricing.

1) Life-cycle costing estimates a product's revenues and expenses over its expected life cycle. The result is to highlight upstream and downstream costs in the cost planning process that often receive insufficient attention. Emphasis is on the need to price products to cover all costs, not just production costs.

b. A concept related to life-cycle cost that is relevant to pricing is whole-life cost, which equals life-cycle costs plus after-purchase costs (operating, support, repair, and disposal) incurred by customers. Reduction of whole-life costs is a strong competitive weapon. Customers may pay a premium for a product with low after-purchase costs.

Stop and review! You have completed the outline for this subunit. Study multiple-choice questions 21 through 24 beginning on page 381.

9.7 PRICING -- CALCULATIONS

Some of the questions pertaining to pricing decisions that the candidate will encounter on the CMA exam focus on actually calculating the appropriate price for a given set of facts. This subunit consists entirely of such questions. Please review Subunit 9.6 before attempting to answer the questions in this subunit.

Stop and review! You have completed the outline for this subunit. Study multiple-choice questions 25 and 26 beginning on page 382.

9.8 RISK MANAGEMENT

1. **The Evolution of Risk Management**

    a. In previous decades, businesses addressed risk management with a "stovepipe" approach. The IMA's Statement on Management Accounting, "Enterprise Risk Management: Frameworks, Elements, and Integration," describes it this way:

    > ... the treasury function focused on risks emanating from foreign currencies, interest rates, and commodities--so called financial risks. An organization's insurance group focused on hazard risks such as fire and accidents. Operating management looked after various operational risks, and the information technology group was concerned with security and systems risks. The accounting and internal audit function focused on risks caused by inadequate internal controls and trends in performance indicators. The general assumption was that executive management had their eye on the big picture of strategic risks facing the enterprise in the short term and over the life of the strategic plan.

    b. This fragmented approach to risk management is unsuitable to the complex and interconnected business environment of the 21st century. The concept of enterprise risk management (ERM) arose to address the current need.

2. **Four Types of Risk**

    a. **Hazard risks** are risks that are insurable. Examples include natural disasters, the incapacity or death of senior officers, sabotage, and terrorism.

    b. **Financial risks** encompass interest-rate risk, exchange-rate risk, commodity risk, credit risk, liquidity risk, and market risk.

    c. **Operational risks** are the risks related to the enterprise's ongoing, everyday operations. Operational risk is the risk of loss from inadequate or failed internal processes, people, and systems.

    1) These failures can relate to human resources (e.g., inadequate hiring or training practices), business processes (poor internal controls), product failure (customer ill will, lawsuits), occupational safety and health incidents, environmental damage, and business continuity (power outages, natural disasters).

    2) Operational risk includes legal risk (making the enterprise subject to civil or criminal penalties) and compliance risk (the risk that processes will not be carried out in accordance with best practices).

    d. **Strategic risks** include global economic risk, political risk, and regulatory risk.

3. **Volatility and Time**

    a. Anytime uncertainty increases, risk increases. Thus, as the volatility or duration of a project or investment increases, so does the associated risk.

4. **Capital Adequacy**

    a. Capital adequacy is a term normally used in connection with financial institutions. A bank must be able to pay those depositors that demand their money on a given day and still be able to make new loans.

    b. Capital adequacy can be discussed in terms of solvency (the ability to pay long-term obligations as they mature), liquidity (the ability to pay for day-to-day ongoing operations), reserves (the specific amount a bank must have on hand to pay depositors), or sufficient capital.

5.   **Probabilities of Risk Exposures**

   a.   Risk can be quantified as a combination of two factors: the severity of consequences and the likelihood of occurrence. The expected value of a loss due to a risk exposure can thus be stated numerically as the product of the two factors.

   1)   EXAMPLE: A company is assessing the risks of its systems being penetrated by hackers.

Event	Potential Monetary Loss		Likelihood		Expected Loss
Minor penetration	$ 1,000,000	×	95%	=	$ 950,000
Unauthorized viewing of internal databases	50,000,000	×	35%	=	17,500,000
Unauthorized alteration of internal databases	2,000,000,000	×	1%	=	20,000,000

   a)   The company considers it almost inevitable that a minor penetration of its systems will take place. However, the expected monetary loss is sustainable.

   b)   By contrast, the other two levels of incident are much less likely but would have a disastrous impact on the firm.

   b.   Obviously, neither the probabilities nor the dollar amounts in an expected loss calculation are precise. If a disastrous penetration of the company's systems did occur, it might induce a loss of more than $2 billion.

   1)   The unexpected loss or maximum possible loss is the amount of potential loss that exceeds the expected amount.

6.   **Strategies for Risk Response**

   a.   **Risk avoidance** is bringing to an end the activity from which the risk arises. For instance, the risk of having a pipeline sabotaged in an unstable region can be avoided by simply selling the pipeline.

   b.   **Risk retention** is the acceptance of the risk of an activity by the organization. This term is becoming synonymous with the phrase "self insurance."

   c.   **Risk reduction** (mitigation) is the act of lowering the level of risk associated with an activity. For instance, the risk of systems penetration can be reduced by maintaining a robust information security function within the organization.

   d.   **Risk sharing** is the offloading of some loss potential to another party. Common examples are the purchase of insurance policies, engaging in hedging operations, and entering into joint ventures. It is synonymous with risk transfer.

   e.   **Risk exploitation** is the deliberate courting of risk in order to pursue a high return on investment. Examples include the wave of Internet-only businesses that crested in the late 1990s and cutting-edge technologies, such as genetic engineering.

7.   **Residual Risk vs. Inherent Risk**

   a.   Residual risk is the risk of an activity remaining after the effects of any avoidance, sharing, or mitigation strategies.

   b.   Inherent risk is the risk of an activity that arises from the activity itself. For example, uranium prospecting is inherently riskier than retailing.

8.   **Benefits of Risk Management**

   a.   Efficient use of resources. Only after risks are identified can resources be directed toward those with the greatest exposure.

   b.   Fewer surprises. After a comprehensive, organization-wide risk assessment has been performed, the odds that an incident that has never been considered will arise are greatly reduced.

   c.   Reassuring investors. Corporations with strong risk management functions will probably have a lower cost of capital.

9.   **Key Steps in the Risk Management Process**

a.   **Step 1 – Identify risks.** Every risk that could affect the success of the organization must be considered. Note that this does not mean every single risk that is possible, only those that have could have an impact on the organization.

1)   Risk identification must be performed for the entire organization, down to its lowest operating units. Some occurrences may be inconsequential for the enterprise as a whole but disastrous for an individual unit.

b.   **Step 2 – Assess risks.** Every risk identified must be assessed as to its probability and potential impact (see item 5.a. on the previous page).

1)   Not all assessments need be made in quantitative terms. Qualitative terms (e.g., high, medium, low) are sometimes useful.

c.   **Step 3 – Prioritize risks.** In large and/or complex organizations, top management may appoint an ERM committee to review the risks identified by the various operating units and create a coherent response plan.

1)   The committee must include persons who are competent to make these judgments and are in a position to allocate the resources for adequate risk response (i.e, chief operating officer, chief audit officer, chief information officer).

d.   **Step 4 – Formulate risk responses.** The ERM committee proposes adequate response strategies (see item 6. on the previous page).

1)   Personnel at all levels of the organization must be made aware of the importance of the risk response appropriate to their levels.

e.   **Step 5 – Monitor risk responses.** The two most important sources of information for ongoing assessments of the adequacy of risk responses (and the changing nature of the risks themselves) are

1)   Those closest to the activities themselves. The manager of an operating unit is in the best position to monitor the effects of the chosen risk response strategies.

2)   The audit function. Operating managers may not always be objective about the risks facing their units, especially if they had a stake in designing a particular response strategy. Analyzing risks and responses are among the normal duties of internal auditors.

10.   **Risk Appetite**

a.   The degree of willingness of upper management to accept risk is termed the organization's risk appetite.

1)   If top management has a low appetite for risk, the risk response strategies adopted will be quite different from those of an organization whose management is willing to accept a high level of risk.

11.   **Liability and Hazard Insurance**

a.   An insurance policy is a contract that shifts the risk of financial loss caused by certain specified occurrences from the insured to the insurer in exchange for a periodic payment called a premium.

1)   Liability insurance provides an organization with financial protection against damage caused to consumers by faulty products or injury to persons suffered on the organization's premises.

2)   Hazard insurance is the same as homeowner's or automobile driver's insurance. It protects the organization against damage caused to its facilities by accident or natural disaster.

12. **Methods of Managing Operational Risk**

    a. As described in item 2.c., operational risks are the risks related to the enterprise's ongoing, everyday operations. Operational risk is the risk of loss from inadequate or failed internal processes, people, and systems.

    b. Operational risk can thus be effectively managed with adequate internal controls, business process reengineering, and business continuity planning.

13. **Financial Risk Management Methods**

    a. An extremely common form of financial risk management is called hedging. **Hedging** is the process of using offsetting commitments to minimize or avoid the impact of adverse price movements.

      1) A person who would like to sell an asset in the future has a long position in the asset because (s)he benefits from a rise in value of the asset. To protect against a decline in value, the owner can enter into a short hedge, i.e., obtain an instrument whose value will rise if the asset's value falls.

      2) A person who would like to buy an asset in the future has a short position in the asset because (s)he benefits from a fall in value of the asset. To protect against a rise in value, the party can enter into a long hedge, i.e., obtain an instrument whose value will rise if the asset's value rises.

      3) Instruments for hedging include options, futures contracts, and swaps. See Subunit 4 in Study Unit 5 for a fuller discussion.

    b. Financial risk can also be addressed through more conventional methods.

      1) For instance, an organization can lower the risk that it will be unable to meet maturing bond obligations by establishing a sinking fund.

      2) Similarly, the risk of being unable to meet maturing short-term obligations can be mitigated. The establishment of policies regarding the terms of short-term investment instruments can ensure that funds will be available when they are needed (a practice called maturity matching).

14. **Qualitative Risk Assessment Tools**

    a. Precise numeric quantification of risk is not necessarily required to have a sound risk management structure. Qualitative tools are crucial for upper and operational management to describe the risks they face.

      1) Risk identification, the very first step in the process, does not lend itself to quantitative techniques. Intuitive and thought-provoking methods are required to identify all the areas of organizational vulnerability.

        a) The first round of risk identifications can begin with a simple question to management at all levels: What aspects of the organization keep you up at night?

        b) A list of generic risk areas can be distributed to inspire managers about possible points of vulnerability in their domains (foreign exchange risk, supply chain risk, regulatory risk, competitive risk, computer hacker risk, etc.).

        c) A brainstorming session among managers is a simple technique to get the risk identification process started.

      2) Risk ranking is also necessarily an intuitive process. Managers have a "feel" for how much risk a given vulnerability presents to their domains.

      3) Risk mapping is a visual tool for depicting relative risks. The probabilities of the identified events can be graphed on one axis and the severity of the consequences on the other.

15. Quantitative Risk Assessment Tools

a.   Value at risk (VaR) is a technique that employs the statistical phenomenon known as the normal distribution (bell curve). The potential gain or loss resulting from a given occurrence can be determined with statistical precision.

    1)   In organizational settings, the potential gain or loss is usually calculated for the 95% confidence level (1.96 standard deviations) or the 99% confidence level (2.57 standard deviations). For example, management can state with 95% confidence that the potential loss associated with a given risk is $3.7 billion.

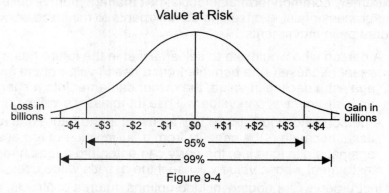

Figure 9-4

b.   Cash flow at risk and earnings at risk are identical in application to VaR. The difference between them is that the dollar amount in question is cash flow or accrual-basis earnings, respectively.

c.   Earnings distributions (in total or on a per-share basis) are also applications of statistical techniques. Just as in the value-at-risk plot above, the potential returns are plotted on the x-axis and the probabilities on the y-axis.

    1)   However, earnings distributions are unlikely to be symmetrical. A skewed distribution is more typical.

16. The COSO ERM Framework

a.   *Enterprise Risk Management – Integrated Framework* (the COSO Framework), published by the Committee of Sponsoring Organizations of the Treadway Commission (COSO) in 2004, provides guidance in the establishment of an ERM program.

b.   The COSO Framework gives the following definition of risk:

    Risk is the possibility that an event will occur and adversely affect the achievement of objectives.

c.   Risk management, at any level of the organization, is

    ... designed to identify potential events that may affect the entity, and manage risk to be within its risk appetite, to provide reasonable assurance regarding the achievement of entity objectives.

d.   Ultimately, risk management applied to the enterprise as a whole can be defined as follows:

    Enterprise risk management is a process, effected by an entity's board of directors, management and other personnel, applied in strategy setting and across the enterprise, designed to identify potential events that may affect the entity, and manage risk to be within its risk appetite, to provide reasonable assurance regarding the achievement of entity objectives.

17. Key Objectives, Components, and Benefits of an ERM Program

   a. **Objectives.** The objective of an ERM program is quite simply to assist the organization in achieving its existing strategic, operational, reporting, and compliance objectives. Risks must be identified and managed in all four of these categories.

      1) Strategic – These are the high-level goals that map out the entity's pursuit of its mission statement.

      2) Operational – These are the entity's goals concerning the efficient and effective deployment of its resources.

      3) Reporting – The entity must have reasonable assurance that its external (and internal) reports are free of material misstatement.

      4) Compliance – The entity must comply with applicable laws and regulations.

   b. **Components.** The COSO Framework identifies eight interrelated components of an ERM program:

- *Internal Environment – Management sets a philosophy regarding risk and establishes a risk appetite. The internal environment sets the basis for how risk and control are viewed and addressed by an entity's people. The core of any business is its people – their individual attributes, including integrity, ethical values, and competence – and the environment in which they operate.*

- *Objective Setting – Objectives must exist before management can identify potential events affecting their achievement. Enterprise risk management ensures that management has in place a process to set objectives and that the chosen objectives support and align with the entity's mission and are consistent with its risk appetite.*

- *Event Identification – Potential events that might have an impact on the entity must be identified. Event identification involves identifying potential events from internal or external sources affecting achievement of objectives. It includes distinguishing between events that represent risks, those representing opportunities, and those that may be both. Opportunities are channeled back to management's strategy or objective-setting processes.*

- *Risk Assessment – Identified risks are analyzed in order to form a basis for determining how they should be managed. Risks are associated with objectives that may be affected. Risks are assessed on both an inherent and a residual basis, with the assessment considering both risk likelihood and impact.*

- *Risk Response – Personnel identify and evaluate possible responses to risks, which include avoiding, accepting, reducing, and sharing risk. Management selects a set of actions to align risks with the entity's risk tolerances and risk appetite.*

- *Control Activities – Policies and procedures are established and executed to help ensure the risk responses management selects are effectively carried out.*

- *Information and Communication – Relevant information is identified, captured, and communicated in a form and timeframe that enable people to carry out their responsibilities. Information is needed at all levels of an entity for identifying, assessing, and responding to risk. Effective communication also occurs in a broader sense, flowing down, across, and up the entity. Personnel receive clear communications regarding their role and responsibilities.*

- *Monitoring – The entirety of enterprise risk management is monitored, and modifications made as necessary. In this way, it can react dynamically, changing as conditions warrant. Monitoring is accomplished through ongoing management activities, separate evaluations of enterprise risk management, or a combination of the two.*

c. **Benefits.** The COSO Framework lists three significant benefits accruing to an organization that adopts an ERM program:

- *Reducing operational surprises and losses – Entities gain enhanced capability to identify potential events and establish responses, reducing surprises and associated costs or losses.*
- *Seizing opportunities – By considering a full range of potential events, management is positioned to identify and proactively realize opportunities.*
- *Improving deployment of capital – Obtaining robust risk information allows management to effectively assess overall capital needs and enhance capital allocation.*

18. **Interaction of Elements**

a. The COSO Framework depicts the interaction of the various elements of an ERM program as a matrix in the form of a cube.

b. The four categories of objectives make up one side, the eight interrelated components make up another, and the organizational units of the entity make up the third. The organization can apply the appropriate approach to each intersection of the three elements, such as control activities for reporting objectives at the division level.

19. **Event Identification**

a. According to the COSO Framework

An event is an incident or occurrence emanating from internal or external sources that affects implementation of strategy or achievement of objectives. Events may have positive or negative impact, or both.

1) Events with a positive impact are considered opportunities, those with negative impact are risks.

b. The COSO Framework has this to say about methods of identifying risks:

An entity's event identification methodology may comprise a combination of techniques, together with supporting tools. For instance, management may use interactive group workshops as part of its event identification methodology, with a facilitator employing any of a variety of technology-based tools to assist participants.

Event identification techniques look to both the past and the future. Techniques that focus on past events and trends consider such matters as payment default histories, changes in commodity prices, and lost-time accidents. Techniques that focus on future exposures consider such matters as shifting demographics, new market conditions, and competitor actions.

c. Specific event identification techniques include the following:

- *Event inventories – These are detailed listings of potential events common to companies within a particular industry, or to a particular process or activity common across industries. Software products can generate relevant lists of generic potential events, which some entities use as a starting point for event identification. For example, a company undertaking a software development project draws on an inventory detailing generic events related to software development projects.*

- *Internal analysis – This may be done as part of a routine business planning cycle process, typically via a business unit's staff meetings. Internal analysis sometimes utilizes information from other stakeholders (customers, suppliers, other business units) or subject matter expertise outside the unit (internal or external functional experts or internal audit staff). For example, a company considering introduction of a new product utilizes its own historical experience, along with external market research identifying events that have affected the success of competitors' products.*

- *Escalation or threshold triggers – These triggers alert management to areas of concern by comparing current transactions, or events, with predefined criteria. Once triggered, an event may require further assessment or an immediate response. For example, a company's management monitors sales volume in markets targeted for new marketing or advertising programs and redirects resources based on results. Another company's management tracks competitors' pricing structures and considers changes in its own prices when a specified threshold is met.*

- *Facilitated workshops and interviews – These techniques identify events by drawing on accumulated knowledge and experience of management, staff, and other stakeholders through structured discussions. The facilitator leads a discussion about events that may affect achievement of entity or unit objectives. For example, a financial controller conducts a workshop with members of the accounting team to identify events that have an impact on the entity's external financial reporting objectives. By combining the knowledge and experience of team members, important events are identified that otherwise might be missed.*

- *Process flow analysis – This technique considers the combination of inputs, tasks, responsibilities, and outputs that combine to form a process. By considering the internal and external factors that affect inputs to or activities within a process, an entity identifies events that could affect achievement of process objectives. For example, a medical laboratory maps its processes for receipt and testing of blood samples. Using process maps, it considers the range of factors that could affect inputs, tasks, and responsibilities, identifying risks related to sample labeling, handoffs within the process, and personnel shift changes.*

- *Leading event indicators – By monitoring data correlated to events, entities identify the existence of conditions that could give rise to an event. For example, financial institutions have long recognized the correlation between late loan payments and eventual loan default, and the positive effect of early intervention. Monitoring payment patterns enables the potential for default to be mitigated by timely action.*

- *Loss event data methodologies – Repositories of data on past individual loss events are a useful source of information for identifying trends and root causes. Once a root cause has been identified, management may find that it is more effective to assess and treat it than to address individual events. For example, a company operating a large fleet of automobiles maintains a database of accident claims and through analysis finds that a disproportionate percentage of accidents, in number and monetary amount, are linked to staff drivers in particular units, geographies, and age bracket. This analysis equips management to identify root causes of events and take action.*

20. **Pervasiveness of ERM**

    a. Before the arrival of ERM, risk management was perceived as simply another line function, concerned only with the adequacy of the organization's hazard and liability insurance.

        1) With risk management recognized as an enterprise-wide function, corporate governance becomes crucial. Each enterprise should establish a risk committee that reports to the board of directors and name a chief risk officer (CRO). The internal audit function must participate in any effective ERM program.

    b. Risk analytics is the use of software tools to calculate risk exposures based on user input. Portfolio management (see Study Unit 4) is an important tool in addressing financial risk.

21. **Cost-Benefit Analysis**

    a. The Application Techniques portion of the COSO Framework provides the following guidance on preparing a cost-benefit analysis:

    Virtually every risk response will incur some direct or indirect cost that is weighed against the benefits it creates. The initial cost to design and implement a response (processes, people, and technology) is considered, as is the cost to maintain the response on an ongoing basis. The costs, and associated benefits, can be measured quantitatively or qualitatively, with the unit of measure typically consistent with that used in establishing the related objective and risk tolerance. A cost–benefit analysis is illustrated [below and on the following page].

    Evaluating the Costs and Benefits of Alternative Risk Responses

    [EXAMPLE:] A supplier to the automotive industry manufactures aluminum suspension modules. The supplier is in a "tandem" relationship with an original equipment manufacturer (OEM), where the vast majority of revenue is generated with the OEM. This OEM traditionally revises its forecasted demand by an average of 20%, always late in the cycle, creating a high degree of uncertainty for the supplier's production and scheduling activities. If the OEM were not to significantly revise demand late in the cycle, the supplier would be able to increase plant utilization by increasing its manufacturing of products for other customers, thereby increasing profitability. The supplier seeks to optimize scheduling and capacity planning for plant utilization to achieve 95% average monthly utilization. Management assessed the most significant risk to this objective – that is, the high level of uncertainty regarding actual demand from the OEM – and assessed costs and benefits of the following risk responses:

    Accept – Absorb the cost of having to respond to late changes in OEM demand, and consider the extent to which it can produce and sell product to other customers within the constraints of the OEM relationship

    Avoid – Exit the relationship with the OEM, and establish relationships with new customers offering more stable demand

    Share – Negotiate a revision to the current contract, stipulating a "take or pay" clause to ensure a certain rate of return

    Reduce – Install a more sophisticated forecasting system, which analyzes external factors (e.g., public information on consumer budgets, OEM and dealership inventories) and internal factors (historical orders from various sources) to better project actual demand from all customers

The following table compares the costs and benefits of these responses. Costs relate predominantly to supply chain management, marketing, information technology, and legal functions. Benefits are expressed using the unit of measure for the objective – plant utilization – and the resulting effect on targeted earnings before interest and taxes (EBIT).

Response	Cost	Description	Benefits
Accept	$750,000	Marketing/sales efforts required to generate additional customers, and additional transportation costs, $750,000	Management predicts it can sell an additional 2% to other customers, bringing utilization up to 82% Effect on EBIT: increase of $1,250,000
Avoid	$1,500,000	Unit price drops 2% due to smaller customers paying less than premium price	Marketing efforts allow utilization of 97%
		$750,000 in increased salary costs for personnel required to identify, win, and sustain new customers	Effect on EBIT: increase of $1,560,000
		$250,000 in increased outbound logistics costs due to larger number of suppliers	
		$500,000 in legal fees to negotiate and finalize new agreements	
Share	$350,000	Unit price drops 5% due to increased pressure from OEM in response to "take or pay" nature of relationship	New contract allows utilization of 99%
		$250,000 in legal fees to negotiate and revise contract agreement	Effect on EBIT: increase of $100,000
		$100,000 to improve data sharing, forecasting, and planning	
Reduce	$1,050,000	Average unit price drops 1% due to smaller customers not paying premium price	Improved forecasting provides sufficient time to win alternative customers for a utilization of 98%
		$500,000 for purchasing new software	Effect on EBIT: increase of $3,170,000
		$50,000 for new software training	
		$500,000 for increased forecasting and analysis	

With this analysis, and considering the likelihood of each alternative and sustainability of results, management decided on [the risk reduction response].

Stop and review! You have completed the outline for this subunit. Study multiple-choice questions 27 through 30 beginning on page 383.

9.9 CORE CONCEPTS

Decision Making

- In decision making, an organization must focus on only **relevant revenues and costs**. To be relevant, the revenues and costs must (1) be made in the future, i.e., not be sunk costs, and (2) differ among the possible alternative courses of action.

- The typical problem for which **marginal (differential or incremental) analysis** can be used involves choices among courses of action. The focus is on incremental revenues and costs, not the totals of all revenues and costs for the given option.

- A special order which might at first be rejected could turn out to be profitable after marginal analysis. Marginal analysis emphasizes incremental costs, highlighting the ability of marginal revenue to **cover fixed costs**.

  - When a manufacturer **has excess production capacity**, there is no opportunity cost to accepting a special order. The company can set a minimum price for the product equal to its variable costs.

  - When a manufacturer **lacks excess production capacity**, the differential (marginal or incremental) costs of accepting the order must be considered. Besides the variable costs of the production run, the firm must consider the opportunity cost of redirecting productive capacity away from (possibly more profitable) products.

- As with a special order, the key variable in a **make-or-buy** (insource vs. outsource) decision is total relevant costs, not total costs; sunk costs are irrelevant; costs that do not differ between the two alternatives should be ignored; and opportunity costs must be considered when idle capacity is not available.

- Marginal analysis also applies to decisions regarding **which products and services** to sell and in what quantities to sell them given the known demand and resource limitations. For example, if the firm can sell as much as it can produce and has a single resource constraint, the decision rule is to maximize the contribution margin per unit of the constrained resource.

- In determining whether to **sell a product** at the split-off point **or process the item further** at additional cost, the joint cost of the product is irrelevant because it is a sunk cost. The sell-or-process-further decision should be based on the relationship between the incremental costs (the cost of additional processing) and the incremental revenues (the benefits received).

Price Elasticity of Demand

- **Price elasticity of demand** measures the sensitivity of the quantity demanded of a product to a change in its price. It can be quantified as:

  Percentage change in quantity demanded ÷ Percentage change in price

- The most accurate method for calculating price elasticity is the **arc method**:

$$\frac{\%\ \Delta Q}{\%\ \Delta P} = \frac{|Q_1 - Q_2| \div |Q_1 + Q_2|}{|P_1 - P_2| \div |P_1 + P_2|}$$

- **Changes in unit volume** follow a predictable pattern based on the price elasticity of demand coefficient:

  - When the coefficient is greater than one, demand is in a **relatively elastic range**, meaning a small change in price results in a large change in quantity demanded.

  - When the coefficient is less than one, demand is in a **relatively inelastic range**, meaning a large change in price results in a small change in quantity demanded.

- **Changes in total revenue** follow a predictable pattern based on the price elasticity of demand coefficient:

  - When demand is in a **relatively elastic range**, a price cut increases total revenue.
  - When demand is in a **relatively inelastic range**, a price increase increases total revenue.

Pricing

- **Pricing objectives** include profit maximization, target margin maximization, volume-oriented objectives, image-oriented objectives, and stabilization objectives.
- **Factors** to consider in pricing decisions are: supply and demand; internal factors, such as marketing-mix strategy and relevant costs; and external factors, such as market type (pure competition, monopolistic competition, etc.) and customer perceptions.
- **Pricing approaches** include cost-based pricing, market-based pricing, competition-based pricing, new product pricing, pricing by intermediaries, and product-mix pricing.
- A **target price** is the expected market price for a product or service, given the company's knowledge of its consumers' perceptions of value and competitors' responses.
- **Life-cycle costing** estimates a product's revenues and expenses over its expected life cycle, from R&D all the way through product phaseout.

Risk Management

- The fragmented, "stovepipe" approach to risk management is unsuitable to the complex and interconnected business environment of the 21st century. The concept of **enterprise risk management (ERM)** arose to address the current need.
- **Four types of risk**: hazard risks, financial risks, operational risks, and strategic risks.
- Anytime **uncertainty** increases, **risk** increases. Thus, as the volatility or duration of a project or investment increase, so does the associated risk.
- **Capital adequacy** can be discussed in terms of solvency (the ability to pay long-term obligations as they mature), liquidity (the ability to pay for day-to-day ongoing operations), reserves (the specific amount a bank must have on hand to pay depositors), or sufficient capital.
- Risk can be quantified as a combination of two factors: the severity of consequences and the likelihood of occurrence. The expected value of a loss due to a risk exposure can thus be stated numerically as the product of the two factors. The **unexpected loss** or **maximum possible loss** is the amount of potential loss that exceeds the expected amount.
- **Strategies** for risk response: risk avoidance, risk retention, risk reduction (mitigation), risk sharing (transfer), and risk exploitation.
- **Residual risk** is the risk of an activity remaining after the effects of any avoidance, sharing, or mitigation strategies. **Inherent risk** is the risk of an activity that arises from the activity itself. For example, uranium prospecting is inherently riskier than retailing.
- **Key steps** in the risk management process: (1) identify risks, (2) assess risks, (3) prioritize risks, (4) formulate risk responses, and (5) monitor risk responses.
- The degree of willingness of upper management to accept risk is termed the organization's **risk appetite**.
- **Liability insurance** provides an organization with financial protection against damage caused to consumers by faulty products or injury to persons suffered on the organization's premises. **Hazard insurance** is the same as homeowner's or automobile driver's insurance. It protects the organization against damage caused to its facilities by accident or natural disaster.

- **Operational risk** is the risk of loss from inadequate or failed internal processes, people, and systems. Operational risk can thus be effectively managed with adequate internal controls, business process reengineering, and business continuity planning.
- An extremely common form of **financial risk management** is called hedging. Hedging is the process of using offsetting commitments to minimize or avoid the impact of adverse price movements. Instruments for hedging include options, futures contracts, and swaps. Financial risk can also be addressed through more conventional methods (bond sinking funds, maturity matching).
- **Qualitative** risk assessment tools:
  - **Risk identification**, the very first step in the process, in particular does not lend itself to quantitative techniques. Intuitive and thought-provoking methods are required to identify all the areas of organizational vulnerability.
  - **Risk ranking** is also a necessarily intuitive process. Managers have a "feel" for how much risk a given vulnerability presents to their domain.
  - **Risk mapping** is a visual tool for depicting relative risks. The probabilities of the identified events can be graphed on one axis and the severity of the consequences on the other.
- **Quantitative** risk assessment tools:
  - **Value at risk (VaR)** is a technique that employs the statistical phenomenon known as the normal distribution (bell curve). The potential gain or loss resulting from a given occurrence can be determined with statistical precision.
  - **Cash flow at risk** and **earnings at risk** are identical in application to VaR, the difference being that the dollar amount in question is cash flow or accrual-basis earnings, respectively.
  - **Earnings distributions** (in total or on a per-share basis) are also applications of statistical techniques. Just as in the value-at-risk plot above, the potential returns are plotted on the x-axis and the probabilities on the y-axis.
- The COSO Framework gives the following **definition of enterprise risk management**:

  Enterprise risk management is a process, effected by an entity's board of directors, management and other personnel, applied in strategy setting and across the enterprise, designed to identify potential events that may affect the entity, and manage risk to be within its risk appetite, to provide reasonable assurance regarding the achievement of entity objectives.

- The **objective** of an ERM program is quite simply to assist the organization achieve its existing strategic, operational, reporting, and compliance objectives. Risks must be identified and managed in all four of these categories.
- The COSO Framework identifies **eight interrelated components** of an ERM program: internal environment, objective setting, event identification, risk assessment, risk response, control activities, information and communication, and monitoring.
- The COSO Framework lists **three significant benefits** accruing to an organization that adopts an ERM program: reducing operational surprises and losses, seizing opportunities, and improving deployment of capital.
- Specific **event identification techniques** include the following: event inventories, internal analysis, escalation or threshold triggers, facilitated workshops and interviews, process flow analysis, leading event indicators, and loss event data methodologies.

QUESTIONS

9.1 Decision Making -- Applying Marginal Analysis

1. What is the opportunity cost of making a component part in a factory given no alternative use of the capacity?

A. The variable manufacturing cost of the component.

B. The total manufacturing cost of the component.

C. The total variable cost of the component.

D. Zero.

Answer (D) is correct. *(CMA, adapted)*
REQUIRED: The opportunity cost of making a component if there is no alternative use for the factory.
DISCUSSION: Opportunity cost is the benefit forgone by not selecting the best alternative use of scarce resources. The opportunity cost is zero when no alternative use for the productive facility is available.

Questions 2 through 4 are based on the following information. Condensed monthly operating income data for Korbin, Inc., for May follows:

	Urban Store	Suburban Store	Total
Sales	$80,000	$120,000	$200,000
Variable costs	32,000	84,000	116,000
Contribution margin	$48,000	$ 36,000	$ 84,000
Direct fixed costs	20,000	40,000	60,000
Store segment margin	$28,000	$ (4,000)	$ 24,000
Common fixed cost	4,000	6,000	10,000
Operating income	$24,000	$ (10,000)	$ 14,000

Additional information regarding Korbin's operations follows:

- One-fourth of each store's direct fixed costs would continue if either store is closed.
- Korbin allocates common fixed costs to each store on the basis of sales dollars.
- Management estimates that closing the Suburban Store would result in a 10% decrease in the Urban Store's sales, while closing the Urban Store would not affect the Suburban Store's sales.
- The operating results for May are representative of all months.

---

2. A decision by Korbin to close the Suburban Store would result in a monthly increase (decrease) in Korbin's operating income of

A. $(10,800)

B. $(6,000)

C. $(1,200)

D. $4,000

Answer (A) is correct. *(CMA, adapted)*
REQUIRED: The effect on operating income of closing the Suburban Store.
DISCUSSION: If the Suburban Store is closed, one-fourth of its direct fixed costs will continue. Thus, the segment margin that should be used to calculate the effect of its closing on Korbin's operating income is $6,000 {$36,000 contribution margin – [$40,000 direct fixed costs × (1.0 – .25)]}. In addition, the sales (and contribution margin) of the Urban Store will decline by 10% if the Suburban store closes. A 10% reduction in Urban's $48,000 contribution margin will reduce income by $4,800. Accordingly, the effect of closing the Suburban Store is to decrease operating income by $10,800 ($6,000 + $4,800).
Answer (B) is incorrect. This amount overlooks the decline in profitability at the Urban Store. Answer (C) is incorrect. This amount assumes that the effect on the Urban Store is a $4,800 increase in contribution margin. Answer (D) is incorrect. Profits will decline.

---

3. Korbin is considering a promotional campaign at the Suburban Store that would not affect the Urban Store. Increasing annual promotional expense at the Suburban Store by $60,000 in order to increase this store's sales by 10% would result in a monthly increase (decrease) in Korbin's operating income during the year (rounded) of

A. $(5,000)

B. $(1,400)

C. $487

D. $7,000

Answer (B) is correct. *(CMA, adapted)*
REQUIRED: The effect on monthly income of an advertising campaign.
DISCUSSION: The $60,000 advertising campaign will increase direct fixed costs by $5,000 per month ($60,000 ÷ 12). Sales and contribution margin will also increase by 10%. Hence, the contribution margin for the Suburban Store will increase by $3,600 ($36,000 × 10%), and income will decline by $1,400 ($5,000 – $3,600).
Answer (A) is incorrect. This amount is the monthly advertising cost. Answer (C) is incorrect. The contribution margin of the Suburban Store will increase by $3,600, which is $1,400 less than the increased advertising cost. Answer (D) is incorrect. This amount omits the 10% increase in variable costs from the calculation.

4. Refer to the information on the preceding page(s). One-half of the Suburban Store's dollar sales are from items sold at variable cost to attract customers to the store. Korbin is considering the deletion of these items, a move that would reduce the Suburban Store's direct fixed expenses by 15% and result in a 20% loss of Suburban Store's remaining sales volume. This change would not affect the Urban Store. A decision by Korbin to eliminate the items sold at cost would result in a monthly increase (decrease) in Korbin's operating income of

A. $(5,200)

B. $(1,200)

C. $(7,200)

D. $2,000

Answer (B) is correct. *(CMA, adapted)*
REQUIRED: The effect on monthly income of eliminating sales made at variable cost.
DISCUSSION: If 50% of the Suburban Store's sales are at variable cost, its contribution margin (sales – variable costs) must derive wholly from sales of other items. However, eliminating sales at variable cost reduces other sales by 20%. Thus, the effect is to reduce the contribution margin to $28,800 ($36,000 × .8). Moreover, fixed costs will be reduced by 15% to $34,000 ($40,000 × .85). Consequently, the new segment margin is $(5,200) ($34,000 direct fixed costs – $28,800 contribution margin), a decrease of $1,200 [$(5,200) – $(4,000)].
Answer (A) is incorrect. This figure is the new segment margin. Answer (C) is incorrect. This figure is the reduction in the Suburban Store's contribution margin. Answer (D) is incorrect. Operating income must decrease.

9.2 Decision Making -- Special Orders

Questions 5 through 7 are based on the following information. The Sommers Company manufactures a variety of industrial valves. Currently, the company is operating at about 70% capacity and is earning a satisfactory return on investment. Management has been approached by Glascow Industries Ltd. of Scotland with an offer to buy 120,000 units of a pressure valve. Glascow manufactures a valve that is almost identical to Sommers' pressure valve; however, a fire in Glascow Industries' valve plant has shut down its manufacturing operations. Glascow needs the 120,000 valves over the next 4 months to meet commitments to its regular customers; the company is prepared to pay $19 each for the valves, FOB shipping point. Sommers' product cost, based on current attainable standards, for the pressure valve is as follows:

Direct materials	$ 5.00
Direct labor	6.00
Manufacturing overhead	9.00
Total cost	$20.00

Manufacturing overhead is applied to production at the rate of $18 per standard direct labor hour. This overhead rate is made up of the following components:

Variable factory overhead	$ 6.00
Fixed factory overhead-direct	8.00
Fixed factory overhead-allocated	4.00
Applied manufacturing overhead rate	$18.00

In determining selling prices, Sommers adds a 40% markup to product cost. This provides a $28 suggested selling price for the pressure valve. The Marketing Department, however, has set the current selling price at $27 to maintain market share. Production management believes that it can handle the Glascow Industries order without disrupting its scheduled production. The order would, however, require additional fixed factory overhead of $12,000 per month in the form of supervision and clerical costs. If management accepts the order, 30,000 pressure valves will be manufactured and shipped to Glascow Industries each month for the next 4 months. Shipments will be made in weekly consignments, FOB shipping point.

5. How many additional direct labor hours would be required each month to fill the Glascow order?

A. 10,000

B. 15,000

C. 30,000

D. 120,000

Answer (B) is correct. *(CMA, adapted)*
REQUIRED: The number of additional direct labor hours required to fill an order.
DISCUSSION: The manufacturing overhead rate is $18 per standard direct labor hour and the standard product cost includes $9 of manufacturing overhead per pressure valve. Accordingly, the standard direct labor hour per finished valve is 1/2 hour ($9 / $18). Therefore, 30,000 units per month would require 15,000 direct labor hours.
Answer (A) is incorrect. This number of hours is found by dividing the direct labor per pressure valve by the manufacturing overhead rate to find the standard direct labor hour per finished valve. Answer (C) is incorrect. The number of pressure valves produced in a month is 30,000. Answer (D) is incorrect. The total number of valves ordered is 120,000.

6. What is the incremental profit (loss) before tax associated with the Glascow order?

A. ($168,000)

B. ($120,000)

C. $552,000

D. $600,000

Answer (C) is correct. *(CMA, adapted)*
    REQUIRED: The incremental profit (loss) before tax in a special order.
    DISCUSSION: The incremental revenue is found by taking the $19 per unit price and multiplying it by the 120,000 units ordered. Then, the variable costs per unit are multiplied by 120,000 to get a $600,000 cost for materials ($5 × 120,000), a $720,000 cost for labor ($6 × 120,000), and a $360,000 cost for overhead ($3 × 120,000). The variable costs are added to the additional fixed overhead cost of $48,000 (4 months × $12,000) to get a total incremental cost of $1,728,000. Then, the total cost is subtracted from the revenue to get an incremental profit before tax of $552,000 ($2,280,000 − $1,728,000).
    Answer (A) is incorrect. A $168,000 loss is found by using a variable overhead rate of $9 per unit. Answer (B) is incorrect. A $120,000 loss is found by using a variable overhead rate of $9 per unit. Answer (D) is incorrect. A $600,000 profit is found by not subtracting the fixed overhead.

7. What is the minimum unit price that Sommers could accept without reducing net income?

A. $14

B. $14.40

C. $20

D. $20.40

Answer (B) is correct. *(CMA, adapted)*
    REQUIRED: The minimum unit price without reducing net income.
    DISCUSSION: The minimum unit price without reducing net income must cover variable costs plus the additional fixed cost. Therefore, the three variable costs of $5.00 for direct materials, $6.00 for direct labor, and $3.00 for variable overhead are added to the additional fixed cost per unit $.40 ($48,000 ÷ 120,000). The total is $14.40.
    Answer (A) is incorrect. Not adding the fixed cost results in $14. Answer (C) is incorrect. Using a variable overhead rate of $9 and ignoring fixed overhead results in $20. Answer (D) is incorrect. Using a variable overhead rate of $9 results in $20.40.

Question 8 is based on the following information. Kator Co. is a manufacturer of industrial components. One of their products that is used as a subcomponent in auto manufacturing is KB-96. This product has the following financial structure per unit:

Selling price	$150
Direct materials	$ 20
Direct labor	15
Variable manufacturing overhead	12
Fixed manufacturing overhead	30
Shipping and handling	3
Fixed selling and administrative	10
Total costs	$ 90

---

8. Kator Co. has received a special, one-time order for 1,000 KB-96 parts. Assume that Kator is operating at full capacity and that the contribution margin of the output that would be displaced by the special order is $10,000. Using the original data, the minimum price that is acceptable for this one-time special order is in excess of

A. $60

B. $70

C. $87

D. $100

Answer (A) is correct. *(CMA, adapted)*
    REQUIRED: The minimum acceptable price.
    DISCUSSION: Given no excess capacity, the price must cover the incremental costs. The incremental costs for KB-96 equal $50 ($20 direct materials + $15 direct labor + $12 variable overhead + $3 shipping and handling). Opportunity cost is the benefit of the next best alternative use of scarce resources. Because acceptance of the special order would cause the company to forgo a contribution margin of $10,000, that amount must be reflected in the price. Hence, the minimum unit price is $60 [$50 unit incremental cost + ($10,000 lost CM ÷ 1,000 units)].
    Answer (B) is incorrect. This amount includes fixed selling and administrative costs. Answer (C) is incorrect. This amount includes fixed manufacturing overhead but omits shipping and handling costs. Answer (D) is incorrect. This amount is based on full absorption cost.

9.3 Decision Making -- Make or Buy

9. In a make-versus-buy decision, the relevant costs include variable manufacturing costs as well as

A. Factory management costs.

B. General office costs.

C. Avoidable fixed costs.

D. Depreciation costs.

Answer (C) is correct. *(CMA, adapted)*
REQUIRED: The relevant costs in a make-versus-buy decision.
DISCUSSION: The relevant costs in a make-versus-buy decision are those that differ between the two decision choices. These costs include any variable costs plus any avoidable fixed costs. Avoidable fixed costs will not be incurred if the "buy" decision is selected.
Answer (A) is incorrect. Factory management costs are unlikely to differ regardless of which decision is selected. Answer (B) is incorrect. General office costs are unlikely to differ regardless of which decision is selected. Answer (D) is incorrect. Depreciation costs are unlikely to differ regardless of which decision is selected.

Questions 10 through 12 are based on the following information. Stewart Industries has been producing two bearings, components B12 and B18, for use in production.

	B12	B18
Machine hours required per unit	2.5	3.0
Standard cost per unit:		
Direct material	$ 2.25	$ 3.75
Direct labor	4.00	4.50
Manufacturing overhead:		
Variable (See Note 1)	2.00	2.25
Fixed (See Note 2)	3.75	4.50
	$12.00	$15.00

Stewart's annual requirement for these components is 8,000 units of B12 and 11,000 units of B18. Recently, Stewart's management decided to devote additional machine time to other product lines resulting in only 41,000 machine hours per year that can be dedicated to the production of the bearings. An outside company has offered to sell Stewart the annual supply of the bearings at prices of $11.25 for B12 and $13.50 for B18. Stewart wants to schedule the otherwise idle 41,000 machine hours to produce bearings so that the company can minimize its costs (maximize its net benefits).

Note 1: Variable manufacturing overhead is applied on the basis of direct labor hours.
Note 2: Fixed manufacturing overhead is applied on the basis of machine hours.

---

10. The net benefit (loss) per machine hour that would result if Stewart accepts the supplier's offer of $13.50 per unit for Component B18 is

A. $.50

B. $(1.00)

C. $(1.75)

D. Some amount other than those given.

Answer (B) is correct. *(CMA, adapted)*
REQUIRED: The net benefit (loss) per machine hour that would result from buying a component.
DISCUSSION: The variable costs of producing B18 total $10.50 ($3.75 + $4.50 + $2.25). Thus, purchasing at $13.50 would result in a loss of $3 per bearing. Given that each bearing requires 3 hours of machine time, the loss is $1 per machine hour.
Answer (A) is incorrect. Subtracting $13.50 from $15.00 and dividing by 3 machine hours results in $.50. Answer (C) is incorrect. Not including variable manufacturing overhead when calculating the costs of producing B18 results in $(1.75) [($8.25 – $13.50) ÷ 3 machine hours]. Answer (D) is incorrect. The loss per machine hour that results from buying a component is $(1.00) [($10.50 – $13.50) ÷ 3].

11. Stewart will maximize its net benefits by

   A. Purchasing 4,800 units of B12 and manufacturing the remaining bearings.

   B. Purchasing 8,000 units of B12 and manufacturing 11,000 units of B18.

   C. Purchasing 11,000 units of B18 and manufacturing 8,000 units of B12.

   D. Purchasing 4,000 units of B18 and manufacturing the remaining bearings.

Answer (D) is correct. *(CMA, adapted)*
   REQUIRED: The combination of purchasing and manufacturing that will maximize net benefits.
   DISCUSSION: Purchasing will increase the company's costs by $3 ($11.25 – $2.25 – $4 – $2) for each B12 bearing, or $1.20 per hour ($3 ÷ 2.5 hrs). Buying B18 will only cost the company an additional $1 per machine hour [($13.50 – $3.75 – $4.50 – $2.25) ÷ 3 machine hours]. Thus, the company should make all the needed B12s and compensate for the machine hours constraint by purchasing B18s. Given that each unit of B12 requires 2.5 hours of machine time, the company can produce the needed 8,000 units in 20,000 hours (2.5 × 8,000). The remaining 21,000 hours (41,000 – 20,000) can then be used for the production of 7,000 B18s (21,000 ÷ 3 hrs.). Because the annual requirement of B18s is 11,000 units, the other 4,000 units will have to be purchased.
   Answer (A) is incorrect. Purchasing 4,800 units of B12 will increase the company's costs by $3 per B12 bearing. Purchasing B18s costs less. The company should not purchase any B12 bearings. Answer (B) is incorrect. Purchasing B12 bearings is not cost effective. By manufacturing all the B12 units needed, the company can also produce 7,000 units of B18. Answer (C) is incorrect. After manufacturing 8,000 units of B12, there are enough hours left to produce 7,000 units of B18, so only 4,000 units of B18 need to be purchased.

12. Assume that Stewart's idle capacity of 41,000 machine hours has a traceable avoidable annual fixed cost of $44,000 that will continue if the capacity is not used. The maximum price Stewart would be willing to pay a supplier for component B18 is

   A. $10.50

   B. $14.00

   C. $14.50

   D. Some amount other than those given.

Answer (D) is correct. *(CMA, adapted)*
   REQUIRED: The maximum price given fixed costs of idle capacity.
   DISCUSSION: If Stewart had sufficient idle capacity to manufacture its annual requirements of both bearings, it would be willing to pay no more than $10.50 ($3.75 + $4.50 + $2.25) for a unit of B18. Since the given fixed cost will continue if the idle capacity is not used, Stewart would increase its costs by paying more than the unit variable cost ($3.75 + $4.50 + $2.25 = $10.50). However, Stewart must purchase some bearings because it has insufficient idle capacity to produce its requirements. The given suppliers' prices for B12 and B18 result in a loss per machine hour of $1.20 and $1.00, respectively. At those prices, Stewart should manufacture all its requirements of B12 and purchase some units of B18. Assuming the given price of B12 is held constant, Stewart would benefit from purchasing B12 only if the loss per hour from buying B18 exceeded $1.20 per hour, or $3.60 per bearing (3 hrs. × $1.20). The maximum price for B18 is thus $14.10 ($10.50 + $3.60).

9.4 Decision Making -- Other Situations

Questions 13 and 14 are based on the following information. Geary Manufacturing has assembled the data appearing in the next column pertaining to two products. Past experience has shown that the unavoidable fixed manufacturing factory overhead included in the cost per machine hour averages $10. Geary has a policy of filling all sales orders, even if it means purchasing units from outside suppliers. Total machine capacity is 50,000 hours.

	Blender	Electric Mixer
Direct materials	$ 6	$11
Direct labor	4	9
Manufacturing overhead at $16 per hour	16	32
Cost if purchased from an outside supplier	20	38
Annual demand (units)	20,000	28,000

13. If Geary Manufacturing desires to follow an optimal strategy, it should produce

A. 25,000 electric mixers and purchase all other units as needed.

B. 20,000 blenders and 15,000 electric mixers, and purchase all other units as needed.

C. 20,000 blenders and purchase all other units as needed.

D. 28,000 electric mixers and purchase all other units as needed.

Answer (B) is correct. *(CMA, adapted)*
REQUIRED: The optimal strategy with respect to producing or purchasing two products.
DISCUSSION: Sales (20,000 blenders and 28,000 mixers) and total revenue are constant, so the strategy is to minimize total variable cost. Each blender requires 1 machine hour ($16 OH ÷ $16 per hour), and each mixer requires 2 machine hours ($32 OH ÷ $16 per hour). For blenders, the unit variable cost is $16 ($6 DM + $4 DL + $6 VOH). For each blender made, the company saves $4 ($20 – $16), or $4 ($4 ÷ 1 hr.) per unit of the constrained resource. The unit variable cost to make a mixer is $32 ($11 DM + $9 DL + $12 VOH). The savings is $6 per mixer ($38 – $32), or $3 ($6 ÷ 2 hours) per unit of the constrained resource. Thus, as many blenders as possible should be made. If 20,000 hours (20,000 units × 1 hour) are used for blenders, 30,000 hours are available for 15,000 mixers. Total variable cost will be $1,294,000 [(20,000 blenders × $16) + (15,000 mixers × $32) + (13,000 mixers × $38)].
Answer (A) is incorrect. Producing 25,000 mixers results in a total variable cost of $1,314,000. Answer (C) is incorrect. Producing 20,000 blenders and no mixers increases costs by $90,000 (15,000 units × $6). Answer (D) is incorrect. The company can produce at most 25,000 mixers.

14. With all other things constant, if Geary Manufacturing is able to reduce the direct materials for an electric mixer to $6 per unit, the company should

A. Produce 25,000 electric mixers and purchase all other units as needed.

B. Produce 20,000 blenders and 15,000 electric mixers, and purchase all other units as needed.

C. Produce 20,000 blenders and purchase all other units as needed.

D. Purchase all units as needed.

Answer (A) is correct. *(CMA, adapted)*
REQUIRED: The optimal strategy if direct materials costs for a product are reduced.
DISCUSSION: Reducing unit direct materials cost for mixers from $11 to $6 decreases unit variable cost to $27 ($6 DM + $9 DL + $12 VOH) and increases the cost savings of making a mixer from $6 to $11, or $5.50 per hour ($11 ÷ 2 hours per unit). Given a cost savings per hour for blenders of $4, the company can minimize total variable cost by making 25,000 mixers (50,000 hours capacity ÷ 2). Total variable cost will be $1,189,000 [(25,000 mixers × $27) + (3,000 mixers × $38) + (20,000 blenders × $20)].
Answer (B) is incorrect. Producing 20,000 blenders and 15,000 mixers results in a total variable cost of $1,219,000. Answer (C) is incorrect. Producing 20,000 blenders results in a total variable cost of $1,384,000. Answer (D) is incorrect. The variable cost of making these items is less than the cost of purchase.

Questions 15 and 16 are based on the following information. Whitehall Corporation produces chemicals used in the cleaning industry. During the previous month, Whitehall incurred $300,000 of joint costs in producing 60,000 units of AM-12 and 40,000 units of BM-36. Whitehall uses the units-of-production method to allocate joint costs. Currently, AM-12 is sold at split-off for $3.50 per unit. Flank Corporation has approached Whitehall to purchase all of the production of AM-12 after further processing. The further processing will cost Whitehall $90,000.

15. Concerning AM-12, which one of the following alternatives is most advantageous?

A. Whitehall should process further and sell to Flank if the total selling price per unit after further processing is greater than $3.00, which covers the joint costs.

B. Whitehall should continue to sell at split-off unless Flank offers at least $4.50 per unit after further processing, which covers Whitehall's total costs.

C. Whitehall should process further and sell to Flank if the total selling price per unit after further processing is greater than $5.00.

D. Whitehall should process further and sell to Flank if the total selling price per unit after further processing is greater than $5.25, which maintains the same gross profit percentage.

Answer (C) is correct. *(CMA, adapted)*
REQUIRED: The processing and selling alternative that is most advantageous.
DISCUSSION: The unit price of the product at the split-off point is known to be $3.50, so the joint costs are irrelevant. The additional unit cost of further processing is $1.50 ($90,000 ÷ 60,000 units). Consequently, the unit price must be at least $5.00 ($3.50 opportunity cost + $1.50).
Answer (A) is incorrect. The joint costs are irrelevant. Answer (B) is incorrect. The unit price must cover the $3.50 opportunity cost plus the $1.50 of additional costs. Answer (D) is incorrect. Any price greater than $5 will provide greater profits, in absolute dollars, even though the gross profit percentage declines.

16. Assume that Whitehall Corporation agreed to sell AM-12 to Flank Corporation for $5.50 per unit after further processing. During the first month of production, Whitehall sold 50,000 units with 10,000 units remaining in inventory at the end of the month. With respect to AM-12, which one of the following statements is true?

A. The operating profit last month was $50,000, and the inventory value is $15,000.

B. The operating profit last month was $50,000, and the inventory value is $45,000.

C. The operating profit last month was $125,000, and the inventory value is $30,000.

D. The operating profit last month was $200,000, and the inventory value is $30,000.

Answer (B) is correct. *(CMA, adapted)*
REQUIRED: The operating profit and inventory value after specified sales of a product.
DISCUSSION: Joint costs are allocated based on units of production. Accordingly, the unit joint cost allocated to AM-12 is $3.00 [$300,000 ÷ (60,000 units of AM-12 + 40,000 units of BM-36)]. The unit cost of AM-12 is therefore $4.50 [$3.00 joint cost + ($90,000 additional cost ÷ 60,000 units)]. Total inventory value is $45,000 (10,000 units × $4.50), and total operating profit is $50,000 [50,000 units sold × ($5.50 unit price – $4.50 unit cost)].
Answer (A) is incorrect. The $3 unit joint cost should be included in the inventory value. Answer (C) is incorrect. The $1.50 unit additional cost should be included in total unit cost. Answer (D) is incorrect. The $3 unit joint cost should be included in the cost of goods sold, and inventory should include the $1.50 unit additional cost.

9.5 Price Elasticity of Demand

17. Long Lake Golf Course has raised greens fees for a nine-hole game due to an increase in demand.

	Previous Rate	New Rate	Average Games Played at Previous Rate	Average Games Played at New Rate
Regular weekday	$10	$11	80	70
Senior citizen	6	8	150	82
Weekend	15	20	221	223

Which one of the following is true?

A. The regular weekday and weekend demand is inelastic.

B. The regular weekday and weekend demand is elastic.

C. The senior citizen demand is elastic, and weekend demand is inelastic.

D. The regular weekday demand is inelastic, and weekend demand is elastic.

Answer (C) is correct. *(CMA, adapted)*
REQUIRED: The true statement about the elasticity of greens fees as indicated by changes in demand related to higher rates.
DISCUSSION: The price elasticity of demand is the percentage change in quantity demanded divided by the percentage change in price. If the elasticity coefficient is greater than one, demand is elastic. If the coefficient is less than one, demand is inelastic. When the percentage changes are calculated as the change over the range (the arc method), the coefficient for senior citizens indicates that demand is elastic:

$$E_d = [(150 - 82) \div (150 + 82)] \div [(\$8 - \$6) \div (\$8 + \$6)]$$
$$= (68 \div 232) \div (\$2 \div \$14)$$
$$= 29.3\% \div 14.3\%$$
$$= 2.05$$

The coefficient for weekends indicates that demand is inelastic:

$$E_d = [(223 - 221) \div (223 + 221)] \div [(\$20 - \$15) \div (\$20 + \$15)]$$
$$= (2 \div 444) \div (\$5 \div \$35)$$
$$= 0.45\% \div 14.3\%$$
$$= 0.0315$$

Answer (A) is incorrect. Weekday demand is elastic. Answer (B) is incorrect. Weekend demand is inelastic. Answer (D) is incorrect. Weekday demand is elastic, and weekend demand is inelastic.

18. If the coefficient of elasticity is zero, then the consumer demand for the product is said to be

A. Perfectly inelastic.

B. Perfectly elastic.

C. Unit inelastic.

D. Unit elastic.

Answer (A) is correct. *(CMA, adapted)*
REQUIRED: The applicable term when the coefficient of elasticity is zero.
DISCUSSION: When the coefficient of elasticity (percentage change in demand/change in price) is less than one, demand is inelastic. When the coefficient is zero, the demand is perfectly inelastic.
Answer (B) is incorrect. Demand is perfectly elastic when the coefficient is infinite. Answer (C) is incorrect. Unitary inelasticity is a meaningless term. Answer (D) is incorrect. Unitary elasticity exists when the coefficient is exactly one.

19. As the price for a particular product changes, the quantity of the product demanded changes according to the following schedule:

Total Quantity Demanded	Price per Unit
100	$50
150	45
200	40
225	35
230	30
232	25

Using the arc method, the price elasticity of demand for this product when the price decreases from $50 to $45 is

A. 0.20

B. 10.00

C. 0.10

D. 3.80

Answer (D) is correct. *(CMA, adapted)*
REQUIRED: The price elasticity of demand using the arc method.
DISCUSSION: A product's price elasticity of demand is measured as the percentage change in quantity demanded divided by the percentage change in price. When price falls from $50 to $45, the coefficient is 3.8, calculated as follows:

$$E_d = [(150 - 100) \div (150 + 100)] \div [(\$50 - \$45) \div (\$50 + \$45)]$$
$$= (50 \div 250) \div (\$5 \div \$95)$$
$$= 20.0\% \div 5.26\%$$
$$= 3.8$$

Answer (A) is incorrect. The 10% decline in price divided by the 50% change in quantity demanded equals 0.20. Answer (B) is incorrect. This figure assumes a 5% change in price. It also does not calculate the change over the sum of the endpoints of the range. Answer (C) is incorrect. The percentage change in price is 0.10.

20. Worldwide, Inc., noticed that they were losing business to other firms. In view of this, the company decided to change its monthly charges for its various telephone services as follows:

	Previous Rate	New Rate
Call waiting	$ 8	$ 4
Caller ID	6	4
International calling	3	1
Internet access	15	13

In response to these price changes, the demand for the above services changed as follows:

	Previous Demand	New Demand
Call waiting	100	150
Caller ID	50	70
International calling	30	40
Internet access	150	160

Using the midpoint method, the price elasticity of demand is the highest for

A. Call waiting.

B. Caller ID.

C. International calling.

D. Internet access.

Answer (B) is correct. *(CMA, adapted)*
REQUIRED: The product with the highest price elasticity of demand using the point method.
DISCUSSION: |Price elasticity of demand measures the responsiveness of demand for a product to a change in price. The coefficient is calculated by dividing the percentage change in quantity demanded by the percentage change in price. The point method uses this formula:

$$E_d = \frac{|Q_1 - Q_2| \div |Q_1 + Q_2|}{|P_1 - P_2| \div |P_1 + P_2|}$$

By convention, elasticity of demand is reported as a positive number. Thus, the calculation for caller ID is as follows:

$$E_d = \frac{|70 - 50| \div |70 + 50|}{|\$4 - \$6| \div |\$4 + \$6|} = \frac{|20 \div 120|}{|\$2 \div \$10|} = \frac{0.167}{0.200} = 0.833$$

Answer (A) is incorrect. The price elasticity of demand for call waiting is only 0.6. Answer (C) is incorrect. The price elasticity of demand for international calling is only 0.286. Answer (D) is incorrect. The price elasticity of demand for Internet access is only 0.452.

9.6 Pricing -- Theory

21. Several surveys point out that most managers use full product costs, including unit fixed costs and unit variable costs, in developing cost-based pricing. Which one of the following is **least** associated with cost-based pricing?

A. Price stability.

B. Price justification.

C. Target pricing.

D. Fixed-cost recovery.

Answer (C) is correct. *(CMA, adapted)*
REQUIRED: The concept least associated with cost-based pricing.
DISCUSSION: A target price is the expected market price of a product, given the company's knowledge of its customers and competitors. Hence, under target pricing, the sales price is known before the product is developed. Subtracting the unit target profit margin determines the long-term unit target cost. If cost-cutting measures do not permit the product to be made at or below the target cost, it will be abandoned.
Answer (A) is incorrect. Full-cost pricing promotes price stability. It limits the ability to cut prices. Answer (B) is incorrect. Full-cost pricing provides evidence that the company is not violating antitrust laws against predatory pricing. Answer (D) is incorrect. Full-cost pricing has the advantage of recovering the full long-term costs of the product. In the long term, all costs are relevant.

22. Which one of the following will **not** occur in an organization that gives managers throughout the organization maximum freedom to make decisions?

A. Individual managers regarding the managers of other segments as they do external parties.

B. Two divisions of the organization having competing models that aim for the same market segments.

C. Delays in securing approval for the introduction of new products.

D. Greater knowledge of the marketplace and improved service to customers.

Answer (C) is correct. *(CMA, adapted)*
REQUIRED: The event that will not occur in a decentralized organization.
DISCUSSION: Decentralization is beneficial because it creates greater responsiveness to the needs of local customers, suppliers, and employees. Managers at lower levels are more knowledgeable about local markets and the needs of customers, etc. A decentralized organization is also more likely to respond flexibly and quickly to changing conditions, for example, by expediting the introduction of new products. Furthermore, greater authority enhances managerial morale and development. Disadvantages of decentralization include duplication of effort and lack of goal congruence.
Answer (A) is incorrect. When segments are autonomous, other segments are regarded as external parties, e.g., as suppliers, customers, or competitors. Answer (B) is incorrect. Autonomous segments may have the authority to compete in the same markets. Answer (D) is incorrect. Decentralizing decision making results in improved service. The managers closest to customers are making decisions about customer service.

23. The most fundamental responsibility center affected by the use of market-based transfer prices is a(n)

    A. Production center.

    B. Investment center.

    C. Cost center.

    D. Profit center.

Answer (D) is correct. *(CMA, adapted)*
    REQUIRED: The most fundamental responsibility center affected by the use of market-based transfer prices.
    DISCUSSION: Transfer prices are often used by profit centers and investment centers. Profit centers are the more fundamental of these two centers because investment centers are responsible not only for revenues and costs but also for invested capital.
    Answer (A) is incorrect. A production center may be a cost center, a profit center, or even an investment center. Transfer prices are not used in a cost center. Transfer prices are used to compute profitability, but a cost center is responsible only for cost control. Answer (B) is incorrect. An investment center is not as fundamental as a profit center. Answer (C) is incorrect. Transfer prices are not used in a cost center.

24. Pazer, Inc., produces portable televisions. Pazer's product manager proposes to increase the cost structure by adding voice-activated volume/channel controls to the television, and also adding three additional repair personnel to deal with products returned due to defects. Are these costs value-added or nonvalue-added?

	Cost of Voice-Activated Controls	Cost of Additional Repair Personnel
A.	Value-added	Value-added
B.	Value-added	Nonvalue-added
C.	Nonvalue-added	Value-added
D.	Nonvalue-added	Nonvalue-added

Answer (B) is correct. *(CMA, adapted)*
    REQUIRED: The correct classification of costs as value-added or nonvalue-added.
    DISCUSSION: The additional cost of the voice-activated controls is a value-added cost because it provides new functionality for the consumer. The cost of additional repair personnel, on the other hand, is nonvalue-added since it is incurred to address deficiencies in quality.
    Answer (A) is incorrect. Costs incurred to compensate for poor quality are nonvalue-added costs. Answer (C) is incorrect. Costs that provide additional functionality for the customer are considered value-added. Answer (D) is incorrect. Costs that provide additional functionality for the customer are considered value-added.

9.7 Pricing -- Calculations

25. The Alpha Division of a company, which is operating at capacity, produces and sells 1,000 units of a certain electronic component in a perfectly competitive market. Revenue and cost data are as follows:

Sales	$50,000
Variable costs	34,000
Fixed costs	12,000

The minimum transfer price that should be charged to the Beta Division of the same company for each component is

    A. $12

    B. $34

    C. $46

    D. $50

Answer (D) is correct. *(CIA, adapted)*
    REQUIRED: The minimum transfer price that should be charged to another division of the same company.
    DISCUSSION: In a perfectly competitive market, market price is ordinarily the appropriate transfer price. Because the market price is objective, using it avoids waste and maximizes efficiency. In a perfectly competitive market, the market price equals the minimum transfer price, which is the sum of outlay cost and opportunity cost. Outlay cost is the variable cost per unit, or $34 ($34,000 ÷ 1,000). Opportunity cost is the contribution margin forgone, or $16 ($50 – $34). Thus, the minimum transfer price is $50 ($34 + $16).
    Answer (A) is incorrect. Given that Alpha Division has no idle capacity, the transfer price to Beta should be the market price of $50 per unit. Answer (B) is incorrect. The opportunity cost needs to be included. Answer (C) is incorrect. The minimum transfer price equals outlay (variable) costs plus opportunity cost, not variable costs plus fixed costs.

26. Finn Products, a start-up company, wants to use cost-based pricing for its only product, a unique new video game. Finn expects to sell 10,000 units in the upcoming year. Variable costs will be $65 per unit and annual fixed operating costs (including depreciation) amount to $80,000. Finn's balance sheet is as follows:

Assets	
Current assets	$100,000
Plant & equipment	425,000

Liabilities & Equity	
Accounts payable	$ 25,000
Debt	200,000
Equity	300,000

If Finn wants to earn a 20% return on equity, at what price should it sell the new product?

A. $75.00

B. $78.60

C. $79.00

D. $81.00

Answer (C) is correct. *(CMA, adapted)*
REQUIRED: The target price for a new product given relevant data.
DISCUSSION: The net income Finn will require is calculated as follows:

Return on equity = Net income ÷ Equity
Net income = Equity × Return on equity
= $300,000 × 20%
= $60,000

The necessary selling price can then be derived:

Net income = [(Selling price – Variable costs) × Units sold] – Fixed costs
Selling price = (Net income + Fixed costs + Variable costs) ÷ Units sold
= ($60,000 + $80,000 + $650,000) ÷ 10,000
= $790,000 ÷ 10,000
= $79 per unit

Answer (A) is incorrect. Improperly applying the return on equity percentage only to current assets results in $75.00. Answer (B) is incorrect. The price would have to be $79. Answer (D) is incorrect. Basing the rate of return on fixed assets rather than equity results in $81.00.

9.8 Risk Management

27. Organizations face several types of risk in pursuit of their strategic objectives. The risk that the treasury function will fail to adequately reconcile the organization's bank statements is an example of

A. Hazard risk.

B. Financial risk.

C. Operational risk.

D. Strategic risk.

Answer (C) is correct. *(Publisher, adapted)*
REQUIRED: The type of risk represented by the failure to reconcile bank statements.
DISCUSSION: Operational risks are the risks related to the enterprise's ongoing, everyday operations. Operational risk is the risk of loss from inadequate or failed internal processes, people, and systems. These failures can relate to human resources (e.g., inadequate hiring or training practices), business processes (poor internal controls), product failure (customer ill will, lawsuits), occupational safety and health incidents, environmental damage, and business continuity (power outages, natural disasters).
Answer (A) is incorrect. Hazard risks are risks that are insurable. Examples include natural disasters, the incapacity or death of senior officers, sabotage, and terrorism. Answer (B) is incorrect. Financial risks encompass interest-rate risk, exchange-rate risk, commodity risk, credit risk, liquidity risk, and market risk. Answer (D) is incorrect. Strategic risks include global economic risk, political risk, and regulatory risk.

28. A landlord owns an office building in the floodplain of the Mississippi River. The landlord has decided to sell the building to a group of investors. The landlord has adopted a risk strategy of

A. Risk exploitation.

B. Risk transfer.

C. Risk avoidance.

D. Risk reduction.

Answer (C) is correct. *(Publisher, adapted)*
REQUIRED: The risk strategy embodied in selling a building in a major river floodplain.
DISCUSSION: Risk avoidance is bringing to an end the activity from which the risk arises. For instance, the risk of having a pipeline sabotaged in an unstable region can be avoided by simply selling the pipeline.
Answer (A) is incorrect. Risk exploitation is the deliberate courting of risk in order to pursue a high return on investment. The building's purchasers are engaging in risk exploitation. Answer (B) is incorrect. Risk transfer, synonymous with risk sharing, is the offloading of some loss potential to another party. Common examples are the purchase of insurance policies, engaging in hedging operations, and entering into joint ventures. Answer (D) is incorrect. Risk reduction (mitigation) is the act of lowering the level of risk associated with an activity. For instance, the risk of systems penetration can be reduced by maintaining a robust information security function within the organization.

29. A firm can mitigate the risk of financial loss from the possible on-the-job injury of one of its employees through

- A. Hazard insurance.
- B. Workers' compensation insurance.
- C. Key employee insurance.
- D. Liability insurance.

Answer (D) is correct. *(Publisher, adapted)*
REQUIRED: The risk mitigation technique for potential loss from employee injury.
DISCUSSION: Liability insurance provides an organization with financial protection against damage caused to consumers by faulty products or injury to persons suffered on the organization's premises.
Answer (A) is incorrect. Hazard insurance is the same as homeowner's or automobile driver's insurance. It protects the organization against damage caused to its facilities by accident or natural disaster. Answer (B) is incorrect. Workers' compensation insurance benefits the injured worker, not the organization. Answer (C) is incorrect. Key employee insurance benefits the organization only in case of the death of a critical member of upper management.

30. Which one of the following is **not** a key component of the COSO Framework for enterprise risk management?

- A. Information and communication.
- B. Internal environment.
- C. Risk mapping.
- D. Control activities.

Answer (C) is correct. *(Publisher, adapted)*
REQUIRED: The item not a key component of the COSO Framework for enterprise risk management.
DISCUSSION: Risk mapping is a visual tool for depicting relative risks. The probabilities of the identified events can be graphed on one axis and the severity of the consequences on the other. It is not a key component of the COSO framework.
Answer (A) is incorrect. Under the information and communication component, relevant information is identified, captured, and communicated. Answer (B) is incorrect. The internal environment sets the basis for how risk and control are viewed and addressed by an entity's people. Answer (D) is incorrect. Control activities are policies and procedures are established and executed to help ensure the risk responses management selects are effectively carried out.

Use the Gleim **CMA Test Prep** Software for interactive testing with **additional multiple-choice questions**!

9.10 ESSAY QUESTION

Scenario for Essay Questions 1, 2

Sonimad Mining Company produces and sells bulk raw coal to other coal companies. Sonimad mines and stockpiles the coal; it is then passed through a one-step crushing process before being loaded onto river barges for shipment to customers. The annual output of 10 million tons, which is expected to remain stable, has an average cost of $20 per ton with an average selling price of $27 per ton.

Management is evaluating the possibility of further processing the coal by sizing and cleaning to expand markets and enhance product revenue. Management has rejected the possibility of constructing a sizing and cleaning plant, which would require a significant long-term capital investment.

Bill Rolland, controller of Sonimad, has asked Amy Kimbell, mining engineer, to develop cost and revenue projections for further processing the coal through a variety of contractual arrangements. After extensive discussions with vendors and contractors, Kimbell has prepared the following projections of incremental costs of sizing and cleaning Sonimad's annual output:

Direct labor (employee leasing)	$600,000 per year
Supervisory personnel (employee leasing)	100,000 per year
Heavy equipment rental, operating, and maintenance costs	25,000 per month
Contract sizing and cleaning	3.50 per ton
Outbound rail freight (per 60-ton rail car)	240 per car

In addition to the preceding cost information, market samples obtained by Kimbell have shown that electrical utilities enter into contracts for sized and cleaned coal similar to that mined by Sonimad at an expected average price of $36 per ton.

Kimbell has learned that 5% of the raw bulk output that enters the sizing and cleaning process will be lost as a primary product. Normally, 75% of this product loss can be salvaged as coal fines. These are small pieces ranging from dust-like particles up to pieces 2 inches in diameter. Coal fines are too small for use by electrical utilities but are frequently sold to steel manufacturers for use in blast furnaces.

Unfortunately, the price for coal fines frequently fluctuates between $14 and $24 per ton (FOB shipping point), and the timing of market volume is erratic. While companies generally sell all their coal fines during a year, it is not unusual to stockpile this product for several months before making any sales.

Questions

1. Prepare an analysis to show whether it would be more profitable for Sonimad Mining Company to continue to sell the raw bulk coal or to process it further through sizing and cleaning. (Note: Ignore any value related to the coal fines in your analysis.)

2. a. Taking into consideration any potential value to the coal fines, prepare an analysis to show if the fines would affect the results of your analysis prepared in Question 1.

   b. What other factors should be considered in evaluating a sell-or-process-further decision?

Essay Questions 1, 2 — Unofficial Answers

1.   The analysis shown below indicates that it would be more profitable for Sonimad Mining company to continue to sell raw bulk coal without further processing. (This analysis ignores any value related to coal fines.)

Incremental Sales Revenue:

Sales revenue after further processing (9,500,000 tons × $36)	$342,000,000
Sales revenue from bulk raw coal (10,000,000 tons × $27)	270,000,000
Incremental sales revenue	$ 72,000,000

Incremental costs:

Direct labor	$ 600,000
Supervisory personnel	100,000
Heavy equipment costs ($25,000 × 12 months)	300,000
Sizing and clearing (10,000,000 tons × $3.50)	35,000,000
Outbound rail freight (9,500,000 tons ÷ 60 tons) × $240 per car	38,000,000
Incremental costs	$74,000,000
Incremental gain (loss)	$ (2,000,000)

2.   a.   The analysis shown below indicates that the potential revenue from the coal fines by-product would result in additional revenue, ranging between $5,250,000 and $9,000,000, depending on the market price of the fines.

1)   Coal fines = 75% of 5% of raw bulk tonnage
            = .75 × (10,000,000 × .05)
            = 375,000 tons

Potential additional revenue:

Minimum: 375,000 tons @ $14 per ton = $5,250,000
Maximum: 375,000 tons @ $24 per ton = $9,000,000

Since the incremental loss is $2 million, as calculated in Question 1 above, including the coal fines in the analysis indicates that further processing provides a positive result and is, therefore, favorable.

b.   Other factors that should be considered in evaluating a sell-or-process-further decision include the

1)   Stability of the current customer market and how it compares to the market for sized and cleaned coal

2)   Storage space needed for the coal fines until they are sold and the handling costs of coal fines

3)   Reliability of cost (e.g., rail freight rates) and revenue estimates, and the risk of depending on these estimates

4)   Timing of the revenue stream from coal fines and impact on the need for liquidity

5)   Possible environmental problems, i.e., dumping of waste and smoke from unprocessed coal

Use **CMA Gleim Online** and **Essay Wizard** to practice additional essay questions in an exam-like environment.

STUDY UNIT TEN
INVESTMENT DECISIONS

(26 pages of outline)

Investment Decisions

Management accountants must be able to help management analyze decisions. This involves making cash flow estimates, calculating the time value of money, and being able to apply discounted cash flow concepts, such as net present value and internal rate of return. Non-discounting analysis techniques are also covered on the CMA exam, as are the income tax implications for investment decision analysis. Candidates will also be tested on such things as ranking investment projects, performing risk analysis, and evaluating real options.

Coverage of investment decisions extends across Study Unit 10.

This study unit is on **investment decisions**. The relative weight assigned to this major topic in Part 2 of the exam is **20%**.

After studying the outline and answering the questions in this study unit, you will have the skills necessary to address the following topics listed in the ICMA's Learning Outcome Statements:

Part 2 – Section D.1. Capital budgeting process

The candidate should be able to:

a. define capital budgeting and identify the steps or stages undertaken in developing and implementing a capital budget for a project
b. identify and calculate the relevant cash flows of a capital investment project on both a pretax and after-tax basis
c. demonstrate an understanding of how income taxes affect cash flows
d. distinguish between cash flows and accounting profits and discuss the relevance to capital budgeting of incremental cash flow, sunk cost, and opportunity cost
e. explain the importance of changes in net working capital in capital budgeting
f. discuss how the effects of inflation are reflected in capital budgeting analysis
g. define hurdle rate
h. identify and discuss qualitative considerations involved in the capital budgeting decision
i. describe the role of the post-audit in the capital budgeting process

Part 2 – Section D.2. Discounted cash flow analysis

The candidate should be able to:

a. demonstrate an understanding of the two main discounted cash flow (DCF) methods, net present value (NPV), and internal rate of return (IRR)
b. calculate the NPV and IRR

    c.   demonstrate an understanding of the decision criteria used in NPV and IRR analyses to determine acceptable projects

    d.   compare NPV and IRR, focusing on the relative advantages and disadvantages of each method, particularly with respect to independent versus mutually exclusive projects and the "multiple IRR problem"

    e.   explain why NPV and IRR methods can produce conflicting rankings for capital projects if not applied properly

    f.   identify assumptions of NPV and IRR

    g.   evaluate and recommend project investments on the basis of DCF analysis

Part 2 – Section D.3. Payback and discounted payback

The candidate should be able to:

    a.   demonstrate an understanding of the payback and discounted payback methods

    b.   identify the advantages and disadvantages of the payback and discounted payback methods

    c.   calculate payback periods and discounted payback periods

Part 2 – Section D.4. Ranking investment projects

The candidate should be able to:

    a.   define independent projects and mutually exclusive projects

    b.   define capital rationing

    c.   rank capital investment projects and recommend optimal investments using the profitability index

    d.   determine when the profitability index would be recommended over the NPV rule

    e.   identify and discuss the problems inherent in comparing projects of unequal scale and/or unequal lives

    f.   identify and explain alternative solutions to the ranking problem, including internal capital markets and linear programming

Part 2 – Section D.5. Risk analysis in capital investment

The candidate should be able to:

    a.   identify alternative approaches to dealing with risk in capital budgeting

    b.   demonstrate an understanding of and calculate certainty equivalents

    c.   distinguish among sensitivity analysis, scenario analysis, and Monte Carlo simulation as risk analysis techniques

    d.   explain why a rate specifically adjusted for risk should be used when project cash flows are more or less risky than is normal for a firm

    e.   explain how the value of a capital investment is increased if consideration is given to the possibility of adding on, speeding up, slowing down, or discontinuing early

    f.   demonstrate an understanding of real options and identify examples of the different types of real options (calculations not required)

Part 2 – Section D.6. Valuation

The candidate should be able to:

    k.   explain the use of sensitivity analysis in valuation

    q.   explain how real options affect the valuation of a company

        Statements a. through j., l. through p., and r. are covered in Study Unit 5.

10.1 THE CAPITAL BUDGETING PROCESS

1. **Capital Budgeting**

   a.   Capital budgeting is the process of planning and controlling investments for long-term projects. It is this long-term aspect of capital budgeting that presents the management accountant with specific challenges.

      1)   Most financial and management accounting topics, such as calculating allowance for doubtful accounts or accumulating product costs, concern tracking and reporting activity for a single accounting or reporting cycle, such as 1 month or 1 year.

      2)   By their nature, capital projects affect multiple accounting periods and will constrain the organization's financial planning well into the future. Once made, capital budgeting decisions tend to be relatively inflexible.

   b.   Capital budgeting applications include

      1)   Buying equipment
      2)   Building facilities
      3)   Acquiring a business
      4)   Developing a product or product line
      5)   Expanding into new markets

   c.   A firm must accurately forecast future changes in demand in order to have the necessary production capacity when demand for its product is strong, without having excess idle capacity when demand slackens.

   d.   A capital project usually involves substantial expenditures.

      1)   Planning is crucial because of possible changes in capital markets, inflation, interest rates, and the money supply.

   e.   As with every other business decision, the tax consequences of a new investment (and possible disinvestment of a replaced asset) must be considered.

      1)   All capital budgeting decisions need to be evaluated on an after-tax basis because taxes may affect decisions differently. Companies that operate in multiple tax jurisdictions may find the decision process more complex. Another possibility is that special tax concessions may be negotiated for locating an investment in a given locale.

2. **Types of Costs Considered in Capital Budgeting Analysis**

   a.   An avoidable cost may be eliminated by ceasing an activity or by improving efficiency.

   b.   A common cost is shared by all options and is not clearly allocable to any one of them.

   c.   A deferrable cost may be shifted to the future with little or no effect on current operations.

   d.   A fixed cost does not vary with the level of activity within the relevant range.

   e.   An imputed cost may not entail a specified dollar outlay formally recognized by the accounting system, but it is nevertheless relevant to establishing the economic reality analyzed in the decision-making process.

   f.   An incremental cost is the difference in cost resulting from selecting one option instead of another.

g. An opportunity cost is the maximum benefit forgone by using a scarce resource for a given purpose and not for the next-best alternative.

   1) In capital budgeting, the most basic application of this concept is the desire to place the company's limited funds in the most promising capital project(s).

   2) An even more important application is the shareholders' opportunity cost of capital. This is the rate of return the company's shareholders could earn by taking their funds and investing them elsewhere at a similar level of risk.

      a) Shareholders' opportunity cost of capital is one choice for a firm's hurdle rate.

h. Relevant costs vary with the action. Other costs are constant and therefore do not affect the decision.

i. A sunk cost cannot be avoided because an expenditure or an irrevocable decision to incur the cost has been made.

   1) An example is the amount of money already spent on manufacturing equipment.

j. The weighted-average cost of capital is the weighted average of the interest cost of debt (net of tax) and the costs (implicit or explicit) of the components of equity capital to be invested in long-term assets. It represents a required minimum return of a new investment to prevent dilution of owners' interests.

   1) The desired rate of return is the minimum that the firm will accept. It may be the opportunity cost of funds, the weighted-average cost of capital, or some other minimum based on, for example, other investment options or the industry average.

3. **The Stages in Capital Budgeting**

   a. Identification and definition. Those projects and programs that are needed to attain the entity's objectives are identified and defined.

      1) For example, a firm that wishes to be the low-cost producer in its industry will be interested in investing in more efficient manufacturing machinery. A company that wishes to quickly expand into new markets will look at acquiring another established firm.

      2) Defining the projects and programs determines their extent and facilitates cost, revenue, and cash flow estimation.

         a) This stage is the most difficult.

   b. Search. Potential investments are subjected to a preliminary evaluation by representatives from each function in the entity's value chain.

      1) Dismal projects are dismissed at this point, while others are passed on for further evaluation.

   c. Information-acquisition. The costs and benefits of the projects that passed the search phase are enumerated.

      1) Quantitative financial factors are given the most scrutiny at this point.

         a) These include initial investment and periodic cash inflow.

      2) Nonfinancial measures, both quantitative and qualitative, are also identified and addressed.

         a) Examples include the need for additional training on new equipment and higher customer satisfaction based on improved product quality.

         b) Also, uncertainty about technological developments, demand, competitors' actions, governmental regulation, and economic conditions should be considered.

d.   Selection. Employing one of the selection models (net present value, internal rate of return, etc.) and relevant nonfinancial measures, the project(s) that will increase shareholder value by the greatest margin are chosen for implementation.

e.   Financing. Sources of funds for selected projects are identified. These can come from the company's operations, the issuance of debt, or the sale of the company's stock.

f.   Implementation and monitoring. Once projects are underway, they must be kept on schedule and within budgetary constraints.

   1)   This step also involves determining whether previously unforeseen problems or opportunities have arisen and what changes in plans are appropriate.

4.   **Steps in Ranking Potential Investments**

a.   Capital budgeting requires choosing among investment proposals. Thus, a ranking procedure for such decisions is needed. The following are steps in the ranking procedure:

   1)   **Determine the asset cost or net investment.**

      a)   The net investment is the net outlay, or gross cash requirement, minus cash recovered from the trade or sale of existing assets, with any necessary adjustments for applicable tax consequences. Cash outflows in subsequent periods also must be considered.

      b)   Moreover, the investment required includes funds to provide for increases in working capital, for example, the additional receivables and inventories resulting from the acquisition of a new manufacturing plant. This investment in working capital is treated as an initial cost of the investment (a cash outflow) that will be recovered at the end of the project (i.e., the salvage value is equal to the initial cost).

   2)   **Calculate estimated cash flows**, period by period, using the acquired assets.

      a)   Reliable estimates of cost savings or revenues are necessary.

      b)   Net cash flow is the economic benefit or cost, period by period, resulting from the investment.

      c)   Economic life is the time period over which the benefits of the investment proposal are expected to be obtained, as distinguished from the physical or technical life of the asset involved.

      d)   Depreciable life is the period used for accounting and tax purposes over which cost is to be systematically and rationally allocated. It is based upon permissible or standard guidelines and may have no particular relevance to economic life. Because depreciation is deductible for income tax purposes, thereby shielding some revenue from taxation, depreciation gives rise to a depreciation tax shield.

   3)   **Relate the cash-flow benefits to their cost** by using one of several methods to evaluate the advantage of purchasing the asset.

   4)   **Rank the investments.**

5.   **Book Rate of Return**

   a.   A common misstep in regard to capital budgeting is the temptation to gauge the desirability of a project by using accrual accounting numbers instead of cash flows.

      1)   Shareholders and financial analysts use GAAP-based numbers because they are readily available.

         a)   The measure usually produced this way is called **book rate of return** or **accrual accounting rate of return**.

$$Book\ rate\ of\ return = \frac{GAAP\ net\ income\ from\ investment}{Book\ value\ of\ investment}$$

      2)   However, net income and book value are affected by the company's choices of accounting methods.

         a)   Accountants must choose which expenditures to capitalize versus which to expense immediately. They also choose how quickly to depreciate capitalized assets.

         b)   A project's true rate of return cannot be dependent on such bookkeeping decisions.

      3)   Another distortion inherent in comparing a single project's book rate of return to the current one for the company as a whole is that the latter is an average of all of a firm's capital projects.

         a)   It reveals nothing about the performance of individual investment choices. Embedded in that number may be a handful of good projects making up for a large number of poor investments.

      4)   For these reasons, book rate of return is an unsatisfactory guide to selecting capital projects.

6.   **Cash Flows**

   a.   Relevant cash flows are a much more reliable guide when judging capital projects, since only they provide a true measure of a project's potential to affect shareholder value.

      1)   The relevant cash flows can be divided into the following three categories:

         a)   **Net initial investment**

            i)   Purchase of new equipment
            ii)   Initial working capital requirements
            iii) After-tax proceeds from disposal of old equipment

         b)   **Annual net cash flows**

            i)   After-tax cash collections from operations (excluding depreciation effect)
            ii)   Tax savings from depreciation deductions (depreciation tax shield)

         c)   **Project termination cash flows**

            i)   After-tax proceeds from disposal of new equipment
            ii)   Recovery of working capital (untaxed)

EXAMPLE

A company is determining the relevant cash flows for a potential capital project. The company has a 40% tax rate.

1) **Net initial investment:**

    a) The project will require an initial outlay of $500,000 for new equipment.

    b) The company expects to commit $12,000 of working capital for the duration of the project in the form of increased accounts receivable and inventories.

    c) Calculating the after-tax proceeds from disposal of the existing equipment is a two-step process.

        i) First, the tax gain or loss is determined.

Disposal value	$ 5,000
Less: tax value	(20,000)
Tax-basis loss on disposal	**$(15,000)**

        ii) The after-tax effect on cash can then be calculated.

Disposal value	$ 5,000
Add: tax savings on loss ($15,000 × .40)	6,000
After-tax cash inflow from disposal	**$11,000**

    d) The cash outflow required for this project's net initial investment is therefore $(501,000) [$(500,000) + $(12,000) + $11,000].

2) **Annual net cash flows:**

    a) The project is expected to generate $100,000 annually from ongoing operations.

        i) However, 40% of this will have to be paid out in the form of income taxes.

Annual cash collections	$100,000
Less: income tax expense ($100,000 × .40)	(40,000)
After-tax cash inflow from operations	**$ 60,000**

    b) The project is slated to last 8 years.

        i) The new equipment is projected to have a salvage value of $50,000 and will generate $62,500 per year in depreciation charges ($500,000 ÷ 8).

        NOTE: On the CMA exam, salvage value is never subtracted when calculating the depreciable base for tax purposes.

        ii) The old equipment has 4 years of service life remaining.

        iii) Unlike the income from operations, the higher depreciation charges will generate a tax savings. This is referred to as the **depreciation tax shield**.

        iv) The tax savings generated by the higher depreciation for the first 4 years is $23,000 [($62,500 − $5,000) × .40] and for the last 4 years is $25,000 [($62,500 − $0) × .40].

    c) The annual net cash inflow from the project is thus $83,000 ($60,000 + $23,000) for the first 4 years and $85,000 ($60,000 + $25,000) for the last 4 years.

3) **Project termination cash flows:**

    a) Proceeds of $50,000 are expected from disposal of the new equipment at the end of the project.

        i) First, the tax gain or loss is determined.

Disposal value	$50,000
Less: tax basis	0
Tax-basis gain on disposal	**$50,000**

        ii) The after-tax effect on cash can then be calculated.

Tax basis gain on disposal	$50,000
Less: tax liability on gain ($50,000 × .40)	(20,000)
After-tax cash inflow from disposal	**$30,000**

    b) Once the project is over, the company will recovery the $12,000 of working capital it committed to the project.

    c) The net cash inflow upon project termination is therefore $42,000 ($30,000 + $12,000).

    b. As the example above indicates, tax considerations are essential when considering capital projects.

7. **Other Considerations**

   a. Effects of inflation on capital budgeting.

      1) Inflation raises the hurdle rate. In an inflationary environment, future dollars are worth less than today's dollars. Thus, the firm will require a higher rate of return to compensate.

   b. Post-investment audits should be conducted to serve as a control mechanism and to deter managers from proposing unprofitable investments.

      1) Actual-to-expected cash flow comparisons should be made, and unfavorable variances should be explained. The reason may be an inaccurate forecast or implementation problems.

      2) Individuals who supplied unrealistic estimates should have to explain differences. Knowing that a post-investment audit will be conducted may cause managers to provide more realistic forecasts in the future.

      3) The temptation to evaluate the outcome of a project too early must be overcome. Until all cash flows are known, the results can be misleading.

      4) Assessing the receipt of expected nonquantitative benefits is inherently difficult.

Stop and review! You have completed the outline for this subunit. Study multiple-choice questions 1 through 7 beginning on page 413.

10.2 DISCOUNTED CASH FLOW ANALYSIS

CMA candidates can expect a variety of questions that will require the use of either Present Value or Future Value tables. The CMA exam will provide the necessary data to answer the question either within the given information of the question itself or through the Time Value tables. Gleim Test Prep Software and Gleim Online will familiarize you with how to use these tables on the actual exam by providing the necessary data within the question and by providing an emulation of how to access the Present/Future Value tables.

1. **Time Value of Money**

   a. A dollar received in the future is worth less than a dollar received today. Thus, when analyzing capital projects, the management accountant must discount the relevant cash flows using the time value of money.

   b. A quantity of money to be received or paid in the future is worth less than the same amount now. The difference is measured in terms of interest calculated using the appropriate discount rate. Interest is the payment received by holders of money from the current consumer to forgo current consumption.

   c. Standard tables have been developed to facilitate the calculation of present and future values. Each entry in one of these tables represents the factor by which any monetary amount can be modified to obtain its present or future value.

   d. The **present value (PV) of a single amount** is the value today of some future payment.

      1) It equals the future payment times the present value of 1 (a factor found in a standard table) for the given number of periods and interest rate.

EXAMPLE

| | Present Value | | |
No. of Periods	6%	8%	10%
1	0.943	0.926	0.909
2	0.890	0.857	0.826
3	0.840	0.794	0.751
4	0.792	0.735	0.683
5	0.747	0.681	0.621

The present value of $1,000, to be received in 3 years and discounted at 8%, is $794 ($1,000 × 0.794).

e.   The **future value (FV) of a single amount** is the amount available at a specified time in the future based on a single investment (deposit) today. The FV is the amount to be computed if one knows the present value and the appropriate discount rate.

1)   It equals the current payment times the future value of 1 (a factor found in a standard table) for the given number of periods and interest rate.

EXAMPLE

Future Value

No. of Periods	6%	8%	10%
1	1.0600	1.0800	1.1000
2	1.1236	1.1664	1.2100
3	1.1910	1.2597	1.3310
4	1.2625	1.3605	1.4641
5	1.3382	1.4693	1.6105

The future value of $1,000 invested today for 4 years at 10% interest will be $1,464 ($1,000 × 1.464).

---

f.   **Annuities**

1)   An annuity is usually a series of equal payments at equal intervals of time, e.g., $1,000 at the end of every year for 10 years.

a)   An **ordinary annuity (annuity in arrears)** is a series of payments occurring at the end of each period. In an **annuity due (annuity in advance)**, the payments are made (received) at the beginning of each period.

i)   Present value. The first payment of an ordinary annuity is discounted. The first payment of an annuity due is not discounted.

ii)   Future value. Interest is not earned for the first period of an ordinary annuity. Interest is earned on the first payment of an annuity due.

b)   The PV of an annuity. A typical present value table is for an ordinary annuity, but the factor for an annuity due can be easily derived. Select the factor for an ordinary annuity for one less period (n − 1) and add 1.000 to it to include the initial payment (which is not discounted).

EXAMPLE

Present Value

No. of Periods	6%	8%	10%
1	0.943	0.926	0.909
2	1.833	1.783	1.736
3	2.673	2.577	2.487
4	3.465	3.312	3.170
5	4.212	3.993	3.791

To calculate the present value of an **ordinary annuity** of four payments of $1,000 each discounted at 10%, multiply $1,000 by the appropriate factor ($1,000 × 3.170 = $3,170).

Using the same table, the present value of an **annuity due** of four payments of $1,000 each also may be calculated. This value equals $1,000 times the factor for one less period (4 − 1 = 3), increased by 1.0. Thus, the present value of the annuity due for four periods at 10% is $3,487 [$1,000 × (2.487 + 1.0)].

The present value of the annuity due ($3,487) is greater than the present value of the ordinary annuity ($3,170) because the payments occur 1 year sooner.

    c) The FV of an annuity is the value that a series of equal payments will have at a certain moment in the future if interest is earned at a given rate.

EXAMPLE

	Future Value		
No. of Periods	6%	8%	10%
1	1.0000	1.0000	1.0000
2	2.0600	2.0800	2.1000
3	3.1836	3.2464	3.3100
4	4.3746	4.5061	4.6410
5	5.6371	5.8667	6.1051

To calculate the FV of a 3-year **ordinary annuity** with payments of $1,000 each at 6% interest, multiply $1,000 by the appropriate factor ($1,000 × 3.184 = $3,184).

The FV of an **annuity due** also may be determined from the same table. Multiply the $1,000 payment by the factor for one additional period (3 + 1 = 4) decreased by 1.0 (4.375 – 1.0 = 3.375) to arrive at a FV of $3,375 ($1,000 × 3.375).

The future value of the annuity due ($3,375) is greater than the future value of an ordinary annuity ($3,184). The deposits are made earlier.

---

    g. A firm's goal is for its discount rate to be as low as possible.

        1) The lower the firm's discount rate, the lower the "hurdle" the company must clear to achieve profitability. For this reason, the rate is sometimes called the **hurdle rate**.

    h. The two most widely used rates in capital budgeting are

        1) The firm's weighted-average cost of capital and
        2) The shareholders' opportunity cost of capital.

    i. A common pitfall in capital budgeting is the tendency to use the company's current rate of return as the benchmark. This can lead to rejecting projects that should be accepted.

        1) EXAMPLE: A firm's current rate of return on all projects is 12%. Its shareholders' opportunity cost of capital is 10%. The company incorrectly rejects a project earning 11%.

    j. The two principal methods for projecting the profitability of an investment are net present value and internal rate of return.

2. **Net Present Value**

    a. The net present value (NPV) method expresses a project's return in **dollar terms**.

        1) NPV nets the expected cash streams related to a project (inflows and outflows), then discounts them at the hurdle rate, also called the desired rate of return.

            a) If the NPV of a project is positive, the project is desirable because it has a higher rate of return than the company's desired rate.

2) EXAMPLE:

a) The company discounts the relevant net cash flows using a hurdle rate of 6% (its desired rate of return).

Period	Net Cash Flow	6% PV Factor	Discounted Cash Flows
Initial Investment	$(501,000)	1.00000	$(501,000)
Year 1	77,000	0.94340	72,642
Year 2	77,000	0.89000	68,530
Year 3	77,000	0.83962	64,651
Year 4	77,000	0.79209	60,991
Year 5	85,000	0.74726	63,517
Year 6	85,000	0.70496	59,922
Year 7	85,000	0.66506	56,530
Year 8	101,800	0.62741	63,870
Net Present Value			**$ 9,653**

b) Because the project has net present value > $0, it is profitable given the company's hurdle rate.

3. Internal Rate of Return

a. The internal rate of return (IRR) expresses project's return in **percentage terms**.

1) The IRR of an investment is the discount rate at which the investment's NPV equals zero. In other words, it is the rate that makes the present value of the expected cash inflows equal the present value of the expected cash outflows.

a) If the IRR is higher than the company's desired rate of return, then the investment is desirable.

2) EXAMPLE:

a) The discounted cash flows used in the NPV exercise above can be recalculated using a higher discount rate (a higher rate will drive down the present value) in an attempt to get the solution closer to $0.

Period	Net Cash Flow	7% PV Factor	Discounted Cash Flows
Initial Investment	$(501,000)	1.00000	$(501,000)
Year 1	77,000	0.93458	71,963
Year 2	77,000	0.87344	67,255
Year 3	77,000	0.81630	62,855
Year 4	77,000	0.76290	58,743
Year 5	85,000	0.71299	60,604
Year 6	85,000	0.66634	56,639
Year 7	85,000	0.62275	52,934
Year 8	101,800	0.58201	59,249
Net Present Value			**$ (10,758)**

b) The higher hurdle rate causes the NPV to be negative. Thus, the IRR of this project is somewhere around 6.5%.

c) Because the company's desired rate of return is 6%, the project should be accepted, the same decision that was arrived at using the net present value method.

4. Cash Flows and Discounting

a. Conceptually, net present value is calculated using the following formula:

$$NPV = \frac{Cash\ Flow_0}{(1+r)^0} + \frac{Cash\ Flow_1}{(1+r)^1} + \frac{Cash\ Flow_2}{(1+r)^2} + \frac{Cash\ Flow_3}{(1+r)^3} + etc.$$

1) The subscripts and exponents represent the discount periods. The variable r is the discount rate.

b. Present value tables are available as a convenient way to discount cash flows.

5. **Pitfalls of IRR**

   a. IRR used in isolation is seldom the best route to a sound capital budgeting decision.

      1) **Direction of cash flows.** When the direction of the cash flows changes, focusing simply on IRR can be misleading.

         a) EXAMPLE: Below are the net cash flows for two potential capital projects.

	Initial	Period 1
Project X	$(222,240)	$240,000
Project Y	222,240	(240,000)

         The cash flow amounts are the same in absolute value, but the directions differ. In choosing between the two, a decision maker might be tempted to select the project that has a cash inflow earlier and a cash outflow later.

         b) The IRR for both projects is 8%, which can be proved as follows:

Project X			Project Y		
$(222,240) × 1.000 = $(222,240)			$ 222,240 × 1.000 = $ 222,240		
240,000 × 0.926 = 222,240			(240,000) × 0.926 = (222,240)		
$ -0-			$ -0-		

         c) Discounting the cash flows at the company's hurdle rate of 6% reveals a different picture.

Project X			Project Y		
$(222,240) × 1.000 = $(222,240)			$ 222,240 × 1.000 = $ 222,240		
240,000 × 0.943 = 226,320			(240,000) × 0.943 = (226,320)		
$ 4,080			$ (4,080)		

            i) It turns out that, given a hurdle rate lower than the rate at which the two projects have the same return, the project with the positive cash flow earlier is by far the less desirable of the two.

            ii) Clearly, a decision maker can be seriously misled if (s)he uses the simple direction of the cash flows as the tiebreaker when two projects have the same IRR.

         d) This effect is known as the multiple IRR problem. Essentially, there are as many solutions to the IRR formula as there are changes in the direction of the net cash flows.

      2) **Mutually exclusive projects.** As with changing cash flow directions, focusing only on IRR when capital is limited can lead to unsound decisions.

         a) EXAMPLE: Below are the cash flows for two potential capital projects.

	Initial	Period 1	IRR
Project S	$(178,571)	$200,000	12%
Project T	(300,000)	330,000	10%

         b) If capital is available for only one project, using IRR alone would suggest that Project S be selected.

         c) Once again, however, discounting both projects' net cash flows at the company's hurdle rate suggests a different decision.

Project S			Project T		
$(178,571) × 1.000 = $(178,571)			$(300,000) × 1.000 = $(300,000)		
200,000 × 0.943 = 188,600			330,000 × 0.943 = 311,190		
$ 10,029			$ 11,190		

            i) While Project S has the distinction of giving the company a higher internal rate of return, Project T is in fact preferable because it adds more to shareholder value.

3) **Varying rates of return.** A project's NPV can easily be determined using different desired rates of return for different periods. The IRR is limited to a single summary rate for the entire project.

4) **Multiple investments.** NPV amounts from different projects can be added, but IRR rates cannot. The IRR for the whole is not the sum of the IRRs for the parts.

6. **Comparing Cash Flow Patterns**

a. Often a decision maker must choose between two mutually exclusive projects, one whose inflows are higher in the early years but fall off drastically later and one whose inflows are steady throughout the project's life.

1) The higher a firm's hurdle rate, the more quickly a project must pay off.
2) Firms with low hurdle rates prefer a slow and steady payback.

b. EXAMPLE: Consider the net cash flows of these two projects:

	Initial	Year 1	Year 2	Year 3	Year 4
Project K	$(200,000)	$140,000	$100,000	–	–
Project L	(200,000)	65,000	65,000	$65,000	$65,000

1) A graphical representation of the two projects at various discount rates helps to illustrate the factors a decision maker must consider in such a situation.

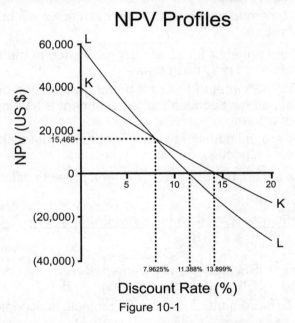

NPV Profiles

Figure 10-1

c. The NPV profile can be of great practical use to managers trying to make investment decisions. It gives the manager a clear insight into the following questions:

1) How sensitive is a project's profitability to changes in the discount rate?

a) At a hurdle rate of exactly 7.9625%, a decision maker is indifferent between the two projects. The net present value of both is $15,468 at that discount rate.

b) At hurdle rates below 7.9625%, the project whose inflows last longer into the future is the better investment (L).

c) At hurdle rates above 7.9625%, the project whose inflows are "front-loaded" is the better choice (K).

2) At what discount rates is an investment project still a profitable opportunity?

a) At any hurdle rate above 13.899%, Project K loses money. This is its IRR, i.e., the rate at which its NPV = $0 (Project L's is 11.388%).

7.   **Comparing NPV and IRR**

a.   The reinvestment rate becomes critical when choosing between the NPV and IRR methods. NPV assumes the cash flows from the investment can be reinvested at the project's discount rate, that is, the desired rate of return.

b.   The NPV and IRR methods give the same accept/reject decision if projects are independent. Independent projects have unrelated cash flows. Hence, all acceptable independent projects can be undertaken.

    1)   However, if projects are mutually exclusive, the NPV and IRR methods may rank them differently if

        a)   The cost of one project is greater than the cost of another.

        b)   The timing, amounts, and directions of cash flows differ among projects.

        c)   The projects have different useful lives.

        d)   The cost of capital or desired rate of return varies over the life of a project. The NPV can easily be determined using different desired rates of return for different periods. The IRR determines one rate for the project.

        e)   Multiple investments are involved in a project. NPV amounts are addable, but IRR rates are not. The IRR for the whole is not the sum of the IRRs for the parts.

    2)   The IRR method assumes that the cash flows will be reinvested at the internal rate of return.

        a)   If the project's funds are not reinvested at the IRR, the ranking calculations obtained may be in error.

        b)   The NPV method gives a better grasp of the problem in many decision situations because the reinvestment is assumed to be in the desired rate of return.

c.   NPV and IRR are the soundest investment rules from a shareholder wealth maximization perspective.

    1)   In some cases, NPV and IRR will rank projects differently.

        a)   EXAMPLE:

Project	Initial Cost	Year-End Cash Flow	IRR	NPV (k=10%)
A	$1,000	$1,200	20%	$91
B	$ 50	$ 100	100%	$41

           i)   IRR preference ordering: B, A
          ii)   NPV preference ordering: A, B

d.   If one of two or more mutually exclusive projects is accepted, the others must be rejected.

    1)   EXAMPLE: The decision to build a shopping mall on a piece of land eliminates placing an office building on the same land.

    2)   When choosing between mutually exclusive projects, the ranking differences between NPV and IRR become very important. In the example above, a firm using IRR would accept B and reject A. A firm using NPV would make exactly the opposite choice.

    e.   The problem can be seen more clearly using a net present value profile. The NPV profile is a plot of a project's NPV at different discount rates. The NPV is plotted on the vertical axis and the rate of return (k) on the horizontal axis.

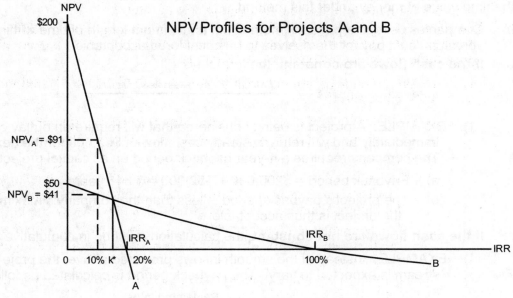

Figure 10-2

        1)   These profiles are downward sloping because a higher discount rate (desired rate of return) implies a lower NPV. The graph shows that, for all discount rates higher than k*, the firm should select project B over A because NPV_B is greater than NPV_A. This preference ordering also results from applying the IRR criterion. Below k*, however, NPV_A is greater than NPV_B, so A should be selected, even though IRR_B is greater than IRR_A.

        2)   These profiles show that IRR will always prefer B to A. NPV will prefer B to A only past some critical discount rate k*.

    f.   The manager concerned with shareholder wealth maximization should choose the project with the greatest NPV, not the largest IRR. IRR is a percentage measure of wealth, but NPV is an absolute measure. Shareholder well-being is also measured in absolute amounts.

        1)   The choice of NPV over IRR is easy to see with a simple example. Assume a choice between investing $1 and receiving $2 or investing $100,000 and receiving $150,000. The IRRs of the projects are 100% and 50%, respectively, which supports the first project. But assume instead that the interest rate is 10%. The NPVs of the projects are $.81 and $36,363, respectively. To select the first project because of the IRR criterion would lead to a return of $.81 instead of $36,363. Thus, the NPV is the better criterion when choosing between mutually exclusive projects.

Stop and review! You have completed the outline for this subunit. Study multiple-choice questions 8 through 15 beginning on page 415.

10.3 PAYBACK AND DISCOUNTED PAYBACK

1.   The **payback period** is the number of years required to return the original investment; that is, the time necessary for a new asset to pay for itself. Note that no accounting is made for the time value of money under this method.

   a.   Companies using the payback method set a maximum length of time within which projects must pay for themselves to be considered acceptable.

   b.   **If the cash flows are constant**, the formula is

$$Payback\ period = \frac{Initial\ net\ investment}{Annual\ expected\ cash\ flow}$$

   1)   EXAMPLE: A project is being considered that will require an outlay of $200,000 immediately and will return a steady cash flow of $52,000 for the next 4 years. The company requires a 4-year payback period on all capital projects.

   a)   Payback period = $200,000 ÷ $52,000 = 3.846 years

   b)   The project's payback period is less than the company's maximum, and the project is thus acceptable.

   c.   **If the cash flows are not constant**, the calculation must be in cumulative form.

   1)   EXAMPLE: Instead of the smooth inflows predicted above, the project's cash stream is expected to vary. The payback period is calculated as follows:

End of Year	Cash Inflow	Remaining Initial Investment
Year 0	$ 0	$200,000
Year 1	48,000	152,000
Year 2	54,000	98,000
Year 3	54,000	44,000
Year 4	42,000	2,000

   a)   At the end of 4 years, the original investment has still not been recovered, so the project is rejected.

   d.   The **strength** of the payback method is its simplicity.

   1)   The payback method is sometimes used for foreign investments if foreign expropriation of firm assets is feared. Even in these circumstances, it is most often used in addition to a more sophisticated method.

   2)   To some extent, the payback period measures risk. The longer the period, the more risky the investment.

   e.   The payback method has two significant **weaknesses**:

   1)   It disregards all cash inflows after the payback cutoff date. Applying a single cutoff date to every project results in accepting many marginal projects and rejecting good ones.

   2)   It disregards the time value of money. Weighting all cash inflows equally ignores the fact that money has a cost.

2. The **discounted payback method** is sometimes used to overcome the second of the drawback inherent in the basic payback method.

    a. The net cash flows in the denominator are discounted to calculate the period required to recover the initial investment.

Period	Cash Inflow	6% PV Factor	Discounted Cash Flow	Remaining Initial Investment
Initial Investment	$ 0	1.00000	$ 0	$200,000
Year 1	48,000	0.94340	45,283	154,717
Year 2	54,000	0.89000	48,060	106,657
Year 3	54,000	0.83962	45,339	61,318
Year 4	42,000	0.79209	33,268	28,050

        1) After 4 years, the project is much further from paying off than under the basic method.

        2) Clearly then, this is a **more conservative** technique than the traditional payback method.

    b. The discounted payback method's advantage is that it acknowledges the time value of money.

        1) Its drawbacks are that it loses the simplicity of the basic payback method and still ignores cash flows after the arbitrary cutoff date.

3. **Other Payback Methods**

    a. The **bailout payback method** incorporates the salvage value of the asset into the calculation. It measures the length of the payback period when the periodic cash inflows are combined with the salvage value.

    b. The **payback reciprocal** (1 ÷ payback) is sometimes used as an estimate of the internal rate of return.

    c. The **breakeven time** is the period required for the discounted cumulative cash inflows on a project to equal the discounted cumulative cash outflows (usually but not always the initial cost).

        1) Thus, it is the time necessary for the present value of the discounted cash flows to equal zero. This period begins at the outset of a project, not when the initial cash outflow occurs.

        2) An alternative that results in a longer breakeven time is to consider the time required for the present value of the cumulative cash inflows to equal the present value of all the expected future cash outflows.

Stop and review! You have completed the outline for this subunit. Study multiple-choice questions 16 through 21 beginning on page 417.

10.4 RANKING INVESTMENT PROJECTS

1. **Capital rationing** exists when a firm sets a limit on the amount of funds to be invested during a given period. In such situations, a firm cannot afford to undertake all profitable projects.

   a. Another way of stating this is that the firm cannot invest the entire amount needed to fund its theoretically optimal capital budget.

      1) Only those projects that will return the greatest NPV for the limited capital available in the internal capital market can be undertaken.

   b. Reasons for capital rationing include

      1) A lack of nonmonetary resources (e.g., managerial or technical personnel)
      2) A desire to control estimation bias (overly favorable projections of a project's cash flows)
      3) An unwillingness to issue new equity (e.g., because of its cost or a reluctance to reveal data in regulatory filings)

2. The **profitability index** (or excess present value index) is a method for ranking projects to ensure that limited resources are placed with the investments that will return the highest NPV.

$$Profitability\ index = \frac{NPV\ of\ future\ cash\ flows}{Net\ investment}$$

   a. EXAMPLE: A company has $200,000 to invest. It can therefore either invest in Project F below or in Projects G and H.

	Initial	Year 1	Year 2	Year 3	Year 4
Project F	$(200,000)	$140,000	$100,000	-	-
Project G	(88,950)	30,000	30,000	$30,000	$30,000
Project H	(88,440)	30,000	28,000	28,000	34,000

      1) Discounting each project at 6% results in the following:

	NPV	Divided by: Initial Investment	Equals: Profitability Index
Project F	$21,020	$200,000	0.105
Project G	15,000	88,950	0.169
Project H	15,218	88,440	0.172

      2) In an environment of capital rationing, the company can see that it should invest first in Project H, then in Project G, and, if new funding is found, last in Project F.

3. **Internal capital market** is a way of referring to the provision of funds by one division of a firm to another division. A division operating in a mature industry that generates a lot of cash can provide funding to another division that is in the cash-hungry development stage.

   a. An advantage is the avoidance of stock issue costs or interest costs on new debt.
   b. A disadvantage is that calling it a "market" is somewhat misleading. The dynamics of the process are more akin to centralized planning and budgeting than to the workings of a free marketplace.

4. **Linear programming** is a technique (now usually computerized) for optimizing resource allocations so as to select the most profitable or least costly way to use available resources.

   a. It involves optimizing an objective function subject to the net of constraint equations.
   b. For example, a linear programming application can maximize NPV for a group of projects in a capital rationing situation (expenditure constraint).

Stop and review! You have completed the outline for this subunit. Study multiple-choice questions 22 through 28 beginning on page 419.

10.5 COMPREHENSIVE EXAMPLES OF INVESTMENT DECISIONS

CMA candidates will be expected to have an understanding of how to calculate net present value (NPV) and internal rate of return (IRR) as well as be able to identify the criteria used to compare, evaluate, and recommend capital projects. You should also have an understanding of how these methods are affected by independent versus mutually exclusive projects. Pay close attention to the requirements to recognize whether the projects are independent.

The two comprehensive examples in this subunit demonstrate the calculations for NPV, IRR, payback period, and the profitability index. Review these examples and then practice answering questions and test yourself on how these problems will be presented on the exam in both multiple-choice and essay questions. If you receive an essay question with a scenario requiring you to provide any or all of these calculations, be prepared to show your work whether you are presented with a spreadsheet or must use the answer box utilizing the word processing tools.

1.   EXAMPLE: Hazman Company plans to replace an old piece of equipment that is obsolete and expected to be unreliable under the stress of daily operations. The equipment is fully depreciated, and no salvage value can be realized upon its disposal. One piece of equipment being considered as a replacement will provide an annual cash savings of $7,000 before income taxes and without regard to the effect of depreciation. The equipment costs $18,000 and has an estimated useful life of 5 years. No salvage value will be used for depreciation purposes because the equipment is expected to have no value at the end of 5 years.

Hazman uses the straight-line depreciation method on all equipment for both book and tax purposes. Hence, annual depreciation is $3,600. The company is subject to a 40% tax rate. Hazman's desired rate of return is 14%, so it will use the 14% column from a present value table.

Analysis of cash flows:

Annual cash savings	$ 7,000	
Less: income taxes (40%)	(2,800)	
After-tax cash savings		$4,200
Historical cost of equipment	$18,000	
Divided by: useful life	÷ 5	
Annual depreciation	$ 3,600	
Times: tax rate	× 40%	
Depreciation tax shield		1,440
Annual after-tax cash inflows		$5,640

a.   **Net present value** = (After-tax cash flows × Present value of an annuity)
         − Net investment
     = ($5,640 × 3.43) − $18,000
     = $19,345 − $18,000
     = $1,345

b. **Internal rate of return.** The goal is to find the discount rate that most nearly equals the net investment.

Net present value at 16% ($5,640 × 3.27)	$ 18,443
Net present value at 18% ($5,640 × 3.13)	(17,653)
Difference	$ 790

Net present value at 16%:	$ 18,443
Initial investment	(18,000)
Difference	$ 443

Estimated increment [($443 ÷ $790) × 2%]	1.1%
Rate used	16.0
Internal rate of return	17.1%

c. **Payback period** = Net investment ÷ After-tax cash flow
= $18,000 ÷ $5,640
= 3.19 years

d. **Profitability index** = NPV of future cash flows ÷ Net investment
= ($5,640 × 3.43) ÷ $18,000
= $19,345 ÷ $18,000
= 1.07

2. EXAMPLE: The management of Flesher Farms is trying to decide whether to buy a new team of mules at a cost of $1,000 or a new tractor at a cost of $10,000. They will perform the same job. But because the mules require more laborers, the annual return is only $250 of net cash inflows. The tractor will return $2,000 of net cash inflows per year. The mules have a working life of 8 years and the tractor 10 years. Neither investment is expected to have a salvage value at the end of its useful life. Flesher Farms' desired rate of return is 6%.

a. **Net Present Value**

	Mules	Tractor
Net cash inflows	$ 250	$ 2,000
Times: present value factor	6.210	7.360
Present value	$1,553	$14,720
Minus: initial investment	(1,000)	(10,000)
Net present value	$ 553	$ 4,720

b. **Internal Rate of Return**

1) Mules: Initial investment ÷ Net cash inflows = $1,000 ÷ $250 = 4

a) On the 8-year line, a factor of 4 indicates a rate of return of approximately 18.7%.

2) Tractor: Initial investment ÷ Net cash inflows = $10,000 ÷ $2,000 = 5

a) On the 10-year line, a factor of 5 indicates a rate of return of approximately 15.2%.

c. **Payback Period**

1) Mules: Initial investment ÷ Net cash inflows = $1,000 ÷ $250 = 4 years
2) Tractor: Initial investment ÷ Net cash inflows = $10,000 ÷ $2,000 = 5 years

d. **Profitability Index**

1) Mules: Present value of cash inflows ÷ Initial investment = $1,553 ÷ $1,000
= 1.553

2) Tractor: Present value of cash inflows ÷ Initial investment = $14,720 ÷ $10,000
= 1.472

e.   The mule investment has the higher IRR, the quicker payback, and the better profitability index.

1)   However, the tractor has the better net present value. The various methods thus give different answers to the investment question.

2)   Either investment will be profitable. Management may decide to let noneconomic factors influence the decision.

a)   For example, the mules will require the use of more laborers. If unemployment in the community is high, management might wish to achieve a social goal of providing more jobs.

b)   Alternatively, a labor shortage might convince management to buy the tractor to reduce labor worries.

Stop and review! You have completed the outline for this subunit. Study multiple-choice questions 29 and 30 on page 422.

10.6   RISK ANALYSIS AND REAL OPTIONS IN CAPITAL INVESTMENT

1.   **Risk analysis** attempts to measure the likelihood of the variability of future returns from the proposed investment. Risk cannot be ignored entirely, but mathematical approaches can be impossible because of a lack of critical information. The following approaches are frequently used to assess risk:

a.   **Informal method.** NPVs are calculated at the firm's desired rate of return, and the possible projects are individually reviewed. If the NPVs are relatively close for two mutually exclusive projects, the apparently less risky project is chosen.

b.   **Risk-adjusted discount rates.** This technique adjusts the rate of return upward as the investment becomes riskier. By increasing the discount rate from 10% to 15%, for example, the expected flow from the investment must be relatively larger or the increased discount rate will generate a negative NPV, and the proposed acquisition/ investment would be rejected. Although difficult to apply in extreme cases, this technique has much intuitive value.

c.   **Certainty equivalent adjustments.** This technique is directly drawn from the concept of utility theory. It forces the decision maker to specify at what point the firm is indifferent to the choice between a certain sum of money and the expected value of a risky sum. The technique is not frequently used because decision makers are not familiar with the concept.

d.   **Simulation analysis.** This method represents a refinement of standard profitability theory. The computer is used to generate many examples of results based upon various assumptions. Project simulation is frequently expensive. Unless a project is exceptionally large and expensive, full-scale simulation is usually not worthwhile.

e.   **Sensitivity analysis.** Forecasts of many calculated NPVs under various assumptions are compared to see how sensitive NPV is to changing conditions. Changing or relaxing the assumptions about a certain variable or group of variables may drastically alter the NPV. Thus, the asset may appear to be much riskier than was originally predicted. In summary, sensitivity analysis is simply an iterative process of recalculated returns based on changing assumptions.

f. The **Monte Carlo technique** is often used in simulation to generate the individual values for a random variable.

1) The performance of a quantitative model under uncertainty may be investigated by randomly selecting values for each of the variables in the model (based on the probability distribution of each variable) and then calculating the value of the solution. If this process is performed a large number of times, the distribution of results from the model will be obtained.

2) EXAMPLE: Suppose a new marketing model includes a factor for a competitor's introduction of a similar product within 1 year. Management estimates there is a 50% chance that this will happen. For each simulation, this factor must be determined, perhaps by flipping a coin or by putting two numbers in a hat and selecting one number. Random numbers between 0 and 1 could be generated. Numbers under one-half reveal a similar product; numbers over one-half reveal no similar product.

g. **The capital asset pricing model (CAPM).** This method is derived from the use of portfolio theory. It assumes that all assets are held in a portfolio. Each asset has variability in its returns. Some of this variability is caused by movements in the market as a whole, and some is specific to each firm. In a portfolio, each security's specific variability is eliminated through diversification, and the only relevant risk is the market component. The more sensitive an asset's rate of return is to changes in the market's rate of return, the riskier the asset. See item 10. in Study Unit 4, Subunit 1.

2. **Real (managerial or strategic) options** reduce the risk of an investment project. A real option is the flexibility to affect the amounts and risk of an investment project's cash flows, to determine its duration, or to postpone its implementation. A real option is ordinarily part of a major (strategic) project and involves real, not financial, assets.

a. The value of a real option is the difference between the project's net present value (NPV) without the option and its NPV with the option. Similarly, the worth of the project (true NPV) equals its NPV without the option plus the value of the option.

1) Moreover, the greater the availability of real options and the uncertainty related to their exercise, the greater the worth of the project. The reason is that increased uncertainty (greater variability of potential cash flows) enhances the likelihood that an option will be exercised and therefore increases its value.

2) Real options are not measurable with the same accuracy as financial options because the formulas applicable to the latter may not be appropriate for the former. Thus, other methods, e.g., decision tree analysis with recognition of probabilities and outcomes and simulations, are used in conjunction with discounted cash flow methods.

a) An approach that exploits the availability of derivatives and other securities that are sensitive to specific risks is the replicating portfolio. This method involves identifying securities trading in efficient public markets with cash flows that are the same as those of the real option. Accordingly, these securities must have cash flows and fair values that respond to the same risks as the real option. Given the known prices of the securities, the firm may calculate the value of the portfolio and, presumably, the real option with the same cash flows.

i) An advantage is that this method does not require estimating a discount rate for a discounted cash flow analysis.

ii) A disadvantage is the need to estimate the effects on cash flows of multiple sources of risk.

b.   Management accountants should be able to determine what real options are embedded in a project, to measure their value, and to offer advice about structuring a project to include such options. The following are among the types of real options:

1)   **Abandonment** of a project entails selling its assets or employing them in an alternative project. Thus, the abandonment value of a project may be approximated. Abandonment should occur when, as a result of an ongoing evaluation process, the entity determines that the abandonment value of a new or existing project exceeds the NPV of the project's future cash flows.

a)   The abandonment option enhances a project's worth by allowing the entity to profit from favorable conditions while allowing it to reduce its risk when conditions are unfavorable. Thus, a project should be designed so that it has multiple decision points and total commitment of resources to project completion is deferred.

2)   The option of making a **follow-up investment** (expansion) may be the factor that renders a project feasible. NPV for the initial project may be negative because its scale is inefficient. For example, a new factory may lack the capacity to be profitable even if it can sell all of its output. However, if demand is expected to increase, a subsequent investment to expand capacity to an efficient scale may be profitable.

3)   The follow-up investment option is based on the assumption that the expansion would not have been possible without the first-stage investment. Otherwise, the entity might have chosen the option to **wait and learn**, that is, to postpone the project (also called a timing option). Postponement permits the entity to undertake the project with greater information and preparation, but it forgoes earlier cash flows and the possible advantage of being first into the market.

4)   Other real options include the following:

a)   The flexibility option to vary inputs, for example, by switching fuels

b)   The capacity option to vary output, for example, to respond to economic conditions by raising or lowering output or by temporarily shutting down

c)   The option to enter a new geographical market, for example, in a market where NPV is apparently negative but the follow-up investment option is promising

d)   The new product option, for example, the opportunity to sell a complementary or a next-generation product even though the initial product is unprofitable

5)   Real options may be viewed as call options or put options. For example, an abandonment option is in essence a put option, and a wait-and-learn option is in essence a call option.

c.   Qualitative considerations. Although real options may often not be readily quantifiable, adding them to a project is always a consideration because doing so is frequently inexpensive and the potential risk reduction is great.

1)   The option is usually more valuable the later it is exercised, the more variable the underlying risk, or the higher the level of interest rates.

Stop and review! You have completed the outline for this subunit. Study multiple-choice questions 31 through 37 beginning on page 423.

10.7 CORE CONCEPTS

The Capital Budgeting Process

- Capital budgeting is the process of **planning and controlling** investments for **long-term projects**. By their nature, capital projects affect **multiple accounting periods** and will constrain the organizations financial planning well into the future. Once made, capital budgeting decisions tend to be relatively inflexible.
- **Stages** in the capital budgeting process are:
  - Identification and definition
  - Search for potential investments
  - Information acquisition
  - Selection
  - Financing
  - Implementation
  - Monitoring
- **Relevant cash flows** are a much more reliable guide when judging capital projects, since only they provide a true measure of a projects potential to affect shareholder value. The relevant cash flows can be divided into three categories:
  - **Net initial investment**
    - Purchase of new equipment
    - Initial working capital requirements
    - After-tax proceeds from disposal of old equipment
  - **Annual net cash flows**
    - After-tax cash collections from operations excluding depreciation effect
    - Tax savings from depreciation deductions
  - **Project termination cash flows**
    - After-tax proceeds from disposal of new equipment
    - Recovery of working capital (untaxed)

Discounted Cash Flow Analysis

- When analyzing capital projects, the management accountant must **discount the relevant cash flows** using the time value of money. A firm's goal is for its discount rate to be **as low as possible**. The lower the firm's discount rate, the lower the hurdle the company must clear to achieve profitability. For this reason, the rate is sometimes called the **hurdle rate**.
- The **net present value (NPV) method** for projecting the profitability of an investment expresses a project's return in dollar terms. NPV nets the expected cash streams related to a project (inflows and outflows), then discounts them at the hurdle rate, also called the desired rate of return.
  - If the NPV of a project is positive, the project is desirable because it has a higher rate of return than the company's desired rate.
- The **internal rate of return (IRR) method** expresses a project's return in percentage terms. The IRR of an investment is the discount rate at which the investment's NPV equals zero. In other words, it is the rate that makes the present value of the expected cash inflows equal the present value of the expected cash outflows.
  - If the IRR is higher than the company's desired rate of return, the investment is desirable.
- **IRR used in isolation** is seldom the best route to a sound capital budgeting decision.
  - When the **direction of the cash flows** changes, focusing simply on IRR can be misleading.

- Often a decision maker must choose between two mutually exclusive projects, one whose inflows are **higher in the early years** but fall off drastically later and one whose inflows are **steady throughout** the project's life.

  - The higher a firm's hurdle rate, the more quickly a project must pay off.
  - Firms with low hurdle rates prefer a slow and steady payback.

Payback and Discounted Payback

- The **payback period** is the number of years required to return the original investment; that is, the time necessary for a new asset to pay for itself. Note that no consideration is made for the time value of money under this method.

- Companies using the payback method set a maximum **length of time** within which projects must **pay for themselves** to be considered acceptable. If the cash flows are not constant, the calculation must be in cumulative form. If the cash flows are constant, this formula can be used:

  Payback period = Initial net investment ÷ Annual expected cash flow

- The strength of the payback method is its **simplicity**.

- The payback method has two significant **weaknesses**.

  - It disregards all cash inflows after the payback cutoff date. Applying a single cutoff date to every project results in accepting many marginal projects and rejecting good ones.

  - It disregards the time value of money. Weighting all cash inflows equally ignores the fact that money has a cost.

- The **discounted payback method** is sometimes used to overcome the second of the drawbacks inherent in the basic payback method. The net cash flows in the denominator are discounted to calculate the period required to recover the initial investment. Clearly, this is a more conservative technique than the traditional payback method.

- The **bailout payback method** incorporates the salvage value of the asset into the calculation. It measures the length of the payback period when the periodic cash inflows are combined with the salvage value.

- The **payback reciprocal** (1 ÷ payback) is sometimes used as an estimate of the internal rate of return.

- The **breakeven time** is the period required for the discounted cumulative cash inflows on a project to equal the discounted cumulative cash outflows (usually but not always the initial cost).

Ranking Investment Projects

- **Capital rationing** exists when a firm sets a limit on the amount of funds to be invested during a given period. In such situations, a firm cannot afford to undertake all profitable projects. **Only those projects** that will return the greatest NPV for the limited capital available in the internal capital market can be undertaken.

- The **profitability index** (or excess present value index) is a method for ranking projects to ensure that limited resources are placed with the investments that will return the highest NPV.

  Profitability index = NPV of future cash flows ÷ Net investment

- **Internal capital market** is a way of referring to the provision of funds by one division of a firm to another division. A division operating in a mature industry that generates a lot of cash can provide funding to another division that is in the cash-hungry development stage.

- **Linear programming** is a technique (now usually computerized) for optimizing resource allocations so as to select the most profitable or least costly way to use available resources. It involves optimizing an objective function subject to the net of constraint equations.

<u>Risk Analysis and Real Options in Capital Investment</u>

- **Risk analysis** attempts to measure the likelihood of the variability of future returns from the proposed investment. Several approaches can be used to **assess risk**.
- Under the **informal method**, NPVs are calculated at the firm's desired rate of return, and the possible projects are individually reviewed.
- With **risk-adjusted discount rates**, the rate of return is adjusted upward as the investment becomes riskier.
- The **certainty equivalent adjustments** technique forces the decision maker to specify at what point the firm is indifferent to the choice between a certain sum of money and the expected value of a risky sum.
- Under **sensitivity analysis**, forecasts of many calculated NPVs under various assumptions are compared to see how sensitive NPV is to changing conditions. Changing or relaxing the assumptions about a certain variable or group of variables may drastically alter the NPV.
- **Simulation analysis** represents a refinement of standard profitability theory. The computer is used to generate many examples of results based upon various assumptions. Project simulation is frequently expensive.
- The **capital asset pricing model** is derived from the use of portfolio theory. It assumes that the return on each asset in a portfolio has variability. In a portfolio, each security's specific variability is eliminated through diversification, and the only relevant risk is the market component.
- **Real (managerial or strategic) options** reduce the risk of an investment project. A real option is the flexibility to affect the amounts and risk of an investment project's cash flows, to determine its duration, or to postpone its implementation.
- The **value of a real option** is the difference between the project's NPV without the option and its NPV with the option.
- Real options are **not measurable with the same accuracy** as financial options because the formulas applicable to the latter may not be appropriate for the former.
- Management accountants should be able to **determine what real options are embedded** in a project, to measure their value, and to offer advice about structuring a project to include such options.
- The following are among the types of real options: abandonment, the option of making a follow-up investment, the option to wait and learn, the flexibility option to vary inputs, the capacity option to vary output, the option to enter a new geographical market, and the new product option.

QUESTIONS

10.1 The Capital Budgeting Process

1. Of the following decisions, capital budgeting techniques would **least** likely be used in evaluating the

    A. Acquisition of new aircraft by a cargo company.

    B. Design and implementation of a major advertising program.

    C. Trade for a star quarterback by a football team.

    D. Adoption of a new method of allocating nontraceable costs to product lines.

Answer (D) is correct. *(CMA, adapted)*
REQUIRED: The decision least likely to be evaluated using capital budgeting techniques.
DISCUSSION: Capital budgeting is the process of planning expenditures for investments on which the returns are expected to occur over a period of more than 1 year. Thus, capital budgeting concerns the acquisition or disposal of long-term assets and the financing ramifications of such decisions. The adoption of a new method of allocating nontraceable costs to product lines has no effect on a company's cash flows, does not concern the acquisition of long-term assets, and is not concerned with financing. Hence, capital budgeting is irrelevant to such a decision.
Answer (A) is incorrect. A new aircraft represents a long-term investment in a capital good. Answer (B) is incorrect. A major advertising program is a high cost investment with long-term effects. Answer (C) is incorrect. A star quarterback is a costly asset who is expected to have a substantial effect on the team's long-term profitability.

2. In equipment-replacement decisions, which one of the following does **not** affect the decision-making process?

    A. Current disposal price of the old equipment.

    B. Operating costs of the old equipment.

    C. Original fair market value of the old equipment.

    D. Cost of the new equipment.

Answer (C) is correct. *(CMA, adapted)*
REQUIRED: The irrelevant factor when making an equipment replacement decision.
DISCUSSION: All relevant costs should be considered when evaluating an equipment-replacement decision. These include the cost of the new equipment, the disposal price of the old equipment, and the operating costs of the old equipment versus the operating costs of the new equipment. The original cost or fair market value of the old equipment is a sunk cost and is irrelevant to future decisions.

3. The term that refers to costs incurred in the past that are **not** relevant to a future decision is

    A. Discretionary cost.

    B. Full absorption cost.

    C. Underallocated indirect cost.

    D. Sunk cost.

Answer (D) is correct. *(CMA, adapted)*
REQUIRED: The past costs not relevant to a future decision.
DISCUSSION: A sunk cost cannot be avoided because it represents an expenditure that has already been made or an irrevocable decision to incur the cost.
Answer (A) is incorrect. A discretionary cost is characterized by uncertainty about the input-output relationship; advertising and research are examples. Answer (B) is incorrect. Full absorption costing includes in production costs materials, labor, and both fixed and variable overhead. Answer (C) is incorrect. Underallocated indirect cost is a cost that has not yet been charged to production.

4. A depreciation tax shield is

    A. An after-tax cash outflow.

    B. A reduction in income taxes.

    C. The cash provided by recording depreciation.

    D. The expense caused by depreciation.

Answer (B) is correct. *(CMA, adapted)*
REQUIRED: The definition of a depreciation tax shield.
DISCUSSION: A tax shield is something that will protect income against taxation. Thus, a depreciation tax shield is a reduction in income taxes due to a company's being allowed to deduct depreciation against otherwise taxable income.
Answer (A) is incorrect. A tax shield is not a cash flow, but a means of reducing outflows for income taxes. Answer (C) is incorrect. Cash is not provided by recording depreciation; the shield is a result of deducting depreciation from taxable revenues. Answer (D) is incorrect. Depreciation is recognized as an expense even if it has no tax benefit.

Questions 5 through 7 are based on the following information. The Moore Corporation is considering the acquisition of a new machine. The machine can be purchased for $90,000; it will cost $6,000 to transport to Moore's plant and $9,000 to install. It is estimated that the machine will last 10 years, and it is expected to have an estimated salvage value of $5,000. Over its 10-year life, the machine is expected to produce 2,000 units per year, each with a selling price of $500 and combined material and labor costs of $450 per unit. Federal tax regulations permit machines of this type to be depreciated using the straight-line method over 5 years with no estimated salvage value. Moore has a marginal tax rate of 40%.

5. What is the net cash outflow at the beginning of the first year that Moore Corporation should use in a capital budgeting analysis?

    A. $(85,000)

    B. $(90,000)

    C. $(96,000)

    D. $(105,000)

Answer (D) is correct. *(CMA, adapted)*
    REQUIRED: The initial net cash outflow that should be used in a capital budgeting analysis.
    DISCUSSION: Initially, the company must invest $105,000 in the machine, consisting of the invoice price of $90,000, the delivery costs of $6,000, and the installation costs of $9,000.
    Answer (A) is incorrect. The amount of $(85,000) erroneously includes salvage value but ignores delivery and installation costs. Answer (B) is incorrect. The amount of $(90,000) ignores the outlays needed for delivery and installation costs, both of which are an integral part of preparing the new asset for use. Answer (C) is incorrect. The amount of $(96,000) fails to include installation costs in the total.

6. What is the net cash flow for the third year that Moore Corporation should use in a capital budgeting analysis?

    A. $68,400

    B. $68,000

    C. $64,200

    D. $79,000

Answer (A) is correct. *(CMA, adapted)*
    REQUIRED: The net cash flows for the third year that would be used in a capital budgeting analysis.
    DISCUSSION: The company will receive net cash inflows of $50 per unit ($500 selling price – $450 of variable costs), or a total of $100,000 per year. This amount will be subject to taxation, but, for the first 5 years, there will be a depreciation deduction of $21,000 per year ($105,000 cost divided by 5 years). Therefore, deducting the $21,000 of depreciation expense from the $100,000 of contribution margin will result in taxable income of $79,000. After income taxes of $31,600 ($79,000 × 40%), the net cash flow in the third year is $68,400 ($100,000 – $31,600).
    Answer (B) is incorrect. The amount of $68,000 deducts salvage value when calculating depreciation expense, which is not required by the tax law. Answer (C) is incorrect. The amount of $64,200 assumes depreciation is deducted for tax purposes over 10 years rather than 5 years. Answer (D) is incorrect. The amount of $79,000 is taxable income.

7. What is the net cash flow for the tenth year of the project that Moore Corporation should use in a capital budgeting analysis?

    A. $100,000

    B. $81,000

    C. $68,400

    D. $63,000

Answer (D) is correct. *(CMA, adapted)*
    REQUIRED: The net cash flow for the tenth year of the project that would be used in a capital budgeting analysis.
    DISCUSSION: The company will receive net cash inflows of $50 per unit ($500 selling price – $450 of variable costs), or a total of $100,000 per year. This amount will be subject to taxation, as will the $5,000 gain on sale of the investment, bringing taxable income to $105,000. No depreciation will be deducted in the tenth year because the asset was fully depreciated after 5 years. Because the asset was fully depreciated (book value was zero), the $5,000 salvage value received would be fully taxable. After income taxes of $42,000 ($105,000 × 40%), the net cash flow in the tenth year is $63,000 ($105,000 – $42,000).
    Answer (A) is incorrect. The amount of $100,000 overlooks the salvage proceeds and the taxes to be paid. Answer (B) is incorrect. The amount of $81,000 miscalculates income taxes. Answer (C) is incorrect. The amount of $68,400 assumes that depreciation is deducted; it also overlooks the receipt of the salvage proceeds.

10.2 Discounted Cash Flow Analysis

8. The net present value (NPV) method of investment project analysis assumes that the project's cash flows are reinvested at the

- A. Computed internal rate of return.
- B. Risk-free interest rate.
- C. Discount rate used in the NPV calculation.
- D. Firm's accounting rate of return.

Answer (C) is correct. *(CMA, adapted)*
REQUIRED: The rate at which the NPV method assumes early cash inflows are reinvested.
DISCUSSION: The NPV method is used when the discount rate is specified. It assumes that cash flows from the investment can be reinvested at the particular project's discount rate.
Answer (A) is incorrect. The internal rate of return method assumes that cash flows are reinvested at the internal rate of return. Answer (B) is incorrect. The NPV method assumes that cash flows are reinvested at the NPV discount rate. Answer (D) is incorrect. The NPV method assumes that cash flows are reinvested at the NPV discount rate.

9. The rankings of mutually exclusive investments determined using the internal rate of return method (IRR) and the net present value method (NPV) may be different when

- A. The lives of the multiple projects are equal and the size of the required investments are equal.
- B. The required rate of return equals the IRR of each project.
- C. The required rate of return is higher than the IRR of each project.
- D. Multiple projects have unequal lives and the size of the investment for each project is different.

Answer (D) is correct. *(CMA, adapted)*
REQUIRED: The circumstances in which IRR and NPV rankings of mutually exclusive projects may differ.
DISCUSSION: The two methods ordinarily yield the same results, but differences can occur when the duration of the projects and the initial investments differ. The reason is that the IRR method assumes cash inflows from the early years will be reinvested at the internal rate of return. The NPV method assumes that early cash inflows are reinvested at the NPV discount rate.
Answer (A) is incorrect. The two methods will give the same results if the lives and required investments are the same. Answer (B) is incorrect. If the required rate of return equals the IRR, the two methods will yield the same decision. Answer (C) is incorrect. If the required rate of return is higher than the IRR, both methods will yield a decision not to acquire the investment.

10. The internal rate of return for a project can be determined

- A. If the internal rate of return is greater than the firm's cost of capital.
- B. Only if the project cash flows are constant.
- C. By finding the discount rate that yields a net present value of zero for the project.
- D. By subtracting the firm's cost of capital from the project's profitability index.

Answer (C) is correct. *(CMA, adapted)*
REQUIRED: The means of finding a project's internal rate of return (IRR).
DISCUSSION: The IRR is a capital budgeting technique that calculates the interest rate that yields a net present value equal to $0. It is the interest rate that will discount the future cash flows to an amount equal to the initial cost of the project. Thus, the higher the IRR, the more favorable the ranking of the project.
Answer (A) is incorrect. The cost of capital is not used in the calculation of the IRR. Answer (B) is incorrect. The IRR can be determined regardless of the constancy of the cash flows. However, it is more difficult to calculate when cash flows are not constant because a trial-and-error approach must be used. Answer (D) is incorrect. There is no relationship between IRR and the profitability index.

11. Brown and Company uses the internal rate of return (IRR) method to evaluate capital projects. Brown is considering four independent projects with the following IRRs:

Project	IRR
I	10%
II	12%
III	14%
IV	15%

Brown's cost of capital is 13%. Which one of the following project options should Brown accept based on IRR?

- A. Projects I and II only.
- B. Projects III and IV only.
- C. Project IV only.
- D. Projects I, II, III and IV.

Answer (B) is correct. *(CMA, adapted)*
REQUIRED: The acceptable projects given a certain cost of capital.
DISCUSSION: When sufficient funds are available, any capital project whose internal rate of return (IRR) exceeds the company's cost of capital should be accepted.
Answer (A) is incorrect. Projects I and II have rates of return lower than the company's cost of capital. Answer (C) is incorrect. The rate of return for Project III also exceeds the company's cost of capital. Answer (D) is incorrect. Projects I and II should be rejected; their rates of return are lower than the company's cost of capital.

Questions 12 through 15 are based on the following information.

The following data pertain to a 4-year project being considered by Metro Industries:

- A depreciable asset that costs $1,200,000 will be acquired on January 1. The asset, which is expected to have a $200,000 salvage value at the end of 4 years, qualifies as 3-year property under the Modified Accelerated Cost Recovery System (MACRS).

- The new asset will replace an existing asset that has a tax basis of $150,000 and can be sold on the same January 1 for $180,000.

- The project is expected to provide added annual sales of 30,000 units at $20. Additional cash operating costs are: variable, $12 per unit; fixed, $90,000 per year.

- A $50,000 working capital investment that is fully recoverable at the end of the fourth year is required.

Metro is subject to a 40% income tax rate and rounds all computations to the nearest dollar. Assume that any gain or loss affects the taxes paid at the end of the year in which it occurred. The company uses the net present value method to analyze investments and will employ the following factors and rates.

Period	Present Value of $1 at 12%	Present Value of $1 Annuity at 12%	MACRS
1	0.89	0.89	33%
2	0.80	1.69	45
3	0.71	2.40	15
4	0.64	3.04	7

12. The discounted cash flow for the fourth year MACRS depreciation on the new asset is

A. $0

B. $17,920

C. $21,504

D. $26,880

Answer (C) is correct. *(CMA, adapted)*
REQUIRED: The discounted cash flow for the fourth year MACRS depreciation deduction on the new asset.
DISCUSSION: Tax law allows taxpayers to ignore salvage value when calculating depreciation under MACRS. Thus, the depreciation deduction is 7% of the initial $1,200,000 cost, or $84,000. At a 40% tax rate, the deduction will save the company $33,600 in taxes in the fourth year. The present value of this savings is $21,504 ($33,600 × 0.64 present value of $1 at 12% for four periods).
Answer (A) is incorrect. A tax savings will result in the fourth year from the MACRS deduction. Answer (B) is incorrect. The amount of $17,920 is based on a depreciation calculation in which salvage value is subtracted from the initial cost. Answer (D) is incorrect. The appropriate discount factor for the fourth period is 0.64, not 0.80.

13. The discounted, net-of-tax amount that relates to disposal of the existing asset is

A. $168,000

B. $169,320

C. $180,000

D. $190,680

Answer (B) is correct. *(CMA, adapted)*
REQUIRED: The discounted, net-of-tax amount relating to the disposal of the existing asset.
DISCUSSION: The cash inflow from the existing asset is $180,000, but that amount is subject to tax on the $30,000 gain ($180,000 – $150,000 tax basis). The tax on the gain is $12,000 ($30,000 × 40%). Because the tax will not be paid until year end, the discounted value is $10,680 ($12,000 × .89 PV of $1 at 12% for one period). Thus, the net-of-tax inflow is $169,320 ($180,000 – $10,680). NOTE: This asset was probably a Section 1231 asset, and any gain on sale qualifies for the special capital gain tax rates. Had the problem not stipulated a 40% tax rate, the capital gains rate would be used. An answer based on that rate is not among the options.
Answer (A) is incorrect. The amount of $168,000 fails to discount the outflow for taxes. Answer (C) is incorrect. The amount of $180,000 ignores the impact of income taxes. Answer (D) is incorrect. The discounted present value of the income taxes is an outflow and is deducted from the inflow from the sale of the asset.

14. The expected incremental sales will provide a discounted, net-of-tax contribution margin over 4 years of

    A. $57,600

    B. $92,160

    C. $273,600

    D. $437,760

Answer (D) is correct. *(CMA, adapted)*
    REQUIRED: The expected net-of-tax contribution margin over 4 years.
    DISCUSSION: Additional annual sales are 30,000 units at $20 per unit. If variable costs are expected to be $12 per unit, the unit contribution margin is $8, and the total before-tax annual contribution margin is $240,000 (30,000 units × $8). The after-tax total annual contribution margin is $144,000 [$240,000 × (1.0 − .4)]. This annual increase in the contribution margin should be treated as an annuity. Thus, its present value is $437,760 ($144,000 × 3.04 PV of an annuity of $1 at 12% for four periods).
    Answer (A) is incorrect. The amount of $57,600 multiplies the annual increase in contribution margin by the tax rate instead of the PV factor. Answer (B) is incorrect. The amount of $92,160 is based on only 1 year's results, not 4. Answer (C) is incorrect. The amount of $273,600 improperly includes fixed costs in the calculation of the contribution margin.

15. The overall discounted-cash-flow impact of the working capital investment on Metro's project is

    A. $(2,800)

    B. $(18,000)

    C. $(50,000)

    D. $(59,200)

Answer (B) is correct. *(CMA, adapted)*
    REQUIRED: The overall discounted-cash-flow impact of the working capital investment.
    DISCUSSION: The working capital investment is treated as a $50,000 outflow at the beginning of the project and a $50,000 inflow at the end of 4 years. Accordingly, the present value of the inflow after 4 years should be subtracted from the initial $50,000 outlay. The overall discounted-cash-flow impact of the working capital investment is $18,000 [$50,000 − ($50,000 × .64 PV of $1 at 12% for four periods)].
    Answer (A) is incorrect. The firm will have its working capital tied up for 4 years, which results in a cost of $18,000 at 12% interest. Answer (C) is incorrect. The working capital investment is recovered at the end of the fourth year. Hence, the working capital cost of the project is the difference between $50,000 and the present value of $50,000 in 4 years. Answer (D) is incorrect. The answer cannot exceed $50,000, which is the amount of the cash outflow.

10.3 Payback and Discounted Payback

16. Jasper Company has a payback goal of 3 years on new equipment acquisitions. A new sorter is being evaluated that costs $450,000 and has a 5-year life. Straight-line depreciation will be used; no salvage is anticipated. Jasper is subject to a 40% income tax rate. To meet the company's payback goal, the sorter must generate reductions in annual cash operating costs of

    A. $60,000

    B. $100,000

    C. $150,000

    D. $190,000

Answer (D) is correct. *(CMA, adapted)*
    REQUIRED: The cash savings that must be generated to achieve a targeted payback period.
    DISCUSSION: Given a periodic constant cash flow, the payback period is calculated by dividing cost by the annual cash inflows, or cash savings. To achieve a payback period of 3 years, the annual increment in net cash inflow generated by the investment must be $150,000 ($450,000 ÷ 3-year targeted payback period). This amount equals the total reduction in cash operating costs minus related taxes. Depreciation is $90,000 ($450,000 ÷ 5 years). Because depreciation is a noncash deductible expense, it shields $90,000 of the cash savings from taxation. Accordingly, $60,000 ($150,000 − $90,000) of the additional net cash inflow must come from after-tax net income. At a 40% tax rate, $60,000 of after-tax income equals $100,000 ($60,000 ÷ 60%) of pre-tax income from cost savings, and the outflow for taxes is $40,000. Thus, the annual reduction in cash operating costs required is $190,000 ($150,000 additional net cash inflow required + $40,000 tax outflow).
    Answer (A) is incorrect. The amount of $60,000 is after-tax net income from the cost savings. Answer (B) is incorrect. The amount of $100,000 is the pre-tax income from the cost savings. Answer (C) is incorrect. The amount of $150,000 ignores the impact of depreciation and income taxes.

17. The capital budgeting model that is generally considered the best model for long-range decision making is the

  A. Payback model.

  B. Accounting rate of return model.

  C. Unadjusted rate of return model.

  D. Discounted cash flow model.

Answer (D) is correct. *(CMA, adapted)*
  REQUIRED: The best capital budgeting model for long-range decision making.
  DISCUSSION: The capital budgeting methods that are generally considered the best for long-range decision making are the internal rate of return and net present value methods. These are both discounted cash flow methods.
  Answer (A) is incorrect. The payback method gives no consideration to the time value of money or to returns after the payback period. Answer (B) is incorrect. The accounting rate of return does not consider the time value of money. Answer (C) is incorrect. The unadjusted rate of return does not consider the time value of money.

18. A characteristic of the payback method (before taxes) is that it

  A. Incorporates the time value of money.

  B. Neglects total project profitability.

  C. Uses accrual accounting inflows in the numerator of the calculation.

  D. Uses the estimated expected life of the asset in the denominator of the calculation.

Answer (B) is correct. *(CMA, adapted)*
  REQUIRED: The characteristic of the payback method.
  DISCUSSION: The payback method calculates the number of years required to complete the return of the original investment. This measure is computed by dividing the net investment required by the average expected cash flow to be generated, resulting in the number of years required to recover the original investment. Payback is easy to calculate but has two principal problems: it ignores the time value of money, and it gives no consideration to returns after the payback period. Thus, it ignores total project profitability.
  Answer (A) is incorrect. The payback method does not incorporate the time value of money. Answer (C) is incorrect. The payback method uses the net investment in the numerator of the calculation. Answer (D) is incorrect. Payback uses the net annual cash inflows in the denominator of the calculation.

19. The length of time required to recover the initial cash outlay of a capital project is determined by using the

  A. Discounted cash flow method.

  B. Payback method.

  C. Weighted net present value method.

  D. Net present value method.

Answer (B) is correct. *(CMA, adapted)*
  REQUIRED: The method of determining the time required to recover the initial cash outlay of a capital project.
  DISCUSSION: The payback method measures the number of years required to complete the return of the original investment. This measure is computed by dividing the net investment by the average expected cash inflows to be generated, resulting in the number of years required to recover the original investment. The payback method gives no consideration to the time value of money, and there is no consideration of returns after the payback period.
  Answer (A) is incorrect. The discounted cash flow method computes a rate of return. Answer (C) is incorrect. The net present value method is based on discounted cash flows; the length of time to recover an investment is not the result. Answer (D) is incorrect. The net present value method is based on discounted cash flows; the length of time to recover an investment is not the result.

20. Which one of the following statements about the payback method of investment analysis is correct? The payback method

  A. Does not consider the time value of money.

  B. Considers cash flows after the payback has been reached.

  C. Uses discounted cash flow techniques.

  D. Generally leads to the same decision as other methods for long-term projects.

Answer (A) is correct. *(CMA, adapted)*
  REQUIRED: The true statement about the payback method of investment analysis.
  DISCUSSION: The payback method calculates the amount of time required to complete the return of the original investment, i.e., the time it takes for a new asset to pay for itself. Although the payback method is easy to calculate, it has inherent problems. The time value of money and returns after the payback period are not considered.
  Answer (B) is incorrect. The payback method ignores cash flows after payback. Answer (C) is incorrect. The payback method does not use discounted cash flow techniques. Answer (D) is incorrect. The payback method may lead to different decisions.

21. The payback reciprocal can be used to approximate a project's

    A. Profitability index.

    B. Net present value.

    C. Accounting rate of return if the cash flow pattern is relatively stable.

    D. Internal rate of return if the cash flow pattern is relatively stable.

Answer (D) is correct. *(CMA, adapted)*
    REQUIRED: The item that can be approximated by a project's payback reciprocal.
    DISCUSSION: The payback reciprocal (1 ÷ payback) has been shown to approximate the internal rate of return (IRR) when the periodic cash flows are equal and the life of the project is at least twice the payback period.
    Answer (A) is incorrect. The payback reciprocal is not related to the profitability index. Answer (B) is incorrect. The payback reciprocal approximates the IRR, which is the rate at which the NPV is $0. Answer (C) is incorrect. The accounting rate of return is based on accrual-income based figures, not on discounted cash flows.

10.4 Ranking Investment Projects

22. The profitability index (present value index)

    A. Represents the ratio of the discounted net cash outflows to cash inflows.

    B. Is the relationship between the net discounted cash inflows less the discounted cash outflows divided by the discounted cash outflows.

    C. Is calculated by dividing the discounted profits by the cash outflows.

    D. Is the ratio of the discounted net cash inflows to discounted cash outflows.

Answer (D) is correct. *(CMA, adapted)*
    REQUIRED: The true statement about the profitability index.
    DISCUSSION: The profitability index, also known as the excess present value index, is the ratio of the present value of future net cash inflows to the initial net cash investment (discounted cash outflows). This tool is a variation of the NPV method that facilitates comparison of different-sized investments.
    Answer (A) is incorrect. The cash inflows are also discounted in the profitability index. Answer (B) is incorrect. The numerator is the discounted net cash inflows. Answer (C) is incorrect. The profitability index is based on cash flows, not profits.

23. The recommended technique for evaluating projects when capital is rationed and there are no mutually exclusive projects from which to choose is to rank the projects by

    A. Accounting rate of return.

    B. Payback.

    C. Internal rate of return.

    D. Profitability index.

Answer (D) is correct. *(CMA, adapted)*
    REQUIRED: The best ranking method when capital is rationed and projects are not mutually exclusive.
    DISCUSSION: The profitability index (PI) is often used to decide among investment alternatives when more than one is acceptable. The profitability index is the ratio of the present value of future net cash inflows to the initial net cash investment. The PI, although a variation of the net present value method, facilitates comparison of different-sized investments.
    Answer (A) is incorrect. The accounting rate of return is a poor technique. It ignores the time value of money. Answer (B) is incorrect. The payback method ignores the time value of money and long-term profitability. Answer (C) is incorrect. The internal rate of return is not effective when alternative investments have different lives.

24. The technique that reflects the time value of money and is calculated by dividing the present value of the future net after-tax cash inflows that have been discounted at the desired cost of capital by the initial cash outlay for the investment is called the

    A. Capital rationing method.

    B. Average rate of return method.

    C. Profitability index method.

    D. Accounting rate of return method.

Answer (C) is correct. *(CMA, adapted)*
    REQUIRED: The technique that divides the present value of future net cash inflows by the initial cash outlay.
    DISCUSSION: The profitability index is another term for the excess present value index. It measures the ratio of the present value of future net cash inflows to the original investment. In organizations with unlimited capital funds, this index will produce no conflicts in the decision process. If capital rationing is necessary, the index will be an insufficient determinant. The capital available as well as the dollar amount of the net present value must both be considered.
    Answer (A) is incorrect. Capital rationing is not a technique but rather a condition that characterizes capital budgeting when insufficient capital is available to finance all profitable investment opportunities. Answer (B) is incorrect. The average rate of return method does not divide the future cash flows by the cost of the investment. Answer (D) is incorrect. The accounting rate of return does not recognize the time value of money.

Questions 25 and 26 are based on the following information. Mercken Industries is contemplating four projects, Project P, Project Q, Project R, and Project S. The capital costs and estimated after-tax net cash flows of each mutually exclusive project are listed below. Mercken's desired after-tax opportunity cost is 12%, and the company has a capital budget for the year of $450,000. Idle funds cannot be reinvested at greater than 12%.

	Project P	Project Q	Project R	Project S
Initial cost	$200,000	$235,000	$190,000	$210,000
Annual cash flows				
Year 1	$ 93,000	$ 90,000	$ 45,000	$ 40,000
Year 2	93,000	85,000	55,000	50,000
Year 3	93,000	75,000	65,000	60,000
Year 4	0	55,000	70,000	65,000
Year 5	0	50,000	75,000	75,000
Net present value	$ 23,370	$ 29,827	$ 27,333	$ (7,854)
Internal rate of return	18.7%	17.6%	17.2%	10.6%
Excess present value index	1.12	1.13	1.14	0.96

25. During this year, Mercken will choose

A. Projects P, Q, and R.

B. Projects P, Q, R, and S.

C. Projects Q and R.

D. Projects P and Q.

Answer (C) is correct. *(CMA, adapted)*
REQUIRED: The investments that will be chosen given capital rationing.
DISCUSSION: Only two of the projects can be selected because three would require more than $450,000 of capital. Project S can immediately be dismissed because it has a negative net present value (NPV). Using the NPV and the profitability index methods, the best investments appear to be Q and R. The internal rate of return (IRR) method indicates that P is preferable to R. However, it assumes reinvestment of funds during Years 4 and 5 at the IRR (18.7%). Given that reinvestment will be at a rate of at most 12%, the IRR decision criterion appears to be unsound in this situation.
Answer (A) is incorrect. The amount of capital available limits the company to two projects. Answer (B) is incorrect. The amount of capital available limits the company to two projects. Answer (D) is incorrect. The profitability index and NPV are higher for R than P.

26. If Mercken is able to accept only one project, the company would choose

A. Project P.

B. Project Q because it has the highest net present value.

C. Project P because it has the highest internal rate of return.

D. Project P because it has the shortest payback period.

Answer (B) is correct. *(CMA, adapted)*
REQUIRED: The project chosen if only one can be undertaken.
DISCUSSION: Because unused funds cannot be invested at a rate greater than 12%, the company should select the investment with the highest net present value. Project Q is preferable to R because its return on the incremental $45,000 invested ($235,000 cost of Q – $190,000 cost of R) is greater than 12%.
Answer (A) is incorrect. Project P has a life of only 3 years, and the high IRR would be earned only for that period and could not be reinvested at that rate in Years 4 and 5. Also, P's NPV is lower than that of Q. Answer (C) is incorrect. Although P's IRR of 18.7% for 3 years exceeds Q's (17.6% for 5 years), the funds from P cannot be invested in Years 4 and 5 at greater than 12%. Answer (D) is incorrect. The payback period is a poor means of ranking projects. It ignores both reinvestment rates and the time value of money.

27. Woods, Inc., is considering four independent investment proposals. Woods has $3 million available for investment during the present period. The investment outlay for each project and its projected net present value (NPV) is presented below.

Project	Investment Cost	NPV
I	$ 500,000	$ 40,000
II	900,000	120,000
III	1,200,000	180,000
IV	1,600,000	150,000

Which of the following project options should be recommended to Woods' management?

    A. Projects I, II, and III only.

    B. Projects I, II, and IV only.

    C. Projects II, III, and IV only.

    D. Projects III and IV only.

Answer (A) is correct. *(CMA, adapted)*
REQUIRED: The acceptable capital projects given net present value.
DISCUSSION: Capital rationing exists when a firm sets a limit on the amount of funds to be invested during a given period. In such situations, a firm cannot afford to undertake all profitable projects. The profitability index (or excess present value index) is a method for ranking projects to ensure that limited resources are placed with the investments that will return the highest net present value (NPV).

$$Profitability\ index = \frac{NPV\ of\ future\ cash\ flows}{Net\ investment}$$

The indexes for Woods' potential projects can thus be calculated as follows:

Project	Investment Cost	Net Present Value	Profitability Index
I	$ 500,000	$ 40,000	0.080
II	900,000	120,000	0.133
III	1,200,000	180,000	0.150
IV	1,600,000	150,000	0.094

Ranked in order of desirability, they are III, II, IV, and I. Since only $3 million is available for funding, only III, II, and I will be selected.
    Answer (B) is incorrect. Project III is more desirable than Project IV. Answer (C) is incorrect. While Project IV is more desirable than Project I, insufficient funding is available to engage Project IV. Answer (D) is incorrect. Projects I and II are also desirable and sufficient funding is available.

28. Capital budgeting methods are often divided into two classifications: project screening and project ranking. Which one of the following is considered a ranking method rather than a screening method?

    A. Net present value.

    B. Time-adjusted rate of return.

    C. Profitability index.

    D. Accounting rate of return.

Answer (C) is correct. *(CMA, adapted)*
REQUIRED: The method considered a project ranking rather than a screening method.
DISCUSSION: The profitability index is the ratio of the present value of future net cash inflows to the initial cash investment. This variation of the net present value method facilitates comparison of different-sized investments. Were it not for this comparison feature, the profitability index would be no better than the net present value method. Thus, it is the comparison, or ranking, advantage that makes the profitability index different from the other capital budgeting tools.
    Answer (A) is incorrect. The net present value (NPV > 0) is a capital budgeting tool that screens investments; i.e., the investment must meet a certain standard to be acceptable. Answer (B) is incorrect. The time-adjusted rate of return is a capital budgeting tool that screens investments; i.e., the investment must meet a certain standard (rate of return) to be acceptable. Answer (D) is incorrect. The accounting rate of return is a capital budgeting tool that screens investments; i.e., the investment must meet a certain standard (rate of return) to be acceptable.

10.5 Comprehensive Examples of Investment Decisions

Questions 29 and 30 are based on the following information. McLean, Inc., is considering the purchase of a new machine that will cost $150,000. The machine has an estimated useful life of 3 years. Assume that 30% of the depreciable base will be depreciated in the first year, 40% in the second year, and 30% in the third year. The new machine will have a $10,000 resale value at the end of its estimated useful life. The machine is expected to save the company $85,000 per year in operating expenses. McLean uses a 40% estimated income tax rate and a 16% hurdle rate to evaluate capital projects.

Discount rates for a 16% rate are as follows:

	Present Value of $1	Present Value of an Ordinary Annuity of $1
Year 1	.862	.862
Year 2	.743	1.605
Year 3	.641	2.246

29. What is the net present value of this project?

A. $15,842

B. $13,278

C. $40,910

D. $9,432

Answer (B) is correct. *(CMA, adapted)*
REQUIRED: The NPV of the new machine.
DISCUSSION: The NPV method discounts the expected cash flows from a project using the required rate of return. A project is acceptable if its NPV is positive. The future cash inflows consist of $85,000 of saved expenses per year minus income taxes after deducting depreciation. In the first year, the after-tax cash inflow is $85,000 minus taxes of $16,000 {[$85,000 – ($150,000 × 30%) depreciation] × 40%}, or $69,000. In the second year, the after-tax cash inflow is $85,000 minus taxes of $10,000 {[$85,000 – ($150,000 × 40%) depreciation] × 40%}, or $75,000. In the third year, the after-tax cash inflow (excluding salvage value) is again $69,000. Also in the third year, the after-tax cash inflow from the salvage value is $6,000 [$10,000 × (1 – 40%)]. Accordingly, the total for the third year is $75,000 ($69,000 + $6,000). The sum of these cash flows discounted using the factors for the present value of $1 at a rate of 16% is calculated as follows:

$69,000 × .862	=	$ 59,478
$75,000 × .743	=	55,725
$75,000 × .641	=	48,075
Discounted cash inflows		$163,278

Thus, the NPV is $13,278 ($163,278 – $150,000 initial outflow).
Answer (A) is incorrect. Ignoring tax on the cash proceeds received from salvage value results in an NPV of $15,842. Answer (C) is incorrect. The amount of $40,910 equals the present value of a 3-year annuity of $85,000 discounted at 16%, minus $150,000. Answer (D) is incorrect. Failing to include the cash proceeds from salvage value results in an NPV of $9,432.

30. The payback period for this investment would be

A. 2.94 years.

B. 1.76 years.

C. 2.09 years.

D. 1.14 years.

Answer (C) is correct. *(CMA, adapted)*
REQUIRED: The payback period for an investment.
DISCUSSION: The payback period is the number of years required for the cumulative undiscounted net cash inflows to equal the original investment. The future net cash inflows consist of $69,000 in Years 1 and 3, and $75,000 in Year 2. After 2 years, the cumulative undiscounted net cash inflow equals $144,000. Thus, $6,000 ($150,000 – $144,000) is to be recovered in Year 3, and payback should be complete in approximately 2.09 years [2 years + ($6,000 ÷ $69,000 net cash inflow in third year)].
Answer (A) is incorrect. This number of years does not consider depreciation. Answer (B) is incorrect. This number of years ignores the tax effects. Answer (D) is incorrect. This number of years results from considering the depreciation as a cash inflow and failing to account for the income tax.

10.6 Risk Analysis and Real Options in Capital Investment

31. Mega, Inc., a large conglomerate with operating divisions in many industries, uses risk-adjusted discount rates in evaluating capital investment decisions. Consider the following statements concerning Mega's use of risk-adjusted discount rates.

I. Mega may accept some investments with internal rates of return less than Mega's overall average cost of capital.

II. Discount rates vary depending on the type of investment.

III. Mega may reject some investments with internal rates of return greater than the cost of capital.

IV. Discount rates may vary depending on the division.

Which of the above statements are correct?

A. I and III only.

B. II and IV only.

C. II, III, and IV only.

D. I, II, III, and IV.

Answer (D) is correct. *(CMA, adapted)*
REQUIRED: The true statement about use of risk-adjusted discount rates.
DISCUSSION: Risk analysis attempts to measure the likelihood of the variability of future returns from the proposed investment. Risk can be incorporated into capital budgeting decisions in a number of ways, one of which is to use a hurdle rate higher than the firm's cost of capital, that is, a risk-adjusted discount rate. This technique adjusts the interest rate used for discounting upward as an investment becomes riskier. The expected flow from the investment must be relatively larger, or the increased discount rate will generate a negative net present value, and the proposed acquisition will be rejected. Accordingly, the IRR (the rate at which the NPV is zero) for a rejected investment may exceed the cost of capital when the risk-adjusted rate is higher than the IRR. Conversely, the IRR for an accepted investment may be less than the cost of capital when the risk-adjusted rate is less than the IRR. In this case, the investment presumably has very little risk. Furthermore, risk-adjusted rates may also reflect the differing degrees of risk, not only among investments, but by the same investments undertaken by different organizational subunits.
Answer (A) is incorrect. Discount rates may vary with the project or with the subunit of the organization. Answer (B) is incorrect. The company may accept some projects with IRRs less than the cost of capital or reject some project with IRRs greater than the cost of capital. Answer (C) is incorrect. The company may accept some projects with IRRs less than the cost of capital or reject some project with IRRs greater than the cost of capital.

32. Sensitivity analysis, if used with capital projects,

A. Is used extensively when cash flows are known with certainty.

B. Measures the change in the discounted cash flows when using the discounted payback method rather than the net present value method.

C. Is a "what-if" technique that asks how a given outcome will change if the original estimates of the capital budgeting model are changed.

D. Is a technique used to rank capital expenditure requests.

Answer (C) is correct. *(CMA, adapted)*
REQUIRED: The true statement about sensitivity analysis.
DISCUSSION: After a problem has been formulated into any mathematical model, it may be subjected to sensitivity analysis, which is a trial-and-error method used to determine the sensitivity of the estimates used. For example, forecasts of many calculated NPVs under various assumptions may be compared to determine how sensitive the NPV is to changing conditions. Changing the assumptions about a certain variable or group of variables may drastically alter the NPV, suggesting that the risk of the investment may be excessive.
Answer (A) is incorrect. Sensitivity analysis is useful when cash flows or other assumptions are uncertain. Answer (B) is incorrect. Sensitivity analysis can be used with any of the capital budgeting methods. Answer (D) is incorrect. Sensitivity analysis is not a ranking technique; it calculates results under varying assumptions.

33. The proper discount rate to use in calculating certainty equivalent net present value is the

A. Risk-adjusted discount rate.

B. Cost of capital.

C. Risk-free rate.

D. Cost of equity capital.

Answer (C) is correct. *(CMA, adapted)*
REQUIRED: The proper discount rate to use in calculating certainty equivalent net present value.
DISCUSSION: Rational investors choose projects that yield the best return given some level of risk. If an investor desires no risk, that is, an absolutely certain rate of return, the risk-free rate is used in calculating net present value. The risk-free rate is the return on a risk-free investment such as government bonds. Certainty equivalent adjustments involve a technique directly drawn from utility theory. It forces the decision maker to specify at what point the firm is indifferent to the choice between a sum of money that is certain and the expected value of a risky sum.
Answer (A) is incorrect. A risk-adjusted discount rate does not represent an absolutely certain rate of return. A discount rate is adjusted upward as the investment becomes riskier. Answer (B) is incorrect. The cost of capital has nothing to do with certainty equivalence. Answer (D) is incorrect. The cost of equity capital does not equate to a certainty equivalent rate.

34. When the risks of the individual components of a project's cash flows are different, an acceptable procedure to evaluate these cash flows is to

A. Divide each cash flow by the payback period.

B. Compute the net present value of each cash flow using the firm's cost of capital.

C. Compare the internal rate of return from each cash flow to its risk.

D. Discount each cash flow using a discount rate that reflects the degree of risk.

Answer (D) is correct. *(CMA, adapted)*
REQUIRED: The acceptable procedure for evaluating cash flows when the risks of individual components of the project's cash flows are different.
DISCUSSION: Risk-adjusted discount rates can be used to evaluate capital investment options. If risks differ among various elements of the cash flows, then different discount rates can be used for different flows.
Answer (A) is incorrect. The payback period ignores both the varying risk and the time value of money. Answer (B) is incorrect. Using the cost of capital as the discount rate does not make any adjustment for the risk differentials among the various cash flows. Answer (C) is incorrect. Risk has to be incorporated into the company's hurdle rate to use the internal rate of return method with risk differentials.

35. Sensitivity analysis is used in capital budgeting to

A. Estimate a project's internal rate of return.

B. Determine the amount that a variable can change without generating unacceptable results.

C. Simulate probabilistic customer reactions to a new product.

D. Identify the required market share to make a new product viable and produce acceptable results.

Answer (B) is correct. *(CMA, adapted)*
REQUIRED: The reason sensitivity analysis is used in capital budgeting.
DISCUSSION: After a problem has been formulated into any mathematical model, it may be subjected to sensitivity analysis, which is a trial-and-error method used to determine the sensitivity of the estimates used. For example, forecasts of many calculated NPVs under various assumptions may be compared to determine how sensitive the NPV is to changing conditions. Changing the assumptions about a certain variable or group of variables may drastically alter the NPV, suggesting that the risk of the investment may be excessive.
Answer (A) is incorrect. Sensitivity analysis is a means of making several estimates of inputs into a capital budgeting decision to determine the effect of changes in assumptions. Answer (C) is incorrect. Sensitivity analysis is not a simulation technique; it is simply a process of making more than one estimate of unknown variables. Answer (D) is incorrect. Sensitivity analysis would not identify the required market share; instead, it would be used to make several estimates of market share to determine how sensitive the decision is to changes in market share.

36. When evaluating a capital budgeting project, a company's treasurer wants to know how changes in operating income and the number of years in the project's useful life will affect its breakeven internal rate of return. The treasurer is most likely to use

A. Scenario analysis.

B. Sensitivity analysis.

C. Monte Carlo simulation.

D. Learning curve analysis.

Answer (B) is correct. *(CMA, adapted)*
REQUIRED: The most appropriate tool for assessing the effect on a capital project of changes in operating income and useful life.
DISCUSSION: Forecasts of many calculated NPVs under various assumptions are compared to see how sensitive NPV is to changing conditions. Changing or relaxing the assumptions about a certain variable or group of variables may drastically alter the NPV. Thus, the asset may appear to be much riskier than was originally predicted. In summary, sensitivity analysis is simply an iterative process of recalculated returns based on changing assumptions.
Answer (A) is incorrect. Scenario analysis is not used for quantitative calculations. Answer (C) is incorrect. Monte Carlo simulation is used to account for an element of randomness. The changes in operating income and life of the project in this situation are under the control of the person running the simulation and thus are not random. Answer (D) is incorrect. Learning curve analysis is used to anticipate the increased rate at which people perform tasks as they gain experience; it is not an appropriate tool for capital budgeting.

37. The relevance of a particular cost to a decision is determined by

A. Riskiness of the decision.

B. Number of decision variables.

C. Amount of the cost.

D. Potential effect on the decision.

Answer (D) is correct. *(CMA, adapted)*
REQUIRED: The determinant of relevance of a particular cost to a decision.
DISCUSSION: Relevance is the capacity of information to make a difference in a decision by helping users of that information to predict the outcomes of events or to confirm or correct prior expectations. Thus, relevant costs are those expected future costs that vary with the action taken. All other costs are constant and therefore have no effect on the decision.

10.8 ESSAY QUESTIONS

Scenario for Essay Questions 1, 2

Kravel Corporation is a diversified company with several manufacturing plants. Kravel's Dayton Plant has been supplying parts to truck manufacturers for over 30 years. The last shipment of truck parts from the Dayton Plant will be made December 31, Year 6. Kravel's management is currently studying three alternatives relating to its soon-to-be-idle plant and equipment in Dayton.

1. Wasson Industries has offered to buy the Dayton Plant for $3,000,000 cash on January 1, Year 7.

2. Harr Enterprises has offered to lease the Dayton facilities for 4 years beginning on January 1, Year 7. Harr's annual lease payments would be $500,000 plus 10% of the gross dollar sales of all items produced in the Dayton Plant. Probabilities of Harr's annual gross dollar sales from the Dayton Plant are estimated as follows:

Annual Gross Dollar Sales	Estimated Probability
$2,000,000	.1
4,000,000	.4
6,000,000	.3
8,000,000	.2

3. Kravel is considering the production of souvenir items to be sold in connection with upcoming sporting events. The Dayton Plant would be used to produce 70,000 items per month at an annual cash outlay of $2,250,000 during Year 7, Year 8, and Year 9. Linda Yetter, Vice President of Marketing, has recommended a selling price of $5 per item and believes the items will sell uniformly throughout Year 8, Year 9, and Year 10.

The adjusted basis of the Dayton Plant as of the close of business on December 31, Year 6, will be $4,200,000. Kravel has used straight-line depreciation for all capital assets at the Dayton Plant. If the Dayton Plant is not sold, the annual straight-line depreciation charge for the plant and equipment will be $900,000 each year for the next 4 years. The market value of the plant and equipment on December 31, Year 10, is estimated to be $600,000.

Kravel requires an after-tax rate of return of 16% for capital investment decisions and is subject to corporate income tax rates of 40% on operating income and 20% on capital gains.

Questions

1. Calculate the present value (at December 31, Year 6) of the expected after-tax cash flows for each of the three alternatives available to Kravel Corporation regarding the Dayton Plant. Assume all recurring cash flows take place at the end of the year.

2. Discuss the additional factors, both quantitative and qualitative, Kravel Corporation should consider before a decision is made regarding the disposition or use of the idle plant and equipment at the Dayton Plant.

Essay Questions 1, 2 — Unofficial Answers

1.   The present values of the expected after-tax cash flows of the three alternatives available to
Kravel Corporation can be calculated as follows:

Alternative 1 – Sell plant to Wasson Industries:

Proceeds from sale of plant		$3,000,000
Salvage value	$ 3,000,000	
Less: adjusted basis	(4,200,000)	
Accrual-basis loss on sale	$(1,200,000)	
Times: tax rate	× 40%	
Tax benefit from loss on sale		480,000
After-tax cash inflow from sale		$3,480,000

Alternative 2 – Lease plant to Harr Enterprises:

	Annual Gross Dollar Sales		Estimated Probability		Expected Value of Sales	
	$2,000,000	×	0.1	=	$ 200,000	
	4,000,000	×	0.4	=	1,600,000	
	6,000,000	×	0.3	=	1,800,000	
	8,000,000	×	0.2	=	1,600,000	
Expected annual gross sales					$ 5,200,000	
Times: portion for lease payment					× 10%	
Variable portion of lease payment					$ 520,000	
Add: fixed portion of lease payment					500,000	
Before-tax cash flow from lease					$ 1,020,000	
Less: income taxes (40%)					(408,000)	
After-tax cash flow from lease					$ 612,000	
Times: PV factor					× 2.798	
Present value of lease payments						$1,712,376
Annual depreciation expense					$ 900,000	
Times: tax rate					× 40%	
Annual depreciation tax shield					$ 360,000	
Times: PV factor					× 2.798	
PV of depreciation tax shield						$1,007,280
Proceeds from sale of plant					$ 600,000	
Salvage value			$ 600,000			
Less: book value @ 12/31/Yr 10			(600,000)			
Accrual-basis g/l on disposal			$ -0-			
Times: tax rate			× 40%			
Tax effect from g/l on sale					-0-	
After-tax cash inflow from sale					$ 600,000	
Times: PV factor					× .552	
PV of proceeds from sale of plant						$ 331,200
Present value of after-tax cash flows						$ 3,050,856

Alternative 3 – Keep plant and produce souvenir items:

Income taxes should be recognized in the years in which the revenues are earned. Tax expense for Years 8 and 9 is therefore $780,000 [($4,200,000 – $2,250,000) × .40].

Year 10 taxes are $1,680,000 ($4,200,000 × .40). Since depreciation expense is included in cost of goods sold, the depreciation tax shield only arises in years when product is sold. The shield for Years 8 and 9 is $360,000 ($900,000 × .40). The shield for Year 10 is $720,000, consisting of the $360,000 arising from cost of goods sold plus $360,000 for the current year when the building is not being used for production.

Since the book value of the plant is expected to equal its salvage value at the end of Year 10, there will be no tax effect from an accrual-basis gain or loss, and thus the relevant cash flow is the entire proceeds.

	Year 7	Year 8	Year 9	Year 10
Sales revenue (70,000 × $5 × 12 months)	$ 0	$ 4,200,000	$ 4,200,000	$ 4,200,000
Less: annual cash outlays	(2,250,000)	(2,250,000)	(2,250,000)	0
Expected annual cash flows	$(2,250,000)	$ 1,950,000	$ 1,950,000	$ 4,200,000
Less: income taxes	0	(780,000)	(780,000)	(1,680,000)
After-tax cash flows	$(2,250,000)	$ 1,170,000	$ 1,170,000	$ 2,520,000
Add: depreciation tax shield	0	360,000	360,000	720,000
Add: termination salvage value	--	--	--	600,000
Net after-tax cash flows	$(2,250,000)	$ 1,530,000	$ 1,530,000	$ 3,840,000
Times: PV factor	× 0.862	× 0.743	× 0.641	× 0.552
Present value of after-tax cash flows	$(1,939,500)	$ 1,136,790	$ 980,730	$ 2,119,680
Net present value of after-tax cash flows				$ 2,297,700

2. While considering its decision regarding the Dayton Plant, Kravel must consider

- That all of Alternative 1's cash flows take place immediately, making it the least risky of the three.

- The adequacy of the cash flows estimates and the appropriateness of the hurdle rate used.

- The timing of cash flows of each of the alternatives in light of the firm's overall cash budget.

- The possibility that the manufacture of truck parts will once again be a profitable use of the plant. Alternative 1 precludes this option permanently and, under Alternative 2, it will not be available until Year 11.

Use **CMA Gleim Online** and **Essay Wizard** to practice additional essay questions in an exam-like environment.

428

APPENDIX A
ICMA CONTENT SPECIFICATION OUTLINES AND CROSS-REFERENCES

The following pages consist of a reprint of the ICMA's Content Specification Outlines (CSOs) and related information for Part 2, effective May 1, 2010. In addition, we have provided cross-references to the Gleim CMA study units. Please use these CSOs as reference material only. The ICMA's CSOs have been carefully analyzed and have been incorporated into 10 study units to provide systematic and rational coverage of exam topics.

We believe we provide comprehensive coverage of the subject matter tested on the CMA exam. If, after taking the exam, you feel that certain topics, concepts, etc., tested were not covered or were inadequately covered, please go to www.gleim.com/feedbackCMA2 or scan the QR code below with your mobile device. We do not want information about CMA questions, only information/feedback about our CMA Review System's coverage.

Be part of something!

Help make Gleim even better with your feedback.

www.gleim.com/feedbackCMA2

Effective May 1, 2010

Content Specification Outlines
Certified Management Accountant (CMA) Examinations

The content specification outlines presented below represent the body of knowledge that will be covered on the CMA examinations. The outlines may be changed in the future when new subject matter becomes part of the common body of knowledge.

Candidates for the CMA designation are required to take and pass Parts 1 and 2.

Candidates are responsible for being informed on the most recent developments in the areas covered in the outlines. This includes understanding of public pronouncements issued by accounting organizations as well as being up-to-date on recent developments reported in current accounting, financial and business periodicals.

The content specification outlines serve several purposes. The outlines are intended to:

- Establish the foundation from which each examination will be developed.
- Provide a basis for consistent coverage on each examination.
- Communicate to interested parties more detail as to the content of each examination part.
- Assist candidates in their preparation for each examination.
- Provide information to those who offer courses designed to aid candidates in preparing for the examinations.

Important additional information about the content specification outlines and the examinations is listed below and on the following page.

1. The coverage percentage given for each major topic within each examination part represents the relative weight given to that topic in an examination part. The number of questions presented in each major topic area approximates this percentage.

2. Each examination will sample from the subject areas contained within each major topic area to meet the relative weight specifications. No relative weights have been assigned to the subject areas within each major topic. No inference should be made from the order in which the subject areas are listed or from the number of subject areas as to the relative weight or importance of any of the subjects.

3. Each major topic within each examination part has been assigned a coverage level designating the depth and breadth of topic coverage, ranging from an introductory knowledge of a subject area (Level A) to a thorough understanding of and ability to apply the essentials of a subject area (Level C). Detailed explanations of the coverage levels and the skills expected of candidates are presented on the following page.

4. The topics for Parts 1 and 2 have been selected to minimize the overlapping of subject areas among the examination parts. The topics within an examination part and the subject areas within topics may be combined in individual questions.

5. With regard to U.S. Federal income taxation issues, candidates will be expected to understand the impact of income taxes when reporting and analyzing financial results. In addition, the tax code provisions that impact decisions (e.g., depreciation, interest, etc.) will be tested.

6. Candidates for the CMA designation are assumed to have knowledge of the following: preparation of financial statements, business economics, time-value of money concepts, statistics and probability.

7. Parts 1 and 2 are four-hour exams and each contains 100 multiple-choice questions and 2 essay questions. Candidates will have three hours to complete the multiple-choice questions and one hour to complete the essay section. A small number of the multiple-choice questions on each exam are being validated for future use and will not count in the final score.

8. For the essay questions, both written and quantitative responses will be required. Candidates will be expected to present written answers that are responsive to the question asked, presented in a logical manner, and demonstrate an appropriate understanding of the subject matter. It should be noted that candidates are expected to have working knowledge in the use of word processing and electronic spreadsheets.

9. Ethical issues and considerations are tested in both Parts 1 and 2. In Part 1, ethics will be tested from the perspective of the individual and in Part 2, from the perspective of the organization.

In order to more clearly define the topical knowledge required by a candidate, varying levels of coverage for the treatment of major topics of the content specification outlines have been identified and defined. The cognitive skills that a successful candidate should possess and that should be tested on the examinations can be defined as follows*:

Knowledge: Ability to remember previously learned material such as specific facts, criteria, techniques, principles, and procedures (i.e., identify, define, list).

Comprehension: Ability to grasp and interpret the meaning of material (i.e., classify, explain, distinguish between).

Application: Ability to use learned material in new and concrete situations (i.e., demonstrate, predict, solve, modify, relate).

Analysis: Ability to break down material into its component parts so that its organizational structure can be understood; ability to recognize causal relationships, discriminate between behaviors, and identify elements that are relevant to the validation of a judgment (i.e., differentiate, estimate, order).

Synthesis: Ability to put parts together to form a new whole or proposed set of operations; ability to relate ideas and formulate hypotheses (i.e., combine, formulate, revise).

Evaluation: Ability to judge the value of material for a given purpose on the basis of consistency, logical accuracy, and comparison to standards; ability to appraise judgments involved in the selection of a course of action (i.e., criticize, justify, conclude).

The three levels of coverage can be defined as follows:

Level A: Requiring the skill levels of knowledge and comprehension.

Level B: Requiring the skill levels of knowledge, comprehension, application, and analysis.

Level C: Requiring all six skill levels – knowledge, comprehension, application, analysis, synthesis, and evaluation.

The levels of coverage as they apply to each of the major topics of the Content Specification Outlines are shown on the following pages with each topic listing. The levels represent the manner in which topic areas are to be treated and represent ceilings, i.e., a topic area designated as Level C may contain requirements at the "A," "B," or "C" level, but a topic designated as Level B will not contain requirements at the "C" level.

*A more thorough explanation of these skills is presented in Appendix C, "Types and Levels of Exam Questions."

CMA Content Specification Overview

Part 2   ***Financial Decision Making***
(4 hours – 100 questions and 2 essay questions)

Financial Statement Analysis	**25%**	**Level C**
Corporate Finance	**25%**	**Level C**
Decision Analysis and Risk Management	**25%**	**Level C**
Investment Decisions	**20%**	**Level C**
Professional Ethics	**5%**	**Level C**

Candidates for the CMA designation are assumed to have knowledge of the following: preparation of financial statements, business economics, time-value of money concepts, statistics and probability. Questions in both parts of the CMA exam will assume that the successful candidate can effectively integrate and synthesize this knowledge with the specific topics covered in the content specification outline.

Below and on the following pages, we have reproduced verbatim the ICMA's Content Specification Outlines (CSOs) for Part 2. We also have provided cross-references to the study units and subunits in this book that correspond to the CSOs' coverage. If one entry appears above a list, it applies to all items in that list.

Part 2 – Financial Decision Making

A. **Financial Statement Analysis (25% - Levels A, B, and C)**

  1. ***Basic Financial Statement Analysis***
    a. Common size financial statements (1.8)
    b. Common base year financial statements (1.8)
    c. Growth analysis (1.8)
    d. Purposes and components of financial statements (1.3 – 1.7)

  2. ***Financial Performance Metrics – Financial Ratios***
    a. Liquidity (2.1, 2.2)
    b. Leverage (2.5)
    c. Activity (2.3)
    d. Profitability (3.1, 3.2)
    e. Market (3.3, 3.4)

  3. ***Profitability analysis***
    a. DuPont analysis (3.2)
    b. Income measurement analysis (3.6)
    c. Revenue analysis (3.6)
    d. Cost of sales analysis (3.6)
    e. Expense analysis (3.6)
    f. Variation analysis (3.6)

  4. ***Analytical Issues in Financial Accounting***
    a. Impact of foreign operations (3.7)
    b. Effects of changing prices and inflation (3.5)
    c. Off-balance sheet financing (3.8)
    d. Cash Flow Statement reconciliation to Income Statement (1.6, 1.7)
    e. Impact of changes in accounting treatment (3.6)
    f. International Financial Reporting Standards (IFRS) (3.9)
    g. Fair value accounting (3.10)
    h. Differences in accounting and economic concepts of value and income (8.5)
    i. Earnings quality (3.5)

B. **Corporate Finance (25% - Levels A, B, and C)**

1. *Risk and return* (4.1)

    a. Calculating return
    b. Types of risk
    c. Relationship between risk and return
    d. Risk and return in a portfolio context
    e. Diversification
    f. Asset pricing models

2. *Managing financial risk* (4.2)

    a. Portfolio management
    b. Hedging
    c. Financial risk management

3. *Financial instruments*

    a. Term structure of interest rates (5.1)
    b. Bonds (5.1)
    c. Debt management (5.1)
    d. Common stock (5.2)
    e. Preferred stock (5.2)
    f. Options and other derivatives (5.4)
    g. Valuation of financial instruments (5.3, 5.4)

4. *Cost of capital*

    a. Weighted average cost of capital (5.6)
    b. Cost of individual capital components (5.6)
    c. Calculating the cost of capital (5.6)
    d. Marginal cost of capital (5.7)

5. *Managing current assets*

    a. Working capital terminology (6.1)
    b. Cash management (6.2)
    c. Marketable securities management (6.3)
    d. Accounts receivable management (6.4)
    e. Inventory management (6.5)
    f. Types of short-term credit (6.6)
    g. Minimizing the cost of short-term credit (6.6)

6. *Raising capital*

    a. Financial markets and regulation (7.1)
    b. Market efficiency (7.1)
    c. Financial institutions (7.1)
    d. Initial public offerings (7.1)
    e. Secondary offerings (7.1)
    f. Dividend policy and share repurchases (7.2)
    g. Private placements (7.1)
    h. Lease financing (7.2)

7. *Corporate restructuring*

    a. Mergers and acquisitions (7.3)
    b. Divestitures (7.3)
    c. Bankruptcy (7.4)

8. ***International finance***

   a. Fixed, flexible and floating exchange rates (7.5)
   b. Managing transaction exposure (7.6)
   c. Financing international trade (7.7)
   d. Transfer pricing tax implications (7.7)
   e. Political risk (7.7)

C. Decision Analysis and Risk Management (25% - Levels A, B, and C)

1. ***Cost/volume/profit analysis***

   a. Breakeven analysis (8.1, 8.2)
   b. Profit performance and alternative operating levels (8.3)
   c. Analysis of multiple products (8.4)

2. ***Marginal analysis***

   a. Sunk costs, opportunity costs and other related concepts (8.5)
   b. Marginal costs and marginal revenue (8.5, 8.6)
   c. Special orders and pricing (9.2)
   d. Make versus buy (9.3)
   e. Sell or process further (9.4)
   f. Add or drop a segment (9.1)
   g. Capacity considerations (9.1 – 9.4)

3. ***Pricing***

   a. Market comparables (9.6)
   b. Setting prices (9.6, 9.7)
   c. Target costing (9.6, 9.7)
   d. Elasticity (9.5)
   e. Product life cycle considerations (9.6)
   f. Market structure considerations (9.6)

4. ***Risk assessment*** (9.8)

   a. Risk identification and exposure
   b. Definition and scope of operational risk, hazard risk, financial risk and strategic risk
   c. Risk mitigation strategies
   d. Enterprise risk management

D. Investment Decisions (20% - Levels A, B, and C)

1. ***Capital budgeting process*** (10.1)

   a. Stages of capital budgeting
   b. Incremental cash flows
   c. Income tax considerations

2. ***Discounted cash flow analysis*** (10.2, 10.5)

   a. Net present value
   b. Internal rate of return
   c. Comparison of NPV and IRR

3. ***Payback and discounted payback*** (10.3, 10.5)

   a. Uses of payback method
   b. Limitations of payback method
   c. Discounted payback

4.　***Ranking investment projects*** (10.4)

    a.　Ranking methods
    b.　Capital rationing
    c.　Mutually exclusive projects

5.　***Risk analysis in capital investment*** (10.6)

    a.　Sensitivity analysis
    b.　Certainty equivalents
    c.　Real options

6.　***Valuation*** (10.6)

    a.　Discounted cash flow models
    b.　Multiples models
    c.　Valuation for acquisitions and divestitures
    d.　Discount rates

E.　Professional Ethics (5% - Levels A, B, and C)

1.　***Ethical considerations for the organization***

    a.　Anti-bribery provisions of the U.S. Foreign Corrupt Practices Act (1.1)
    b.　Provisions of IMA's Statement on Management Accounting, "Values and Ethics: From Inception to Practice" (1.2)
    c.　Corporate responsibility for ethical conduct (1.2)

APPENDIX B
ICMA SUGGESTED READING LIST
(AS PRINTED IN THE ICMA'S 2012 RESOURCE GUIDE)

The ICMA suggested reading list that follows is reproduced to give you an overview of the scope of Part 2. You will not have the time to study these texts. Our CMA Review System is complete and thorough and is designed to maximize your study time. Candidates are expected to stay up-to-date by reading articles from journals, newspapers, and professional publications.

NOTE: Edition numbers and publication dates may not be current, but we prefer that you focus entirely on Study Units 1-10 in this book to help you pass Part 2 of the CMA exam.

Part 2 – Financial Decision Making

Financial Statement Analysis

Mackenzie Bruce, Coetsee Danie, Njikizana Tapiwa, Chamboko Raymond, Colyvas Blaise, and Hanekom Brandon, *2012 Interpretation and Application of International Financial Reporting Standards*, John Wiley & Sons, Hoboken, NJ, 2012.

Gibson, Charles H., *Financial Reporting & Analysis*, 12th edition, South-Western Cengage Learning, Mason, OH, 2011.

Subramanyam, K.R., and Wild, John L., *Financial Statement Analysis*, 10th edition, McGraw Hill, New York, NY, 2009.

Corporate Finance

Brealey, Richard A., Myers, Stewart C., and Allen, Franklin, *Principles of Corporate Finance*, 10th edition, McGraw Hill, New York, NY, 2011.

Van Horn, James C., and Wachowicz, John M. Jr., *Fundamentals of Financial Management*, 13th edition, FT/Prentice-Hall, Harlow, England, 2009.

Decision Analysis and Risk Management

Blocher, Edward J., Stout, David E., and Cokins, Gary, *Cost Management: A Strategic Emphasis*, 5th edition, McGraw Hill, New York, NY, 2010.

Horngren, Charles T., Datar, Srikant, Rajan, Madhav, *Cost Accounting: A Managerial Emphasis*, 14th edition, Prentice-Hall, Upper Saddle River, NJ, 2012.

COSO, The Committee of Sponsoring Organizations of the Treadway Commission, 2004, *Enterprise Risk Management – Integrated Framework*.

Moeller, Robert R., *COSO Enterprise Risk Management*, 2nd edition, John Wiley & Sons, Inc., Hoboken, NJ, 2011.

IMA, 2006, *Enterprise Risk Management: Frameworks, Elements, and Integration*, www.imanet.org/resources_and_publications/research_studies_and_statements/statements_on_management_accounting.aspx (members only).

IMA, 2007, *Enterprise Risk Management: Tools and Techniques for Effective Implementation*, www.imanet.org/resources_and_publications/research_studies_and_statements/statements_on_management_accounting.aspx (members only).

Investment Decisions

Brealey, Richard A., Myers, Stewart C., and Allen, Franklin, *Principles of Corporate Finance*, 10th edition, McGraw Hill, New York, NY, 2011.

Van Horn, James C., and Wachowicz, John M. Jr., *Fundamentals of Financial Management*, 13th edition, FT/Prentice Hall, Harlow, England, 2009.

Professional Ethics

IMA, 2008, *Values and Ethics: From Inception to Practice*, www.imanet.org/resources_and_publications/research_studies_and_statements/statements_on_management_accounting.aspx (members only).

United States Department of Justice, *Lay-person's Guide to Foreign Corrupt Practices Act*, www.justice.gov/criminal/fraud/fcpa/docs/lay-persons-guide.pdf.

APPENDIX C
TYPES AND LEVELS OF EXAM QUESTIONS

The following is based on an excerpt from the ICMA's Resource Guide for the CMA exam, printed in 2012.

TYPES OF EXAM QUESTIONS

All multiple-choice items within the CMA parts 1 and 2 are of the 4-option multiple-choice type, with one and only one correct answer for each question. There are, however, a number of variations on this type of item used in the CMA exams. In the examples below, the term "stem" refers to all the information that precedes the answer options or alternatives.

Closed Stem Item

This item type is characterized by a stem that is a complete sentence which concludes with a question mark. The options may be complete or incomplete sentences.

Example:

Which one of the following would have the effect of increasing the working capital of a firm?

a. Cash payment of payroll taxes payable.
b. Cash collection of accounts receivable.
c. The purchase of a new plant, financed by a 20-year mortgage.
d. Refinancing a short-term note with a 2-year note.

Key = d

Sentence Completion Item

This type of item is characterized by a stem that is an incomplete sentence. The options represent conclusions to that sentence.

Example:

If a product's elasticity coefficient is 2.0, this means the demand is

a. perfectly elastic.
b. elastic.
c. inelastic.
d. perfectly inelastic.

Key = b

Except Format

This type of item is employed when you are required to select the option that does not "fit." In this case, three of the options will fit or be defined by the stem, and one option (the correct option) will not fit. A variation on this type of question is to use the word **not** instead of **except** in the stem, in the form of "Which one of the following is **not**...".

Example:

All of the following are considered tangible assets **except**

a.   real estate.
b.   copyrights.
c.   prepaid taxes.
d.   accounts receivable.

Key = b

Most/Least/Best Format

This type of item requires you to select an option which is either better or worse than the others. In all cases, the correct answer represents the collective judgment of experts within the field.

Example #1:

Which one of the following **best** describes a production budget?

a.   It is based on required direct labor hours.
b.   It includes required material purchases.
c.   It is based on desired ending inventory and sales forecasts.
d.   It is an aggregate of the monetary details of the operating budget.

Key = c

Example #2:

Which one of the following is **least** likely to help an organization overcome its communication problems between the Accounting Department and other departments?

a.   Job rotation.
b.   Cross-functional teams.
c.   Written policies and procedures.
d.   Performance appraisals.

Key = d

QUESTION LEVELS

In addition to the variety of item formats previously described, the CMA exams present test items at varying cognitive levels. These levels range from questions that require a recall of material to questions that require a sophisticated understanding such that you must apply your knowledge to a novel situation, or judge the value of information as it may apply to a particular scenario. A description of each of these levels, along with sample questions, appears below and on the following pages. The cognitive level required for each major topic area of the CMA exams is shown in the Topic/Resource outline.

Level A
This cognitive level represents the "lowest" or most basic level, and includes items that require the recall of facts and the recognition of principles. This level includes the categories of knowledge and comprehension.

Knowledge: This is the lowest level of learning. Items in this category are those that require the recall of ideas, material, or phenomena related to the topic of interest. In these questions, you will be asked to define, identify, and select information.

Example:

A market situation where a small number of sellers comprise an entire industry is known as

a. a natural monopoly.
b. monopolistic competition.
c. an oligopoly.
d. pure competition.

Key = c

To correctly respond to the item above, you must recall the textbook definition of an oligopoly.

Comprehension: Items in this category require you to grasp the meaning of the material presented in some novel way. A question testing for comprehension describes some principle or fact in words different from those used in textbooks and often uses a situation as a way to present the idea. In order to answer the item correctly, you must recognize the principle demonstrated in the problem; memory alone will not be sufficient for identifying the correct answer.

Example:

Social legislation is frequently criticized for being inefficient because the agencies

a. use flexible rather than rigid standards.
b. rely heavily on the free market to allocate resources.
c. rarely consider the marginal benefits relative to the marginal costs.
d. enforce their policies too leniently.

Key = c

In order to answer this item correctly, you must know something about the issues or principles in connection with social legislation. Other questions dealing with this level of testing are those that ask you to identify an option which best explains, illustrates, or provides an example of the concept in question.

Level B

This cognitive level includes items that test for the application of material to novel situations and the ability to analyze or break down information into its component parts. Items that require application or analysis are included in this level.

Application: Items in this category measure understanding of ideas or content to a point where you can apply that understanding to an entirely new situation. The objective of these items is to test whether you can use the knowledge in an appropriate manner in a real-life situation.

Example:

The balance sheet for Miller Industries shows the following.

Cash	$ 8,000,000
Accounts Receivable	13,500,000
Inventory	7,800,000
Prepaid Expenses	245,000
Property, Plant, & Equipment	4,700,000

Based on this information, what are the Total Current Assets for this firm?

a. $21,500,000
b. $29,300,000
c. $29,545,000
d. $34,245,000

Key = c

Rather than rely on memory or comprehension alone, the situation presented in this item requires you to draw on your knowledge of the calculation of Total Current Assets and apply that knowledge to the particular data presented in the problem. Other items dealing with this level of testing might ask you to identify a specific situation requiring a certain course of action, or the most appropriate procedure or steps to apply to a particular problem.

Analysis: Analysis involves the ability to break down material into its component parts so that its organizational structure can be understood. It involves the ability to recognize parts, as well as the relationships between those parts, and to recognize the principles involved. Items in this category ask you to differentiate, discriminate, distinguish, infer, and determine the relevancy of data.

Example:

A firm is considering the implementation of a lock-box collection system at a cost of $80,000 per year. Annual sales are $90 million, and the lock-box system will reduce collection time by 3 days. The firm currently is in debt for $3,000,000. If the firm can invest the funds designated for the lock-box at 8%, should it use the lock-box system? Assume a 360-day year.

a.   Yes, it will produce a savings of $140,000 per year.
b.   Yes, it will produce a savings of $60,000 per year.
c.   No, it will produce a loss of $20,000 per year.
d.   No, it will produce a loss of $60,000 per year.

Key = c

In this item, you are presented with a novel situation and asked to identify the data that are relevant to the problem at hand, which in this case involves the determination of the savings or loss of implementing a lock-box type of collection system. You are required to apply principles to determine savings or loss, and then to make an analysis of the outcomes of the alternative courses of action.

Level C

This cognitive level is considered the "highest" or most challenging level, and includes items that require you to evaluate information.

Evaluation: Items in this category are those that require the ability to judge the value of material for a given purpose, based on definite criteria. These questions include those that ask you to appraise, conclude, support, compare, contrast, interpret, and summarize information.

Example:

A home services organization has been using the straight-line depreciation method for calculating the depreciation expenses of its equipment. Based on recently acquired information, the firm's assistant controller has altered the estimated useful lives of the equipment. The corresponding changes in depreciation result in a change from a small profit for the year to a loss. The assistant controller is asked by the controller to reduce by half the total depreciation expense for the current year. Believing he is faced with an ethical conflict, the assistant controller reports the problem to the Board of Directors. In accordance with **IMA's Statement of Ethical Professional Practice**, which one of the following is the correct evaluation of the assistant controller's action?

a.   The assistant controller's action was appropriate as an immediate step.
b.   The assistant controller's action would have been appropriate only if other alternatives had first been tried.
c.   The assistant controller's action was not appropriate under any circumstances.
d.   Not enough information has been given to evaluate the assistant controller's action.

Key = b

The situation presented in this item requires you to evaluate the course of action that the assistant controller has taken. Option b is the correct option. While the assistant controller's action is appropriate, the situation may be resolved by less drastic means first. You are asked to make a judgment on the appropriateness of the actions to the situation described, and answer the question on the basis of this information.

444

INDEX

CPA CPA CPA

GLEIM CPA REVIEW SYSTEM

All 4 sections, including Gleim Online, Review Books, *Test Prep Software Download*, *Simulation Wizard*, Audio Review, *CPA Review: A System for Success* Booklet, plus bonus Book Bag.

$989.95 x _____ = $_____

Also available by exam section (does not include Book Bag).

CMA CMA

GLEIM CMA REVIEW SYSTEM

Includes: Gleim Online, Review Books, *Test Prep Software Download*, Audio Review, *Essay Wizard*, *CMA Review: A System for Success* Booklet, plus bonus Book Bag.

$739.95 x _____ = $_____

Also available by exam part (does not include Book Bag).

CIA CIA

GLEIM CIA REVIEW SYSTEM

Includes: Gleim Online, Review Books, *Test Prep Software Download*, Audio Review, *CIA Review: A System for Success* Booklet, plus bonus Book Bag.

$824.95 x _____ = $_____

Also available by exam part (does not include Book Bag).

EA EA

GLEIM EA REVIEW SYSTEM

Includes: Gleim Online, Review Books, *Test Prep Software Download*, Audio Review, *EA Review: A System for Success* Booklet, plus bonus Book Bag.

$629.95 x _____ = $_____

Also available by exam part (does not include Book Bag).

EQE EQE

"THE GLEIM EQE SERIES" EXAM QUESTIONS AND EXPLANATIONS

Includes: 5 Books and *Test Prep Software Download*.

$112.25 x _____ = $_____

Also available by part.

CPE CPE

GLEIM ONLINE CPE

Try a FREE 4-hour course at gleim.com/cpe
- Easy-to-Complete
- Informative
- Effective

Contact
GLEIM® PUBLICATIONS
for further assistance:

gleim.com
800.874.5346
sales@gleim.com

SUBTOTAL $_____
Complete your
order on the
next page

GLEIM PUBLICATIONS, INC.

P. O. Box 12848　Gainesville, FL 32604

TOLL FREE:　800.874.5346
LOCAL:　352.375.0772
FAX:　352.375.6940
INTERNET:　gleim.com
EMAIL:　sales@gleim.com

Customer service is available (Eastern Time):
8:00 a.m. - 7:00 p.m., Mon. - Fri.
9:00 a.m. - 2:00 p.m., Saturday
Please have your credit card ready,
or save time by ordering online!

SUBTOTAL (from previous page) $_____
Add applicable sales tax for shipments within Florida. _____
Shipping (nonrefundable) 14.00

TOTAL $_____

Email us for prices/instructions on shipments outside the 48 contiguous states, or simply order online.

NAME (please print) _____

ADDRESS _____ Apt. _____
(street address required for UPS/Federal Express)

CITY _____ STATE _____ ZIP _____

____ MC/VISA/DISC/AMEX ____ Check/M.O.　Daytime Telephone (____)_____

Credit Card No. _____ - _____ - _____

Exp. ____/____　Signature _____
Month / Year

Email address _____

1. We process and ship orders daily, within one business day over 98.8% of the time. Call by 3:00 pm for same day service.
2. Gleim Publications, Inc. guarantees the immediate refund of all resalable texts, unopened and un-downloaded Test Prep Software, and unopened and un-downloaded audios returned within 30 days. Accounting and Academic Test Prep online courses may be canceled within 30 days if no more than the first study unit or lesson has been accessed. In addition, Online CPE courses may be canceled within 30 days if no more than the Introductory Study Questions have been accessed. Accounting Practice Exams may be canceled within 30 days of purchase if the Practice Exam has not been started. Aviation online courses may be canceled within 30 days if no more than two study units have been accessed. This policy applies only to products that are purchased directly from Gleim Publications, Inc. No refunds will be provided on opened or downloaded Test Prep Software or audios, partial returns of package sets, or shipping and handling charges. Any freight charges incurred for returned or refused packages will be the purchaser's responsibility.
3. Please PHOTOCOPY this order form for others.
4. No CODs. Orders from individuals must be prepaid.

Subject to change without notice. 07/12

For updates and other important information, visit our website.

gleim.com

GLEIM KNOWLEDGE TRANSFER SYSTEMS®